*Now available

MINOR PROPHETS

PART 2

MICHAEL H. FLOYD

The Forms of the Old Testament Literature

VOLUME XXII

*Rolf P. Knierim, Gene M. Tucker, and
Marvin A. Sweeney, editors*

WILLIAM B. EERDMANS PUBLISHING COMPANY
GRAND RAPIDS, MICHIGAN / CAMBRIDGE, U.K.

© 2000 Wm. B. Eerdmans Publishing Co.
255 Jefferson Ave. S.E., Grand Rapids, Michigan 49503 /
P.O. Box 163, Cambridge CB3 9PU U.K.

Printed in the United States of America

05 04 03 02 01 00   7 6 5 4 3 2 1

Library of Congress Cataloging-in-Publication Data

Floyd, Michael H.
Minor Prophets. Part 2 / Michael H. Floyd.
p.   cm.   (The Forms of the Old Testament literature: v. 22)
ISBN 0-8028-4452-9 (pbk.)
1. Bible. O.T. Minor Prophets — Criticism, Form.
I. Title.   II. Series.
BS1560.F56   2000
224′.90663 — dc21   99-29802
CIP

CONTENTS

ABBREVIATIONS AND SYMBOLS

I. MISCELLANEOUS ABBREVIATIONS AND SYMBOLS

BCE	Before the Common Era
cf.	*confer* (compare)
ch(s).	chapter(s)
contd.	continued
Diss.	Dissertation
ed.	editor(s), edited by; edition
e.g.	*exempli gratia* (for example)
esp.	especially
et al.	*et alii* (and others)
fasc.	fascicle
Fest.	*Festschrift*
idem	the same
i.e.	*id est* (that is)
lit.	literally
LXX	Septuagint
ms(s).	manuscript(s)
MT	Masoretic Text
n(n).	note(s)
p(p).	page(s)
repr.	reprint(ed)
rev.	revised
Tiq soph	*Tiqqun sopherim*
tr.	translator(s), translated by
v(v).	verse(s)
vol(s).	volume(s)
→	the arrow indicates a cross reference to another section of the commentary
§	section, paragraph

II. PUBLICATIONS

AB	Anchor Bible
ABD	*Anchor Bible Dictionary* (ed. D. N. Freedman et al.; 6 vols.; New York: Doubleday, 1992)
AfO	*Archiv für Orientforschung*
AJSL	*American Journal of Semitic Languages and Literatures*
AnBib	Analecta biblica
AOAT	Alter Orient und Altes Testament
ASTI	*Annual of the Swedish Theological Institute*
ATANT	Abhandlungen zur Theologie des Alten und Neuen Testaments
ATD	Das Alte Testament Deutsch
AThD	Acta Theologica Danica
ATSAT	Arbeiten zu Text und Sprache im Alten Testament
AUM	Andrews University Monographs
AzT	Arbeiten zur Theologie
BBB	Bonner biblische Beiträge
BEATAJ	Beiträge zur Erforschung des Alten Testaments und des Antiken Judentums
BetM	*Beth Mikra*
BHS	K. Elliger and K. Rudolph, eds., *Biblia Hebraica Stuttgartensia* (Stuttgart: Deutsche Bibelstiftung, 1977)
Bib	*Biblica*
BibLeb	*Bibel und Leben*
BibOr	Biblia et orientalia
BibS (N)	Biblische Studien (Neukirchen, 1951-)
BIS	Biblical Interpretation Series
BJS	Brown Judaic Studies
BKAT	Biblischer Kommentar Altes Testament
BN	*Biblische Notizen*
BSac	*Bibliotheca Sacra*
BT	*The Bible Translator*
BTB	*Biblical Theology Bulletin*
BWAT	Beiträge zur Wissenschaft vom Alten Testament
BZ	*Biblische Zeitschrift*
BZAW	Beihefte zur Zeitschrift für die alttestamentliche Wissenschaft
CAT	Commentaire de l'Ancien Testament
CBC	Cambridge Bible Commentary
CBET	Contributions to Biblical Exegesis and Theology
CBQ	*Catholic Biblical Quarterly*
EBib	*Études bibliques*
ErIs	*Eretz Israel*
EstBib	*Estudios bíblicos*
ETL	*Ephemerides theologicae lovanienses*
EvQ	*Evangelical Quarterly*

EvT	*Evangelische Theologie*
FOTL	Forms of the Old Testament Literature
FRLANT	Forschungen zur Religion und Literatur des Alten und Neuen Testaments
FThSt	Freiburger Theologische Studien
GKC	*Gesenius' Hebrew Grammar* (ed. E. Kautzsch; 2nd ed.; trans. A. E. Cowley; Oxford: Clarendon, 1910)
GTJ	*Grace Theological Journal*
HAR	*Hebrew Annual Review*
HAT	Handbuch zum Alten Testament
HDR	Harvard Dissertations in Religion
HSM	Harvard Semitic Monographs
HTR	*Harvard Theological Review*
HUCA	*Hebrew Union College Annual*
ICC	International Critical Commentary
IEJ	*Israel Exploration Journal*
Int	*Interpretation*
IntCom	Interpretation: A Bible Commentary for Teaching and Preaching
ITC	International Theological Commentary
JBL	*Journal of Biblical Literature*
JETS	*Journal of the Evangelical Theological Society*
JJS	*Journal of Jewish Studies*
JNES	*Journal of Near Eastern Studies*
JNSL	*Journal of Northwest Semitic Languages*
JRT	*Journal of Religious Thought*
JSOT	*Journal for the Study of the Old Testament*
JSOTSup	Journal for the Study of the Old Testament, Supplements
JSS	*Journal of Semitic Studies*
JTS	*Journal of Theological Studies*
KAT	Kommentar zum Alten Testament
KHC	Kurzer Hand-Commentar zum Alten Testament
MGWJT	*Monatsschrift für Geschichte und Wissenschaft des Judentums*
NAB	*New American Bible*
NBE	Nueva Biblia Española
NCB	New Century Bible
NEB	*New English Bible*
NedTTs	*Nederlands theologisch tijdschrift*
NIB	*The New Interpreter's Bible* (ed. L. Keck et al.; 12 vols.; Nashville: Abingdon, 1994-)
NICOT	New International Commentary on the Old Testament
NIV	*New International Version*
NJB	*New Jerusalem Bible*
NJPS	*New Jewish Publication Society Version (Tanakh: A New Translation of the Holy Scriptures according to the Traditional Hebrew Text)*

NRSV	*New Revised Standard Version*
OBO	Orbis biblicus et orientalis
Or	*Orientalia*
OTL	Old Testament Library
OTM	Old Testament Message
OTS	*Oudtestamentische Studiën*
OTWSA	*Ou-Testamentiese Werkgemeenskap in Suid-Afrika*
POS	Pretoria Oriental Series
PTMS	Pittsburgh Theological Monograph Series
RB	*Revue biblique*
RevScRel	*Revue des Sciences Religieuses*
RHPR	*Revue d'histoire et de philosophie religieuses*
RSR	*Recherches de science religieuse*
RST	Regensburger Studien zur Theologie
RSV	*Revised Standard Version*
RTR	*Reformed Theological Review*
SB	Sources bibliques
SBib	*Sémiotique et Bible*
SBLDS	Society of Biblical Literature Dissertation Series
SBLMS	Society of Biblical Literature Monograph Series
SBS	Stuttgarter Bibelstudien
SBT	Studies in Biblical Theology
ScrHier	Scripta hierosolymitana
SSN	Studia semitica neerlandica
ST	*Studia theologica*
StEv	*Studia Evangelica*
SWBA	Social World of Biblical Antiquity Series
TBC	Torch Bible Commentaries
TBT	*The Bible Today*
TBü	Theologische Bücherei
TD	*Theology Digest*
TDOT	G. J. Botterweck, H. Ringgren, and H.-J. Fabry, eds., *Theological Dictionary of the Old Testament* (trans. D. E. Green et al.; 16 vols.; Grand Rapids: Eerdmans, 1974-)
TOTC	Tyndale Old Testament Commentary
TQ	*Theologische Quartalschrift*
TTS	Trierer theologische Studien
TynBul	*Tyndale Bulletin*
TZ	*Theologische Zeitschrift*
UBSMS	United Bible Societies Monograph Series
VT	*Vetus Testamentum*
VTSup	*Vetus Testamentum, Supplements*
WBC	Word Biblical Commentary
WMANT	Wissenschaftliche Monographien zum Alten und Neuen Testament
ZAW	*Zeitschrift für die alttestamentliche Wissenschaft*
ZTK	*Zeitschrift für Theologie und Kirche*

Editors' Foreword

This book is the eleventh in a series of twenty-four volumes planned for publication. The series eventually will present a form-critical analysis of every book and each unit of the Old Testament (Hebrew Bible) according to a standard outline and methodology. The aims of the work are fundamentally exegetical, attempting to understand the biblical literature from the viewpoint of a particular set of questions. Each volume in the series will also give an account of the history of the form-critical discussion of the material in question, attempt to bring consistency to the terminology for the genres and formulas of the biblical literature, and expose the exegetical procedure in such a way as to enable students and pastors to engage in their own analysis and interpretation. It is hoped, therefore, that the audience will be a broad one, including not only biblical scholars but also students, pastors, priests, and rabbis who are engaged in biblical interpretation.

There is a difference between the planned order of appearance of the individual volumes and their position in the series. While the series follows basically the sequence of the books of the Hebrew Bible, the individual volumes will appear in accordance with the projected working schedules of the individual contributors. The number of twenty-four volumes has been chosen for merely practical reasons that make it necessary to combine several biblical books in one volume at times, and at times to have two authors contribute to the same volume. Volume XIII is an exception to the arrangement according to the sequence of the Hebrew canon in that it omits Lamentations. The commentary on Lamentations will be published with the second of two volumes on the book of Psalms.

The initiation of this series is the result of deliberations and plans that began some twenty years ago. At that time the current editors perceived the need for a comprehensive reference work that would enable scholars and students of the Hebrew scriptures to gain from the insights that form-critical work had accumulated throughout seven decades, and at the same time to participate more effectively in such work themselves. An international and interconfessional team of scholars was assembled and has been expanded in recent years.

Several possible approaches and formats for publication presented themselves. The work could not be a handbook of the form-critical method with some examples of its application. Nor would it be satisfactory to present an encyclopedia of the genres identified in the Old Testament literature. The reference work would have to demonstrate the method on all of the texts, and identify genres only through the actual interpretation of the texts themselves. Hence, the work had to be a commentary following the sequence of the books in the Hebrew Bible (the Kittel edition of the *Biblia hebraica* then and the *Biblia hebraica stuttgartensia* now).

The main purpose of this project is to lead the student to the Old Testament texts themselves, and not just to form-critical studies of the texts. It should be stressed that the commentary is confined to the form-critical interpretation of the texts. Consequently, the reader should not expect here a full-fledged exegetical commentary that deals with the broad range of issues concerning the meaning of the text. In order to keep the focus as clearly as possible on a particular set of questions, matters of text, translation, philology, verse-by-verse explanation, etc. are raised only when they appear directly relevant to the form-critical analysis and interpretation.

The adoption of a commentary format with specific categories for the analysis of the texts rests upon a conclusion that has become crucial for all form-critical work. If the results of form criticism are to be verifiable and generally intelligible, then the determination of typical forms and genres, their settings and functions, has to take place through the analysis of the forms in and of the texts themselves. This leads to two consequences for the volumes in this series. First, each interpretation of a text begins with the presentation of the *structure* of that text in outline form. The ensuing discussion of this structure attempts to distinguish the typical from the individual or unique elements, and to proceed on this basis to the determination of the *genre,* its *setting,* and its *intention.* Traditio-historical factors are discussed throughout this process where relevant; e.g., is there evidence of a written or oral stage of the material earlier than the actual text before the reader?

Second, the interpretation of the texts accepts the fundamental premise that we possess all texts basically at their latest written stages — technically speaking, at the levels of the final redactions. Any access to the texts, therefore, must confront and analyze that latest edition first, i.e., a specific version of that edition as represented in a particular text tradition. Consequently, the commentary proceeds from the analysis of the larger literary corpora created by the redactions back to any prior discernible stages in their literary history. Larger units are examined first, and then their subsections. Therefore, in most instances the first unit examined in terms of structure, genre, setting, and intention is the entire biblical book in question; next the commentary treats the individual larger and then smaller units.

The original plan of the project was to record critically all the relevant results of previous form-critical studies concerning the texts in question. While this remains one of the goals of the series, it had to be expanded to allow for more of the research of the individual contributors. This approach has proved to be important not only with regard to the ongoing insights of the contributors but also in view of the significant developments that have taken place in the field in recent years. The team of scholars responsible for the series is committed to following a basic design throughout the commentary, but differences of emphasis and even to some extent of approach will be recognized as more volumes appear. Each author will ultimately be responsible for his own contribution.

The use of the commentary is by and large self-explanatory, but a few comments may prove helpful to the reader. This work is designed to be used alongside the Hebrew text or a translation of the Bible. The format of the interpretation of the texts, large or small, is the same throughout, except in cases where the biblical material itself suggests a different form of presentation. Individual books and major literary corpora are introduced by a general bibliography referring to wider information on the subjects discussed and to works relevant for the subunits of that literary body. Whenever available, a special form-critical bibliography for a specific unit under discussion will conclude the discussion of that unit. In the outline of the structure of units, the system of sigla attempts to indicate the relationship and interdependence of the parts within that structure. The traditional chapter and verse divisions of the Hebrew text, as well as the versification of the *Revised Standard Version,* are supplied in the right-hand margin of the outlines.

In addition to the commentary on the biblical book, this volume includes a glossary of the genres discussed in the commentary. Many of the definitions in the glossary were prepared by Professor Sweeney, but some have arisen from the work of other members of the project on other parts of the Old Testament. Each subsequent volume will include such a glossary. Eventually, upon the completion of the commentary series, all of the glossaries will be revised in the light of the analysis of each book of the Old Testament and published as Volume XXIII of the series. The individual volumes will not contain special indices, but the indices for the entire series will be published as Volume XXIV.

The editors acknowledge with appreciation the contribution of numerous persons and institutions to the work of the project. All of the contributors have received significant financial, secretarial, and student assistance from their respective institutions. In particular, the editors have received extensive support from their universities. Without such concrete expressions of encouragement the work scarcely could have gone on. At Claremont, the Institute for Antiquity and Christianity has from its own inception provided office facilities, a supportive staff, and the atmosphere that stimulates not only individual but also team research. Emory University and the Candler School of Theology have likewise provided tangible support and encouragement. The editors are particularly indebted to Jacqueline E. Lapsley of Princeton Theological Seminary for her extraordinary editorial assistance in the preparation of this volume while she was a graduate student at Emory University, and to Dr. and Mrs. J. E. Williams for their generous financial support of our work.

ROLF P. KNIERIM
GENE M. TUCKER
MARVIN A. SWEENEY

AUTHOR'S PREFACE

It has now been several decades since the Old Testament Form Criticism Project was conceived and the Forms of the Old Testament Literature series began publication. In the meantime biblical scholarship has changed. The methods of modern historical scholarship, including form criticism, have been radically doubted, and there is no longer any consensus about the function of a commentary. In view of these changes, a work that purports to be a form-critical commentary probably needs to explain itself.

Form criticism is based on two insights of Hermann Gunkel: (1) that our understanding of any text is inevitably based on some concept of its genre; and (2) that the genres of Old Testament literature are more closely related to oral tradition than those of modern European literature. Early form critics also tended to assume that the contents as well as the forms of most texts were rooted in oral tradition. The identification of genre thus became instrumental in the traditio-historical quest for earlier versions of the material contained in the text. From the ideal form of the genre one could supposedly deduce what the original, presumably oral form of the text must have been.

All quests for the original forms of biblical texts have rightly been called into question, but this does not discredit Gunkel's basic insights. In fact, biblical scholarship's shift from a predominantly historical to a predominantly literary approach does nothing to diminish the importance of form criticism's main concerns. From a literary-critical perspective it can also be argued that the interpretation of any text entails some concept of its genre. Genre categories are always operative, consciously or subconsciously, in our understanding of language. For literary interpretation, the real issue is thus not whether the question of genre matters, but whether it is to be intentionally and explicitly addressed. When biblical scholarship does so with respect to its particular literary corpus, as I have done here with respect to some of the prophetic books, Gunkel's other claim also remains largely vindicated. As it turns out, many genres of Old Testament literature — or at least many of the prophetic genres that I have investigated here — are indeed more closely related to oral tradition than the genres of modern European literature.

This conclusion means only that biblical writers tended to pattern what they wrote on what they heard. It does not necessarily imply that there were earlier oral versions of any texts now contained in the Bible. Nor does it necessarily imply that any earlier oral versions, even if they once existed, are now recoverable from the final forms of biblical texts. When pursued as a primarily literary discipline, form criticism is mainly concerned with the genre of the final form of the text, and the question of whether the text had any historical antecedents is taken up if and only if the final form of the text provides some basis on which to do so. Sometimes the final form of a prophetic text is by definition predicated on the existence of earlier prophecies, and in such cases it may be helpful to pursue the historical question of what those earlier prophecies were, but only as far as the available information actually allows, and only in order to understand the final form of the text.

Although I take a primarily literary approach to form criticism, I have not found it possible to make a radical distinction between literature and history. Unlike the early form critics, I do not see the quest for the original form of the text as an integral part of the discipline. Unlike many contemporary literary critics, however, I do not see how an interpreter can avoid the historical questions that are inevitably raised by literary analysis itself. If language is always understood with reference to some social context, so is literature; and in the case of ancient documents literary interpretation thus entails some kind of historical investigation. Such historical investigation is the means to a literary end, however, not an end in itself.

Neither is form-critical analysis an end in itself. Consideration of genre is a key part of the interpretive process, but only a part. Form-critical analysis, of the sort that is undertaken here, focuses on this one aspect of interpretation at the expense of all the rest, in order to be of assistance to those who undertake the entire process. I thus imagine that readers wrestling with the meaning of a text from one of the prophetic books treated in this volume will eventually need to ask about its genre. If they do not want to conduct this part of the process from scratch, they may be helped by consulting this commentary. They will find in it a point of departure for their reflection on this one particular aspect of interpretation.

In the sections labeled "Text," there are preliminary analyses of only those text-critical and translation problems that have some direct bearing on form-critical issues, using the *Revised Standard Version* as a general point of reference. In the sections labeled "Structure," "Genre," and "Setting," readers have not only my considered opinion regarding the genre and the social context in which it was conventional, but also the literary structure analysis on which my opinion is based, and often a report of other scholarly opinions as well. If they do not find my conclusion persuasive, they will have information on which to base an alternative conclusion. They can thus bring an informed view of the text's genre to the larger consideration of its meaning. In the sections labeled "Intention," I have tried to signal the general direction in which the previously stated genre classification might take the readers' reflection on the text.

The textual analysis presented in these pages thus does not pretend to be a complete interpretation. The entire discussion specializes in form-critical issues, on the assumption that their clarification will make a signal contribution to the overall task of interpretation. The technicalities are validated by the creativity of the more complete interpretations that they help other readers to generate.

In working at this project off and on for many years, I have become indebted to more people than I can thank here. Some, however, cannot go unmentioned. While I was teaching at Texas Wesleyan University, President Jon Fleming and Dean Ronald Ballard encouraged me and allowed me time to begin this work. Parts of this volume were completed on various sabbatical leaves supported by the Trustees of the Episcopal Theological Seminary of the Southwest and the Conant Fund of the Episcopal Church's Board for Theological Education. Before the Seminary became completely computerized, page upon page was typed by Nancy Mourette Bose, our Faculty Secretary. Ehud Ben Zvi, Robert Haak, Roy Melugin, David Petersen, and Marvin Sweeney kindly gave preliminary versions of various sections a critical reading. (They are not to be implicated in any of my mistakes.) The onerous chore of final proofreading was shared by Webster Gibson and Mikail McIntosh-Doty. Pat Booher and Rob Cogswell, from the Library staff at the Seminary of the Southwest, have provided the most competent and agreeable research support that any writer could wish for.

Last but not least, I express my appreciation for the patience and good humor of my family: my wife April, who unwittingly married into this project; and my children Simeon, Hannah, and Joel, who have grown up thinking that it was a permanent part of my vocation.

San José, Costa Rica   MICHAEL H. FLOYD
May 11, 1999

NAHUM

Bibliography

E. Achtemeier, *Nahum–Malachi* (IntCom; Atlanta: John Knox, 1986); L. Alonso Schökel and J. L. Sicre Diaz, *Profetas: Comentario,* vol. 2 (NBE; Madrid: Cristiandad, 1980); W B. Becking, "Is het boek Nahum een literaire eenheid?" *NedTTs* 32 (1978) 107-24; K. J. Cathcart, *Nahum in the Light of Northwest Semitic* (BibOr 26; Rome: Biblical Institute Press, 1973); D. L. Christensen, "The Book of Nahum: The Question of Authorship within the Canonical Process," *JETS* 31 (1988) 51-58; idem, "The Book of Nahum as a Liturgical Composition: A Prosodic Analysis," *JETS* 32 (1989) 159-69; R. J. Coggins, "Nahum," in Coggins and S. P. Esther Re'emi, *Israel among the Nations: Nahum, Obadiah, Esther* (ITC; Grand Rapids: Eerdmans; Edinburgh: Handsel, 1985); K. Elliger, *Das Buch der zwölf Kleinen Propheten,* vol. 2 (4th ed.; ATD 25/2; Göttingen: Vandenhoeck & Ruprecht, 1959); F. O. García-Treto, "The Book of Nahum," *NIB* 7:593-619; A. Haldar, *Studies in the Book of Nahum* (Uppsala: Lundequistska Bokhandeln, 1947); F. Horst, "Nahum," in T. H. Robinson and Horst, *Die Zwölf Kleinen Propheten* (2nd ed.; HAT 14; Tübingen: Mohr [Siebeck], 1954); P. Humbert, "Le problème du livre de Nahoum," *RHPR* 12 (1932) 1-15; J. Jeremias, *Kultprophetie und Gerichtsverkündigung in der späten Königszeit Israels* (WMANT 35; Neukirchen-Vluyn: Neukirchener, 1970); C.-A. Keller, "Nahoum," in R. Vuilleumier and Keller, *Michée, Nahoum, Habacuc, Sophonie* (CAT 11b; Neuchâtel: Delachaux & Niestlé, 1971); W. A. Maier, *The Book of Nahum* (Saint Louis: Concordia, 1959); K. Marti, *Das Dodekapropheton* (KHC 13; Tübingen: Mohr [Siebeck], 1904); R. D. Patterson and M. E. Travers, "Literary Analysis and the Unity of Nahum," *GTJ* 9 (1988) 45-58; B. Renaud, "La composition du livre de Nahoum: Une proposition," *ZAW* 99 (1987) 198-219; J. J. M. Roberts, *Nahum, Habakkuk, and Zephaniah* (OTL; Louisville: Westminster/John Knox, 1991); W. Rudolph, *Micha, Nahum, Habakuk, Zephanja* (KAT 13/3; Gütersloh: Mohn, 1975); H. Schulz, *Das Buch Nahum* (BZAW 129; Berlin: de Gruyter, 1973); K. Seybold, *Profane Prophetie* (SBS 135; Stuttgart: Katholisches Bibelwerk, 1989); J. M. P. Smith, "Nahum," in Smith, W. H. Ward, and J. A. Bewer, *A Critical and Exegetical Commentary on Micah, Zephaniah, Nahum, Habakkuk, Obadiah, and Joel* (ICC; Edinburgh: T. & T. Clark, 1911); R. L.

Smith, *Micah–Malachi* (WBC 32; Waco: Word, 1984); K. Spronk, "Synchronic and Diachronic Approaches to the Book of Nahum," in *Synchronic or Diachronic? A Debate on Method in Old Testament Exegesis* (ed. J. C. de Moor; *OTS* 34; Leiden: Brill, 1995) 159-86; M. A. Sweeney, "Concerning the Structure and Generic Character of the Book of Nahum," *ZAW* 104 (1992) 364-77; A. S. van der Woude, "The Book of Nahum: A Letter Written in Exile," *OTS* 20 (1977) 108-26; J. D. W. Watts, *The Books of Joel, Obadiah, Jonah, Nahum, Habakkuk and Zephaniah* (CBC; Cambridge: Cambridge University Press, 1975).

Chapter 1

THE BOOK AS A WHOLE

Structure

The book of Nahum is largely concerned with a particular historical event: the fall of Nineveh to the combined forces of the Babylonians and Medes in 612 BCE. Scholars differ widely in their understanding of the document and of how it is related to this event. Some maintain that Nahum, unlike many prophetic books, did not go through successive stages of redaction. In their view the book is all of one piece, written by a single author sometime after the conquest of Thebes in 663 (an event that is retrospectively described in 3:8-10) but before the fall of Nineveh in 612. Scholars who share this view are by no means agreed, however, in their opinions on the nature of the document. Becking sees it simply as the prophet's means of publicizing his revelations concerning Nineveh's doom (pp. 122-24). Haldar sees it as a propagandistic tract written by Judahite cultic personnel in the late seventh century, conjuring up the prospect of liberation in order to foment popular opposition to Assyrian domination (pp. 147-49). Van der Woude sees Nahum as a letter from someone of northern Israelite descent whose ancestors were exiled by the Assyrians. This letter was supposedly written to Judahite coreligionists to comfort them during the reign of Manasseh when Assyrian influence on Judah was at its harshest (van der Woude, 124).

In contrast with such views, other scholars regard the book of Nahum as the product of redaction, resulting from the gradual editorial expansion of an original core of prophecies predating the fall of Nineveh. Again, however, there is little agreement even among those who share this general approach. Some see liturgical influence as a major factor in the book's formation, and others do not. Some think that the redactional process would have been finished relatively soon after 612 (e.g., Rudolph, 144-45), but others think that it extended on into the exilic or even postexilic period (e.g., Elliger, 2-3). Some define the original core in terms of one type of prophetic speech, while others define it in terms of another type.

For example, Humbert holds that prophecies anticipating Nineveh's defeat — prophecies that were perhaps originally intended for ritual proclamation — were soon afterward augmented with other materials to form the liturgy for a victory celebration ("Le problème," 3-4). Rudolph rejects the possibility of a cultic setting altogether (pp. 144-45), while Horst argues more guardedly that the original prophecies were edited soon after the event they foretold, not to form a liturgy per se but to be publicly read in a liturgical context (pp. 153-55).

Scholars who advocate some form of redactional theory are far from agreement on which parts of the book belonged to the original core and which were later additions. For example, Schulz (pp. 17-18) sees the prophecies of salvation addressed to Judah as the basic core, rather than the prophecies of punishment addressed to Assyria. This view stands diametrically opposed to that of Jeremias (pp. 48-53), who argues that the prophecies of punishment are the oldest material and that they were originally addressed to Judah rather than to Assyria.

There is likewise little unanimity regarding either the main parts of the book or the whole that they make up. For example, Roberts finds four major sections (1:2–2:1; 2:2-14; 3:1-17; 3:18-19) that together form a repeated announcement of Yahweh's impending judgment on Assyria (pp. 37-38). In contrast, Renaud finds five somewhat different sections (1:2-8; 1:9–2:3; 2:4-11; 2:12–3:17; 3:18-19) that collectively project the defeat of Nineveh onto an eschatological screen, so that it becomes the emblem of the final defeat of evil at the end of time (pp. 211-18). Sweeney, differing yet again, finds only three main sections (1:2-10; 1:11–2:1; 2:2–3:19), which he regards as a refutation speech of the sort that typically occurs in prophetic disputations, challenging the assumption that Yahweh is powerless by attributing the fall of Nineveh to him (pp. 374-77). No wonder Coggins (pp. 6-7) casts doubt on the very possibility of structural analysis — even as he proceeds to lay out his own somewhat different seven-section scheme!

The differences of opinion, of which those cited above are only a partial sample, are too numerous and diverse to address individually here. In raising the question of Nahum's overall nature and design and of the book's relation to the historical event on which it is largely focused, I will limit myself to the kinds of conclusions that can be drawn from a structural analysis of the book's final form, which after all constitutes the primary evidence. In view of a total lack of scholarly consensus, the structure analysis presented here can only be tentative. It will nevertheless serve heuristically as the ground on which to reconsider some of the larger questions of interpretation. I will discuss other scholarly theories only insofar as they reach conclusions based on similar grounds.

The superscription (1:1) describes this document as "a *maśśā'* (*RSV* 'oracle') concerning Nineveh," and "the book *(sēper)* of the revelation *(hǎzôn; RSV* 'vision') of Nahum." I will return to a consideration of what can be more specifically deduced from such terminology. Suffice it to note at the outset that the title (1:1a) relates the entire composition to the fate of Nineveh, regardless of whether this is explicit in any particular part of it. The subtitle (1:1b) further identifies the document as a written composition that is related to a revelation once mediated through a prophet named Nahum. My analysis of the main body thus focuses on two issues: (1) how the book as a whole presents the fall of Nineveh; and (2) how the book as a written composition relates to prophetic activity traditionally associated with the figure of Nahum, prophetic activity that may have initially involved written or oral communication. I consider these two issues in the light of what one can learn from examining the overall format of the main body, the various perspectives from which the fall of Nineveh is viewed, and the way in which the description of this event develops and progresses.

5

With respect to format, the first major section of the book (1:2–2:11) is addressed to a general audience, including but not limited to both Judahites and Assyrians. It recounts the fall of Nineveh from start to finish in 2:1-11, presenting it as a particular case of the way in which Yahweh generally treats his enemies (1:2-10), and as the eventual outcome of a historical process initiated by Yahweh long ago (1:11-14). More specifically, the announcement of Nineveh's fall serves to confirm previous prophecies (1:12-13) regarding the end to which the Assyrians' departure from Jerusalem in 701 (1:11) would inevitably lead, in accord with primordial precedent (1:2-10).

The second major section of the book (2:12–3:19) is addressed only to the Assyrians. The fall of Nineveh, which is episodically recounted in the progression from unit to unit, is presented as an event that has happened (3:13-19) to vindicate the claims of contemporary observers regarding the current international situation and Yahweh's involvement in it (2:12–3:7). More specifically, the announcement that Nineveh's once powerful commercial and ruling classes have disappeared into thin air (3:16) corroborates the prophetic claim that Yahweh is punishing Nineveh precisely because of the economic exploitation and political treachery that have characterized its dealings with other nations (3:1-4); the announcement that a mortally wounded king is the only remaining vestige of Assyrian leadership (3:18-19) corroborates the prophetic claim that Yahweh has doomed Assyria precisely because of its royal family's predatory behavior (2:12-14); and the announcement that Nineveh's defenses are irreparably breached (3:13-15a) corroborates the observation that the city's fortifications have become ripe for the taking (3:12).

The second section also presents the fall of Nineveh as happening in accord with the precedent set when the once invincible city of Thebes was previously overthrown by the Assyrians themselves (3:8-12). Just as Thebes was once subjected to a reversal of historical roles by the Assyrians, so that the conquerors became the conquered, the Assyrians are now being subjected to a similar reversal by a new imperial power.

When considered in terms of their contrasting perspectives, the two sections can be seen as complementary. The first section describes how the fall of Nineveh looks from a perspective that is predominantly Judahite in its orientation but also international in its scope. Viewed from this standpoint, the event is construed in the light of both older mythic traditions concerning Yahweh's primordial exploits and older prophetic traditions concerning Yahweh's past dealings with the Assyrians. The second section then goes back over the same ground in an extended flashback. It describes how the fall of Nineveh looks from a perspective that is predominantly Assyrian in its orientation but also broad enough in its scope to include Judah. Viewed from this standpoint, the event is construed in the light of both contemporary prophetic assessments of the situation and commonsense judgments regarding the Assyrians' inability to maintain the status quo indefinitely. These two perspectives differ somewhat in their respective assessments of how and why Nineveh fell, but they converge in portraying Yahweh as the one who is chiefly responsible for bringing this about.

The two sections are also complementary with respect to the overall development and progression in the description of Nineveh's fall. This event is first described, from the initial cry of alarm at the enemy's approach to the final deportation of the captives, at the conclusion of the first section (2:2-11). The second section then recapitulates the same progression, from the initial enemy threat (2:12-13) to the final dispersion of the survivors (3:18), but in a way that repeatedly thrusts readers into the middle of the action and each time brings them a little closer to the final outcome. This has an effect that is not unlike a parody of the death scene from an opera or classical drama, in which the main character has already reached the point of death but keeps reviving for one more farewell speech or one more aria before collapsing again and continuing to die.

As each unit of the second section begins, the fall of Nineveh is already in progress; and as each unit ends, no matter how far the devastation has progressed, the ultimate point of defeat has yet to be reached. The persistent repetition of this device shows it to be a deliberate compositional feature of this section within the larger framework of the book as a whole. The entire composition is designed first to tell the reader that Nineveh has been destroyed just as prophecies foretold, and then to bring the reader again and again to the point at which this prophesied outcome is an ever more foregone conclusion, although its utter completion remains to be seen.

From the foregoing observations regarding the format of the book's main body, the differing perspectives from which the fall of Nineveh is viewed, and the way in which the description of this event progresses and develops, one can draw some general conclusions about how the book presents the fall of Nineveh to its readers, and how the book depends on previously existing prophetic traditions.

First, the fall of Nineveh is presented from a retrospective standpoint as an event that has recently happened. At the same time it is presented as an event to be vicariously relived again and again, and as an event that maintains its relevance for succeeding generations, because it is a concrete historical example of a recurring situation in which Yahweh typically acts the same way. As creator of the world he can influence cosmic forces in favor of those who cooperate with him in maintaining a just world order, and he can influence cosmic forces to the detriment of those who oppose him in this regard. As the first section moves from this broad theological generalization about a particular pattern of divine involvement in human affairs to the specific case of Nineveh's overthrow, readers are challenged to consider whether their current situation might not be another instance of Yahweh's acting in accord with this same pattern, in which case they are also challenged to consider whether they belong among Yahweh's allies or among his foes.

In moving from a general description of how Yahweh treats his enemies and allies to a specific historical case, the book uses a device that requires readers to hesitate in identifying the cast of characters. At the outset readers know only that any characters they may meet will have something to do with Nineveh (1:1a). When characters are finally introduced, all are initially addressed or described without being named, which puts readers in the position of having to tell one from another by means of such meager distinctions as

7

their differing grammatical genders, while also trying to figure out the historical identity of each. The historical identities are eventually made explicit, but not before readers have had to form some tentative ideas on this score just to make provisional sense of the unfolding text. When each character is finally named, some readers may have to revise their earlier assumptions about who this is.

It gradually becomes clear that there are three main dramatis personae: a feminine character (1:11-13), who turns out to be a personification of Judah (2:1); a masculine character (1:14), who is not conclusively identified until the end of the book as the king of Assyria (3:18-19); and another feminine character (2:2), who turns out to be a personification of Nineveh (2:8; 3:7). The process of trial and error through which readers must go to identify these characters leaves a distinct impression of the uncertainties that are inevitably involved in any attempt to identify a particular historical situation with a general pattern of divine activity.

Second, the fall of Nineveh is presented as an event that looks pretty much the same no matter which of the book's perspectives its readers might tend to share. They might view this event from the perspective in which Yahweh's agency is explicitly acknowledged and prophetic revelation is held in high regard, as in the first section. Or they might view it from the perspective in which Yahweh's agency is not so widely recognized and prophetic revelation is no more highly regarded than commonsense observation, as in the second section. From either standpoint the Assyrians appear to have been caught in the interplay of historical forces with which human beings must from time to time interact, but over which humans have little control; and in the process the Assyrians have received their just deserts. It is implied that readers who see this have tacitly recognized Yahweh, but readers do not have to confess the God of Israel in order to grasp the universally comprehensible moral significance of Assyria's overthrow.

Third, the fall of Nineveh is presented as an event in which one can discern Yahweh's involvement through two different but mutually informative kinds of prophetic activity. Such prophetic insight can derive from studying the records of older prophecies concerning past events, as is the case in the first section of the book; it can also derive from intuitive analysis of contemporary affairs, as is the case in the second section. The book thus models for its readers the way in which they are to use it in discerning how Yahweh might be involved in their own situation. On the one hand they are to study the book as the record of a prophecy concerning a past event, thus learning how to recognize the pattern of divine activity that is evident in the fall of Nineveh. On the other hand they are to analyze their own situation intuitively, to see if they might discern this same pattern within the flux of current events.

With regard to the question of whether and to what extent the finished form of Nahum depends on previously existing prophetic traditions, the format of the book's first section is the primary source of information. It describes Nineveh's fall in 612 (2:1-11) as the fulfillment of two older prophecies (1:12-13 and 1:14) concerning the eventual outcome of an event that happened nearly a century earlier, i.e., the Assyrians' departure from Jerusalem in 701

(1:11; → 1:11-14, Text). This section thus presupposes the existence of previously existing traditions that were concerned with what this mysterious departure portended, based on prophecies made sometime after 701 but well before 612. The book itself, composed sometime after 612, is predicated on the assumption that the fall of Nineveh showed these older prophecies to have been more or less correct in their view of what would finally result from the Assyrians' retreat.

It is therefore probable that 1:12-13 and 1:14 are based on prophecies that originated sometime during the century prior to the composition of the book as a whole. Little more can be said with any certainty about the book's tradition history. Although both 1:12-13 and 1:14 are modeled on conventional types of prophetic speech, it is unlikely that either now remains in its original form (→ 1:11-14, Structure). It is therefore difficult to reach any conclusion regarding whether the older prophecies were oral or written, or how they were transmitted. It is possible that other parts of the book are also based on older traditions, but since they are not presented as such in the final form of the book, it is difficult to distinguish any material that is traditional from material that is not. Although many of the book's individual units have generic forms that are typical of independently existing prophetic speeches, this does not necessarily mean that these units ever existed independently (→ 1:2–2:11, Setting; also 2:12–3:19, Setting).

With regard to the formation of prophetic books in general, scholars usually assume that the original core of prophetic tradition can be attributed to the prophetic figure for whom the book is named. On this assumption one could suppose that the tradition underlying 1:12-13 and 1:14 derives from Nahum himself, and that the book into which this tradition has been incorporated is the work of a later anonymous author. It is conceivable, however, that the tradition underlying 1:12-13 and 1:14 derives from an anonymous prophetic figure, and that the book into which it has been incorporated is the work of Nahum. It is even conceivable, if the prophecies underlying 1:12-13 and 1:14 date to a time rather long after the event they serve to interpret, that Nahum was responsible for both the original prophecies and the book into which they were subsequently incorporated. Because the superscription is in third person biographical rather than first person autobiographical style, the first of these three possibilities is more probable than the other two. Since we know next to nothing about Nahum and his career as a prophet, however, deciding among these possibilities would not enhance our understanding of the text to any great extent.

From an analysis of the compositional form, this appears to be a book about a revelation received by a prophet sometime during the seventh century, a revelation concerning the long-range implications of the Assyrians' retreat from Jerusalem in 701. The book was written sometime after the fall of Nineveh in 612 by someone who had studied the record of the earlier revelation and who saw this event as the fulfillment of what the earlier revelation had anticipated. The book, which at some point became associated with the name of Nahum, was written to show that Nineveh had fallen in accord with what had earlier been foreseen, and to deduce what later generations could generally learn from this. The document is in this sense "the book of the revelation *(ḥāzôn)* of Nahum" (1:1b; on the meaning of *ḥāzôn* [*RSV* "vision"] in this context, → 1:1, Structure). We have now to consider in what sense it is also a *maśśā'* (1:1a; *RSV* "oracle").

Genre

Many commentators continue to regard the book of Nahum as a collection of prophetic speeches and poems that are lumped together only because they all relate in some way to the theme of Assyria's decline and fall (e.g., Seybold, 19; Roberts, 9-11, 37-38). In its overall arrangement such a document is not supposed to follow the conventions of any particular genre. As the structure analysis of the book's major sections will show, however, the individual units of the text are carefully organized into a recurring conventional pattern, and compositions formed in accord with this pattern were typically used to teach the lessons that could be learned from the past when viewed through prophetic eyes (→ 1:2–2:11; 2:12–3:19). The book of Nahum, in each of its two main parts, bears the generic stamp of the (→) prophetic historical exemplum. The issue is thus not whether the book is organized along generic lines, but whether the book as a whole bears the stamp of the same genre as its subsidiary sections, or perhaps of some similar genre. Past scholarship has not often given due consideration to the issue of the genre of the parts in relation to the genre of the whole. When it has, only two of the resulting theories have managed to gain any measure of acceptance. The book as a whole has been described as an extended eschatological hymn and as a prophetic liturgy.

According to the first of these two theories, the book becomes a kind of eschatological vision because of the way in which prophecies concerning the historical event of Nineveh's fall have been redacted to give them an eschatological significance (e.g., Schulz, 99-101; Renaud, 213-18). Like the figure of Babylon in the book of Revelation, the personification of Nineveh here becomes a symbol of all that is evil; and the overthrow of Nineveh thus represents the consummate deliverance of Yahweh's elect through his final defeat of the forces of evil at the end of time (e.g., B. S. Childs, *Introduction to the Old Testament as Scripture* [Philadelphia: Fortress, 1979] 443-46). For supporting evidence those who hold this view often adduce the reference to Judah's enemy as *bĕlîyā'al* (*RSV* "the wicked") in 2:1b (cf. 1:11), arguing that this casts Nineveh in the role of Belial, a satanic figure who often figures prominently in late postexilic eschatological scenarios (e.g., Jeremias, 14-15; Renaud, 203). The thesis depends primarily, however, on the argument that the introduction in 1:2-8 is a hymn that serves to "eschatologize" the battle description running through the rest of the book, action that would otherwise seem to remain on an earthly historical plane.

Both of these arguments are untenable. There is no evidence that the term *bĕlîyā'al* had come to denote a personification of evil by the time Nahum is generally supposed to have reached its final form (Sweeney, 366-67). In both 2:1 and 1:11 this word can only have the meaning that it ordinarily denoted before it became a proper name, i.e., "self-destructive lawlessness" (→

10

1:11-14, Structure). The use of this term thus does not automatically carry with it any eschatological connotations. More importantly, however, the function of 1:2-8 in the book as a whole cannot be accurately described as an "eschatologizing" one.

Despite the scholarly consensus that 1:2-8 provides a hymnic introduction to the book as a whole, it is doubtful that this is so (→ 1:2-10, Genre). It is therefore problematic to assume that Nahum's description of Nineveh's defeat is rhetorically comparable to the descriptions of Yahweh's victories in the Psalms. Even if this were the case, however, for two reasons one cannot really say that 1:2-8 adds an eschatological dimension to the action in the rest of the book. First, the description in 1:2-8 is itself not eschatological in any strict sense. There is undoubtedly an allusion to Yahweh's primordial combat with the forces of chaos in 1:4, but this mythic precedent is the basis on which the text describes how he may generally act at any time (1:2-3, 7-8), not how he will specifically act at the end of time. The description in 1:2-8 shows no trace of an *Urzeit-Endzeit* polarity. Second, the present compositional form of the book as a whole does not develop conceptually from the specific case of Nineveh's fall to its broader theological implications, even if such thinking was originally the impetus for the redactor to elaborate on prophecies concerning this event. The book now moves conceptually in precisely the opposite direction, from broad generalizations regarding a pattern of divine activity to a specific historical case of it. The point is not to add to Nineveh's defeat any larger dimension of meaning that was once not perceived, nor to make it the symbol of something yet to come, but to present this event as a concrete temporal actualization of an eternal divine potential. The book as a whole thus cannot be characterized as an extended eschatological hymn.

The other theory, that the book is a prophetic liturgy, is also problematic. Following Humbert ("Essai d'analyse," 269-72; "Le problème," 3-4), several scholars have argued that the shift from one addressee to another, which occurs at various points throughout the book, is symptomatic of the way in which various officiants and members of the congregation typically respond to one another in worship (e.g., G. Fohrer, *Introduction to the Old Testament* [tr. D. E. Green; Nashville, Abingdon, 1968] 449-51). On closer examination, however, this turns out not to be the case. The composition of Nahum does not actually entail the quasi-dramatic alternation of voices that is generally characteristic of liturgy, but only a single prophetic voice that is alternately directed to various different addressees (J. H. Eaton, *Vision in Worship* [London: SPCK, 1981] 14-21). Some scholars have therefore retreated to a weaker form of the liturgical theory, arguing that Nahum is a composition designed for liturgical recitation rather than a liturgy per se (e.g., Watts, 5-6; Christensen, "Liturgical Composition," 168-69). Other scholars, however, would now go no farther than Coggins, who grants that "a good deal of the material in the book shows affinities with what appears to be 'cultic usage,'" but concludes that this may only imply "an indebtedness to the language of the cult" (p. 10).

Although the theory of Nahum as a prophetic liturgy has not proved tenable in its original form, in its modified form it poses a question that still remains open: Is this the type of composition that was intended to be publicly read or recited in a liturgical context? This may be the case because both of its two major sections have the same genre as texts like Deut 32 and Ps 78, poems that were presumably intended for such liturgical usage. From this fact it does not necessarily follow that (→) 1:2–2:11 and (→) 2:12–3:19 were used in a liturgical setting, or that together they form a composition used in a liturgical setting. In the final analysis one must account not only for the resemblance between the main body (1:2–3:19) and such prophetic didactic psalms but also for the relationship between the superscription (1:1) and the main body (1:2–3:19). On this level, as well as the level of the main body itself, the book of Nahum and this group of psalms may no longer be comparable.

The liturgical theory also calls attention to a prominent feature of the text that requires explanation, regardless of how the question of Nahum's liturgical recitation is finally resolved. Taken together, the book's individual units may not constitute integral parts of a prophetic liturgy; but considered separately, each of them could conceivably have a setting in the cult or royal court. As the analysis of the individual units will show, nearly all of them use rhetorical conventions of direct address resembling those that are at home in some kind of ritual or ceremonial context — the kind of symbolically defined context, for example, in which a character personifying the city of Nineveh is at least figuratively present, or perhaps even played by an actor, and can thus be apostrophized or dramatically addressed by a prophet of Yahweh (as is the case with respect to the five individual units in 2:2–3:17). This fact does not necessarily mean that the individual units with such traits ever existed independently, or that they were ever actually used in a cultic setting. Nor does this fact necessarily have any direct bearing on the question of whether the book as a whole was designed for liturgical recitation (→ 1:2–2:11, Setting). If, however, one proposes that the book was designed for some other purpose, one must also explain why the book consistently employs the kinds of direct address that reflect the symbolically represented presence of characters personifying nations and cities.

Sweeney has proposed that the main body of Nahum resembles the kind of refutation speech that typically forms part of a (→) prophetic disputation (pp. 374-77). This avoids some of the problems associated with the theories of Nahum as an eschatological hymn or prophetic liturgy, but it does not reckon sufficiently with the phenomenon of alternating direct addressees. Sweeney's proposal is also problematic because a disputation usually includes an explicit statement of the position or attitude with which the prophet wishes to contend (→ Hag 1:2-11, Genre), and such a statement is lacking here. Sweeney argues that the issue in dispute is implied in the introductory unit (1:2-10), which imputes to the audience the opinion that Yahweh has no power over world affairs. After contending with the audience on this point, the prophet attempts to refute it in the rest of the book (1:11–3:19) by showing the fall of Nineveh to be an act of Yahweh. Without any explicit indication that 1:2-10 is in fact contentious, however, it is difficult to tell whether it should be taken in this way. The introductory unit might just as plausibly be taken as an axiomatic assertion that Yahweh has the power to destroy his enemies and protect his allies, thus giving rise to the question of who his enemies and allies are. The rest of the book might then be seen as a response to this open question, showing (among other things) that these roles can be reversed over time. In any case the theory of a prophetic refutation speech does not adequately explain the conventions of direct address that are such a striking feature of Nahum.

Sweeney identifies the addressees as Assyria, Judah, Nineveh, and the Assyrian king, but it is difficult to tell what kind of rhetorical situation he imagines for a prophetic disputation that would include all these parties. In what context might a prophet even fictively engage an audience that is Assyrian as well as Judahite, attempting to disabuse both groups of a commonly held opinion regarding Yahweh's power or lack thereof? The setting of a prophetic disputation is usually conceived as a prophet's face-to-face encounter with a live audience, in which an attempt is being made to change the group's opinion or attitude (A. Graffy, *A Prophet Confronts His People* [AnBib 104; Rome: Biblical Institute Press, 1984] 118-24). Some of the texts that have been classed as prophetic disputations are probably fictional examples of the genre that were never actually used in such a setting, but even in these cases an element of verisimilitude is maintained with respect to the way the audience is characterized, so that one can still realistically imagine the speaker in a face-to-face encounter with the kind of group that a prophetic disputant might have confronted. This is hardly the case with regard to Nahum.

Of course one can never actually address an entire nation or city, but one might nevertheless conceivably address a group as "Judah" or "Nineveh" if the occasion were one on which they might be recognized as representatives of the whole population. Granting such hyperbole here, it is still difficult to see in Nahum any reflection of the kind of situation in which a prophetic disputation might realistically occur. For Nahum to be categorized as even a fictional example of this genre, one would have to imagine an occasion on which representatives of an imperial power like Assyria might gather with representatives of a small state like Judah, and might find themselves confronted by a prophet who attempts to disabuse them of their common misconceptions regarding the god of the smaller nation — an occasion on which the imperial king might also be present in person and not only allow his subjects to be insultingly condemned but also suffer himself to be pronounced as good as dead! Because such a scenario is so unrealistic, and because the text also lacks any explicit statement of a position to refute, it is difficult to see how Nahum can be regarded as a refutation speech from a prophetic disputation.

In view of the difficulties entailed by attempts to classify the genre of Nahum as an extended eschatological hymn, a prophetic liturgy, and a prophetic refutation speech, we now turn back to the information given in the superscription, which identifies the book of Nahum as "a *maśśā'* concerning Nineveh" (1:1a). The *RSV* rather neutrally translates this term as "oracle," thus reflecting the impasse reached by scholars in attempting to understand *maśśā'* on the basis of its etymology. Weis has broken this impasse with a more form-critical approach to the problem, providing a definition that is helpful in understanding the form and function of this book as a whole. On the basis of his study the genre of Nahum can be more adequately described in a way that is consistent with the text's own self-designation.

Weis finds *maśśā'* to be a genre term that applies to both a type of prophetic speech and a type of prophetic literature, and in the latter case it can apply to works of prophetic literature as a whole or in part. Examples of this genre show great formal diversity, but a particular cluster of basic elements is generally found in most of them: (1) oracular speech of Yahweh; (2) reports of past and/or present events; and (3) commands and/or prohibitions directly addressed to the audience, sometimes within the context of what the prophet says in Yahweh's name and sometimes within the context of the prophet's own words. The function of this combination of elements is generally to explain how some previously communicated expression of the divine will is now being realized, or is about to be realized, in the realm of human affairs. The audience is thus informed about what Yahweh is doing in the present time on the basis of what he was once revealed to be doing at an earlier time, and also given some direction concerning an appropriate response on their part (Weis, 273-74). Defined thus, a *maśśā'* is a kind of revelation that serves to interpret the present applicability of a previous revelation. Weis therefore suggests that one appropriate translation for *maśśā'* would be "prophetic interpretation of revelation."

In the case of Nahum there is a report of a past event in 1:11; there are speeches of Yahweh representing previously revealed expressions of the divine will in 1:12-14, as well as other speeches of Yahweh explaining how these older prophecies are presently being fulfilled in 2:12–3:7; and in 2:1-2 and 3:14-15 there are commands urging the audience to take appropriate measures in response to Yahweh's initiatives. The book as a whole thus shows the basic elements that are characteristic of the MAŚŚĀ', and together these elements function as a prophetic interpretation of revelation.

This genre classification obviates some fallacious presuppositions that have occasionally thwarted efforts to explain the literary form of Nahum. Some have assumed that a prophetic book with literary compositional integrity cannot also be the product of redaction (e.g., Becking, 122-24; Patterson and Travers, 58); or that literary compositional integrity in the final form of a prophetic book precludes the delineation of any previously existing prophetic traditions on which the book might have been based (e.g., Christensen, "Question of Authorship," 57). A demonstration of literary compositional integrity, however, does not in itself resolve the question of whether or to what extent the text is redactional. One must also ask what kind of compositional integrity and what kind of redactional activity are involved. For example, a *maśśā'* is a type of prophetic literature that is defined in terms of a previously existing prophecy, and it is thus a literary genre whose compositional form often incorporates within it some citation of this previous prophecy. Precisely because Nahum has the kind of literary compositional integrity that is characteristic of a *maśśā'*, it is possible to identify this prophetic book as a later author's elaboration of older prophecies, and to find traces of these older prophecies in 1:12-13 and 1:14 (although Weis himself regards Nahum as an exception in this regard [pp. 151-60]; → Structure).

In view of the great formal diversity that is allowed by the above definition of the *maśśā'*, it is important to note not only how each example of the genre fits the basic description but also how each example's distinctive qualities modify the basic form and function. Nahum also has other prominent features that make it a unique example of this genre, and these pose two issues that need further clarification.

First, although the *maśśā'* is defined flexibly enough to allow the basic elements of the genre to combine with other elements in various configurations, in this particular case the basic elements combine with others so as to assume a rather different generic form in each of the book's two major sections. The analysis below presents both 1:2–2:11 and 2:12–3:19 as examples of the (→) prophetic historical exemplum. In what sense do two prophetic historical exempla make a *maśśā'*?

The two genres are not all that different. The prophetic historical exemplum asks the audience to view the past in a certain way, so as to reveal patterns of divine activity still operative in the present. The *maśśā'* directs the audience to engage the present in a certain way because Yahweh is acting in accord with a pattern revealed in the past. Both of these rhetorical strategies are at work throughout Nahum, but one appears to predominate when the book is viewed in terms of its two main sections and the other appears to predominate when it is viewed as a whole. When the two main sections are considered separately, the textual features that unify the parts of each section and distinguish the sections from each other are emphasized. Viewing the text from this standpoint, one notices that the two sections represent two different ways of learning a lesson from the past (→ Structure), and the rhetorical strategy of the prophetic historical exemplum is foregrounded. When the two main sections are considered as integral parts of the book as a whole, however, their common features and their complementary differences are emphasized. Viewing the text from this standpoint, one notices that these two different ways of learning from the past have basically the same implications for how to engage the present, and the rhetorical strategy of the *maśśā'* is foregrounded. In their complementary relationship with each other, the two prophetical historical exempla are thus integrated into the *maśśā'* of the whole.

Second, the conventions of direct address remain to be explained. If the book is a literary composition, why does it use the kinds of direct address that seem, at least on first glance, to reflect the kind of symbolically defined context in which ritual is performed — a scene populated by characters personifying nations, cities, and kings, to each of whom this prophetic voice speaks in turn? Do such rhetorical conventions mean that the book was intended to be read or recited in the cult or royal court? Moreover, how are such rhetorical conventions consistent with the design of a *maśśā'*? In a *maśśā'* the commands are supposed to direct the people of Yahweh in their response to what he is currently doing, but in Nahum there is apparently just one command of this sort (2:1b). Most of the commands describing reactions to Yahweh are actually addressed to Nineveh (2:2; 3:14-15). The theory of Nahum's being a *maśśā'* may at first seem to be as problematic in this regard as the theory of its being a prophetic disputation, but this does not finally turn out to be the case.

Because the *maśśā'* is also a form of (→) prophetic speech, even a fictional literary adaptation of the genre — like the one here — remains a realistic reflection of the way in which prophetic discourse was actually conducted. In order to understand the rhetorical conventions that are operative in Nahum, one must therefore ask if there are situations in which a prophet might function in the way that is generally implied by the *maśśā'* form, and in the process have occasion to use this kind of direct address. In what situation might a prophet be called to assess Yahweh's involvement in the immediate situation, informed by the history of Yahweh's involvement in such situations, and then give advisory directives regarding the community's response? In what situation of this kind might a prophet also have occasion to address either persons who were actually the designated official representatives of nations and cities or symbolic personifications of nations and cities?

This is Isaiah's situation during the Assyrian siege of Jerusalem in the reign of Hezekiah (2 Kgs 18:13–19:37). After the siege is begun Hezekiah sends a delegation to Isaiah, asking him to intercede on Jerusalem's behalf. Isaiah replies in the form of an oracle assuring Hezekiah that the Assyrians will be prompted to leave, that the siege will thus fail, and that the Assyrian king will eventually be killed. This oracle advising Hezekiah not to surrender is directly addressed to him, but Isaiah does not speak it to him in person. He speaks it to the king's representatives, who are then to take the message to the king (2 Kgs 19:6-7).

Again, when Hezekiah has prayed for deliverance, Isaiah sends him another oracular message. This one is also directly addressed to Hezekiah, though delivered by messengers and not spoken to him in person by the prophet (2 Kgs 19:20-34). The oracular speech addressed to Hezekiah contains within it an oracular speech addressed directly to the Assyrian king, informing him that Yahweh, who has given him his past victories, is now going to send him defeat (2 Kgs 19:21-28). The Assyrian king does not actually receive this message, for it is neither spoken to him personally by Isaiah nor delivered to him through messengers. Although directly addressed to the Assyrian king, it is to be spoken in the presence of Hezekiah. The Assyrian king is present in the sense that he is encamped with his army outside the city wall, but not in the sense that he is ever within earshot of the words ostensibly addressed to him. The words ostensibly addressed to the Assyrian king are actually for Hezekiah's benefit.

Isaiah does not formulate a prophecy that has the form of a *maśśā'* per se, but throughout the story he is involved in prophetic activity that has basically the same function as this form of prophetic speech. He attempts to assess Yahweh's involvement in the immediate situation, informed by the historical precedent of how Yahweh defended Jerusalem in the time of David (2 Kgs 19:34). In so doing, he in effect advises Hezekiah regarding the appropriate course of action for the community to take.

This is the kind of situation into which Nahum draws its readers and makes them participants. As they become accustomed to the gradually emerging scene, readers find themselves in a city threatened by siege. The prophetic voice always plays a role that, like Isaiah, is attempting to assess Yahweh's involvement in the immediate situation on the basis of historical precedent. It first addresses itself, again like Isaiah, to a character playing the role of Judah's designated representative (1:11–2:1 [*RSV* 1:11–1:15]). Through this representative the prophetic voice sends to Judah the message that Yahweh is delivering them, just as he previously said he would. Within the message sent to Judah, as in Isaiah's message sent to Hezekiah, there is an oracle directly addressed to the Assyrian king (1:14) but not actually spoken in his presence.

At this point the prophetic voice assumes a role that is not directly comparable with the role of Isaiah in 2 Kgs 18:13–19:37, but one that is nevertheless still in keeping with the general situation of a city threatened by siege. It assumes the role of a sentinel stationed on Jerusalem's city wall (→ 2:1-11, Genre), announcing the arrival of messengers bringing the good news that Assyria has been defeated, and that the threat of siege has thus vanished (2:1). The same prophetic voice then suddenly switches into an ironic mode, still playing the role of a sentinel but now pretending to be on Nineveh's city wall. It thus announces to the character personifying Nineveh that the city has come under siege (2:2). The prophetic voice then continues in this vein for the rest of the book (2:2–3:19), addressing mostly the same personification of Nineveh and reinforcing its ironic assumption of the sentinel role (→ 3:13-17, Genre), but also addressing again the character of the Assyrian king (3:18-19). Like the first speech addressed to the character of the Assyrian king (1:14), the speeches in 2:2–3:19 addressed to Nineveh and to him are never actually meant for their ears. They are rather meant to be overheard by the character playing the role of Judah's representative and are actually for Judah's benefit.

Although the conventions of direct address used in Nahum are somewhat similar to ones that might also be used in a ritual setting, they neither entail ritual acts nor reflect a cultic tableau. They rather reflect a crisis situation in which prophets could become involved in public affairs, actually addressing themselves to the officially designated representatives of their own community, and in the process also figuratively addressing themselves to symbolic personifications of their enemies. The book of Nahum is a fictional but realistic representation of such a situation. The prophetic voice addresses itself to a character who is a representative of Judah, and in the process also addresses itself to characters who are symbolic personifications of Nineveh and the king of Assyria. The scene shifts from the time when Jerusalem was besieged by the Assyrians to the time when Nineveh's defeat signaled that this would never threaten to recur. There is also a move from one locale to another and a concomitant reversal of status as the scene shifts from the locale of Jerusalem, where the Assyrians are the besiegers, to the locale of Nineveh, where the Assyrians are the besieged. Throughout these changes the same prophetic voice speaks in various modes from the same general background situation of a city threatened by siege.

When Nahum's conventions of direct address are understood in this way, they are consistent with the design of a *maśśā'*. Although most of the commands are ostensibly addressed to Nineveh (2:2; 3:14-15), they nevertheless serve to show Yahweh's people how to respond to what he is currently doing. They are ironic commands that are figuratively addressed to the symbolic personification of Nineveh but are actually intended for the benefit of the character representing Judah. They urge Nineveh to take protective measures, but in a

17

context that underscores how futile such measures have become — like cries to throw a life preserver to a person who has already drowned and been pulled from the water (→ 3:13-17, Structure). In effect they underscore the hopelessness of Nineveh's situation, and thus reinforce the command directed explicitly to Judah, to "keep your feasts" (2:1b), and thus join in the joyful worldwide response to the news of Assyria's overthrow (3:19b).

Setting

When the conventions of direct address in Nahum are understood in this way, the idea of the book's being initially designed for liturgical reading or recitation becomes considerably less compelling — though of course all Scripture eventually came to be used in this way. When seen in the context of the individual units or the two main sections of the book, the cases of direct address in Nahum could conceivably be of a ritual sort. When seen in the context of the book as a whole, however, it is evident that they are not. This negative conclusion regarding a liturgical setting means that the book of Nahum is not a direct or particularly helpful source of information about cultic prophecy, but it nevertheless has some indirect bearing on this subject. It challenges some of the rather simplistic dichotomies in terms of which the discussion of cultic prophecy has sometimes been carried out.

At least with respect to preexilic times, cultic prophets are often assumed to have been chauvinistic promisers of national salvation who thought that Yahweh would always preserve his people at the expense of other nations, and noncultic prophets are assumed to have been moralistic presagers of national doom who realized that Yahweh's justice transcended all national distinctions. On this basis Nahum has been called a cultic prophet just because this book celebrates Judah's liberation from Assyrian tyranny (e.g., Fohrer, *Introduction*, 449-51), and on a similar basis attempts have been made to rescue him from this charge by arguing conversely that — contrary to the obvious impression given in the book's final form — he originally prophesied Yahweh's punishment of Judah (e.g., Jeremias, 20-42).

The text itself, however, resists being straitjacketed into either side of this dichotomy. It certainly presents a message of salvation for Judah, but this message is neither rooted in cultic practices nor based on the assumption that Yahweh will always favor his own people over other nations. It appears to be rooted in a noncultic type of prophetic activity, and it is based on a quite different and more complex set of assumptions, such as: both Yahweh's people and other nations can become either his allies or his enemies; the status of any nation as an ally or enemy of Yahweh can change over time; and one nation can be inadvertently affected by the consequences of another's choice in this regard. The stereotype of the noncultic prophet as one who traffics only in jeremiads is thus called into question, and so is the converse stereotype of the cultic prophet as one who has an overly optimistic monopoly on promises of salvation.

On the whole the book of Nahum is conditioned by the necessity of ex-

18

plaining momentous current events in terms of Yahweh's unfolding purpose. This reflects a setting in which prophets were called on to provide, or felt compelled to volunteer, their perception of Yahweh's involvement in the present world situation. Kings and their advisers, or other such groups of leaders, were typically the recipients of this information. They might request such prophetic assistance in private consultation (Jer 38:14) or through go-betweens (Jer 37:3-10), and prophets might confront kings with unsolicited advice in the course of their daily duties (Isa 7:1-9) or give information to a group of leaders assembled for the purpose of receiving it (Ezek 8:1–11:25).

The book more specifically reflects a setting in which prophets attempted to understand Yahweh's present purposes through their study of what previous prophets had discerned, basing these attempts on their observations concerning whether and how previous prophecies had materialized. They studied prophecies that seemed not to have been fulfilled when they were first proclaimed to see if they might now be coming to fulfillment. They also studied prophecies that seemed to have been fulfilled when they were first proclaimed to see what could be learned from them as validated precedents.

In the case of Nahum the earlier prophecies (1:12-14) regarding the significance of the Assyrians' departure from Jerusalem (1:11) might well have seemed questionable in view of what a minor setback this actually was for Assyria's control of Judah. Although Jerusalem was spared when they left, the yoke of Judah's bondage was hardly broken in accord with 1:12-13; and although Sennacherib was killed about twenty years later, Assyrian royal power did not immediately collapse in accord with 1:14. Signs of potential weakening in Assyria's power, like the revolts intermittently fomented by the Babylonians during the seventh century, would have nevertheless kept some interest in these prophecies alive. Not until the reign of Josiah, however, when Judah managed to assert a measure of independence and Nineveh was finally overthrown, could any plausible claims have been made regarding their fulfillment. The book of Nahum not only makes such claims; it also reinforces them by presenting revelations contemporary with the fall of Nineveh, asserting that this is an act of Yahweh. With his own prophetic insight regarding the events of 612, the author confirms his predecessor's prophetic insight regarding the plan of Yahweh incipient in the events of 701.

The author presents his conclusions, based on his study of older prophetic traditions, in the form of a written document. In order to produce such a written document through this kind of study, a person would need to have scribal training and would probably belong to a group that kept written records of older prophecies. Prophets belonging to such groups wrote books like Nahum to be studied among themselves, and to be used for the instruction of public officials and others who needed to learn the lessons of the past in order to govern and guide their people in the present.

With regard to the composition history of Nahum, it is possible to identify only the approximate span of time over which it was produced. The prophecies that underlie 1:12-13 and 1:14 came sometime after 701 but well before 612, and the final form of the book came sometime after 612. There were perhaps some intervening stages of development, but these cannot be determined with any certainty. It is possible, for example, that the prophecies of punishment in (→) 2:12-14 and (→) 3:1-7 were proclaimed in some form at a point after Nineveh was threatened by siege but before the city's final defeat. This does not necessarily follow, however, from the fact that these units are identifiable as prophecies of punishment. It is also possible that they were composed for their present literary context (→ 2:12–3:19, Setting). It is difficult to say just how soon after 612 the book would have reached its final form. The text shows no sign of the bitter consternation that later resulted when the Babylonians, who had been hailed as Yahweh's means of rectifying the misrule of the Assyrians, turned out to be just as oppressive (→ Hab 1:2-17). The book thus perhaps reached its final form before the Babylonian hegemony extended to include Judah, within about a decade after 612.

Intention

Modern commentators often describe the book of Nahum as "nationalistic" and make disparaging comments about the immorality of its "vengeful" sentiments. Interpretations of this sort are problematic in two major respects. First, they assume incorrectly that Nahum's joy over Assyria's downfall stems from a chauvinistic theology, for which it is axiomatic that any enemy of Judah is an enemy of Yahweh. I have already noted some of the ways in which the book is designed precisely to challenge any tendency on the part of its readers to make such an equation. Second, such critiques of Nahum imply that modern theology has some better way of describing divine involvement in international affairs, which is hardly the case. Modern theology has generally tended to avoid this subject by relegating theological statements to the realm of human emotion, or to deal with it provisionally by using admittedly inadequate Marxist categories. Nahum rubs many modern commentators the wrong way because it exposes this deficiency.

The book of Nahum presents the fall of Nineveh in 612 as the culmination of a plan instigated by Yahweh. This plan was in accord with his power and ability, manifest from creation, to maintain a just world order. It began with an event whose potential could be seen only through prophetic eyes, with the Assyrians' departure from Jerusalem in 701. In light of these antecedents, the fall of Nineveh signaled Yahweh's intention to restore to Judah and Israel a status like the one they enjoyed before their sins made Yahweh send the Assyrians against them. Yahweh's decision to destroy the Assyrians, and thus to use them no longer as instruments of his purpose, was motivated by their self-aggrandizing abuse of their power over subject nations. They have become liable to defeat, just like the overweening imperial powers that they themselves have overthrown. Along with those who joyfully behold the spectacle of their overthrow, the Assyrians must learn the lesson of why their great power has now come to nothing.

The book of Nahum is designed to get its readers to relive this historical process, which appears from hindsight to be the fulfillment of originally uncertain revelations. They can thereby learn to discern whether God is doing something similar in their own day. Readers are thus led to examine the contemporary situation for similarly uncertain signs of the same kind of divine action: A tyrant has been vanquished in what appears to be part of God's plan to deliver his people from the fatal historical consequences of their own sins, and to secure for them a form of existence that is appropriate under the newly emerging historical conditions. This plan appears to be carried out as part of a larger process in which all worldly powers, including the people of God, are being held accountable for their actions. The principalities and powers should thus be able to see that their dominance is subject to the same moral contingencies as the dominance of those whom they displaced. If they fail to see this, they will find themselves confronting the Lord of history as their enemy, and the world will rejoice as their power comes to nothing.

Readers of Nahum are first of all challenged to discern whether and how this pattern is applicable. In the process of discovering its applicability they are further challenged to discern whether they themselves are among God's enemies and, if so, they are encouraged not to remain in that condition.

Bibliography

P. Humbert, "Essai d'analyse de Najoum 1:2–2:3," *ZAW* 44 (1926) 266-80; C.-A. Keller, "Die theologische Bewältigung der Geschichtlichen Wirklichkeit in der Prophetie Nahums," *VT* 22 (1972) 399-419; J. L. Mihelic, "The Concept of God in the Book of Nahum," *Int* 2 (1948) 199-207; R. Weis, "A Definition of the Genre *Maśśā'* in the Hebrew Bible" (Diss., Claremont Graduate School, 1986); W. C. van Wyk, "Allusions to 'Prehistory' and History in the Book of Nahum," in *De fructu oris sui (Fest.* A. van Selms; ed. I. H. Eybers et al.; POS 9; Leiden: Brill, 1971) 222-32.

Chapter 2

THE SUPERSCRIPTION (1:1)

Structure

I. Main title		1:1a
A. General designation: *maśśa'*		1:1aα
B. Specification: concerning Nineveh		1:1aβ
II. Subtitle		1:1b
A. General designation: book of the vision . . .		1:1bα
B. Specification: of Nahum the Elkoshite		1:1bβ

Genre

Nahum opens with a variation on the kind of PROPHETIC SUPERSCRIPTION that can also be found at the beginning of Isaiah, Jeremiah, Amos, Obadiah, and Habakkuk. This kind of prophetic superscription is characterized by the form: "the *x* of *y*," in which *x* represents some term for prophetic revelation, such as *ḥăzôn* ("vision," as in Isa 1:1 and Obad 1), *maśśā'* (*RSV* "oracle," as in Hab 1:1), or *dibrê* ("words of," as in Jer 1:1 and Amos 1:1), and *y* represents the name of the prophet. The other basic type of prophetic superscription is characterized by its use of the (→) prophetic word formula ("the word of Yahweh that came to *y*"). The former emphasizes the identity of the prophet who received a particular kind of revelation, while the latter emphasizes that the revelation had an authentically divine origin.

The superscription of Nahum is distinctive in two respects. First, the conventional form described above is shown by its subtitle rather than its main title. The main title first identifies the subject of the revelation, the city of Nineveh, before giving the name of the prophet who received the revelation. Second, two complementary terms are used for the type of revelation that is presented here. It is described not only as a *maśśā'* (*RSV* "oracle") but also as a *sēper ḥăzôn* ("book of vision"). The term *sēper* ("book") indicates that this revelation takes the form of a written document. This document contains a

22

maśśā' concerning Nineveh that is capable of generating prophetic insight *(ḥăzôn)* when it is read and studied (→ Book as a Whole, Genre).

The use of the term *ḥăzôn* has led some commentators to hold that some or all of the book, particularly the vivid descriptions of battle in chs. 2 and 3, derive from prophetic experience that is visionary in the strict sense. The term itself, however, does not necessarily denote this. The root *ḥzh* is used in prophetic superscriptions both as a noun to describe the content of the revelations contained in the main body of the book and as a verb to describe the mode of receiving those revelations. It is applied to prophetic books that contain some material explicitly derived from visions along with some material that is not (e.g., Amos 1:1; Isa 1:1), and to prophetic books that contain no material explicitly derived from visions (e.g., Obad 1; Hab 1:1). Since there are no explicit indications of visionary experience in Nahum, such as vision report formulas (→ prophetic vision report), it is likely that in this case the term *ḥăzôn* refers to prophetic insight in general, possibly but not necessarily including any paranormal visionary experience. The kind of vivid description found in chs. 2 and 3 could certainly have some other derivation.

Nahum is identified here as "the Elkoshite," but this gentilic designation of his village or clan is otherwise unknown. Other prophetic superscriptions similarly identify prophets in terms of the place or family from which they originally came (e.g., Jer 1:1; Amos 1:1; Mic 1:1). In these cases the concern for the prophet's origins is typically complemented by a concern for his historical situation, which is expressed by specifying the reigns of kings in which he was active. In the case of Nahum the stipulation that the revelation concerns Nineveh may have a similar function, indicating that Nahum was active during those years when momentous things were happening with regard to this city, i.e., the years leading up to its fall in 612 BCE.

Setting

Such superscriptions were the work of scribal groups engaged in the preservation and historical study of prophecy's relics and records. The particularities of this superscription further reflect a group whose horizon of interest extended to include the historical study of some aspects of international relations.

Intention

This superscription is devised so as to classify this prophetic book historically with regard to a hierarchy of factors: its subject matter, the prophet whose words on that subject were recorded therein, the place from which this prophet came, and, by implication, the time when he was active. Such scholarly classification presents this document as a record of revelation that can in turn become revelatory for studious readers and interpreters (→ Book as a Whole, Genre).

23

Bibliography

G. Tucker, "Prophetic Superscriptions and the Growth of a Canon," in *Canon and Authority* (ed. G. W. Coats and B. O. Long; Philadelphia: Fortress, 1977) 56-70.

Chapter 3

THE FIRST MAJOR SECTION
OF THE BOOK (1:2–2:11 [*RSV* 1:2–2:10]
AND ITS INDIVIDUAL UNITS

A PROPHETIC CHALLENGE TO OPPONENTS OF YAHWEH,
1:2–2:11 (*RSV* 1:2–2:10)

Structure

I. Interrogation affirming the futility of opposing Yahweh	1:2-10
A. Inferential questioning concerning the capacity for opposing Yahweh	1:2-6
B. Inferential questioning concerning the consequences of opposing Yahweh	1:7-10
II. Interpretation of a past event	1:11-14
A. Statement reporting the departure of an enemy of Yahweh	1:11
B. Prophecies interpreting the significance of this departure	1:12-14
1. The event as a portent of salvation for Judah	1:12-13
2. The event as a portent of punishment for Assyria	1:14
III. Announcements showing the fulfillment of these prophecies	2:1-11
A. Announcement of the arrival of a messenger bringing Judah news of the enemy's overthrow	2:1
B. Extended announcement of an attack against Nineveh resulting in the city's defeat and destruction	2:2-11

Modern scholarship has been largely concerned with the reconstruction of an alphabetical acrostic in ch. 1, recently focusing on the more limited possibility of a partial alphabetical acrostic in 1:2-8, but this endeavor entails severe problems that now necessitate its reconsideration (→ 1:2-10, Structure). In any case it is commonly observed by scholars with varying opinions on the nature and extent of this acrostic that 1:9-10 is closely related in form and content to 1:2-8, as a summary and hortatory application of what has previously been said about Yahweh's characteristic treatment of his enemies (e.g., Humbert, "Le problème," 6-7; Elliger, 5; Rudolph, 156-57; Schulz, 13; Becking, 112; Coggins, 27-28; Sweeney, 369-72; Hieke, "Anfang II," 17). 1:2-8 and 1:9-10 are thus widely seen as subunits with a close affinity (→ 1:2-10, Structure). Beyond this, rhetorical shifts of various kinds give fairly clear and widely recognized indications of the dividing points between the other basic segments of the text in this section of the book.

Nah 1:11 is set off as a separate segment by a shift at 1:12 from the description of action to the quotation of oracular speech. The two speeches of Yahweh in 1:12-13 and 1:14 are distinguished from one another by their respective introductions, by their contrasting content, and by a change at 1:14 in the grammatical gender of the addressee from feminine singular to masculine singular. At 2:1 direct discourse is abandoned in favor of an announcing style ("behold!"), and the relatively brief announcement in 2:1 is differentiated from the extended announcement in 2:2-11 primarily by a change in content, from proclamation of the prospect of peace to notification of an imminent attack. As the narration in 2:4-11 describes in some detail the disastrous outcome of the attack that is heralded in 2:2, it becomes apparent that these two announcements also differ with respect to the identity of their feminine singular addressees. The first is addressed to Judah, and the second to Nineveh (2:9). The narration breaks off after 2:11, and the beginning of a new section is signaled by the shift in 2:12 to a taunting question. Scholars widely agree on these points of structural division, but they have fundamental differences of opinion regarding both the nature of the resulting textual segments and their overall configuration.

Such differences of opinion stem largely from the fact that the various addressees, to which these textual segments are directed, are not explicitly identified. They are distinguished only by their grammatical number and gender, and characterized by roles that are very minimally defined. Many scholars have attempted to specify the historical identity of these addressees on the basis of external criteria by placing each segment in the context of some well-known event. Such appeals to history have remained inconclusive, however, because the description in each segment of text is so brief and so vague that it can hardly constitute a direct reference to any particular event. This approach has not only reduced the text to a hodgepodge; it has also resulted in confusion regarding the nature of the hodgepodge. It would thus seem better to follow the lead of the text itself and to try to identify the characters gradually on the basis of internal criteria as the book unfolds. This is possible if the analysis of characterization becomes an integral part of the structure analysis describing the basic units of the text and their overall configuration (→ 1:11-14, Structure; 2:1-11, Structure). It is also possible to situate this overall configuration historically, even though each subunit of the text is in itself ambiguous with regard to its historical context.

26

As for the overall configuration, scholars generally agree on only two things: (1) that this section begins with a hymn (1:2-8); and (2) that this hymn is followed by a series of prophetic speeches addressed to various characters. With regard to the nature of this combination of elements there are generally two alternative views, each of which has many variations. On the one hand, some see in such a sequence the reflection of a liturgical process (e.g., Humbert, "Essai d'analyse," 269-72; de Vries, 479-81; Eaton, *Vision in Worship*, 15-21); on the other hand, some see in it only a more or less topically organized collection of prophecies (e.g., Elliger, 7-16; Keller, 116-26; Roberts, 42-67). Rather than pursue either of these alternatives, the structure analysis presented here begins by reexamining the two points of agreement that they both presuppose and from which they both proceed. Below I dispute the identification of 1:2-8 as a hymn, and I also argue that 1:2-6 and 1:7-10 form the main subdivisions of 1:2-10, rather than 1:2-8 and 1:9-10 (→ 1:2-10, Genre). At this point I will reconsider the organizing principle of 1:11–2:11. Is this part of the book just a series of individual speeches, regardless of whether the series might also be further characterized as a kind of liturgical responsory or a kind of prophetic anthology? Or are the components of this section organized in some other way?

The crux of the matter is how 1:11 is to be understood. Many suppose that this verse is the kind of accusation that generally pertains to prophecies of punishment. When 1:11 is read in this way, however, an element of discontinuity is introduced between this verse and the following prophecy in 1:12-13, despite the fact that the text's formal features seem to signal just the opposite. Continuity is suggested by the fact that both 1:11 and 1:12-13 have a feminine singular addressee. When 1:11 is viewed as an accusation, however, any sense of continuity is lost.

If the feminine singular addressees in 1:11 and 1:12-13 are the same, it is difficult to see how these two subunits are otherwise connected because the deliverance that is promised her in 1:12-13 could hardly follow from the accusation that is leveled against her in 1:11. If 1:11 and 1:12-13 are addressed to the same feminine character, they must have been uttered at different times and under very different circumstances. A common addressee would certainly be the only reason for joining such an accusation to such a prophecy of salvation (although Sweeney, for example, attempts to discern a more profound link on this basis, pp. 371-72).

If the feminine singular addressees in 1:11 and 1:12-13 are different, the situation is no less problematic. It is perhaps plausible to imagine that one feminine character might be accused of harboring opposition to Yahweh (1:11), and that another feminine character might conversely be promised deliverance from enemy oppression (1:12-13), but it is difficult to see how there could be such an abrupt shift in rhetorical stance without any overt signal to this effect. Moreover, if the addressees were different there would be even less of a reason for joining such an accusation to such a prophecy of salvation (though Graham, for example, attempts to discern a more profound link on this basis, pp. 44-46).

When 1:11 is read as an accusation, it seems to have more thematically in common with the prophecy of punishment in 1:14 than with the prophecy of salvation in 1:12-13, despite the fact that the text itself gives no formal indication of such an affinity. To some scholars 1:12-13 has even seemed intrusive or extraneous enough to warrant a drastic rearrangement of the text into a supposedly more original form, so that 1:11 is followed directly by 1:14 (e.g., Marti, 315-16; Schulz, 15-16; Jeremias, 20-25; Seybold, 20-22, 32; Hieke, "Anfang II," 16-19). There is no text-critical warrant for this arbitrary change, however, and it also gives rise to a puzzling incongruity. If 1:11 and 1:14 are directly linked, why does the former have a feminine singular addressee and the latter a masculine singular addressee? If 1:11 and 1:14 form a subunit, this would imply that the grammatical markers of gender and number are used arbitrarily, without any consistency at all. Despite these problems such dubious rearrangements of the text have become the basis for various far-reaching but divergent theories concerning the original core and subsequent editions of the book of Nahum (e.g., Jeremias, 48-53; Schulz, 102-10; Seybold, 19-34).

Such speculation is useless without first explaining how the present form of the text is arranged, and then asking whether this affords any basis on which to suppose that it ever had an earlier form. The primary task is to explain the compositional structure of the text as we now have it, but when one assumes 1:11 to be an accusation this task becomes virtually impossible. Past scholarly work on Nahum shows that this assumption leads inevitably to fragmentation and even rearrangement of the text. The only way out of this impasse is to ask whether 1:11 could be something other than an accusation and, if so, how it then might be related to the subunits that follow.

In analyzing the compositional form of 1:11-14 one must consider two major factors: (1) the similarities and differences in gender and number; and (2) the spare but still definitive description of each character's role. When one gives due consideration to both factors, the coherence and consistency of 1:11-14 become evident. 1:11 speaks to a feminine character about a masculine character who is cast in the role of Yahweh's enemy. 1:12-13 speaks similarly to a feminine character about a masculine character who is again cast in the role of Yahweh's enemy, promising her that Yahweh will deliver her from this enemy's domination. 1:14 then speaks to a masculine character who is yet again cast in the role of Yahweh's enemy, announcing that Yahweh will destroy him.

This suggests that 1:11 serves to introduce both 1:12-13 and 1:14. It sets the scene by presenting the two main characters, one masculine and one feminine, who are each in turn informed of their contrasting fates. Since there is nothing to indicate that the feminine singular addressee of 1:11 is different from the feminine singular addressee of 1:12-13, there is no reason to suppose that they are not one and the same. Vv. 11-14 thus provide a particular instance of what is generally described in 1:2-10, giving a specific example of how Yahweh destroys his enemies and protects his friends.

One should also note, however, that the contrasting fates of the two main characters are the result of a reversal in their interrelationship. Yahweh will "no more" *(lō' 'ôd)* afflict the feminine character with the masculine character's domination (v. 12), which implies that Yahweh previously counted the

28

masculine character as his friend and the feminine character as his enemy. Similarly, Yahweh will "no more" *(lō' 'ôd)* extend the influence *(zr' šēm; RSV* "perpetuate the name") of the masculine character, which implies that Yahweh was previously involved in establishing the masculine character's power at the expense of the feminine character. Now, however, the tables are turned. The feminine character is to be liberated, and the masculine character is to be conquered.

Nah 1:11 is a pivotal verse not only because it introduces the two characters in 1:11-14, whose fates exemplify the theological generalizations in 1:2-10, but also because it describes the point at which the reversal in their interrelationship first became evident. One should understand 1:11 as a report of the event that signaled this turning point, whose implications for weal and woe are subsequently drawn out in 1:12-14. This report is addressed to the same feminine character who continues to be addressed in 1:12-13, and it describes something done by the same masculine character who is directly addressed in 1:14. V. 11 can be read in this way if its main verb, *yṣ'*, is understood to mean not "come out" (so *RSV* and most commentators), but rather "depart" (→ 1:11-14, Text). V. 11 thus reports the "departure" of the masculine character, who came to punish the feminine character on Yahweh's behalf but left without succeeding, thus showing that he had begun to lose favor with Yahweh.

After 1:11-14 comes a new but not altogether independent unit, 2:1-11. This unit consists of two notices or announcements, a relatively brief one (2:1) addressed to a feminine character identified as Judah, and a somewhat longer one (2:2-11) addressed to another initially unidentified feminine character, who is subsequently identified as the city of Nineveh (2:9). In 2:1 the arrival of a messenger is heralded, bringing Judah the news that her former enemy is being destroyed. In 2:2-3 Nineveh is warned of an impending attack, and in 2:4-11 this warning is extended by a narrative account of the attack and its outcome, describing the city's overthrow in graphic detail.

This unit proclaims that the prophecies in 1:12-13 and 1:14, regarding the implications of the "departure" reported in 1:11, are now being fulfilled; and it does so in a way that begins to give some historical specificity to this section overall. In 1:12-13 the "departure" is seen as a sign that the masculine character will eventually lose control over the feminine character, and in 2:1 Judah is told that this has happened, thus retroactively identifying the feminine character in 1:11-14 as Judah. In 1:14 the "departure" is seen as a sign that Yahweh will eventually obliterate the masculine character, focusing on the destruction of his family (i.e., *zr' miššiměkā* [*RSV* "perpetuation of your name"]) and temple-palace (*bêt 'ĕlōhêkā* [*RSV* "the house of your gods"]), and in 2:2-11 the overthrow of Nineveh is described with attention to the destruction of its ruling family (2:8) and its temple-palace (*hêkāl*, 2:7b). The event announced in 2:2-11 thus appears to fulfill what was prophesied in 1:14. This suggests that the masculine character in 1:11-14 and the feminine personification of Nineveh in 2:2-11 are closely associated, though not exactly identical. The masculine character in 1:11-14 might then be a personification of the Assyrian king (→ 1:11-14, Structure), complementing the feminine personification of his capital city in 2:2-11. Such an association is only suggested at this point,

29

however, and it remains to be seen whether it will be confirmed as the rest of the book unfolds (→ Book as a Whole, Structure; cf. the subsequent direct address of the Assyrian king in 3:18).

Nineveh's attacker is not explicitly identified but is only characterized in 2:2a as a *mēpîṣ* (*RSV* "shatterer"). In the rest of this unit and the rest of the book, however, Nineveh is described as suffering total defeat. The event that is announced in 2:2-11 thus can only be the attack of Nineveh in 612 BCE by the Babylonians and Medes that resulted in the city's destruction. This section thus portrays the fall of Nineveh as the conclusion of a historical process that began when the Assyrian king once "departed" from Judah (1:11), an event that portended to the prophetic eye not only the eventual liberation of Judah from Assyrian domination (1:12-13; 2:1) but also the downfall of the Assyrian imperial regime itself (1:14). The "departure" in question is most probably the retreat of Sennacherib from his unsuccessful siege of Jerusalem in 701 BCE during the reign of Hezekiah (2 Kgs 18:13–19:37).

In sum, this section of the book is made up of three units. The first (1:2-10) gives a general description of how Yahweh destroys his enemies and protects his friends. The second (1:11-14) gives a specific example of how this general principle applies under changing historical circumstances. It singles out a particular past event as the occasion for a reversal of these two roles. Judah was once among Yahweh's enemies, and the Assyrians were then his allies. At that time Yahweh used the Assyrians to punish his own people. Sennacherib's unsuccessful siege of Jerusalem in 701, however, signaled a decisive shift. This event marked the beginning of a long historical process, through which Judah would eventually assume the role of Yahweh's favored ally, and Assyria would conversely assume the role of Yahweh's doomed enemy. The third unit (2:1-11) asserts that this process has now reached its previously prophesied conclusion. The fall of Nineveh in 612 fulfills the prophetic claim that Judah would one day be free from Assyrian domination, and the corresponding prophetic claim that the Assyrian kingship would one day meet its end.

Genre

This section is generically complex. It consists of three units, each of which has a recognizable generic structure of its own. It begins with a prophetic interrogation (→ 1:2-10, Genre), continues with a prophetic symbolic interpretation of a past event (→ 1:11-14, Genre), and concludes with a prophetic sentinel report (→ 2:1-11, Genre). The question is whether these three compositional forms assume some other generic shape as they combine to form this section of the book. As a composition designed to draw presently applicable theological generalizations from past historical experience, this section strongly resembles such didactic historical poems as Deut 32 and Ps 78.

This section has the following characteristics in common with Deut 32 and Ps 78: (1) The audience is directly addressed in a way that induces them to reflect on patterns of divine activity in history. All three texts have an intro-

30

duction that engages the audience in this way (→ 1:2-10, Structure; cf. Deut 32:1-7; Ps 78:1-8), but they differ considerably in the extent to which they subsequently reinforce this relationship with the audience. Ps 78 abandons direct address after its introduction and does not revert to it again; Deut 32 has direct address at the beginning, at a couple of points in the middle (vv. 17b-18, 38b), and at the end (v. 43); Nah 1:2–2:11 maintains direct address throughout but signals shifts from one addressee to another with changes in grammatical gender and number. (2) Past events are reported or narrated. Again, this similarity is subject to considerable variation. This section of Nahum gives only a brief report of one event, referring obliquely to the departure of Sennacherib from Jerusalem in 701 (1:14). Deut 32 recounts Israel's wandering in the wilderness and their entry into the promised land, describing the origins of Israel's tendency to be unfaithful to Yahweh (vv. 8-18). Ps 78 tells much the same story but adds episodes concerning events from the time of the tribal league and the establishment of the Davidic monarchy (vv. 9-72). (3) The past is prophetically interpreted in terms of patterns of divine activity that still impinge on the present. This can be expressed through third person narration of divine activity, as is the case in Ps 78; or it can also be expressed through various combinations of such narration and oracular speech of Yahweh, as is the case in Deut 32 and Nah 1:2–2:11.

All three of these texts analyze the past in terms of the same basic pattern of divine activity: When Yahweh's people reject him, he punishes them by giving their enemies the upper hand. But when these enemies get too overbearing, he reverses the situation by punishing them instead, thus saving his people in spite of themselves. This pattern is discerned from a variety of mythic and historical contexts, and is brought to bear on the audience's present situation in a variety of ways. In any case, the basic function of such texts is to show that Yahweh is presently acting in a way that is comparable with how he has typically acted in the past, and thus lead the audience to reassess the current state of their relationship with Yahweh. This kind of composition can be described as a PROPHETIC HISTORICAL EXEMPLUM. (Cf. the somewhat different discussions of genre in A. F. Campbell, "Psalm 78: A Contribution to the Theology of Tenth Century Israel," *CBQ* 41 [1979] 76-77; and S. Carillo Alday, "Género literario del Cántico de Moisés," *EstBib* 26 [1967] 69-76.)

This particular example of the genre has two distinctive features that set it apart from the other two examples with which it is compared above. First, Nah 1:2–2:11 shows a particular style of direct address that is not evident in either Deut 32 or Ps 78. Second, this section of Nahum claims not only that a certain pattern of divine activity from the past is repeating itself in the present, but also that certain prophecies to this effect are now being fulfilled.

All three texts engage the audience in a manner that is reminiscent of both wisdom and prophetic traditions. Each sounds like a teacher addressing a group of disciples, and at the same time like a prophet addressing a public gathering. Didactic methods are used for the prophetic task of making nations aware of Yahweh's involvement in their affairs (→ 1:2-10, Genre; J. R. Boston, "The Wisdom Influence upon the Song of Moses," *JBL* 87 [1968] 198-202; H. J. Kraus, *Psalms 60–150* [tr. H. C. Oswald; Minneapolis: Augsburg,

1989] 122-26). Above and beyond this, the use of direct address in this section of Nahum is distinctive in two respects.

First, the latter part of this section is addressed both to characters representing a foreign nation (i.e., Assyria in 1:14; 2:2-11) and to a character representing Yahweh's people (i.e., Judah in 1:11-13; 2:1), informing this foreign nation of its coming doom and conversely informing Yahweh's people of their resulting deliverance. This manner of speaking is not typical of the prophetic historical exemplum but is rooted in another closely related type of prophetic activity that is also reflected in the text of Nahum (→ Book as a Whole, Genre).

Although this sort of direct address is atypical, it is not incompatible with the basic intent of the prophetic historical exemplum. This is evident from the way in which the identities of the addressees are initially not disclosed but are gradually made explicit as the book unfolds. Before any historically specific names are given to some of the characters in this section (i.e., Judah in 2:1; Nineveh in 2:9), the audience is left in the position of tentatively trying to imagine just who these characters might be on the basis of their rather skimpily defined roles. Even by the end of this section, the identity of the masculine singular character remains somewhat ambiguous (→ Structure). This keeps the composition from playing into any preconceptions the audience might have about the roles of the good guys and bad guys in their particular historical situation. As long as the audience remains uncertain about which character(s) they can identify with, they will keep trying to relate to them all in a variety of ways. This serves to reinforce the didactic intent of the prophetic historical exemplum, which is for the audience to reassess their relationship with Yahweh in the light of his involvement in their present situation. The text makes a definite claim about what the fall of Nineveh shows regarding the status of Judah as Yahweh's ally and the status of Assyria as Yahweh's enemy, but it does not want the audience from Judah to assume too quickly that they belong in the category of Yahweh's allies.

Second, this section of Nahum draws a lesson from the past that is somewhat different from the lesson drawn by Deut 32 and Ps 78. These other examples of the prophetic historical exemplum aim to show that a certain pattern of divine activity from the past is repeating itself in the present. Nah 1:2–2:11 shares this aim, but it also shows that this repetition is being confirmed by the fulfillment of prophecies that foretold it. This section is thus in large part structured on the basis of a progression from prophecy (1:11-14) to fulfillment (2:1-11; → Structure). In this regard this section of Nahum resembles certain kinds of historical narratives, including such prophetic legends as Isa 37:9-38 (see also the additional "historical demonstration narratives" adduced by S. J. de Vries in *Prophet against Prophet* [Grand Rapids: Eerdmans, 1978] 54-56), as well as parts of more extended historiographical compositions like the Deuteronomistic History (G. von Rad, "The Deuteronomic Theology of History in I and II Kings," in *The Problem of the Hexateuch and Other Essays* [tr. E. W. Trueman Dicken; New York: McGraw-Hill, 1966] 205-21). These narratives express not only their authors' views of Yahweh's involvement in past events but also the conviction that their authors' retrospective views of Yahweh's involvement in past events are consistent with prospective views of prophets who were directly involved in those events. Such texts present models of prophetic discernment by showing how one can learn from prophets of the past how to identify the kinds of things that Yahweh might be doing in the present. This particular example of the prophetic historical exemplum thus teaches that its audience should make the same use of this text that this text makes of the prophecies contained within it.

In this case it is possible to recognize the fact of dependence on older traditions but not to reconstruct with any certainty the form in which they were previously transmitted. As noted above, this section of Nahum is designed to show that the fall of Nineveh fulfills previous prophecies regarding the Assyrians' departure from Jerusalem nearly a century earlier. It therefore presupposes the existence of older prophecies formulated sometime after the Assyrian retreat but prior to the fall of Nineveh, prophecies claiming that the retreat portended the kind of thing that finally came to pass when the Babylonians and Medes razed Nineveh. 1:12-13 and 1:14 are presented as oracles expressing the substance of these older prophecies, but there is no reason to suppose either that these verses now contain the original forms of these older prophecies or that these verses afford any basis on which to reconstruct the original forms of these older prophecies (→ 1:11-14, Genre).

Setting

This kind of composition reflects a context in which historical records and prophetic traditions were preserved and studied. The author would also be familiar enough with mythic traditions to make creative use of them, as well as knowledgeable in the area of international affairs. These clues suggest that a text of this sort might well have been produced by a prophet schooled in wisdom who functioned as an adviser to public officials. It is thus probably a written composition intended for scribal readers, but its rhetoric is not of the sort that aims only at such an audience. This compositional form represents the attempt of a prophet to disseminate the results of his historical study and divinatory reflection in a manner that rouses public concern about the theological significance of current events. It is designed to loosen the audience's adherence to any prejudices they may have, so that its own viewpoint will be more readily received. It thus appears to be intended for group instruction of some kind.

It is not possible to say anything more specific on the basis of this section alone. It is probable that compositions like Deut 32 and Ps 78 were lyrically recited as an integral part of a liturgy — perhaps a covenant renewal liturgy — by someone assuming the ritual role of a prophetic teacher (Kraus, *Psalms 60–150*, 122). Nonetheless, from the fact that this section is generically comparable with such poems it does not necessarily follow that it was used in the same way. Deut 32 and Ps 78 take shape as more or less self-contained compositions, but this section assumes the same shape as it also forms part of a larger literary whole. In this case the identification of the genre is therefore not a sufficient basis on which to assume that this part of the text

33

ever existed independently, or that it ever had a setting distinct from the setting of the book as a whole. The same principle applies to each individual unit in relation to this section.

On the one hand, the three component units all have generic forms that were typically at home in the setting of prophetic public oratory. On the other hand, in this particular sequence these forms readily assume yet another generic form that was probably at home in a somewhat different setting, the lyrical recitation of prophetic ritual instruction. It is perhaps theoretically possible that this section's component units each existed independently as prophetic speeches of different kinds, and that they were subsequently combined in the form of a cult lyric. It seems unlikely, however, that three prophetic speeches designed for various purposes and occasions would so readily lend themselves, as prefabricated units, to forming an altogether different kind of prophetic communication designed for an altogether different purpose and occasion. (This would be fortuitous indeed!) Moreover, although each of the units in this section has the form of an independently existing prophetic speech, there is a good deal of interdependence with respect to content ($\rightarrow$ Structure; see also the discussion below of each individual unit's structure). All this raises sharply the question of whether the units in this section ever existed independently of the section itself.

It seems likely that we have here something analogous to the modern literary convention of a letter within a novel, sent by one of the story's characters to another. Such a letter may in fact have the form of an independently existing genre, but this does not mean that it ever existed independently of the novel that contains it. Despite its apparent generic integrity, the letter was always an integral part of a larger generic whole, and this is evident from the way it functions to further the development of the novel as such. Similarly, although we have here three units that each appears to have some generic integrity, they may nevertheless have all been integral parts of a larger generic whole from the beginning.

What is true of each unit in this regard is also true of the entire section. Although it has the form of an independently existing genre, and although this genre was probably used for ritual instruction in a liturgical context, this particular example of the genre may never have existed independently in such a setting. This is strongly suggested by the fact that this section assumes the generic form of a prophetic historical exemplum within the larger literary context of the entire book, as part of a larger generic whole, and by the way in which it serves to develop that larger generic whole as such. The setting of this section would thus be identical with the setting of the book as a whole, and it is unlikely that the book was meant for liturgical recitation ($\rightarrow$ Book as a Whole, Genre and Setting).

Intention

This text leads its audience to consider whether they should see their present situation in terms of an antecedent pattern of divine activity. This pattern, which has been symbolized in myths dealing with Yahweh's primordial containment and control of the watery forces of chaos, is seen to be operative in one particularly telling historical case. This unit has in view the whole course of relations between the Israelite kingdoms and the Assyrian empire, focusing on two events: the departure of the Assyrian army from Judah after an unsuccessful siege of Jerusalem in 701, and the overthrow of the Assyrian capital, Nineveh, by the Medes and Babylonians in 612. Yahweh's involvement in this course of events is prophetically discerned to be congruent with this pattern: Although Yahweh sometimes punishes his own people by subjugating them to a foreign power, he eventually turns against the foreign power. This happens because the foreign power develops enough hubris to keep them from carrying out their historical mission in accord with Yahweh's purpose. Thus the utter destruction of Yahweh's people is avoided not because of anything they have done to deserve this but because Yahweh is determined to maintain them as witnesses of his intention to redeem the world he created (cf. Deut 32:19-42; Isa 10:5-14; etc.).

The main point is never to cease to identify oneself with Yahweh's people, even when he has punished them for opposing him; and beyond this never to oppose Yahweh at all, so as not to incur his terrible wrath. To apply this insight one must try to divine whether Yahweh is now acting in accord with this paradigmatic pattern, as he proved to be doing in the events leading up to the fall of Nineveh.

Bibliography

W. R. Arnold, "The Composition of Nahum 1:1–2:3," *ZAW* 19 (1901) 225-65; S. J. de Vries, "The Acrostic of Nahum in the Jerusalem Liturgy," *VT* 16 (1966) 476-81; W. C. Graham, "The Interpretation of Nahum 1:9–2:3," *AJSL* 44 (1927-28) 37-48; T. Hieke, "Der Anfang des Buches Nahum I," *BN* 68 (1993) 13-17; idem, "Der Anfang des Buches Nahum II," *BN* 69 (1993) 15-20.

A PROPHETIC INTERROGATION OF THOSE WHO WOULD PRESUME TO OPPOSE YAHWEH, 1:2-10

Text

The sense of vv. 8-10, particularly v. 10, is difficult. When the probable Hebrew *Vorlage* of the LXX is compared with the MT, it appears that one is not a corruption of the other, but rather that they are both variants of a common ancestor. It is thus not possible to patch up the MT with occasional reference to the LXX, but at the same time it is unlikely that the hypothetical original can now be recovered from the complex welter of their similarities and differences. It is thus prudent to stay with a literal translation of the MT that, though somewhat cumbersome, is not nearly as far-fetched as some of the speculative emendations that have been proposed (for a sample of which see Schulz, 12-13, n. 34).

In accord with the ordinary norms of Hebrew grammar, the feminine singular suffix attached to *māqôm* ("place") in v. 8a is best read with reference to the nearest preceding feminine singular noun, i.e., *ṣārâ* ("opposition"; *RSV* "trouble") in v. 7a. The sense of vv. 8-9 can then be rendered as follows:

> (8) With an overwhelming flood he will put an end to the place
> [of opposition],
> and pursue his enemies into darkness.
> (9) What would you plot against Yahweh?
> It is he who puts an end to [such plots].

The inevitability of a bad end for any who would dare to oppose Yahweh is then underscored in v. 10 by mixing several metaphors. V. 10a reads literally, "For unto thorns are entanglements, and like their drink are drunkards," but in view of the context the entire verse may be more idiomatically rendered as follows:

> (10) For even as thorns are entangled,
> and drunkards are [drunk] like their drink,
> they are consumed like dried-out chaff.

The gist seems to be that Yahweh's enemies will come to the same withering end as dried-out chaff, and will do so just as naturally and inexorably as thorns grow entangled and drunkards drink. These metaphors imply, moreover, that Yahweh's enemies bring such a destructive fate on themselves.

Structure

I. Inferential questioning concerning the capacity for opposing Yahweh	1:2-6
A. Basic assertion: description of Yahweh	1:2-5
1. Aspects of Yahweh's nature	1:2-3a
a. His vengeful anger toward his foes	1:2
1) Characteristic attributes	1:2a
a) He is a jealous and avenging God	1:2aα
b) He is an avenging and wrathful Lord	1:2aβ
2) Characteristic actions	1:2b
a) He takes vengeance on his adversaries	1:2bα
b) He keeps wrath for his foes	1:2bβ
b. His patient determination to execute justice	1:3a
1) Characteristic attributes	1:3aα
a) Slow to anger	1:3aα[1]
b) Great in might	1:3aα[2]
2) Characteristic action: he does not clear the guilty	1:3aβ

For about a century a scholarly consensus has generally held that the main body of Nahum opens with an alphabetical acrostic (Christensen,

"Acrostic Reconsidered," 17-19), although opinions have diverged considerably regarding its precise form and extent. Earlier forms of this hypothesis required that much of the text in ch. 1 and the beginning of ch. 2 be emended or excised to create a poem in which the initial letters of the lines spelled out the entire Hebrew alphabet. According to the more recent consensus it is generally agreed that the acrostic sequence covers only half the alphabet, from *aleph* to *kaph*, and that it extends only through 1:8. Even in this more moderate form the hypothesis of an alphabetical acrostic is dubious for a couple of reasons. First, there are no convincing text-critical grounds for the emendations and rearrangements of the text that are necessary in order to find lines beginning with *daleth, zayin, yodh*, and *kaph*. Second, even if such emendations and rearrangements were warranted, there are extraneous lines that do not fit the alphabetical sequence, so that the lines supposedly creating the sequence occur at irregular intervals. The whole notion of an acrostic that spells out only half of something is questionable to begin with. It is even more questionable to suppose that an acrostic sequence can be established by arbitrarily ignoring the presence of those lines whose initial letters happen not to fit into it. This would vitiate any plausible concept of the acrostic as a poetic form.

Nogalski grants these points but attempts to circumvent them. He argues that a truly alphabetical acrostic was once redactionally prefixed to the collected prophecies of Nahum, but this acrostic form subsequently became distorted when further material was added and changes were made in the redactional process of making the book of Nahum an integral part of the Book of the Twelve (pp. 198-201). This hypothesis begs the more fundamental question, however, of whether it is necessary to suppose either of these steps in accounting for the present compositional form of Nah 1:2-10. If one can show that the present form of this unit is based on a pattern that, on the one hand, does not entail its ever having existed as an alphabetical acrostic and, on the other hand, includes by definition the material that Nogalski supposes to have been added secondarily, such redactional scenarios become superfluous and hence dubious. The hypothesis of a partial alphabetical acrostic in 1:2-8, in whatever form, has outlived any heuristic usefulness it once had. It should now be abandoned, or at least held in abeyance, to see if the form of 1:2-10 might be more satisfactorily described on some other basis (Floyd, 421-30).

When the view of this unit is not colored by the presuppositional filter of the alphabetical acrostic hypothesis, it becomes evident that a more fundamental organizing principle is operative within and beyond that part of the text that is commonly held to be based on this form. Vv. 2-8 cannot be regarded as a self-contained unit because of the way in which vv. 9-10 are connected with v. 8. In v. 9 a theme begun in v. 8, the theme of Yahweh's "making an end" of his foes, is continued by reiterating the very same phrase *('śh kālâ);* and v. 10 is explicitly connected with v. 9 by the subordinate conjunction *kî* (which the *RSV* leaves untranslated; → Text). Although v. 11 also reiterates a theme begun in v. 9, the theme of "plotting against Yahweh" *(ḥšb 'l/'l yhwh)*, a change of addressee indicates the start of something new here (Sweeney, 369-72). Vv. 2-10 thus form a unit that is connected with the unit beginning in v. 11 but is also distinct from it (so Marti, 308-13; Horst, 157-59; Schulz, passim). When structural analysis makes this fact its starting point rather than the supposed acrostic in 1:2-8, a pattern more basic than any acrostic sequence emerges.

This structural pattern is defined by the recurrences of the same basic compositional elements in vv. 2-6 and vv. 7-10. These basic elements include, first, a portrayal of Yahweh through a set of statements (vv. 2-5, vv. 7-8) alternately describing his attributes (vv. 2-3a, v. 7) and his theophanic actions (vv. 3b-5, v. 8). This portrayal is then followed by a rhetorical question (v. 6a, v. 9aα) and additional statements that summarize and reiterate the foregoing description of Yahweh (v. 6b [cf. vv. 2-5], vv. 9aβ-10 [cf. vv. 7-8]).

The elements common to both vv. 2-6 and vv. 7-10 are interrelated similarly in each case. In both of these subunits the initial description of Yahweh (vv. 2-5, vv. 7-8) functions as an assertion, from which the answer to the rhetorical question (v. 6a, v. 9aα) is to be inferred. Subsequent statements (v. 6b, vv. 9aβ-10) serve as corollaries to the initial assertion concerning Yahweh, summarizing and further nuancing the description of his attributes and theophanic actions, so as to reiterate and reinforce the point that is essential for inferring a true answer to the question. The overall rhetorical shape of both vv. 2-6 and vv. 7-10 may thus be characterized as inferential questioning.

These two subunits differ mainly in the way the rhetorical questions are formulated. In v. 6a the question is indirectly posed in the third person singular, but in v. 9aα it is directly addressed to the audience in the second person plural. In view of the fact that the structures of vv. 2-6 and vv. 7-10 are otherwise so fundamentally similar, this difference constitutes a variation on their common form. In the transition from the first instance of inferential questioning to the second, this shift from indirect to direct interrogation serves to intensify the involvement of the audience in the overall process. The issue of opposing Yahweh is first entertained impersonally, as it might apply to anyone in general (v. 6a); the audience is then confronted with the issue directly, as it may apply to them in particular (v. 9aα).

As the rhetorical pattern of inferential questioning in vv. 2-6 is repeated in vv. 7-10, the two dominant motifs in the former are synthesized in the latter. The two dominant motifs in vv. 2-6 are Yahweh's punishment of his enemies (vv. 2-3a) and his stormy subjugation of the waters of chaos (vv. 3b-5; cf. Horst, 157). In vv. 7-10 these are synthesized by describing Yahweh's punishment of his enemies in terms of "an overwhelming flood" and banishment into "darkness" (i.e., the netherworld; Cathcart, 58-59). The primordial creative defeat of chaos thus becomes paradigmatic for describing how Yahweh handles those who oppose him on the stage of human history.

As the historical and cosmic dimensions of Yahweh's capacity to dispose of his foes become more clearly delineated, the focus of the rhetorical questioning simultaneously shifts. The interrogation moves from raising the issue of whether anyone in general could withstand Yahweh to the issue of whether this particular audience is to be counted among his allies or among his opponents.

Genre

A consensus of scholarly opinion has long held that this introductory unit is basically a (→) psalm, and more specifically a (→) hymn of praise. This view has often been closely related to the view that the unit forms an alphabetical acrostic, since acrostics usually embody some form of psalm poetry. Even those who question the acrostic hypothesis, however, have generally concurred in describing this unit as a hymn (e.g., R. L. Smith, 71-72). This categorization rests primarily on the unmistakable similarity between the way Yahweh is described in vv. 2-8, making heavy use of participial and adjectival predicates, and the way he is typically described in hymns. The kind of material found in vv. 9-10 is not particularly hymnlike, however, and this has led some to characterize them as an addition to vv. 2-8, indicating a specifically prophetic adaptation of the hymn form (Horst, 158-59; Rudolph, 156-57; Schulz, 10-14; Becking, 108-12; etc.). Since Gunkel the prophetic nature of this hymnic unit has often been seen to lie in the supposedly eschatological content of its description (pp. 242-43), but more recently its prophetic nature has also been seen to lie in the way the description of Yahweh in vv. 2-8 has been expanded in vv. 9-10. This expansion has been variously characterized as a ritual question-and-answer addressed by a prophetic cultic functionary to a congregation (Humbert, "Essai d'analyse," 267-68), a "gnomic exhortation" urging the audience of the prophetic speaker to take the message of the hymn to heart (de Vries, 478-80), a public pronouncement intimating the promise of Judah's deliverance from Assyria (Rudolph, 156-57), etc.

The alphabetical acrostic hypothesis is questionable enough also to render questionable the corollary assumption that this unit embodies some form of psalm poetry. Although it contains a description of Yahweh that is undeniably hymnlike, this unit does not have the kind of structure that is typical of a hymn. In particular, it lacks the other basic element, the imperative call to praise (R. L. Smith, 67). This lack would not in itself disqualify any text from being classified as a hymn, for a few examples of the genre do consist solely of hymnic description without any call to praise (e.g., Ps 93). In this case, however, we have not only the absence of this key element, but also the prominent presence of another element that is not typical of hymns, the rhetorical question. The hymnlike description of Yahweh is twice combined with a rhetorical question (v. 6a, v. 9aα), and the effect of repeatedly combining such description with interrogatives is quite different from the effect of its being combined with imperatives. Here the hymnlike description assumes a function other than praise.

In this text descriptive statements are used for the purpose of inferential questioning in a way that is not characteristic of the hymn genre. Here the descriptive statements comprise a set of axiomatic assertions about Yahweh's nature, from which the implications provoked by the rhetorical questions are to be drawn. The descriptive statements thus constitute the basic message of the text, and the questions serve the subsidiary role of drawing out their implications for the audience. The questions follow from the descriptive statements, both formally and materially. In hymns, however, it is generally the other way around. The calls to praise constitute the basic message of the text, and the descriptive statements serve the subsidiary role of substantiating and reinforcing the audience's response to these invitations to participate in the liturgy. This is indicated by the way in which the descriptive statements are generally formulated as motive clauses that are grammatically dependent on the commands of the calls to praise. In hymns descriptive statements are typically subordinate to the other most prominent element, the call to praise. In this text, however, the other most prominent element, the rhetorical question, is subordinate to the descriptive statements.

Not only the repeated questioning is significant here but also the shift from impersonally formulated questioning in v. 6a to confrontationally formulated questioning in v. 9aα. Impersonally formulated questions of the sort represented by v. 6a figure occasionally in hymns (e.g., Pss 76:8 [*RSV* 7]; 147:17), although they are very rare. None of the psalms that are commonly classified as hymns, however, shows any questioning of the congregation in second person plural direct address of the sort found in v. 9aα. This also shows that despite the hymnlike description in vv. 2-8, 1:2-10 is in the final analysis something quite different from a hymn.

The rhetorical strategy of inferential questioning is essentially aphoristic (cf. de Vries's description of the vv. 9-10 as "gnomic exhortation," 478-80). It can be found in individual proverbs of a rather pragmatic nature (e.g., Prov 18:14; 20:6; 27:4), but it can also serve to convey a specifically theological message in a variety of generic contexts, ranging from wisdom (e.g., Job 23:13a; 36:22-23) to prophecy (e.g., Amos 3:8; Isa 50:9), including cultic poetry (as in the hymns with rhetorical questions cited above). In various speeches from Job the combination of theological description and rhetorical questions can take a more complex shape, in which case it can either become part of a larger compositional form (e.g., Job 9:4-12) or assume a more or less independent form of its own (e.g., Job 26:2-14).

Because Nah 1:2-10 combines theological description of Yahweh and rhetorical questions for the purpose of prophetic confrontation, it can be called a PROPHETIC INTERROGATION (Floyd, 436-37). This genre belongs to the realm of prophetic discourse not because it conveys any directly oracular or revelatory message but because of the divinatory function it assumes in relation to the overall compositional context (→ 1:2–2:11).

Setting

This kind of prophetic interrogation reflects two conventional modes of expression. As indicated by the texts from Proverbs cited above, inferential questioning serves a didactic function and is generally characteristic of scribal wisdom. Because of the confrontational shift that is evident here, from third person in v. 6a to second person in v. 9aα, this particular example of inferential questioning also reflects the kinds of accusatory confrontations that prophets often had with both individuals and the people at large as they communicated disconcerting revelations that required the addressees to reassess their attitude

41

or behavior (e.g., Isa 7:13; 22:1b, 16; Jer 4:30; Ezek 18:2, 25, 29; cf. Pss 50:16; 52:3 [*RSV* 1]). Such confrontations might occur in a variety of contexts, as a prophet announced divine punishment to an individual, in a communal complaint liturgy occasioned by the threat of an enemy attack, in other kinds of rituals (such as covenant renewal; see H. J. Kraus, *Psalms 1–59* [H. C. Oswald; Minneapolis: Augsburg, 1988] 1:490-91), etc.

Many scholars have continued to hold some variation on the view Humbert advanced more than half a century ago ("Essai d'analyse," 269-72) that this unit reflects a cultic setting. More recently, for example, de Vries has attempted to envision how this text might form part of the Jerusalem temple liturgy (p. 479), and Coggins has more cautiously described it as the adaptation of a cultic form (pp. 19-20). Most claims of this sort are predicated on the prior assumption that 1:2-10 basically fits the description of a hymn, a genre with a cultic setting. Although there are good reasons to reject this assumption and to classify this unit as a prophetic interrogation rather than a hymn (→ Genre), it is still not implausible to suppose that this text may reflect a cultic setting.

Such a supposition is problematic, however, because we know so little about how the ancient liturgies were actually conducted, and because this text does not conform very well with the little that we do know. In particular, the confrontational questioning of v. 9 appears anomalous in view of the few facts that are available. Humbert imagined this verse as a kind of versicle and response, in which an officiant would ask the congregation, "What do you ascribe to Yahweh?" (reading *tšḥbwn* instead of *tḥšbwn*), and the people would reply, "He annihilates [opposition]!" etc. But this kind of spoken exchange does not resemble very closely the few descriptions that we have of the people's responsive participation in worship (e.g., 2 Chr 7:3; cf. Ps 136). De Vries has proposed that vv. 9-10 form an exhortation spoken by a liturgical leader, urging the people to take to heart the message of vv. 2-8. Such an exhortation is virtually unparalleled, however, and it is doubtful that hymnic description generally served the liturgical function of providing a basis for exhortation. Ps 95 might be adduced as an example of an exhortation based on hymnic description, but it is the only example, and its hortatory conclusion (Ps 95:7b-11) is not based on the same kind of accusatory questioning as Nah 1:9-10.

With respect to the hypothesis of a cultic setting, one may say that prophets probably did confront liturgical assemblies with accusatory questioning (e.g., Ps 50:16). In doing so, they may well have adapted from scribal wisdom the convention of inferential questioning — as they often adapted conventional forms of expression from various settings — but there is no direct evidence of this. Even if some prophetic interrogation may have taken place in a cultic context, however, Nah 1:2-10 has particular features that make it very difficult to suppose that this text ever had such a setting, or even that it was adapted from a form of speech with a primarily cultic setting.

Christensen has given the cultic setting hypothesis a somewhat different twist. He attempts to show that 1:2-10 shares with the rest of the book a distinctive kind of prosodic consistency ("Liturgical Composition," 161-67); and he claims that this precludes the possibility of 1:2-10 ever having existed as an independent prophetic speech with a setting of its own. According to

Christensen such prosodic consistency, in and of itself, shows 1:2-10 and the rest of the book to be all of one piece. The entire book was not redacted from previously existing units of prophetic tradition but written from scratch to be sung in some liturgical context ("Question of Authorship," 57-58).

This argument is dubious in several respects. First, even if one can show Nahum to have the same prosody throughout, this would not necessarily mean that it was entirely produced in the same compositional process. Redactors could certainly have composed additions with the same prosody as the prophetic traditions with which they were working. Second, from the fact that all or part of Nahum is sophisticated poetry it does not necessarily follow that it had some liturgical function. In addition to cultic poetry ancient Israel also had religious but noncultic poetry, as well as profane poetry (as Seybold has emphasized in arguing that Nahum's poetry belongs to the profane category [pp. 54-64]). Third, this unit's well-wrought poetic form does not necessarily indicate that it was composed as a purely literary piece without any prophetic rhetorical function and that it never existed as an independent speech. In its present literary context 1:2-10 serves to introduce a section of the book (→ 1:2–2:11), but this does not necessarily mean that this kind of compositional form could not also have had a somewhat different rhetorical function of its own. The examples from Job cited above (→ Genre), particularly Job 26:2-14, show that this sort of inferential questioning could be extended to form an independent speech. Although the situation portrayed in the book of Job is no doubt fictional, the conversation between Job and his friends is probably a somewhat realistic representation of a kind of actually occurring public discussion.

Thus despite Christensen's argument it is quite possible to imagine that a poetic composition like 1:2-10 may have once been uttered as a prophetic speech on a public occasion, although it is unlikely that this particular example of the genre ever had such an independent setting (→ 1:2–2:11, Setting). A prophetic interrogation might have been spoken on any public occasion, perhaps to a congregation gathered for worship, but probably not as part of the liturgy itself (just as Amos's speeches in the sanctuary at Bethel [Amos 7:10-17] and Jeremiah's speech at the temple in Jerusalem [Jer 26:1-9] were presumably not integral parts of the liturgies celebrated in those places).

Intention

The superscription (1:1) has identified this book as a prophecy concerning Nineveh, but by the end of this unit it is not yet clear how the text is related to this theme. Nor is it even clear who the addressees are. It is only clear that Yahweh implacably destroys his enemies, and conversely protects his friends. This text aims, first, to evoke in all who hear or read these words the realization that opposing Yahweh is as futile as opposing the power that orders creation out of chaos. Above and beyond this, the text aims for its audience to reconsider what constitutes an enemy of Yahweh, whether they might not fall into this category, and whether this might not be something for them to avoid at all costs.

Bibliography

W. R. Arnold, "The Composition of Nahum 1:1–2:3," *ZAW* 19 (1901) 225-65; D. L. Christensen, "The Acrostic of Nahum Reconsidered," *ZAW* 87 (1975) 17-30; idem, "The Acrostic of Nahum Once Again: A Prosodic Analysis of Nahum 1:1-10," *ZAW* 99 (1987) 409-15; S. de Vries, "The Acrostic of Nahum in the Jerusalem Liturgy," *VT* 16 (1966) 476-81; M. Floyd, "The Chimerical Acrostic of Nahum 1:2-10," *JBL* 113 (1994) 421-37; H. Gunkel, "Nahum 1," *ZAW* 11 (1893) 223-44; J. Nogalski, "The Redactional Shaping of Nahum 1 for the Book of the Twelve," in *Among the Prophets* (JSOTSup 144; ed. P. R. Davies and D. J. A. Clines; Sheffield: JSOT Press, 1993) 193-202; A. van Selms, "The Alphabetic Hymn in Nahum 1," *OTWSA* 12 (1969) 33-45.

PROPHETIC INTERPRETATION OF
AN ENEMY'S DEPARTURE, 1:11-14

Text

The *RSV* follows many commentators in rendering 1:11 as a negative question. This requires importing into this verse the final word from 1:10, however, and then changing it from *mālē'* to *hălō'*. Neither of these changes has any good text-critical warrant. Also, the sense of the main verb, *yāṣā'*, is better rendered as "departed from" rather than *RSV* "come out from" (so Rudolph, 158-59; Becking, 113; Roberts, 53; etc.). This verse would thus read: "One who plots evil against Yahweh, who counsels self-destructive lawlessness, has departed from you" (→ Structure).

The text of 1:12 is uncertain in many respects (cf. LXX), but in any case the perfect forms of the verbs *gzz* (niphal, "be cut off"), *'br* ("pass over"), and *'nh* ("afflict") are not in the kind of sequence that would impute to them a future meaning. They should therefore be translated with some past or perfect tense, in contrast with the *RSV*'s somewhat inconsistent rendering of the first two in the future and the third in the past. The verse would thus read: "Although strong and so numerous, they were cut off and [they] disappeared; and [although] I have afflicted you, I will afflict you no more."

Structure

I. Report of a past event: the departure of an enemy
   of Yahweh   1:11
   A. The action: departure   1:11aα
   B. The agent: double characterization   1:11aβb
      1. One who plots evil against Yahweh   1:11aβ
      2. One who counsels lawlessness   1:11b
II. Prophetic interpretation of this event   1:12-14
   A. The event as a portent of salvation: speech of Yahweh   1:12-13

1. Introduction (messenger formula):
   thus says Yahweh . . .   1:12aα
2. Speech proper   1:12aβ-13
   a. Report of what happened: though strong
      and numerous, the enemy was forced to leave   1:12aβ
   b. Statement of Yahweh's purpose   1:12b-13
      1) Negatively expressed: I will no longer
         afflict you   1:12b
      2) Positively expressed: I will liberate you
         from your bondage to this enemy   1:13
B. The event as a portent of punishment:
   speech of Yahweh   1:14
   1. Introduction: Yahweh has commanded
      concerning you   1:14aα
   2. Speech proper: announcement of punishment   1:14aβb
      a. Description of punishment   1:14aβbαβ¹
         1) Effect of Yahweh's action:
            your name will no more be perpetuated   1:14aβ
         2) Yahweh's action   1:14b
            a) I will cut off the images from the
               temple of your gods   1:14bα
            b) I will make your grave   1:14bβ¹
      b. Motivation: for you are contemptible   1:14bβ²

This unit contains a statement (1:11) followed by two prophecies (1:12-13; 1:14). Each of the two prophecies has its own introductory formula (v. 12aα, v. 14aα). Both the statement (1:11) and the first of the two prophecies (1:12-13) directly address an unidentified feminine character, and the second prophecy (1:14) directly addresses an unidentified masculine character. The structure of the unit is dramatic only in the sense that it involves direct address of one character and then another by a prophetic voice, without explicitly identifying either addressee. As the text progresses from each of its three main parts to the next, both the masculine and feminine characters are more fully developed in terms of Yahweh's contrasting intentions for each of them.

Many interpreters read v. 11 as a charge against the feminine character whom it addresses, taking the main verb *yṣ'* in the sense of "come out." She is thus accused of being the source from which opposition to Yahweh has emerged: "From you [it] has come out." Some also tendentiously emend the text, as the *RSV* does, to bring out this sense (→ Text). Such an interpretation may at first seem plausible in view of what precedes v. 11, but it does not remain so in view of what follows. The preceding unit (1:2-10) concludes with the admonitory question, "What would you plot (*ḥšb*) against Yahweh?" (v. 9aα). The recurrence of the same verb in v. 11 may at first lead the reader to suppose that the addressee is now being implicated in someone's "plotting (*ḥšb*) against Yahweh." But when other factors are taken into account, particularly the alternation in the addressees' gender and number, this supposition appears untenable.

The admonitory question in v. 9aα is formulated in the second person masculine plural, but the statement in v. 11 is formulated in the second person feminine singular. If v. 11 accused any person or group with the same offense that this person or group had just been warned about in v. 9aα, there would be no reason for such a change in person and gender. Moreover, if the feminine character in v. 11 were being implicated in opposition to Yahweh, she would become liable to complete annihilation (v. 9aβ; cf. v. 8), but this turns out not to be the case. In vv. 12-13 she is promised just the opposite, namely, that Yahweh will put an end to her affliction and liberate her. It is thus improbable that v. 11 makes the feminine character an accomplice in plotting against Yahweh.

In vv. 12-13 the feminine character is directly addressed in the second person singular with a prophecy concerning a masculine enemy who is described in the third person — both singular and plural — as one who opposes both her and Yahweh. If this section of Nahum has any coherence, v. 11 must be taken similarly. In v. 11, as well as in vv. 12-13, the feminine character is being addressed in the second person singular with a statement concerning an enemy of her and of Yahweh, who is described in the third person masculine singular.

The analysis presented here thus interprets the statement in v. 11 not as an accusation of the feminine character but as a reminder of an event that once happened to her. The addressee and the event itself are minimally described. The role of the feminine character is defined only by a pronominal suffix (*mimmēk,* "from you"), and the reader is left with no clue regarding her identity — unless, perhaps, the convention of personifying a people or their capital city as a feminine figure is being tacitly invoked, but this remains to be seen. The event is described only in terms of the verb *yṣ'*, as a "departure" (→ Text). In v. 11 the feminine character is thus being reminded that the masculine character once "departed from" her.

In contrast, this masculine character is more fully described. With two epithets he is cast in the role of "one who plots evil against Yahweh" and "one who counsels *bĕlîyā'al*" (*RSV* "villainy"). The first of these epithets simply denotes that he is an enemy of Yahweh, but the meaning of the second is less clear. From problematic assumptions about the meaning of the term *bĕlîyā'al,* which also occurs in 2:1, some have drawn unwarranted conclusions regarding the identity of this enemy.

In late biblical times *bĕlîyā'al* came to designate a mythic personification of evil, and Belial thus became the name of a satanic figure. This meaning has sometimes been imputed to the term here, on the assumption that an earthly kingdom is being cast in such a mythic role or that Nahum generally portrays eschatological conflict (e.g., Horst, 159; Watts, 106). The epithet applied to the departing enemy, *yō'ēṣ bĕlîyā'al,* is thus understood as "Belial's counselor," i.e., Belial's right-hand man; and 2:1 is understood as a reference to Belial himself (Cathcart, 33, 35).

Two considerations militate against this sort of reading, one historical and the other grammatical. First, the mythic personification of Belial appears to have been a rather late development, and there is no good reason to suppose that *bĕlîyāʻal* had assumed this meaning by the time Nahum was composed. There is no evidence of a satanic figure named Belial in biblical or extrabiblical literature from earlier than the third century BCE (see the data presented by T. J. Lewis, "Belial," *ABD* 1:655-56), and most scholars would date the final edition of Nahum to the late seventh or early sixth century. A few have held that parts of the book are postexilic, but this generally entails a date no later than the fifth century (e.g., Seybold, 32). How could 1:11 and 2:1 show a use of this word that remains unparalleled at the time when Nahum was written and becomes well attested only some two centuries later?

Second, although it is grammatically possible to parse the participle *yōʻēṣ* as a substantive in the construct state, in which case *bĕlîyāʻal* could assume a possessive sense, it is unlikely that these two words form a construct chain. It is more likely that this phrase has the same grammatical structure as its counterpart, *ḥōšēb rāʻâ*, because the former stands in apposition to the latter (as Sweeney observes [p. 368], although his analysis attributes to *ḥōšēb* and *yōʻēṣ* a gerundlike meaning that Hebrew participles do not normally have [GKC §116]). For semantic reasons *ḥōšēb rāʻâ* cannot be read as a construct phrase. The noun *rāʻâ* ("evil") is rather the direct object of the participle *ḥōšēb* ("one who plots"). If *bĕlîyāʻal* is likewise taken as the direct object of the participle *yōʻēṣ*, it is unlikely that *bĕlîyāʻal* would denote a personification. The epithet *ḥōšēb rāʻâ* refers not to "the Evil One's plotter" but to one who devises schemes that have the nature of evil. The epithet *yōʻēṣ bĕlîyāʻal* would thus similarly refer not to "Belial's counselor" but to one who devises policies that have the nature of *bĕlîyāʻal*.

In 1:11 *bĕlîyāʻal* must thus denote something well within the range of what it ordinarily meant before it ever became a nickname for the devil. (If this is the case here, the same is also the case in 2:1.) Through intensive discussion the sense of this word has lately come into sharper focus, although its etymology remains controversial (→ Bibliography). The noun *bĕlîyāʻal* denotes behavior that offends any fundamental and widely recognized moral norm, because of which offenders are destined to be destroyed. It also connotes that offenders are headed for Sheol, which simply means that they are bound to die, and not — as Emerton rightly insists (pp. 216-17) — that they are, in the modern vernacular, "going to hell."

Rosenberg describes an act of *bĕlîyāʻal* as "a transgression of a basic behavioral norm which in Israel is seen in terms of the violation of the covenantal relationship between the individual, community, and God" (p. 38). Largely on this basis Sweeney concludes that the offender described in 1:11 must be Judahite (pp. 371-72). A review of Rosenberg's own data shows, however, that acts of *bĕlîyāʻal* are not necessarily limited to offenses committed by Israelites against the laws of the covenant between Yahweh and his people. They also encompass any human beings' transgressions of the moral norms inherent in the order of creation (e.g., Prov 6:12-15; 16:27; 19:18; Job 34:17-19). Such transgressions may perhaps be described as violations of the covenant in the broadest sense, i.e., "the everlasting covenant between God and every living creature of all flesh upon the earth" (Gen 9:16; cf. Hos 2:20 [*RSV* 18]). Acts of *bĕlîyāʻal* are hardly limited, however, to violations of the covenant in

47

the narrower sense, i.e., the covenant between Yahweh and his people. The phrase *yōʾēṣ bĕlîyāʿal* may thus be roughly translated as "one who counsels self-destructive lawlessness" (→ Text), and the terminology itself does not necessarily connote anything about the nationality of the masculine character to whom this epithet is applied.

In the final analysis v. 11 is a brief report, reminding its unidentified feminine addressee of a departure once made by a masculine character. This masculine character is generally identified as an enemy of Yahweh, and more specifically as the kind of enemy that threatens the moral order of creation, whom Yahweh therefore "annihilates with an overwhelming flood" and "pursues into darkness" (1:8).

The following prophecy, which is also addressed to the feminine character (1:12-13), elaborates on the significance of the event reported in 1:11. As this elaboration unfolds, it becomes apparent that the masculine character personifies a group, as he is indiscriminately described here in both singular and plural terms. (In v. 12a note the plural verb *nāgōzû* ["be cut off"] agreeing with the plural forms *šĕlēmîm* ["strong"] and *rabbîm* ["many"] in the preceding adversative clause from the same verse, and also the singular verb *ʿābār* ["pass away"] agreeing with the singular participles of the epithets from v. 11.) His "departure" is described as a development with four underlying and far-reaching implications.

First, the departure of this group is portrayed as a defeat that was unlikely because of their superior strength (v. 12a). Second, the defeat of this group is portrayed as a result of Yahweh's battle with the cosmic forces of chaos. It is denoted with the same verb that was previously used to describe the flood wielded by Yahweh against his enemies (cf. *ʿābār* [*RSV* "pass away"] in v. 12aβ and *šeṭep ʿōbēr* [*RSV* "overwhelming flood"] in v. 8a). Third, the unlikely defeat of this group is described as the sign of a change in Yahweh's treatment of the feminine character, signaling that he will "no longer afflict" her (v. 12b). This implies that Yahweh was responsible for the group's attack of the feminine character in the first place, as well as for their subsequent defeat and departure from her. Fourth, in bringing about the departure Yahweh intends not just to relieve the affliction of the feminine character in this one instance, but also to make a fundamental change in the relationship between the masculine and feminine characters. The departure means that the group represented by the masculine character will now no longer be able to keep the feminine character in subjection (v. 13).

The following prophecy (v. 14), which is addressed to the masculine character, announces that the event reported in v. 11 marks the beginning of the end for the group that he represents. He will not only lose control over the feminine character (v. 13); in accord with Yahweh's decree he will also eventually be destroyed. The summary accusation leveled against the masculine character (v. 14bβ²) is very vague ("you are contemptible" [*RSV* "vile"]), and does not add anything to the development of this character above and beyond the impression given by the two epithets in v. 11b ("one who plots evil against Yahweh" and "one who counsels self-destructive lawlessness"). The punishment is described with enough specificity, however, to provide another clue to the identity of the masculine character. The three things that are mentioned in v. 14bαβ[1] — posterity, temple, and tomb — are typically important aspects of royal status. Thus the enemy who departed in defeat, who was once sent by Yahweh to put the feminine character in subjection, who is now being made by Yahweh to lose control over her, and who will soon be destroyed by Yahweh, appears to be a foreign king.

Genre

This part of Nahum is generally assumed to be a redactional pastiche of material originally belonging to the genres of (→) prophecy of punishment (v. 14) and (→) prophecy of salvation (vv. 12-13). In line with the attempt to read v. 11 as an accusation, it is often included with v. 14 in the prophecy-of-punishment category, although opinions diverge as to whether these two verses were originally part of the same prophetic speech, and whether the feminine singular addressee in v. 11 and the masculine singular addressee in v. 14 have the same identity (→ 1:2–2:11, Structure). Although vv. 12-13 do indeed resemble a prophecy of salvation, and although v. 14 also resembles a prophecy of punishment, it is questionable whether this section can be adequately described in terms of redacted prophecies from these two genres.

For the reasons of both form and content discussed above, v. 11 is not to be taken as an accusation addressed to someone whom Yahweh is about to punish. It is rather a report addressed to the female character whose salvation is announced in vv. 12-13, recounting the "departure" of the male character whose punishment is announced in v. 14 (→ Structure). The report in v. 11 is thus the dominant element in this unit, which the prophecies in both vv. 12-13 and v. 14 serve to explicate. One must thus formulate the question of genre in terms of whether there is anything conventional about this particular combination of elements.

It is perhaps possible, as most recent commentators have generally supposed, that vv. 12-13 and v. 14 once existed outside their present literary context as independent prophetic speeches. In their present form, however, they are hardly comprehensible as such. Each depends, in its own way, on the information provided by the two epithets in v. 11 concerning the identity of the masculine character.

Without reference to "one who plots evil against Yahweh, one who counsels self-destructive lawlessness," there is no antecedent for the masculine singular pronominal subject of the verb *'ābār* ("pass away") in v. 12a, nor any antecedent for the third person pronominal suffixes in v. 13. These epithets obviously do not give enough information about the masculine character to deduce his specific historical identity, but without this information the audience would have absolutely no idea of just whose strong and numerous forces have been rendered impotent (v. 12a), or just whose yoke will be broken off in order to free the feminine character from bondage (v. 13). Similarly, without this information Yahweh's decision not to let the masculine character afflict the feminine character any longer (v. 12b) would be inexplicable.

49

In v. 14 there is likewise little motivation for the punishment that is pronounced against the masculine character. The final clause (v. 14bβ^2) says only that he is "contemptible" (*qll; RSV* "vile"), which is forceful but hardly specific. It is the foregoing description of the masculine character's offenses, i.e., "plotting evil against Yahweh" and "counseling self-destructive lawlessness," that provides the accusatory basis for the punishment pronounced against him in v. 14. V. 14bβ^2 serves only as a summarizing conclusion for what has already been spelled out in v. 11. Without the information given in v. 11, the audience would have no idea of what makes the masculine character so "contemptible."

If vv. 12-13 and v. 14 ever existed as independent prophetic speeches, they have been so extensively modified to follow v. 11 that their original formulation is no longer discernible. This is not to gainsay the previous observation that vv. 12-13 and v. 14 resemble prophecies of salvation and prophecies of punishment, respectively. It is rather to underscore the necessity of reformulating the form-critical question in terms of whether it was conventional to use such forms of prophetic speech (1:12-13 and 1:14) as integral parts of a larger generic whole (1:11-14), in which they served to explicate the report of an event that had already happened (1:11).

In this regard it is instructive to compare Nah 1:11-14 with Ezek 24:1-14, although these two texts have significant differences as well as similarities. In broad outline Ezek 24:1-14 has three basic features. First, there is a report of an event that has already happened: "The king of Babylon has laid siege to Jerusalem" (v. 2b). Second, the significance of this event is interpreted with reference to a symbolic metaphor, i.e., a stew pot whose contents will be boiled away and whose insides will become rusted out. Third, the consequences of the event are spelled out in terms of this metaphor through prophecies that mostly announce a now inevitable punishment for Jerusalem, but also hint at the eventual possibility of salvation beyond this punishment: Like the contents of the pot, the inhabitants of Jerusalem will be boiled away in the fire of the Babylonian conquest; and like the pot itself, Jerusalem will be left empty to become rusted out — but with the possibility that the same fire will also eventually burn the rust away and make the pot clean and usable again.

Nah 1:11-14 is basically similar to Ezek 24:1-14 in several major respects. First, there is a report of an event that has already happened: "He [the masculine character] has departed from you [the feminine character]" (v. 11). Second, the significance of this event is interpreted with reference to a symbolic metaphor, which is in this case connoted by the first of the two epithets applied to the masculine character: "one who plots evil against Yahweh." The connotations of this phrase are defined in the previous unit (1:2-10), which states that Yahweh will "make a full end" of those who "plot against" him (1:9a), and that he typically "makes a full end" of such enemies by wielding an "overwhelming flood" against them (1:8). In 1:11-14 the significance of the past event is thus interpreted with reference to a particular kind of symbolic metaphor, the mythic archetype of Yahweh's victorious struggle with the cosmic forces of chaos. Third, the consequences of this past event are spelled out in terms of this metaphor with prophecies concerning the fate of its two participants (1:12-14). In accord with this mythic archetype the departure of the masculine character, who had "plotted evil against Yahweh," is seen as the beginning of a historical process through which Yahweh will eventually "make a full end" of this opponent (1:14; cf. 1:8) and conversely show his goodness toward "those who take refuge in him" (1:12-13; cf. 1:7).

Despite these telling similarities, Ezek 24:1-14 and Nah 1:11-14 are not of exactly the same genre. Ezek 24:1-14 is a (→) report of prophetic revelation in which the prophet was commissioned by Yahweh to formulate the report of an event, describe the symbolic metaphor in terms of which the event's significance is to be interpreted, and deliver prophecies spelling out the consequences of the event thus interpreted. In Nah 1:11-14 there is no corresponding narration of how this unit's revelatory message first came to the prophet, nor any account of his being commissioned by Yahweh to deliver it. Nah 1:11-14 is rather like the speech Ezekiel might have given if he had simply conveyed to his audience what Yahweh told him to say, without explicitly mentioning anything about how Yahweh first revealed it to him and directed him to deliver it.

Nah 1:11-14 thus has basically the same form as the revelation that the prophet is commissioned to communicate in Ezek 24:1-14. There are additional differences, but these amount only to variations on a common form. For example, the function of direct address is more complex in Nah 1:11-14. In Ezek 24:1-14 the report of the past event in v. 2b is not formulated in the second person, as is the corresponding report in Nah 1:11. Moreover, in communicating the message revealed in Ezek 24:1-14 the prophetic voice is addressed to only one audience, while in Nah 1:11-14 the prophetic voice has two different addressees. These differences are due largely to the fact that Ezekiel's audience is limited to the people of Yahweh, and his scope is correspondingly limited to their fate at the hands of the Babylonians; but Nahum's audience includes a foreign king (→ Structure), and his scope is correspondingly broadened to include the fall of this foreign power (1:14).

In drawing out the significance of a symbolically interpreted past event, Ezek 24:1-14 mostly utilizes the rhetorical conventions of just one form of prophetic speech, the prophecy of punishment. In similarly drawing out the significance of a symbolically interpreted past event, Nah 1:11-14 by contrast utilizes the rhetorical conventions of two different forms of prophetic speech, the prophecy of salvation (1:12-13) and the prophecy of punishment (1:14). Moreover, the prophecy of punishment in 1:14 is more specifically a (→) prophecy of punishment against a foreign nation, a genre that may entail an apostrophe ostensibly addressed to foreigners but actually designed to be overheard by the prophet's local constituency (→ Zeph 2:5-7, Setting). This is probably the case here because this unit as a whole, including the initial report of the past event itself in 1:11, is predominantly addressed to the feminine character, thus showing that it is primarily concerned with Yahweh's intention to liberate her from this foreign oppressor. Although 1:14 is ostensibly addressed to the masculine character, this prophecy does not really express any concern for his fate as such. In the context of the unit as a whole it rather indicates a concern with how his demise will favorably affect the prospects of the feminine character (→ Book as a Whole, Genre).

The rhetorical pattern of Nah 1:11-14 is thus slightly different from, and a bit more complex than, the rhetorical pattern of the revelation that the prophet is commissioned to communicate in Ezek 24:1-14. Ezek 24:1-14 nevertheless attests to a convention of prophetic discourse with essentially the same form as Nah 1:11-14, as does Ezek 17:1-24 when compared with Nah 1:11-14 in the same qualified way. This form is characterized by the following combination of elements but, as Ezek 17:1-24 shows, they need not occur in this particular order: (1) a brief report of a past event (cf. Ezek 17:11-15), (2) whose significance is interpreted with reference to some kind of symbolic metaphor (cf. Ezek 17:2-10), and (3) whose unfolding consequences are described using prophetic speeches of various types (cf. Ezek 17:16-24). This genre of prophetic discourse may be called a PROPHETIC SYMBOLIC INTERPRETATION OF A PAST EVENT.

Setting

Comparison with Ezek 24:1-14 may at first suggest that this genre serves only to interpret past events that have been recorded in written form, for Yahweh first commands Ezekiel to write down the summary statement of what happened, so that it can then be explicated by the ensuing prophecies (Ezek 24:2). Ezek 24:1-14 appears to be atypical in this regard, however. Ezek 17:1-24 and Nah 1:11-14 give no indication that written records play any similar ancillary role in providing a report of the event that is to be interpreted. On the contrary, the reporting statement in Ezek 17:1-24 is explicitly part of what is to be "said" in the prophetic speech that Ezekiel is commissioned to deliver in public (v. 12); and this would also appear to be the case in Nah 1:11-14, because the reporting statement is expressed in the form of direct address, as if it were similarly to be spoken in public.

The use of this genre, the prophetic symbolic interpretation of a past event, certainly presupposes that the event in question is remembered, but this could come about in a variety of ways. Remembrance of an event, whether it happened recently or long ago, might be due to its having become a matter of written record, as in the case of Ezek 24:1-14, but such remembrance might also be due to the prominence attained by the event in popular living memory. Even if a written record were instrumental in preserving the remembrance of an event, the minimal reporting statement that is typical of this genre (e.g., Ezek 17:12; Nah 1:11) would appear to be based more on the memory sustained by the record than on the record itself. Such a report may in effect be a summary statement of what a prophet found out from a document, but without its being quoted or even directly derived from the document itself.

The use of this genre reflects a situation in which a past event seems portentous but ambiguous, and a prophet attempts to resolve the ambiguity by communicating a symbolically charged revelation. In some cases prophetic symbolic action has much the same function. For example, in the conflict between Jeremiah and Hananiah (Jer 28), their disagreement concerns the significance of a particular event, namely, the plundering of the Jerusalem temple and first deportation to Babylon in 596 BCE. They have conflicting prophetic insights that are expressed in terms of disagreement over the way in which this event is comparable to a particular symbolic stereotype. Hananiah maintains that this event was imposed by Yahweh, but only as a temporary setback that is now in the process of being reversed. He therefore insists on breaking the wooden yoke that Jeremiah has been wearing as a sign of Yahweh's intention to subject Judah to Babylonian control, to show just the opposite, that Babylon's power over Judah is in the process of disintegrating. In order to affirm that this event was just the first stage in Yahweh's plan for the complete subjection of Judah to Babylon, Jeremiah then replaces the wooden yoke with an unbreakable iron one.

When a prophet presents a symbolic interpretation of a past event like the one in Nah 1:11-14, the symbolic prototype is not defined by an object like a yoke, or by a public act like Hananiah's breaking the yoke, but by verbal imagery. In the case of Nah 1:11-14 this verbal imagery is based on a mythic archetype, but in the case of Ezek 24:1-14 and Ezek 17:1-24 it is based on allegories involving familiar domestic objects (i.e., a stew pot) or native fauna and flora (i.e., eagles, cedar trees, and vines). In any case, however, the objects and gestures of many prophetic symbolic actions have basically the same function as the verbal imagery of a prophetic symbolic interpretation of a past event. By relating the event to the symbol, whether the symbol is verbally described or dramatically enacted, the pattern of Yahweh's involvement in the ongoing course of history is disclosed.

The illuminating parallel provided by Jer 28 does not mean that a prophetic symbolic interpretation of a past event necessarily presupposes a setting marked by prophetic conflict. In Jer 28 both Jeremiah and Hananiah agree that the intervention of the Babylonians is somehow yokelike, and they disagree over what the symbol shows about the significance of this event. In Nah 1:11-14 there is no indication of any conflict over what the mythic archetype shows about the event reported in v. 11. The form of this unit simply reflects a situation in which the theological significance of this event would remain ambiguous without the prophetic insight that emerges from interpreting it in terms of the mythic archetype. The genre concerns past events that have been remembered as turning points of some kind but whose implications for the present and future are uncertain and remain to be seen.

Although this unit has an identifiable generic structure, and although this generic structure is typical of an independently existing kind of prophetic speech with a particular setting, it is unlikely that this particular example of the genre ever existed independently in such a setting (→ 1:2–2:11, Setting).

Intention

This unit aims for its audience to identify with the unnamed feminine character whom it primarily addresses. They are to understand their present situation and future prospects as the unfolding result of Yahweh's involvement in a historical process that began with a particularly portentous event. A superior enemy

53

force, personified here as an unnamed masculine character, once nearly over-whelmed the feminine character as part of Yahweh's plan to punish her. This enemy, however, became too ruthless and overbearing to serve Yahweh's pur-pose any longer. That he departed without managing to destroy her should therefore be seen in terms of Yahweh's pattern of containing and finally de-stroying the primordial forces of chaos. The departure was a sign not only of Yahweh's intention to deliver her on that occasion but also of his intention to protect her from then on and ultimately to free her from this evil enemy. She thus need not fear that this enemy's power will continue. On the contrary, his total destruction is to be expected.

Bibliography

J. A. Emerton, "Sheol and the Sons of Belial," *VT* 37 (1987) 214-18; V. Maag, "B^{e}lija'al im Alten Testament," *TZ* 221 (1965) 287-99; R. Rosenberg, "The Concept of Biblical 'Belial,'" in *Proceedings of the Eighth World Congress of Jewish Studies (1981), Division A: The Period of the Bible* (Jerusalem: World Union of Jewish Studies, 1982) 35-40; D. W. Thomas, "*b^{e}lîya'al* in the Old Testament," in *Biblical and Patristic Studies in Memory of Robert Pierce Casey* (ed. J. N. Birdsall and R. W. Thomson; Freiburg: Herder, 1963) 11-19.

PROPHECIES ARE BEING FULFILLED! 2:1-11
(*RSV* 1:15–2:10)

Structure

I. Announcement of salvation for Judah	2:1
A. Report of the appearance of a messenger of peace	2:1aα
B. Twofold command to celebrate	2:1aβ
1. Keep your feasts!	2:1aβ^1
2. Fulfill your vows!	2:1aβ^2
C. Explication	2:1b
1. Promise: never again shall self-destructive lawlessness threaten to overwhelm you	2:1bα
2. Rationale: it is utterly cut off	2:1bβ
II. Announcement of punishment for Nineveh	2:2-11
A. Report of an enemy campaign: a shatterer has come up against you	2:2aα
B. Fourfold command to prepare for siege	2:2aβb
1. Man the ramparts!	2:2aβ
2. Watch the road!	2:2bα
3. Gird your loins!	2:2bβ^1
4. Collect all your strength!	2:2bβ^2

This unit consists of two parts, 2:1 and 2:2-11, that are largely parallel in their form but contrasting in their content. Each part directly addresses a female character, as indicated by the second person feminine singular forms in v. 1aβb and v. 2aα. First comes an announcement of something that has happened (v. 1aα, v. 2aα), followed by commands directing the addressee to take an appropriate course of action (v. 1aβ, v. 2aβb). Then there is a prophetic explication of this turn of events (v. 1b, v. 3) that provides a rationale for such commands. This explication describes the significance of what is initially announced (v. 1aα, v. 2aα), relating it to what has been prophesied in 1:11-14 concerning the nature of Yahweh's involvement in the overall situation. The second part differs from the first by adding in 2:4-11 a narrative continuation of what is announced in 2:2aα, recounting the final outcome.

The first part of this unit (2:1) begins by announcing the arrival of a messenger of peace (v. 1aα). As commands are issued regarding an appropriately festive response (v. 1aβ), the feminine character to whom these commands are addressed is explicitly identified as Judah. The explication (v. 1b) further describes the messenger's proclamation of peace in terms of the event reported in 1:11 and the salvation prophesied in 1:12-13. In 1:11-13 the departure of the masculine character (v. 11) is taken to portend that the forces of "self-destructive lawlessness" (bĕlîyā'al [RSV "villainy"]) have been "cut off" ('br), so that the feminine character will "never again" (lō' 'ôd) be threatened by them (vv. 12-13). In 2:1b Judah similarly receives word that "all such self-destructive lawlessness" (bĕlîya'al kullô [RSV "the wicked"]) has indeed now been utterly "cut off" ('br), so that Judah will "never again" (lō' 'ôd) be threatened by it. As the fulfillment of the prophecy in 1:12-13 is announced in 2:1, the feminine character to whom 1:11-13 was addressed is also retrospectively identified as Judah.

Although the second part of this unit (2:2-11) is also addressed to an initially unidentified feminine character, a radical change in content suggests that this announcement is no longer addressed to Judah. Judah has just been promised in 2:1 that she will not be attacked, and 2:2 announces precisely the opposite, namely, that the addressee is being attacked. The attacker confronting the unidentified feminine addressee is likewise unidentified, and is described only as a mēpîṣ (RSV "shatterer," although "scatterer" would perhaps be a better translation of this term). The announcement itself (v. 2aα) is appropriately followed by commands to take proper measures in preparation for the enemy on-

slaught (v. 2aβb). The explication (v. 3) puts this attack into a broad historical
and theological perspective. It is part of Yahweh's plan to reverse a historical
process in which his people, including all Israel and not just Judah, have long
been at the mercy of their plundering foes.

The explication in 2:3 thus describes the attack announced in 2:2aα in
terms of what is reported in 1:11 and what is prophesied in 1:12-14. In 1:11-14
the departure of the masculine character is taken to portend that the feminine
character — who can now be identified as Judah — will no longer be afflicted
by Yahweh with subjection to yokes and bonds such as his. In 2:3 the attack
announced in 2:2 is described in terms of Yahweh's taking decisive action
against all those who have plundered his people. The second feminine character, who is addressed in 2:2 with the announcement of an attack against her,
cannot simply be equated with the masculine character addressed in 1:14, but
the attack against the second feminine character is described in 2:3 as the fulfillment of the punishment prophesied for this masculine character in 1:14.

Unlike the first part of this unit (2:1), the second part (2:2-11) continues
with an impressive narrative description (2:4-11) of what happens as a result of
the event that is initially announced (2:2aα). Vv. 4-11 tell how the defensive
measures commended to the feminine character in 2:2aβb are finally of no
avail, as she is overrun and destroyed by the *mēpîṣ*. Well into this narrative the
defeated feminine character is identified, almost in passing, as Nineveh (2:9).
This disclosure retroactively gives greater historical specificity to the background of both this unit and the preceding unit. The masculine character, who
is mentioned in 1:11-13 and directly addressed in 1:14, is the Assyrian king;
and the second feminine character, who is directly addressed in 2:2-11, is his
capital city.

The two units in 1:11–2:11 thus have in view the whole course of Assyrian intervention in the affairs of both the northern and the southern kingdoms,
from around the last half of the eighth century to the final decades of the seventh century BCE. The fall of Nineveh is seen as Yahweh's decisive reversal of
the historical process of Assyrian domination, which he had originally intended for the punishment of his people. This reversal was foreshadowed in
the departure of the Assyrian troops, who in 701 had besieged Jerusalem but
had left without taking the city (2 Kgs 18:13–19:37). Assyrian hegemony had
resulted in chaotic disruption of the world order rather than peaceful stability.
The failure of the Assyrians to take Jerusalem signaled that they had in effect
become enemies of Yahweh and could no longer serve his purpose. This event
thus portended the doom of the Assyrian kingship (1:11-14), and the fall of
Nineveh became the context in which this prophecy of punishment finally
came to be fulfilled (2:2-11).

Genre

The generic form of this unit derives from the metaphor of the prophet as sentinel. It was the job of the sentinel to keep watch on the city wall, or at some
other vantage point, and to look for the approach of messengers (2 Sam 18:24-

27) or other persons (2 Sam 13:34), as well as for troop movements (1 Sam 14:16; Lam 4:17). When the sentinel saw something, he then had to interpret its significance (2 Kgs 9:17-20) and, if need be, to issue directives concerning an appropriate response.

The prophetic role might be analogously defined in terms of keeping informed about contemporary developments, interpreting them in the light of Yahweh's purpose as signs of the times, and announcing them so as to evoke an appropriate response (Isa 21:6-10; 52:7-10; Jer 6:17; Ezek 3:17-21; 33:2-9; Mic 7:4, 7; Hab 2:1). A prophetic speech conceived in terms of this analogy might take the form of a sentinel's report, beginning with *hinnēh* ("behold!") and the announcement of a messenger's approach, as in Nah 2:1aα (cf. Isa 52:7), or simply with the announcement of troop movements, as in Nah 2:2aα (cf. Isa 21:9a). The initial announcement might be followed by commands directing an appropriate response, as in Nah 2:1aβ and 2:2aβb (cf. Isa 52:9a; Jer 6:17a). A specifically prophetic adaptation of this speech form would also include some explication of the announced developments in the light of Yahweh's involvement in the situation, as in Nah 2:1b and 2:3 (cf. Isa 21:9b-10). As this unit has all these elements, one may aptly describe it as a PRO-PHETIC SENTINEL REPORT (→ Hab 1:5-11).

Setting

The very concept of the prophet as sentinel presupposes the kind of social situation in which one could be well informed regarding contemporary political and military developments. The prophet who identified with this concept would probably have moved in circles that had some access to the reports of the messengers for whom sentinels would actually be watching. For example, this particular unit presupposes the kind of news that a real messenger would have brought to Jerusalem, informing the city that the Assyrian capital had been attacked.

In at least one instance the prophet's role as sentinel is prominently associated with the prophet's function as intercessor in communal complaint liturgies (Hab 2:1; → Hab 1:2-17; 3:1-19; cf. Ps 5:4 [*RSV* 3]). Such an association cannot be extended into a general description of the background of the prophet as sentinel, nor can it be taken as a general description of the setting of the prophetic sentinel report. It does suggest, however, that this concept of the prophetic role and this genre of prophetic speech generally pertained to a context in which prophets functioned as advisers to public leaders concerning current affairs (cf. Isa 37:1-4; Jer 37:3; Ezek 20:1). This manner of speaking served to make a prophet's view of some recent development a matter of public concern.

Although this unit has an identifiable generic structure, and although this generic structure is typical of an independently existing kind of prophetic speech with a particular setting, it is unlikely that this particular example of the genre ever existed independently in such a setting (→ 1:2–2:11, Setting).

Intention

This unit substantiates what has generally been said about Yahweh's treatment of his enemies (1:2-10), as this generalization has been applied to a specific historical case, but a historical case in which the participants have until now remained more or less anonymous (1:11-14). This unit announces that present events are actually working out in accord with the foregoing prophetic interpretation (1:12-14) of a particular past event (1:11), as it also identifies the participants in the historical case in question. The protagonist is Israel, personified by a feminine character representing the kingdom of Judah; and the antagonist is Assyria, personified by a masculine character representing the Assyrian king as well as a feminine character representing the Assyrian capital of Nineveh.

The audience is meant to understand that although Yahweh used Assyria to destroy the northern kingdom of Israel, and although he also subjected Judah to Assyrian control, this did not necessarily mean either that Yahweh recognized Assyria as the embodiment of divine justice or that Yahweh intended to obliterate his people altogether. Long ago during the reign of Hezekiah, in the Assyrians' departure from Jerusalem, Yahweh signaled that he would eventually overthrow the Assyrians and begin to restore all that they had taken from Israel. Current developments are now bearing out this prophetic interpretation of the departure, and because of Nineveh's overthrow Judah can begin to celebrate the prospect of freedom. Such divine involvement in human affairs is predicated on Yahweh's power as creator to control and contain the forces of chaos.

Bibliography

P. Humbert, "La vision de Nahoum 2,4-11," *AfO* 5 (1928-29) 14-19.

Chapter 4

THE SECOND MAJOR SECTION OF THE BOOK (2:12–3:19 [*RSV* 2:11–3:19]) AND ITS INDIVIDUAL UNITS

A CHALLENGE TO NINEVEH'S HUBRIS, 2:12–3:19 (*RSV* 2:11–3:19)

Structure

Although many scholars would recognize the blocks of text that figure in this outline as units of some kind, there is virtually no unanimity concerning either their nature or their overall configuration. The extent to which opinions differ in this regard can be illustrated by the following random sample of the diverging views.

Humbert ("Problèmes," 8-9 and passim) construes 2:12-14 as a prophecy of punishment introduced by a mock lamentation, 3:1-7 as a prophecy of

59

punishment introduced by a dirge, 3:8-17 as a satire, and 3:18-19 as another mock lamentation; and he understands this sequence to reflect a liturgical process.

Schulz (pp. 92, 101-2) views 2:12–3:19 as a redactionally unified composition that brings together two originally somewhat disparate elements: a two-part cycle of eschatological divine judgments (2:12-14; 3:4-6) and a mock lamentation over Nineveh (3:7-18). Part of a song describing the destruction of Nineveh (3:1-3) has been interpolated into this redactional unit, and a conclusion has been added (3:19) in order to relate this section of the book to the foregoing section.

Keller (pp. 101-2) sees this section of the book as a continuation of the battle description begun in 2:2-11 (*RSV* 1-10). He regards 2:2–3:19 as a long prophetic poem divided into nine strophes, some of which coincide with the textual units delimited in the outline above and some of which do not. In his view this poem was designed to announce the fall of the city and to bring this about through its incantatory force.

In contrast, Rudolph (pp. 165-87) finds relatively little compositional integrity here. He sees 2:12-14 as the mocking conclusion of the prophetic vision described in 2:2-11. 3:1-7 is a woe oracle, and 3:8-19 a mélange of originally unrelated utterances brought together under the rubric of sealing Nineveh's fate.

Roberts (pp. 37-38) sees 2:12-14 as part of a larger oracle beginning in 2:2, directed against the Assyrian king. 3:1-17 forms a "*hôy* oracle" against Nineveh; and 3:18-19, another oracle against the Assyrian king, constitutes a separate concluding section.

The issue of the compositional structure of this section of the book comes to a head in the question of whether there is a fundamental division at 2:12 and, if so, what its nature is. A number of commentators, like Rudolph and Roberts, would rather see 2:12-14 as a conclusion for the description of the sacking of Nineveh in 2:4-11. Two things militate against this view, however.

First, the description in 2:4-11 forms an integral part of the unit (→) 2:1-11 (*RSV* 1:15–2:10), and this unit does not need such elements as the mock lamentation in 2:12-13 or the announcement of punishment in 2:14 to form a unit with the recognizable generic profile of an extended sentinel report. Second, although 2:12-14 does pick up in the middle of what is described in 2:4-11, the same is true for most of ch. 3 as well. If this is the determining factor, then all the material in 2:4–3:19 belongs together as a single unit, as Keller maintains. That most of the commonly recognized units in 2:12–3:19 contain some kind of reprise on the battle description in 2:4-11 suggests, above all, that they all have something in common and, moreover, that by virtue of this commonality they collectively stand together in the same relationship vis-à-vis 2:1-11.

The heuristic supposition of a major subdivision of the book at 2:12 thus begins with the basic observation that the parts of this section all hang together by virtue of their reiteration, in various ways, of something that has already been communicated at the conclusion of the book's first major section. The substantiation of this supposition requires some consideration of whether and how the various units of 2:12–3:19 are interrelated in additional ways, as well as some consideration of how this section's connection with 2:1-11 figures in the composition of the book as a whole. The structure analysis of the (→) book as a whole has already taken up the latter consideration, and the following discussion will take up the former consideration.

This section begins with two prophecies claiming that the attack on Nineveh is a manifestation of Yahweh's intention to punish Assyria for having a king who "preys on" *(trp)* other nations (2:12-14), and for Nineveh's "prostituting" *(znh)* herself in the conduct of international relations by "selling" *(mkr)* and thus exploiting other nations (3:1-7). As a consequence of these offenses the city will be destroyed and its survivors will be subjected to degrading humiliation. These two prophecies are linked with respect to their dominant themes by a catchword. Both the ill-gotten gains resulting from the Assyrian king's mistreatment of his victims (2:13b) and Nineveh's self-prostitution (3:1b) are termed *ṭerep* ("prey"; *RSV* "booty").

Nineveh is next questioned as to whether she may have presumed to be immune from this fate, and is disabused of any such delusive fantasies by a comparison with Thebes (3:8-12). Just as the apparently invincible power of Thebes nevertheless proved vulnerable to the Assyrians, the apparently invincible power of Nineveh will also prove vulnerable to some other rival. Nineveh's seemingly impregnable fortifications, like the first figs of the season, are actually ripe for devouring.

This section concludes with two speeches announcing that events have turned out much as the two initial prophecies foretold. The first announcement (3:13-17) reports that the damage inflicted on Nineveh is so great that the city can never regain the capacity to defend itself. The second announcement (3:18-19) discloses that the survivors are in exile, scattered and leaderless, as it anticipates the imminent and certain death of the Assyrian king. Like the two initial prophecies, these two concluding announcements are thematically linked by a catchword. Both the city's incapacity to recover from the damage and the king's incapacity to recover from his wound are described in terms of how this affects the "people" (*'am*, 3:13a [*RSV* "troops"]; → 3:13-17, Text; 3:18b).

The composition of this section thus develops through three phases. In the first phase (2:12–3:7) the downfall of Assyria is well underway, and this is shown to be in accord with the will of Yahweh, focusing first on the elimination of the Assyrian king and his line (2:12-14), and then on the overthrow of Nineveh, the capital city (3:1-7). The second phase (3:8-12) questions whether Nineveh's presumed invincibility has any basis in reality, citing Thebes as a recent example of a presumably invincible city that was nevertheless overthrown. In the third phase (3:13-19) Assyria is falling, and it is announced that this is happening in accord with the previously revealed will of Yahweh, focusing first on the overthrow of Nineveh, the capital city (3:13-17), and then on the elimination of the Assyrian king (3:18-19). The compositional development thus progresses from prophecy (2:12–3:7) to fulfillment (3:3:13-19), by way of a pivotal section (3:8-12) that emphasizes that there is historical precedent for the overthrow of the seemingly permanent status quo. The thematic transition from kingship (2:12-14) to capital city (3:1-7) in the prophecy phase corresponds chiastically with the thematic transition from capital city (3:13-17) to kingship (3:18-19) in the fulfillment phase. The prophecy of the kingship's end specifically includes the stipulation that royal "messengers" *(mal'ākayik)* will no longer go out from Nineveh (2:14b), and the announcement of this prophecy's fulfillment correspondingly concludes with the observation that the "news" *(šimăkā)* of Nineveh's defeat is reaching the rest of the world.

Although this section is not basically narration, a narrative sequence is implied in the order of its units. The temporal perspective of each unit partly overlaps with the next, in such a way that the entire series progresses from a point in time prior to the fall of Nineveh to a point in time after this event. The first unit (2:12-14) begins with a question presupposing that Nineveh's security has been threatened, and on this basis proceeds to anticipate the eventual demolition of the city's military capability, the annihilation of its royal house, the removal of any opportunity for it to victimize other nations, and the silencing of its communications. As the next unit (3:1-7) opens, Nineveh is under attack but is not yet totally defeated. Many have been slain, but the survivors have not yet reached the point of experiencing the degradation to which victors typically subject their captives.

The third unit (3:8-12) reaches back to the precedent of Thebes' survivors being led into captivity, and thus implies that the same fate will inevitably happen to Nineveh's survivors. This remains to be seen, however, for the Assyrians have not quite yet lost control of the city. They are still holding on, but the main fortifications have now grown weak enough to fall — like ripe figs — at the slightest shake.

The fourth unit (3:13-17) reports that the city's defenses are being destroyed more quickly than they can be repaired, and that the loss of population is too great to be restored. In effect, Nineveh has thus lost the battle. The fifth and final unit (3:18-19) begins with a disclosure that the survivors have indeed been taken into exile, and ends still anticipating the death of the mortally wounded Assyrian king.

Every unit of this section, each in its own way, extends the description of what has already happened and what is yet to happen in the ongoing process of prophecy and fulfillment. As a whole, this section recapitulates the foregoing brief description in 2:2-11 of basically the same progression. The announcement that "the scatterer" *(mēpîṣ; RSV* "shatterer") has attacked (2:2) finally progresses to the announcement that the Assyrians have been "scattered" (3:18b; *nāpōṣû* [so *RSV* and *BHS*]). The thematic development of this section thus unfolds in a context that also includes an episodic and impressionistic representation of the fall of Nineveh, and is thus brought into a direct relationship with the recapitulation of this particular course of events.

Genre

This section is generically complex. It consists of five units, each of which has a recognizable generic structure of its own: two (→) prophecies of punishment against a foreign nation (2:12-14; 3:1-7), a (→) prophetic interrogation (3:8-12), a (→) mock sentinel report (3:13-17), and a (→) mock dirge (3:18-19). As noted above (→ Structure), these units are arranged so as to constitute an extended reprise of the brief description of Nineveh's overthrow in 2:2-11 (*RSV* 1-10). As they combine to serve this function vis-à-vis the battle description in the previous section, the question is whether they also collectively assume any particular generic form. When 2:12–3:19 is viewed in this light, its overall form can be seen to resemble that of the first section in several major respects.

The first section engages the audience to get them to reflect on the present significance of Yahweh's involvement in a past event. Inferential questioning (1:2-10) and various kinds of direct address are used to get the presumably Judahite audience to reflect on the present significance of the Assyrians' departure from Jerusalem in 701, an event that now portends their deliverance from Assyrian domination (1:11-14). The second section continues in much the same vein, also using inferential questioning (3:8-9) and only one kind of direct address for a similar purpose. The second section consists entirely of speeches that, like 1:14 and 2:2-11, are ostensibly directed to foreigners but are meant to be overheard by a Judahite audience. As in 2:2-11, a feminine personification of the city of Nineveh is addressed in 2:12–3:17; and as in 1:14, the king of Assyria is addressed in 3:18-19. These devices get the ostensibly Ninevite audience to reflect on the current significance of the Assyrians' defeat of Thebes in 663 (3:10), an event that now portends the Assyrians' own defeat (3:11-12).

In the second section, as in the first, Yahweh's involvement in Assyria's rise and fall is described as conforming to a pattern of divine activity with a primordial precedent. The mythic allusions in 1:4 recall Yahweh's ability to control the watery forces of chaos and to subdue them whenever they threaten his maintenance of a just world order. On the historical scene Yahweh can similarly use the nations for his own ends, but then subdue them whenever they threaten his maintenance of a just world order (1:8-9). In the first section the Assyrians' failure to take Jerusalem is seen as a turning point marking the recurrence of this pattern. Yahweh had previously used the Assyrians as his agents to punish Judah; but now that they have dared to oppose him, he will destroy them as he once subdued his watery foes (1:11-14).

In the second section the fall of Thebes is seen as a similar turning point in the recurrence of a similar mythic pattern, but one that signals the Assyrians' ascent rather than their decline. The status of Thebes is described in terms of keeping the Nile's waters at bay (3:8), thus implying that the power of Thebes is a manifestation of the same divine power that maintains the world order. The defeat of Thebes in turn implies that they no longer serve the divine purpose and are hence being treated as enemies. Their conquerors (i.e., the Assyrians) are thus taking their place as agents of this divine power. Like

Yahweh's mythic exploits, the fall of Thebes provides a precedent for the kind of historical turnabout through which the Assyrians are being deprived of their dominant role.

The first section is designed to show that prophecies about the eventual outcome of the Assyrians' departure from Jerusalem (1:11-14) are being fulfilled in the fall of Nineveh (2:1-11 [*RSV* 1:15–2:10]). The second section is similarly designed to show that prophecies claiming Yahweh's responsibility for the fall of Nineveh (2:12–3:7) are being fulfilled in the way that this event has now actually come about (3:12-19).

Despite these similarities there is also a significant difference between the first and the second sections of Nahum. Each induces the audience to draw a somewhat different kind of lesson from past events. In the first section the Assyrians' departure from Jerusalem has a significance that is prophetically discerned, a significance that is described in terms of the ongoing relevance of past prophecies and with explicit reference to Yahweh's involvement in the event. This raises the issue of whether the audience will share the prophetic perception of what Yahweh is currently doing. In the second section, however, the overthrow of Thebes has a significance that is more or less self-evident, a significance that is described in terms of historical probability and without any explicit reference to Yahweh's involvement in the event. This raises the issue of whether the audience will continue to hold the historically improbable assumption of an unchanging status quo.

Comparison of the first and second sections shows that they are basically the same kind of PROPHETIC HISTORICAL EXEMPLUM (→ 1:2–2:11 [*RSV* 1:2–2:10], Genre). Their main difference is due to the fact that the second section serves as a reprise and extension of the subunit with which the first section concludes (2:4-11), as a speech fictively addressed to the Assyrians concerning the loss of their capital city and king. In keeping with this convention of direct address, this section refrains from arguments based ultimately on either revelations received by Yahweh's prophets or claims about Yahweh himself. The historical lesson is not grounded primarily on knowledge of Yahweh because Assyrians, by definition, do not know Yahweh.

This speech does claim that Yahweh is responsible for the fate now befalling the Ninevites, and that this can be verified by the fulfillment of prophecies concerning the fall of Nineveh. Its main thrust, however, is to upbraid the Assyrians for not learning the lesson of their own history, which should have been obvious whether or not they realized that Yahweh was in control of it. By fictively addressing the Ninevites in this vein, this speech informs its Judahite audience that their God is in control of the present international situation even though the imperial powers do not recognize him. It presents to its Judahite audience the negative example of a nation that inadvertently finds itself in opposition to Yahweh, because it did not learn from its own historical experience the lesson of its limitations.

Setting

Prophetic historical exempla, such as Deut 32 and Ps 78, were probably used as ritual instruction lyrically recited by a prophetic teacher in a liturgical context (→ 1:2–2:11 [*RSV* 1:2–2:10], Setting). One cannot assume, however, that this section of the book had the same setting as these other poems just because it shares with them the same generic form. In this particular case the identification of the genre is not a sufficient basis on which to identify the setting because the text is so composite. This section comprises five units, each of which has the form of an independently existing type of prophetic speech that could conceivably have its setting in the realm of prophetic public oratory (see the discussion below of each individual unit). It is perhaps theoretically possible that this section's component units each existed independently as prophetic speeches of different kinds, and that they were subsequently combined to form this section. It seems unlikely, however, that five prophetic speeches designed for various purposes and occasions would so readily lend themselves, as prefabricated units, to forming an altogether different kind of prophetic communication designed for an altogether different purpose and occasion.

This improbability raises the question of whether the units in this section ever existed independently outside the context of the section itself, and what is true of each unit in this regard may also be true of this entire section. Although it has the form of an independently existing genre, and although this genre was probably used for ritual instruction in a liturgical context, this particular example of the genre may never have existed independently in such a setting. This is strongly suggested by the fact that this section assumes the generic form of a prophetic historical exemplum within the larger literary context of the entire book, as an imitation and extension of the preceding section, and as part of a larger generic whole. The setting of this section would thus be identical with the setting of the (→) book as a whole.

Intention

The intention of this section is threefold. First, it informs its audience that the battle of Nineveh is turning out in accord with Yahweh's intention that the Assyrians' mistreatment of their subject nations should not go unpunished. They may therefore join in the international celebration of Nineveh's suffering the same cruel fate to which she subjected others. Second, the audience is also assured that Yahweh's involvement in the fall of Nineveh is not just wishful thinking from their own local perspective, but an act of divine justice that can be universally perceived as such, even if Judah alone realizes that their God Yahweh is responsible. Third, the text sets before its audience the negative example of a nation that has not taken to heart the lessons of its own past.

65

YAHWEH IS REQUITING THE CITY WHOSE KING HAS PREYED ON HIS VICTIMS, 2:12-14 (*RSV* 11-13)

Structure

I. Accusation: a place compared with the lair of a
predatory lion   2:12-13
  A. Taunt: rhetorical question implying that the lair
is no longer secure   2:12
  B. Description of the king lion as an effective provider
for his pride   2:13
II. Announcement of punishment: speech of Yahweh   2:14
  A. Challenge formula: behold, I am against you   2:14aα^1
  B. Oracle formula: says Yahweh of hosts   2:14aα^2
  C. Description of punishment   2:14aβb
    1. Loss of armed might   2:14aβ
      a. Yahweh's action: I will burn chariots . . .   2:14aβ^1
      b. Consequences: the sword will devour
your young . . .   2:14aβ^2
    2. Loss of victims   2:14b
      a. Yahweh's action: I will cut off your prey . . .   2:14bα
      b. Consequences: the voice of your messengers
shall no more be heard   2:14bβ

The beginning of this unit is indicated by a rhetorical shift from the foregoing description of destruction to questioning, and by a simultaneous shift in content. The latter is evident in the introduction of a new metaphor that is operative throughout this unit, comparing an unidentified imperial city with the lair of a predatory lion. Despite these signals of a new section, the city is addressed in the same second person feminine singular form as Nineveh was in the preceding subunit (2:2-11 [*RSV* 1-10]), thus suggesting that they are one and the same.

The description is formulated primarily in terms of the vehicle in vv. 12-13, i.e., in terms of the king lion's bringing back his kill to feed the mates and children of his pride; and it is formulated primarily in terms of the tenor in v. 14, i.e., in terms of the city's loss of such a capacity to prey on conquered peoples. The principal points of comparison are established by the reiteration of *kĕpirîm* in both v. 12a and v. 14aβ, so that the city's inhabitants are metaphorically represented by the "young lions" of the pride; and also by the similar repetition of words derived from the root *ṭrp* in v. 13a (*ṭōrēp; RSV* "tore"), v. 13b (*ṭerep* and *ṭĕrēpâ; RSV* "prey" and "torn flesh"), and v. 14b (*ṭarpēk; RSV* "your prey"), so that the city's subjects are compared with the prey of the king lion.

This metaphor functions to provide the derogatory imagery in terms of which the city is first accused of enriching its own royal house by its exploitative imperialistic conquests (vv. 12-13), and is then informed that Yahweh will deprive the city of its power to act this way (v. 14). The heart of the accusation in v. 13 corresponds in its two main parts with the two main parts of the announcement of punishment in v. 14. The description in v. 13a of the king lion as a dynastic progenitor, providing for his harem and the offspring who will succeed him, corresponds with the announcement in v. $14a\beta^2$ that the "young lions" or princes will be killed. Similarly, the description in v. 13b of the king lion as a hunter, who amasses a plentiful supply of meat for his pride, corresponds with the announcement in v. 14b that the supply of prey will be cut off.

The initial taunt serves both to introduce the metaphor in terms of which this whole unit is formulated and to locate the announcement of punishment temporally. The mocking question in v. 12 suggests that the inviolability of the city is already threatened, but the announcement of judgment in v. 14 indicates that its final destruction is yet to happen. This unit thus reflects a point in time before Nineveh had actually fallen, but after the city's security had become so compromised that this outcome seemed inevitable.

Genre

This unit is basically a PROPHECY OF PUNISHMENT AGAINST A FOREIGN NATION ($\rightarrow$ Zeph 2:5-7, Genre), but one that is distinguished by the formulation of its accusation in terms of a TAUNT. Because this element situates the pronouncement of Yahweh in the midst of something that is already happening ($\rightarrow$ Structure), the speech as a whole serves not so much to anticipate what will happen as to identify it as an action of Yahweh, so that the outcome will be seen to have happened in accord with his purpose.

Setting

Prophecies of punishment against foreign nations were often spoken on some momentous occasion in the life of Jerusalem's royal court or cult ($\rightarrow$ Zeph 2:5-7, Setting). This is the sort of speech that might have been made in response to the news that an attack on Nineveh was imminent, perhaps on the occasion of some special public celebration of this development, or in the context of some regularly recurring ceremonial event at which such critical international developments were given public attention.

This unit has the form of a type of prophetic speech that could exist independently in its own setting, but this does not necessarily mean that this unit ever existed independently in such a setting ($\rightarrow$ 2:12–3:19 [*RSV* 2:11–3:19], Setting).

Intention

This unit identifies the attack threatening the imperial city of Nineveh as a crisis caused by Yahweh, through which he is bringing deliverance to his own people and redressing the Assyrian king's predatory abuse of his power for the aggrandizement of his dynasty and capital at the expense of innocent victims.

Bibliography

→ Zeph 2:5-7, Bibliography.

YAHWEH IS REQUITING THE CITY THAT HAS PROSTITUTED ITSELF, 3:1-7

Text

In view of the dominant metaphor in this unit (→ Structure), a more literalistic translation of 3:4 is preferable to the *RSV*, such as: "And all for the countless harlotries of the harlot, the good-looking one, the mistress of sorceries, who sells nations for her harlotries and peoples for her sorceries." This follows Dahood's analysis of a causal *beth*, while rejecting the attempts made by him and Winton Thomas to find here some root other than *mkr* ("sell"; *RSV* "betray"). See M. J. Dahood, "Causal *beth* and the root *mkr* in Nahum 3.4," *Bib* 52 (1971) 395-96; D. Winton Thomas, "The Root *mkr* in Hebrew," *JTS* 37 (1936) 388-89; idem, "A Further Note on the Root *mkr* in Hebrew," *JTS* 3 (1952) 214. The verb in question is simply *mkr*, used here in a metaphorical sense, whose larger connotations become evident in the light of the overall context.

In 3:7b the second person feminine singular form of the MT, *lāk* ("for you"), should be retained instead of preferring the third person feminine singular form of the LXX ("for her"), as the *RSV* does.

Structure

I. Accusation: fall of a city compared with the punishment
   of a harlot   3:1-4
   A. Mock lament   3:1
      1. Woe cry   3:1aα
      2. Its object: the bloody city full of lies and booty   3:1aβbα
      3. The lamentable state of the city: no end to the
         predation!   3:1bβ
   B. Description of attack: impressions of the fighting   3:2-3
      1. The sound and movement of the chariotry   3:2
      2. The appearance of the weapons   3:3a
      3. The heaviness of the casualties   3:3b
   C. Reason for the disaster   3:4
      1. Basic statement: all because of the harlot's
         countless harlotries   3:4aα

This unit begins with an accusation directed against an initially unidentified city (vv. 1-4), sarcastically lamenting that the city is now suffering the consequences of having acted like a "harlot" *(znh)* in the sphere of international relations. This is followed by an announcement of punishment addressed directly to the same city (vv. 5-7), which finally turns out to be Nineveh (v. 7aβ), informing her of Yahweh's intention to humiliate her publicly, describing the measures he will take in terms of this same metaphor as punishments appropriate for such harlotry.

The accusatory function of vv. 1-4 emerges only gradually, as this subunit begins on a note of ironic ambiguity. From the way the city is characterized in v. 1, it is not clear whether she is bloody because of the bloodshed that she has inflicted on others, or because of the bloodshed that others are inflicting on her. It is likewise not clear whether the city is full of lies and booty because she has deceived and plundered others, or because others are deceiving and plundering her. It is thus not clear whether the initial "woe" is a sincere cry of lament exclaimed over an oppressed city in distress, or a sarcastic mock lament exclaimed over an oppressing city that deserves to be in distress. The description of the city under attack (vv. 2-3) at first seems to resolve this ambiguity in favor of the former possibility, but then in v. 4 it turns out that all this destruction comes as retribution for the city's harlotlike mistreatment of other peoples. Vv. 1-3 are ostensibly a true lament, but one that is finally given a sarcastic twist by the addition of v. 4. This subunit turns out to be accusatory in the sense that it describes Nineveh as suffering a fate that she has brought on herself, as the well-deserved consequence of her international infidelity.

Nineveh is being charged with behavior that is metaphorically compared with "harlotry" *(znh)*. This charge is linked with the description of Nineveh's destruction in terms of the excessiveness of both the city's culpable actions and their consequences. The "fullness" *(mĕlē'â)* of the city's lies and booty (v. 1b) corresponds with the consequent "heaviness" *(kōbed; RSV* "heaps") of the casualties (v. 3a), just as "no lack" *(lō' yāmîš)* of plunder (v. 1b) corresponds with the consequent "endlessness" *('ên qēṣeh)* of the dead bodies (v. 3b). Similarly, the "countlessness" *(rōb)* of the city's harlotries (v. 4a) corresponds with the consequent "greatness" *(rōb)* of the carnage (v. 3b; *RSV* "hosts").

The term for "harlotry" *(znh)* applies to the behavior not only of a common whore but also of an adulterer, and even extends to include a general sort of infidelity in relationships (P. Bird, " 'To Play the Harlot': An Inquiry into an Old Testament Metaphor," in *Gender and Difference in Ancient Israel* [ed. P. Day; Minneapolis: Fortress, 1989] 75-94). The closely related offense of "sorcery" *(kšp; RSV* "charm") can simply entail the practice of magic, but it may also extend to include any corrupting influence. The archetypical "harlot," in the sense that applies here, is Jezebel, who was also infamous for her "sorceries" (2 Kgs 9:22). She unjustly exploited the resources of defenseless persons (1 Kgs 21:1-16), with which she supported national policies that were contrary to Yahweh's purposes for Israel as his people. Nineveh has similarly exploited defenseless peoples by expropriating their wealth and sending them into captivity, which is what *mkr* ("sell"; *RSV* "betray") connotes here (→ Text; cf. Gen 45:4; Amos 2:6). With such ill-gotten gains Nineveh has similarly pursued imperial policies that were contrary to Yahweh's purposes for Assyria as a world power.

The punishment that is announced for the city is initially described in terms that are consistent with the metaphor of "harlotry" (v. 5), taking the humiliating measures that were deemed appropriate treatment for an adulterer (cf. Hos 2:5, 11-12 [*RSV* 3, 9-10]); but the description is then extended in terms of the similarly dehumanizing actions to which a defeated city's survivors were usually subjected by their captors (v. 6; cf. Isa 20:1-6; Rudolph, 178). Upon beholding this great spectacle (v. 5b), world opinion will confirm the justness of Yahweh's action (v. 7). The rhetorical question of the witnesses suggests that no one will be found to mourn Nineveh's defeat (v. 7a), and in conclusion Yahweh echoes their sentiments, as he confronts Nineveh with another rhetorical question similarly suggesting that it will be impossible to find anyone to comfort the survivors (v. 7b).

The initial mock lament (vv. 1-4) serves to introduce the metaphor that is operative in this unit and also to locate the announcement of punishment temporally in relation to the events it describes. This speech comes just after that point in the fighting when defeat has become inevitable, the point at which this sort of "lamentation" would be in order, but before the humiliation of the survivors (vv. 5-7) that would take place only when the fighting has finally stopped.

Genre

This unit contains elements of the (→) dirge, but they are satirically adapted to form the kind of accusation that — in combination with an announcement of punishment — is typical of the PROPHECY OF PUNISHMENT AGAINST A FOREIGN NATION. Because the pronouncement of Yahweh is situated in the midst of something that is already happening (→ Structure), the primary point of the speech as a whole is not to anticipate the defeat of Nineveh as such, but to identify it as an event in which Yahweh is decisively involved.

Setting

→ 2:12-14 (*RSV* 11-13).

Intention

This unit describes the spectacular defeat of Nineveh and the consequent public humiliation of the survivors as the well-deserved fate that the Assyrians have brought on themselves, in which Yahweh's power and justice are manifest to all the world. Such punishment is appropriate in view of the ways in which the Assyrians have prostituted themselves in the exercise of their imperial prerogatives, abusively exploiting the human and material resources of conquered peoples.

Bibliography

→ Zeph 2:5-7, Bibliography.

THE CITY IS INTERROGATED FOR PRESUMING TO BE INVINCIBLE, 3:8-12

Structure

I. Rhetorical question asserting that Nineveh is no better
   than Thebes on the Nile   3:8aα

Although the addressee of the opening question is not identified, there is no indication of any change in this regard from the previous unit. It is therefore the city of Nineveh that is figuratively asked to imagine its present prospects in the light of what previously happened to the city of Thebes (v. 8aα). A comparison is then drawn (vv. 8aβ-12), suggesting that the same discrepancy experienced by Thebes, between apparent invincibility and actual vulnerability (vv. 8aβ-10), will also be experienced by Nineveh (vv. 11-12).

Thebes is portrayed as a focal point from which cosmic power radiates. Its actual geographical location, as a "city by the Nile," is made emblematic of the divine power to control the waters (v. 8aβb), the power that must be exercised in order for life and a just world order to exist — a central theme of ancient Near Eastern cosmologies. A correspondence is then drawn between Thebes as a manifestation of this divine power and Thebes as center of political power, the power by means of which the nations are governed (v. 9). In the seventh century Thebes was the city from which Ethiopia ruled over Egypt, uniting these two states and such neighboring peoples as Put and Libya in a strong imperial confederation. Despite this strength, Thebes was overthrown (v. 10) — as Nineveh well knows, since the Assyrians were the ones who took Thebes in 663 BCE.

The initial question thus mockingly presupposes a negative answer, insinuating that there is no reason for the Ninevites to think that they could not suffer the same fate that they themselves inflicted on Thebes. To deny this possibility is to be divorced from reality, and in this regard is comparable to being in a drunken stupor (v. 11a). To those in such a state of denial Nineveh may appear to be an invincible fortress (v. 11b); but in reality the city is as vulnerable as a ripe fig that, with just a little shake, will drop right into the waiting open mouth of its devourer (v. 12).

Genre

This unit has a taunting tone, but it is not on this account necessarily a (→) taunt in any strict sense (cf. Num 21:27-30), nor a prophetic adaptation of this genre (cf. Isa 14:4-23). The genre is evident from its recapitulation of the same combinations of elements found in (→) 1:2-10, namely, the combination of a rhetorical question with statements providing the information from which the answer is to be inferred. In contrast to the statements given in 1:2-10, which describe attributes of Yahweh, the statements given here compare Thebes with Nineveh. They nevertheless function similarly.

The answer to the leading question is to be inferred through the logic of inverse proportionality on which the comparison is based: If Thebes, whose defenses were virtually invulnerable, went into captivity and exile, then how much more should Nineveh, whose defenses are ripe for destruction, be vulnerable to the same fate. This unit thus has the same essentially aphoristic character as 1:2-10, and it serves the same confrontational function. It is thus a PROPHETIC INTERROGATION (→ 1:2-10, Genre).

Setting

In contrast with 1:2-10, which could conceivably have been spoken before the kind of public gathering to which it is ostensibly addressed (→ 1:2-10, Setting), this prophetic interrogation was not meant to be spoken in the presence of its addressee, the city of Nineveh. It rather reflects the kind of setting in which Nineveh could have been fictively personified and spoken to (→ Book as a Whole, Genre).

This unit has the form of a type of prophetic speech that could exist independently in its own setting, but this does not necessarily mean that this unit ever existed independently in such a setting (→ 2:12–3:19 [*RSV* 2:11–3:19], Setting).

Intention

In confronting its ostensible addressee, contextually identified as Nineveh, this unit conveys to those who actually hear it the message that no political power, no matter how strong, is immune to the kind of defeat that befell Thebes — least of all Nineveh in its present condition. As Nineveh confronts the prospect of suffering the same fate that she once inflicted on Thebes and many others, the audience is implicitly reminded that the exercise of imperial power is contingent on the maintenance of a just world order. To suppose otherwise is a self-deluding attempt to escape historical reality.

FURTHER RESISTANCE IS USELESS, 3:13-17

Text

The *RSV* translates 3:13aα as an insult to the machismo of Nineveh's armed forces: "Behold, your troops are women." Although a similar reading is given by other versions and many commentators, it is nevertheless problematic. In the ancient social context the courage and strength of enemy troops could indeed be impugned by labeling them "women" (cf. Isa 19:16; Jer 51:30), but there are two reasons for supposing that this is not the case here.

First, the term *'am* (lit. "people"; *RSV* "troops"), when applied to a city or locality, normally refers to its entire population, not just to the military segment of it (e.g., Jer 29:16, 25; Ruth 4:9; Zeph 1:11). The word can take on the particular connotation of military personnel, but usually in contexts where this is made explicit by the surrounding description (e.g., 1 Sam 11:11; 1 Kgs 20:10; Num 20:20). Second, in light of the overall context of this unit, it is unlikely that Nah 3:13aα is a sarcastic observation to the effect that Nineveh's troops have become cowardly and weak. The subsequent statements concerning the destruction of the city's gates and bars (3:13aβb) do not have such a derisive and insinuating tone. They simply provide a rather straightforward description of some effects of the fighting. Thus in all probability the point of v. 13aα is a similarly straightforward one: The city's manpower has been decimated. Hence the ironic commands to replenish the population in 3:15bβ (→ Structure).

All things considered, it is better to render 3:13aα somewhat literally as "your people are women," taking this as a description of the extent to which the men of the city have been killed off (cf. 3:3), leaving a population that consists largely of noncombatant females (cf. Isa 3:25–4:1).

Structure

This unit continues to be addressed directly to the personified city of Nineveh. It begins by reporting the damage done by an enemy onslaught to both the city's population (v. 13aα) and its points of access (v. 13aβb). This is followed by calls to restore the city's capability to withstand a siege by replenishing its water supply (v. 14aα) and building up its fortifications (v. 14aβb), as well as by augmenting its depleted population (v. 15b).

The commands urging such remedial measures are followed not by the kinds of motivations that would actually encourage compliance with them but by assertions of their ineffectiveness. Any attempts to restore Nineveh's readiness for siege are futile because the destruction will encompass not only the city's defenses but also its very capacity to furnish the materials for building them (v. 15). Any attempts to repopulate the city are similarly futile, because even those social classes whose size is supposedly the index of a city's wealth and power are actually a drain on the city's resources. Like a plague of locusts, they get all they can for themselves and then fly away (vv. 16-17). Given Nineveh's dysfunctional social system, an increase in the power structure would actually decrease the city's capacity to defend itself. Nineveh's defensive efforts are doomed because of both the overwhelming force of the enemy offensive from without and the undermining force of the degenerate social tendencies from within.

The destructive effects of these external and internal forces are linked by a locust metaphor, using the two terms *yeleq* (*RSV* "locust") and *'arbeh* (*RSV* "grasshopper") with reference to basically the same kind of insect. First the effects of the enemy's fire and sword are described in terms of their "devouring like the locust" (v. 15a). The following command to augment the population is couched in the same terms ("multiply like the locust!"), thus implying that the defensive measure of increasing the population will have much the same impact as the enemy offense (v. 15b). This implication is explicitly reinforced by subsequent comparison of both the burgeoning merchant class and the bloated ruling class with swarms of locusts. The military destructiveness that is coming at Nineveh from the outside is thus identified with the social self-destructiveness that is eating at Nineveh from the inside.

This unit takes the form of a rallying cry addressed to the beleaguered city, but an ironic one because it is in effect a statement of why this would be useless.

Genre

The form of this unit derives from the kind of speech a sentinel would make, whether announcing observations made from some vantage point to rouse a city under attack (Ezek 33:2-3) or spreading information gathered through reconnaissance regarding the attack of a city (Jer 48:19-20). Such a speech would primarily entail a brief description of the situation (2 Sam 18:24b-25a; 2 Kgs 9:17a), perhaps introduced with the interjection *hinnēh* ("behold!"; 2 Sam 13:34). This report would often be followed by signals or commands directing the people to make an appropriate response or take appropriate measures (Jer 6:17; 31:6; Isa 52:8-9). The structure of Nah 3:13-17 is based on this combination of elements, but the commands grow increasingly ironic as the futility of heeding them is repeatedly underscored (→ Structure). This unit is therefore a MOCK SENTINEL REPORT (→ Zech 11:1-3, Genre).

Setting

The sentinel report itself originated in the context of military operations and civil defense. Prophets borrowed this convention and employed it — though not necessarily in the ironic fashion that is evident here — in the context of prophetic public oratory (→ Nah 2:1-11 [*RSV* 1:15–2:10]; Hab 1:5-11). In this particular case the form does not actually convey to the Ninevites, to whom it is ostensibly addressed, any message about their threatened situation. The message that it relates would hardly be news to them. It rather serves to provide its Judahite audience, as they overhear it fictively spoken to Nineveh personified, with an assessment of the reason for Nineveh's present vulnerability to enemy attack (→ Book as a Whole, Genre).

The person who could make such an assessment in the midst of a crisis would have to be well informed about international affairs and would view analysis of international affairs as an aspect of the prophetic role. This unit thus reflects a setting in which a prophet, acting in a capacity metaphorically analogous to the role of a sentinel, publicly communicated his assessment of the current international scene. Such a speech might well have been delivered on a ceremonial occasion in the life of Jerusalem's royal court or cult, at which the news of such a momentous event as the attack of Nineveh was celebrated.

This unit has the form of a type of prophetic speech that could exist independently in its own setting, but this does not necessarily mean that this unit ever existed independently in such a setting (→ 2:12–3:19 [*RSV* 2:11–3:19], Setting).

Intention

The speaker impersonates a Ninevite sentinel, ironically warning the city that all attempts to defend themselves against attack are futile, thus informing the Judahite audience that internal social decay has made Nineveh vulnerable to her external enemies.

THE KING OF ASSYRIA IS FINISHED, 3:18-19

Structure

I. Description of the Assyrians' distress	3:18-19a
A. Distress of the king's subjects	3:18
1. Condition of the ruling class: shepherds and nobles asleep	3:18a
2. Consequences for the people as a whole: scattered on the mountains with no one to gather them	3:18b
B. Distress of the king himself: a serious wound with no one to assuage it	3:19a
II. Description of the international reaction	3:19b
A. Reaction proper: all who hear the news clap their hands	3:19bα
B. Explication (rhetorical question): who hasn't been subjected to your wickedness?	3:19bβ

The first part of this unit addresses the king of Assyria in terms of an analogy between the condition of his subjects and the condition of his own person. The body politic, as it were, is weakened by the failure of its leadership system, and there is no "shepherd" alive or alert enough to regroup the scattered flock (v. 18). The king is similarly incapacitated by a grievous wound that nothing can heal (v. 19a). The second part of the unit describes to the king the reaction of those who hear the news that both he and his empire are on the verge of total collapse. All will clap (v. 19aα) because there is no one whom Assyrian rule has not affected adversely (v. 19bβ).

Genre

A (→) dirge mourns the death of an individual, typically describing how the deceased person lived and died, and sometimes directly addressing the deceased person as if he or she were still present. A (→) lamentation similarly mourns the fate of a community that has suffered some catastrophe such as plague or defeat, typically comparing its former peace and prosperity with the present desolation. This unit basically resembles a dirge, as it accosts the fatally wounded Assyrian king with the mournful prospect of his impending death; but in this case the distinction between dirge and lamentation becomes somewhat blurred. Since the fate of Assyria as a whole is inescapably tied to the fate of the king, the description of the king's impending death is an integral part of the crisis now faced by the people as a whole, whose desolation is described in terms of their being left leaderless. In place of the conventional expressions of sorrow, this unit substitutes the description of a joyful response on the part of those who hear the news of Assyria's distress. This shows it to be an ironic adaptation of the genre and hence a MOCK DIRGE (Elliger, 21; Horst, 166).

Setting

The dirge itself originated in the context of funerary mourning, and prophets adapted the genre to announce the prospect of certain death for both individuals and nations. This ironic version of the genre utilizes a convention of direct address according to which a foreign enemy is fictively addressed before a domestic audience (→ Book as a Whole, Genre). The king of Assyria could have been fictively addressed in this manner on some ceremonial occasion of the royal cult or court, at which the prospect of the empire's imminent fall was celebrated.

This unit has the form of a type of prophetic speech that could exist independently in its own setting, but this does not necessarily mean that this unit ever existed independently in such a setting (→ 2:12–3:19 [*RSV* 2:11–3:19], Setting).

Intention

As the Judahite audience overhears the king of Assyria being informed of his imminent defeat and death, they are led to participate in the international outbreak of joy that is sure to follow.

HABAKKUK

Bibliography

E. Achtemeier, *Nahum–Malachi* (IntCom; Atlanta: John Knox, 1986); L. Alonso Schökel and J. L. Sicre Diaz, *Profetas: Comentario,* vol. 2 (NBE; Madrid: Cristiandad, 1980); L. Boadt, *Jeremiah 26–52, Habakkuk, Zephaniah, Nahum* (OTM 10; Wilmington, Del.: Michael Glazier, 1982); D. R. Bratcher, "The Theological Message of Habakkuk: A Literary-Rhetorical Analysis" (Diss., Union Theological Seminary [Richmond, Va.], 1984); W. H. Brownlee, "The Composition of Habakkuk," in *Hommages à André Dupont-Sommer* (ed. A. Caquot and M. Philonenko; Paris: Adrien-Maisonneuve, 1971) 255-75; B. S. Childs, *Introduction to the Old Testament as Scripture* (Philadelphia: Fortress, 1979) 447-56; J. H. Eaton, *Obadiah, Nahum, Habakkuk and Zephaniah* (TBC; London: SCM, 1961); K. Elliger, *Das Buch der zwölf Kleinen Propheten,* vol. 2 (3rd ed.; ATD 25/2; Göttingen: Vandenhoeck & Ruprecht, 1956); D. E. Gowan, "Habakkuk and Wisdom," *Perspective* 9 (1968) 157-66; idem, *The Triumph of Faith in Habakkuk* (Atlanta: John Knox, 1976); A. H. J. Gunneweg, "Habakuk und das Problem des leidenden *ṣdyq,*" *ZAW* 98 (1986) 400-415; R. D. Haak, *Habakkuk* (VTSup 44; Leiden: Brill, 1992); T. Hiebert, "The Book of Habakkuk," *NIB* 7:623-55; F. Horst, "Habakkuk," in T. H. Robinson and Horst, *Die Zwölf Kleinen Propheten* (2nd ed.; HAT 14; Tübingen: Mohr [Siebeck], 1954); P. Humbert, *Problèmes du livre d'Habacuc* (Mémoires de l'Université de Neuchâtel 18; Neuchâtel: Secrétariat de l'Université, 1944); J. G. Janzen, "Eschatological Symbol and Existence in Habakkuk," *CBQ* 44 (1982) 394-414; J. Jeremias, *Kultprophetie und Gerichtsverkündigung in der späten Königszeit Israels* (WMANT 35; Neukirchen-Vluyn: Neukirchener, 1970); P. Jöcken, *Das Buch Habakuk* (BBB 48; Cologne: Peter Hanstein, 1977); idem, "War Habakuk ein Kultprophet?" in *Bausteine biblischer Theologie (Fest.* G. J. Botterweck; ed. H.-J. Fabry; BBB 50; Cologne: Peter Hanstein, 1977) 319-32; C.-A. Keller, "Habacuc," in R. Vuilleumier and Keller, *Michée, Nahoum, Habacuc, Sophonie* (CAT 11b; Neuchâtel: Delachaux et Niestlé, 1971); K. Marti, *Das Dodekapropheton* (KHC 13; Tübingen: Mohr [Siebeck], 1904); E. Nielsen, "The Righteous and the Wicked in Habaqquq," *ST* 6 (1953) 54-78; B. Peckham, "The Vision of Habakkuk," *CBQ* 48 (1986) 617-36; J. J. M. Roberts, *Nahum, Habakkuk, and Zephaniah* (OTL; Louisville:

Westminster/John Knox, 1991); W. Rudolph, *Micha, Nahum, Habakuk, Zephanja* (KAT 13/3; Gütersloh: Gerd Mohn, 1975); M. A. Sweeney, "Structure, Genre, and Intent in the Book of Habakkuk," *VT* 41 (1991) 63-83; W. H. Ward, "Habakkuk," in J. M. P. Smith, Ward, and J. A. Brewer, *A Critical and Exegetical Commentary on Micah, Zephaniah, Nahum, Habakkuk, Obadiah, and Joel* (ICC; Edinburgh: T. & T. Clark, 1911).

Chapter 1

THE BOOK AS A WHOLE

Structure

Habakkuk is commonly divided into three main sections: a dialogue in which the prophet twice addresses Yahweh (1:2-4 and 1:12-17) and Yahweh twice replies (1:5-11 and 2:1-4 [+5?]); a series of woe oracles (2:6-20); and a psalm (3:1-19). The book is better understood, however, in terms of three differently defined sections: a complaint (1:2-17) concerning the fulfillment of a previously proclaimed prophecy that is cited within the complaint (1:5-11); a

81

report of an oracular inquiry (2:1-20); and a psalmodic representation of prophecy (3:1-19). The reasons for preferring these structural divisions are presented in the analysis of each section below. The main consideration here is how these three sections cohere in forming the book as a whole.

The theme of unjust imperial domination is common to all sections of the book; but each treats this theme in a somewhat different way so as to indicate a progression in the way Yahweh is understood to be involved in the world situation. The first section (1:2-17) wrestles with the issue of whether Yahweh's claim to have granted the Babylonians their dominant position implicates him in the injustice that they have perpetrated. In the second section (2:1-20) Yahweh affirms that the imperialists have lost all claims to legitimacy by greedily pursuing conquest for its own sake and that he has therefore destined them to fall. The third section (3:1-19) expresses the hope that Yahweh will eventually deliver his people from the invaders, who are likened to the chaos monster once defeated by Yahweh in primordial combat, and claims that this pattern of divine action is beginning to repeat itself within the historical process. When the book is read as a whole, the reader gets the impression that the imperial power in all three sections is one and the same.

This impression is reinforced by describing the imperial power's mistreatment of the conquered people with a common vocabulary and imagery throughout. For example, the evil forces "gather" their subjects (*'sp;* 1:9b; 1:15aβ; 2:5bβ) and "sweep over" them (*'br;* 1:11aβ; 3:10aβ). They are perhaps more impressively described as insatiably devouring their victims, using imagery that connotes the mythic figure of the chaos monster (*'kl* ["eat"], 1:8b; 3:14b; *bl'* ["swallow"], 1:13b; cf. 2:5bα). Some have argued that reading the book as a whole serves to generalize its historical references beyond the particularities of any specific time and place (e.g., Childs, 452-53), but it is just the opposite. Since the imperial power in the first section is explicitly identified as the Babylonians (1:6; *RSV* "Chaldeans"), and since the otherwise unnamed imperial power in all three sections is one and the same, the historical reference of the book as a whole becomes particularized in terms of Judah's Babylonian crisis (Nielsen, 75-77; → Setting).

The second section of the book (2:1-20) provides a solution for the problem posed in the first section (1:2-17). A prophecy has become problematic because of the way it has been fulfilled. The prophecy in question proclaimed that Yahweh had ordained the rise of Babylon as a world power (1:5-11), and the rise of Babylon has indeed come to pass. Because of the unusually despotic way in which the Babylonians established their hegemony, however, this claim now seems to make Yahweh responsible for the unjust order that they have so brutally established. In such a situation a commitment to justice cannot be reconciled with faith in Yahweh. The report of the oracular inquiry in 2:1-20 addresses this dilemma. It characterizes the Babylonians as a nation that has let greed get the better of them, so that their goal has become conquest for its own sake, and they tyrannically mistreat their defeated subjects. In the process they have become self-deluded concerning the real source of their power, which they attribute to themselves rather than to God. They can thus no longer serve Yahweh's purpose and are well on their way to self-destruction (2:4-5).

The outcome of the oracular inquiry described in 2:1-20 reinterprets the prophecy in 1:5-11 by reaffirming its basic claim while also adding qualifications that are intended to avoid its problematic implications. Yahweh can be seen as responsible for Babylon's rise, as the oracle in 1:5-11 asserts, but not for the injustice that has accompanied the imposition of their rule. If one recognizes that Babylon is now destined to fall and trusts that Yahweh will eventually bring about this destiny, faith in him as Lord of history can become compatible with a commitment to justice. If Yahweh's reply to the inquiry is written down and studied in relation to current developments, events will turn out so as to authenticate this reinterpretation. Signs of Babylon's approaching overthrow already show that Yahweh ultimately governs the course of history justly, thus also retrospectively vindicating the claim that he ordained their ascendancy to begin with.

A relationship between 3:1-19 and 2:1-20 is established by the way in which the oracular inquiry is announced in 2:1. The prophet states two reasons for undertaking the inquiry: first, to see what Yahweh will say to him (v. 1bα); and second, to see what his own reaction will be (v. 1bβ). His overall objective is to see whether the "corrective" in Yahweh's reply (*tôkaḥat; RSV* "complaint") will alter the adverse attitude expressed by the prophet in the initial complaint (1:2-17). After complying with the period of critical reflection enjoined on the prophet by Yahweh's directives concerning the reception of the reply (2:2aβb), the prophet may change his mind. The report of Yahweh's reply portrays him as addressing himself to the prophet in a highly apologetic way, and one might argue that this mode of address in itself implies the prophet's acceptance of Yahweh's corrective (→ 2:1-20), so that the book's thematic progression from doubt to faith is for all practical purposes completed by the end of ch. 2. There is perhaps some evidence of a version of Habakkuk that included only chs. 1–2, i.e., the Qumran scroll 1QpHab, but the reason for the omission of ch. 3 in this particular type of *pesher* commentary is not at all clear (see W. H. Brownlee, *The Midrash Pesher of Habakkuk* [SBLMS 24; Missoula, Mont.: Scholars Press, 1979] 218-19). In any case, what follows in ch. 3 is an explicit indication of the prophet's reaction to Yahweh's reply. Judging from the confidence that it expresses in Yahweh's intention to deliver his people from Babylonian oppression, the prophet has indeed accepted Yahweh's correction. From the retrospective vantage point of ch. 3, the doubts expressed in ch. 1 appear to have been at least somewhat transcended. One can thus read 3:1-19 as an integral part of the book, in which case the superscription in 1:1 applies to it as much as to the preceding material (→ Genre).

Nonetheless, 3:1-19 also has a quasi-independent status that is indicated by its having a superscription of its own (3:1). The nature of its independence is evident from the rubrics for liturgical performance that are contained in part of this superscript (3:1b), as well as in the postscript (3:19b). These rubrics show that ch. 3 functions in a dual capacity, as part of the book but also — unlike the rest of the book — as part of the cult's repertoire of psalmody. (The reappearance of the Prayer of Habakkuk in the book of Odes, appended to the Psalter in the LXX, also attests to this latter function.) When the poem in 3:2-

19a is liturgically performed, it does not lose either its identification with Habakkuk or the connotations of its context in the book as a whole. It serves rather as a liturgically dramatized epitome of what Habakkuk prophesied and of the overall message of the book that is named for him.

The three major sections of Habakkuk are simply juxtaposed. They are linked in a thematic progression but not by narration. The substance of the thematic development implies, however, a kind of narrative sequence (cf. Childs, 452). The starting point of the prophecy is 1:5-11, which would have been proclaimed when the armies of Babylon were first looming on Judah's horizon. Then, with the actual imposition of Babylonian control, comes the recognition of this prophecy's problematic implications as these are expressed in the complaint that now contains it (1:2-17). In order to resolve this dilemma, the prophet seeks the additional revelation (2:1) reported in 2:2-20. The transcription and study of this revelation, in accord with Yahweh's directives (2:2aβb), leads to the recognition that the deliverance promised in it is beginning to happen. This recognition is finally expressed in the form of another complaint (3:2-19a), along with the hope that Yahweh will bring what he has begun to its completion. The book as a whole thus serves to represent a historical process, in which the prophet is the central figure, but not an explicitly interconnected sequence of actions or events.

Genre

Most scholars view the whole of Habakkuk as somehow liturgical. A few have denied that there is anything cultic about either the whole book or its individual sections. For example, Keller views the entire document as the record of the prophet's personal encounter with Yahweh, written down and published in compliance with the divine command in 2:2aβ (*Habacuc,* 138-39; cf. Jöcken, "War Habakuk ein Kultprophet?" 326-32). The majority, however, have recognized that Habakkuk is largely made up of liturgical poetry with a cultic setting (i.e., 1:2-17 and 3:2-19a) and have thus supposed that the whole book is similarly connected with the cult. There is a diverse and wide range of opinion with regard to the nature of this connection. Critics variously hold that the book in its entirety is a prophetic liturgy (e.g., Humbert, 280-96; G. Fohrer, *Introduction to the Old Testament* [tr. D. E. Green; Nashville and New York: Abingdon, 1968] 483; Nielsen, 59); that the core of the book is a prophetic liturgy for the proclamation of divine judgment (1:2-17) that has been supplemented and redacted in accord with a rather different liturgical concept (Jeremias, 55-110); that the book is in part a liturgy (1:2–2:4) with other materials appended (e.g., Elliger, 24-26, 43, 51); that the book contains no liturgy per se but cultic materials arranged for liturgical reading (Horst, 167); that the book is a loose collection of diverse materials, some of cultic origin, that have been brought together by virtue of their common theme, namely, the downfall of the godless (O. Eissfeldt, *The Old Testament: An Introduction* [tr. P. R. Ackroyd; New York and Evanston: Harper & Row, 1965] 420); that although the book has the form of a simple complaint, it is a literary imitation of a liturgical form rather than an actual liturgy (Haak, 11-20); etc.

Many of these diverse conclusions regarding the liturgical nature of Habakkuk have been influenced more by stereotypical preconceptions concerning cultic prophecy in general than by specific indications in the present text of a particular prophetic role. They also seem to share the presupposition that works containing cultic materials can attain compositional integrity only by forming some kind of liturgy. Both aspects of the matter stand in need of reconsideration.

Parts of Habakkuk do indeed reflect a cultic prophetic role and are therefore probably liturgical. 1:2-17 and 3:2-19a are not simply complaints, or even communal complaints. They are more specifically prophetic complaints, in the sense that the supplicant is acting in the capacity of an intermediary between the divine and human realms. In both cases their specifically prophetic nature is evident not only from the way in which the supplicant's plight becomes identified with the plight of the people at large, so that the anticipated deliverance encompasses them all. It is also evident from the way in which the anticipation of deliverance is grounded in prophetic apperception of a less than self-evident divine reality. Whatever else one might say about cultic prophecy in general, there is explicit although sparse evidence of prophetic participation in at least some kinds of complaint rituals (→ 1:2-17, Setting; 3:1-19, Setting). In view of this evidence it is probable that these two sections of the book were once parts of complaint liturgies led by a prophet.

At the same time, however, it is clear that the book itself is not in the form of a liturgy, primarily because 2:1-20 does not fit this description. The prophetic practice of oracular inquiry, which this section reflects, may have been in some cases intimately connected with the cult. Sometimes the announcement of a prophet's intention to undertake such an inquiry may have been made in a cultic context, and sometimes the oracle obtained through the inquiry may also have been ritually recited. A report of oracular inquiry in itself, however, would not have had any outright liturgical function. It would rather have served to inform the study of such prophetic practices and the traditions on which they were based (→ 2:1-5, Setting).

Habakkuk thus contains liturgical materials without assuming the form of a liturgy, but it does not necessarily follow that the book has no formal integrity as a literary work. The question is whether the three sections of the book, related as they are in theme and sequence, assume some form that is not of the same genre as any of the individual sections themselves. The superscription (1:1) labels the book as a *maśśā'* (*RSV* "oracle"). Weis has shown that this is a genre term that can be applied to a kind of prophetic speech, to sections of a work of prophetic literature, or to prophetic literary works in their entirety. Although the genre has considerable flexibility of form, it generally contains such elements as these that are particularly relevant to the case of Habakkuk: (a) a speech of Yahweh disclosing how his will is becoming manifest in human affairs; (b) directives concerning behavior or attitudes that are appropriate in response to what Yahweh is doing; and (c) a grounding of these directives in human acts or events that manifest Yahweh's activity or purpose. These elements are often combined so as to show that Yahweh is presently acting in accord with some previous prophecy that is usually cited within the larger literary context but not necessarily included within the *maśśā'* itself (Weis, 273-74). This genre generally serves to provide its audience with insight into their historical situation and with specific directions about how to react to contemporary developments because of the way Yahweh is perceived to be working out his purpose.

The three sections of Habakkuk are interrelated so as to comprise the basic elements of a *maśśā'*. The complaint in 1:2-17 presents the prophecy in 1:5-11 as problematic, thus introducing the oracular inquiry reported in 2:1-20 as the means of qualifying and reauthenticating it (cf. Weis's somewhat different analysis, 161-65). The revelation reported in 2:2-20 discloses that Yahweh's will is becoming manifest in the increasing inevitability of the Babylonians' fall, due to their greed and hubris (a). It calls for those committed to justice to maintain their faith in Yahweh's intention to restore it. The prophecy is thus to be written down and studied, to discern in unfolding events the signs of its coming to pass (b). The attitude encouraged by this prophecy is grounded in the growing recognition of the international community that Babylon is doomed in accord with Yahweh's purpose (c). In 3:2-19a the prophet's exemplary faith is further grounded in his discernment of a sign, within the realm of human events, that Yahweh's deliverance from Babylonian tyranny is actually underway (3:3-7). The basic elements of the *maśśā'* are evident in 2:1-20, but the form is more fully developed in the interrelationship of the whole book's three main sections, particularly in the relation of 1:2-17 to 2:1-20. The book as a whole can thus be classified as a Maśśā', in accord with its superscription (1:1).

One of the main functions of a *maśśā'* is to persuade the audience to change their attitude toward their situation, and hence to change their behavior, by altering their perception of Yahweh's involvement in their situation. This particular example of the genre attempts to bring about a change on the part of its audience by having the central prophetic character undergo such an alteration of perception while simultaneously promoting the identification of the audience with this prophetic character. The prophet cannot resolve the revelation that the Babylonian crisis is Yahweh's doing with his own experience of it as something antithetical to Yahweh's basic nature. Even as the privileged intermediary between Yahweh and the people, he must be convinced through a divine corrective to reinterpret this revelation in a particular way. He thus serves not only as the extraordinary mediator of a prophetic message but also as the prime example of how an ordinary person becomes convinced of that message. The transformation that the prophet undergoes with respect to the ambiguities of divine involvement in the Babylonian crisis thus becomes a model for the kind of transformation that it is possible for the reader to undergo with respect to the ambiguities of divine involvement in other similar situations (→ Intention).

Setting

Two somewhat different kinds of social activity are reflected in the book as a whole. On the one hand, the generic forms of (→) 1:5-11 and (→) 2:1-5 reflect prophetic concern with the interpretation of momentous historical developments. Texts written in these forms are indicative of prophetic attempts to divine Yahweh's role in particular events. They are also indicative of prophetic attempts to reflect critically on the ambiguities of this type of divination by studying the written records of its practice. On the other hand, the generic forms of 1:2-17 and 3:2-19a reflect prophetic attempts to express the significance of revelations received, as well as of critical reflections on them, in the context of worship. Such texts are indicative of the ritual representation of prophetic insights through psalmodic performances on specific cultic occasions.

The book as a whole thus reflects a setting in which mantic scribalism and prophetic psalmody overlapped. It is difficult to tell whether this overlap was generally characteristic of some particular institutional context in late preexilic times, or whether it resulted from a somewhat unusual combination of both kinds of activity in one and the same prophetic role. It is likewise difficult to tell just how much Habakkuk himself was involved in the production of the book that bears his name, and to what extent he himself may have played the distinctive prophetic role that emerges from the book as a whole.

All of the book's three major sections are dominated by an autobiographical first person perspective. It is possible that the "I" is actually Habakkuk himself, and the book can be read coherently assuming that the first person point of view is none other than the prophet's own. If so, one may suppose that Habakkuk lived in Judah during the late seventh and early sixth centuries (cf. the legendary account in Bel and the Dragon, 33–39). Sometime around the beginning of the seventh century's final decade, after the overthrow of Nineveh in 612 BCE signaled the decline of Assyrian might, he would have communicated the prophecy in 1:5-11 heralding Yahweh's designation of the Babylonians as the nation to supersede Assyria as the region's dominant superpower. Sometime after 605, when the Babylonians first intervened directly in Judah or perhaps in reaction to the first deportation from Jerusalem in 596, the harsh reality of Babylonian control would have occasioned second thoughts on the part of Habakkuk about this earlier prophecy of his, thoughts that he expressed in 1:2-17. Sometime thereafter, in order to resolve his doubts, he undertook the oracular inquiry reported in 2:1-20.

The terminus ad quem for Habakkuk's involvement is determined by the way in which both 2:1-20 and 3:2-19a claim that Babylon's power has already shown signs of weakening. This claim suggests that both texts were composed around the middle of the sixth century when conflict among Nebuchadnezzar's successors destabilized the empire internally and the Persians began to make themselves felt externally. The prophet Habakkuk could conceivably have been responsible for nearly all of the book bearing his name, producing the material contained in 1:2-17, 2:1-20, and 3:2-19a over a period of years sometime between ca. 610 and 550 BCE. As a mantic scribe he could have had a direct hand in recording and reinterpreting his own prophecies (→ 2:1-5, Setting).

It is also possible that Habakkuk's autobiographical "I" is in some or all cases a fictive representation. In this event, judging from what we know about the pseudepigraphical formation of prophetic books in general, it is likely that at least the initial oracle 1:5-11 was composed by Habakkuk, and that some or all of the subsequent reinterpretive prophetic activity was done anonymously by others. In any case, because the superscriptions in 1:1 and 3:1a have a biographical rather than an autobiographical form, it is unlikely that Habakkuk himself was finally responsible for the book as such. Even if he composed virtually all of the three major sections, there was probably a subsequent final redaction by someone else. Nothing indicates that the book took a long time to assume its final form, and the final redaction can therefore be dated to a time shortly after the composition of its latest component part, around the middle of the sixth century.

Intention

The book aims to involve its readers in the reeducation of Habakkuk, who is characterized as a prophet from the time of the Babylonian crisis. The three major sections represent successive states in the development of this character by presenting the records of his involvement in two kinds of prophetic activity: complaint liturgies and oracular inquiry. Readers can identify with the protagonist as he struggles in these two ways to reconcile what has been revealed concerning Yahweh's involvement in the crisis with his own experience. They may thus learn something of how to reconcile what the book reveals concerning Yahweh's involvement in this kind of situation with their own experience.

In 1:2-17 readers are allowed to overhear the prophet's articulation of the problem that confronts him, as he attempts to serve as the intermediary between Yahweh and the people. It has been revealed that Yahweh, in his capacity as supreme ruler of creation, has given the Babylonians world dominion — although they obviously know nothing of Yahweh and think that their superiority is of their own making. The prophet has experienced the imposition of Babylonian control, however, as nothing but oppression and degradation. Such involvement on Yahweh's part could serve the purpose of justice only if it were meant to be a punishment that would teach his people a lesson. But it seems instead that Yahweh rules unjustly, and his way of delegating power implies that humanity was ultimately made for exploitation.

Yahweh's own clarification of the problem, which the prophet sought and received, is related in 2:1-20. Yahweh explains that the injustice perpetrated by the Babylonians does not derive from their having been assigned a dominant role in world affairs, but from the way they have played this role. They have assumed that conquest and exploitation are in themselves justifiable, and they have not acknowledged their responsibility to rule the nations fairly. It is in the nature of things that those who get so greedy and self-deluded will in time destroy themselves. Conversely, recognizing that Yahweh's involvement in world affairs makes history a moral process, those who remain committed to justice will live.

Yahweh further points out that the nations have generally grasped the basic principle that an empire that rules as Babylon has ruled is doomed to fall. This recognition amounts to a tacit recognition of Yahweh's agency, even by those who do not know him, and in effect implies that he is universally acknowledged. The prophet and the people can live in some realistic hope of their eventual deliverance from Babylonian oppression not just because Yahweh has said on the record that he will cause this deliverance to happen but also because of the worldwide recognition that there is a tendency toward justice at work within the historical process.

Hab 3 presents the script for a ritual dramatization of the prophet's reaction to Yahweh's explanation in 2:2-20. Readers thus do not simply overhear this expression of the new attitude that informs the prophet after Yahweh's corrective. They are invited to try on this attitude for themselves through vicarious dramatic impersonation of the prophetic character. The prophet is now persuaded that Yahweh initially commissioned the Babylonians for world domination, that Yahweh is presently in the process of bringing about their downfall, and that both actions are consistent with Yahweh's status as the just ruler of all things in heaven and earth. There is still no self-evident basis for the prophet's hope of liberation, however. There are only some intimations of an imminent convulsive change in the world order; and, given Yahweh's involvement in the situation, this change is likely to be of a particular sort. It will be a re-creation of the world order that recapitulates the process through which Yahweh created the world to begin with. Just as he then did battle with the forces of evil and chaos in order to establish the possibility of a just existence for all creatures, so will he now do battle with the tyrannical oppressor to reestablish this possibility for all, and thus bring about the deliverance of his people. In reality there is ample evidence that the power of chaos and evil is still strong, and the prospect of the conflict that must be endured to overcome it is fearful. But there is still good reason to hope.

The thematic development of the book as a whole finally focuses the readers' attention on those contemporary situations in which injustice is so all-pervasive that it seems to derive not just from the human capacity for malice and self-deception but from the very way in which the world works. Hopefulness then expires because the world itself seems made for injustice. The revelation that God created heaven and earth may only aggravate such situations, particularly when God's people move beyond the innocuous affirmation of this notion in principle and attempt to affirm it in concrete historical terms. God may then become implicated in the injustice, or the oppressors may appear to attain divine legitimation, but in any case the attitude of hopelessness is only reinforced.

There are grounds for objecting to such hopelessness, but they can only be discovered by questioning God about his apparent cooperation with injustice. In response God points to the commonsense observation that oppressors tend to overstep themselves, and to the universal if sometimes vague realization that they thereby lose their legitimacy. Such a response implies that oppressors can succeed only by usurping a sovereign power greater than their own, and this implication makes room for hope in the capacity of that power to renew the world order. Commitment to justice is thus not finally opposed to faith in the divine creator but rather ultimately springs from it. The book of Habakkuk emphasizes, however, that there is nothing self-evident about this insight. It is a hard-won realization that is reached as prophetic souls dare to let God correct what they claim to know of him, and as God's people dare to follow suit.

Bibliography

C. A. Keller, "Die Eigenart der Prophetie Habakuks," *ZAW* 85 (1973) 156-67; E. Otto, "Die Theologie des Buches Habakuk," *VT* 35 (1985) 274-95; R. D. Weis, "A Definition of the Genre *Maśśā'* in the Hebrew Bible" (Diss., Claremont Graduate School, 1986).

Chapter 2

THE SUPERSCRIPTION (1:1)

Structure

I. Title: *maśśā'*	1:1aα
II. Specification: relative clause	1:1aβb
A. Predicate describing the mode of revelation:	
which he saw . . .	1:1aβ
B. Subject identifying the recipient of the revelation	1:1b
1. Name of recipient: Habakkuk	1:1bα
2. Appositional designation of the recipient's role:	
the prophet	1:1bβ

This heading entitles the whole book as a *maśśā'*, i.e., a prophetic interpretation of revelation (→ Book as a Whole, Genre). It is further specified that this *maśśā'* was "seen" (*ḥzh*) by a prophet named Habakkuk. The use of the term *ḥāzâ* (*RSV* "he saw") to describe how the prophet apprehended what was revealed to him has led some to suppose that the prophet is here being characterized as a "seer" in the narrow, technical sense of the word, i.e., as one who sees visions. It is in turn supposed that the book grew out of some kind of paranormal visionary experience. The root *ḥzh* can refer to the phenomenon of clairvoyance, but it can also be used in a less specific way to describe the perception of revelation in general. It is therefore used to entitle prophetic books that mix material that is specifically visionary with material that is revelatory in a more general sense (e.g., Amos 1:1; Isa 1:1), as well as prophetic books containing nothing that is particularly visionary (e.g., Obad 1).

Two contextual factors suggest that *ḥzh* has its more general sense here. First, there are no vision report formulas or other such explicit indicators of paranormal visionary experience (→ prophetic vision report). The only serious candidate for such an indicator, the verb *rā'îtî* (*RSV* "I saw") in 3:7a, denotes the plainly visible effects of Yahweh's appearance on the world scene, rather than the prophet's apperception of things that are in principle not nor-

mally visible to others, or of Yahweh himself (cf., e.g., Amos 7:1; Isa 6:1; →
Hab 3:1-19, Structure). Second, the terms for seeing are so prominent throughout Habakkuk as to constitute a leitmotif. In ch. 1 the use of these terms helps
to develop a theme of conflicting perspectives as they describe a discrepancy
between the way in which Yahweh would have the prophet perceive the situation and the way in which the prophet would have Yahweh perceive it. (The
roots r'h ["see"] and nbṭ ["look"] occur repeatedly in [→] 1:2-17 [vv. 3aα,
5aα, 13abα].) In ch. 2 the use of such terms helps to develop a contrasting
theme of converging perspectives as the prophet comes to understand that
Yahweh's view of the situation both includes and relativizes what he has seen.
(The root r'h reappears in 2:2bα, and ḥāzôn occurs twice in 2:2-3; → 2:1-20,
Structure.) The prophet is thus enabled to see things from Yahweh's more
comprehensive viewpoint.

In 1:1 ḥāzâ thus describes the prophet's imaginatively envisioning the
hidden significance of events, rather than clairvoyance per se. The distinctive
formulation of 1:1 serves to introduce this kind of prophetic perception as a
central theme of the book as a whole.

Genre

This is a PROPHETIC SUPERSCRIPTION, of which there are two main types. One is
distinguished by its use of the (→) prophetic word formula ("the word of
Yahweh that came to . . . ," e.g., Hos 1:1). The other is distinguished by its use
of a term for prophetic revelation, such as dibrê ("words of," e.g., Amos 1:1),
ḥāzôn ("vision," e.g., Obad 1), or maśśā᾽ (RSV "oracle," e.g., Nah 1:1), plus
the name of the prophet. The former type puts relatively more emphasis on
Yahweh as the source of the prophet's revelation, while the latter type — of
which this superscription is an example — puts relatively more emphasis on
the prophet as the recipient and medium of the revelation. When compared
with other examples of its type, this superscription appears to be distinctively
formulated. The name of the prophet appears within the context of a subordinate clause modifying the term for revelation, rather than within the more typical context of a construct phrase grammatically bound to the term for revelation (e.g., Isa 1:1; Jer 1:1; Amos 1:1; Obad 1; Nah 1:1). Making the name the
subject of a verb denoting prophetic perception emphasizes the prophet's intermediary role to an even greater extent.

Superscriptions of both types often include further information regarding the time of the prophet's activity, his provenance, or his genealogy (e.g.,
Jer 1:1-3). In contrast, the superscription in Hab 1:1 shows no elaboration of
this sort. It is as if the reference to the Babylonians in 1:6 is sufficient to put
the whole work into some kind of historical context, so that the title need not
be concerned with such things.

Setting

Prophetic superscriptions were the creation of scribal groups that were concerned with the preservation, study, and ongoing reinterpretation of the records of prophetic revelation.

Intention

This heading serves not only to introduce the book as a document associated with a prophet named Habakkuk but also to introduce Habakkuk as a prophet with a particular significance. He was exemplary in the way that he proved his discernment of Yahweh's true purpose in a particular historical situation.

Bibliography

G. Tucker, "Prophetic Superscriptions and the Growth of a Canon," in *Canon and Authority* (ed. G. W. Coats and B. O. Long; Philadelphia: Fortress, 1977) 56-70.

Chapter 3

THE FIRST MAJOR SECTION
OF THE BOOK (1:2-17)
AND ITS INDIVIDUAL UNITS

**THE PROPHET MAKES A COMPLAINT ABOUT THE
FULFILLMENT OF AN EARLIER PROPHECY, 1:2-17**

Structure

Within ch. 1 and continuing into ch. 2 there is an alternation between the prophet's speaking on his own behalf and his speaking on Yahweh's behalf. As

94

this section of the book opens, the prophet is addressing Yahweh. The prophet's prayer is interrupted at 1:5, where Yahweh himself suddenly starts speaking — not to the prophet in particular but to a group audience. At 1:12 the prophet again begins addressing Yahweh, and at 2:2 Yahweh speaks again — this time directly addressing the prophet himself. As ch. 2 opens, the nature of Yahweh's speech to the prophet is explicitly described in the reporting narration of v. 2aα as a "response" ('nh) of some kind. The overall interpretation of Habakkuk depends to a considerable extent on just what kind of "response" this is thought to be, and on whether the speech of Yahweh in 1:5-11 is thought to be a response of the same sort. The virtually unanimous consensus of recent opinion holds that the speech of Yahweh beginning at 2:2aβ is Yahweh's reply to the issues raised by the prophet in 1:12-17, and that the speech of Yahweh in 1:5-11 is similarly Yahweh's reply to the issues raised by the prophet in 1:2-4. Commentators thus frequently characterize the first section of the book as a dialogue between Habakkuk and Yahweh, and it is even represented as such in the editorial headings of several modern translations (e.g., *NIV* and *NJB*). Some considerations of both form and content suggest otherwise, however.

With regard to form, it is significant that there is no narrative element between the prophet's speech in 1:2-4 and the speech of Yahweh in 1:5-11, like the reporting narration between the prophet's speech in 1:12-17 and the speech of Yahweh that begins at 2:2aβ. Bratcher has noted (p. 72) that Habakkuk features introductions of various kinds at the beginning of each major section, except at 1:5. There are superscriptions at 1:1 and 3:1, fragments of autobiographical narration in 2:1, and quotation formulas at 2:2aα and 2:6bβ, but nothing similar at 1:5. The absence of any such marker at 1:5 suggests that this transition is not of the same sort as these other explicitly marked transitions. Childs has further observed (pp. 451-52) that these same introductory elements constitute a framework for the book as a whole, shaping it into something like a biographical account. The overall structure of Habakkuk is indeed characterized by a kind of implicit narrative progression (→ Book as a Whole), but the lack of any explicit or implicit indication of sequencing at 1:5 suggests that the relationship between 1:5-11 and its context is more of an interruption than a progression.

With regard to content, the catchwords and phrases that are repeated in 1:2-17 provide prominent clues concerning the conceptual relationships among its constituent units. The word *ḥāmās* (*RSV* "violence") is a term for the trouble that confronts the prophet (1:3a), about which he has vainly petitioned Yahweh (1:2b), as well as a term for the general impact of the Babylonians' advance (1:9a). The presence of the Babylonians, as it is described in 1:5-11, is thus identified as the cause of the predicament that provokes the prophet's complaint in 1:2-4 (Sweeney, 67). A similar effect is achieved by the repetition of the verbal pair *r'h* (*RSV* "see") and *nbṭ* (*RSV* "look upon"). These are terms for various processes of perception, and they are used to describe how the prophet is made to experience evil (1:3a), how one is to discern Yahweh's involvement in world affairs (1:5a), and how Yahweh himself recognizes intolerable wickedness (1:13). The experience of Yahweh as a contributor to injustice, as described in 1:2-4, is thus identified with the realization that Yahweh's divine power is manifest in the rise of Babylon, as described in 1:5-11. This linkage is in turn tied to the conviction that Yahweh's involvement in injustice is ultimately incompatible with his true character, as expressed in 1:12-17.

Much the same line of thought is reflected in a catch phrase that combines the nominal subject *mišpāṭ* (*RSV* "justice") with the verbal predicate *yṣ'* (*RSV* "go further, proceed"). It is twice used to denote the injustice that results from Yahweh's indifference to the prophet's plea, once stated negatively (1:4a, "justice never goes forth"), and once again stated positively (1:4b, "justice goes forth perverted"). The same terms reappear in the ironic portrayal of Babylonian "justice" as self-serving (1:7b, "their justice . . . proceed[s] from themselves") and hence no justice at all. The injustice in which Yahweh is implicated in 1:2-4 is thus identified with the injustice perpetrated by the Babylonians in 1:5-11 (Sweeney, 68), and this identification is in turn tied to the conviction that Yahweh's involvement with the Babylonians will somehow make for justice (1:12b; *RSV* "judgment") in the long run.

There are still more repetitions of this sort (e.g., the use of *rāšā'* ["wicked"] and *ṣaddîq* ["righteous"] in both 1:4b and 1:13b), but these three examples suffice to show the general conceptual relationship among the individual units of ch. 1. In 1:2-4 the prophet complains about injustice, and he charges Yahweh not only with allowing it (1:2) but also with direct involvement in it (1:3; note the hiphil forms as well as the clauses of consequence). The next unit interrupts the prophet's complaint in order to provide a kind of etiological explanation, in Yahweh's own words, of just who the perpetrators of the injustice are, as well as just how Yahweh himself is involved. Finally, in 1:12-17, the complaint resumes by raising the question of whether this reign of injustice is meant to be a correctional punishment (*hôkîaḥ*, 1:12b; *RSV* "chastisement") and hence a temporary phenomenon in accord with the belief in Yahweh's justness; or whether it will continue indefinitely in the general nature of things (*tāmîd*, 1:17b; *RSV* "forever") and hence calls Yahweh's justness into question.

From the standpoint of form as well as content, 1:5-11 can hardly be a response to the prophet's questioning in 1:2-4. It is not even addressed to the prophet but to some other unidentified group. Moreover, the developments described in 1:5-11 are logically the presupposition on which the questions in 1:2-4 are based, rather than conclusions to be drawn from them. Asserting that Yahweh's control over world history is demonstrated in his assigning international dominance to the Babylonians, the prophecy in 1:5-11 has come true with a vengeance. Precisely for this reason the prophet makes his complaint in 1:2-4 + 12-17. The impact of this prophecy's fulfillment on the prophet, and on the people of Yahweh whom he represents, has been so destructive that Yahweh's own integrity has been called into question. The things that Yahweh says in 1:5-11 are not in reply to Habakkuk's complaint. They are rather what the complaint is all about (Gowan, *Triumph*, 36). There is thus no dialogue between Habakkuk and Yahweh in this section of the book (Sweeney, 64) but rather a complaint addressed by the prophet to Yahweh (1:2-4 + 12-17), interrupted by the quotation of a previous prophecy (1:5-11) on whose fulfillment the complaint is predicated (cf. Bratcher, 72-74; Sweeney, 66-68).

This complaint comes to an end at 1:17, and the narrative introduction in 2:1 marks the start of a new section. The sense in which the speech of Yahweh beginning at 2:2aβ constitutes a "response" to the prophet remains to be seen (→ 2:1-20, Structure).

Genre

Following Gunkel's suggestive lead, Humbert worked out in detail the proposition that Hab 1:2–2:5 is a prophetic liturgy. By means of this generic category Gunkel sought to explain certain portions of prophetic books, characterized by sudden rhetorical shifts in speaker and/or addressee, in terms of the dramatic exchange that generally pertains to ritual. The spoken parts of Israelite liturgy, as reflected in the cultic poetry of the psalms, would typically involve the leader of the congregation and the people and sometimes choral groups as well. They would alternately respond to one another as they collectively engaged in the ritual process of speaking and listening to Yahweh. In such a context the leader might function as a prophetic intermediary, speaking sometimes to Yahweh on behalf of the people and sometimes to the people on behalf of Yahweh.

This phenomenon is most clearly evident in those complaint psalms that explicitly contain an oracular reply to pleas and questions directed toward Yahweh (e.g., Pss 85, 12, 14). It is also indirectly reflected in those complaint psalms that do not explicitly contain such an oracular reply but nevertheless seem to presuppose some overt indication of divine favor, as they shift suddenly from petitions for Yahweh's response to thanks and praise for his having responded (e.g., Pss 6, 22, 28, 31, 57). Gunkel drew a parallel between the dramatic dialogue of the complaint liturgy, as reflected in such psalms, and several prophetic texts, particularly Mic 7:7-20 and Isa 33. Humbert similarly analyzed the first part of Habakkuk as consisting of a communal complaint spoken to Yahweh by the prophet on behalf of the people (1:2-4), an oracular response of Yahweh addressed through the prophet to the people as a whole (1:5-11), a second complaint spoken to Yahweh by the prophet on behalf of the people (1:12-17), and a response of Yahweh addressed to the prophet as their representative (2:1-5).

Humbert's position continues to have influence (e.g., Elliger, 25-26; Eaton, *Vision,* 58-61; Boadt, 167), but it does not satisfactorily explain the relationship between the elements of complaint and oracular speech in Hab 1 and 2. For one thing, the parallel on which this theory depends takes no account of such narrative elements as are found in 2:1-2aα. The complaint psalms that contain oracles, as well as the examples of prophetic liturgy proposed by Gunkel, more often than not present speeches of Yahweh without any narrative introduction — even the speech report formula "(thus) says Yahweh" is usually lacking. It would seem contrary to the nature of liturgy as a genre to contain anything but the spoken parts of a ritual, as they would be dramatically iterated in the actual performance of worship, and perhaps in addition some rubrics directing how such speeches should be rendered. Indeed, there is no parallel in either the complaint psalms or Gunkel's exemplary prophetic liturgies to the autobiographical report of receiving a revelation in Hab 2:1-2aα.

Eaton (*Vision,* 60-61) compares this narration with the introduction to the pronouncement of an oracle in Ps 85:9 (*RSV* 8), and one might mention further the similar introduction in Ps 2:7. These examples are not really analogous, however. The autobiographical report in (→) Hab 2:1-5 describes a situation in which the issues of whether Yahweh will respond, what he will say, and how this prophet will react are all open questions. In contrast Pss 85:9 and 2:7 reflect a situation in which the pronouncement of a prophecy is ritualized; and such matters are therefore, in the nature of the case, more or less prescribed in advance. These psalms provide a kind of script for the enactment of a prophetic drama, in accord with which the action can be played again and again. In contrast, Hab 2:1-5 recounts the reception of a prophetic revelation as it happened once upon a time.

Another problem with the liturgy hypothesis emerges in connection with the relationship of 1:5-11 to 1:2-4. According to Humbert's theory one must suppose (1) that both exchanges between the prophet and Yahweh would have taken place on one and the same occasion, (2) that 1:5-11 is a direct reply to 1:2-4, and (3) that 1:5-11 is moreover a particular kind of reply, i.e., a prophecy of salvation. If one also supposes that the oppressor described in 1:12-17 is to be identified with the conquering Babylonian empire described in 1:5-11 — as is necessary in view of the fact that there is no other antecedent for the pronominal references to the oppressor in 1:12-17 — it is very difficult to maintain all three of these suppositions at once. First, it is hard to see 1:5-11 as a description of anything that might portend salvation for the beleaguered "righteous one" (*ṣaddîq*) in 1:2-4. There is little salvific potential in this unrelieved portrayal of total conquest and destruction (→ 1:5-11). Even if one grants that 1:5-11 might amount to a prophecy of salvation, little sense can be made of it as such in the overall context. How could the Babylonians be announced in the first exchange as the imminently expected liberators, and then be denounced in the second exchange as the already subjugating persecutors? This difficulty can be resolved by supposing — as many commentators have — that the first and second exchanges reflect different historical situations. But then one would have to abandon the idea of a liturgy here, or at least qualify the hypothesis to claim that the text reflects the pattern of a prophetic liturgy without actually constituting one (so Horst, 173).

Because of such problems, most commentators have not categorized Hab 1:2–2:5 as a prophetic liturgy outright but have instead described this part of the book as a series of four prophetic speeches, perhaps from various historical situations, now arranged in the pattern of a dramatic exchange that may be reminiscent of liturgical dialogue (so Marti, 331-33; Horst, 172-80; Rudolph, 200; Keller, *Habacuc,* 137; Bratcher, 51-139 passim; Brownlee, "Composition," 260-64; Alonso Schökel and Sicre Diaz, 1096-97; Roberts, 87-112; etc.). Such a proposal, however, does not really resolve the two most problematic aspects of the dialogue hypothesis. As a "reply" to the issues raised in 1:2-4, 1:5-11 is altogether inapt. And although 2:1-5 begins in a dramatic mode (2:1), this serves to characterize its speaker as the mediator of the ensuing speech of Yahweh (2:2-20), thus introducing a kind of reporting narration (2:2aα) that is anomalous in the context of a dialogue (→ 2:1-5). In the final analysis, the compositional form of this section of Habakkuk cannot be defined in terms of a dramatic exchange, liturgical or otherwise.

The genre should instead be identified on the basis of the following propositions: (1) 1:2-17 is an unreported speech of the prophet to Yahweh, and thus stands apart from the reported speech of Yahweh to the prophet that begins in ch. 2; and (2) the speech of the prophet to Yahweh in 1:2-17 is interrupted in 1:5-11 by the quotation of a previously proclaimed oracle addressed to a group audience (→ Structure). Generic classification must therefore define the kind of speech that is found in 1:2-17, and in the process explain the function of the interruption in 1:5-11.

Following Humbert, many commentators have noted that (→) 1:2-4 and (→) 1:12-17 resemble complaint psalms. By virtue of these similarities 1:2-17 may on the whole be described as a kind of PROPHETIC COMPLAINT. This particular example of the genre is distinctive, however, not only because of the way it is interrupted in 1:5-11 but also because of the way in which the complaint is predicated on what this interruption says. The complaint protests the injustice of the conquest that is described in 1:5-11 as it also accuses Yahweh of being involved in precisely the way that is claimed in 1:5-11 (→ Structure). The complaint thus presupposes that the developments prophesied in 1:5-11 have come to pass, and it serves to question the implications of their theological significance. The genre of 1:2-17 may thus be more particularly described as a PROPHETIC COMPLAINT ABOUT THE FULFILLMENT OF AN ORACLE.

Other significant examples of this genre include Jer 15:10-18 and Ps 89. This "confession" of Jeremiah is a prophetic complaint that also quotes a previous prophecy (15:13-14; cf. 17:3-4) in order to reflect on its failure to be completely fulfilled (Floyd, "Prophetic Complaints," 407-15). In Ps 89 a previously pronounced oracle concerning the eternal election of the Davidic dynasty is quoted (vv. 4-5, 20b-38 [RSV 3-4, 19b-37]; cf. 2 Sam 7:11b-16) in order to reflect on the significance of the monarchy's overthrow (M. H. Floyd, "Ps LXXXIX: A Prophetic Complaint about the Fulfillment of an Oracle," VT 42 [1992] 442-57). The definitive characteristic of the genre is that a previously proclaimed prophecy is quoted within the context of a complaint, so that the complaint serves to explore what is implied by the way in which the prophecy has been fulfilled or has failed to be fulfilled. In the case of Jer 15:10-18, the problem is that something predicted has only partly come to pass. In the case of Ps 89, the problem is that something predicted and confirmed through long historical experience is now no longer in effect. In the case of Hab 1:2-17, the problem is that something predicted has indeed come to pass, but in such a way as to question the justness of Yahweh even as it demonstrates the predictive accuracy of his prophet.

Setting

The two other examples of this genre given above point toward two different but interrelated settings. Because Ps 89 is a self-contained variation on the basic form of the (→) complaint, comparison with it suggests a cultic setting. As further evidence for the likelihood of such a setting, Pss 60 and 108 can be cited. The verbatim recurrence of the same oracular speech of Yahweh in both texts (Ps 60:8-10 [*RSV* 6-8] = Ps 108:8-10 [*RSV* 7-9]) shows that it is being quoted, and at least in the case of Ps 60 it appears that the complaint is occasioned by a problem in the fulfillment of this oracle: the nation's historical situation is no longer what the prophecy promised (Ps 60:3-5, 11-12 [*RSV* 1-3, 9-10]). Ps 60 thus provides an example of a prophetic complaint about the fulfillment of an oracle, the cultic performance of which is highly probable.

Some critics think that the "confessions" of Jeremiah are also complaints with a cultic setting (e.g., H. Graf Reventlow, *Liturgie und prophetisches Ich bei Jeremia* [Gütersloh: Mohn, 1963] 205-57), but most regard them as the products of subsequent retrospective reflection on Jeremiah's life and work on the part of either the prophet himself or his later interpreters (A. H. J. Gunneweg, "Konfessionen oder Interpretation im Jeremiabuch," *ZTK* 67 [1970] 395-416). In the particular case of Jer 15:10-18, such a setting is suggested by the distinctive way in which the complaint form is used. Because it serves to reinterpret a previously proclaimed oracle, the complaint form here attests to a situation in which scribes reflected on the significance of earlier prophecies for later times, and the results of their reflection were imaginatively expressed in a form adapted from the conventions of cultic poetry.

These two settings, the cult and groups of mantic scribes, should not be regarded as mutually exclusive since the personnel of both would have come from basically the same social group (S. Mowinckel, *The Psalms in Israel's Worship* [tr. D. R. Ap-Thomas; 2 vols.; New York: Abingdon, 1967] 2:90-95, 105-9). They may even be considered interdependent in the sense that the use of the complaint form, as the ideational structure in which to express the reinterpretation of prophecy, would presuppose that complaints concerning the fulfillment of oracles were actually performed in the cult. The quotation of previously extant oracles within complaint psalms would conversely presuppose some mantic reflection on the implications of this ritual practice for the analysis of prophetic divination. As Hab 1:2-17 functions within the final form of the text (→ Book as a Whole), its setting lies in the practice of prophetic reinterpretation. The capacity of this unit to serve such a function is directly dependent, however, on the liturgical performance of such prophetic complaints in a cultic setting, and this example of the genre might well have once been used in this way.

This section of the book was composed in reaction to some devastating Babylonian intervention in Judah's internal affairs, but it seems not to reflect the total destruction of 587 BCE. It was thus composed between 605 and 587, at some point during the years in which Judah first paid tribute to Babylon (605-602), then experienced Babylonian reprisals for refusing to pay tribute (605-598), and finally suffered defeat and the imposition of a puppet ruler at the hands of the Babylonians.

Intention

This text expresses the desire to confront a peculiar dilemma: Conditioned by the exigencies of a given historical situation, the fulfillment of a particular prophetic claim about the nature of Yahweh's involvement in world affairs has turned out to be theologically problematic in the context of subsequent historical developments. The identification of Babylonian power as a manifestation of Yahweh's divine power (1:5-11) posed no great problem as long as the Babylonians represented the subject nations struggling against Assyrian tyranny; but once the Babylonians assumed the role of imperial overlords, that same identification resulted in Yahweh's appearing to have commissioned the new oppressor. Simply by virtue of its being addressed to Yahweh, the complaint in 1:2-17 acknowledges the very principle on which the problematic prophecy was originally predicated, namely, that Yahweh is the controlling influence in world history. The prophet and all the supplicants represented by him thus depend utterly and ultimately on Yahweh alone.

As the complaint reproaches Yahweh, it affirms the collective recent experience of him as a perpetrator of injustice as it also expresses the hope that some recategorization of this experience will be forthcoming. Yahweh's response might enable the Babylonians' ruthlessness to be perceived as their own perversion of Yahweh's sending them to be world rulers, or as something that despite its presently destructive effects will ultimately serve the cause of justice.

Bibliography

J. H. Eaton, *Vision and Worship: The Relation of Prophecy and Liturgy in the Old Testament* (London: SPCK, 1981); M. H. Floyd, "Prophetic Complaints about the Fulfillment of Oracles in Habakkuk 1:2-17 and Jeremiah 15:10-18," *JBL* 110 (1991) 397-418; H. Gunkel, "The Close of Micah: A Prophetical Liturgy," in *What Remains of the Old Testament and Other Essays* (tr. A. K. Dallas; New York: Macmillan, 1928) 115-49; idem, "Jesaia 33, eine prophetische Liturgie," *ZAW* 42 (1924) 177-208.

THE PROPHET ACCUSES YAHWEH
OF RESPONSIBILITY FOR INJUSTICE, 1:2-4

Structure

I. Reproach implicating that Yahweh is responsible for injustice 1:2-4a
   A. Allegations concerning the nature of Yahweh's involvement 1:2-3
      1. Charge of culpable inactivity   1:2
         a. Question concerning Yahweh's failure to respond:
            how long?   1:2a
         b. Description of the effect: indifference to violence   1:2b

This unit begins with questions describing what Yahweh *does not* do, i.e., respond to the supplicant's pleas (v. 2). It then describes by the same means what Yahweh *does* do, i.e., cause the supplicant to experience evil. In the course of this shift, from focusing on the negative effects of Yahweh's inactivity to the equally negative effects of his activity, the scope of the description is also enlarged, as it moves from a portrayal of how the supplicant's personal situation is affected to a portrayal of how the wider social situation is affected. Yahweh's unresponsiveness to this supplicant's cry not only shows him to be indifferent to the "violence" *(ḥāmās)* that besets the supplicant (v. 2); it also implicates him in the spread of strife throughout the society (v. 3). Yahweh is therefore evidently to blame for the current breakdown of social norms (v. 4a). In conclusion this overall breakdown is described in terms of the "wicked" *(rāšāʿ)* attacking the "righteous" *(ṣaddîq;* v. $4b\alpha$), and the result of this antagonism is in effect the same as the result of Yahweh's aforementioned culpable activity and inactivity (vv. 2-4a), i.e., injustice (v. $4b\beta$). Yahweh is thus identified as one who sides with the wicked, and conversely identified as one who opposes the righteous.

Genre

As is evident from the typical elements of invocation, description of trouble, plea for deliverance, and reproach, this is a COMPLAINT. Because of the extent to which reproach becomes the dominant element, with all the others combining to serve its accusatory function, this unit provides a somewhat unusual example of the genre. There is an ironic reversal of the more usual relationship among these elements. The form would ordinarily include a petition requesting

Yahweh's help, but in this case there is only reproach for Yahweh's chronic in-attentiveness to such petitions, insinuating that Yahweh actually favors the wicked. This variation on the complaint form is particularly suited to the pro-phetic purpose of probing the divine reality. Although the supplications are ex-pressed in the first person singular, in the style of an individual complaint, the prayer as a whole is occasioned by a crisis that affects the entire society. Al-though the supplicant initially focuses only on the way in which this crisis af-fects his personal situation, the concern of the complaint gradually extends to encompass a wider context. The supplicant is thus speaking as the people's representative, in the capacity of an intermediary between them and Yahweh. Because this is generally a prophetic role, this text may be more specifically characterized as a PROPHETIC COMPLAINT.

Setting

Psalms of this genre were typically used in communal complaint liturgies (e.g., 2 Chr 20:1-30). It is difficult to say whether this unit could ever have existed independently from its compositional context in Hab 1:2-17, and thus difficult to say whether it could have functioned in a liturgical setting where the com-plaint was not specifically concerned with the fulfillment of a prophecy (→ 1:2-17, Setting). This unit may well have once been an independent prophetic speech, but nothing about the text requires one to suppose so.

Its focus on the local scene is often contrasted with the focus elsewhere on Babylon and the international scene. The crisis that occasions this com-plaint is certainly described as having a direct and devastating impact on the prophet and his immediate surroundings, but nothing suggests either that the crisis is confined to the local situation or that its genesis lies there. Thus any conclusion about the independence of this unit, based on the supposition that its concerns are purely domestic, goes beyond the evidence.

The description of trouble is phrased in the stereotypical terminology of the complaint (Humbert, 10-11), and although this description undoubtedly came to expression in response to some particular historical circumstances, the same description could well apply to any situation in which legal norms and customary standards of decency have broken down. By virtue of this unit's present literary context it now describes a crisis caused by Babylonian aggres-sion (Johnson, 261; Sweeney, 74). Any attempt to specify some other original historical setting on the basis of references in this unit alone also goes beyond the evidence.

Intention

Because of the way in which Yahweh has treated the prophet, both bringing on him the present predicament and ignoring his pleas for change, the prophet blames the Holy One for the injustice that now besets the community at large. Yet, in turning to Yahweh with his complaint, the prophet also indicates a desire to test whether these outward appearances truly reflect the underlying divine reality.

Bibliography

J. G. Harris, "The Laments of Habakkuk's Prophecy," *EvQ* 45 (1973) 21-29; M. D. Johnson, "The Paralysis of Torah in Habakkuk i 4," *VT* 35 (1985) 257-66; H. Schmidt, "Ein Psalm im Buche Habakuk," *ZAW* 62 (1949-50) 52-63.

A PROPHECY CONCERNING YAHWEH'S ROLE IN WORLD AFFAIRS, 1:5-11

Text

The first person verb form used by the *RSV* in 1:5b ("I am doing a work") is based on the LXX, and the MT actually uses the impersonal expression *pô'al pō'ēl,* which means in effect that "a work is in progress" (Bratcher, 141, n. b; Keller [*Habacuc,* 149] adduces other ancient versions in support of a similar sense). The LXX is of course not amiss in assuming that this "work" is attributable to Yahweh, but in the MT Yahweh's involvement remains implicit until v. 6. There Yahweh first explicitly claims agency.

The main point of v. 11 is clear from its conclusion in v. 11b, but the translation of v. 11a is difficult. I understand it to mean that the Babylonians have "violated" (*ḥlp; RSV* "sweep by"; cf. Isa 24:5) the "spirit" (*rûaḥ; RSV* "wind") of Yahweh's divine commission, and in thus overstepping their assigned role they have "transgressed" (*wayya'ăbōr; RSV* "go on"). They "whose own might is their god" have thus "incurred guilt" (*wĕ'āšēm; RSV* "guilty men").

Structure

I. Call to attend to the international situation	1:5
A. Commands	1:5a
1. Concerning visual perception: look and see!	1:5aα
2. Concerning attitudinal reaction: wonder and be astounded!	1:5aβ
B. Motivation	1:5b
1. Main reason: a work is in progress	1:5bα
2. Subsidiary reason: secondhand reports are insufficient	1:5bβ
II. Announcement of Yahweh's commissioning the Babylonians for world dominance	1:6-11
A. Announcement proper	1:6

1. Self-description of Yahweh's action:
   lo, I am rousing . . .   1:6aα^1
2. Object of his action   1:6aα^2bα
   a. Object proper: the Chaldeans   1:6aα^2
   b. Elaboration   1:6aβbα
      1) First appositional phrase: that bitter
         and hasty nation   1:6aβ
      2) Second appositional phrase: who march
         through the breadth of the earth   1:6bα
3. Yahweh's purpose in rousing the Chaldeans:
   for them to seize the habitations of others   1:6bβ
B. Extended description of the Chaldeans   1:7-11
   1. Aspects of their character   1:7-10
      a. Salient attributes   1:7-8
         1) In general terms   1:7
            a) Dread and terrible   1:7a
            b) A law unto themselves   1:7b
         2) In specific military terms: crack chariotry   1:8
      b. Their modus operandi   1:9-10
         1) In general terms   1:9a
            a) To promote violence   1:9aα
            b) To inspire terror   1:9aβ
         2) In specific military terms: their invincible
            sieges   1:9b-10
   2. Summary appraisal: the Chaldeans are guilty
      of self-deification   1:11

This unit begins with someone directly addressing a group, as is shown by the initial plural commands to "look" and "see," in contrast with the previous unit, where the prophet directly addresses Yahweh. There is at first no self-reference on the part of the speaker that would indicate just who it might be (→ Text). In v. 6 a first person pronoun finally appears in a formula that is characteristic of prophetic oracular speech in the name of Yahweh (P. Humbert, "La formule hébraïque en *hineni* suivi d'un participe," repr. in *Opuscules d'un hébraïsänt* [Mémoires de l'Université de Neuchâtel 26; Neuchâtel: Secrétariat de l'Université, 1958] 54-59). Thus, as the prophet begins to speak on Yahweh's behalf to a group (v. 5a), he first calls attention to important international developments that must be seen to be believed. At the same time he also attempts to evoke an attitude of wonder toward these events and then proceeds to interpret them in terms of Yahweh's own intentions.

The events in question are the conquests by which the Neo-Babylonian empire ("the Chaldeans") gained control of most of the ancient Near East in the latter part of the seventh century BCE. According to the prophetic interpretation of Yahweh's purpose, the Babylonians' rise to power is part of Yahweh's plan for the world (v. 6), despite the fact that they rule as though might makes right (vv. 7-8), and despite their conduct of warfare being rather brutal (vv. 9-10). They are of course not aware that they serve Yahweh's purpose, and they thus exercise the prerogatives of their empowerment without ever intending to be subservient to its divine source. Because their motivations are so self-serving, they in effect put themselves in place of God and thus become guilty of self-deification (v. 11).

Genre

When seen as the announcement of an action of Yahweh directed specifically against either Judah or some particular group within Judah, this unit has been classified as a (→) prophecy of punishment (e.g., Jeremias, 80; Gowan, *Triumph*, 24; Roberts, 94). When seen as the announcement of an action of Yahweh directed against Judah's foes, thus leading to Judah's liberation, it has been classified as a (→) prophecy of punishment against a foreign nation (e.g., Eaton, *Obadiah*, 88-90; cf. Jöcken, "War Habakuk ein Kultprophet?" 326), or even a (→) prophecy of salvation (e.g., Haak, 14). The text itself, however, does not describe the Babylonian conquest as being directed specifically against either Judah or Judah's foes. It rather describes their conquest as having an impact on all the nations in general. This unit is therefore concerned to assert that Yahweh stands behind the emergence of Babylon as a dreaded world power, rather than to draw out the implications of this development for the weal or woe of any nation or party in particular. Hence it is questionable whether any of the above-mentioned generic categories applies here (C.-A. Keller, "Die Eigenart der Prophetie Habakuks," *ZAW* 85 [1973] 158).

The first concern of this unit is simply to call attention to a particular international development (1:5) and then to interpret its theological significance for the prophet's audience (1:6-11). There is of course no earthly vantage point from which one can literally "look among the nations," but in urging his audience to do so the prophet is metaphorically assuming a particular role, the role of a sentinel. A sentinel would keep watch on a city wall, on a watchtower, or on the outskirts of a military encampment to monitor the approach of all parties (2 Sam 13:34; 18:24b-25a), particularly the approach of any military force (2 Kgs 9:17-20). A sentinel's duties might also include the gathering of reports brought by travelers concerning things that have happened farther away (Isa 21:6-7; Jer 48:19). On the basis of such observations a sentinel might initiate the community's response with various appropriate directives, depending on the nature of the news (Jer 6:17; 31:6; 48:20). When a prophet metaphorically assumed the sentinel's role, these directives might be predicated on divinatory perceptions regarding the involvement of Yahweh in contemporary events (Isa 52:8-9).

This unit shows the following distinctive formal traits that are characteristic of the prophet's playing a sentinel's role: (1) announcement of a recent historical development, first in very general terms (1:5bα), then in specifically military terms (1:8, 9b-10; cf. 1 Sam 14:16; Nah 2:2 [*RSV* 1]; Lam 4:17; Isa 21:9a); (2) a command concerning the appropriate response, which in this case is simply wonder (1:5aβ; cf. Jer 6:17a; Nah 2:1aβ, 2b [*RSV* 1:15aβ; 2:1b];

Ezek 3:17); and (3) an interpretation of the announced development in terms of Yahweh's involvement (1:6; cf. Isa 21:9b-10; Nah 2:1b, 3 [*RSV* 1:15b; 2:2]). This cluster of elements shows that 1:5-11 is an instance of the PROPHETIC SENTINEL REPORT (→ Nah 2:1-11 [*RSV* 1:15–2:10]; Zech 11:1-3).

Setting

The sentinel report itself originated in the context of military operations and civil defense. Prophetic borrowing of this convention reflects the courtly milieu in which reports of international developments were circulated and studied by those who advised official decision makers. This particular text must have been composed sometime after such intelligence reports had made the Babylonians' great destructive capacity evident, but before they had completely replaced the Assyrians and their Egyptian allies as the dominant power in the ancient Near East. This prophecy was thus probably proclaimed just before this decisive shift in the balance of power at the end of the seventh century BCE, represented by such crucial events as the Battle of Haran in 609 and the Battle of Carchemish in 605. Shortly after this transition, as a consequence of the Babylonians' directly intervening in Judah, this prophecy was incorporated into the surrounding prophetic complaint of which it is now an integral part (→ 1:2-17).

Intention

The general aim of this text is to impart to its courtly audience the results of prophetic divination concerning Yahweh's role in foreign affairs. It asserts more specifically that Yahweh should be seen as the instigator of the new world order being established by the Babylonians, even if the effect of their rule on subject peoples makes their assumption of this imperial role morally ambiguous. The charge of self-deification, with which this prophecy concludes, suggests that the Babylonians will unwittingly serve Yahweh's purpose without ultimately attaining his favor.

THE PROPHET QUESTIONS YAHWEH'S COMPATIBILITY WITH INJUSTICE, 1:12-17

Text

As *BHS* indicates, the MT reading of 1:12aβ^2 is counted as one of the traditional Tiq soph. According to most versions of this tradition, the original reading of *l' tmwt* ("you shall not die") was altered to the present reading of *l' nmwt* ("we shall not die") because the scribes found the former to be theologically objectionable. The value of this tradition for text-critical purposes is highly debatable (C. McCarthy, *The Tiqqune Sopherim* [OBO 36; Freiburg: Universitätsverlag; Göttingen: Vandenhoeck & Ruprecht, 1981]), and it is difficult to imagine how the sentiment that God is undying could be theologically problematic from any orthodox standpoint, ancient or modern. If meant ironically, as is often the case in the reproachful rhetoric of the complaint, a statement like "you shall not die" could well be loaded with sarcasm and could perhaps have been found objectionable for this reason. In this particular instance the Tiq soph reading can only be preferred on such a highly speculative basis, and in the following analysis I therefore retain the MT reading (cf. McCarthy, 105-11). Read either way, v. 12aβ² fulfills much the same function in the compositional structure of 1:12-17, partly making up the expression of trust that is a characteristic element of the complaint genre.

Structure

I. Affirmation of confidence: invocation of Yahweh by
name and epithet   1:12
  A. Rhetorical question attributing to Yahweh a consistent
character: are you not as before?   1:12aα
  B. Inferential expressions of trust   1:12aβb
    1. Declaration of hope for deliverance: we shall
not die!   1:12aβ
    2. Apologetic explanations of Yahweh's purpose in
rousing the Babylonians   1:12b
      a. It will eventually make for justice   1:12bα
      b. It serves as chastisement   1:12bβ
II. Reproach   1:13-17
  A. Attribution to Yahweh of incompatibility with injustice   1:13a
    1. Incapacity to condone evil: expressed in terms of
visual perceptiveness   1:13aα
    2. Inability to countenance wrong   1:13aβ
  B. Inferential questioning of Yahweh's apparent
responsibility for injustice   1:13b-17
    1. Questions concerning the reason for complicity
with evil   1:13b
      a. Why countenance the faithless?   1:13bα
      b. Why condone oppression of the righteous
by the wicked?   1:13bβ
    2. Elaboration in terms of an extended fishing simile   1:14-17
      a. Question of why humanity seems made for
domination   1:14-16
        1) Basic statement of comparison: humanity
like fish and crawling things   1:14
        2) Extension of comparison   1:15-16
          a) The imperialist fisherman gloatingly
takes his catch   1:15

| | b) | He worships the technological means of exploitation | 1:16 |
| | b. | Question of whether such domination will go on indefinitely | 1:17 |

In this unit the prophetic spokesman addresses Yahweh, first expressing confidence in his moral integrity (v. 12) and then upbraiding him for the present situation that seems to deny strongly any such integrity (vv. 13-17). The same structure is evident in both v. 12 and vv. 13-17, but in each case it is used for a rhetorically different purpose. Each begins by attributing some quality to Yahweh (v. 12aα, v. 13a), and then draws out something that may be inferred from such an attribution (v. 12aβb, vv. 13b-17). If Yahweh's character is indeed consistent with his past history of just dealings (v. 12aα), then his people may expect to survive the Babylonian oppression (v. 12aβ); and that oppression will moreover turn out to be consistent with some just purpose of his (v. 12b). Similarly, if Yahweh is indeed incapable of condoning evil (v. 13a), why does the reign of injustice seem to be such an ongoing part of the way things are (vv. 13b-17)?

The basic structure of the unit thus shows a tendency to generalization as it treats issues raised concretely by the present crisis in terms of Yahweh's characteristic attributes. The extended simile in 1:14-17 serves to accentuate this tendency as it compares the present crisis with certain aspects of the created order of things. In contrast with the complaint in 1:2-4, the inclusion of an affirmation of confidence along with a reproach serves to heighten the expectation that something will happen to resolve the moral problem posed by Yahweh's rousing the Babylonians. But the nature of the relationship between the affirmation of confidence and the reproach also serves to deepen the problem.

The issue of Yahweh's moral integrity, which is initially seen only in terms of his involvement in a particular historical situation, comes to be seen here in terms of his involvement with creation as a whole. On the one hand Yahweh has a record of acting justly, as both creator and savior. But on the other hand his complicity with the Babylonians seems symptomatic of a divine responsibility for injustice that is built into the order of creation: Humanity seems to be made like fish and other "lower" creatures — incapable of effective self-determination and hence subject by nature to domination and exploitation. The unit ends by questioning whether this is indeed the way things are and how long Yahweh will allow them to be so.

Genre

This unit contains a combination of elements that is characteristic of the COMPLAINT: an invocation of Yahweh expressed within an affirmation of trust, a description of trouble expressed within a reproach, and a plea for deliverance implicit in the final questions. Because these elements are combined in such a way as to press a theological problem that has been generated by the fulfill-

109

ment of a prophecy (→ 1:2-17), this instance of the complaint genre may be further distinguished as a PROPHETIC COMPLAINT.

Setting

This unit presupposes both the prior fulfillment and the foregoing quotation of the prophecy in 1:5-11 (→ 1:2-17). Pronominal elements whose antecedents lie back in the preceding unit serve to link v. 12b with Yahweh's announcement of his rousing the Babylonians in v. 6a, as a description of his underlying motives. The same phenomenon also serves to identify the Babylonians with the fisherman in vv. 14-17, comparing their treatment of the nations (vv. 9-10) with his treatment of his catch (vv. 15-17), as well as their worship of their own military capacity (v. 11) with his worship of his means of exploitation (v. 16). This unit therefore does not show evidence of any independent existence prior to the composition of the chapter as a whole. There is no reason to suppose that it might have been used in any kind of communal complaint setting, other than the one in which the chapter as a whole might have been used, i.e., an occasion of complaint concerning the fulfillment of the prophecy in 1:5-11 (→ 1:2-17, Setting).

Intention

As the prophetic spokesman approaches Yahweh on the people's behalf, he seeks to instill in them the confidence that Yahweh will do something to resolve the problem of his moral integrity. At the same time the prophet imparts to them his awareness of how radical any such action must be: It will entail a new kind of world in which the sort of brutal imperialism represented by the Babylonians will no longer exist.

Bibliography

→ 1:2-4.

Chapter 4

THE SECOND MAJOR SECTION
OF THE BOOK (2:1-20)
AND ITS INDIVIDUAL UNITS

THE PROPHET REPORTS HIS RECEPTION OF YAHWEH'S REPLY TO HIS INQUIRY, 2:1-20

Text

The *RSV* and other modern versions translate *tôkaḥtî* in v. 2b as "my complaint," apparently assuming that it refers back to the complaints in 1:2-17. This translation is problematic, however, for the word has this meaning nowhere else. It refers neither to cultic complaints of the sort represented by 1:2-17, for which there are other terms such as *śîaḥ,* nor to complaining in general. The word ordinarily means "reproof" or "correction," and so on. It should be taken in this sense here, and its pronominal suffix is best understood as a so-called objective genitive. The prophet therefore expresses his intention "to see what [Yahweh] will say to me, and how I will respond to my being corrected" (cf. *NIV*'s alternate reading and *NEB*). In other words, he expects that he will be disabused of his former attitude by what Yahweh will say to him (→ Setting).

Structure

I. Announcement of oracular inquiry		2:1
A. Description of the prophet's preparation in terms of a sentinel metaphor		2:1a
1. Waiting on the watchtower		2:1aα
2. Standing on the bulwark		2:1aβ
B. Statement of the prophet's objectives		2:1b
1. To receive Yahweh's reply		2:1bα

This section of Habakkuk has two main parts. The first, beginning at 2:1, is primarily concerned with Yahweh's response to a revelation sought by the prophet. The second consists largely of a series of "woe" speeches, beginning at 2:6. Scholars disagree both with regard to the nature and extent of these two units, and with regard to whether and how they are related. Scholars generally agree that Yahweh's reply to the prophet reaches its climax in v. 4. Some would also include all of v. 5 within that reply (e.g., Ward, 13-14; Horst, 178-79; Rudolph, 214-17; Bratcher, 112), in which case v. 6a would furnish the introduction to the series of "woes" that make up the rest of the chapter. Some would regard v. 5bα as the end of Yahweh's reply to the prophet (e.g., Humbert, 15-17; Brownlee, "Composition," 163-65; Boadt, 184), so that vv. 5bβ-6a form the introduction to the following unit. Still others would limit Yahweh's reply to v. 4 (e.g., Marti, 335-36; Elliger, 38-39; Eaton, *Obadiah,* 94; Keller, *Habacuc,* 156-60; Watts, 132-36), thus making 2:5-6a the introduction to the "woes." Regardless of how they come down on this question, the majority of commentators regard the "woes" as a distinctly different section of the book, having little directly to do with Yahweh's preceding reply to the prophet. Some have observed that the "woes" provide concrete examples of Yahweh's general statement in vv. 4a-5 regarding the fate of the greedy one, but each of these same commentators views the nature of the connection between Yahweh's reply and the "woes" rather differently (Boadt, 183; Bratcher, 196-97, 208-9; and Sweeney, 71-72).

A determination of the boundary between the two main parts of this section, as well as an assessment of their relationship, depends in large part on how one reads vv. 4, 5, and 6. According to the interpretation presented here, v. 4 is the point at which the substance of Yahweh's reply begins. The prophet has previously announced his intention to await a revelation from Yahweh (v. 1). When Yahweh responds, his speech begins with directions concerning the transcription of the revelation that is about to follow, together with an exhortation to await its realization (vv. 2-3). Then comes the oracle sought by the prophet (v. 4), expressed in terms of a contrast between the fate of a person whose greed (*napšô; RSV* "soul") leads him astray and the fate of a person committed to justice, who still remains faithful to Yahweh (→ 2:1-5, Text).

By virtue of both form and content, all of v. 5 is an integral part of Yahweh's oracular reply to the prophet. With respect to form, it is explicitly linked to v. 4 by the conjunctive expression *wĕ'ap kî (RSV* "moreover"). With respect to content, it elaborates on the theme of being led astray by greed (v. 4a) with a description of how this happens. A taste for wine, when overindulged, can give a man such delusions of grandeur that he is bound to fall; and a taste for conquest, when overextended to cosmic proportions, can likewise predispose a conqueror to make fatal mistakes. Insatiability of both sorts leads to obliviousness, which in turn leads to self-destruction. Avarice, like a drunken stupor, can hardly inform realistic behavior. The elaboration in v. 5 completes the contrast between the greedy and the just begun in v. 4. The person who combines a commitment to justice with faithfulness to Yahweh will live (v. 4b), but a person with an insatiable greed for conquest becomes like death itself (v. 5b).

Although v. 6 marks both a change of subject and a shift in style, it is nevertheless explicitly connected with the oracular reply of Yahweh in vv. 4-5. The pronominal elements in v. 6a would be unintelligible without referring back to antecedents there. Who are *'ēlleh kullām* (*RSV* "all these") if not the nations and peoples described as the victims of imperialism in v. 5? Who is he whom they proceed to mock, if not the the *geber yāhîr* (*RSV* "arrogant man") addicted to conquest in v. 5, who is in turn to be identified with the person led astray by greed in v. 4? With respect to content, v. 6a is thus a direct continuation of vv. 4-5, linking 2:6-20 closely with the first part of the chapter.

Moreover, there is no indication of any change of speaker at this point. The rhetorical question in v. 6a serves to introduce the long speech of "all peoples and nations" in vv. 6b-20, but the text gives no reason to suppose that the reporter of what the nations are saying is anyone other than Yahweh. The speech of Yahweh that begins to be reported in v. 2 thus extends through vv. 6-20 all the way to the end of the chapter, and the overall structure of this section is based on the rhetorical frame of direct discourse within direct discourse: Within his report of a revelation sought and received from Yahweh (2:1-20), the prophet quotes Yahweh's reply (2:2-20); and within his reply to the prophet (2:2aβ-20), Yahweh quotes the outcry of the nations (2:6-20). By concluding his reply to the prophet with this report of world opinion, Yahweh is reinforcing the parenetic note sounded at the outset. The directive in v. 3, to wait in hope for the fulfillment of the oracle in vv. 4-5, is made more persuasive by identifying the main point of this oracle with the universally recognized perception of the world situation that is described in vv. 6-20.

A tendency not to treat this section as a coherent whole is evident in the frequent attempts to emend and explain away the grammatical and phraseological connections by which the two main parts of ch. 2 are bound together in vv. 4-6. This tendency is largely rooted in two hypotheses. According to the already discussed idea of a dialogue between the prophet and Yahweh (→ 1:2-17, Structure), scholars have sought in ch. 2 a speech of Yahweh that relates as a reply to 1:12-17, just as 1:5-11 supposedly relates as a reply to 1:2-4. Many have found 2:1-5 or 2:1-4 to be a pericope suitable for completing the dialogue, which has in turn led to the supposition of a fundamental division between the dialogue and the "woe" speeches, despite some disagreement over just where to locate the boundary between them. The foregoing analysis of 1:2-17 has attempted to show the shortcomings of this hypothesis, arguing that 1:2-17 is better understood as a prophetic complaint occasioned by the fulfillment of the previously proclaimed prophecy that is cited in 1:5-11 (→ 1:2-17, Genre). There is thus no reason to regard any part of ch. 2 as the conclusion to a dialogue. This section rather marks the start of something new, a report of how the prophet sought and received a revelation from Yahweh, a revelation of which the "woe" speeches in 2:6-20 can be considered an integral part.

Another impediment to seeing any close link between 2:1-5 and 2:6-20 is the hypothesis that the "woe" speeches represent a distinctive kind of prophetic speech. If one assumes that these are the sorts of speeches that Yahwistic prophets would typically make to their own people, it is utterly incongruous for them to be introduced in v. 6a as words in the mouths of gentile nations (e.g., Humbert, 18-19; Ward, 15; Horst, 180; Rudolph, 222; Jeremias, 57-58). Those who share this assumption have thus taken the "woe" speeches out of their present literary context and have attempted to read them as prophecies proclaimed at various times by Habakkuk or some other prophet against various foreign nations, or even against Judah. This approach proceeds not on the basis of the supposedly artificial introductory characterization of the "woe" speeches in v. 6a, but on the basis of a historical question: Against whom, and in what historical circumstances, was each of these "woes" once directed by some prophetic speaker? (For a review of some of the many proposals, see Jöcken, *Habakuk*, 403-501.)

The analysis of the "woe" speeches presented below (→ 2:6-8) argues that they are not basically prophecies but are rather examples of the (→) reproof speech, a genre deriving from the sphere of wisdom. Like many rhetorical conventions that were not distinctively prophetic, this manner of speaking could certainly be adapted by prophets for their own purposes. It is not surprising that a reproof speech would figure in the composition of a prophetic speech or text, in view of the extent to which both learned and popular wisdom overlapped with the practice of prophecy (D. F. Morgan, *Wisdom in the Old Testament Traditions* [Atlanta: John Knox, 1981] 63-93). This same convention was more at home, however, in other areas of community life, where it could also be employed for various ordinary purposes. It is thus not at all incongruous for such speeches to be placed on the lips of the nations in general.

It is conceivable that some of the "woe" speeches may have once existed independently outside their present literary context, and perhaps even conceivable that they could have once been used to prophesy against some foreign power, or against some king or party in Judah. It is probably pointless to speculate about this, however, not only because all the "woe" speeches lack much in the way of historical specificity, but also because they may never have served any particularly prophetic function to begin with. It is certainly beside the point to object that Gentiles would not have actually recognized Yahweh as the cause of Babylon's fall, or admitted the futility of idols. The element of personification in v. 6a shows that this is a fictional representation of an expression of international opinion, not a report of what any particular group of Gentiles ever actually said. It is more relevant to ask what sense it might have made to imagine the nations as characters voicing such opinions, and to ask whether any significant degree of verisimilitude was intended. These questions can only be answered in taking a closer look at the overall arrangement of the "woe" speeches in 2:6b-20.

Two distinctive features set off the first four "woe" speeches from the fifth. The structure of the fifth varies the order of the basic elements that is common to the other four. Variation is immediately evident from the changed position of the "woe" cry itself, which stands at the head of the first four units but comes in the middle of the fifth, although the order of other elements is also affected (→ 2:18-20, Structure). In addition, there is verbatim repetition in the first and the fourth of the "woe" speeches (in v. 8b and v. 17b), a reprise that functions like an *inclusio* to bracket vv. 6b-17 from vv. 18-20. The former subsection has only the earth and all humanity in view (note *'ādām* [*RSV* "men"] and *'āreṣ* [*RSV* "earth"] in both v. 8b and v. 17b), while the latter has the whole cosmic scheme of heaven and earth in view (v. 20). The former is relatively more concerned with what the present means for the future, while the latter is relatively more concerned with what the future means for the present (2:18-20, Structure). The former initiates and carries on the international outcry that is introduced in v. 6a, while the latter calls for this outcry to cease (*has* [*RSV* "keep silence"], v. 20). These progressions — from part of the cosmos to its whole, from future expectations to present immediacy, and from the beginning and middle of an action to its end — all show that the fifth and final "woe" speech stands in relation to its four predecessors as their climax and conclusion (cf. Bratcher, 169-70; Sweeney, 73).

The first four "woe" speeches themselves are also interrelated in a particular way. Both the first and the fourth illustrate the general ethical principle of just retribution through a reversal of circumstances. Those who have extorted and plundered others will themselves be extorted and plundered by their victims (vv. 6b-8). Similarly, those who have made their neighbors drink to the neighbors' disadvantage will themselves be made to drink to their own disadvantage (vv. 15-17). The only difference is that in the second case it is Yahweh who brings this reversal about and thus restores the balance of justice (v. 16b).

Both the second and third "woes" illustrate another general ethical principle: the futility of attempting a worthy end by corrupt means. Any effort to secure one's house with the proceeds from exploitation will only result in its insecurity, for the house itself will then testify to the exploitation (vv. 9-11). Similarly, any effort to found a city through bloodshed will only result in its eventual downfall, for such efforts perpetuate the very dynamic that destroys cities (vv. 12-14). The only difference is that in the second case Yahweh is the one who renders it futile to use illegitimate means toward a legitimate end, and thus restores the balance of justice. The overall arrangement of the first four "woes" serves evidently to correlate the practical recognition of two basic ethical principles with the practical recognition of Yahweh's agency (cf. Bratcher, 209).

The "woe" speeches in 2:6b-20 are thus not just a group of separate items strung together in a series, but integral parts of a compositional form designed to develop a line of thought (Elliger, 48), which can be construed in terms of three points corresponding to the three major subdivisions, vv. 6b-11, 12-17, and 18-20. (1) Even from a relatively superficial earthly perspective, which considers only the outward reality of the situation, the Babylonians are bound to fall because they have violated fundamental moral principles. By transgressing the Golden Rule and by trying to reach good ends by evil means, they have brought the moral order of the world into discord — a discord that must eventually be harmonized at the expense of those who initially caused it. (2) From a somewhat more profound earthly perspective that looks behind the outward reality for the inner meaning of events, Yahweh is the one who is bringing about the downfall of Babylon, acting in his capacity as the author and sustainer of the world's moral order. He has built these fundamental principles into the fabric of creation, and he rectifies their violation through the historical process. Recognition of history as a moral process is thus tantamount to recognition of Yahweh as the ruler of creation. Such recognition amounts to indirect knowledge of Yahweh through the apprehension of his *kābôd* (*RSV* "glory," v. 14a), if not direct knowledge of Yahweh himself. (3) When the recognition that Babylon's fall is inevitable is put in a cosmic perspective, embracing both the unseen heavenly realms and the visible earthly realm, the prospect becomes epiphanic. From this perspective such an event as Babylon's fall discloses the divine reality at work in the human sphere. The Babylonians' idolatrous legitimation of their rule is thereby exposed as a self-deluding and hence unsuccessful attempt at their own self-deification (→ 2:18-20). Recognition of history as a moral process thus carries within itself the potential of Yahweh's becoming universally recognized as sole ruler of the universe.

The figurative placement of this line of thought on the lips of the nations shows considerable theological reflection. Its starting point is the realization of the international community that the dominant superpower is now about to fall because of a moral imperative that amounts to a divine decree. The implications of this development are followed out in light of the fact that the Babylonians have legitimated their rule on the basis of the same idolatrous customs that are also generally practiced by their gentile victims. The nations' consensus of opinion regarding Babylon thus stands in a virtually antithetical tension with their own common religious practices — a tension whose resolution implies the universal recognition of Yahweh. Such an international outcry, when it is introduced in a rhetorical question as the conclusion of Yahweh's speech to the prophet, asserts that world opinion already tacitly recognizes what Yahweh has explicitly revealed to the prophet (2:4-5) and thus makes the prospect of waiting for the oracle's fulfillment all the more reasonable. As the prophet's audience beholds him being thus persuaded, they are in turn persuaded that it would be reasonable to emulate the prophet in his acceptance of this revelation.

The fictional representation of the outcry of the nations in 2:6-20 would not fulfill its own rhetorical objectives if it were not a plausible reflection of the actual climate of international opinion around the turn of the sixth century. It is intended to be realistic in this sense. In describing the nations' acknowledgment of Yahweh and their rejection of idolatry it does not, however, purport to express any consciously held attitudes or beliefs on the part of the Gentiles. Such description serves rather to take the implications of international opinion, interpreted from a Yahwistic perspective, to their ultimate conclusion (cf. Pss 97:6-7; 98:2-3; 1 Sam 4:7-8).

When the function of 2:6-20 is clarified, the second major section of Habakkuk appears to consist primarily of a long speech by Yahweh (2:2aβ-20) that comes in response to the prophet's waiting for a revelation (2:1-2aα).

Yahweh first explains that the word which he is about to give will not seem immediately applicable. It must therefore be recorded and studied in order to discern the time when it will actually come to pass (2:2aβ-3). Then follows Yahweh's pronouncement on the situation, portending doom for those whose greed for conquest has led them astray, but hope for those who remain both committed to justice and faithful to Yahweh (2:4-5). Finally, Yahweh challenges the prophet to accept this pronouncement and live in hope of its fulfillment. Such a faith stance is reasonable not only because of the actual state of world opinion but also because of the theological conclusion to which its implications ultimately lead (2:6-20).

Genre

This section consists basically of a brief announcement of the prophet's intention to await a revelation from Yahweh (2:1), followed by a lengthy report of Yahweh's reply (2:2-20). It thus retains the overall shape of a REPORT OF AN ORACULAR INQUIRY (→ 2:1-5, Genre). This particular example of the genre is somewhat unusual, however, because of the way in which the terse oracular reply (2:4-5) is nearly overshadowed by the directives and persuasive elements that frame it so extensively (2:2aβ-3 + 6-20). The relative prominence of these elements shows that this section is concerned not just with recounting the outcome of an oracular inquiry. A heavy apologetic emphasis is also evident. The oracle itself is apparently so problematic that considerable attention must be given to its authentication, not only in the process of reporting its revelation but also in the very process of its being revealed.

Such reports focus typically on the prophet as a privileged intermediary between the divine and human realms, emphasizing that the prophet is privy to Yahweh's counsel in ways that other ordinary mortals are not. In this case, however, the report is designed and extended so as to reverse this tendency, emphasizing instead that the prophet may have much the same difficulties as his human audience when it comes to understanding and accepting a revelation, even a revelation that the prophet himself has received.

This effect is achieved by reducing the narrative element to the barest minimum (→ 2:1-5, Genre). The initial bit of reporting narration (2:2aα) is structurally prominent (II.A) and thus serves to establish at the outset a clear rhetorical distinction between the revelation addressed by Yahweh to the prophet and the report addressed by the prophet to his audience. The narration remains so sparse, however, that this rhetorical distinction quickly gets blurred. By the time the outcry of the nations begins to be quoted in a subsequent bit of reporting narration (2:6a), the audience may well not retain a clear idea of just who is speaking to whom. Such scanty narrational markers as 2:2aα and 2:6a can scarcely sustain over time any distinct awareness of such a complicated rhetorical relationship as direct discourse within direct discourse. By this point the audience may no longer realize that Yahweh is quoting to the prophet the taunts of the peoples, and that the prophet is in turn quoting Yahweh to them. The audience may instead be getting the impression that Yahweh is speaking directly to them. They are thus being challenged to accept the revelation in much the same way as the prophet.

This impression is reinforced by the ambiguous way in which the outcry of the nations ends with a call for "silence!" predicated on the assertion that "Yahweh is in his holy temple" and addressed to "all the earth" (2:20b). There is nothing to suggest a change of speaker in the stylistic variations with which the final "woe" speech begins (→ 2:18-20, Structure), but the way in which it concludes may well leave readers wondering. The nations' taunting of their oppressor is suddenly brought to an end by contrasting an idol with Yahweh. The idol is neither alive nor numinous (2:19b), but Yahweh reveals himself enthroned in majesty as living Lord of the universe (2:20a). This contrast then evokes a call for "all the earth" to reverence Yahweh in silence — but by whom is this call spoken?

Since there is no explicit indication of a new speaker, the nations would presumably continue in this role. But do they then turn suddenly from taunting their oppressor to address themselves with a command? This kind of change seems unlikely. Thus, alternatively, does Yahweh at this point cease to quote the international outcry and resume the rhetorical stance which he had previously assumed in 2:2aβ-6bα[1], i.e., the stance of speaking for himself? If so, why does he not also go back to directly addressing the prophet, in accord with the conventions of the oracular inquiry that obtain in 2:2aβ-6bα[1], instead of turning to address "all the earth"? Why would Yahweh make third person references to himself in such a quasi-hymnic context? In view of the quasi-hymnic nature of v. 20, perhaps it is instead possible that the prophet here resumes the rhetorical stance with which he initiated the report in 2:1-2aα, i.e., the stance of informing his audience about Yahweh. The prophet would thus be turning again to his audience, assuming the role of one who leads the people in hymnic praise of Yahweh, calling on them to acknowledge Yahweh as the source of the revelation imparted in the reply to the prophet's inquiry (2:2aβ-19). The resumption of this rhetorical stance would explain the command to revere Yahweh in v. 20b, but it also raises a problem with respect to the characterization of the addressees as "all the earth." The recipients of a hymnic call to praise are appropriately addressed in this way (e.g., Pss 96:1b; 98:4a; 100:1), and so are the addressees of some kinds of prophetic speech (cf., e.g., Zech 2:17 [*RSV* 13]; → Zech 2:10-17 [*RSV* 6-13]), but it is anomalous for the audience of a prophetic report to be imagined in such terms. It is also difficult to suppose that v. 20a marks an intrusion on the part of the prophet, in view of the grammatical coordination that explicitly binds it and the foregoing variation on the "woe" speech (vv. 18-19) — where he is presumably not the primary speaker — into a single unit (vv. 18-20).

There may be still other possibilities, but in any case the text of 2:1-20 remains irresolvably ambiguous with regard to who has the final word. Such ambiguity is in accord with the overall design of this section, which serves to establish and then to blur the distinction between two different rhetorical standpoints: the standpoint of Yahweh, from which he identifies the universal belief in the inevitability of Babylon's doom with the revelation that he has disclosed to the prophet; and the standpoint of the prophet, from which he imparts this disclosure to his audience. All such distinctions coalesce in the epiphanic climax with which this section concludes, as each of the human parties — the nations, the prophet, and the prophet's audience — hears itself called by some finally unidentifiable voice to join with the other parties in acknowledging the universal sovereignty of Yahweh. As a result, readers find themselves directly confronted by Yahweh's reply to the prophet, almost as if it were addressed to them in the first place.

Setting

This text reflects the conduct of an oracular inquiry (→ 2:1-5, Setting), but reports of such inquiries were neither produced nor utilized in the course of conducting this divinatory practice. Reports of oracular inquiries were rather a means of subsequently publicizing and reflectively interpreting their outcome. Several textual details reflect various aspects of the social context in which these reports were composed and circulated. The command in 2:3a, to transcribe the revelation in order to study it, shows that this text grew out of a group that kept records of prophecies and studied prophetic lore. The parenesis (2:3b) and persuasion (2:6-20) that frame the substance of the oracle itself (2:4-5) suggest that this was a group that engaged in critical reflection concerning the authentication of prophecy as well as its theological implications. A text like this would probably have been the product of such critical reflection, composed as a means of communicating the retrospectively considered significance of the oracular inquiry it describes.

The significance of this particular inquiry is signaled in the prophet's announcement of his intention to await a revelation from Yahweh (2:1). His purpose is not just to see what Yahweh will say to him (2:1bα) but also to see how he will react to a *tôkaḥat* from Yahweh (2:1bβ; → Text). This word can mean "rebuke" or "reproof," i.e., criticism for doing something wrong; but it can also mean "correction," i.e., reform of mistaken beliefs and behavioral habits. The term applies in the former sense to what the nations are characterized as doing in 2:6-20 as they taunt the Babylonians with reproof speeches (→ 2:6-8, Genre). It applies in the latter sense to the overall effect of Yahweh's reply on the prophet and particularly to the persuasive effect of Yahweh's citing the nations' reproof of the Babylonians. The outcome of the oracular reply is thus being interpreted in terms of how it "corrected" the prophet's former mistaken assessment of Yahweh's complicity in Babylonian domination (→ 1:2-17). As a result of the critical reflection and study that are implied by the command to transcribe the revelation (2:3a), the prophet's mind is changed.

It is questionable whether the "woe" speeches in 2:6b-20 ever existed independently, outside their present literary context, before they were incorporated into this report of oracular inquiry. Various theories to this effect have been proposed, supposing that the "woe" speeches exemplify a rhetorical convention whose original use was different from the use to which the text now puts them. There is considerable disagreement over whether the "woe" speeches exemplify a kind of prophetic oracle or a kind of wisdom saying, and over the original form they supposedly once assumed (cf., e.g., Gerstenberger, 256-62; Brownlee, "Composition," 268-69; Jeremias, 67-75). Nevertheless, those who hold such theories generally agree that the "woe" speeches originated and formerly circulated in a setting different from the one that produced the final form of the text, and that they were subsequently adapted for use in their present literary context through a redactional process.

Although prophetic literature could and often did develop in this way, there is no compelling reason to suppose that this particular text did so. As reproof speeches (→ 2:6-8, Genre), the "woes" were not only apt for their present use as representations of the international outcry, they were also at home within the kind of group that produced this text. This manner of speaking was conventional among scribal groups that studied prophetic lore and composed such theologically reflective reports of oracular inquiry as it expressed the kind of "correction" (tôkaḥat) that their mantic study was intended to inculcate. There is thus nothing to indicate that these "woe" speeches ever existed in some other form, or that they ever served any purpose other than the one they presently serve. The futility of attempting to find allusions to historical contexts — besides the Babylonian crisis that is the historical context for the book as a whole — is underscored by the mixed and divergent results: various scholars have read the same sayings in reference to the Assyrians, Egyptians, Arabs, Greeks, Seleucids, and Scythians, not to mention various parties within Judah (Jöcken, Habakuk, 1-289 passim). Only one piece of hard evidence has any bearing on this question, namely, the fact that one of the "woes" (2:12-14) appears to be a pastiche of excerpts from other prophetic texts (cf. Mic 3:10; Jer 51:58; Isa 11:9). But this evidence also points precisely toward the composition of these "woe" speeches in the same kind of setting that produced the text in its final form: a scribal group occupied with the study of prophetic records.

Intention

This section presents the prophet as both an authentic intermediary between Yahweh and his people and an example for them to emulate in each of the four following respects. First, the prophet turns to Yahweh in the expectation that he will be shown how to reconcile the apparent conflict between a commitment to justice and faith in Yahweh as Lord of history. Second, he expects that he will have to authenticate Yahweh's response through critical discussion and searching reflection, and he accordingly learns from Yahweh that the applicability of the revelation may be discerned only through transcribing and studying it. Third, it is revealed to him that the Babylonians have already forfeited all claims to legitimacy because of their greed, and that one can avoid being caught up in their self-destruction by remaining convinced that Yahweh is justly in the process of bringing about their downfall. Fourth, the prophet submits this conviction to the test of reason and world opinion, finding that the nations also recognize the inevitability of Babylon's fall for reasons that call their own idolatrous religion — of the same sort that is practiced by the Babylonians — into question.

THE PROPHET ANNOUNCES AN ORACULAR INQUIRY AND RECEIVES A REPLY, 2:1-5

Text

The witness of the versions is not of much help in clarifying the notorious problems of 2:4-5a (P. J. M. Southwall, "A Note on Habakkuk ii.4," *VT* 19 [1969] 614-17), not least because the LXX text has considerable uncertainties of its own (e.g., J. Ziegler, "Konjektur oder überlieferte Lesart? Zu Hab 2,5 *katoinomēnos*] *katoiomenos*," *Bib* 33 [1952] 366-70). The MT has been made to seem more problematic than it actually is by the supposition that the antithesis expressed in 2:4 requires v. 4a to be formally analogous to v. 4b. Such antitheses do not necessarily entail strict parallelism, however, as countless examples in Proverbs attest. One can make tolerable sense of the MT by recognizing that in v. 4a *nepeš* has roughly the same meaning that it has in v. 5a, i.e., "appetite" or "greed," rather than "soul," etc. (so *RSV*). Greed is thus the thematic as well as the grammatical subject of v. 4a, and the antithesis in v. 4 is therefore based on a contrast between the effect of someone's being greedy and the effect of a just person's faithfulness. The theme of greed is then developed further in v. 5 (cf. S. Schreiner, "Erwägungen zum Text von Hab 2:4-5," *ZAW* 86 [1974] 538-42). If one further assumes that the pronominal suffixes in *napšô bô* have an indefinite antecedent (see the examples of this phenomenon cited by J. A. Emerton, "The Textual and Linguistic Problems of Habakkuk II.4-5," *JTS* 28 [1977] 15), v. 4a can be translated as follows: "It has become swollen, it does not go straight, i.e., one's appetite within himself," or more idiomatically, "Someone's appetite, once grown greedy, leads him astray." This rendering takes the prepositional phrase *bô* to modify not the noun *nepeš* but the verb *yšr,* further qualifying its figurative description of the dynamic "locomotive" effect of the *nepeš* on the total personality. (This point is effectively shown by Janzen, 62-68, but his further conclusions seem dubious.) With 2:4 understood in this way, v. 5a appears to provide a specific example of how a particular kind of greed, adduced by a particularly addictive substance, can lead one astray: "Moreover, because wine is treacherous, a man becomes greedy and will not succeed."

Structure

122

A. Introduction with speech report formula   2:2aα
B. Speech of Yahweh   2:2aβ-5
    1. Directions concerning reception of the revelation   2:2aβ-3
       a. Making a record   2:2aβ-3a
         1) Order to transcribe the revelation   2:2aβb
           a) Commands   2:2aβ
             (1) Write it down!   2:2aβ^1
             (2) Inscribe it on tablets!   2:2aβ^2
           b) Statement of purpose: that the one
               who reads it may run   2:2b
         2) Motivation   2:3a
           a) The revelation applies to a future time   2:3aα
           b) Its fulfillment is coming soon   2:3aβ^1
           c) It will turn out to be true   2:3aβ^2
       b. Directions to await the fulfillment of the
         revelation   2:3b
         1) Conditional command   2:3bα
           a) Condition: if it seems slow . . .   2:3bα^1
           b) Command proper: wait!   2:3bα^2
         2) Motivation   2:3bβ
           a) Positively stated: it will surely come   2:3bβ^1
           b) Negatively stated: it will not delay   2:3bβ^2
    2. Revelation contrasting the fate of the greedy
      with the fate of the just   2:4-5
       a. Basic statement   2:4
         1) The fate of one who becomes greedy:
           to be led astray   2:4a
         2) The fate of a just person who remains
           faithful: to live   2:4b
       b. Elaboration on the fate of the greedy   2:5
         1) The fate of an arrogant man   2:5a
           a) Cause: wine is treacherous   2:5aα
           b) Effect: a man becomes arrogant   2:5aβ^1
           c) Outcome: he does not succeed   2:5aβ^2
         2) Identification of the arrogant with the greedy   2:5b
           a) Characterization of the arrogant man:
               having greed as wide as Sheol   2:5bα^1
           b) Manifestation of his greed   2:5bα^{2}β
             (1) Generally described: an appetite
                 insatiable as Death   2:5bα^2
             (2) Specifically described in terms
                 of international relations: limitless
                 accumulation of conquered
                 nations and peoples   2:5bβ

As this unit opens the prophet is still speaking, but not to Yahweh. He instead announces that he will seek a revelation from Yahweh (2:1). The process of making such an inquiry is described through metaphorical comparison of the prophet with a sentinel. He will be on the lookout and wait in patience to see what will happen (cf. Hos 9:8; Isa 21:6-12; Jer 6:17; Ezek 3:17; 33:1-9). The prophet's divinatory procedures are described proleptically in the form of direct speech regarding what he is about to do, rather than retrospectively in the form of narration reporting what he has done. This device imparts a dramatic quality to the beginning of this unit (Eaton, *Obadiah*, 95-96).

Narration in the proper sense begins with the reporting of Yahweh's reply in v. 2aα. Yahweh's speech contains a prophecy (2:4-5) that is prefaced with some directions about having it recorded (2:2aβ-3). It is to be written down on tablets so that its authentication will be a matter of record when it is eventually fulfilled at some indefinite future time (2:2aβ²). The command to "write!" has as its object *ḥāzôn,* which means literally "vision" (so *RSV*). Such terminology is perhaps confusing because the following dictum of Yahweh (2:4-5) hardly seems "visionary," especially in comparison with other more graphically descriptive parts of the book (e.g., 1:5-11; 3:8-15). Some have therefore supposed that the *ḥāzôn* in question lies outside this section and have identified it with one of these other pericopes. Although 1:5-11 does mention "seeing" *(r'h)* Yahweh at work among the nations, this unit can hardly be the object of the command in 2:2aβ. The prophecy to be written down has yet to be fulfilled, but the fulfillment of 1:5-11 is the occasion for the prophetic complaint in (→) 1:2-17. And although 3:8-15 is obviously visionary in the sense that it springs from a vivid imagination, nothing indicates that it originated from experience that was visionary in any strict sense (→ 3:1-19). In sum, there is no report of a vision as such in Habakkuk, and here *ḥāzôn* must thus have its well-attested and more general meaning, i.e., "revelation," in which case it refers to the oracle of Yahweh in 2:4-5.

Just as the figure of the sentinel is used in connection with the reception of revelation (2:1a), the figure of the runner is used in connection with the transcription of revelation (2:2b). The runner was both a messenger (2 Sam 18:24; cf. 2 Chr 30:6, 10) and a herald of the king's approach (2 Sam 15:1; 1 Kgs 1:5). The concept of running thus lent itself to describing metaphorically the medium through which Yahweh's works and words were announced, whether this were a natural process (Ps 147:15) or a prophetic revelation (Jer 23:21; 51:31). Here this image is applied to the studious reader of the prophecy, who is intended to "run" with it, both in the sense of disseminating the message to others and in the sense of interpreting it in relation to ongoing events, acting as a harbinger of Yahweh's increasingly evident approach. The metaphor itself does not imply that the text of the revelation need be brief (contra, e.g., Ward, 13; Brownlee, "Placarded Revelation," 320; Eaton, *Obadiah,* 96). It rather connotes the way in which Yahweh's reply is to be treated during the time between its initial revelation and its eventual actualization in the course of events: In the form of a written record it is to be read, studied, and interpreted, looking for signs of its fulfillment in contemporary developments. Such activity would be a manifestation of the hopeful patience that Yahweh further urges on the prophet (2:3b), in view of the distinct possibility that the revelation may not seem immediately and self-evidently applicable to either the present situation or the prophet's imminent prospects.

At the heart of Yahweh's revelation stands a single, somewhat aphoristic saying (2:4), to which is added a brief elaboration (2:5), after which Yahweh continues speaking in a rather different vein (2:6-20; → 2:1-20, Structure). The saying draws an antithetical contrast between the fate of a person who lets greed get the upper hand and the fate of a person who remains faithfully committed to justice. The former will somehow go wrong, but the latter will live (→ Text). The subsequent elaboration in v. 5 gives further specificity to the decidedly negative but still rather vague description of greed's effects in v. 4. There is additional description of the dynamics of greed's influence, the end to which it leads, and the identity of the greedy one in the present context. The basic statement of greed's negative effects (v. 4a) is juxtaposed with a statement about alcohol's negative effects (v. 5a), as if to suggest a similarity between greed and drunkenness. In both cases overconsumption leads to intoxicating delusions of grandeur, which in turn lead to failure. The end to which greed finally comes is portrayed through the mythic imagery of the death monster (v. 5bα) that seizes victims in its maw and swallows them into its netherworld belly, Sheol. By virtue of their insatiability, greed and death are thus much alike and affect people in much the same way. Finally the greedy one, drunk with self-deluding arrogance and consuming himself to death, is explicitly identified with an imperial power engaged in a program of limitless conquest (v. 5bβ).

Genre

This unit reflects the customary practice of a prophet's seeking a revelation from Yahweh. This kind of divination was often occasioned by some issue of public importance and often done at the request of community leaders (e.g., 1 Kgs 14:1-18; 2 Kgs 8:7-15; Jer 21; 42–43). The text touches on the two main aspects of this matter as it first describes how the revelation was sought (2:1) and then what the divine response was (2:2-20). Each aspect of the matter is represented differently, however. The initial announcement of the prophet's intention to inquire of Yahweh is cast in a dramatic form (as Horst [178] has recognized in calling 2:1 a prophetic soliloquy [Selbstgespräch]), whereas the following report of Yahweh's reply is cast in narrative form. Although the unit as a whole is not pure narration, this combination creates in effect a narrative sequence. From the preliminary preparations to the resulting oracle, the action unfolds in accord with the sequence in which this kind of divination was actually carried out. In the final analysis this unit is thus a REPORT OF AN ORACULAR INQUIRY.

Two of its distinctive features deserve further comment: the already mentioned combination of dramatic speech with narrated speech, and the autobiographical style. Both the initial announcement in 2:1 and the speech report in 2:2-20 are expressed from an autobiographical or first person point of view. The first person viewpoint serves in some examples of this genre to emphasize the closeness of the relationship between the prophet and Yahweh (e.g., Ezek 14:1-11; 20:1-44). The difference between the prophet's relationship with Yahweh and his audience's relationship with Yahweh is thus underscored in terms of the people's dependence on the prophet for knowledge of Yahweh. Here the combination of drama with narration serves to mitigate this tendency. This combination orients the protagonist toward the action in a particular way. The seeking of the revelation is described prospectively, while the reception of the revelation is described retrospectively. There is thus no account of how the prophet actually received the divine response but rather a structural ellipsis at precisely that point in the narrative sequence, which leaves the prophet's private experience shrouded in mystery. This hiatus in the narration also introduces an element of suspense by dramatizing the waiting. Will Yahweh reply? What will he say? What would an apt response to him entail? By showing such expectancy the prophet models the attitude that is being commended to the audience by the report. In this case the autobiographical style serves to underline that the prophet and his people are basically in the same situation when it comes to accepting this seemingly implausible oracle as a revelation truly from Yahweh, even though the prophet is in some mysterious fashion also the intermediary between them and Yahweh. The prophet's attempt to resolve his crisis of faith thus becomes an example, with which the audience of this report is meant to identify.

Setting

Such reports as this grew out of the custom of making oracular inquiry, but there is no evidence that they were ever used in the course of the inquiry itself. Reports of oracular inquiry were composed and circulated in a setting once removed from the actual practice of this kind of divination.

Some scholars have relegated this unit to a cultic setting (e.g., Humbert, 17-18, 280-83; Eaton, *Vision,* 54-61) but without clearly defining the relationship between the practice of oracular inquiry and the conduct of liturgy. Although it seems that the process of seeking and receiving an oracle from Yahweh was sometimes ritually dramatized in the context of a complaint liturgy (e.g., Pss 12, 108), this prophetic practice was not necessarily performed in connection with any liturgy at all. One might simply seek a prophet out and ask her or him to inquire of Yahweh, and the prophet would then go and communicate with Yahweh (whatever that might entail) and bring back Yahweh's reply (e.g., Jer 42–43; 2 Kgs 3:4-20). The intention of making an oracular inquiry could be announced in a cultic setting, particularly in the context of a complaint ritual, without the inquiry itself being part of the rite (e.g., Pss 5, 85).

In the case of Hab 2:1-5, the announcement itself is more like those made in a cultic context (e.g., Pss 5:4 [*RSV* 3]; 85:9a [*RSV* 8a]) than those made in a noncultic context (e.g., Jer 42:4). The terms in which the prophet's preparations are described, however, suggest a kind of divinatory procedure that would be incompatible with cultic practices (cf. 2 Kgs 3:15). The sentinel

metaphor is vague, but it clearly emphasizes the waiting — which could sometimes take days (Jer 42:7)! It is difficult to imagine that a service could be held
up indefinitely, perhaps for days on end, until whenever the prophet might receive the revelation sought for. Moreover, the part of Yahweh's speech that is
quoted in 2:2-5 bears little resemblance to oracles that appear to have been ritually recited (cf. Pss 12:6 [RSV 5]; 108:8-10 [RSV 7-9]). The announcement in
Hab 2:1 is thus of the sort that might have been made in a cultic context; but
the oracular reply itself, which is reported in 2:2-20, is not of the sort that
would have been recited as part of a rite in a cultic context.

One can thus characterize this report as a much abbreviated, highly se-
lective, and intentionally interpretive account of a divinatory process that was
probably initiated by the prophet's announcement on a liturgical occasion but
subsequently carried out under other circumstances over some extended period
of time. The autobiographical style may of course be a fictive device, but it is
precisely the characteristics of selectivity and tendentiousness that give this
account the ring of an authentic prophetic memoir (H. W. Wolff, *Hosea* [tr.
G. Stansell; Hermeneia; Philadelphia: Fortress, 1974] 57-58). In any case this
text is the product of concentrated reflection on the prophet's involvement
with a particular oracular inquiry, on the part of either the prophet himself or
someone who wished to represent him. It was not designed to tell the whole
story, but only to mention some facets of the process and to dwell at length on
others — above all on Yahweh's reply. Thus it would convey a particular interpretation of the inquiry to people who were concerned with its import but who
were not privy to the divinatory process itself.

For what class of persons would such a report have been composed, and
what was the nature of their concerns? Some further inferences may be drawn
from the directions given in Yahweh's speech concerning the transcription of
his reply to the prophet (2:2aβb). The resulting document should not be confused with the present text, which describes the initial impetus for making a
transcription. Nor should the context in which the transcription would have
been used be automatically identified with the context in which the present report of its origins would have been used. If these two contexts were not one
and the same, however, they would have at least been closely related. Since
this text consists largely of an extended "verbatim" account of Yahweh's reply,
its composition may well have depended on the prior transcription of the revelation itself in compliance with Yahweh's command. Any conclusions drawn
regarding the setting of the transcription will thus afford some clues regarding
the setting of the report that we now have, shedding some light on how it came
to be composed.

Brownlee has proposed that the transcription of the revelation to
Habakkuk can be understood as something analogous to Isaiah's writing a
motto on a sign — the motto with which his newborn son was named, portending the fall of Syria and Israel to Assyria (Isa 8:1-4). This copy of the prophecy
would thus be an object of public display, somewhat like a poster carried in a
picket line or a banner in a procession, and its setting would be definable
within the realm of prophetic symbolic action. There are obviously some similarities between these two cases, but the parallel is not exact. The argument for

their fundamental comparability depends on three dubious assumptions. First, it is assumed that the revelation to be copied by Habakkuk is roughly as brief as the motto given to Isaiah, and thus that it includes only 2:4, or at most 2:4-5. Yahweh's command to Habakkuk, however, states explicitly that *tablets* (plural!) will be required to record the revelation, and it is possible that Yahweh's speech also includes 2:6-20 (→ 2:1-20, Structure). Second, the assumption that the term *b'r* (*RSV* "make plain") refers to making big, clear letters, of the sort that one would write on a sign, is questionable (D. T. Tsumura, "Hab. 2:2 in the Light of Akkadian Legal Practice," *ZAW* 94 [1982] 294-95). Finally, it is assumed that the metaphorical allusion to "running" in v. 2b implies a text that can be read "on the run," i.e., at a glance; but this imagery more likely implies the ongoing prophetic scrutiny of the transcription in view of the signs of the times (→ Structure; cf. J. M. Holt's somewhat different critique in "'So He May Run Who Reads It,'" *JBL* 83 [1964] 298-302). All things considered, the making and use of a document from the revelation given to Habakkuk is not particularly comparable to Isaiah's public demonstration with a sign. It is something more like Jeremiah's making a scroll at Yahweh's command (Jer 36:1-4; cf. Isa 30:8, which shows that "tablet" and "scroll" should not be considered incompatible in this regard).

One can imagine such transcription as the penultimate step in the long and complex process that stands behind the composition of the report beginning in 2:1-5. It probably began in a cultic context with the prophet's announcement of his intention to seek a revelation from Yahweh (2:1). He would then have undertaken the kind of preparation described metaphorically in the announcement, waiting for Yahweh's reply. After receiving the revelation, he would have made a transcription of it in accord with the divine command, consisting of at least 2:2aβ-5, a document that was to be read and studied in anticipation of the oracle's eventual fulfillment. After concentrated reflection on the entire process a brief preface was devised, consisting of the initial announcement plus a concisely formulated bit of reporting narration (2:2aα), explicitly describing the origin of the oracle as Yahweh's response to a prophetic inquiry. It is difficult to say whether 2:6-20 was included in the original transcript of Yahweh's reply, or whether it was added in the process of composing the report to draw out the theological implications of the reply. In any case this text was produced by a scribal group that recorded and studied prophetic lore, a group with which the prophet himself had some association, or to which he perhaps even belonged.

Intention

This unit reports a prophecy that speaks to the unjust amassing of wealth and power by a greedy imperial conqueror. It asserts that such imperialism is contrary to the order of things and thus ultimately self-defeating. This situation is not in accord with the divine will and thus cannot continue indefinitely. Although an oracle to this effect is divinely revealed to the prophet, it is not self-evidently true. It can only be authenticated by remaining faithfully committed to the cause of justice and by also remaining faithfully committed to Yahweh as the author of justice while waiting to see whether the perpetrators of injustice will indeed be overthrown. By his willingness to wait on the Lord, the prophet exemplifies the attitude of faithfulness that the revelation itself commends.

Bibliography

W. S. Brownlee, "The Placarded Revelation of Habakkuk," *JBL* 82 (1963) 319-25; M. H. Floyd, "Prophecy and Writing in Habakkuk 2,1-5," *ZAW* 105 (1993) 462-81; J. G. Janzen, "Habakkuk 2:2-4 in the Light of Recent Philological Advances," *HTR* 73 (1980) 53-78; A. S. van der Woude, "Der Gerechte wird durch seine Treue leben: Erwägungen zu Habakuk 2:4-5," in *Studia Biblica et Semitica* (*Fest.* T. C. Vriezen; ed. W. C. van Unnik and A. S. van der Woude; Wageningen: H. Veenman & Zonen, 1966) 367-75.

YAHWEH'S DESCRIPTION OF THE INTERNATIONAL OUTCRY AGAINST THE OPPRESSOR: THE FIRST "WOE" SPEECH, 2:6-8

Structure

I. Introduction to a series of five "woe" speeches:
description of an international consensus — 2:6
  A. Rhetorical question asserting that there is an
international consensus of negative opinion
regarding the imperialist aggressor — $2{:}6a\alpha\beta^1$
    1. Initial characterization of its expression in terms
of a well-formulated speech against the oppressor — $2{:}6a\alpha$
    2. Additional characterization of its expression in
terms of allusive mockery — $2{:}6a\beta^1$
  B. Formula of direct quotation — $2{:}6a\beta^2$
II. First in a series of five "woe" speeches — 2:6b-8
  A. Designation of negative behavior — 2:6b
    1. "Woe" cry — $2{:}6b\alpha^1$
    2. Characterization of one who behaves negatively:
two participial clauses — $2{:}6b\alpha^2\beta$
      a. Whoever accumulates stolen goods — $2{:}6b\alpha^2$
      b. Whoever becomes overobligated — $2{:}6b\beta$
  B. Consequences of such behavior: described by a
rhetorical question with direct address — 2:7
    1. Reaction of the victims — 2:7a
      a. Of those with onerous obligations:
they will arise — $2{:}7a\alpha$

    b. Of those who are potentially threatening:

        they will awake   2:7aβ

  2. Fate of the offenders: you will be plundered   2:7b

C. Rationale: a *kî* clause continuing direct address   2:8

  1. Basic statement: in terms of a role reversal   2:8a

    a. The oppressors have plundered their victims   2:8aα

    b. The victims will then plunder their oppressors   2:8aβ

  2. Elaboration on the cause of this reversal   2:8b

    a. Because of human bloodshed   2:8bα^1

    b. Because of the violence done   2:8b$\alpha^2\beta$

      1) In general: to the earth   2:8bα^2

      2) In particular: to cities and their inhabitants   2:8bβ

As a continuation of the speech of Yahweh begun in 2:2aβ-5, this unit is linked to its predecessor by the pronominal elements in 2:6a referring back to antecedents in 2:5. The plural subject *'ēlleh kullām* (*RSV* "all these") refers back to the conquered nations and peoples mentioned in v. 5bβ, and the singular object suffix on the prepositions *'al* (*RSV* "against") and *lĕ* (*RSV* "of") refers back to the imperialistic aggressor described in v. 5abα. The introduction itself consists of a rhetorical question asserting that the conquered nations hold a common view of their oppressor. The expression of this view is figuratively described as a great chorus of nations and peoples, whose participants are all speaking out against their abuse by their imperial overlord. The nations and peoples thus personified are not just crying out in anguish, however. They are voicing the kind of speeches that an accomplished user of language would compose (i.e., a *māšāl* [*RSV* "taunt"]). These speeches are further characterized as "mockery" (*mĕlîṣâ; RSV* "derision") and "allusiveness" (*ḥîdôt; RSV* "scoffing"). They are thus apt for use in the diplomatically delicate context of protesting against an oppressor who — even if the oppressor's doom seems already inevitable — still holds some power.

Then follows the first (2:6b-8) in a series of five directly quoted speeches, each of which is similarly structured. The first part of this speech (2:6b) begins with the cry *hôy* (*RSV* "woe!"), exclaimed in reaction to certain kinds of negative behavior, i.e., accumulating stolen goods and incurring more obligations than can possibly be met. The cry *hôy* is basically an exclamation that voices a range of reactions to the inscrutable misfortunes inherent in the human condition. When exclaimed by those suffering such misfortune, it expresses the speakers' dismay at their own fate ("Too bad for us!"). When exclaimed by others, it expresses the speakers' dismay at the fate of those suffering, thus connoting the speakers' sympathy and solidarity with the sufferers ("Too bad for Jack, our departed brother, and for his family!"). If the suffering in question is well deserved, the "woe" cry takes on an ironic connotation that is tantamount to condemnation ("Too bad for Jack the Ripper!"). Because the "woe" cry is in this case exclaimed in reaction to those who behave in certain negative ways, thus bringing the inevitable consequences on themselves, it takes on such an ironic sense here (see J. G. Williams, "Irony and Lament: Clues to Prophetic Consciousness," *Semeia* 8 [1977] 51-74). The exclamation *hôy* conjures up the prospect of a fate that would be lamentable if it were not well deserved — but it is. This element of the unit (v. 6b) is thus a mock expression of dismay (cf. Gowan, *Triumph,* 59-62).

The first part of each "woe" speech includes a participial clause in addition to *hôy,* or in this case a pair of participial clauses (2:6b). Because participial formulations are altogether ambiguous with respect to grammatical person, there is no explicit element of direct address inherent in the combination of *hôy* plus participle (→ Genre). In this case, however, the interjection of the rhetorical question *'ad-mātay* ("for how long?") foreshadows the way in which the agent is directly addressed in the second part of the speech (2:7) as the consequences of his behavior are spelled out: "Don't you realize that your victims will eventually arise and threaten you?" In the third part of the speech (2:8) the inevitability of such a development is explained in terms of the principle of just reversal (2:8a) and in terms of additional factors that make this principle all the more applicable (2:8b): "You have plundered them, so they will plunder you." This is bound to be the case, particularly because of the bloodshed and violence that have accompanied the plundering.

Genre

Like each of the similar units that follow in the series (vv. 9-11, 12-14, 15-17, 18-20), this unit has generally been regarded as a form of prophetic speech and categorized as a (→) woe oracle. This genre has been defined in terms of a combination of the "woe" cry and a substantive denoting an evildoer or a class of evildoers, which often takes the form of a plural active participle. Westermann (pp. 189-94) proposed that the woe oracle was basically a curse, but this theory has not found much acceptance. There has instead been considerable debate over whether this genre is to be understood as a prophetic adaptation of mourning customs (Clifford, Williams, and Janzen), or as a prophetic adaptation of a traditional kind of proverbial saying concerning the unfortunate fate of evildoers (Gerstenberger and Whedbee).

According to the former theory, the function of *hôy* in a woe oracle derives from its primary function in a dirge, as an expression of grief and sympathy. For those who hold this view the woe oracle addresses directly those who do certain bad things as it also condemns them by conjuring up in advance the lamentable end to which God will eventually bring them. According to the latter theory, the function of *hôy* derives instead from its role as an antonymic counterpart to *'ašrê* (whose root means "fortunate") in a type of proverbial saying about the just deserts of behaving in various ways. The formulation *'ašrê* plus substantive describes the fortunate lot of those who do certain good things (e.g., Prov 8:32, 34; Pss 1:1; 128:1); and the formulation *hôy* plus substantive is conversely supposed to describe the unfortunate lot of those who do certain bad things. For those who hold this view the woe oracle is not directly addressed to the kinds of evildoers that it describes, and its basic message is not one of divine retribution for them. It is rather a kind of categorical proposition, which affirms that certain kinds of evildoers naturally come to a bad end just because of the way things are.

131

Undercutting these two alternatives, Roberts has more recently argued that *hôy* does not in itself communicate either an attitude of mournfulness or a sense of misfortune's natural inevitability. It is rather just a neutral interjection, much like "hey!" or "ah!" in English, with which speakers get the attention of their audiences. The formulation *hôy* plus substantive is thus a kind of emphatic direct address ("hey, you!") in which the addressees are designated and often further characterized by the substantive. He thus proposes renaming this genre more neutrally as the "*hôy* oracle" (Roberts, "Form," 294-300).

Several issues have emerged from this scholarly debate that directly affect the generic classification of the "woe" speeches in Habakkuk. First, there is the semantic question of whether *hôy* is a neutral exclamation, or whether it has a fuller meaning. If *hôy* has a fuller meaning, there is the closely related question of whether it refers primarily to funerary mourning or to the inevitably unfortunate consequences resulting from certain kinds of bad behavior, etc. Second, there is the grammatical question of whether *hôy* indicates direct address, and of whether its linkage with a substantive necessarily indicates direct address of any person or group that may be designated by the substantive. Third, there is the larger question of whether the occurrence of *hôy* or the occurrence of the formulation *hôy* plus substantive provides in itself a sufficient basis on which to define any particular generic form.

In support of his argument that *hôy* is simply a neutral exclamation, Roberts calls attention to one case in which any presentiment of either doom or misfortune seems unlikely: Isa 55:1 ("Form," 297-98). In this instance *hôy* introduces the invitation to a free banquet: "*Hôy!* Every one who thirsts, come to the waters; and whoever has no money, come, buy and eat!" This example does indeed show that the semantic range of *hôy* must be in some respects broader than that of the English word "woe," since there is nothing particularly "woeful" about the prospect that is opened up for Yahweh's people by the prophecy in Isa 55:1-13. Among some forty-seven occurrences of the word *hôy,* however, Isa 55:1 represents only a very few cases in which "woe" or something similar seems an altogether inappropriate translation. This fact hardly suggests that *hôy* is just a neutral attention-getter.

As a basic English equivalent, "alas" might be somewhat better than "woe," since it semantically encompasses more of a sense of sorrow and pity than "woe" does, without generally including the overtones of condemnation that "woe" can sometimes convey (cf. Williams's preference for the term "alas oracle" over the term "woe oracle"). At any rate, although *hôy* may well need to be translated in a variety of contextually appropriate ways, it invariably expresses a reaction to a situation that is somehow sorrowful, or at least potentially so. This is even the case in Isa 55:1, where *hôy* signals not that the invitation to a free banquet is sorrowful, but that a failure to accept the invitation would be. In Isa 55:1 *hôy* expresses the reaction of the prophetic speaker to the possibility that he goes on to describe in 55:2a, that the people will keep doing just the opposite of what they are now being invited to do: "Alas! . . . Why do you keep spending your money for that which is not bread, and your labor for that which does not satisfy?" Here, in relation to the commands in 55:1, *hôy* thus has the force of an emphatic "please!"

With regard to whether *hôy* has a more specific primary sense, the theory that *hôy* can be defined as the antonym of *'ašrê* must be discounted simply because there is no direct evidence that *hôy* was ever actually used in this way. The only two examples adduced were created by emending Isa 3:10-11 and Eccl 10:16-17 in ways that have little or no text-critical warrant (Gerstenberger, 261). Such readings of these two texts would never have been conceivable were it not for the hypothetical necessity of finding examples to justify this preconceived theory. It is unlikely that *hôy* and *'ašrê* could serve analogous semantic functions since these two terms are not grammatically analogous to begin with (*'ašrê* stands in a construct relationship with any subsequent substantive while *hôy* is paratactically juxtaposed with whatever follows it). Without any more substantial examples of *hôy* functioning as the antonym of *'ašrê*, there is no real basis for supposing that such a relationship defines the primary sense of *hôy*. The exclamation *hôy* thus does not connote anything in particular with regard to the natural inevitability of wrongdoing's unfortunate consequences.

The other theory, that *hôy* is the most elemental form of a *qînâ* or "dirge," has somewhat stronger support. Narrative descriptions of *hôy* being used in this way (e.g., 1 Kgs 13:30; Jer 22:18; 34:5) show that it could serve as a means of expressing a mourner's grief. In some prophetic contexts, where there is also some other indication that the conventions of mourning are being adapted to describe the effects of divine punishment, it is reasonable to suppose that *hôy* carries with it some connotations of a mourner's cry (e.g., Jer 22:13 [*hôy*], 18 [*spd*]; Amos 5:1-3 [*qînâ*], 18 [*hôy*]; 6:1 [*hôy*]; Mic 2:1 [*hôy*], 4 [*nhh*]). In other contexts, however, it seems rather far-fetched to suppose that *hôy* connotes anything specifically funerary. In Jer 47:6, for example, *hôy* becomes part of an extended image, in which the personified "sword of Yahweh" is figuratively addressed. It is doubtful that this use of *hôy* entails any implication of mourning for the sword's metaphorical "death." It rather expresses distress in reaction to the grievous harm that the sword can wreak and thus reinforces the immediately ensuing call for it to return to its scabbard.

Although *hôy* could indeed serve as a mourner's cry, this usage cannot be regarded as either the primary usage from which all others derive, or the usage in terms of which all others are to be defined. In view of the widely varying contexts in which *hôy* occurs, it rather appears that *hôy* was a more general expression of grief, sorrow, concern, pity, etc., which also attained the specialized function of a mourner's cry when uttered specifically in reaction to death. It could thus express not only the sentiment of a dirge *(qînâ)* in the context of funerary mourning *('bl)* but also the kind of "groaning" *('nh)* with which fishers and farmers might react to a severe drought (Isa 29:1-2 [*hôy* and *ta'ănîyâ wa'ănîyâ*]; cf. 19:5-10 [*'nh*]); or the trepidation one might feel in the face of an overwhelming force like a flood (Isa 17:12); or the "fear" *(ḥărādâ)* and "awe" *(paḥad)* with which one might anticipate the onset of a potentially constructive but difficult time, as a woman anticipates the eventually fruitful but nevertheless difficult pains of labor (Jer 30:5-8), etc. Thus *hôy* is an exclamation that generally expresses a range of reactions appropriate to a calamity, or to the threat of a calamity. It expresses a range of sentiments including but not limited to funerary mourning.

133

With respect to the question of whether *hôy* entails direct address, it is clear that *hôy* often occurs in this rhetorical context, but scholars have debated whether this is necessarily the case (Hillers, 185). Roberts has argued that *hôy* creates a vocative relationship with any substantive that follows it ("Form," 298-300). His argument is based largely on the assumption that *hôy* in the context of a dirge is always addressed to the dead person being mourned. In support of this assumption he adduces David's apostrophe of Jonathan in his dirge on the death of both Jonathan and his father, Saul (2 Sam 1:26), as well as David's outcry on the death of his son Absalom (2 Sam 19:1 [*RSV* 18:33]). The first of these examples does indeed show that the dead could be addressed in a dirge, and the example of David's dirge on the death of Abner (2 Sam 3:33-34) might also be cited in this regard. It is questionable whether David's outcry for Absalom counts as a dirge in any proper sense, or whether it is rather just an exclamation of grief. In any case, it is difficult to see what these cases show regarding *hôy* since *hôy* does not occur in any of them. Roberts nevertheless concludes that such funerary exclamations as *hôy 'āḥî* (1 Kgs 13:30; Jer 22:18; 34:5) self-evidently entail direct address ("Alas, my brother!") because one can automatically assume that they follow the same convention as the examples of dirges without *hôy*.

It does not necessarily follow from the particular examples cited by Roberts that a dirge is by definition addressed to the person whose death it mourns, nor does it necessarily follow that any occurrence of *hôy* in a funerary context necessarily conforms to such a convention. In prophetic adaptations of the dirge convention the dirge itself is not always addressed to those whose doom it proleptically mourns (e.g., Jer 9:16-21 [*RSV* 17-22]; Amos 5:1-2). Moreover, it is not clear that the funerary exclamation *hôy 'āḥî* is directly addressed to the departed brother ("Alas, my brother!"). In Jer 22:18 this phrase parallels the similar expression *hôy hōdô*, which cannot entail direct address because of the third person masculine singular suffix attached to the noun, and thus must be translated, "Alas! His majesty!" This example raises the question of whether *hôy 'āḥî* should not be similarly translated, "Alas! My brother!" rather than, "Alas, my brother!" as simply an expression of grief in reaction to the brother's death rather than an expression of grief directly addressed to the dead brother.

In further support of his argument that *hôy* entails direct address, Roberts has attempted to clarify the rhetorical situation in a group of texts that would seem most likely to contravene this claim, namely, texts in which the substantive following *hôy* is modified by relative clauses in third person form. Roberts shows successfully, as does Hillers, that this phenomenon is not syntactically incompatible with the same substantive's being directly addressed in the second person. This point may be granted, but it does not necessarily follow that the substantive's status as a vocative is defined solely or even primarily by the occurrence of *hôy* itself. In every one of the examples adduced there is at some point at least one explicit second person marker, either verbal or pronominal; and it is the presence of such markers, rather than *hôy*, that indicates the substantive's vocative status.

Several other occurrences of *hôy*, all identified by Roberts as exceptions to his claim, show that *hôy* does not necessarily create a vocative relationship with any substantive that follows it (e.g., Isa 10:5; 17:12; 28:1). Isa 18:1-2 perhaps provides the strongest evidence against Roberts's argument. In this case the singular noun following *hôy* clearly cannot be a vocative (i.e., "the land of whirring wings") because plural commands explicitly identify a group of others as the ones being directly addressed (i.e., the "messengers" commanded to go there).

In and of itself *hôy* is thus ambiguous with respect to grammatical person. On the one hand a speaker can address it directly to another individual or to a group, in which case it becomes part of a vocative expression. On the other hand a speaker can also exclaim it without addressing it to anyone in particular, in which case it becomes a kind of soliloquy that is overheard. This ambiguity can be resolved only when pronouns and verbs additionally provide enough explicit information about grammatical person to clarify the overall rhetorical situation.

Given these rather different rhetorical possibilities, *hôy* can assume a wide variety of compositional functions in texts with very different structures, and the components of the formulation *hôy* plus substantive can be related to each other in a wide variety of ways. It is thus unlikely that either *hôy* or the formulation *hôy* plus substantive could in itself provide a sufficient basis on which to define any particular generic form. It is therefore necessary to take a case-by-case approach to the texts in which *hôy* figures prominently, looking for the larger structural typicalities in terms of which they might be generically classified.

The "woe" speech in Hab 2:6b-8 has structural elements in common with the four "woe" speeches that follow in 2:9-20. All five "woe" speeches contain the three following elements, and in all but the last of the "woe" speeches these elements occur in the following order: (1) the "woe" cry plus at least one active participle, together with various other elements that fill out the predicate in each participial clause; (2) a description of the negative consequences of the behavior denoted by the participle(s), sometimes in the form of an indicative statement and sometimes in the form of a rhetorical question; and (3) a conclusion describing the final outcome of these negative consequences so as to provide a rationale or explanation for the overall process. What kind of speech is defined by such a structure?

It is first pertinent to note that the text does not present these "woes" as prophetic speech per se. As noted above, the "woes" comprise a quotation within a quotation: The narration quotes Yahweh (2:2), and within this frame of discourse Yahweh then quotes the conquered nations, figuratively placing these words in their mouths (2:6a). The "woes" spoken by the nations are collectively characterized in three ways by the introduction in 2:6a. They are first of all said to constitute a "saying" (*māšāl; RSV* "taunt"). To this rather broad categorization two more qualifications are subsequently added. This "saying" of the nations is further described as distinctive on account of its "mockery" or "satire" (*mĕlîṣâ; RSV* "derision") and its "hidden significance" or "allusiveness" (*ḥîdôt; RSV* "scoffing").

The first and most general of these terms, *māšāl*, refers basically to any skilled use of language. It can thus apply to prophetic speech in particular or to any other highly specialized use of language (hence the *RSV*'s contextually appropriate translation), but even in such particular applications the term still retains its basic and more general sense (A. R. Johnson, *"māšāl,"* in *Wisdom in Israel and in the Ancient Near East* [*Fest.* H. H. Rowley; ed. M. Noth and D. Winton Thomas; VTSup 3; Leiden: Brill, 1955] 162-69). By speaking a *māšāl* the nations are thus characterized as using some specialized kind of speech. In the overall context of Yahweh's reply to the prophet (2:2-20) this *māšāl* serves to show that the nations recognize, through reflection on their own historical experience, insights much the same as those that have been divinely revealed to the prophet (→ 2:1-20, Structure). The "woes" are thus represented as a specialized kind of speech that is capable of expressing theological insights much like prophecy does; but they are not prophecies, strictly speaking.

The outcry of the nations (2:6b-20) amounts to "mockery" or "satire" *(mĕlîṣâ)* because of the way "woe" functions ironically in each of its constituent units (→ Structure). With the initial "woe" cry, each of these speeches begins as if to express the speaker's dismay over some current or prospective misfortune affecting either the speaker or some fellow human being(s), but the ensuing participial clauses describe those who behave so as to deserve unfortunate consequences, thus giving the initial cry an ironic twist.

The outcry of the nations (2:6b-20) also consists of speeches that are loaded with "allusiveness" or "hidden significance" *(ḥîdôt),* in the sense that they are only implicitly directed against their imperialistic conqueror. They are formulated so as not to accuse anyone overtly. These speeches rather posit certain categories of negative behavior and then engage their addressee in such a way that he is led to implicate himself in such wrongdoing. When directed against their Babylonian overlords (2:6a), the five "woe" speeches add up to an indictment that robs Babylonian rule of any claim to legitimacy, but the charge is insinuated rather than asserted.

These particular "woe" speeches have an indirectly accusatory rhetorical strategy that is based on combining *hôy* with direct address in a distinctive way. As noted above, *hôy* itself remains ambiguous with respect to grammatical person, unless or until this ambiguity is resolved with some explicit pronominal or verbal indicator. The combination of *hôy* plus a masculine singular active participle, which is characteristic of these "woe" speeches, is likewise ambiguous with respect to grammatical person because participles — unlike other forms of the verb — are by definition marked only for gender and number. This ambiguity is not resolved until the participial clause unfolds a bit further, and pronominal elements within its predicate provide some explicit information. In every case these pronominal markers are masculine singular in agreement with the gender and number of the preceding participle, and they are also — at least initially — in the third person. The "woe" speeches in Habakkuk are thus distinctively characterized by their initially impersonal formulation.

Then comes a switch to second person direct address. In a couple of cases this change occurs before the end of the participial clause. In the first "woe" speech the switch is accomplished by the interjection of a quick rhetorical question (*'ad-mātay,* "how long?"; v. 6a), and in the fourth "woe" speech by a second person pronominal suffix (*ḥămatkā,* "your wrath" [*RSV* "his wrath"]; v. 15a). In these two cases use of second person direct address continues on into the second part of the speech, where the consequences of the action described by the participle are spelled out. In the first speech the rhetorical question in v. 6a is followed by another rhetorical question in v. 7, formulated with second person pronominal suffixes; and in the fourth speech the second person pronominal suffix in v. 15a is followed in v. 16 with a sentence begun by a second person verb (*śāba'tā; RSV* "you will be sated").

In other cases the switch does not happen until the second part of the speech as the consequences of the action described by the participle are spelled out. In the second "woe" speech the description of consequences begins with a second person verb form (*yā'aṣtā; RSV* "you have devised shame"; v. 10a) and continues with second person pronominal suffixes. In the third and fifth speeches the consequences are described in the form of a rhetorical question (v. 13, v. 18). It is therefore typical and constitutive for the "woe" speeches in Habakkuk to begin on a note of ambiguity with respect to grammatical person, to resolve this ambiguity in favor of an impersonal statement formulated in the third person, and then to switch to second person direct address — the fifth and final "woe" speech being a climactic variation on this pattern that, by virtue of its having been reiterated four times, is by then well established (→ 2:1-20, Structure; 2:18-20).

The rhetorical effect of this compositional structure is particularly appropriate within the overall context of 2:6-20. The *hôy* plus participle formulation first plays mockingly on the conventions of expressing dismay, condemning a kind of reprehensible behavior with an impersonal statement that invites the hearer's assent without directly accusing or threatening anyone. Then, just as he is beginning to identify with the speaker's attitude of moral condemnation, the hearer is directly addressed with further description of this behavior and its consequences, as if to imply that he is caught up in this cause-and-effect process, and thus guilty. The hearer's own sense of morality is thus turned back on him in a self-incriminating way, and this effect is reinforced by the concluding *kî* clause that grounds the cause-and-effect process in a basic principle regarding either the order of things or the nature of Yahweh's involvement in human affairs. This type of indirectly accusatory speech is an apt form with which to characterize the outcry of the nations against their doomed but still powerful conqueror.

The exclamation *hôy* is an important element in the structure of these speeches, and it is crucial for the attainment of their distinctive rhetorical effect. It is not their most distinctive element, however, and thus it does not in itself determine their genre. The "woe" speeches of Habakkuk are primarily defined in terms of the way they combine a participially described bad action with its inevitably negative consequences, and they thus have a basic affinity with similarly structured proverbial sayings (e.g., Prov 21:17; 22:8; cf. Jeremias, 69-70; Hiebert calls these "woe" speeches "proverbial sayings" ["Book of Habakkuk," 647]). Such sayings occur often in the context of a contrast between the fortunate prospects of those who do good and the conversely

137

unfortunate consequences of those who do evil (e.g., Prov 10:17; 11:15, 19, 28; 13:3, 13; 24:24-25; 28:13, 19), but not always (e.g., Prov 26:6, 27; 29:1). Habakkuk's "woe" speeches consistently describe the consequences, using some form of direct address while these proverbial sayings generally do not; but since such proverbial sayings can also utilize rhetorical questions (e.g., Prov 14:22; cf. Hab 2:7a, 13, 18a), one should not see this contrast as absolute. The distinctive use of direct address in the "woe" speeches also bears comparison with the (→) wisdom instruction, which similarly employs elements of direct address (e.g., calls to attention, commands, prohibitions, and rhetorical questions) in order to gain the hearer's consideration of some general rule regarding the fate of evildoers (e.g., Prov 20:9; 23:29-31 [*RSV* 32-35]).

Habakkuk's "woe" speeches do not exactly fit the generic category of either the proverbial saying or the wisdom instruction, but such comparison locates the search for their genre within the ample pale of wisdom (cf. Gowan, "Habakkuk and Wisdom," 161-63). The identification of the international outcry in 2:6-20 as a kind of wisdom speech is further indicated by the fact that the combination of terms with which it is characterized in 2:6a (i.e., *māšāl, mĕlîṣâ,* and *ḥîdôt*) is precisely the same combination of terms that is used in Prov 1:6 to describe what one learns to understand through training in wisdom. The "woe" speeches can thus be generically defined as some kind of wisdom speech, which contrasts with proverbial sayings and wisdom instructions in the following specific ways. While proverbs and instructions generally define a link between various categories of behavior and their adverse effects, the "woe" speeches identify a given situation as a particular case in which this linkage applies concretely. Whereas proverbs and instructions describe both the commission and the consequences of certain evil actions in the abstract and rather impersonally, the "woe" speeches actually call someone to account for acting in this way and admonish that person regarding the results. The proverbial sayings and wisdom instructions thus constitute the theory that these "woe" speeches put into practice (cf. Jeremias, 72-74).

The wisdom tradition calls such praxis "reproof" (*tôkaḥat,* from the root *ykḥ;* cf. the related noun *tôkêḥâ*). This term is humanly applied to a parent's scolding of a child (e.g., Prov 15:5), a teacher's rebuke of a student (e.g., Prov 5:12b-13), and one person's admonition of a fellow (e.g., Ps 141:5). It is also applied to God's chastisement of human beings individually (e.g., Ps 39:12 [*RSV* 11]), as well as of nations, including his own people, whether through prophets (e.g., Isa 37:4; Ezek 3:26) or through the vicissitudes of history (e.g., Jer 2:19; Pss 94:10; 149:7). In Hab 2:6-20 the nations are metaphorically portrayed as speaking in accord with this convention, reproving their Babylonian overlord for his abuse of power but in an oblique way as behooves the underdogs. The genre of their discourse may thus be called a REPROOF SPEECH.

This type of speech might occur within a wide variety of social contexts, ranging from informal family conversation to more formal public deliberations and oratory (→ Setting). The particulars of this form could vary accordingly, with regard to length as well as complexity. The basic elements are (1) statement of a rule or maxim regarding the consequences of some particular type of behavior, and (2) direct address of a person or group as the party presently liable to be suffering the consequences of such behavior. The use of *hôy* in Habakkuk's reproof speeches is thus incidental to the definition of their genre and is rather due to the use of the genre in this particular context. By using a mock expression of dismay to identify certain types of behavior as morally reprehensible, the writer characterizes the attitude with which the conquered nations address their tyrannical ruler as a combination of disdain and circumspection.

The reproof speech is not a prophetic genre. Here it has been adapted for a prophetic purpose, though not in the sense that a prophet is speaking it directly to someone in order to reprove that person in Yahweh's name. Rather, the prophet describes Yahweh's attribution of such speeches to the nations (2:6-20) as part of what Yahweh says to him in response to his waiting for a revelation (2:2-20). In the context of this reply these speeches serve to persuade the prophet to accept the seemingly implausible statement at its core (2:4-5; → 2:1-20, Structure). The prophet thus uses Yahweh's description of the nations' reproving their conqueror to show how Yahweh's reply was in effect a "reproof" *(tôkaḥat)* for him (2:1bβ), disabusing him of his faithlessness.

Setting

This fictional representation of the international outcry reflects the relatively stylized delivery of reproof speeches in public settings, although they might be informally uttered in domestic conversation as well. There are references to "reproof" *(ykḥ)* in Proverbs, suggesting that it could occur in the course of scribal instruction (Prov 1:25, 30; 5:12-13; 10:17; 15:31-32), but these references include no explicit description of what was involved. Some of the dialogue between Job and each of his three companions is described as "reproof" (e.g., Job 19:5; 32:12), and their attempts to persuade Job of his own responsibility for his misfortune thus afford an example of how reproof functioned in a wisdom context.

The first of their speeches to Job, delivered by Eliphaz (4:2–5:27), is specifically said by Job to entail "reproof" (6:25b-26a). Although this speech is longer and more complex than any of the "woe" speeches in Hab 2:6b-20, its composition includes the same basic elements: (1) a participially formulated rule regarding the consequences of certain kinds of wrongdoing (Job 4:8); (2) direct address of Job as one who is suffering the consequences of such behavior (5:10); and (3) summary description of the outcome in the form of a *kî* clause, grounding this cause-and-effect process in a basic principle concerning the natural order of things (5:16-17). The appearance of a reproof speech within the discussion of Job and his three acquaintances suggests that prominent members of the community may have used this genre in their deliberations concerning morality and social status.

The rhetorical convention of reproof could be adapted for the purpose of prophetic confrontations. This convention is evident, for example, in the speech with which Samuel announced to Saul the rejection of his kingship by Yahweh (1 Sam 15:22-23). This speech is very similar to the "woe" speeches from Habakkuk with regard to its basic elements, but in the speech of Samuel these elements are ordered much as they are in the variation on the Habakkuk "woe" speech pattern in 2:18-20. First comes the element of direct address, a rhetorical question implicating Saul (1 Sam 15:22a; cf. Hab 2:7, 18a); then follows a statement of the rule or maxim that Saul has contravened (1 Sam 15:22b; cf. Hab 2:7, 19); then comes a description of the outcome formulated as a *kî* clause, grounding Yahweh's rejection of Saul in the basic principle of fair retribution (1 Sam 15:23; cf. Hab 2:8, 18b). In Samuel's speech the negative consequences of Saul's behavior are described within this concluding rationalization as the climax of the speech rather than within the rule itself.

Although the situation portrayed in Hab 2:6a is not altogether unlike either of these two settings, it more closely resembles yet another setting in which reproof played a major role. A couple of prophetic references describe reproof as something that took place "in the gate" (Amos 5:10; Isa 29:21), thus showing that citizens could call their community or its leaders to account by delivering a speech in this public forum. By the use of reproof speeches the chorus of international dissent is characterized in terms of a forum of world opinion, in which the community of conquered nations confront their imperial overlord much as members of a local community might reprove their rulers "in the gate."

The setting of the reproof speech itself should not be confused with the setting of this fictional representation of a reproof speech. This fictional representation (Hab 2:6-20) has been incorporated into the prophet's report of the reply to his oracular inquiry (2:2-20), and such a composition would have had its setting within some scholarly group concerned with the theological issues raised by prophecy. It reflects the group's concern with figuring out how world opinion regarding divine purposes in history might be related to prophetic perceptions of Yahweh's involvement in human affairs.

Intention

Like each of the "woe" speeches in the entire series, this unit has a twofold intention. In general, it aims first to portray the nations as having reached a certain realization regarding the legitimacy and limitations of Babylonian power. It further aims to present world opinion on this score as a corroboration of Yahweh's message to the prophet. More specifically, this unit insinuates that the Babylonians have ruled by robbery and false pretense, making pledges that they could never keep. Like thieves and false contractors in general, they will eventually get a rise out of those who have been continually robbed and defrauded. Such a reaction has in fact already set in, and because of the violence and bloodshed caused by the Babylonians, the process will inevitably play itself out in accord with the universal principle of just reversal: The plunderers will become the plundered. Universal reason thus bears out what Yahweh told the prophet. Because of greed, Babylonian power has forfeited all its claims to legitimacy and is hence as good as gone.

Bibliography

R. E. Clements, "The Form and Character of Prophetic Woe Oracles," *Semitics* 8 (1982) 17-29; R. J. Clifford, "The Use of *Hôy* in the Prophets," *CBQ* 28 (1966) 458-64; E. Gerstenberger, "The Woe-Oracles of the Prophets," *JBL* 81 (1962) 249-63; D. R. Hillers, "*Hôy* and *Hôy* Oracles: A Neglected Syntactic Aspect," in *The Word of the Lord Shall Go Forth* (*Fest.* D. N. Freedman; ed. C. L. Meyers and M. O'Connor; Winona Lake, Ind.: Eisenbrauns for the American Schools of Oriental Research, 1983) 185-88; W. Janzen, *Mourning Cry and Woe Oracle* (BZAW 125; Berlin: de Gruyter, 1972); E. Otto, "Die Stellung der Wehe-Worte in der Verkündigung des Propheten Habakuk," *ZAW* 89 (1977) 73-107; J. J. M. Roberts, "Form, Syntax, and Redaction in Isaiah 1:2-20," *Princeton Seminary Bulletin* 3 (1982) 293-306; G. Wanke, "'ôy und hôy," *ZAW* 78 (1966) 215-18; C. Westermann, *Basic Forms of Prophetic Speech* (tr. H. C. White; Philadelphia: Westminster, 1967) 190-94; J. W. Whedbee, *Isaiah and Wisdom* (Nashville: Abingdon, 1971) 80-110; J. G. Williams, "The Alas-Oracles of the Eighth Century Prophets," *HUCA* 38 (1967) 75-91.

THE SECOND "WOE" SPEECH, 2:9-11

Structure

I.	Designation of negative behavior	2:9
	A. "Woe" cry	2:9aα[1]
	B. Characterization of one who behaves negatively	2:9aα[2]b
	1. Participial clause: whoever gets evil gain for his house	2:9aα[2]β
	2. Twofold clause of purpose	2:9b
	a. To set his nest on high	2:9bα
	b. To be safe from harm's reach	2:9bβ
II.	Consequences of such behavior: direct address	2:10
	A. Its effect on the perpetrator's "house": the shame of having destroyed many peoples	2:10abα
	B. Its effect on the perpetrator himself: his life is forfeit	2:10bβ
III.	Rationale: twofold *kî* clause	2:11
	A. The stone laments being part of a corrupt house	2:11a
	B. The beam responds in kind	2:11b

This unit is permeated by a metonymical extension of the word "house" *(bayit)*, by which it comes to mean not only "dwelling" but also "household," "family," "lineage," etc. When applied to a king, as it is by implication here, the word also comes to mean "dynasty," and hence to connote the whole imperial power structure on which dynastic control is based.

The pericope begins with a mock expression of dismay (2:9) decrying anyone who would protect his house by evil means. An unidentified addressee — who is known from the larger context to be the greedy oppressor described in 2:4-5 — is subsequently implicated in this misdeed by two allegations: (1) that his house bears the shame of its existence having cost the life of many nations (2:10abα), and (2) that the integrity of his own life is thereby put in question (2:10bβ). Attempts to protect one's house by evil deeds have these self-defeating consequences because the various components of the house itself figuratively realize just how corrupt its makeup is (2:11). In other words, even those who make up the house recognize that attempts to secure it through ill-gotten gains are eventually self-defeating. The prospective downfall of the whole house and its master is thus grounded in the basic principle that the end does not justify the means.

The conquered nations are here voicing their opinion that because the imperial dynasty has attempted to establish its security through the unjustifiable destruction of many peoples, its existence is put in question. This analysis of the situation corroborates what Yahweh has revealed to the prophet concerning the despot's imminent downfall due to his insatiable absorption of nations and peoples (2:4-5).

Genre, Setting, and Intention

→ 2:6b-8.

THE THIRD "WOE" SPEECH, 2:12-14

Structure

I. Designation of negative behavior	2:12
A. "Woe" cry	2:12aα^1
B. Characterization of one who behaves negatively: two participial clauses	2:12aα^{2}b
1. Whoever builds a town with blood	2:12aα^{2}β
2. Whoever founds a city on iniquity	2:12b
II. Consequences of such behavior: a rhetorical question	2:13
A. Verbless clause identifying the effective agent: Yahweh of hosts	2:13a
B. Twofold clause of result	2:13b
1. Peoples labor only for fire	2:13bα
2. Nations weary themselves for naught	2:13bβ
III. Rationale: a *kî* clause	2:14
A. Basic statement: the earth to be filled with the knowledge of Yahweh's glory	2:14a
B. Metaphorical elaboration: as the waters cover the sea	2:14b

This unit begins with a mock expression of dismay (2:12) denouncing anyone who would promote urban settlement by violent means. Such a program is then imputed to an unidentified addressee — who is known from the larger context to be the greedy oppressor described in 2:4-5 — with a rhetorical question affirming that all such efforts are destined for futility (2:13bβ) and destruction (2:13bα) in accord with Yahweh's overall design (2:13a). The actualization of this norm thus constitutes a manifestation of Yahweh's glory. Those who grasp the underlying principle, that even a good end cannot be sustained by evil means, thus in effect have knowledge of Yahweh's glory. The increasing realization on the part of the world community that this principle is becoming ever more evident in the course of human events will thus lead to universally shared insight regarding the nature of Yahweh (2:14).

The conquered nations are here voicing their opinion that the imperialistic program of forced resettlement, pursued by the Babylonians in continuity with their Assyrian predecessors (cf. Nah 3:1), is too bloody and vicious for Yahweh to let it finally succeed. They are also admitting that their unanimous acceptance of the conviction is tantamount to universal acknowledgment of Yahweh. This analysis of the situation corroborates what Yahweh has revealed to the prophet concerning the reconcilability of a commitment to justice with a faithful acknowledgment of Yahweh's lordship over history (2:4-5).

Genre, Setting, and Intention

→ 2:6b-8.

THE FOURTH "WOE" SPEECH, 2:15-17

Structure

I. Designation of negative behavior	2:15
A. "Woe" cry	2:15aα¹
B. Characterization of one who behaves negatively	2:15aα²b
1. Two participial clauses	2:15aα²β
a. Whoever makes his neighbor drink	2:15aα²β¹
b. Whoever makes them drunk	2:15aβ²
2. Clause of purpose: to gaze on their shame	2:15b
II. Consequences of such behavior: direct address	2:16
A. Basic statement: being satisfied with contempt instead of glory	2:16aα
B. Elaboration in terms of role reversal: the one who makes his neighbor drink is made to drink	2:16aβb
1. Initiation of the reversal: twofold command to drink and stagger	2:16aβ
2. Description of the reversal itself	2:16b

This unit is permeated with the same imagery of drinking that was previously used to describe Babylon's downfall. The point of the reference to wine in 2:5aα is to compare the inevitably adverse results of its overconsumption with the inevitably adverse consequences of Babylon's greed for conquest. Here Babylon's treatment of the nations is being compared with drunken debauchery. Their intent is, as it were, to get their neighbors drunk and take advantage of them. Midway through the unit there is a role reversal, which brings with it a shift in imagery. The Babylonians, who are making their neighbors drink, will themselves be made to drink. The image of drinking the dregs from Yahweh's cup (e.g., Ps 75:9 [*RSV* 8]; Isa 51:17, 22; Jer 25:15) is conjured up to show Babylon in the process of getting its just deserts from Yahweh.

The passage begins with a mock expression of dismay decrying anyone who would debauch his neighbor with drinking (2:15). An unidentified addressee — who is known from the larger context to be the greedy oppressor described in 2:4-5 — is then implicated in this misbehavior by the allegation that his participation in the drinking bout will not turn out as expected. Babylon will get no advantage over its neighbors but will instead only earn their contempt (2:16aα). The decline of Babylon is the result of a role reversal that Yahweh is bringing about (2:16aβb). The Babylonians have drunkenly set their own downfall in motion not only because of the way in which they have mistreated fellow human beings from various regions (2:17aα), but also because of the way in which they have mistreated other creatures (2:17aβ). Their mistreatment of humanity and all earthly creation is finally redescribed (2:17b) in a verbatim repetition of 2:8b, which links this fourth "woe" with the first (2:6b-8) in the series of five (→ 2:1-20, Structure).

The conquered nations are here voicing their opinion that the Babylonians' deceptive attempts to take advantage of their neighbors are so contemptible as to offend the moral order of creation, and so unfair as to ensure that

Yahweh will turn the tables on them. This analysis of the situation corroborates what Yahweh has revealed to the prophet concerning the cosmic proportions and inevitable deadliness of Babylon's insatiability (2:5).

Genre, Setting, and Intention

→ 2:6b-8.

THE FIFTH AND FINAL "WOE" SPEECH, 2:18-20

Structure

I. Consequences of idolatry: twofold rhetorical question making parallel affirmations	2:18
A. First affirmation of idolatry's unprofitability	2:18aα
1. Question proper: what profit?	2:18aα^1
2. Rationale expressed in a *kî* clause: its maker shaped it	2:18aα^2
B. Second affirmation of idolatry's unprofitability	2:18aβb
1. Question proper: [what profit] is an image and teacher of lies?	2:18aβ
2. Rationale	2:18b
a. *Kî* clause: the worker trusts in his own creation	2:18bα
b. Purpose clause: to make mute idols	2:18bβ
II. Designation of idolatry as negative behavior	2:19-20
A. Mock expression of dismay	2:19a
1. "Woe" cry	2:19aα^1
2. Characterization of one who behaves negatively: twofold participial clause in parallelism	2:19aα^{2}β
a. Whoever says to wood, "Awake!"	2:19aα^2
b. [Whoever says] "Arise!" to mute stone	2:19aβ
B. Elaboration in terms of a contrast between an idolatrous image and Yahweh	2:19b-20
1. The idolatrous image	2:19b
a. Mock acclamation of its theophanic potential: this gives revelation?!	2:19bα^1
b. Further characterization	2:19bα^{2}β
1) Exterior: overlaid with gold and silver	2:19bα^2
2) Interior: no breath in it	2:19bβ
2. Yahweh	2:20
a. Characterization: cosmic king in his heavenly palace	2:20a
b. Directive acclaiming his theophanic presence: silence before him, all the earth!	2:20b

This last of the five "woes" is composed of the same basic elements as its four predecessors, but here they are combined differently in order to conclude this section of the book (→ 2:1-20, Structure). The sequence of the two most basic elements in the reproof speech is reversed, so that the part accosting the addressee with the consequences of his deeds — in this case a rhetorical question (2:18) — precedes the mock expression of dismay decrying such behavior (2:19-20). Moreover, the element of rationale (expressed with a *kî* clause) is in this case integrated with the description of the consequences into a single subunit, rather than appended to the description of consequences as a subunit of its own. This structural change introduces an element of contrast, emphasizing the difference between the progression from present events to future consequences (which is characteristic of the four preceding "woe" speeches) and the movement from future consequences back to present events in this "woe" speech.

An unidentified addressee — who is known from the larger context to be the greedy oppressor described in 2:4-5 — is implicated in the practice of idolatry by means of a rhetorical question affirming its unprofitability (2:18). It is unprofitable because it involves the worship of one's own works (2:18aα), which amounts to a particularly insidious kind of self-deification. Whatever is revealed by such a self-deluding practice must be false (2:18aβb). A mock expression of dismay next denounces anyone who would worship in this way (2:19a) by addressing an earthbound inanimate object as if it had power on a cosmic scale over human affairs (2:19b). By contrast, Yahweh is an unseen heavenly reality whose cosmic power is awesomely evident over all the earth (2:20).

The conquered nations are here voicing their opinion that the imperialists' religion is symptomatic of their fatal misperception of reality. In the stupor of their self-delusion they cannot see the one who is really in control. Precisely because they have worshiped their own power, they are now bound to lose it. This analysis of the situation corroborates what Yahweh has revealed to the prophet concerning the self-destructive potential of the oppressor's hubris (2:4-5).

Genre, Setting, and Intention

→ 2:6b-8.

Chapter 5

THE THIRD MAJOR SECTION OF THE BOOK (3:1-19)

THE PRAYER OF HABAKKUK, 3:1-19

Text

Hiebert (*God of My Victory*, 13) has proposed an emendation of *ḥayyêhû* (*RSV* "renew it") in v. 2bβ[1], changing this piel singular imperative of *ḥyh* with its masculine singular pronominal suffix to the second person masculine singular perfect form of the same verb, *ḥîyîtā* ("you sustained life"). This is potentially important for the form-critical classification of ch. 3 as a complaint (→ Genre) since it would remove the only overtly petitionary element in the text. Unlike some other rather speculative proposals that are easily dismissed (e.g., J. Reider, "Etymological Studies in Biblical Hebrew," *VT* 4 [1954] 283-84; cf. Margulis, 413), this one claims the versional support of the LXX. Hiebert argues that the sense of the MT is problematic because there is no clear antecedent for the pronominal suffix and because the piel of *ḥyh* invariably takes an inanimate object. He therefore resorts to the LXX, where he finds the Greek noun *zōōn* ("living things") to be the most likely counterpart to the Hebrew verb. Retroverting this Greek noun into the Hebrew *ḥayyôt* ("living things"), he observes that the LXX translator must have misread the second person masculine singular piel perfect form of *ḥyh* as *ḥayyôt* because of their similar consonantal spellings (the consonantal cluster *ḥyt* would orthographically represent both words).

This proposal is untenable for several reasons. First, the pronominal suffix does have an antecedent in the masculine singular noun *poʿal* (*RSV* "work") from the preceding line. Moreover, the piel of *ḥyh* can and does take inanimate objects, such as stone structures (1 Chr 11:8; Neh 3:34 [*RSV* 4:2]) and the cosmic order (Neh 9:6). Hiebert dismisses this evidence because it comes from "late" texts (*God of My Victory*, 152, n. 12), and he is arguing that Hab 3 is "early." Such reasoning is circular. Even more problematic is the way in which Hiebert uses the LXX here. At this point the Greek text reflects not just a He-

147

brew text with variant readings different from the MT, but a Hebrew text with a poetic form that is different from and structurally more complex than the MT. It is neither obvious nor probable that the Greek noun *zōōn* reflects an underlying Hebrew form that is the counterpart to the verb *ḥayyêhû* in the MT. One must also somehow account for the future passive verb in the LXX, *gnōsthēsē* ("you shall be known").

The overall problem of the relationship between the LXX and MT of v. 2b cannot be resolved here. It is sufficient for our purposes to point out that the Hebrew text reflected in the LXX would most likely have a second person masculine singular *imperfect* form, corresponding to the Greek future form, and not a perfect as Hiebert maintains. Such a Hebrew verb might well be taken in its jussive sense and thus constitute a petitionary element — less direct than the imperative of the MT but a petitionary element nevertheless — as is often the case in complaint psalms (e.g., Pss 5:12 [*RSV* 11]; 7:10 [*RSV* 9]; 59:9 [*RSV* 8]; 83:16 [*RSV* 15]; 139:19). Regardless of what might finally prove to be the best text here, one cannot claim that recourse to the LXX obviates the necessity of reckoning with a petitionary element in v. 2.

Structure

I. Superscription	3:1
A. Title	3:1a
1. General designation: prayer	3:1aα
2. Specification: of Habakkuk the prophet	3:1aβ
B. Elaboration: according to Shigionoth	3:1b
II. Main body: the prayer proper	3:2-19a
A. The prophet's request: direct address	3:2
1. Invocation of Yahweh	3:2aα
a. Report of the prophet's having heard about Yahweh	$3:2a\alpha^1$
b. Report of the prophet's fearful reaction to Yahweh's work	$3:2a\alpha^2$
2. Petitions	3:2aβb
a. For Yahweh to act in the course of events	3:2aβ
1) To renew his work	$3:2a\beta^1$
2) To make it known	$3:2a\beta^2$
b. For Yahweh to show mercy in his anger	3:2b
B. Narration of Yahweh's compliance with the prophet's request	3:3-19a
1. Yahweh's renewal and manifestation of his work in accord with the request in v. $2a\beta^1$	3:3-7
a. Account of Yahweh's theophany	3:3-6a
1) Aspects of Yahweh's advent	3:3-5
a) Whence he comes: Teman and Mt. Paran	3:3a
b) The accompanying cosmic signs: glory and praise	3:3b

The poem in 3:2-19a is framed by a superscription in 3:1 and a postscript in 3:19b that identify this poem as the *tĕpillâ* (*RSV* "prayer") of Habakkuk (v. 1a) and specify how it is to be performed liturgically (vv. 1b, 19a). A comparison and contrast is thereby set up between the foregoing material in chs. 1–2 and the material in ch. 3 with respect to both the prophetic message and its mode of presentation. The poem in 3:2-19a is to be identified with the prophet Habakkuk, perhaps because he was thought to have authored it (→ Setting), but more importantly because its view of Yahweh's problematic involvement in world affairs and its attitude of faith in Yahweh's intention to establish justice and deliver his people are essentially similar to the view and attitude expressed in the prophecies that are associated with Habakkuk in chs. 1–2. In contrast with the prophetic message of chs. 1–2, however, which is expressed in the form of a *maśśā'* (1:1), the prophetic message of ch. 3 may or may not be included under this rubric. It may be read as part of the *maśśā'* (→ Book as a Whole, Genre) but may also be sung separately as liturgical psalmody.

The initial invocation of Yahweh (3:2) programmatically introduces the rest of the composition (3:3-19a). The prophet calls on Yahweh (3:2aα) to establish a contrast between, on the one hand, the divine activity (Yahweh's *po'al;* RSV "work") and, on the other hand, the prophet's perception of (*šāma'tî;* RSV "I have heard") and reaction to (*yārē'tî;* RSV "I fear") that activity. Thus in response to the subsequent narration of Yahweh's coming to judge the earth (3:6a), the prophet reports (3:7) that he has "seen" (*rā'îtî*) some local manifestation of the earth's frightened trembling at Yahweh's approach (3:6b). Likewise, in response to the narration of Yahweh's struggle with chaos (3:8-9, 12-15), the prophet reports (3:16) that he has "heard" (*šāma'tî*) the noise of the battle, and that he has reacted to hearing it — just as the whole cosmos has reacted to "seeing" (*rā'û*) it (3:10-11) — with frightened trembling.

In this introductory verse the prophet also petitions Yahweh for two things (3:2aβb), and the two subunits that make up the rest of the poem proceed to illustrate Yahweh's acting in accord with these petitions. In compliance with the twofold request that Yahweh renew his activity and make himself known in the course of events (3:2aβ), the account of Yahweh's theophany (3:3-6) describes Yahweh's power becoming manifest on the earthly plane in terms of an international shake-up (3:6). In compliance with the request that Yahweh remember to show mercy even in his anger (3:2b), the account of Yahweh's battle with chaos (3:8-9, 12-15) describes this struggle for the stability of the cosmos as an expression of Yahweh's anger toward the forces of chaos in general (3:8a) and toward the wicked nations in particular (3:12, 13b), as well as a means of his mercifully saving his people (3:13a).

When one views the two episodes of narration (3:3-7 and 3:8-19a) in relation to the prophet's introductory invocation of Yahweh (3:2), the nature of their interrelationship becomes evident. The first episode (3:3-7) follows from a request for Yahweh to renew his involvement in human affairs (3:2aβ) in accord with the mythic archetypes that have shaped Yahweh's reputation (3:2aα[1]). It concludes with the prophet's attestations to such involvement on Yahweh's part, based on his own observations concerning some disturbance to the south (3:7). The second episode (3:8-19a) follows from a request for Yahweh to express in the historical process not just his wrath but also his mercy (3:2b) — a prospect whose potential ambiguity leaves the prophet fearful (3:2aα[2]). It concludes with the prophet's affirmation that, although the situation remains ambiguous and he remains fearful, Yahweh will indeed eventually comply with this request (3:16-19a). This affirmation is based largely on hearsay, however. Unlike the prophet's attestation that Yahweh has begun to act, which is based on his own observations of the current world scene, his confidence in a favorable outcome is based only on what he has previously heard regarding Yahweh's character. He trusts that things will turn out in accord with the same mythic archetype that was evident to him from the start. The first episode of the narration therefore recounts Yahweh's provisional compliance with part of what the prophet requested, on the basis of which the second segment can proceed to recount Yahweh's eventual compliance with all of what the prophet requested.

The same interrelationship is evident from the way in which the two episodes are linked to each other within a continuous narrative progression. The conclusion of the theophany episode is linked with the beginning of the combat episode by their use of the same imagery to describe the earth's reaction to Yahweh, i.e., the shaking of the mountains (v. 6aβ, v. 10aα). The conclusion of the theophany episode is likewise linked with the conclusion of the combat episode by their use of the same imagery to describe Yahweh's treatment of the earth and the nations, i.e., Yahweh's taking his stand on the earth and thereby overturning the international order (v. 6aα, v. 12). The prophet's observations confirming that Yahweh has come to judge the nations (v. 7) thus provide the basis on which he further supposes that Yahweh has begun to attack the forces of chaos and that he will defeat them and deliver his people. The combat episode finally recapitulates its beginning (v. 15; cf. v. 8), thus leaving the prophet and his audience in the middle of the whole story. But because the eventual outcome has already been projected on the basis of what has transpired thus far, the prophet can affirm his confidence in Yahweh's eventual deliverance (vv. 16b-19).

The two episodes have differences that indicate some development, as the narration progresses, in both the scenic scope and the characterization of the prophetic role. Although the perspective in the first episode extends to include the heavens (v. 3b), it is nevertheless largely earthbound and local in its focus. (Note the purely earthly response in v. 6b to Yahweh's action, and the realistic use of place-names in v. 3a and v. 7.) The perspective in the second episode is, in contrast, relatively cosmic and universal. (Note the inclusion of the heavens and the depths, along with the earth, in the response to Yahweh described in vv. 10-11; and note also in vv. 13b-14 the characterization of Judah's enemy in terms of the mythic archetype of the chaos monster rather than in terms of any national or political name.) In the first episode the prophetic "I" stands alone, and Yahweh is described with relatively objective and impersonal third person forms. In the second episode a social dimension is added with the inclusion of the congregational "us" (v. 16), and Yahweh is described in direct address with relatively subjective and personal second person forms. As the narration progresses from recounting what Yahweh evidently has done to recounting what he hopefully will do, the scenic scope is broadened to show his local and particular activity on Judah's behalf as an event with potentially cosmic and universal implications. The characterization of the prophetic role simultaneously grows more complex as the nature of the prophet's relationship with Yahweh and with the people is made more explicit, so that the prophet's function as an intermediary between the divine and human realms is gradually heightened.

The prophet's concluding statement (3:16-19a) begins in the same way that Yahweh was addressed initially, i.e., with the prophet's declaration that he has "heard" (*šāma'tî;* v. 16aα; cf. v. 2aα), thus harking back to the very beginning of the poem. But now the prophet has not only heard of how Yahweh acts. He has also seen some evidence that Yahweh has begun to act in the present situation in just the same way that he has acted before. Although the prophet is shaken by the ambiguity of what has happened thus far (v. 16a), because Yahweh's involvement in human affairs is potentially dangerous for all concerned, he nevertheless expresses his intuition that salvation will result (v. 16b). The description of dearth in v. 17 similarly harks back to the description of plague and pestilence as part of Yahweh's retinue in the theophany episode (v. 5). Conditions of drought and famine are thus interpreted as signs of Yahweh's involvement in the world situation on behalf of his people. As portents of salvation they constitute a cause for rejoicing. When the world order is threatened, Yahweh's people — like the wild deer — can depend for their strength and safety on him alone (v. 19a).

Genre

The generic classification of 3:1-19 involves determining both the kind of poem that appears in 3:2-19a and the kind of text that is produced by the addition of the annotations in 3:1 and 3:19b.

With regard to the poem itself, Humbert (pp. 24-28) made an attempt to describe it in terms of Gunkel's categories of psalms (H. Gunkel, *The Psalms* [tr. T. M. Horner; Philadelphia: Fortress, 1967]). He observed that this text describes Yahweh in ways that are reminiscent of the genre (→) hymn of praise, but that it also contains elements that are characteristic of the (→) complaint, such as: (a) invocation of Yahweh (v. 2aα), (b) petition for deliverance (v. 2aβb), (c) description of trouble (vv. 16b-17), and (d) affirmation of confidence (vv. 16b, 18-19). Subsequent discussion has tended to emphasize one of these two aspects of the text over the other.

Cross (pp. 157, 164) and Hiebert (*God of My Victory,* 83-120) have followed Albright (pp. 5-9) in emphasizing the essentially hymnic nature of the poem, either minimizing the effect of the complaint elements or emending them away. Mowinckel (pp. 7-9) strongly criticized Albright's approach to the text, and several have followed him in emphasizing the overall coherence of the poem in the form of a complaint (e.g., Gowan, *Triumph,* 69-70; Eaton, "Origin and Meaning," 159; Margulis, 437-40). Both sides in this debate seem to agree that vv. 3-15 constitute some kind of core unit, but they disagree as to its origin and nature. Cross and Hiebert regard the mythic motifs of theophany and combat as indications of an affinity with Canaanite epic traditions, and on this basis they classify this unit as a divine warrior hymn and a victory hymn, respectively. Those who acknowledge the dominance of the complaint ele-

ments tend to regard vv. 3-15 as a record of the prophetic vision mentioned in
1:1 and 2:2-3 (e.g., Rudolph, 239-43; Elliger, 51; Gowan, *Triumph*, 80-82;
Horst, 183-86). The views of both sides in this debate are problematic enough
to preclude any settlement of the question by arguing either for one side or
against the other.

The theory that the hymnic description in this unit is based on a prophetic vision is untenable for several reasons. The use of the term *ḥāzôn* (*RSV*
"vision") in 1:1 and 2:2-3 does not necessarily indicate any clairvoyance on
the prophet's part, for this term can have the general meaning of "revelation"
as well as the more specific meaning of "vision." The general meaning is more
likely here (→ 1:1; 2:1-5, Structure). Some advocates of this theory cite the
prophet's description of his queasiness as evidence of his having had some
paranormal visionary experience (e.g., Horst, 183-84; Eaton, *Obadiah*, 116;
Rudolph, 241), but queasiness could certainly have some other etiology. The
main problem with this view is that it goes against what the text explicitly says
in this regard. The prophet's discomfort is specifically attributed to what he
has *heard,* not what he has seen.

The prophet claims to have seen not Yahweh himself or even the earth's
trembling at his coming but only the impact of such tremors on the tents of
Cushan and Midian (v. 7). The prophet's report of his having seen this disturbance is an important part of the poem, for these trembling tents
metonymically represent the initial impact of Yahweh's activity on the earthly
scene as a whole. The prophet's claim to have seen them thus counts as evidence of Yahweh's growing involvement in human affairs, but precisely because this disturbance is in principle the kind of thing that is observable to all.
The prophet has also perceived within this development some hidden significance, which becomes the basis for his hope that things will eventually turn
out in accord with what he has heard. The narrative description here is perhaps
visionary in a very general sense, i.e., imaginative, and it is based on prophetic
intuitions regarding the significance of what the prophet has observed. The
prophet's observations themselves, however, are not based on any experience
that is visionary in the strict sense of the word, as is explicitly the case in some
other prophetic texts (e.g, Isa 6; Amos 7:1-3; → Zech 2:8-17, Genre).

Judging from what the text itself says, the prophet's intuitions and hopes
derive from what he has heard about Yahweh. Just as there is nothing particularly paranormal about what he has seen, there is nothing particularly paranormal about what he has heard. Rather, the prophet's interpretation of the brute
historical facts is based on what he has heard regarding Yahweh's "work"
(*po'al,* v. 2aα; cf. v. 16aα[1]), i.e., on mythic accounts of Yahweh's great deeds.
Cross and Hiebert have therefore rightly asserted an affinity between the description in this unit and the Canaanite mythic traditions. The generic classification that they have deduced on this basis is dubious, however, for several
reasons. On the one hand the existence of the divine warrior hymn or victory
hymn as a genre has not been sufficiently established; and on the other hand,
even if one grants the existence of such a genre, this text does not meet the
principal criterion that has been proposed for it.

Neither Cross's divine warrior hymn nor Hiebert's victory hymn is defined in terms of a conventional literary form with a typical structure. They point instead to a cluster of mythic motifs. This way of defining the genre is problematic in view of the fact, which they themselves have amply documented, that these same motifs can cluster in a wide variety of formally quite heterogeneous texts, such as the hymn of praise in Ps 114, the royal complaint in Ps 89, and the Ugaritic mythic accounts of Baal's exploits (Cross, 147-57) — and even, as Albright pointed out (p. 5), in the annalistic account of the victory of Rameses II at Kadesh. A generic affinity is claimed for these different sorts of texts because they all contain narrative that supposedly follows the conventions of epic recital. It now goes without saying that many kinds of biblical texts draw on an extensive repertoire of mythic motifs that were common throughout the ancient Near East and were expressed in terminology that is particularly characteristic of the Canaanite mythic traditions as represented by the texts from Ugarit. One may also grant that the various kinds of compositions that have been lumped together under the rubric of the divine warrior hymn or the victory hymn all tend to show a particular cluster of mythic motifs, thus treating the common theme of victory from a variety of divine and human perspectives. It does not necessarily follow, however, that they all belong to the same generic class.

Such a conclusion would make the categorical mistake of assuming that a common content entails a common form. This is precisely the issue that emerges when one compares Hab 3:2-19a with other alleged representatives of the divine warrior or victory hymn. Although Habakkuk's prayer obviously contains the mythic motifs that are supposed to constitute this genre, the form of the narration in 3:2-19a bears little resemblance to the conventions of epic recital that are supposed to give this group of quite heterogeneous texts its rather minimal formal coherence. If the Ugaritic myths of Baal's exploits provide any indication of those conventions — and they must of course be seen as paradigmatic examples — it is not typical for the narrators either to involve themselves in the story by using the first person or to address the story's divine characters directly by using the second person. Yet the first of these features is an essential characteristic of both narrative episodes in 3:2-19a (see v. 7 in 3:3-7 and vv. 16-19a in 3:8-19a), and the second is an essential characteristic of the latter narrative episode (3:8-19a). In sum, the texts that have been adduced as examples of the divine warrior or victory hymn do not actually define a generic classification, but rather constitute a grouping of texts on the basis of a common thematic content. Even though in some respects one may rightly compare 3:2-19a with the texts in this group, still other aspects of its content, as well as significant formal differences, remain to be explained.

In order to reach a satisfactory explanation, it is first necessary to reconsider a point on which all sides in the debate seem to agree. Most scholars regard vv. 3-15 as a hymnic core, framed in v. 2 and vv. 16-19a with elements of complaint. On closer inspection, however, vv. 3-15 do not actually constitute a viable subunit that is unqualifiedly hymnic. The commonly accepted analysis ignores the structural analogy between vv. 3-15 and vv. 16-19a. The self-report of the prophet in v. 7 concludes the theophany episode in vv. 3-6 in much the same way that the soliloquy in vv. 16-19a concludes the combat episode in vv.

8-15. When vv. 3-15 are treated as a separate subunit distinct from vv. 16-19a, v. 7 appears to be a quite intrusive anomaly. Bratcher at least recognizes this difficulty, which others pass over in silence. He observes that "the introduction of the first person into this lengthy description of God [i.e., vv. 3-15] is abrupt and difficult to fit into the context" (p. 289, n. g). Rather than revise his structural analysis, however, he attributes the incongruity to textual corruption — despite his own admission that the textual witnesses are all in agreement at this point! The incongruity is only apparent, however. It can be obviated by showing that v. 7 is part of a recurring pattern, in which vv. 3-7 and vv. 8-19a form subunits that are structurally parallel. Each begins with an account of both Yahweh's action (vv. 3-6a, vv. 8-9 + 12-15) and the world's reaction (v. 6b, vv. 10-11) and concludes with the prophet's first person report of his own perceptions (v. 7, vv. 16-19a).

Moreover, the introduction in v. 2 does not simply frame the two parallel subunits in vv. 3-7 and vv. 8-19a. Each of these subunits is narrated somewhat differently because of the way in which each is materially predicated on different requests in v. 2αβb (→ Structure). The narration in the first episode (vv. 3-6) describes the divine action as something that is already initiated and disclosed, in response to the prophet's asking Yahweh to renew and reveal his work (v. 2αβ). The narration in the second episode (vv. 8-15) describes the continuation and outcome of the same divine action as something that is yet to happen, in response to the prophet's asking Yahweh to be merciful in his fury (v. 2b). It is therefore misleading to describe 3:2-19a in terms of a hymnic core (vv. 3-15) framed by elements of complaint. Elements of complaint and hymnic description are interpenetrating throughout, and the elements of complaint are structurally dominant in the sense that they govern the way in which the hymnlike description of Yahweh's actions is narrated. The poem in 3:2-19a is thus best characterized as a PROPHETIC COMPLAINT.

This section of Habakkuk is not just a complaint, however. It is a complaint that has been annotated so as to associate it with a particular historical figure and a particular mode of cultic performance. The first part of the superscription (3:1a) labels 3:2-19a as a poem pertaining to the prophet Habakkuk — the same prophet who, in the superscription to the book as a whole (1:1), has been identified with an oracle concerning the encroachment of the Babylonians (1:6b; → 1:5-11). The rest of the superscription (3:1b) and the entire postscript (3:19b) are concerned with the liturgical rendition of the complaint psalm in 3:2-19a. The meaning of v. 1b (*RSV* "according to Shigionoth") is obscure, as is the enigmatic *selâ* (vv. 9a, 13b), but both are generally thought to refer to some aspect of musical performance. The subscript stipulates further that this complaint is to be sung with string accompaniment (cf. 1 Chr 15:21), as is also the case with other psalms (e.g., Pss 4:1; 6:1; 54:1; 67:1; 76:1; cf. 61:1 [all *RSV* superscriptions]). On the one hand, these classificatory annotations do not radically transform the genre of Hab 3:1-19 into something altogether different from the complaint in 3:2-19a since they function partly to preserve the complaint's ongoing use in the liturgical role that such psalms were generally designed to play (→ Setting). On the other hand, these annotations serve other functions as well, so that it does not suffice to define the genre of ch. 3 as a whole simply in terms of the complaint that it contains.

Childs ("Psalm Titles") has suggested that such annotations, as they appear in the headings of the Psalms, are essentially exegetical. The identification of a particular psalm with a particular historical figure — most notably David, but others as well — indicates that it is to be read in the context of either a particular occasion or the general circumstances of that person's life. Childs thus proposes that texts with such headings be considered a kind of midrash. This observation regarding one general function of psalm headings helps to explain at least part of what is involved here in the similar identification of the complaint in Hab 3:2-19a with the historical figure of the prophet Habakkuk. This identification amounts to an exegetical commentary as it indicates that the sense of the complaint can be clarified by reading it in light of the situation faced by Habakkuk during the Babylonian crisis. There is more to the matter, however, that finally makes midrash an inapt generic classification for the chapter as a whole.

The identification of 3:2-19a with Habakkuk does indeed have an exegetical function, as it calls for the complaint to be interpreted in light of what generally happened to the prophet. But it also has a historiographical function as it conversely invites the reader to fill in the fragmentary biography of Habakkuk with information derived from the complaint. As the complaint dramatizes the prophet's exemplary faith and hope in Yahweh, despite the questionable justness of Yahweh's involvement in the situation, it elucidates an aspect of the prophet's role that is evident but not much emphasized in the autobiographical snippets preserved in chs. 1–2 (→ 2:1-5, Intention). Moreover, the combination of rubrical directions for the complaint's ritual performance with its attribution to a particular prophet reflects not only the practice of prophets' participation in cultic events, proclaiming to the congregation in a variety of ways how God is involved in their present situation. This combination also reflects the ongoing ritual performance of some forms of cultic poetry, conceived as a type of prophetic activity in its own right.

Prophecy and psalmody overlap here in much the same way that they overlap in the Chronicler's description of worship at Jerusalem's royal sanctuary. On the one hand, an inspired spokesman who apprises the people of Yahweh's favorable intentions, in the context of a complaint ceremony occasioned by enemy attack, is called a "prophet" (2 Chr 20:14-17; cf. 20:20). On the other hand, those whom David appointed to hereditary positions as psalmodists in Yahweh's sanctuary are also said to "prophesy" (from the same root, *nb'*; 1 Chr 16:1-8). Prophecy and psalmody therefore merge in the ongoing ritual representation of what past prophets once said and did on particular cultic occasions. Psalmody thus conceived entails not merely the repeated recitation of a repertoire of sacred songs, but also the periodic representation of past prophetic acts in which historically prominent prophetic figures — such as David and his seer Asaph — expressed their insights concerning Yahweh's involvement in the events of their own day (2 Chr 29:30). The same insight is thereby rendered potentially applicable to similar subsequent situations.

The genre designation of Hab 3:1-19 should encompass the complexity of the interrelationships among the superscription, the postscript, and the prophetic complaint that they both annotate. The term *midrash* is perhaps applicable to the exegetical function of the annotations, but it does not do justice to their additional historiographical and liturgical functions. Since the term *midrash* properly refers only to certain kinds of exegetical commentary (G. G. Porton, "Defining Midrash," in *The Study of Ancient Judaism* [ed. J. Neusner; New York: KTAV, 1981] 55-92), it should not be extended to apply to a text like Hab 3. The term PROPHETIC PSALMODY SCRIPT is alternatively proposed to describe this literary phenomenon: the sort of poetic composition that would have been spoken by a prophet on a particular liturgical occasion, transcribed and catalogued to identify it with a particular prophet and his historical situation, so as to make it both readable for purposes of mantic exegesis and performable by cultic singers as a ritual reactualization of previously efficacious prophetic activity.

Setting

The complaint itself (3:2-19a) has a compositional form that is typical of the cult. The prophet comes before a group of compatriots gathered for worship to express preternatural insights regarding Yahweh's involvement in the crisis now confronting their nation. By recognizing mythic archetypes of divine activity in the dynamics of this threatening situation, the prophet discerns some signs of Yahweh's favorable intentions that are far from self-evident. The poem gives voice to a prophetic character, learned in mythology, who is leading a complaint liturgy occasioned by an enemy invasion.

There is evidence of prophets assuming such a role, at least in preexilic times. There are some direct references to the involvement of prophets in cultic activities (e.g., 2 Kgs 23:2), and several psalms afford examples of cultic poetry containing oracular or other prophetic elements (see A. R. Johnson, *The Cultic Prophet in Ancient Israel* [2nd ed.; Cardiff: University of Wales Press, 1962] 60-75; idem, *The Cultic Prophet and Israel's Psalmody* [Cardiff: University of Wales Press, 1979]). More specifically, there is a complete description of a complaint liturgy in 2 Chr 20:1-19, already mentioned above, in which a prophet plays a prominent role alongside the king. Although the king leads the prayer of complaint in this particular case, the Psalms offer examples of specifically prophetic prayers of complaint (e.g., Pss 60, 89; → Hab 1:2-17). Hab 3:2-19a would have thus have had a cultic setting in a complaint liturgy led by a prophet.

Although this cultic role of prophets is relatively well attested, its social background remains obscure. It is not clear, for example, whether the prophetic function of officiating at the royal sanctuary on state occasions was generally the prerogative of those seers who served as the king's advisers, as it was in the case of Nathan (1 Kgs 1:32-40). It is likewise not clear whether or how prophets were associated with the guilds of psalmographers and psalmodists attached to the royal sanctuary and various other cultic establishments, whose compositional forms were readily appropriated by court prophets (S. Mowinckel, "Cult and Prophecy," in *Prophecy in Israel* [Issues in Religion and Theology 10; ed. D. L. Petersen; tr. J. L. Schaaf; Philadelphia: Fortress; London: SPCK, 1987] 83-97). Finally, it is also not clear how the groups that composed and compiled psalmodic texts, or the groups that preserved and recomposed prophetic texts, were related to scribal institutions or schools of wisdom — although obviously some modicum of scribal skill and training would be necessary for the ongoing activity of both sorts of groups (S. Mowinckel, "Psalms and Wisdom," in *Wisdom in Israel and in the Ancient Near East* [*Fest.* H. H. Rowley; ed. M. Noth and D. Winton Thomas; VTSup 3; Leiden: Brill, 1955] 204-24; cf. J. C. VanderKam, "The Prophetic-Sapiential Origins of Apocalyptic Thought," in *A Word in Season* [*Fest.* W. McKane; ed. J. D. Martin and P. R. Davies; JSOTSup 42; Sheffield: JSOT Press, 1986] 163-76).

It is therefore difficult to determine precisely the social context in which the text of the poem in 3:2-19a would have been transmitted as the record of a prophetic complaint, or the setting in which the annotations in 3:1 and 3:19a would have been added. Judging from comparison with the headings in the Psalms, these annotations are characteristic of the psalmodic conventions of the Second Temple period. During this time the concept of psalmody as a prophetic activity, ritually representing the mantic expressions of the Davidic dynasty's seers, came to the fore (R. J. Tournay, *Seeing and Hearing God with the Psalms* [tr. J. E. Crowley; JSOTSup 118; Sheffield: JSOT Press, 1991] 34-67). Both the performance conventions and the prophetic conception of Second Temple psalmody may have had preexilic antecedents, however. The setting of the annotated text is thus not necessarily limited to the Second Temple's guilds of psalmodists, although in its present form it reflects the usage of these groups.

It is possible that the complaint in 3:2-19a was composed and/or recited by the prophet Habakkuk for a particular cultic event at some point in the Babylonian crisis during the late sixth century. We cannot be certain of this, however. The identification of the complaint with Habakkuk in 3:1a is a genuinely historical classification, but its significance must be assessed in terms of the general limitations and conventions of ancient historiography in representing the direct discourse of persons from the past. Since the means of verbatim transcription were next to nothing, it was conventional for historians to compose appropriate speeches representing what particular persons were supposed to have said on particular occasions. It is therefore possible that this complaint was composed by someone other than Habakkuk, either before or after his time, and eventually identified with him by those who preserved other records associated with him (chs. 1–2). It may then have become included among these records because it appeared to summarize authentically his message and because it did so in a form that enabled his message to have ongoing cultic representation.

Reviving Albright's theory of the early origin of Hab 3, Hiebert maintains that it antedates the time of Habakkuk by some five to six centuries, and that its cultic setting was specifically the old southern sanctuary of the proto-Israelite tribal league (*God of My Victory*, 120-24). He adduces three lines of argumentation: (1) grammatical forms peculiar to early Hebrew indicate a date of composition sometime between the thirteenth and tenth centuries; (2) heavy indebtedness to Canaanite mythic tradition indicates composition in the earliest phase of Israel's religious development during the premonarchial period, when Canaanite cultural influence was strongest; and (3) references to specific historical sites toward the south, such as Teman and Mt. Paran, evoke the traditional theme of Israel's original encounter with Yahweh at some holy place between Egypt and Canaan, and thus constitute an allusion to a Late Bronze Age sanctuary of Yahweh in southern Transjordan.

All of these arguments are problematic. The antique grammatical forms do not occur in a concentration heavy enough to necessitate the poem's antiquity. It is possible that they are the result of archaizing literary diction rather than the remnant of genuinely early Hebrew (see D. A. Robertson, *Linguistic Evidence in Dating Early Hebrew Poetry* [SBLDS 3; Missoula, Mont.: Society of Biblical Literature, 1972] 135-56 passim, whose conclusions are misrepresented by Hiebert). The linguistic evidence is thus inconclusive. As for Canaanite cultural influence during the premonarchial period, many would argue that the Israelite tribal league was a countercultural development, and that Canaanite influence was much stronger during the monarchial period than prior to it (e.g., N. Gottwald, *The Tribes of Yahweh* [Maryknoll, N.Y.: Orbis, 1979]). In any case there are clear-cut instances of the use of Canaanite mythic motifs in nearly every phase of Israel's literary history, from earliest times down to the late Second Temple period, and it is difficult to see why this phenomenon necessitates an early date in the case of Hab 3.

Finally, the occurrence of a mythic motif in a poem hardly requires the poem to be as old as the motif. The theme of Yahweh's coming from the south — whether the area is identified by the place-name of Teman (Hab 3:3a), Paran (Hab 3:3a; Deut 33:2a), Seir (Deut 33:2a; Judg 5:4a), or Edom (Judg 5:4a) — may well reflect the historical reality of a pre- or proto-Israelite sanctuary in southern Transjordan. In this particular case, however, the motif is being used to interpret an event that is contemporary from the perspective of the poem's speaker. He has seen the effects of some disturbance on the dwelling of the land of Midian (3:7) — whether this disturbance be a natural disaster or a political upheaval of some kind — and these are metaphorically identified as the effects of Yahweh's awesome "work," about which he has heard (3:2-6). The speaker indicates explicitly that this mythic tradition regarding Yahweh's "ways" is an ancient one (3:6bβ), and that he is witnessing a renewed manifestation of Yahweh's characteristic activity that has taken years to reappear (3:2b). The poem itself thus reflects an awareness of its not being as old as the traditional mythic motif that it utilizes — which makes Hiebert's conclusion concerning the historical significance of the place-names in 3:3a rather difficult to sustain.

The tenuousness of Hiebert's case illustrates the problems that emerge from pressing the issue of setting — whether social or historical — beyond what the evidence will bear. One can only say that the poem in 3:2-19a reflects the practice of prophets leading complaint liturgies, and that it may have been produced by Habakkuk himself or by some other anonymous prophetic figure.

At some point before or during the final redaction of the book the prayer became associated with other traditions pertaining to Habakkuk, as an apt summary expression of what he stood for, and was given the annotations in 3:1 and 3:19b. Before the Babylonian crisis was resolved the complaint in ch. 3 was incorporated, along with its annotations, into the final form of the book.

Intention

The main purpose of the complaint itself is to express the prophet's functioning in a crisis situation as an intermediary between Yahweh and the assembled audience. As the people's representative he beseeches Yahweh to deliver them from the threat of foreign domination, and as Yahweh's representative he reveals to the people that this deliverance has already begun to happen, as he models before them the attitude of hope that constitutes the appropriate response to this divine initiative. The prophet's confidence is based on his having seen some sign in the current situation of a pattern of action that is typical of Yahweh: a shake-up of the world order that entails his people's deliverance from injustice. Just as Yahweh once defeated the forces of chaos and evil to establish and maintain a just world order, so he is now rejoining that battle to restore such an order. The hardships of the present situation are the birth pangs of a new age, and are thus even warrants for the hope of eventual deliverance.

In its present annotated form the complaint further purports to complement the rather sketchy record of Habakkuk in chs. 1–2 and to provide an alternative means of communicating its significance. The complaint fills out the previous record in two major respects. First, it dramatizes the prophet's positive reaction to what Yahweh said in reply to the oracular inquiry (2:2b). More specifically, it shows his compliance with Yahweh's exhortation to wait in hope for the eventual vindication of his justness (2:3b). Second, the complaint also dramatizes the prophet's discernment of a sign that Yahweh has begun to fulfill his promise concerning the doom of the greedy and the vindication of the faithful (2:4), in accord with the divine command to write the promise down and study it in the light of unfolding events (2:2aβ-3). Directions for the ongoing ritual performance of this complaint provide for the dissemination and reactualization of Habakkuk's ideas through the musical rendition of this prayer, as well as through exposition of the written text.

Bibliography

W. F. Albright, "The Psalm of Habakkuk," in *Studies in Old Testament Prophecy* (*Fest.* T. H. Robinson; ed. H. H. Rowley; Edinburgh: T. & T. Clark, 1950) 1-18; U. Cassuto, "Chapter iii of Habakkuk and the Ras Shamra Texts," in *Biblical and Oriental Studies* (tr. I. Abrahams; 2 vols.; Jerusalem: Magnes, 1973-75) 2:3-15; B. S. Childs, "Psalm Titles and Midrashic Exegesis," *JSS* 16 (1971) 137-50; F. M. Cross, *Canaanite Myth and Hebrew Epic* (Cambridge: Harvard University Press, 1973); J. H. Eaton, "The Origin and Meaning of Habakkuk 3," *ZAW* 76 (1964) 144-71; H. M. I. Gevaryahu, "Biblical

Colophons: A Source for the 'Biography' of Authors, Texts, and Books," in *Congress Volume: Edinburgh, 1974* (VTSup 28; Leiden: Brill, 1975) 42-59; T. Hiebert, *God of My Victory* (HSM 38; Atlanta: Scholars Press, 1986); W. A. Irwin, "The Mythological Background of Habakkuk, Chapter 3," *JNES* 15 (1956) 47-50; B. Margulis, "The Psalm of Habakkuk: A Reconstruction and Interpretation," *ZAW* 82 (1970) 409-41; S. Mowinckel, "Zum Psalm des Habakuk," *TZ* 9 (1953) 1-21.

ZEPHANIAH

Bibliography

E. Achtemeier, *Nahum–Malachi* (IntCom; Atlanta: John Knox, 1986); L. Alonso Schökel and J. L. Sicre Diaz, *Profetas: Comentario,* vol. 2 (NBE; Madrid: Cristiandad, 1980); I. J. Ball, "The Rhetorical Shape of Zephaniah," in *Perspectives on Language and Text (Fest.* F. I. Andersen; ed. E. W. Conrad and E. G. Newing; Winona Lake, Ind.: Eisenbrauns, 1987) 155-65; idem, *A Rhetorical Study of Zephaniah* (Berkeley: Bibal, 1988); E. Ben Zvi, *A Historical-Critical Study of the Book of Zephaniah* (BZAW 198; Berlin: de Gruyter, 1991); R. A. Bennett, "The Book of Zephaniah," *NIB* 7:659-704; A. Berlin, *Zephaniah* (AB 25A; New York: Doubleday, 1994); B. S. Childs, *Introduction to the Old Testament as Scripture* (Philadelphia: Fortress, 1979); J. H. Eaton, *Obadiah, Nahum, Habakkuk and Zephaniah* (TBC; London: SCM, 1961); R. Edler, *Das Kerygma des Propheten Zefanja* (FThSt 126; Freiburg: Herder, 1984); K. Elliger, *Das Buch der zwölf Kleinen Propheten,* vol. 2 (6th ed.; ATD 25/2; Göttingen: Vandenhoeck & Ruprecht, 1967); G. Gerleman, *Zephanja: Textkritisch und literarisch untersucht* (Lund: Gleerup, 1942); F. Horst, "Zephanja," in T. H. Robinson and Horst, *Die Zwölf Kleinen Propheten* (3rd ed.; HAT 14; Tübingen: Mohr [Siebeck], 1964); P. R. House, *Zephaniah: A Prophetic Drama* (JSOTSup 69; Sheffield: Almond, 1988); A. S. Kapelrud, *The Message of the Prophet Zephaniah: Morphology and Ideas* (Oslo: Universitetsforlaget, 1975); C.-A. Keller, "Sophonie," in R. Vuilleumier and Keller, *Michée, Nahoum, Habacuc, Sophonie* (CAT 11b; Neuchâtel: Delachaux & Niestlé, 1971); G. Krinetzki, *Zefanjastudien* (RST 7; Frankfurt: Peter Lang; Bern: Herbert Lang, 1977); G. Langohr, "Rédaction et composition du livre de Sophonie," *Muséon* 89 (1976) 51-73; N. Lohfink, "Zephaniah and the Church of the Poor," *TD* 32 (1985) 113-18; K. Marti, *Dodekapropheton* (KHC 13; Tübingen: Mohr [Siebeck], 1904); F. Martin, "Le Livre de Sophonie [Première Partie]," *SBib* 39 (1985) 1-22; idem, "Le Livre de Sophonie [Seconde Partie]," *SBib* 40 (1985) 5-20; B. Renaud, "Le livre de Sophonie: le Jour de YHWH thème structurant de la synthèse rédactionelle," *RevScRel* 60 (1986) 1-33; J. J. M. Roberts, *Nahum, Habakkuk, and Zephaniah* (OTL; Louisville: Westminster/John Knox, 1991); W. Rudolph, *Micha, Nahum, Habakuk, Zephanja* (KAT 13/3; Gütersloh: Mohn, 1975); L. Sabottka, *Zephanja* (BibOr 25; Rome: Biblical Institute

Press, 1972); K. Seybold, *Satirische Prophetie* (SBS 120; Stuttgart: Katholisches Bibelwerk, 1985); J. M. P. Smith, "Zephaniah," in Smith, W. H. Ward, and J. A. Brewer, *A Critical and Exegetical Commentary on Micah, Zephaniah, Nahum, Habakkuk, Obadiah, and Joel* (ICC; Edinburgh: T. & T. Clark, 1911); R. L. Smith, *Micah–Malachi* (WBC 32; Waco: Word, 1984); M. A. Sweeney, "A Form-Critical Reassessment of the Book of Zephaniah," *CBQ* 53 (1991) 388-408; J. D. W. Watts, *The Books of Joel, Obadiah, Jonah, Nahum, Habakkuk and Zephaniah* (CBC; Cambridge: Cambridge University Press, 1975); M. Weigl, *Zefanja und das "Israel der Armen": Eine Untersuchung zur Theologie des Buches Zefanja* (Klosterneuburg: Österreichisches Katholisches Bibelwerk, 1994).

Chapter 1

THE BOOK AS A WHOLE

Structure

Although modern scholars have found it difficult to agree on the delineation of basic units in certain parts of Zephaniah (Berlin, *Zephaniah,* 17-20), they have nevertheless generally agreed with regard to the overall organization of the book. It is commonly divided into three sections based on three standard prophetic themes: judgment for Judah and Jerusalem (1:2–2:3), judgment for the nations (2:4–3:8), and salvation for both Judah and the nations (3:9-20; Childs, *Introduction,* 458). Some recent descriptions of Zephaniah's overall compositional form have continued to utilize this tripartite framework (e.g., Achtemeier, 69; Alonso Schökel and Sicre Diaz, 1110-11; Martin, 3; Ben Zvi, 325-46; Bennett, 669), occasionally modifying it in certain respects (e.g., Lohfink, 114-17; Roberts, 161-63), but cracks have begun to appear in the consensus (Renaud, 2-3; R. Rendtorff, *The Old Testament: An Introduction* [tr. J. Bowden; Philadelphia: Fortress, 1986] 234; Weigl, 230-33; → 2:1–3:13, Structure). Seeking an alternative to the oversimplified thematic contrasts of judgment versus salvation and Judah versus the Gentiles, other recent studies have described the book's structure in a diverse variety of ways.

Paul House has argued that Zephaniah is a "prophetic drama" (pp. 55-89). By this description he means not that this text ever served as the script for a stage play, but that Yahweh and the prophet are two distinctly different characters whose alternating speeches constitute dramatic action. This action develops as the "Day of Yahweh" theme progresses through phases analogous to those of a narrative plot sequence. After the theme is introduced (1:1-7), its complications appear (1:8–2:11) and then come to a head (2:12–3:5) so as to reach a climactic resolution (3:6-13) and final conclusion (3:14-20), in much the same way that the events within a story generally move through conflict to reach a climax in which the conflict is resolved.

House's attempt to do something different is refreshing, but his basic premise is fundamentally flawed. In trying to distinguish the prophet and Yahweh as two different dramatic characters he does not reckon sufficiently with the way in which various conventions of oracular speech serve precisely to blur this distinction. When a human being impersonates a god, in order to bring a revelation from the deity, the character of the divine source of this revelation becomes to some extent identified with the character of its human transmitter. Most prophetic speech is thus characterized by the lack of any fine line between the prophet's speaking for Yahweh and the prophet's speaking for himself or herself. The absence of any such differentiation is evident, for example, in the way that prophetic speech often alternates indiscriminately between describing the divine agency in first person from the perspective of Yahweh himself and in third person from the prophet's own perspective (Roberts, 161). It is also reflected in the way that first person speech of Yahweh is not always tagged with any of the various oracular formulas, such as "thus says Yahweh" *(kōh 'āmar yhwh)* or "oracle of Yahweh" *(nĕ'um yhwh).* That such formulas are optional shows considerable diffidence about the explicit indication of human intermediation, even though such intermediation is always involved in the communication of a revelation. In sum, no clear distinction is generally made between the divine and human elements in prophetic speech. There are some exceptions to this generalization, such as (→) prophetic complaints in which the prophet addresses Yahweh directly, but in these cases the identification of the genre provides a basis on which such a distinction can be made.

According to House, Zephaniah has no dramatic dialogue in the strict sense, i.e., Yahweh and the prophet do not address each other. They rather take turns speaking about such main themes as the Day of Yahweh. In order for this hypothesis to work, House would have to develop some specific criteria for distinguishing the speech of Yahweh from the speech of the prophet and then utilize these criteria consistently. Any criteria that he may have developed, however, remain tacit, and in this regard his analysis lacks consistency. If alternation between speech of Yahweh and speech of the prophet were indeed the text's most fundamental contrast, then why would Yahweh in the same breath refer to himself in both first and third person, as House supposes in several instances (e.g., 1:2-6 and 1:17, and 3:6-13)? Why would Yahweh have to report in the third person that he himself is speaking by using the standard oracular speech report formulas, as House requires of him at several points (e.g., 1:2; 1:10; 2:9; 3:20)? How could the prophet ever speak in the first person on Yahweh's behalf, which would have to be the case in 2:5bβ according to House's analysis, although House tries to avoid this incongruity by his unconvincing treatment of this clause as direct discourse (p. 121)? Because of such inconsistencies House's structure analysis finally breaks down, along with the prophetic drama hypothesis that is based on it. (Cf. the similar attempt of Martin to make a systematic distinction between the speech of Yahweh and the speech of the prophet ["Première Partie," 3-5], which also finally breaks down for much the same reason, although he at least notes such inconsistencies and does not characterize the alternation as "dramatic.")

Berlin alternatively presents her exposition of the text according to the subdivisions in one of the most important Masoretic mss. (the Leningrad Codex), describing this approach as a more or less arbitrary measure and denying that these subdivisions shed any light on the overall composition of the book (*Zephaniah,* 17-23). In taking such an approach she appears to conceive of structural analysis in historical rather than literary terms as an attempt to reconstruct the stages of the book's redactional development. With respect to structure in the literary sense, she only asserts that the book is "a unified work" without discussing any specific means of describing what this unity might consist of: "Viewing [the book] as a whole yields an interpretation much more interesting and compelling than viewing it as a collection of separate parts"

(*Zephaniah,* 23). It thus appears that Berlin would make no methodological distinction between synchronic analysis of the interrelated parts that now make up the book's final form and diachronic analysis of the separate parts that once constituted the stages in which it was redacted. In rejecting any possibility of the latter, she seems to think that one must also reject any possibility of the former.

Berlin's agnostic stance toward structural analysis of any kind is perhaps symptomatic of the current state of biblical scholarship. The field is presently polarized between those who view it as a primarily historical discipline and thus emphasize diachronic analysis at the expense of synchronic analysis, and those who view it as a primarily literary discipline and thus emphasize synchronic analysis at the expense of diachronic analysis. In a time of such polarization one might well feel, like Amos (5:13), that whoever is wise will keep silent. I take a different stance in this study, however. My analysis here assumes, along with Berlin, that a prophetic book is first of all to be understood as a literary whole. Unlike Berlin, however, I also assume that such understanding requires synchronic analysis of the parts that make up the whole and of how they are interrelated. Only on this basis can one then determine whether any diachronic analysis, of a sort that might show something about the text's redactional history, is warranted. The possibility of such diachronic analysis cannot be either affirmed or denied a priori but must be determined case by case.

Using rhetorical methods, Ball has attempted a synchronic analysis of Zephaniah, focusing in his earlier work on the individual parts of the book (*Rhetorical Study*) and in his later work on the book as a whole ("Rhetorical Shape"). Ball stands in the long line of those who define rhetoric in a narrow sense as the embellishment or ornamentation of language. His brand of rhetorical analysis is thus concerned mostly with looking for stylistic flourishes in patterns of sound (e.g., assonance and alliteration), in diction (e.g., reiterated idiomatic expressions and verbal roots), and in phraseology (e.g., parallelism and *inclusio*). By observing the ways in which such patterns combine, he draws conclusions regarding the division of the text into its basic units. He proposes that 2:1-7 forms a template for the organization of the whole book, which consists of three subunits that are thematically and structurally parallel to the other main sections of the book: as a warning of the impending Day of Yahweh, 2:1-3 corresponds to 1:2-18; in describing the destruction of Judah's enemies, 2:4 corresponds with 2:8-18; and in progressing from "woe" to salvation, 2:5-7 corresponds with 3:1-20 ("Rhetorical Shape," 164).

There is little to quarrel with in Ball's description of textual details. His work provides a fund of careful observation that any student of Zephaniah can ill afford to neglect. The main problem is that Ball's approach lacks any criteria for determining which of the many things noted by him are more salient indications of how the composition is organized. For example, he substantiates the correspondence between 2:5-7 and 3:1-20 by noting that (1) both begin on the same sad note of "woe" and end on the same glad note of "restoration," (2) both show the same eight key terms presented in the same sequence, as well as the same four key terms not presented in the same sequence, and

(3) both describe the remnant of Judah as benefiting from Yahweh's favor and the destruction of enemies, although in 2:1-7 the enemies are external (the Philistines) and in 3:1-20 they are internal ("your proudly exultant ones"). The two sections of text do indeed have these things in common, but they also have some other important features that go altogether unnoticed in drawing such a correspondence.

For example, the commands in 3:8 and 3:14 seem to mark major turning points in the sense that they emphatically introduce some new element into the discourse. They do not figure at all in Ball's analysis of 3:1-20 because there is nothing that particularly corresponds with them in 2:5-7. They do, however, correspond with commands at other turning points such as 2:1-3, 1:7, and 1:11. Might not the connection between all these commands be stronger than the connections noted by Ball between the parts of 2:1-7 and parts of the rest of the book, so that they are finally more determinative for its overall structure? There is obviously some kind of connection between the "woe" in 2:5 and the "woe" in 3:1, but why does such repetition necessarily indicate the start of two corresponding units? Could it not be that they, as well as the other patterns noted by Ball, might rather indicate subdivisions within units defined on some other basis — units perhaps initiated by the very commands that Ball's analysis does not regard as important factors in the book's overall composition? Any literary text is likely to show many striking features and patterns of language. Which of these are more determinative for its structure on the whole and what makes them so? Ball's analysis does not really reckon with this issue (nor does Lohfink in his even less substantiated claim that dominant themes recur so as to form a palindrome in each of the book's three sections [pp. 114-17]).

In attempting a synchronic analysis of the book as a whole, I also take a basically rhetorical approach. This approach differs from Ball's, however, in two major respects. First, it defines rhetoric more comprehensively as the adept use of conventions of discourse, rather than as stylistic embellishment. Second, it therefore uses a particular criterion to distinguish those features and patterns of language that are especially determinative for the overall structure from those that are less so, namely, the criterion of whether specific features and patterns of language are characteristic of any particular conventions of discourse. The kind of rhetorical analysis pursued in this study thus enters the domain of form criticism by raising the question of the genres evident in the text. The approach taken here does not, however, move immediately to the diachronic question of the text's redaction history, as form criticism sometimes has done. I first attempt to clarify the literary genres used in the text's final form, and only then do I go on to ask whether this form-critical analysis provides any basis for supposing that the text may have existed in any earlier versions and any basis for describing the forms that these earlier versions may have taken. Although my conclusions in this study differ somewhat from those of Sweeney, particularly with regard to the overall organization of 2:1–3:20, my approach is methodologically similar to his.

The superscription (1:1) identifies this book as a revelation received from Yahweh by a prophet named Zephaniah, who lived in the reign of Josiah, king of Judah (i.e., about the second half of the seventh century BCE). It does not identify the prophet as the author of the book, nor does it present the book as a document whose composition was contemporaneous with the prophetic activity of Zephaniah. On the contrary, the book presents the revelation to Zephaniah retrospectively, from the standpoint of an unidentified author for whom "the days of Josiah" are at least to some extent past history. The book thus purports to be written by someone other than Zephaniah sometime after the reign of Josiah, but to convey the message revealed to Zephaniah during that time. The superscription's retrospective viewpoint raises a number of historical questions: Was there really a prophet named Zephaniah who was active during the reign of Josiah? If so, how long did it take for someone else to write the book that claims to record his message? How could such an author know anything about revelations received by Zephaniah in an earlier time, and how accurate could the available record be? What was the nature of the author's interest in past prophecies, and how does this inform the composition of the book? Such questions can be addressed only to the extent that the text itself, in its final form, affords a basis on which to do so (→ Genre, Setting).

The first main section of the book (1:2-18) begins by announcing that Yahweh will sweep away all living things on earth and so remove corruption from the cult of Jerusalem (1:2-6). It then urges the addressees to expect such a disaster because their leaders and various sectors of their society have accepted false beliefs and followed foreign practices (1:7-18). As a consequence of their observing a "day of Yahweh," whether it be sacrificial feast (1:7-10) or communal complaint (1:11-18), there will come a "Day of Yahweh." All manner of cultic devotions to Yahweh thus become signs pointing to a time when he will deepen their foreign entanglements (1:8b) and their closely interrelated domestic socioeconomic problems (1:11b) into a disaster of cosmic proportions (1:10, 13-18).

Next the addressees are urged to return to Yahweh before this disaster is fully realized and humbly to seek to understand what he is doing, so that in meeting their doom they might not be wholly destroyed (2:1-3). Beyond the catastrophe there lies the hope of a new future for those who perceive the nature of Yahweh's involvement in the historical process (2:4–3:13). As he destroys the present world order and re-creates a new one (2:7–3:10), Yahweh is eliminating those regimes that threaten the security of his people in their land, both regional rivals (2:4-11) and distant imperial powers (2:12-15), thus assuring a place for a remnant of his people (2:7, 9b). Because Judah has had a long history of ignoring Yahweh's correctives and failing to perceive the purposes of Yahweh in the rise and fall of nations (3:1-7), Judah will share the same fate as its foes. The people are nevertheless urged to await the Day of Yahweh in hope (3:8a) because the disintegration of the present world order offers all humanity the opportunity to make a new beginning (3:8b-9). In this context of universal renewal the repentant remnant of Yahweh's people is also offered the opportunity of becoming a new Israel, whose corporate existence is characterized by purity in worship, humility toward Yahweh, simplicity of life, honesty in conduct, and safety from enemies (3:11-13).

Finally, the addressees are urged to be glad even now about such future

170

prospects (3:14) because Yahweh has already begun to transform both the world order and the mode of his people's existence within it. He has already taken measures, on the foreign as well as the domestic scene, that portend the completion of this process. Because of what has already happened, both externally with regard to Judah's enemies (3:15a) and internally with regard to Judah's cultic institutions (3:18), they can trust that Yahweh's promise to restore a remnant of his people (3:19a, 20), in the context of restoring all humanity (3:19b), will be victoriously fulfilled (3:16-17).

Genre

The superscription (1:1) establishes a distinction between the retrospective standpoint from which the book presents the prophecy of Zephaniah and the time in which the prophet is supposed to have received his revelation. Throughout the rest of the book (1:2–3:20) this revelation is nevertheless presented in accord with the conventions of direct address customarily used in prophetic public speaking. The book thus consistently addresses its readers in much the same way that a prophet would have addressed a live audience of hearers. In assessing the genre of the book as a whole, one must give due consideration to both fundamental aspects of its overall structure: Its author assumes an explicitly retrospective stance toward the prophecies of Zephaniah, and yet the author also addresses these prophecies to his readers as if they were hearing them firsthand.

Ben Zvi characterizes the author in a way that emphasizes the former aspect at the expense of the latter. He presupposes that the author's assumption of a historiographer's role precludes his also playing a prophetic role: "The author does not claim to be a prophet. He or she wrote a book about the word of YHWH that came to a prophet in the past, and writing a book about the prophecies putatively delivered by a prophet at a certain time in the past is clearly a different activity than prophesying" (p. 349). Such a sharp distinction between prophecy and historiography is not warranted. For example, historiographical narratives can also be prophetic (e.g., Haggai; → prophetic history). In this particular case the dual nature of the text is evident from the double function served by the superscription (1:1) in relation to the main body (1:2–3:20).

On the one hand, the superscription provides an introductory summary of information explicitly indicated by the oracle formulas in 1:2-3, 1:10, 2:9, and 3:8, and by the speech report formula with which the book concludes. That is, it summarily indicates that Zephaniah once spoke various oracles "in the days of Josiah," oracles that claimed to address his contemporaries with revelations from Yahweh concerning their destiny. On the other hand, the superscription also labels the entire document produced by the author as "the word of Yahweh," a single revelation expressed in the present text's representation of Zephaniah's oracles. It thus also expresses the author's own claim to have discerned in his study of Zephaniah's oracles a revelation now addressed to the readers of this book, a revelation that similarly concerns their destiny. The superscription characterizes not only Zephaniah as a prophet who received an authentic revelation for the people of his own time, but also the author as one who has retrospectively recognized Zephaniah's authenticity and who has therefore put Zephaniah's prophecies into a particular form so that readers of a later time can see how this revelation also applies to them.

The superscription thus implies that the author has a prophetic capacity, deriving from both his study of the traditions relating to Zephaniah and his own creativity, through which "the word of Yahweh" reaches the readers of this text. By addressing his readers with the same forms of direct address that Zephaniah himself might well have used in speaking to his contemporaries, the author joins his voice with the voice of Zephaniah and asserts that he is reiterating basically the same prophetic message that Zephaniah first articulated "in the days of Josiah." The text is thus not just a transcript of oracles from a particular time in the past. It is also a means of divinatory communication regarding Yahweh's involvement in the later time of the author and his readers, whether they come from his own or some future generation. Its scribal composer is likewise not just an archivist but also an author who casts the received traditions concerning Zephaniah into a new form, thus aspiring to play much the same kind of prophetic role vis-à-vis his readers that Zephaniah is supposed to have played vis-à-vis his hearers.

Even though the author assumes a retrospective stance with regard to the prophetic activity of Zephaniah, he views his own historical horizon as converging with the future proclaimed by the prophet. In other words the author identifies himself as someone who comes after Zephaniah, someone who reiterates the same message to a later generation, someone who reaffirms that Zephaniah's prophecies have begun to be fulfilled in the intervening course of events, and someone who is still living within the process of those prophecies finally coming to complete fulfillment.

The book was initially aimed at readers of the author's own generation, to persuade them to see themselves at the same point along this historical continuum. It is addressed primarily to the people of Yahweh, but its message concerns all peoples alike. The message thus also pertains to any Gentiles of the author's day and time who might recognize Yahweh's universality and thus be open to such persuasion. The book urges its addressees to share its perception of the current world situation, a perception that the author purports to have appropriated from an earlier prophet. Through this document the author intends his readers to discern and confirm for themselves, in the unfolding course of events, the same signs of Yahweh's involvement and overall purpose first discerned by Zephaniah.

Although the book was initially aimed at the author's generation, it was not intended only for readers of the author's own time. The book is designed to teach a lesson to readers of any time, and it is therefore cast largely in the form of exhortations (1:7–3:20) designed to persuade readers that the initially announced punishment of Yahweh (1:2-6) serves a basically educational purpose that is relevant both to its own time and to other times.

Even as Yahweh makes his people face the ruinous consequences of their sins, he also goes to extreme lengths to get them to understand what this shows about his more basically favorable intentions toward them, and to get them to behave in a way that makes for their eventual well-being. The book's own term for such an experience is *mûsār* (3:2a, 7a; *RSV* "correction"). The word refers to a punishment applied when a lesson has not been learned, in hopes that the lesson will finally be taken to heart (e.g., Prov 15:10; 22:15). When *mûsār* is used in connection with prophecy, it can refer to both a prophet's attempts to instruct the people concerning Yahweh's will (e.g., Jer 35:13; 32:33) and a prophetically interpreted punishment brought on the people by Yahweh in hopes that they can be reeducated for their own good (e.g., Jer 2:30; 30:14; Ezek 5:15; Hos 5:2; cf. Hos 10:10). In addition, and above all, *mûsār* refers to the process of reforming instruction that extends from generation to generation, from parent to child and from teacher to disciple (e.g., Prov 1:8a; 4:1a).

By virtue of the book's predominantly parenetic form, Zephaniah is characterized as a prophet of Yahweh's *mûsār* for his own time, and the book also shows itself to be conceived as a text performing the same function for the next generation. The text thus establishes a paradigm for further extending the same educational process from generation to generation. Later readers, whose historical horizon is no longer delimited by the outcome of events that happened in "the days of Josiah," are invited to imagine their world situation in terms of any typological correspondence it may have with the world situation described in the book and to ask whether a similar pattern of divine involvement might not be evident in current events. The author's retrospective presentation of Zephaniah's prophecies, from which standpoint they appear to have been partly fulfilled, serves as a basis on which readers of a later age may also find their world to be illumined and thus gain prophetic insight concerning divine initiatives that are coming to fulfillment in their own day and time.

Sweeney has suggested that Zephaniah belongs to the genre of (→) prophetic exhortation (pp. 406-8). This term aptly describes much of the book's main body (1:2–3:20), but it does not adequately describe the nature of the text as a whole. More specifically, it captures little of the relationship between the superscription (1:1) and the main body and does not reckon with the fact that the exhortation proper (1:7–3:20) is predicated on a (→) prophecy of punishment (1:2-6). There is no well-established term for this sort of text, which belongs to prophecy because it is designed to be revelatory, as well as to wisdom because it is also designed to be didactic and historiographical. I here propose that this text be provisionally classified as a PROPHETIC INSTRUCTION to indicate that it represents a scribal author's representation of an earlier prophet's revelation, expressed in an oracular form for the theological reeducation of its addressees (cf. M. A. Sweeney, "The Book of Isaiah as Prophetic Torah," in *New Visions of Isaiah* [ed. R. F. Melugin and M. A. Sweeney; JSOTSup 214; Sheffield: Sheffield Academic Press, 1996] 50-67).

Setting

The primary concern here is with the setting in which the final form of the book was produced, but since the final form claims to derive from a revelation received by an earlier prophet, any determination of the setting necessarily entails a consideration of the relationship between the present text and any previous prophetic activity on which it may be based. From the foregoing observations regarding the author's role, it is evident that documents like this one would have been written by scribes who did not regard themselves as merely curators of transcribed oracles and historians of Israel's prophets, though their role included both of these functions. These scribes also saw themselves as making a creative contribution to the transmission of prophetic traditions, a contribution that was prophetic in its own right. If the book of Zephaniah was produced in the context of such a prophetically inspired scribal group, it is relevant to ask whether parts of the text embodying their contribution might be distinguished from parts of the text embodying older traditions associated with Zephaniah himself. If so, the authenticity of the older traditions might be independently assessed, and any significant differences between their express concerns and those of their later scribal redactors might also be clarified.

The text of Zephaniah has been subjected to numerous studies attempting to winnow the wheat of the prophet's original sayings from the chaff of later additions. In order to make such a distinction the text has typically been divided into segments, largely on the basis of thematic distinctions (e.g., Langohr, "Le livre," 26-27; idem, "Rédaction," 51; Krinetzki, 1-222; Edler, 1-110; Seybold, 13-20). Pericopes dealing with punishment are thus separated from those dealing with salvation, pericopes whose scope is universal are separated from those whose scope is more particularistic, pericopes dealing with foreign nations are separated from those dealing with Judah, pericopes dealing specifically with the Day of Yahweh are separated from those that describe punishment in other terms, etc. The resulting segments are then dated, some to Zephaniah's time because of their emphasis on themes that are supposedly more germane to the latter half of the seventh century, and others to exilic or postexilic times because of their emphasis on themes that are supposedly more germane to these periods. Finally, theories are developed about the stages in which the various textual pieces were first assembled, supplemented with additional pieces, and then reassembled to produce the present text.

Much form-critical work on Zephaniah has proceeded from this kind of historical criticism, taking only the pericopes judged to be the prophet's original sayings as the basic units for form-critical analysis (e.g., Langohr, "Rédaction," 64-67; Krinetzki, 1-222; Edler, 111-204; Seybold, 21-62). This interdependence of methods assumes not only that earlier segments of the text can be separated from later segments on the basis of thematic contrasts, but also that the earlier segments exhibit the marks of oral prophetic speech in its purest forms, and that the later additions exhibit either the degeneration or the artificial elaboration of these forms in the process of scribal redaction.

When Zephaniah is initially approached in terms of its final compositional form (→ Structure), asking whether the present text actually affords any basis on which to suppose that it ever existed in any earlier versions and then asking whether it also affords any basis on which to reconstruct the forms that such earlier versions might have taken, it becomes difficult to justify this way of doing historical and form-critical analysis. First, it is apparent that the final compositional form often serves precisely to integrate the kinds of the-

174

matic contrasts that historical criticism has usually attempted to dissociate. It is therefore difficult to treat such contrasts as signs of seams joining textual sources from different periods. Moreover, it is also apparent that the book as a whole is no less dependent than its individual units on forms that are typical of oral prophetic speech. Although the book is obviously a written document, its main body (1:2–3:20) consistently employs the rhetoric of a prophet addressing a live audience. The possibility of separating the words originally spoken by Zephaniah from subsequent redactional material is thus highly doubtful. Ben Zvi has reached a similar conclusion but on a different basis (pp. 291-95, 357-58), and similar doubts have also been expressed by others whose approaches have led them to grasp something of the overall compositional form, e.g., Keller (p. 180) and Kapelrud (pp. 13-40).

In this regard it should also be noted that more than a century of effort has not led to any substantial agreement concerning the original words of Zephaniah versus secondary additions (see Edler's convenient tabular survey of the widely varying opinions, pp. 261-63). Nor do the various theories concerning the stages of the redactional process converge to any significant extent (cf., e.g., Krinetzki, 223-38; Langohr, "Rédaction," 51-63; Renaud, 24-33). In view of how difficult it has proved to distinguish redactional material from original prophecies, some scholars have alternatively supposed that the book simply reports what Zephaniah said without much, if any, secondary reworking (e.g., Keller, 180; Kapelrud, 13-40; Watts, 155; Bartel, 321-26; cf. Ball, *Rhetorical Study,* 285-87). If the author were merely a transcriber of Zephaniah's words, however, there would be no need for the self-consciously retrospective viewpoint created by the superscription (→ Genre; cf. Ben Zvi, 11-12).

The originality of the prophet, the creativity of the author, and the temporal distance between them are all factors to reckon with. One must therefore approach the book as a text that purports to have been produced over a span of time, through a process that began with Zephaniah's prophesying, continued with the preservation of traditions concerning his prophecies, and culminated in the work of the author who composed the text's final form. There is no explicit information with regard to whether the process also involved other persons along the way, although this is certainly possible, and there is no basis on which to distinguish the respective contributions made by the various participants in this process. In this case historical criticism cannot separate earlier from later sources, but must rather attempt to determine the extent of the time span over which the whole text could have come into being, asking whether it is likely that the book was composed in the way that its superscription implies (i.e., from received traditions regarding the prophecies of Zephaniah rather than from scratch). The question of setting thus becomes specifically defined in terms of the social context from which such productivity could have emerged during this particular period of time.

The book as a whole envisions a historical process of Yahweh's punishment and — emerging from within this process of punishment and extending beyond it — an interpenetrating process of Yahweh's salvation (cf. Martin, "Première Partie," 5-6). The process of punishment encompasses the disintegration of the whole world order on which earthly life depends, but it focuses on the elimination of alien cults from the royal sanctuary in Jerusalem and on Yahweh's consequent annihilation of the religious and political leaders who have imposed on Judah this worship of foreign gods (3:3-4, 11b). The process of salvation begins in the midst of this crisis when some of Yahweh's people respond to his call and return to him, in order to learn what he is teaching them through Judah's devastation. It extends to include the regathering of the scattered remnant of Yahweh's people into a new Israel that will occupy the whole region in which they once lived but within a transformed order of earthly existence that is no longer characterized by the invidious national and cultural differences of the past.

A particular development is singled out as an act of Yahweh that is especially significant in terms of both the process of punishment and the process of salvation, signaling that each has reached a critical stage. This development is initially described as an excommunicatory purge of foreign elements from the cult of Jerusalem, but it soon becomes evident that this purge extends to include the elimination of all leaders in politics or commerce who are directly or indirectly responsible for the predominance of such foreign influences. In 1:2-18 this development is prospectively described as part of Yahweh's impending punishment (1:4b-6). In 2:1–3:13 the same development is again prospectively described (3:3-4, 11b), but as part of Yahweh's impending transformation of Judah and the whole world order, in which the people are urged to participate by returning to faithfulness in Yahweh alone. In 3:14-20 this event is retrospectively described as a past development, indicating that this transformation is already underway and that it therefore promises to reach completion.

At the conclusion of the book Judah has experienced something of the promised purge of the cult (3:18; → 3:14-20, Text), which in view of the preceding description has a double significance. On the one hand it signals the beginning of a worldwide political and socioeconomic crisis in which Judah will undergo deprivation and eventually be reduced to a scattered remnant. On the other hand it signals the beginning of a cosmic transformation in which this scattered remnant will be restored to its place in a new kind of world, where they will have no national enemies and thus be able to coexist prosperously and peacefully with other peoples of the earth.

The cultic purge that signals this cosmic revolution is strikingly similar to the purge of the Jerusalem temple cult instigated ca. 621 BCE by King Josiah (2 Kgs 23:4-14), in whose reign the superscription (1:1) locates the prophetic activity of Zephaniah. The development that the book describes as a cosmic turning point is thus probably to be identified with the Deuteronomic reform of Josiah, so that the main sections of the text have an implied narrative sequence in relation to this historical event. From the standpoint of the book's first section (1:2-18) the reform is yet to happen. From the standpoint of the book's second section (2:1–3:14) the reform has still not happened, but some of the larger ripple effects that are supposed to form its context have become evident. In particular it appears that Assyria is about to go the way of Ethiopia (→ 2:12-15). From the standpoint of the book's third section (3:14-20) something along the lines of the promised reform has happened (3:18; → 3:13-20, Text), which warrants the eventual fulfillment of all that has been prophesied.

Viewed from the shifting perspective of the book as a whole, Josiah's reform has such mixed consequences because of Judah's long entanglement in foreign alliances. Although the expulsion of foreign gods and their functionaries may have indicated a measure of freedom, made possible by the weakening of Assyrian hegemony, it could hardly extricate Judah from the dynamics of the crumbling world order on which such alliances had long been based. Although the reform was a sign of repentance, it could not avert Judah's being dragged down in the international chaos that would inevitably follow Assyria's downfall. The reform had positive significance not because it could avert Judah's destruction, but because it embodied a religious attitude that could provide a basis for the future continuing existence of Yahweh's people in some radically redefined form. The ideal of repentance, as a process of turning to Yahweh for reeducation in the course of defeat, would serve to establish their identity under the conditions of the new world order that he was in the process of bringing about. Seen in a cosmic context Josiah's purge had mythic connotations. It signaled a massive attempt on Yahweh's part to reverse the kind of world order that had existed since Babel, characterized by conflict and confusion (→ 2:1–3:13, Structure). It began an attempt on Yahweh's part to bring about the same kind of ideal world order that he had originally intended to realize by means of the Flood (→ 1:2-18, Structure).

It is likely that the formation of this book had its impetus in prophecies of Zephaniah concerning the significance of Josiah's Deuteronomic reform. Although it is not possible to identify with certainty any of Zephaniah's original sayings, it is probable that there were such sayings, and that traditions regarding them were preserved and transmitted (cf. Ben Zvi, 291-95, 357-58). The rhetorical forcefulness of the text depends on its being recognized as the record of a prophetic figure whose perceptions were known to have stood the test of time. Otherwise there would have been no basis for the kind of scribal activity that produced the book, and no basis for its having been received as authoritative. The production of the book can thus be described in terms of a time span beginning in the last quarter of the seventh century.

There is no way to determine whether the book's view of the Deuteronomic reform, as an event signaling both the inevitability of dispersion and the hope of restoration, is rooted in the traditions about Zephaniah on which the book is based, or whether it resulted from subsequent scribal reinterpretation of those traditions. Several scholars have argued that there are no a priori reasons why the prophet could have interpreted the Deuteronomic reform in such a fashion during the reign of Josiah (cf., e.g., Scharbert, 239-49; Haak, "Zephaniah in Seventh-Century Judah"; idem, "Zephaniah's Oracles against the Nations"; Sweeney, 404-6). We cannot tell whether Zephaniah actually did so, however, since we cannot tell which if any particular parts of the extant text have come directly from the prophet himself.

The book's view of Judah, as a people destined for both dispersion and restoration, could of course have been retrojected into the text as a *vaticinium post eventu* by an exilic or even a postexilic redactor (cf. Ben Zvi, 347-53). Nothing in the text itself, however, requires its being given an exilic or postexilic date. Exile and restoration need not have already happened in order for such events to be imagined as real future possibilities. As for exile, the notion that the southern kingdom would one day suffer the same fate as the northern kingdom, and for much the same reasons, was commonplace. As for restoration, the decline of Assyria created a political situation in which the small states of the Levant could plausibly entertain such nationalistic aspirations in anticipation of a new world order.

It is possible that the book of Zephaniah "prophesies" exile and/or restoration ex post facto, but it is equally possible that the book anticipates both developments from a late preexilic perspective (cf. the range of opinions described by Williams, 77-86). It is therefore difficult to determine the end of the time span over which the book was produced. The final redaction could have been as early as the beginning of the sixth century. In this case the book would have helped its initial readers to understand the tragic events in which they were being caught up as a transformative and hence ultimately hopeful process. The final redaction could also have been much later, well into the postexilic period. In this case the book would have invited its initial readers to imagine themselves in the crisis situation of the late seventh and early sixth centuries, and thereby come to understand their living in a restored Judah as the still evolving outcome of the Deuteronomic reform. If the book were completed prior to the exile, so that it originally served the former function, it would have subsequently assumed the latter function in the course of the Second Temple period.

The overall arrangement of the book of Zephaniah reflects scribal study of the traditions associated with the prophet, in whatever form they may have first been recorded, in order to see whether Zephaniah's perception of the reform's portentous significance was borne out as Judah suffered through the turmoil surrounding and following the downfall of Assyria. Such study would have been undertaken by members of mantic scribal groups, whose existence in Judah is attested from at least as early as the seventh century (M. H. Floyd, "Prophecy and Writing in Habakkuk 2,1-5," *ZAW* 105 [1993] 477-80; D. W. Jamieson-Drake, *Scribes and Schools in Monarchic Judah* [JSOTSup 109; SWBA 9; Sheffield: Almond Press, 1991] 136-59).

Ben Zvi suggests that texts like the book of Zephaniah were produced in order for their scribal authors to gain a monopoly on authentic revelation, undercutting the authority of prophets who still claimed to know the revelation of Yahweh from immediate experience rather than textual interpretation. The production of prophetic writings might indeed make such a power play possible, but this social function is not necessarily inherent in the phenomenon of written prophecy itself. Mantic writing could also have been motivated by the scribes' recognition that, in their desire to know divine wisdom, they had something in common with prophets who received revelations and spoke oracles. The words of such prophets were therefore worthy of being recorded and studied in order to learn from them how to recognize patterns of divine activity (Floyd, "Prophecy and Writing," 480). In this particular case the common interest is conceived in terms of *mûsār* (*RSV* "correction"; 3:2, 7). Zephaniah is characterized as a prophet concerned with this aspect of divine wisdom, which was also a typical concern of scribes (→ Genre). There is no evidence that the

178

author of Zephaniah aims to disqualify prophetic revelation through immediate experience, although in the context of a closed canon Zephaniah could join other prophetic texts in having this effect.

In sum, the book of Zephaniah appears to have been composed in a school of mantic wisdom. In this social context scribes recorded, studied, and reflected on traditions associated with the late-seventh-century prophet Zephaniah in light of later developments. The book expresses an anonymous scribal author's interpretation of the historical process initiated by the Josianic reform, informed by Zephaniah's leading ideas as well as the subsequent scribal study of those ideas. The text is designed so that readers locate themselves at a particular point in this historical process, in the immediate aftermath of the reform around the beginning of the sixth century. From this vantage point readers are invited to contemplate both the inevitability of exile and the promise of restoration. This may be a reflection of the author's own historical location, but it may also be the fictive creation of an exilic or postexilic author.

Intention

The book reflects its anonymous scribal author's conviction that the unfolding course of events had shown Zephaniah's interpretation of Josiah's reform to be more or less on target. Informed by Zephaniah's insights, this event could be retrospectively viewed as the beginning of a worldwide upheaval through which Yahweh would destroy both Judah and the age-old mode of national existence that made violence and injustice inevitable. In the process Yahweh would also create a whole new mode of earthly existence in which a transformed Israel could live in peace and righteousness. Such an authentication of Zephaniah's perceptions depends, in turn, on the author's own prophetic perception of Yahweh's continuing involvement in human affairs. The text is designed so that its initial readers would be encouraged to confirm the author's view through their own experience of recent developments, and subsequent readers would be encouraged to see if they could discern any similar patterns of divine activity in the events of their day.

Modern readers who aspire to the kind of interpretation invited by the text might be led to ask, for example, whether some recent event that has been catastrophic for the religious establishment might also portend the potentially fruitful disintegration of the current world order. In the context of such a crisis might God not be creating the possibility of a new kind of identity for his people as he also creates a new and better kind of world for all people to live in?

Bibliography

A. Bartel, "The Historical Background to the Prophecies of Zephaniah 1–2" [in Hebrew with English summary], *BetM* 50 (1972) 320-26; R. Haak, "Zephaniah in Seventh-Century Judah," unpublished paper read at the Albright Institute for Archeological Research, Jerusalem, March 18, 1993; idem, "Zephaniah's Oracles against the Nations," unpublished paper read at the Chicago Society for Biblical Research, Feb. 2, 1992; G. Langohr, "Le livre de Sophonie et la critique d'authenticité," *ETL* 52 (1976) 1-27; J. Scharbert, "Zefanja und die Reform des Joschija," in *Künder des Wortes* (*Fest.* J. Schreiner; ed. L. Ruppert; Würzburg: Echter, 1982) 237-53; D. L. Williams, "The Date of Zephaniah," *JBL* 82 (1963) 77-88.

Chapter 2

THE SUPERSCRIPTION (1:1)

Structure

Genre

This is a PROPHETIC SUPERSCRIPTION of the type that is also common to the books of Hosea, Micah, and Joel, characterized by the use of the PROPHETIC WORD FORMULA ("the word of Yahweh that came to *x*") in its title. Other prophetic books begin with titles consisting of some term for prophetic revelation in a construct relation with the name of the prophet, such as "the words of *(dibrê) x,*" or "the vision of *(ḥăzôn) x,*" or "the *maśśā'* (*RSV* "oracle") of *x*." In the former case there is relatively more emphasis on asserting the divine origin of the revelation than on naming the prophetic intermediary, although these two aspects of the matter are necessarily inseparable since there is no divine revelation without a human intermediary (Wolff, *Hosea,* 4).

Setting

Such superscriptions were used by scribal groups who made it their business to preserve and study records of prophecy. The emphasis of the title shows some concern with an issue that was important in Deuteronomic circles: whether prophets who spoke in the name of Yahweh were really representatives of his will (Deut 13:1-5; 18:15-22). The form of 1:1 may thus reflect an origin in such circles, which were apparently active from the late preexilic on into the postexilic period (E. W. Nicholson, *Deuteronomy and Tradition* [Philadelphia: Fortress, 1967] 83-118).

Intention

The structure of 1:1 shows an aim not only to title the book so as to emphasize its truly divine and authentically Yahwistic origin, but also to classify the prophet and his work in terms of their historical period, "in the days of Josiah," i.e., the late seventh century. The superscription also indicates the self-conception of the author as one who has the prophetic capacity of testing an earlier prophet's insights (→ Book as a Whole, Structure).

The inclusion of the four previous generations in Zephaniah's genealogy emphasizes his descent to an extent that is unparalleled in any other prophetic superscription. Some have supposed that this Zephaniah is to be identified with one of the other biblical persons with the same name (e.g., 2 Kgs 25:18; Zech 6:10; 1 Chr 6:36). Such suppositions are possible but difficult to substantiate (Williams, 85-88). It has been more specifically debated whether the Hezekiah that heads Zephaniah's four-generation genealogy was the eighth-century Judahite king of the same name. If so, the genealogy would serve to link Zephaniah back with the religious reforms that Hezekiah had supposedly attempted (2 Kgs 18:1-8) — the same sort of reforms that King Josiah carried out in Zephaniah's own day, and which Deuteronomistic circles continued to advocate on into the postexilic period (Heller). Royal ancestry would be consonant with the subsequent focus on the royal court and household (1:8aα).

It has also been debated whether the designation of Zephaniah's father as *kûšî* (*RSV* "Cushi") indicates that the prophet was of African descent (Rice; Anderson, 54-55; Bennett, 670-72). This word is an ethnic term that means literally "a Cushite," but it could also serve as a proper name or nickname for an Israelite that presumably had a Cushite ancestry (cf. Jer 36:14; Ps 7:1 [*RSV* superscription]). If so, this would be consonant with the pivotal historical role that is subsequently assigned to Yahweh's overthrow of the Cushites in the main body of the book (Zeph 2:12; *RSV* "Ethiopians"; → 2:12-15, Structure) and also consonant with the subsequent designation of "the rivers of Cush" (3:10; *RSV* "the rivers of Ethiopia") as the southernmost extent of the cosmic context in which Yahweh acts (→ 2:1–3:13, Structure).

In any case, the genealogy functions in connection with the historical periodization to show that Zephaniah's prophecies regarding events of his own day should be seen not only from the retrospective standpoint of the author of the book but also in light of antecedent events that happened generations earlier.

Bibliography

R. W. Anderson Jr., "Zephaniah ben Cushi and Cush of Benjamin: Traces of Cushite Presence in Syria-Palestine," in *The Pitcher Is Broken* (*Fest.* G. W. Ahlström; ed. S. W. Holloway and L. K. Handy; JSOTSup 190; Sheffield: Sheffield Academic Press, 1995) 45-70; J. Heller, "Zephanjas Ahnenreihe (Eine redaktionsgeschichtliche Bemerkung zu Zeph. 1:1)," *VT* 21 (1971) 102-4; G. Rice, "The African Roots of the Prophet Zephaniah," *JRT* 36 [1979] 21-31; G. Tucker, "Prophetic Superscriptions and the Growth of a Canon," in *Canon and Authority* (ed. G. W. Coats and B. O. Long; Philadelphia: Fortress, 1977) 56-70; D. L. Williams, "The Date of Zephaniah," *JBL* 82 (1963) 76-88; H. W. Wolff, *Hosea* (tr. G. Stansell; Hermeneia; Philadelphia: Fortress, 1974).

Chapter 3

THE FIRST MAJOR SECTION OF THE BOOK (1:2-18) AND ITS INDIVIDUAL UNITS

ALL THE EARTH WILL BE PUNISHED ON THE DAY OF YAHWEH, 1:2-18

Structure

Commentators differ on the delimitation of this section and its constituent units, as well as the overall organization. Particularly when the dominant concern has been to extricate Zephaniah's own words from later additions, data relevant to the overall compositional structure have sometimes been relegated to a secondary status and hence overlooked. Even so, recent commentators with widely diverging presuppositions about the nature and extent of the prophet's original contribution have tended to recognize that some well-defined organizational principle is at work here (compare, e.g., Keller, 187-96; Renaud, 4-6; Elliger, 58-67; and Kapelrud, 21-31). The differences in their attempts to describe this principle have centered on three closely interrelated questions: (1) how the announcement of punishment in vv. 2-6 is connected with the following material on the Day of Yahweh, (2) how vv. 7-18 are structured, and (3) whether 2:1-3 should be regarded as the conclusion of 1:2-18 or the beginning of a new section.

The answers to these questions depend largely on the analysis of 1:7-18. Many scholars take the announcement of the nearness of the Day of Yahweh in v. 7 and its reiteration in v. 14 to indicate a fundamental division between vv. 7-13 and vv. 14-18 (e.g., Alonso Schökel and Sicre Diaz, 1116; Nel, 163-66; Roberts, 174-85; Sweeney, 395-96), assuming that vv. 7-18 are basically an announcement of the Day of Yahweh. Against this assumption it is to be noted that, although the Day of Yahweh theme is obviously prominent in this passage, the primary function of vv. 7-18 is not to announce or even describe the day. This theme is rather a secondary element that is completely subordinate to the hortatory elements of the text. The initial announcement of the nearness of the Day of Yahweh (v. 7b) is subordinated by the conjunction $k\hat{\imath}$ ("for") to the preceding command in v. 7a, and thus forms part of its motivation. Adverbial phrases that locate actions "on that day," "at that time," etc. (vv. 8a, 9a, 10a, 12a, 18a) all modify imperfect or *waw*-consecutive perfect verbs narrating future events and are thus incorporated into the narratives (vv. 8-10, 12-18) that serve to extend the motivations (vv. 7b, 11b) of the commands in v. 7a and v. 11a. All references to the "day" in vv. 14-16, including the announcement of its nearness in v. 14a, the description of its "sound" in v. 14b, and the series of attributive statements in vv. 15-16, form an interlude in the narration of vv. 12-18. This interlude has a double function (→ 1:11-18, Structure). On the one hand it serves as a conclusion to the first segment of this narrative (vv. 12-16), in which the effects of Yahweh's punishment are described from a Judeocentric perspective. On the other hand, it serves to establish links with the preceding narrative in vv. 8-10, not only by reiterating the announcement that the Day of Yahweh is near (v. 14a; cf. v. 7bα) but also by providing a reprise description of its dread sounds (v. 14b; cf. v. 10). All references to the Day of Yahweh thus figure as subordinate elements in an essentially parenetical rhetorical pattern that is common to vv. 7-10 and vv. 11-18.

This pattern begins with directives that resemble forms of address associated with cultic observances (vv. 7a, 11a). Both of these commands are initially posed as if to invite the addressees to participate in customary observances with which they are familiar — in the first case a sacrificial celebration of Yahweh's presence and in the second case a solemn complaint about an economic crisis that threatens the community's well-being. Because of the way these invitations are subsequently developed, however, the addressees are further urged to see their participation in each of these observances as the beginning of a story that — because of the nature of Yahweh's involvement in the course of events — leads inevitably to a disastrous conclusion.

On the one hand, the theme of the Day of Yahweh gives some continuity to the development of this rhetorical pattern, since it applies both to the occasion in which the addressees are initially invited to participate and to the disastrous outcome of the narration that subsequently unfolds. On the other hand, the Day of Yahweh theme can apply to both situations only because it is capable of ironically shifting its meaning. It applies initially to both the sacrificial celebration and the solemn complaint, in the sense that both provide occasion for a day devoted to the worship of Yahweh. It also applies to the terrible consequences that follow from each of these observances, in the sense that Yahweh's activity becomes manifest in this turn of events. The rhetorical pattern in vv. 7-18 thus exploits an ambiguity in the phrase "Day of Yahweh" — a day devoted to the worship of Yahweh versus a time when Yahweh acts — as a means of urging the addressees to extend their recognition of Yahweh's presence in the cult to a realization of the destructive potential of his involvement in current events (Y. Hoffman, "The Day of the Lord as a Concept and a Term in the Prophetic Literature," *ZAW* 93 [1981] 37-50).

The relationship between vv. 2-6 and vv. 7-18 is both formal and conceptual. The punishment announced in vv. 2-6 is first described from a worldwide perspective (vv. 2-3) and then from the local perspective of Judah and Jerusalem (vv. 4-6). The exhortation that follows in vv. 7-18 is conversely first developed from the local perspective of Judah and Jerusalem (vv. 7-16) and then from a worldwide perspective (vv. 17-18). This formal correspondence is based on the mythic conceptualization of Jerusalem as the local earthly manifestation of the cosmic heavenly reality of Yahweh's reign (e.g., Pss 48, 87). Whatever happens to Jerusalem is thus a microcosmic indication of the macrocosmic state of affairs. Within this conceptual framework the function of vv. 7-18 vis-à-vis vv. 2-6 is to get the addressees to realize that the seeds of the impending disaster announced in vv. 2-6 are already sown in the current course of events.

Zeph 2:1-3 is an exhortation to repent that, though predicated on this realization, is motivated by the subsequent revelation of the possibility of a new beginning (→ 2:1–3:13). Thus although 1:2-18 leads up to and opens onto a new section in ch. 2, 2:1-3 is the beginning of this new section rather than the conclusion of 1:2-18 (Nel, 166-67; Ball, *Rhetorical Study*, 114; Sweeney, 397-98). The point of 1:2-18 is to realize what the nature of the present situation actually is. Ch. 2 begins to deal with what should then be done and also explains why (Keller, 197-99; Renaud, 4-6).

Genre

This unit consists basically of a prophecy of punishment (→ 1:2-6, Genre) that has been considerably extended by an exhortation (vv. 7-18). The exhortation elaborates on the initial announcement of what Yahweh's intends to do to persuade the addressees of its plausibility. The exhortation is largely an extension of the initial prophecy of punishment, in that it continues making the same kind of first person statements of what Yahweh intends to do (vv. 8aβ-9, 12, 17a). The exhortation elaborates on these oracular statements by combining them with third person statements describing the effects of Yahweh's actions (vv. 10, 13-16, 17b-18), organizing both kinds of statements in narrative sequences (vv. 8-10, 12-18), and using these narratives of future events to extend the motivations (vv. 7b, 11b) of the commands (vv. 7a, 11a) on which the exhortation is based. The exhortation (vv. 7-18) thus reinforces and further develops the prophecy of punishment (vv. 2-6) that it serves to extend, so that this section as a whole can also be defined as a PROPHECY OF PUNISHMENT.

It is not unusual for prophecies of punishment to include hortatory elements, such as the call to attention, "hear this word!" (e.g., Amos 4:1; Isa 1:10; Jer 2:4; Mic 3:9). The call to attention can be varied by combining it with other generic elements, like the dirge in Amos 5:1-2. Cultic directives, such as the (→) call to communal complaint, can likewise be used to introduce an announcement of punishment (e.g., Joel 1:2-14) or used within the announcement of punishment itself (e.g., Isa 14:31; 23:1-14; 32:11-14; Jer 6:26; 25:34; 49:3). This text is distinctive because its cultic directives (vv. 7a, 11a) are not incorporated into the announcement of punishment (vv. 2-6) in such ways. Rather, each command initially stands apart from any description of divine punishment as an invitation to an event that is assumed to evoke a more or less favorable response from the addressees. It is the subsequent narration that transforms their favorable response into a realization that divine punishment is the consequence of present conditions in which they are implicated.

Setting

As a speech addressed primarily to inhabitants of Jerusalem (v. 11a), this section reflects the convention of prophetic oratory before a public audience. From the few explicit descriptions of such speech making, it is evident that prophets sometimes took advantage of cultic assemblies at major sanctuaries to gain a forum for their words (e.g., Jeremiah at Jerusalem [Jer 26] and Amos at Bethel [Amos 7:10-17], the latter text suggesting that public speeches were made at Bethel [7:11], although it actually reports a prophecy that appears to have been addressed privately to an individual there).

Several features of this section suggest specifically that it reflects the convention of a prophet opportunistically addressing a group gathered in Jerusalem to take part in some cultic event. First, the whole form of this text reflects the mythic concept of Jerusalem as a microcosmic representation of a macrocosmic reality, a concept preeminently at home in the cult. Second, the prophetic exhortation is based on cultic forms of address, and its rhetorical pattern is characterized by the metaphorical expansion of concepts drawn from familiar cultic experiences to describe manifestations of divine activity transcending the cultic sphere.

Although this section reflects the practice of prophetic oratory on a cultic occasion, there is no way of telling whether it was actually spoken in such a setting, or whether the text is a literary adaptation of this oratorical convention (→ Book as a Whole, Setting).

Intention

This section informs readers who identify with its Judahite addressees that they are included in an impending world-shattering catastrophe. It attempts to persuade them that although this catastrophe lies in the future, it grows ineluctably out of mundane things that are already happening, such as their indifference to the corruption of their cultic practices and their business-as-usual attitude toward moral issues raised by their worsening economic situation. The terms in which this persuasion is cast show a concern to apply the conception of the world that is symbolized within the cult — where Yahweh is present as king — to the world as it is experienced socioeconomically.

Bibliography

H. Irsigler, *Gottesgericht und Jahwetag: Die Komposition Zef 1,1–2,3 untersucht auf der Grundlage der Literarkritik des Zefanjabuches* (ATSAT 3; St. Ottilien: Eos, 1977); P. J. Nel, "Structural and Conceptual Strategy in Zephaniah, Chapter 1," *JNSL* 15 (1989) 155-67.

YAHWEH'S PUNISHMENT OF ALL EARTHLY LIVING THINGS, 1:2-6

Structure

I. Announcement of punishment for everything on earth — 1:2-3
  A. Basic statement — 1:2
    1. Description of punishment — 1:2abα
      a. Yahweh's action: I will sweep away — 1:2aα
      b. Its objects: everything on earth — 1:2aβbα
    2. Oracle formula — 1:2bβ
  B. Elaboration — 1:3
    1. Redescription of punishment — 1:3abβ^1
      a. Its effects on all sentient beings — 1:3aα
        1) Described in terrestrial terms — 1:3aα^1
          a) Yahweh's action: I will sweep away . . .
          b) Its objects: humanity and other animals
        2) Described in extraterrestrial terms — 1:3aα^2
          a) Yahweh's action: I will sweep away . . .

b) Its objects
  (1) Birds of heaven
  (2) Fish of the sea

b. Its effects on humanity in particular	1:3aβbβ^1
1) Described in terms of one group	1:3aβ
a) Yahweh's action: I will overthrow . . .	1:3aβ^1
b) Its objects: the wicked	1:3aβ^2
2) Described in terms of all humanity	1:3bαβ^1
a) Yahweh's action: I will cut off . . .	1:3bα
b) Its objects: humanity	1:3bβ^1
2. Oracle formula	1:3bβ^2
II. Announcement of punishment for Judah and Jerusalem	1:4-6
A. Basic statement: description of punishment in terms of its effects on Yahweh's people as a whole	1:4a
1. Yahweh's action: I will stretch out my hand . . .	1:4aα^1
2. Its objects	1:4aα^{2}β
a. In general: Judah	1:4aα^2
b. In particular: all inhabitants of Jerusalem	1:4aβ
B. Elaboration: description of punishment in terms of how it affects particular groups	1:4b-6
1. Yahweh's action: I will cut off from this place . . .	1:4bα
2. Its objects	1:4bβ6
a. In particular	1:4bβ-5
1) Vestiges of the Baal cult	1:4bβ
2) Idolatrous priests	1:5a
3) Devotees of astral cults	1:5bα
4) Yahweh worshipers who also worship Milcom	1:5bβ
b. In general: those unfaithful to Yahweh	1:6
1) Positively described: those who have turned from Yahweh	1:6a
2) Negatively described: those who do not seek or inquire of Yahweh	1:6b

Although the structures of vv. 2-3 and vv. 4-6 are not parallel in every respect, they are similar enough to develop analogous lines of thought concerning Yahweh's actions on a worldwide scale and his treatment of Judah. Analogous lines of thought emerge from the way in which the text proceeds with its description of the objects of Yahweh's action. On a worldwide scale he will bring destruction on everything, but especially on earthly animal life and — because of the wicked — on humanity in particular. Similarly, on a local scale he will bring destruction on Judah as a whole, but particularly on the inhabitants of Jerusalem and — because of the openly apostate — on the unfaithful in their midst (Ball, *Rhetorical Study,* 45-62; Alonso Schökel and Sicre Diaz, 1114; Nel, 155-59). In both cases the infractions of some lead to disaster for all.

A conceptual basis for this line of thought is established by clear allusions in vv. 2-3 to Gen 1–11. The Flood Story, like Zeph 1:2-3, describes a scene from which all living things are eliminated from "the face of the earth" (Gen 6:7; 7:4; cf. 8:8), and both use the same term *'sp* in an unusual sense ("sweep away") to describe this elimination (Gen 8:21). Like the account of creation in Gen 2, Zeph 1:3 plays on the etymological similarity between the word for humanity *('ādām)* and the word for the earth *('ădāmâ)* from which humanity was made (Gen 2:7; cf. 3:17-19). With respect to the kinds of animal life, Gen 1 uses the same series as v. 3, but in reverse order (M. De Roche, "Zephaniah i 2-3: The 'Sweeping' of Creation," *VT* 30 [1980] 104-9).

The structure of v. 3 interrelates these allusions to various aspects of Gen 1–11 in a particular way. In v. 3 the plot of the Creation Story is, in effect, reversed. This verse forms an elaboration on a counterstatement of the divine promise with which the Flood Story concludes (i.e., v. 2; cf. Gen 8:21b-22; 9:11). This elaboration then goes on to specify the effect of the reversal in terms of its impact on the wicked. The allusions thus conform to an antitype of the entire primeval history, which turns both the plot and the conclusion of the creation and flood stories inside out (much as Paul's comparison of Adam and Christ [Rom 5:12-21] turns the story of the fall in Gen 3 inside out). Such allusive description recasts the role that human wickedness plays in the stability of the world.

The primeval history shows, among other things, that the order of creation is not fundamentally jeopardized by any divine reaction to the evil aspects of human nature. The point of the antitype is that the world can, however, be at least partly undone through a divine reaction to the failure of humanity to accept its collective responsibility for maintaining justice. The mythic allusions in this unit put its announcement of punishment under the rubric of "some are guilty, but all are responsible." Thus it is that some wicked persons can bring about the destruction of the underlying social and ecological relationships on which all sentient life depends. By analogy, some of Jerusalem's inhabitants who have been unfaithful can bring about the destruction of the underlying religious and socioeconomic relationships on which Judah's total existence depends (vv. 4-6).

Viewed as an antitype of the entire primeval history, the mythic allusions in vv. 2-3 might well connote the possibility of some survivors (Eaton, 139-40; Alonso Schökel and Sicre Diaz, 1114) — although these would certainly be, in contrast with Noah and his party, a rather unheroic lot. There is no explicit mention of survivors here, but the possibility of a "lowly remnant" appears in ch. 2. The mythic background created by v. 2 thus not only provides a conceptual basis for the kind of punishment that is described from vv. 2 to 6 through the rest of ch. 1. It also gives an introduction to further developments in ch. 2.

Although the analogous lines of thought in vv. 2-3 and vv. 4-6 depend on such a mythic conceptuality, and although the analogous relationship of vv. 2-3 and vv. 4-6 likewise reflects the mythic conception of Jerusalem as the microcosmic representation of the macrocosmic reality (→ 1:2-18, Structure), it does not follow that the disasters described in vv. 2-3 are just an overblown description of Judah's prospective misfortunes, in which they are exaggerated to cosmic proportions. An element of verisimilitude becomes evident in ch. 2, which contains prophecies of punishment addressed both to Judah's immediate neighbors and to the surrounding world powers, as well as recurrent references to cities that have been depopulated and settled areas that have reverted to open range land. The opening of ch. 1 thus has in view a veritable collapse of the world order as its ancient readers would have conceived such a crisis, involving a deterioration of international and social relationships as well as economic and ecological relationships. As part of this worldwide process, there is also a collapse of the state of Judah involving a deterioration of its religious and civic institutions as well as its social fabric.

Genre

This is a PROPHECY OF PUNISHMENT that shows the basic elements of this type of prophetic speech: an announcement of punishment that often includes a description of Yahweh's role and the results of his punitive actions, together with the reasons for his intervention that are often expressed in the form of accusations. Unlike many examples of this genre, this text incorporates the element of accusation and the element of the reasons for divine intervention into the announcement of punishment itself, rather than structurally distinguishing them from one another. There is accusatory description of those groups within human society at large (v. 3aβ) and within the society of Judah (vv. 4bβ-6) that have elicited Yahweh's vehement reactions against humanity as a whole.

As in other examples of the genre, this unit combines first person speech of Yahweh with third person speech about Yahweh. The shift, which comes at v. 5b, does not coincide with any major differentiation of structural or generic elements. There is thus no sharp distinction drawn between those parts of the prophecy that reflect the prophet's complete identification with God and those parts that reflect more of a sense of the prophet's own personal identity. The oracle formulas (vv. 2bβ, 3bβ[2]) function stylistically to bracket vv. 2-3 from vv. 4-6 (cf. Sweeney, 394-95), but since Yahweh clearly continues speaking after v. 3, it is evidently not their role to distinguish oracular from nonoracular speech. Thus even when the prophet purports to speak words directly from Yahweh's mouth, which can be indicated in a variety of ways, the mediation of the prophet's own personality is tacitly acknowledged (see G. Tucker, "Prophetic Speech," *Int* 32 [1978] 43).

Setting

As a type of public speech, the prophecy of punishment could be delivered in a wide variety of situations, ranging from confrontations provoked by a prophet (e.g., Isa 7:3-9) to consultations instigated by a request from someone else (e.g., 1 Kgs 22:1-28). The genre was often spoken to anyone who happened to be found in the streets, squares, or gates of a city. Two aspects of this particular example of the genre help us to be a bit more specific. First, it is primarily directed against both priestly and lay participants in certain religious practices: an officially established cult of Baal alongside the officially established cult of

Yahweh (v. 4b), popular devotion to astral deities (v. 5a), the profession of oaths to Yahweh along with oaths to another god (v. 5b), and the abandonment of the oracles of Yahweh altogether (v. 6). Second, it is informed by ancient Near Eastern mythological traditions.

The voice that speaks these words is thus characterized in terms of two roles. It plays the part of the prophetic antagonist of the royal sanctuary, like Amos, Isaiah, and Jeremiah, and also the role of the mythographer. The implied audience is a group to whom official policies concerning the state cult are directly relevant and a group that can recognize mythic allusions. The occasion for such a speech might well have been a cultic gathering (cf. Jer 26:1-7).

Although this unit reflects a convention of prophetic speech, there is no way of telling whether it was actually spoken in the kind of setting where such speech was typical, or whether the text is a literary adaptation of this convention (→ Book as a Whole, Setting).

Intention

This text announces the extensive collapse of what appears from Judah's perspective to be the order of creation, focusing on Jerusalem as the center of both the national life and the cosmos. It also informs its readers that Yahweh will bring about this collapse because many of Judah's conventional cultic practices actually represent the sort of human evil that the ancient myths have described as capable of threatening human existence and undoing the world. Such information is meant to arouse collective concern for the overall situation, based on the realization that the fate of all depends on the assumption of a collective responsibility for the policies and customs of some.

PREPARE FOR YAHWEH'S DAY OF SACRIFICE! 1:7-10

Structure

I. Call to acknowledge the divine presence	1:7
A. Command: silence!	1:7a
B. Twofold motivation	1:7b
1. Announcement of an approaching holy day	1:7bα
2. Description of Yahweh's preparation for sacrifice	1:7bβ
a. Readying the victim	1:7bβ^1
b. Consecrating the guests	1:7bβ^2
II. Narration of things to come	1:8-10
A. Yahweh's action	1:8-9
1. Narrative introduction	1:8aα
a. Recounting verb *(wĕhāyâ)*	1:8aα^1
b. Adverbial phrase: on the day of Yahweh's sacrifice	1:8aα^2

2. Prophecy of punishment   1:8aβ-9
  a. Against those that adopt a particular mode
    of dress   1:8aβb
    1) Action proper: I will punish   1:8aβ¹
    2) Its objects: those who adopt foreign attire   1:8aβ²b
      a) In particular   1:8aβ²
        (1) Officials
        (2) Royal household
      b) In general: all who so dress   1:8b
  b. Against those that behave in a particular way   1:9
    1) Action proper: I will punish   1:9aα¹
    2) Its objects   1:9aα²b
      a) Characterized in terms of their religious
        behavior: those who perform the rite of
        leaping over the threshold   1:9aα²β¹
      b) Future event formula: on that day   1:9aβ²
      c) Characterized in terms of their moral
        behavior: those who fill their master's
        house with violence and fraud   1:9b
B. Effects of Yahweh's action   1:10
  1. Narrative introduction   1:10aα¹
    a. Recounting verb *(wĕhāyâ)*
    b. Future event formula: on that day
    c. Oracle formula: says Yahweh   1:10aα²
  2. Description in terms of sounds and locales   1:10aβb
    a. A cry from the Fish Gate   1:10aβ¹
    b. A wail from the Second Quarter   1:10a
    c. A loud crash from the hills   1:10b

This unit begins with a command to acknowledge with reverence the presence of Yahweh (v. 7a) — a command even if it is based on a noun rather than an imperative verb. This command is ambiguous in the sense that it is cast in terms that might refer to the cultic manifestation of Yahweh's presence, but also to manifestations of his agency in a noncultic context. (Compare, e.g., Ps 114, which calls attention to Yahweh's presence in the saving event of crossing the sea, and Ps 46:9-11 [*RSV* 8-10], which calls attention to the presence that is manifest in cultic representation of such events.) The following motivation (v. 7b) first nudges the meaning of the command toward the cultic possibility: A day of sacrifice is approaching, for which the victim has been prepared and the invited guests have been sanctified. Another possibility is already evident, however, in that Yahweh himself is said to have made these preparations — which means that this sacrificial celebration is not of the usual sort.

The ensuing narration (vv. 8-9) then proceeds to recount what will happen on this approaching day, in such a way as to push the meaning toward the noncultic side, resulting in an ironic reversal. The ambiguity of the term *pqd* (*RSV* "punish"), which has about the same range of meaning as the English expression "take care of," retards this shift, but it eventually becomes clear that the day will feature Yahweh's punishment of high officials, including the royal household, and all others who have likewise been swayed by foreign influences. The punishment will come as a catastrophe whose effects are described in terms of the sounds of destruction and lamentation emanating from various places within Jerusalem's city limits (v. 10).

The narration thus plays on the double meaning of the phrase *yôm zebaḥ,* moving from a sense with cultic connotations ("day of sacrifice") to a sense with noncultic connotations ("day of slaughter"). As it turns out, it is not a holy day that has been announced, on which the people of Judah will feast as invited guests, but rather a day of destruction, on which some unnamed enemy forces will be invited by Yahweh to treat the people of Judah as their victims.

Genre

Although this unit consists largely of a (→) prophecy of punishment (vv. 8aβ-10), this speech of Yahweh is incorporated within a narrative of future events (vv. 8-10) that extends the motivation (v. 7b) of a command (v. 7). Although v. 7 is similar to the directives that call for various actions and attitudes from worshipers in the (→) hymn of praise, the motive clauses (v. 7b) are different from those usually found in this context. Here the motive clauses deal with Yahweh's preparations for sacrifice rather than Yahweh's praiseworthy attributes, and the preceding command may thus rather derive from the repertoire of directives given by those in charge of sacrifices (cf. 1 Sam 16:5). V. 7 may thus be compared with the (→) priestly torah that was sometimes ironically parodied by prophets (e.g., Amos 4:4-5). Although v. 7a has close parallels in Hab 2:20 and Zech 2:17 (*RSV* 13), these parallels show that the command for "silence!" can occur in various generic contexts (→ Hab 2:18-20; Zech 2:10-17 [*RSV* 6-13]), and thus that the genre of this particular unit does not depend on the nature of the command alone.

The verb form *wĕhāyâ* ("and it will happen that . . .") with an adverbial phrase (vv. 8a, 10aα) commonly indicates a continuation in narration of various kinds (e.g., Gen 38:5; Exod 16:5; 1 Sam 13:22; 16:16; 1 Kgs 2:37; 2 Kgs 4:10). Here, however, the sections introduced by this expression do not form the continuation of any foregoing story. They rather form a narrative that is coordinated with the preceding motive clauses (v. 7b), as if to extend them while also moving into another mode of discourse. The substance of the narration is a first person speech of Yahweh (vv. 8aβ-9, 10aβ-b) that is coordinated with narrative introductions (vv. 8aα, 10aα) to form an account of what Yahweh intends to do.

This combination amounts to a command with a rationale for adhering to it, which is basically (→) parenesis. The unusual structure of the rationale shows that the function of the genre here is more complicated than simply urging the addressees to do as they are told. The forcefulness of the command is predicated on a recategorization of experience, which the unusual combination of elements is designed to achieve. By recounting an unexpected outcome for the kind of cultic occasion with which the command would have been initially associated, this passage transposes a type of cultic activity from the category of behavior that is generally beneficial to a category of behavior that is just the opposite. Combined with such exposition, the command calls on its addressees to prepare themselves for the hitherto unexpected, but now nevertheless inevitable, negative consequences of their cultic practices. The inclusion of a speech of Yahweh shows this unit to be parenesis with an oracular warrant, and hence a PROPHETIC EXHORTATION.

Setting

The coherence of this unit depends on the recognition that the initial command could refer to a cultic manifestation of divine presence, but the text as a whole is not cultic communication. It is rather a public alert to the disastrous consequences of certain customary behavior — both cultic and noncultic — practiced preeminently by the royal household and court. This speech thus reflects conventions of prophetic public address, but there is no way of telling whether it was actually spoken publicly, or whether the text is a literary adaptation of this convention (→ Book as a Whole, Setting).

Intention

This unit is designed to change the mind of its readers regarding their presently respectable public piety. It grabs their attention as would-be participants in a sacrificial celebration, only to recount how such participation will lead to disaster. They are meant to realize that the cult is actually a misrepresentation of Yahweh. For a true representation they should look instead to the sacrificial slaughter that he is about to make of the leading citizens, with mournful ramifications for the whole population.

PREPARE FOR YAHWEH'S DAY OF RECKONING! 1:11-18

Structure

I. Call to lament	1:11
A. Call proper	1:11a
1. Command: wail!	1:11aα
2. Designation of addressees: inhabitants of the Mortar	1:11aβ
B. Twofold motivation: description of economic conditions	1:11b
1. Merchant class is gone	1:11bα
2. Money changers are cut off	1:11bβ
II. Narration of things to come	1:12-18
A. Described from Judah's perspective	1:12-16

1. Yahweh's action — 1:12
   a. Narrative introduction — 1:12aα
      1) Recounting verb *(wĕhāyâ)* — 1:12aα¹
      2) Future event formula: at that time — 1:12aα²
   b. Prophecy of punishment — 1:12aβb
      1) Preliminary investigation — 1:12aβ
         a) Action proper: I will search — 1:12aβ¹
         b) Its object: Jerusalem — 1:12aβ²
      2) Subsequent findings — 1:12b
         a) Action proper: I will punish — 1:12bα¹
         b) Its objects: the men who . . . — 1:12bα²β
            (1) Characterized with respect to
                their general condition: thickening
                on their lees — 1:12bα²
            (2) Characterized with respect to their
                relationship with Yahweh: doubters
                of his capacity to effect good or ill — 1:12bβ
2. Effects of Yahweh's actions — 1:13-16
   a. Narrative introduction: recounting verb
      (wĕhāyâ) — 1:13aα¹
   b. Description of devastation — 1:13aα²-16
      1) In terms of economic deprivation — 1:13aα²b
         a) Loss of possessions — 1:13aα²β
            (1) Goods plundered — 1:13aα²
            (2) Houses laid waste — 1:13aβ
         b) Fruitless activity — 1:13b
            (1) Houses built but not lived in — 1:13bα
            (2) Vineyards planted but no wine drunk — 1:13bβ
      2) In terms of defeat: the Day of Yahweh — 1:14-16
         a) Reiterated announcement of its nearness
            (cf. 1:7b) — 1:14a
         b) Reiterated description of its dread sounds
            (cf. 1:10aβb) — 1:14b
         c) Further description of its adverse effects — 1:15-16
            (1) Listing of negative attributes — 1:15-16a
                (a) Basic definitional statement:
                    a day of wrath is that day — 1:15a
                (b) Elaboration: a day of . . . — 1:15b-16a
                    α. Distress and anguish — 1:15bα¹
                    β. Ruin and devastation — 1:15bα²
                    γ. Darkness and gloom — 1:15bβ¹
                    δ. Clouds and thick darkness — 1:15bβ²
                    ε. Trumpet blast and battle cry — 1:16a
            (2) Designation of what is adversely
                affected — 1:16b
                (a) Fortified cities — 1:16bα
                (b) Lofty battlements — 1:16bβ

B. Described from a cosmic perspective   1:17-18
  1. Yahweh's action $1:17a\alpha^1$
    a. Action proper: I will bring distress
    b. Its object: humanity
  2. Effects of Yahweh's action $1:17a\alpha^2$-18
    a. Described with respect to humanity
      in general $1:17a\alpha^2$-$18a\beta^1$
      1) Stated positively in terms of bodily
         harm $1:17a\alpha^2b$
         a) Stated actively in terms of inflicted
            disability $1:17a\alpha^2\beta$
            (1) Effect proper: they shall walk
               like the blind $1:17a\alpha^2$
            (2) Reason: because they have sinned
               against Yahweh $1:17a\beta$
         b) Stated passively in terms of violent
            dismemberment: their blood shall be
            poured out like dust, and their flesh
            like dung   1:17b
      2) Stated negatively with respect to wealth:
         silver and gold cannot deliver them on
         that day $1:18a\beta^1$
    b. Described with respect to all the earth in
      general $1:18a\beta^2b$
      1) Basic statement: in the fire of Yahweh's
         jealous wrath all the earth will be consumed $1:18a\beta^2$
      2) Motivation: reiteration of Yahweh's intention
         to destroy all that inhabits the earth (cf. 1:2-3)   1:18b

The composition of this unit basically resembles the composition of its predecessor (→ 1:7-10, Structure), with similar elements combined in a similar way. The main difference is the double aspect of the narration of things to come in 1:12-18 (cf. 1:8-10). In this case future prospects are described once from Judah's perspective (vv. 12-16) and then again from a cosmic perspective (vv. 17-18). This mirrors the same double aspect that is shown by the prophecy of punishment in (→) 1:2-6. This unit thus has features in common with both 1:2-6 and 1:7-10 that bind all three together as a major section of the book (→ 1:2-18, Structure).

Unlike the command of "silence!" that begins 1:7-10, this unit begins with a command to "wail!" that is addressed to a particular group. They are called *yōšbê hammaktēš* (*RSV* "inhabitants of the Mortar"). In view of the immediately preceding narration (v. 10), which describes a "wail" (*yĕlālâ*, derived from *yll*) emanating from a particular quarter of Jerusalem, the addressees of the command to "wail" (*hêlîlû*, also derived from *yll*) would seem to be characterized as living in some part of the city. This locale cannot now be identified with any certainty, but the latter part of v. 11 suggests that it was an area where commercial and financial activities were centered. By verbalizing one of the nouns from the preceding series of calamitous sounds in v. 10 ("cry," "wail," and "loud crash") and by continuing the series of specific urban locales from which such sounds will come ("the Fish Gate," "the Second Quarter," "the hills," and "the Mortar"), 1:11-18 evidently picks up where 1:7-10 leaves off. In the previous unit's progression from a command (v. 7a) to a motivation (v. 7b) extended by narration (vv. 8-10), the joyful expectation of festivity has been turned into a mournful reaction to calamity. This unit recapitulates the same progression from a command (v. 11a) to a motivation (v. 11b) extended by narration (vv. 12-18) in order to describe more specifically both this mournful reaction and the calamity that occasions it.

Like its counterpart in 1:7-10, this unit also plays on the double meaning of the command with which it begins. The initial imperative *hêlîlû* ("wail!") is ambiguous in the sense that it could refer either to the sort of mourning that would accompany an irrecoverable loss (e.g., Mic 1:8-16) or to the sort of public complaint ritual that would be characterized by prayer for deliverance from some communal crisis (e.g., Joel 1:13-14). The following motivation (v. 11b) suggests the latter, for it describes an economic crisis that might — like natural disaster, plague, or military attack — be the occasion for a liturgy of communal complaint (Wolff, "Aufruf"). This fact does not entirely resolve the ambiguity of the command, however, because the motivation itself is also ambiguous. The phrase *'am kĕna'an* could literally refer to "the people of Canaan," as well as to "traders" (so *RSV*). In this context these words could connote a process of depopulation, as well as a cessation of commercial activity. The ensuing narration (vv. 12-18) further explains what is happening so as to push the meaning of the command away from a call to complaint and more toward a call to mourn while at the same time giving an ironic twist to the initially suggested meaning. The wailing will come in response to a total liquidation of goods and households so severe that there will be no prospect of successful rebuilding or replanting for a long time to come.

The root cause of this destruction lies in civic corruption that is described in terms of a vinic metaphor. Because the phrase *haqqōp'îm 'al-šimrêhem* (*RSV* "thickening upon their lees") in v. 12 can connote both the maturation and the spoilage of wine (D. J. Clark, "Wine on the Lees," *BT* 32 [1981] 241-43), it suggests that the community's ostensibly well-developed commerce is actually or potentially corrupt. The narration thus transforms the meaning of the phrase "Day of Yahweh," moving from the designation of a day of supplication addressing Yahweh to a time when Yahweh acts to establish justice (cf. Amos 5:18-24). As it turns out, the economic crisis will be the occasion for a "Day of Yahweh," but in the sense that Yahweh will deepen it into a condition that no amount of money can help (v. 18), rather than in the sense that he will be open to petitions for help.

Genre

This unit has basically the same combination of generic elements as (→) 1:7-10. First comes a directive (v. 11) that is potentially a (→) call to communal complaint, which impresses the reader as such until the unit's subsequent development makes clear that this is more of a call to mourn. The subsequent development entails extended narration (vv. 12-18) that begins with the formulaic usage of *wĕhāyâ* ("and it shall happen") plus the temporal adverbial phrase *bā'ēt hahî* ("at that time"). It continues with much third person description, but also utilizes elements of first person oracular speech of Yahweh (vv. 12, 17), which shows that the future is being recounted as a (→) prophecy of punishment.

Some loosely call vv. 14-18 a "hymn" on the Day of Yahweh (e.g., Fensham). Such a designation captures the fact that the poetic form of this passage is in many respects exquisitely crafted, in ways that bear some superficial resemblance to the hymnic description in psalms. There is little generic similarity, however, between these verses and a (→) hymn of praise — not even those examples of the genre that Gunkel designated eschatological hymns, such as Pss 68, 98, and 149 (Gunkel, 344).

The "Dies irae" in vv. 14-18 is an integral part of the narration in vv. 12-18, which serves to persuade the addressees to adhere to the foregoing directive in v. 11 while at the same time bringing about a shift in the significance of this directive. It first appears that the audience is being urged to participate in a communal complaint ceremony occasioned by an economic crisis. But, as it turns out, there is no use petitioning Yahweh for relief because the economic crisis is only the beginning of a larger cosmic crisis that Yahweh himself has instigated. By recounting an unexpected outcome for the occasion with which the command would have been initially associated, this passage also changes the significance of certain commercial activities in which the wider society is currently engaged. The absence of these activities is initially regarded as the symptom of the crisis; but these same activities come eventually to be regarded as the cause of the crisis because they were conducted as if their moral consequences made no difference to Yahweh (v. 12). The command, combined with this sort of narrative exposition, thus serves to encourage preparation for the unexpected but nevertheless inevitable results of such commercial corruption. This unit is basically parenetical, and the incorporation of oracular speech of Yahweh into the (→) parenesis shows it to be more specifically a PROPHETIC EXHORTATION.

Setting

This unit is thematically dominated by a call to mourn and therefore plays on the conventions of public mourning (cf. Amos 5:16-19) by voicing a dirge proleptically, as it were (cf. Amos 5:1-2). It reflects the practice of adapting such conventions for the purposes of prophetic public speech. There is no way of telling whether this unit was ever actually spoken in public, or whether the text is a literary adaptation of this prophetic practice (→ Book as a Whole, Setting).

Intention

This unit attempts to change the mind of its addressees about the economic downturn to which it refers. It initially involves them as would-be participants in a liturgy of prayer for relief, thus reflecting a common presupposition that economic recovery can be expected. The narration of an outcome that precludes both the return of economic productivity and the exercise of any clout of wealth leads the addressees toward a reversal of their attitude concerning the extent of the crisis, its cause, and the nature of Yahweh's involvement in it. Things will have to get a lot worse before they get any better because Jerusalem's citizenry has prospered through corruption. Contrary to the expectations of many, Yahweh does act for good and for ill — in this case for ill.

Bibliography

F. C. Fensham, "The Poetic Form of the Hymn of the Day of the Lord in Zephaniah," in *Studies in Old Testament Prophecy* (ed. W. C. van Wyk; *OTWSA* 13-14; Potchefstroom: OTWSA, 1975) 9-14; H. Gunkel, *Einleitung in die Psalmen* (1933; repr. Göttingen: Vandenhoeck & Ruprecht, 1966); H. W. Wolff, "Der Aufruf zur Volksklage," *ZAW* 76 (1964) 48-56.

Chapter 4

THE SECOND MAJOR SECTION
OF THE BOOK (2:1–3:13)
AND ITS INDIVIDUAL UNITS

EXHORTATION TO REPENT IN VIEW OF THE COMING
DAY OF YAHWEH, 2:1–3:13

Structure

Commentators generally agree on the basic parts of this section. Most recognize 2:1-3, 2:5-7, 2:8-10, and 2:13-15 as the units of ch. 2, differing only with regard to whether 2:4 belongs with 2:1-3 or 2:5-7, and whether 2:11 and 2:12 constitute fragmentary separate units or belong with 2:8-10 and 2:13-15, respectively. As for the part of ch. 3 that presently concerns us, most likewise recognize some kind of division after 3:5, 3:8, and 3:13, differing with regard to whether 3:1-5 and 3:6-8 belong together as a single unit, and whether 3:11-13 is more closely connected with the remainder of ch. 3 than with the material that precedes it. The main problem is thus not how to delimit the units themselves but how to describe their overall organization and compositional inter-relationship.

One issue is whether 2:1-3 concludes the material in ch. 1 or starts a new section (→ 1:2-18, Structure). Because 2:1-3 is clearly motivated by the announcement of punishment against Philistia in v. 4, which is in turn linked with the prophecy of punishment against the seacoast as the "land of the Philistines" in 2:5-7, most scholars concerned with the overall compositional form have regarded 2:1-3 as the beginning of a unit extending into ch. 2, rather than as the conclusion the material in ch. 1 (e.g., Keller, 197-99; Renaud, 11-14; Ball, *Rhetorical Study,* 114-22; Sweeney, 397-99; Weigl, 99-121; Ryou, 283-85; but cf. Alonso Schökel and Sicre Diaz, 1118; Roberts, 189-90; etc.). Coherence has been imputed to 2:4-15 because it identifies certain nations according to some pattern, such as a program of foreign policy (Christensen, "Zephaniah 2:4-15," 677-82) or a traditional concept of ethnic origins and sociocultural differences (Berlin, "Zephaniah's Oracle," 181-83); and some have noted that the repetition of *hôy* (*RSV* "woe!") at 2:5 and 3:1 creates a parallel between the prophecies concerning foreign nations in 2:5-15 and the prophecy concerning Judah in 3:1-7 (e.g., Elliger, 74-75; Ryou, 284). Beyond such observations regarding various prominent formal features of this section, there is general agreement that 3:9 marks a fundamental division, separating a part of the book defined by its overall concern with punishment from the following part (3:9-20) contrastingly defined by its overall concern with salvation.

This view of how chs. 2–3 are organized, as a series of prophecies of punishment (2:4–3:8) followed by a series of prophecies of salvation (3:9-20), is problematic in several respects (Renaud, 2-3; Sweeney, 389-90). In particular, it depends on the classification of 3:1-8 as a prophecy of punishment against Judah, which results in a rather forced reading of 3:8 as an announcement of punishment. A charge of failure to repent, like the one found in 3:1-7, can serve as the accusation in a prophecy of punishment, but it does not always do so (→ 3:1-7, Genre). Further, although an announcement of punishment is typically connected to an accusation with *lākēn* ("therefore"), the mere occurrence of this word does not necessarily indicate this kind of connection.

The main problem, however, is that announcements of punishment are not typically based on imperatives like the one in 3:8. Even if one could adduce some formal parallel to show that a command of some kind could serve this function, it is difficult to imagine how a command to "wait" or "hope" *(hkh)* could do so. Rudolph (pp. 289-90) argues that *hkh* must have a threatening sense here, but this word does not have such connotations in any of its biblical contexts (C. Barth, *"chākhāh," TDOT* 4:359-63). It is also difficult to see the rest of 3:8 as part of an announcement of punishment for Judah since it is actually concerned not with Judah in particular but with the nations in general

(Weigl, 231). To make v. 8b refer to Judah one must make a wholly unwarranted emendation, changing *'ălêhem* ("upon them") to *'ălêkem* ("upon you"). To the same end the last clause of v. 8b is often excised on the grounds that it is supposedly a secondary addition, to avoid its description of Yahweh's judgment as encompassing "all the earth," or the phrase *kol-hā'āreṣ* is tendentiously rendered as "the whole land" rather than "all the earth."

In sum, 3:8 is not an announcement of punishment against Judah, because it neither announces punishment nor focuses on Judah. This observation raises the question of whether the overall compositional structure of this part of the book might be based on something other than a contrast between prophecies of punishment and prophecies of salvation. As a way into this question, we may first ask what 3:8 is, and how it relates to 3:1-7 within the surrounding context. In answering this question the main contours of this section's overall structure will begin to emerge, revealing a context in which the previously noted prominent features aptly fit. Once one sees the overall structure, some of the details that various commentators have found rather puzzling will perhaps seem less so.

As a command to foster a particular attitude toward Yahweh, in connection with what is happening on the day when Yahweh acts, 3:8 has an affinity in both form and content with 2:1-3 (cf. Ryou, 284-85). In 2:1-3 the people are urged to take joint action in seeking Yahweh in order to mitigate the punishment that is coming upon Judah and Jerusalem on "the day of Yahweh's wrath" (1:2-18). In 3:8 they are urged to wait in hope for what Yahweh will bring to completion on the "day of [Yahweh's] arising" (v. 8a), because the nations will then be chastised (v. 8b) in order to restore the primal unity that the human race once enjoyed among themselves and in relation to Yahweh (v. 9; → 3:8-13, Structure). These two similar passages are conceptually related to one another in that those who heed the call to repent (2:1-3) can begin to look toward the Day of Yahweh in hope because the judgment that is coming on Judah is part of a larger plan of destruction and subsequent restoration that Yahweh is carrying out with respect to all the nations (3:8-9).

All of the prophecies in this section, whether they announce punishment or salvation, are aligned in series that are subordinated to commands. The series in 2:4-15 is subordinated to the commands in 2:1-3 (Ryou, 325-26), and the series in 3:8b-13 to the command in 3:8a. The whole of this section can thus be seen as an exhortation, with 2:1-3 and 3:8a as the two main structural poles around which the rest of the material is organized (cf. Marti, 366-76; also Sweeney, 399-402). The initial call to repentance (2:1-3) is predicated on the possibility that all those who "seek Yahweh" *(bqš yhwh)* may avert total destruction (2:3b). This possibility is then substantiated in terms of an imminent transformation in the world order (2:4-15). With respect to the region immediately surrounding Judah, the neighboring nations that have long posed a threat to Judah's territorial integrity will be eliminated, thus leaving space in which the repentant remnant of Judah can dwell secure (2:4-11). With respect to the larger sphere of imperial hegemonies and the international balance of power, the empire that Yahweh has long used to maintain order has reached the limits of its term. The Assyrians' strength is declining, and their capital of

Nineveh is on its way to total destruction because they have vainly imagined themselves to be playing an entirely self-directed role (2:12-15). The demise of Assyria, the superpower to which Judah has long been in effect a vassal state, creates the possibility of a new international balance of power more favorable to Judah.

Because of the near total chaos that such a world transformation initially entails, Judah cannot hope to survive intact. Because of Judah's long history of infidelity to Yahweh, its perpetration of injustice, and its failure to heed prophetic warnings, due in large part to a failure of leadership, it is now too late to have any hope of Judah's maintaining its identity as such (3:1-7). In the overall process Judah must either disappear or undergo transformation. The possibility of transformation is open to those who now heed the call to seek Yahweh. In the context of Yahweh's restoration of humanity in general, those in Judah who remain faithful through the crisis have the prospect of surviving and constituting a new Israel. As a repentant people, their past sins will no longer be held against them, and they will dwell in peace (3:8-13).

Viewed in this context, the prophecies in 2:4-15 appear to describe major aspects of the world transformation that Yahweh is bringing about in order to explain why this crisis is a hopeful prospect for the repentant survivors of Judah's destruction. In their overall arrangement these prophecies against foreign nations reflect the interplay of two concepts. On the one hand this particular geographical configuration represents the two spheres of influence that typically impinged on Judah in distinctively different ways: the sphere constituted by Judah's dealings with its immediate neighbors, who were all of the same relatively small size and strength, and the sphere constituted by the interference of larger superpowers from outside the immediate area. On the other hand this same configuration also represents the four points of the compass (Ryou, 323-25). Philistia (2:4-7) is an immediate neighbor to the west, and Moab and Ammon (2:8-11) are immediate neighbors to the east. The Ethiopians or Cushites (kûšîm, 2:12) represent an imperial power to the south, and Assyria is an imperial power to the north (2:13-15). The various nations mentioned in 2:4-15 represent the totality of the world situation viewed from Judah's perspective, with simultaneous reference to both the two main geopolitical categories into which other nations fall and the four cardinal directions in which they lie.

As a result of Yahweh's redefinition of the international boundaries and balance of power (2:4-15), the remnant of Judah may enjoy the restoration of a "Pax Davidica" (3:9-13), but not if the people of Yahweh refuse to share the prophetic perception of the process they are currently caught up in as they have often done in the past (3:1-7). Precisely because some in Judah will come to realize that their predicament is due to unheeded prophecies, they will be able to grasp that it is now Yahweh's prophetically revealed plan for them to undergo the impending punishment faithfully and hopefully, and thus survive to begin anew. In this sense the charge of failure to repent in 3:1-7 can serve as the basis for an exhortation to await the Day of Yahweh in hope (3:8-10), as indicated by connecting the former to the latter with lākēn ("therefore").

Questions have been raised about the specific nations mentioned in this section, the way in which some of them are described, and the overall function of this particular geographical configuration. Why is the land of the Philistines called "Canaan" (2:5bα), when Philistia never constituted more than a small part of the territory that bore this name? Why is Edom, the nation most often vilified for opposing Judah, not mentioned among Judah's neighboring enemies? Why are the Ethiopians or Cushites *(kûšîm)* made to represent the center of imperial power to the south (3:12) when the Egyptians typically posed a far greater threat to Judah throughout most of its history and would seem the more obvious candidates for this role?

Christensen ("Zechariah 2:4-15," 677-82) has suggested that the prophecies in 2:4-15 served as a theological rationale for conquests planned by King Josiah of Judah, during whose reign Zephaniah is supposed to have prophesied (1:1). Christensen assumes that Josiah aimed to regain control of the territory once ruled by David, ranging from Philistia on the west to Ammon and Moab on the east (2:4-11), and he argues that this prophecy legitimated Josiah's imperialistic aims in terms of Yahweh's decision to punish these nations. Yahweh's intention to create an international context that allowed such local expansion had begun to be evident in the overthrow of the Ethiopians some thirty to forty years earlier, i.e., the Ethiopian dynasty whose rule over Egypt came to an end when the Assyrians defeated Thebes in 663 BCE. In just the same way that Yahweh wielded the Assyrians as his "sword" in order to defeat Egypt's Ethiopian rulers (2:12), he will also use some other power as his "outstretched hand" to overthrow the Assyrians themselves (2:13-15), leaving Judah free to take control of neighboring territory without interference from any more distant imperial power. Because pressure placed by the succeeding Egyptian dynasty on the region to the south would have prevented Josiah from attacking Edom, that nation is not listed among those that he aspires to conquer.

Christensen's interpretation of 2:4-15 is problematic in several respects. First, it should be noted that the argument for a connection between this prophecy and Josiah's supposed plans of eastward and westward expansion is largely circular. This text itself is the main evidence that has been adduced for Josiah's having had such plans (E. Ben Zvi, "History and Prophetic Texts," in *History and Interpretation* [*Fest.* J. H. Hayes; ed. M. P. Graham, W. P. Brown, and J. K. Kuan; JSOTSup 173; Sheffield: Sheffield Academic Press, 1993] 113-20). Berlin's objection that prophecies against foreign nations do not generally function to justify territorial expansion (*Zephaniah,* 119-20) is not particularly well taken in view of the military settings in which this genre could be used (→ 2:5-7, Setting). She also notes, however, that though there is no direct evidence of Josiah's having attempted to expand either eastward or westward, there is direct evidence of his having made forays northward (e.g., 2 Kgs 23:15-20). If Zephaniah were indeed concerned with legitimating Josiah's military exploits, it is odd that there is no mention of this relatively well-attested and ideologically important development (*Zephaniah,* 119-20; cf. Ben Zvi, "History and Prophetic Texts," 117-18).

Christensen's interpretation is also weakened by the fact that Judah is not characterized in 2:4-15 as a victor. Philistia, Moab, and Ammon are to be possessed not by Judah as such but by the "remnant" *(šĕʾērît, yeter)* of Judah

(2:7a, 9b). In defense of Christensen's reading, Sweeney argues that these terms do not refer to the surviving former citizens of a Judah that no longer exists, but instead describe the Josianic kindgom of Judah as a nation emerging from the chastisement of past subjection to foreign control and aspiring to reunify with the former northern kingdom (p. 404). In view of the overall context such a reference seems highly unlikely. Although Yahweh's punishment of Judah is aimed specifically at removing various corrupt factions from within the kindgom (1:4-6; 1:12-13; 3:11bα), it is emphatically stated that Judah's punishment is to happen in the course of a punishment affecting "all humanity" (1:3b; cf. 1:17a) in which "all the earth will be consumed" (1:18b; 3:8a). Because Yahweh has repeatedly tried to impose on other nations the kind of punishment that would serve as an example motivating Judah to repent, but to no avail (3:6-7), Judah is not exempt from this process.

The implication is clearly that the people of Judah must now learn from their own direct experience the hard lesson that they have failed to learn from the experience of other nations. The concept of "remnant" is a positive one in the sense that it connotes the possibility of a new beginning after Judah's destruction, so that the destruction is really a creative though painful transformation, but not in the sense of implying that Judah will remain intact (Gerleman, 118; G. W. Anderson, "The Idea of the Remnant in the Book of Zephaniah," *ASTI* 11 [1977-78] 11-14). Judah must undergo the same kind of destructive punishment that Yahweh is inflicting on all the nations in order to participate in the restoration that Yahweh is also planning for all humanity (3:9; cf. 3:19), and in the process they will become "a people humble and lowly" (3:12a; cf. 2:3) who can assume their rightful place in the world without being threatened by either their former neighboring rivals or any outside imperial power. A text that assumes such a fate for Judah could hardly serve to legitimate its battle plans.

Berlin suggests alternatively that although 2:4-15 generally reflects the international situation of the late seventh century, this prophecy was not primarily designed to describe any particular set of historical events during that time. The nations in 2:4-15 are rather selected and characterized in accord with the same categories of ethnic and cultural affinity on which the great genealogy of Noah's descendants in Gen 10 is based ("Zephaniah's Oracle," 181-83; also *Zephaniah,* 120-24). The children of Japheth (Gen 10:2-5), who comprise the maritime peoples, appear only in a cameo role as *'iyê haggôyim* (2:11b [*RSV* "the lands of the nations"]; cf. Gen 10:5). The main contrast is between the children of Shem (Gen 10:21-31), who comprise the nomadic and often pastoral peoples, and the children of Ham (10:6-20), who comprise the urban and sedentary peoples. As a descendant of Abraham through Peleg and Eber (11:10-26; cf. 10:21, 25), Judah is the sole representative of the children of Shem. The children of Ham are represented by Cush (Ethiopia) and Canaan (10:6). Moab, Ammon, and Philistia are all characterized as children of Ham by virtue of their being associated with Canaan, as is Assyria by virtue of Nineveh's having been built by Nimrod, a son of Cush (10:8-12). The text thus basically describes the overthrow of the Hamite urban empire of Assyria, so that Shemite Judah can use the neighboring territory of its former enemies for pasture. It thus reflects "the natural antipathy between nomads and sedentary peoples . . . that is expressed in the antipathy between Ham and Shem (and Japheth) in Gen 9:25-27" (Berlin, *Zephaniah*, 122; cf. B. Oded, "The Table of Nations [Genesis 10] — A Socio-cultural Approach," *ZAW* 98 [1986] 14-32). Egypt and Edom are not mentioned because they were not implicated in a composition directed primarily against the Assyrians and their allies.

Berlin's reading rightly considers the possibility that this section of the book may, like (→) 1:2-18, be informed by mythic allusions to the primeval history in Gen 1–11. Throughout this section of Zephaniah there is indeed a strong emphasis on the theme of ruined cities whose sites become a wasteland occupied by wild animals, no longer useful to humans except for the purpose of grazing flocks and herds. This theme has connotations that derive from intertextual connections with Gen 1–11, but the allusions to Gen 10 found by Berlin seem somewhat forced. There are more explicit allusions to another part of the primeval history, suggesting that this section's all-pervasive theme of urban decay is not to be read primarily in terms of the sociocultural conflict between nomadic Shemites and urban Hamites.

First, it should be noted that this text does not overtly characterize nations in terms of their eponymous or primeval ancestry. Only the Ammonites are described in explicitly patronymic terms as the *běnê 'ammôn* ("sons of Ammon"; 2:8a, 9a). Of the eight remaining references to specific peoples, three are explicitly gentilic rather than patronymic, i.e., the "Cherethites" (2:5a), "Philistines" (2:5b), and "Ethiopians" (2:12). Otherwise the terminology for the nations is ambiguous with respect to whether it is patronymic or gentilic.

There is also some familial terminology in a reference to the remnant of Yahweh's people as "the house of Judah" (*bêt yěhûdâ*, 2:7) and in a reference to the later generations of those scattered by Yahweh as "the daughter of my dispersed ones" (*bat-pûṣay*, 3:10), but both of these expressions are conditioned more by immediate contextual factors than by allusive intertextual connections. In the first instance Judah's characterization as "the *house* of Judah" (2:7a) corresponds to their taking up residence in "the *houses* of Ashkelon" (2:7b), suggesting that this process of urban dispossession may take a generation or so. In the second instance the personification of those scattered from Babel by Yahweh as the "daughter of my dispersed ones" (3:10) corresponds to the subsequent personification of Judah as the "daughter of Zion" (3:14), thus indicating that the descendants of the scattered Judeans are destined for resettlement in Jerusalem, and that this prospect is to be celebrated as a woman or "daughter" would typically join her fellows in leading the community's celebration of a great victory (→ 3:14-17). Although this text sometimes describes things in familial and transgenerational terms, and although it is also partly based on a typological correspondence with events in primeval times (see below), there is no discernible emphasis on direct lineal descent from primeval ancestors. There is therefore no pattern of reference in Zeph 2:1–3:13 that clearly corresponds with the genealogical categories informing Gen 10.

Moreover, when Gen 10 and other genealogical texts from Genesis are examined in detail, some of the lines of descent traced by Berlin seem dubious.

Although Nineveh is indeed said to have been built by Nimrod, a descendant of Ham through Cush, the Assyrians themselves are explicitly listed among the descendants of Shem (Gen 10:22). A similar difficulty emerges with the identification of Moab and Ammon as descendants of Ham. They, along with Judah, do not figure at all in Gen 10. In order to see where these two nations fit into the genealogical scheme one must read further, tracing not only the descent of Abraham and his nephew Lot from Shem through Eber and Peleg in 11:10-28, but also the descent of Moab and Ammon from Lot in 19:30-38, as well as the descent of Judah from Abraham through Isaac and Jacob throughout the rest of Genesis. With this larger picture in view, it is evident that although Moab and Ammon are the offspring of an incestuous union between Lot and his daughters, they are nevertheless clearly direct descendants of Shem, just as Judah and Edom are.

Berlin claims that the comparison of Moab and Ammon with the cities of Sodom and Gomorrah associates these two nations with Canaan because these two cities are said to mark the borders of Canaan in Gen 10:19, thus identifying them virtually as "western Canaanites" and hence descendants of Ham. It is difficult to see how such a comparison can turn the Moabites and Ammonites from Shemites into ersatz Canaanites. These nations and cities are being compared with respect to their ruination, not their ethnicity. Moreover, other cities besides Sodom and Gomorrah (i.e., Admah and Zeboiim) are also involved in the description of Canaan's boundaries in Gen 10:19, cities whose histories were also proverbially associated with some catastrophe (e.g., Deut 29:23; Hos 11:8). If Zeph 2:8-10 were meant to describe the destruction of Moab and Ammon so as to allude to Gen 10:19 and thereby affiliate these two nations with Canaan, why are these other cities not mentioned? On its face, might the comparison with Sodom and Gomorrah in Zeph 2:9 not allude more to Gen 19:1-28 than to Gen 10:19? Also, it is not clear from the description in Gen 10:19 whether Sodom, Gomorrah, and these other cities mark the boundary of Canaan by falling just within it or just beyond it. In the latter case, how would any comparison of Moab and Ammon with Sodom and Gomorrah bring these nations within the pale of Canaan? If Judah is understood to be characterized in this section of Zephaniah as a descendant of Shem on the basis of the line of descent that unfolds from Gen 11, it is difficult to see why the characterization of Moab and Ammon should not be established on the same basis. How can the tenuous possibility of an implicit connection between Zeph 2:9 and Gen 10:19 controvert the explicit and direct information that is given elsewhere in Genesis regarding the genealogy of Moab and Ammon? If it can, is not Judah's identity as a Shemite also rendered uncertain? Although the status of the *ʾîyê haggôyim* ("islands of the nations") as descendants of Japheth is not in question (Gen 10:5), there are similar difficulties with Berlin's supposition that their primary function here is to represent this branch of Noah's family tree (see below).

Berlin's claim that this text is based on a fundamental contrast between the Hamite urban bad guys, who hail from Assyria and its supposedly "Canaanite" allies, and the Shemite seminomadic good guys, who hail from Judah, is not finally persuasive. Her analysis nevertheless rightly calls attention to the necessity of reckoning with mythic factors, as well as historical and political factors, in understanding the way the nations are characterized in this text's portrayal of the world situation. The all-pervasive theme of ruined urban sites grazed by animals cannot be satisfactorily explained in terms of the natural antipathy between city dwellers and nomadic shepherds, as this antipathy may be expressed in Genesis's genealogy of humanity's ancestors, but this theme does have other mythic connotations.

These connotations become evident when another prominent theme is connected with Yahweh's explicit statement in Zeph 3:9 regarding his overall purpose in destroying the old world order and creating a new one. The destruction of cities, in terms of which the old order's demise is largely described, is closely related to the theme of the nations' overbearing pride; and the possibility of Judah's taking its rightful place in a new world order is conversely related to the theme of their attaining humility. In the case of the Philistines, the destruction of their cities is only implicitly attributed to their pride; but the fault of pride is clearly suggested by the fact that those from Judah who "seek humility" (*bqš 'nwh*, 2:3bα), and who are thus enabled to withstand the day of Yahweh's wrath (2:3bβ), are the ones who will take over the abandoned houses of the Philistine cities (2:7bα). In the case of Moab and Ammon, their cities will become like Sodom and Gomorrah precisely because of "their pride" (*gě'ônām*, 2:10a). In the case of Assyria, Nineveh will be destroyed because of an overweening sense of inviolability (2:15a). In the case of Judah, the "oppressing city" (*hā'îr hayyônâ*, 3:1b) of Jerusalem is to undergo a transformation that entails the removal of its "proudly exultant ones" (*'allîzê ga'ăwâ*, 3:11bα), so that they shall no longer be "haughty" (*lěgābhâ*, 3:11bβ) but rather a "people humble and lowly" (*'am 'ānî wādāl*, 3:12a). Yahweh's purpose thus entails a reversal of the human tendency to hubris, a tendency whose etiology is recounted in terms of building a proud city in the story of the Tower of Babel (Gen 11:1-9).

There is a clear allusion to this mythic story in Yahweh's statement that his punishment of all nations is intended to bring about a transformation of human nature. He will "purify" *(brr)* the "speech" *(śěpâ)* of the peoples (3:9a), in the sense of restoring to them the capacity to act "with one accord" (*šěkem 'ehād*, 3:9bβ[2]; cf. Gen 11:6), precisely the capacity that was lost when Yahweh disrupted humanity's unified attempt to build a towering city, confused their "speech" (*śěpâ*, Gen 11:9a), and scattered them over the face of the earth. Thus the overall transformation of the world order described in Zeph 2:1–3:13 that serves as the basis for urging Yahweh's people to be transformed in the process is to be understood as an antitype of the Tower of Babel (Ball, *Rhetorical Study,* 296; R. L. Smith, 142), just as the exhortation in (→) 1:2-18 to prepare for this divine initiative is based on an antitype of the Flood. The ruined urban sites in this section of Zephaniah correspond typologically to the unfinished city on the plain of Shinar (Gen 11:8b), signifying Yahweh's reversal of the scattering and confusion that began with humanity's attempt to build such proud cities. This reversal will result in a return to the kind of conditions that once existed earlier in the days of Enoch and Lamech when city dwellers and nomadic herders lived together in a society undisrupted by the kind of hubris represented by the Tower of Babel (Gen 4:17-20). When the remnant of Judah finally takes full possession of the promised land of Canaan, including the part once occupied by the Philistines, they will become a society composed of both shepherds and city dwellers living together in peace (Zeph 2:7).

In this section of Zephaniah Judah's international seventh-century context is viewed through a mythic lens as the antitype of Babel. In bringing down the Assyrian hegemony Yahweh is unleashing a cataclysm in which Judah will nearly be destroyed; but the same cataclysm also opens up the possibility of a new and more just world order in which the remnant of Judah will enjoy a favorable position. When 2:4-15 is seen in this light, one aspect of Christensen's interpretation is convincing, namely, his explanation of the cursory mention of Ethiopia (i.e., Cush) in 2:12. Christensen views v. 12 as a reference to the defeat of Egypt's Ethiopian dynasty by the Assyrians at Thebes in 663 BCE ("Zephaniah 2:4-15," 681). This event is described as a development brought about by Yahweh in the past (→ 2:12-15), as if to say that just as Yahweh formerly caused the defeat of Egypt's Ethiopian rulers by the Assyrians (2:12), he will now cause the defeat of the Assyrians by some other unnamed nation (2:13-15).

Haak objects to such an interpretation because the defeat of Egypt's Ethiopian dynasty was not an event contemporary with the career of Zephaniah "in the days of Josiah ben Amon, king of Judah" (1:1). He therefore proposes an alternative identification for the *kûšîm* in 2:12 as a tribal group on Judah's southwestern border, and yet another alternative identification for *kûš* in 3:10 ("'Cush' in Zephaniah," in *The Pitcher Is Broken* [*Fest.* G. W. Ahlström; ed. S. W. Holloway and L. K. Handy; JSOTSup 190; Sheffield: Sheffield Academic Press, 1995] 240-44). Others have similarly suggested various alternative identifications for the land and people of Cush (Ball, *Rhetorical Study,* 141, 244-52). Such proposals are problematic in several respects. For example, it is beside the point to object that the defeat of the Ethiopian dynasty did not happen in the time of Zephaniah, because there is no claim that it did. Rather, this event is described as a past victory that has already been won by Yahweh, and thus constitutes a precedent for his imminent overthrow of Assyria.

Arguing along the same line, Berlin asks: "Would this piece of 'ancient history,' which did not directly involve Judah, really have been relevant to Zephaniah's audience?" (*Zephaniah,* 120). She seems to assume a negative answer to this rhetorical question, but there is no rule that limits prophets to dealing only with current events. Indeed, there is clear evidence from another text that the defeat of Egypt's Ethiopian dynasty was considered relevant by a constituency concerned with Judah's international situation in the late seventh century, even though this event happened some forty years earlier. In Nah 3:8-13 the defeat of Thebes by the Assyrians is portrayed as a precedent that portends the subsequent overthrow of the Assyrians themselves. The same idea is implied in Zephaniah by the juxtaposition of 2:12 with 2:13-15, but in 2:12 it is also explicitly asserted that Yahweh himself defeated the Ethiopians "by my sword," thus implying further that the Assyrian conquerors were instrumental in carrying out his will. The recognition that Yahweh once made Assyria victorious against the Ethiopian dynasty thus provides a warrant for the recognition that because of the changed international situation, he is now about to bring Assyria down. The concept informing Zeph 2:12-15 is thus similar to the concept informing Isa 10:5-12. The Assyrians can unwittingly serve as Yahweh's agents for a time, but when they have served his purpose he will punish them for their hubris.

In view of the mythic scope of 2:1–3:13 both the people called the *kûšîm* in 2:12 and the land called *kûš* in 3:13 are more probably to be identified with Ethiopia than with any other locale. If Yahweh is about to "change the speech of the peoples to a pure speech" (3:9a), his action would begin at some place on the outward perimeter of the primeval dispersion from Babel and extend back to the place where human speech first became confused. It would thus begin at a place that from a Judeocentric perspective could represent the southern end of the world; and it would extend back to Shinar in Mesopotamia, a place that from the same perspective could represent the northern end of the world. In 2:12-15 the action of Yahweh is described as having begun in Cush (2:12) and as eventually extending to Nineveh in Assyria (2:13). As a result of Yahweh's worldwide action the primal unity of the human race will finally be restored through universal worship of Yahweh. Offerings will then be brought to Yahweh from as far as the primeval dispersion extended, i.e., from "beyond the rivers of Cush" (3:10). There may have been other peoples and lands called Cush, but none loomed as large in the history of the ancient Near East as Ethiopia, and none was as apt to play the role of Cush in such a mythic scenario as Zeph 2:1–3:13 (Bennett, 691). It is also possible that the reference to Zephaniah as a descendant of "Cushi" in (→) 1:1 indicates his Ethiopian ancestry. (See R. W. Anderson Jr., "Zephaniah ben Cushi and Cush of Benjamin: Traces of Cushite Presence in Syria-Palestine," in *The Pitcher Is Broken* [*Fest.* G. W. Ahlström; ed. S. W. Holloway and L. K. Handy; JSOTSup 190; Sheffield: Sheffield Academic Press, 1995] 45-70; also J. D. Hays, "The Presence and Influence of a Black Nation in the Bible: A Study of the Cushites," *BSac* 153 [1996] 270-80.)

The geographical references in this whole section, including the particular nations mentioned in 2:4-15, are thus finally to be explained by a combination of factors. First, as mentioned above, there are the two main geopolitical categories in terms of which the world order was historically defined from Judah's seventh-century perspective: the smaller, rival, neighboring nations; and the larger, stronger, more distant imperial powers. Second, as also mentioned above, the directional categories of the four points of the compass are simultaneously operative. In view of the allusion to Gen 11:1-9, however, these categories should not be defined merely in terms of historical geography. They should also be mapped out in relation to the main contours of "the face of the earth," over which primeval humanity was scattered from the central location of Shinar (Gen 11:1-9) as described in the mythical geography of Genesis.

As noted above, in terms of the simultaneously operative geopolitical and directional categories, Moab and Ammon represent neighboring rivals to the east of Judah, and the Philistines represent neighboring rivals to the west. It may be true that Judah did not have to reckon much with Edom under the historical conditions of the late seventh century, but in any case there is no need for the mention of a southern neighbor in this scheme, but rather for a southern imperial power.

In view of the mythical geography of Genesis, the characterization of these neighbors on the east-west axis assumes an added dimension. The punishment of Moab and Ammon is compared with the punishment of Sodom and Gomorrah primarily in terms of the infertile alkaline soil connoted by a reference to "salt" (*melaḥ,* 2:9aβ; cf. Gen 19:25-26). The fate of Moab and Ammon is thus described in terms of their becoming like the dry terrain around the Dead Sea, from which a vast desert extends eastward into Arabia. The Philistines are conversely characterized as inhabitants of the relatively well-watered seacoast *(ḥebel hayyām);* and they are also called a "nation of Cherethites" (2:5a), i.e., Cretans, thus identifying them with those who live further westward in the islands of the Mediterranean. The neighboring nations on the east-west axis thus also represent two types of human society: those who live on the land, whether its soil be arable or desert; and those who live by the sea, whether on continental coastland or island. (The east-west axis is similarly described as extending from Arabia [*šĕbā' ûsĕbā'*] to the isles [*'iyîm*] in Ps 72:10, and from the desert [*midbār*] to the isles [*'iyîm*] in Isa 42:11-12.) It is evident from the summary statement in Zeph 2:11 that Yahweh's activity embraces the gods and peoples of both types, ranging from those who live land-locked over "all the earth" *(kol . . . hā'āreṣ)* to those from "all the island nations" *(kōl 'iyê haggôyim)* with access to the sea. (For similar parallels between *'ereṣ* ["earth" or "land"] and *'iyîm* ["isles"] see Isa 42:4; Ps 97:1; Esth 10:1.)

In contrast with the role of Moab and Ammon, the role of Philistia is further defined by its identification as "Canaan" (2:5bβ), a designation with a double meaning. On the one hand, this term can refer to the land Yahweh promised to Abraham as Israel's inheritance (Gen 17:8), so that noting the Philistines' presence in part of Canaan accuses them in effect of illegitimately occupying some of the land that is rightfully Israel's. The Philistines thus represent Canaan in the sense that they were historically the main obstacle to Israel's control of the land. On the other hand, the term *kĕna'an* can also refer, in its various forms, to the merchant class. The prospect that Yahweh will completely destroy "Canaan, land of the Philistines" (2:5bβ), thus echoes the earlier announcement (1:11b) that Jerusalem's "merchants" or "traders" (lit. "people of Canaan") are completely destroyed. By virtue of this double meaning something that has happened in Judah's internal domestic sphere is linked with something that is happening in the external international sphere. The economic crisis through which Judah has lost its merchant class is part of the same process in which the part of Canaan occupied by the Philistines is being restored to Yahweh's people.

Assyria and Ethiopia represent the distant imperial powers on the north-south axis partly for historical reasons. From a late-seventh-century Judahite perspective the point at which Assyrian hegemony reached its greatest extent, i.e., the Assyrian defeat of Egypt's Ethiopian dynasty, was ironically also the point at which Assyrian power finally became overextended. It is thus implied in 2:12 that the fall of Thebes in 663 BCE marked the beginning of the end for Assyria. In view of the antitype created by the allusion to the Tower of Babel in 3:9, it is also mythically significant that Assyria is cast in the role of the empire from the north and Ethiopia in the role of the empire from the south. Nineveh, the capital of Assyria, was built by Nimrod, the first *gibbōr* (*RSV* "mighty man"), who came from Cush to establish his kingdom in the cities of Shinar (Gen 10:8-11). It is thus singularly appropriate that Yahweh's reversal of the scattering and linguistic confusion that began at Shinar would culminate with the destruction of Nineveh.

The role of the southern empire is played by Ethiopia rather than Egypt partly for the historical reason that Egypt had actually been ruled by an Ethiopian dynasty, whose defeat by Assyria was perceived as a sign that Assyria itself would soon be defeated (see above). Moreover, according to the mythical geography of Genesis it appears that Ethiopia, not Egypt, stands opposite Mesopotamia on the world axis. In Gen 2:10-14 the river flowing from Eden is said to form four other great rivers. The precise identities of these rivers and of the regions demarcated by them remain controversial, but in any case it is clear that in this cosmological scheme Ethiopia ("Cush") and Assyria stand poles apart.

When the formal features and geographical details of 2:4-15 are considered within the context of 2:1–3:13, they can be seen to cohere and form integral parts of this section as a whole.

Genre

This section consists of various generic forms, including a (→) prophetic call to repentance, (→) prophecies of punishment against foreign nations, a (→) prophetic charge of failure to repent, and a (→) prophecy of salvation; but in its entirety it is basically a PROPHETIC EXHORTATION. A similarly mixed form has already been encountered in 1:7-18, where the elements of exhortation are subordinated to the prophecy of punishment in 1:2-6 (→ 1:2-18, Structure). Here, in contrast, the elements of exhortation are dominant, and the prophecies of punishment and salvation are all subordinate to them. The function of the prophetic exhortation in 1:7-18 is to bring about agreement with the prophetic perception on which the foregoing announcement of punishment is based. Its function here is rather to foster a change in the religious attitudes and practices of the people, once they have begun to reach such agreement.

Setting

Several of the generic forms that make up this prophetic exhortation have affinities with the cult, particularly with the liturgy of communal complaint. The commands in 2:1-3 may derive from the (→) call to communal complaint (depending on how one reads the somewhat obscure semantics of the imperatives in 2:1), and (→) prophecies of punishment against foreign nations could also

213

be used in this same setting (→ 2:5-7, Setting). Some have argued that the (→) prophetic call to repentance had as its setting the cultic context of covenant renewal (e.g., Brueggemann). Prophetic exhortation as such, however, including exhortation to repent, was not necessarily limited to a cultic setting. It was just as likely to occur in the streets or at the city gates. Examples include Jer 17:19-27, 18:1-11, and 22:1-9. This unit adheres to conventions of prophetic public speaking, but there is no way of telling whether it was ever actually spoken in public, or whether it is a literary adaptation of such conventions (→ Book as a Whole, Setting).

Intention

This section aims to change the attitudes and practices of its addressees, so that they will seek Yahweh alone (2:3; cf. 1:6). It thus attempts to instill the recognition that though the refusal to heed previous prophetic calls for repentance will result in Yahweh's destruction of Judah, there is still reason to change. The reason is made evident by describing what will happen to Judah in the larger context of the world transformation that Yahweh is bringing about. He is redefining the international order and balance of power, in the process of restoring the primal cultural and religious unity of the human race so as to eliminate both the nearby enemies of his people and their more distant imperial overlords. Within this new world order there is ample room for a remnant who, because they have turned to Yahweh and share the prophetic awareness of what he is doing, will form the nucleus of a newly reconstituted Israel. Those who repent on this basis can therefore look to the day of destruction in hope, with the expectation of eventually living unmolested in the land that Israel once controlled at its greatest extent. They can find this new future only in terms of the salvation that Yahweh is effecting for all humanity, in which the God of Israel becomes manifest as the God of all peoples.

Bibliography

A. Berlin, "Zephaniah's Oracle against the Nations and an Israelite Cultural Myth," in *Fortunate the Eyes That See* (*Fest.* D. N. Freedman; ed. A. A. Bartelt et al.; Grand Rapids: Eerdmans, 1995) 175-84; W. Brueggemann, "Amos IV 4-13 and Israel's Covenant Worship," *VT* 15 (1965) 1-15; D. L. Christensen, "Zephaniah 2:4-15: A Theological Basis for Josiah's Program of Political Expansion," *CBQ* 46 (1984) 669-82; D. H. Ryou, *Zephaniah's Oracles against the Nations: A Synchronic and Diachronic Study of Zephaniah 2:1–3:8* (BIS 13; Leiden: Brill, 1995.

CALL TO REPENTANCE BEFORE
THE DAY OF YAHWEH, 2:1-4

Structure

I. Exhortation to repent	2:1-3
A. Call to repent	2:1-3bα
1. Order to assemble	2:1-2
a. Commands: come together and assemble!	2:1a
b. Accusatory address: shameless nation	2:1b
c. Temporal conditions	2:2
1) Before you are driven away . . .	2:2a
2) Before Yahweh's fierce anger comes on you	2:2bα
3) Before the day of Yahweh's wrath comes on you	2:2bβ
2. Order to seek Yahweh's will	2:3
a. First command: seek Yahweh!	2:3aα
b. Addressees: you humble of the land who do his commands	2:3aβ
c. Second command: seek righteousness!	2:3bα^1
d. Third command: seek humility!	2:3bα^2
B. Potential result: perhaps you may be hidden on the day of Yahweh's wrath	2:3bβ
II. Motivation: announcement of punishment for Philistia	2:4
A. For Gaza: desertion	2:4aα
B. For Ashkelon: desolation	2:4aβ
C. For Ashdod: expulsion	2:4bα
D. For Ekron: uprooting	2:4bβ

This unit is based on two sets of commands (vv. 1-2 and v. 3abα) that are followed by a description of the possible result of heeding them (v. 3bβ) and motivated by the announcement in v. 4 of a disaster that is about to befall the Philistines (Ryou, 296). The addressees of the first set of commands are identified only as "you shameless nation," which seems to presuppose that they are still the same group from "Judah and Jerusalem" that was addressed in ch. 1. Although the translation of the imperative in 2:1a is somewhat uncertain, and textual difficulties likewise make much of 2:2a uncertain (see *BHS*), it is nevertheless clear that some sort of immediate response is being urged on this group, before the already unfolding crisis described in ch. 1 grows any deeper. The use of *bĕṭerem lō'* in 2:2b, which combines the sense of "before" and "so that . . . not . . ." (Gerleman, 28), may connote the possibility of averting the full brunt of the disaster if the commands in v. 1 are heeded, as does *'ûlay* ("perhaps") in v. 3bβ if the entire sequence of commands is heeded.

The addressees of the second set of commands are characterized as *kol-'anwê hā'āreṣ*. Because *'ereṣ* can mean "land," this phrase can be understood to mean "all you humble of the land" (so *RSV*) in keeping with the book's intermittent focus on Judah and Jerusalem (1:4-13; 3:1-7; etc.). Because the same word can also mean "earth," this phrase can alternatively be understood to mean "all you humble of the earth" in keeping with the book's intermittent focus on the worldwide international scene (1:1-3, 17-18; 3:8-10; etc.). The question regarding the sense of *'ereṣ* is closely related to another question regarding the relationship between the "shameless nation" addressed in v. 1 and "the humble" addressed in v. 3. Some scholars have found this shift in the characterization of the addressees to be problematic and have thus concluded that the present text consists of commands addressed to different groups at different times (Ryou, 326-28).

It is not necessary to resort to such hypotheses if the commands are understood just as they are presented, i.e., semantically linked in terms of their sequence (cf. Weigl, 103-4). The "humble" in v. 3 are those from the "shameless nation" of the land of Judah, who have heeded the initial call in v. 1 to "assemble." Precisely by their active compliance with this command of Yahweh *(mišpāṭô p'l),* they show themselves to be seekers of the "humility" *('ănāwâ)* by virtue of which they are characterized as "the humble of the land" *('anwê hā'āreṣ).*

The primary emphasis is thus on those from Judah who demonstrate their humility by their responsiveness to the prophetic directives spoken in Yahweh's name. As this section progresses this responsive group is urged to see their repentance as part of a worldwide process in which people from other nations also discover and turn to the God of Israel. The commands in v. 3 thus look forward to what is prophesied concerning the nations in 2:11 and 3:9, and those who respond to these commands are also in this sense among "the humble of the earth."

The repetitive and hence emphatic use of *bqš* ("seek"), which can technically refer to oracular inquiry, suggests that such a discovery can be made by attending to prophecies — like those that precede and follow these commands. The potential result of such "seeking" may be not the total aversion of the coming disaster but some protection from it (v. 3bβ).

The whole call to repentance (vv. 1-3) is predicated on the threat of worldwide punishment prophesied in 1:2-17, and on the prophetic assessment of the extent to which Judah is implicated in the coming disaster. The announcement of punishment for Philistia (v. 4) motivates this call by reiterating with greater specificity the prophecy of punishment for the whole earth, initially focusing on only one sector of Judah's international context. As the rest of ch. 2 unfolds, various other sectors of the international context are also considered, after first taking up this one again in vv. 5-7 (Ryou, 326).

Genre

The sequence of commands in this unit is tantamount to a call for a fundamental change of attitude. This effect is evident not only from the kinds of actions that are commanded but also from the changing characterization of the addressees. This call is based on the possibility that those who turn to Yahweh and seek truly to discern his will can survive the currently worsening crisis (cf. Hunter, 259-71; Tångberg, 102-3; Ryou, 329-33). This is therefore a PROPHETIC CALL TO REPENTANCE.

Setting

Raitt views this genre as an adaptation of that part of a covenant renewal ceremony in which the covenant mediator called for the people's renewed affirmation of their relationship with Yahweh on the basis of covenant law. The prophets supposedly took this manner of speaking and put it to a more general use. Even if the texts that are crucial for this hypothesis (e.g., Exod 19:5-6) do indeed reflect genuinely early tradition rather than later Deuteronomistic influence, it is nevertheless evident that the majority of textual examples from both early and late periods do not explicitly involve covenant terminology or concepts. It seems more likely that calls to covenant renewal would thus have constituted a special case of a more general phenomenon, rather than the main paradigm from which all examples of the call to repentance were subsequently derived.

The immediately preceding prophetic exhortation (1:7-18) plays on the connotations of directives that are at home in the cultic activities of festival sacrifice and communal complaint. The directive that is emphasized in this unit, to "seek" Yahweh, can similarly refer to the cultic activity of participating in a communal complaint (e.g., Ps 27:8; cf. 2 Chr 7:14), and to the quest for a profound sense of Yahweh's purpose that might animate such devotion (e.g., Hos 5:15; S. Wagner, *"biqqēsh," TDOT* 2:236-39). Like (→) 1:7-10 and 1:11-18, speeches of the sort represented by this unit may have been spoken to a group gathered for some cultic occasion, but not as an actual part of the liturgy for which they were assembled.

This unit conforms to one of the conventions of prophetic public speaking on a cultic occasion, but there is no way of telling whether it was ever actually spoken in public, or whether it is a literary adaptation of this convention (→ Book as a Whole, Setting).

Intention

This unit urges its implicitly Judahite addressees to take communal action, and thereby show their willingness to turn to Yahweh in the midst of the impending crisis. By remaining faithful to Yahweh as their situation worsens, they will begin a process through which Judah's destruction may be mitigated. Moreover, the vast cosmic disintegration, of which Judah's imminent destruction is symptomatic, may also begin to be reversed.

Bibliography

A. V. Hunter, *Seek the Lord! A Study of the Meaning and Function of the Exhortations in Amos, Hosea, Isaiah, Micah, and Zephaniah* (Baltimore: St. Mary's Seminary and University, 1982); T. M. Raitt, "The Prophetic Summons to Repentance," *ZAW* 83 (1971) 30-49; D. H. Ryou, *Zephaniah's Oracles against the Nations: A Synchronic and Diachronic Study of Zephaniah 2:1-3:8* (BIS 13; Leiden: Brill, 1995); K. A. Tångberg, *Die prophetische Mahnrede: Form- und traditionsgeschichtliche Studien zum prophetischen Umkehrruf* (FRLANT 143; Göttingen: Vandenhoeck & Ruprecht, 1987).

YAHWEH WILL DESTROY PHILISTIA, 2:5-7

Structure

I. Announcement of Yahweh's action against Philistia — 2:5
  A. Introduction — 2:5abα
    1. Lamentation — 2:5a
      a. "Woe" cry — $2:5a\alpha^1$
      b. Double designation of those affected — $2:5a\alpha^2\beta$
        1) Inhabitants of the seacoast — $2:5a\alpha^2$
        2) Nation of the Cherethites — 2:5aβ
    2. Reason for lamentation: direct address — 2:5bα
      a. Basic statement: the word of Yahweh is
        against you — $2:5b\alpha^1$
      b. Double designation of addressees — $2:5b\alpha^2$
        1) Canaan
        2) Land of the Philistines
  B. Announcement proper: I will destroy you until
    no inhabitant is left — 2:5bβ
II. Effects of Yahweh's action against Philistia — 2:6-7
  A. With respect to Philistia itself: you will become
    pastureland — 2:6
  B. With respect to Judah — 2:7
    1. Description of the effect itself — 2:7abα
      a. In terms of the region in general:
        the seacoast will belong to the remnant of
        Judah as their pasture — 2:7a
      b. In terms of a particular city: in the houses of
        Ashkelon they will lie down in the evening — 2:7bα
    2. Rationale for this outcome: Yahweh their God
      will take care of them and restore them — 2:7bβ

Because this unit is concerned with the Philistines, it elaborates on the immediately preceding announcement of the Philistines' punishment in 2:4, which motivates the call to repentance in 2:1-3. There is no sharp division between 2:4 and 2:5-7, but rather a shift in rhetorical emphasis marked by the interjection *hôy* ("woe!") as the prophetic discourse concerning Philistia continues. Because this unit is also the first in a series of prophecies concerning various other surrounding nations (2:5-15), it furthermore links the call to repentance in 2:1-4 with the entire international situation that begins to be portrayed here. The punishment of the surrounding nations, beginning with Philistia, thus becomes part of the motivation for Judah's repentance. The point is not that Judah's change of heart will result in the nations being punished instead. It is rather that Judah's repentance is happening in the context of a cosmic upheaval affecting Judah and its neighbors alike. Judah thus has not only the prospect of some survivors but also the hope of existing in a world that is free from the oppressive influence that other nations have exerted in the past.

As part of the cosmic upheaval envisioned in ch. 1, Yahweh intends to destroy and utterly depopulate the major urban centers of Philistia (vv. 4-5), so that the region will not be fit for much more than subsistence pastoralism (v. 6b). The area will thus be ripe for occupation by even the decimated remnant of Judah, who will then be in a position to take over the herding and reoccupy the deserted urban sites (v. 7a). The theological rationale for these changes (v. 7b) makes use of the term *pqd* (*RSV* "be mindful"), the same term used in 1:8-9 to denote Yahweh's intention to destroy Judah (*RSV* "punish"), thus showing that the punishment and the potential restoration of Judah are envisioned as parts of the same divinely instigated historico-cosmic process.

Genre

The "woe" cry that begins this unit is generally regarded as a hallmark of the (→) woe oracle. In this case, however, the initial woe cry functions not as a distinctive genre element identifying 2:5-7 as a "woe" oracle (→ Hab 2:6-8, Genre) but as a stylistic device evoking a mood of lamentation and establishing a parallel between the prophecies concerning foreign nations in 2:5-15 and the prophecy concerning Judah in (→) 3:1-7. This unit is more like a (→) prophecy of punishment.

The latter typically announces that Yahweh is bringing misfortune on some person or group and accuses that person or group in order to provide a reason for his doing so. In this case there is an announcement of punishment but without any separate accusation as such. It is only in view of the larger context that the reason for Yahweh's action against Philistia, which an explicit accusation would typically provide, becomes evident. As 2:5-7 comes to be seen in relation to the following prophecies concerning Judah's other neighbors, and also in relation to the Mesopotamian and North African superpowers with which they were from time to time allied, it becomes evident that these are all being characterized as Judah's enemies (Berlin, "Zephaniah's Oracle," 176-77). Their enmity is the reason for Yahweh's opposition. This unit is thus to be identified as a PROPHECY OF PUNISHMENT AGAINST A FOREIGN NATION.

Setting

Prophecies of punishment against foreign nations functioned in a variety of settings that were all concerned in some way with international affairs. Prophecies of this sort could be spoken to representatives of foreign nations by prophets of Yahweh, who either journeyed abroad to meet such representatives or received them as envoys from abroad, in order to influence foreign authorities. Such prophecies could also be addressed to a general audience so as to promulgate the prophet's view on the theological significance of some international development. They could also be ostensibly addressed to foreign enemies but spoken in the hearing of the prophet's own people. In this situation prophecies against foreign nations could in effect communicate to Yahwistic audiences the favorable impact that the foreigners' punishment would have on them.

With regard to 2:5-7 the last of these possibilities seems most pertinent, particularly in view of the promise that the remnant of Judah will possess the deserted Philistine territory (2:7). This text reflects the kind of prophetic speech that served to assure a Judahite audience, as they overheard a message ostensibly addressed to a foreign enemy, that Yahweh's punishment of this enemy would be to their own advantage (Roberts, 197). In the preexilic period prophecies of this sort were typically pronounced when the community was threatened militarily, in the context of a communal complaint liturgy conducted under royal auspices (e.g., Ps 60:8-10 [*RSV* 6-8]; Lam 4:21-22), or in the context of the king's public preparations for battle, or even in course of conducting a battle (e.g., Num 22–24; 1 Sam 15:2-3; 1 Kgs 20:26-30). As the description in 1 Kgs 19:14-28 suggests, the line between these sorts of occasions may not have always been clear-cut, and in any case there is nothing that would limit the language of this unit to any particular one of these alternatives.

Although 2:5-7 adheres to a particular convention of prophetic speech, there is no way to tell whether it was ever spoken in public, or whether it is a literary adaptation of this convention (→ Book as a Whole, Setting). Moreover, in view of how 2:5-7 is incorporated into this entire section of the book, on the one hand as an elaboration on the motivation in 2:4 of the call to repentance in 2:1-3, and on the other hand as the first in a series of prophecies against foreign nations (2:5-15), it is difficult to say whether this unit ever existed independently outside the literary context of this section (→ 2:1–3:13). Although it resembles the kind of prophecies that were typically directed against nations opposing Israel and Judah, this unit did not necessarily originate in the context of conflict between Judah and the Philistines. It may have been literarily composed as part of this section, in which case it would serve to interpret an international situation characterized by a long history of antagonism between these two peoples.

Intention

This text motivates the Judahite addressees, to whom it is implicitly and obliquely directed, to respond to the call to repentance in 2:1-3. As they overhear the punishment ostensibly announced to the Philistines, they are assured that Yahweh will bring a Judahite remnant through the impending crisis. He will enable them to become part of a world order in which the age-old threat of Philistine enmity will not be a fact of life. The Philistines will no longer be a nation, and Judah will be left in full possession of its patrimonial territory.

Bibliography

A. Berlin, "Zephaniah's Oracle against the Nations and an Israelite Cultural Myth," in *Fortunate the Eyes That See* (*Fest.* D. N. Freedman; ed. A. A. Bartelt et al.; Grand Rapids: Eerdmans, 1995) 175-84; D. L. Christensen, *Transformations of the War Oracle in Old Testament Prophecy* (HDR 3; Missoula, Mont.: Scholars Press, 1975); J. H. Hayes, "The Usage of Oracles against Foreign Nations in Ancient Israel," *JBL* 87 (1968) 81-92; D. Petersen, "The Oracles against the Nations: A Form-Critical Analysis," in *Society of Biblical Literature 1975 Seminar Papers* (ed. G. MacRae; 2 vols.; Missoula, Mont.: Scholars Press, 1975) 1:39-61; P. R. Raabe, "Why Prophetic Oracles against the Nations?" in *Fortunate the Eyes That See* (*Fest.* D. N. Freedman; ed. A. B. Beck et al.; Grand Rapids: Eerdmans, 1995) 236-57; D. H. Ryou, *Zephaniah's Oracles against the Nations: A Synchronic and Diachronic Study of Zephaniah 2:1–3:8* (BIS 13; Leiden: Brill, 1995).

YAHWEH WILL REQUITE MOAB AND AMMON, 2:8-11

Text

Along with many commentators the *RSV* translates the *kî* clause in v. 11 in the future tense, but the first verb is a perfect *(rāzâ)* and the second is coordinated with it as a *waw*-consecutive imperfect *(wayyištaḥăwû)*. Both would normally be translated with some past or perfect tense, just like the verbs of the very same sort in the preceding *kî* clause in v. 10b. In view of the overall context, in which this *kî* clause substantiates Yahweh's being characterized in the preceding verbless clause as "terrible" *(nôrā')*, it might best be rendered in the present tense so as to indicate a characteristic action of Yahweh that he has demonstrated in the past and continues to demonstrate: "For [Yahweh] famishes all the gods of the earth, and all . . . bow down to him."

Structure

I. Accusation: first person report of Yahweh	2:8
A. Reporting verb: I have heard . . .	2:8aα^1
B. Offenses witnessed by Yahweh	2:8aα^{2}b
1. Twofold basic designation	2:8aα^{2}β
a. Taunts of Moab	2:8aα^2

221

This prophecy is about the Moabites and Ammonites but is not addressed directly to them. It thus contrasts with the preceding prophecy concerning the Philistines, which refers to Philistia in the second person. This prophecy differs further from its predecessor in making an explicit accusation. Moab and Ammon are charged with "taunting" *(ḥrp)* and "boasting" *(gdp)*, two activities that involve considerably more than just bad-mouthing someone. This pair of terms can refer to the whole range of injuries that enemies inflict on each other, including but not limited to verbal wounds, and together they represent every aspect of aggression. As a consequence of their aggressiveness, Moab and Ammon are to suffer a severe penalty. In contrast with the land of Philistia, which at least will remain pastorally viable, these two nations will become as desolate as the proverbial cities of Sodom and Gomorrah (Gen 19:24-25), and everything of any value will be confiscated by the remnant of Judah.

Yahweh's action against the Moabites and Ammonites is shown by the oath in v. 9aα to be grounded in a direct expression of the divine will and is given an explicitly theological rationale in vv. 10-11. The precise meaning of the term *rāzâ* (*RSV* "famish") is obscure in this context, but it shows that Yahweh's retaliatory action somehow diminishes all other gods and requires that the stability of creation be reaffirmed — not unlike what is described in Ps 82 — therefore commanding the respect of even the most far-flung nations (v. 11b). Yahweh's punishment of Moab and Ammon is thus described in terms of a revamping of creation in which Yahweh is already involved as one specific part of the same process of cosmic disintegration and renewal that is described more generally in 1:2-3. This is also shown by characterizing the beneficiaries of Yahweh's action not as the same "people" of Yahweh against whom the Moabites and Ammonites committed aggression, but as the "remnant" *(šĕʾērît)* and the "survivors" *(yeter)* of Yahweh's people (v. 9b). The punishment of Moab and Ammon is thus part of the same process in which Judah is also to be punished and the world order is to be reconstituted, so that the repentant remnant of Yahweh's people can live in peace.

Genre

This is a PROPHECY OF PUNISHMENT AGAINST A FOREIGN NATION — in this case two foreign nations — a genre whose basic aspects I discussed in connection with the preceding unit (→ 2:5-7, Genre). A distinctive feature of this particular example is the concluding summary-appraisal. Some commentators (e.g., Rudolph, 281-82; cf. Roberts, 201-2; Ben Zvi, 312-13) regard all or part of vv. 10-11 as a later addition to vv. 8-9 and thus as material extraneous to this unit. Considerations of both form and content, however, suggest that vv. 10-11 are an integral part of the prophecy that begins in vv. 8-9.

With respect to content, it is the attribute of Yahweh's "terribleness" *(nôrāʾ)* that forms the conceptual link between the description of his action against Moab and Ammon (vv. 8-11aα) and the explication of this action in terms of Yahweh's subjection of all gods and his recognition by all peoples (v. 11aβb). This attribute is often associated with both the victories of Yahweh and his people over foreign kingdoms (e.g., Ps 76:13 [*RSV* 12]; cf. Ps 47:3 [*RSV* 2]) and Yahweh's supremacy over the other gods (e.g., Ps 96:4; cf. Ps 89:8 [*RSV* 7]), so that these are virtually two sides of the same conceptual coin. Yahweh's punishment of a foreign kingdom and his supremacy over the other gods are explicitly integrated in the attribute of his terribleness — as they are here — in Exod 15:11. In the thematic progression of this unit as a whole, vv. 10-11 thus follow naturally from vv. 8-9 (cf. J. Cales, "L'authenticité du Sophonie II, 11 et son contexte primitif," *RSR* 10 [1920] 355-57).

With respect to form, vv. 10-11 constitute the kind of summary-appraisal that can also be found in wisdom literature (e.g., Prov 1:19; Job 8:13; Eccl 7:23), as well as in prophetic speeches from Isaiah, whether in the context of a prophecy of punishment against a foreign nation (e.g., Isa 14:26-27) or some other genre (e.g., Isa 28:29). As in these other instances, this element here serves to summarize and appraise the foregoing material. In this case the actions of Moab and Ammon, as well as the reaction of Yahweh, are redescribed in terms of more general attributes: their pride and his terribleness. The implications of Yahweh's reaction are then drawn out in terms of his status vis-à-vis the other gods and other nations. Vv. 10-11 serve a double rhetorical function, on the one hand articulating the general presuppositions on which the foregoing characterization of Yahweh and his antagonists is based, and on the other hand forming the climax of this unit as a whole. There is no a priori reason to regard material with such a rhetorical function as secondary.

Setting

Childs has suggested that prophetic speeches which include a summary-appraisal should be seen in relation to wisdom schools ("Isaiah," 136), and Whedbee has noted the additional possibility of a cultic setting in some instances (p. 78). This unit does show a capacity for theological reflection in mythical terms, which was generally characteristic of wisdom schools. As a prophecy of punishment against a foreign nation, it might also have been used in the context of a complaint liturgy (→ 2:5-7, Setting). These are not mutually exclusive possibilities, in the sense that a prophecy might be scholastically formulated for cultic presentation. Moreover, the use of language from both cultic and scholastic contexts does not necessarily require that the speech itself be located in either setting. Just as prophets could use the kinds of directives employed in the cult to compose a noncultic speech (→ 1:2-17, Setting), a prophet might also use the forensic rhetoric generally heard in scribal schools to compose a speech that was not intended for such a school.

The element of summary-appraisal is thus not very telling with respect to the setting of any particular prophecy, at least in comparison with the genre classification of the unit as a whole. As a prophecy of punishment against a foreign nation, this pericope resembles speeches typically made in rites reacting to the threat of enemy attack (→ 2:5-7, Setting). This resemblance does not necessarily mean, however, that this unit originated as a speech occasioned by a particular Moabite-Ammonite attack. It could be a literary adaptation of this prophetic practice (→ Book as a Whole, Setting).

Moreover, in view of how 2:8-11 forms part of a series of prophecies against foreign nations (2:5-15) that together make up the motivation of the call to repentance in 2:1-3, it is difficult to determine whether this unit ever existed independently outside the literary context of this section (→ 2:1–3:13). Within such a context it would be part of an attempt to assess the overall international situation, focusing specifically on the antagonism that was often characteristic of Judah's relations with the Moabites and Ammonites.

Intention

This text motivates the Judahite addressees, to whom it is implicitly directed, to respond to the call to repentance in 2:1-3. It discloses to them that Yahweh will bring some Judahite survivors through the impending crisis and incorporate them into a new world order. This new order is in many ways a reversal of the presently disintegrating one as it entails a transformation of the earthly international relationships that have generated enmity between Judah and their neighbors, particularly Moab and Ammon. It also entails a transformation of the corresponding heavenly relationships between the gods of the nations. As Yahweh debilitates the other gods, Yahweh's people will no longer be tempted to worship them, and even the most distant nations will come to acknowledge the power of Israel's God.

Bibliography

→ 2:5-7; also B. S. Childs, *Isaiah and the Assyrian Crisis* (SBT 2/3; London: SCM, 1967); J. W. Whedbee, *Isaiah and Wisdom* (Nashville: Abingdon, 1971).

YAHWEH IS BRINGING ON ASSYRIA THE SAME DEVASTATION HE HAS BROUGHT ON ETHIOPIA, 2:12-15

Structure

I. Statement concerning Ethiopia: a taunt	2:12
A. Direct address: you, too, Ethiopians!	2:12a
B. Description of punishment: they are slain by my sword	2:12b
II. Prophecy concerning Assyria: description of punishment	2:13-15
A. Yahweh's actions	2:13
1. Against the region of the north: he will stretch out his hand	2:13aα
2. Against the nation of Assyria: he will destroy it	2:13aβ
3. Against the city of Nineveh: he will make it a desolate desert	2:13b
B. Effects of Yahweh's actions	2:14-15
1. Described in terms of conditions on the site of Nineveh: its ruins will be inhabited only by animals	2:14
2. Described in terms of an observer's reaction: a taunt	2:15
a. Characterization of the city	2:15a
1) Definitional statement: this is the city . . .	2:15aα[1]

2)	Itemization of its traits	$2:15a\alpha^2\beta$
	a) Exultant	
	b) Dwelling secure	
	c) Thinking of itself as self-sufficient	
	and invulnerable	$2:15a\beta$
b.	Exclamation over Nineveh's fate	$2:15b$
	1) Its condition: What a desolate lair for	
	animals!	$2:15b\alpha$
	2) Reaction of passers-by: all hiss and	
	shake their fist!	$2:15b\beta$

The brief reference to Ethiopia, with which this unit begins (v. 12), is a transition piece. Together with the quickly following treatment of Assyria, it signals both a continuing connection with the preceding unit and a shift of concern, away from Judah's immediate neighbors toward the North African and Mesopotamian regional centers of power from which imperial overlords often dominated the area of Syria-Palestine. The pivot on which this shift turns is the immediately preceding summary-appraisal in vv. 10-11, which describes Yahweh's treatment of Ammon and Moab in terms of how he generally treats even the most far-flung nations and their gods. This generalization leads naturally to the mention of particular kingdoms that lie outside the surrounding area of Judah's immediate neighbors. Ethiopia and Assyria represent this larger sphere of influence as nations representing the ancient Near Eastern centers of power in North Africa and Mesopotamia.

Ethiopia is mentioned in passing as an imperial power from the south, but the focus of attention is obviously more on Assyria as an imperial power from the north. This focus is perhaps because Yahweh's punishment of Ethiopia is assumed to have happened already. Although v. 12 is usually translated in the future tense (so *RSV*), its unusual grammatical structure offers other possibilities. The subject of this verbless sentence is the second person plural vocative, but the predicate concludes with an appositional pronoun in the third person plural. Although v. 12 is grammatically coordinated with what precedes it in v. 11 by *gam* (*RSV* "also") and with what follows in v. 13 by *wĕ* ("and"; Ryou, 303), the effect of its own disjunctive construction is — among other things — to remove it from the verbal sequence. Outside such a sequence, this sort of clause would normally be taken to describe presently existing circumstances. Thus vv. 11b-13a might be translated: "And all the outlying nations . . . bow down to [Yahweh]. Also you Ethiopians! (They are [already] slain by my sword!) And he will stretch forth his hand against the north. . . ."

Read in this way, v. 12 becomes a rhetorical aside alluding to the defeat of Ethiopia, assuming that this event is common knowledge and thus needs no *prophetic* description (Bennett, 691). The aside also serves to identify this historical development as an action of Yahweh, whose overthrow of this southern nation can be seen to signal that a great transformation has already begun, one that will eventually include his overthrow of a northern nation also. The unit thus focuses mainly on the eventual fate of Assyria.

Attention is concentrated on the downfall of the capital city, Nineveh, as representing the destruction of the entire region and the entire kingdom. In contrast with Philistia, where cities will largely revert to pastureland and become inhabited by pastoralists from the remnant of Judah (2:6-7), the site of Nineveh will become an uninhabited wilderness and remain a lonely ruin, available to herds but inhabited chiefly by wild animals (vv. 13-14).

Some commentators separate v. 15, as a speech that looks back on the fall of Nineveh, from the prophecy in vv. 13-14, which anticipates this event. Although the rhetoric of taunting usually assumes that some misfortune has already taken place, there are a number of reasons to suppose that this is not the case here. First, the demonstrative pronoun that constitutes the subject of v. 15a refers back to, and thus connects v. 15 rather closely with, the preceding reference to Nineveh in v. 13b. Second, v. 15 has a function in relation to the conclusion of this unit that is analogous to the function of the summary-appraisal (vv. 10-11) in the conclusion of the preceding unit (→ 2:8-11). It serves to identify the root causes of the actions taken by Yahweh, and to summarize the description of their effect. V. 15bα summarizes vv. 13b-14 by its repeated references to both the "desolation" *(šmh)* and the "beasts" *(ḥyh)* that are "lying down" *(rbṣ)* as conditions characteristic of the ruined site. Third, in concluding the prophecy concerning Assyria with a speech like the one in v. 15, the unit becomes framed by the same taunting rhetoric with which it is begun in v. 12. Finally, it is generally characteristic of the preceding chapter, in its combination of commands with narration of future events, to describe Yahweh's actions in terms of a process that is already underway and heading toward a particular outcome (→ 1:2-18, Structure). This is also the case with respect to the preceding unit, where Yahweh's future action against Moab and Ammon is identified with action that he is already taking against the gods of the nations (→ 2:8-11, Text). For all these reasons v. 15 should be regarded as an integral part of one and the same prophecy concerning Assyria (vv. 13-15), which proleptically celebrates the disaster announced in vv. 13-14 as if it had already come to pass (cf. Ryou, 303-4). A sarcastic climax is achieved by the ironic juxtaposition of the high expectations that might have conventionally been held for a city like Nineveh (v. 15a) with the fate that Yahweh actually has in store for it — the fate that he will bring about someday soon (v. 15b).

Genre

This is basically a PROPHECY OF PUNISHMENT AGAINST A FOREIGN NATION (→ 2:5-7) directed against Assyria. Yahweh's punishment of Ethiopia is tauntingly cited as something that has already happened, thus indicating that the doom prophesied for Assyria will likewise come to pass. This unit is a somewhat atypical representative of its genre. It neither makes any direct accusation of the nation to be punished nor gives any explicit indication of how their punishment might benefit Judah. The kind of taunting that is in this case directed against Assyria (v. 15) appears as a subsidiary element in some other examples of the genre (e.g., Isa 37:21-29; Ezek 28:9). Here it functions as a variant on, or substitute for, the more basic elements that are missing. The characterization of Nineveh as a city that gloatingly thinks of itself as self-sufficient and invulnerable amounts to an accusation of hubris for which the tragic downfall described in vv. 13-14 is the inevitable consequence. By identifying with the reaction of the anonymous passer-by, the audience hearing this speech would identify themselves with all those who would be relieved by the overthrow of Assyria (cf. Nah 3:19b) and thus see in Nineveh's destruction some implicit sign of their own deliverance.

Setting

This unit reflects the practice of prophesying in the royal sanctuary or court so as to interpret the international situation (→ 2:5-7, Setting). This royal milieu is further reflected in the text's vantage point on events far removed in time and space, which assumes the availability of diplomatically reported information. Although the text conforms to this convention of prophetic speech, there is no way of telling whether it was actually spoken in public, or whether it is a literary adaptation of the convention (→ Book as a Whole, Setting).

Moreover, because 2:12-15 forms part of a series of prophecies against foreign nations (2:5-15) that together make up the motivation of the call to repentance in 2:1-3, it is difficult to determine whether this unit ever existed independently outside the literary context of this section (→ 2:1–3:13). Although this unit resembles prophecies typically proclaimed in the royal sanctuary or court to interpret the international situation, it did not necessarily originate as a speech delivered in direct reaction to some particular international event. It may rather have been literarily composed as part of a larger attempt to assess the overall course of international relations at a particular turning point, focusing specifically on the probability that the Assyrians would suffer a reversal of the fate that they had previously inflicted on the Ethiopians.

Intention

This text motivates the Judahite addressees, to whom it is implicitly directed, to respond to the call to repentance in 2:1-3. It assures them that Yahweh will destroy Assyria to create a new world order in which Judah will be safe and secure. This new order is in many ways a reversal of the presently disintegrating one, as it entails a transformation of earthly international relations, particularly the tendency of the North African and Mesopotamian empires to dominate the Levant. The repentant remnant of Judah can expect to be free from this sort of interference and more particularly from the domination that Assyria has long imposed. The prospect of taunting the tyrant's fall (v. 15) portends the victory celebration that is eventually in store, as does the already accomplished defeat of the Ethiopians (v. 12).

Bibliography

→ 2:5-7.

JERUSALEM AND ITS LEADERS ARE CHARGED WITH THEIR FAILURE TO REPENT, 3:1-7

Structure

I. Introductory lamentation	3:1
A. "Woe" cry	3:1aα
B. Characterization of the affected	3:1aβb
1. Rebellious and defiled	3:1aβ
2. The oppressing city	3:1b
II. Accusation	3:2-7
A. Basic statement	3:2
1. The city's incorrigibility	3:2a
a. Not heeding any voice	3:2aα
b. Not accepting correction	3:2aβ
2. The city's faithlessness	3:2b
a. Not trusting in Yahweh	3:2bα
b. Not drawing near to God	3:2bβ
B. Elaboration	3:3-7
1. Specific indications of faithlessness	3:3-5
a. Corrupt leadership	3:3-4
1) Officials like lions	3:3a
2) Judges like wolves	3:3b
3) Prophets: wanton and faithless	3:4a
4) Priests: profane and lawless	3:4b
b. Contrast between Yahweh and such characters	3:5
1) Yahweh's traits	3:5abβ^1
a) His justness	3:5a
(1) Described in a positive statement: he is righteous	3:5aα
(2) Described in a negative statement: he does no wrong	3:5aβ
b) His constancy	3:5bαβ^1
(1) Described in a positive statement: he gives justice every morning	3:5bα
(2) Described in a negative statement: he does not fail	3:5bβ^1
2) The basic trait of the unjust: they know no shame	3:5bβ^2
2. Specific indications of incorrigibility	3:6-7
a. Yahweh's attempts to call the city back	3:6-7a

1) His punishment of the nations   3:6
   a) The nations themselves in general   3:6a
     (1) Yahweh's action: I have cut off . . .   3:6aα
     (2) Its effect: fortresses are ruined   3:6aβ
   b) The cities of the nations in particular   3:6b
     (1) Yahweh's action: I have laid
       waste their streets   3:6bα
     (2) Its effect: cities are desolate
       and uninhabited   3:6bβ
2) Yahweh's treatment of the city   3:7a
   a) His speaking to them   3:7aα
     (1) Introductory verb: I said . . .   3:7aα^1
     (2) Speech of Yahweh to the city:
       Surely you will fear me and
       accept correction   3:7aα^2
   b) His intention: so that all I have done
     will not be lost sight of   3:7aβ
b. The people's heedlessness: they were all
the more eager to make their deeds corrupt   3:7b

In v. 1 the initial cry of "woe," portending an unfavorable future, is exclaimed over an unnamed party that is first designated in broadly pejorative terms as *mōr'â* ("a rebellious one") and *nig'ālâ* ("a defiled one"), and then more specifically identified as *hā'îr hayyônâ* ("the oppressing city"). In v. 2 the substance of this negative characterization is spelled out so as to imply that the city in question is Jerusalem, whose poor prospects are due to its failure to heed Yahweh's calls for change (v. 2a) and its failure to be true to Yahweh (v. 2b). Each aspect of this twofold charge is subsequently elaborated in greater detail, but in reverse order (vv. 3-7). The elaboration on Jerusalem's faithlessness (vv. 3-5; cf. v. 2b) attributes it primarily to a failure of leadership (vv. 3-4; cf. 1:4b, 8). The corrupt governance "in its midst" (*bĕqirbāh,* v. 3a), which prevents the city from "drawing near" (*qārēbâ,* v. 2b) to God, is sharply contrasted with the manifestations of Yahweh's divine justice that are also "in its midst" (v. 5a). The elaboration on Jerusalem's incorrigibility (vv. 6-7) focuses on its inability to discern Yahweh's will in the chaotic course of international events (v. 6) and its concomitant failure to hear Yahweh's simultaneous calls for changes that could lead to a new and more hopeful future (v. 7a). By not seeing in the prophetically interpreted world situation any reason to cease their corrupt ways (v. 7b), the city shows itself unwilling to "accept correction" (*lqḥ mûsār,* v. 7a; cf. v. 2a).

Some see a fundamental division after 3:5 because at v. 6 there is a change from third person speech of the prophet to first person oracular speech of Yahweh and because there is also a change in focus, shifting from Jerusalem to the nations. The alternation between third and first person prophetic speech is generally characteristic of this section as a whole, however (cf. 2:4-7 and 2:13-15 in third person, and 2:8-12 in first person). And although the nations are mentioned at 3:6, it is only by way of developing the theme already stated

230

in 3:2 that Judah has not "accepted correction." Yahweh has indicated what he can do through various international developments, but his people persist in refusing to repent (Renaud, 17-19). There is a change at v. 6, but not of a sort that indicates a new unit. It rather serves to mark off subsections within 3:1-7 (Marti, 372; Ben Zvi, 314-17; cf. Sweeney, 401-2; Ryou, 305-8).

Genre

Although this unit begins with the interjection that is characteristic of the (→) woe oracle (i.e., *hôy; RSV* "woe"), it does not conform to the conventions of this genre in other respects. In particular, this unit includes no explicit description of the lamentable fate lying in store for the group or persons over whom the woe cry is exclaimed as a consequence of their bad behavior. In this case the woe cry is thus a stylistic device rather than a genre element. It serves to create a parallel between the indictment of Jerusalem in this unit (3:1-7) and the foregoing series of three prophecies against foreign nations (2:5-15), which likewise begins with a "woe" cry (→ 2:1–3:13, Structure; cf. Ryou, 334-43).

This unit is a PROPHETIC CHARGE OF FAILURE TO REPENT. The basic elements of this type of prophetic speech include a description of some prophetically discerned sign of divine activity, along with a disparaging description of the people's inability to accept the prophetic perception and respond accordingly. These elements are often combined in a grammatical construction that employs an adversative conjunction, usually *wĕlō'* ("but not"), but in this case *'ākēn* ("yet" or "nevertheless"). For example, Amos 4:6-11 consists of a series of prophecies in this form: "I did thus and so, yet *(wĕlō')* you did not return to me, says Yahweh." The descriptive elements may be expressed positively or negatively (e.g., Jer 5:3) and may be cast in first person oracular speech of Yahweh (e.g., Isa 30:15-16) or third person speech of the prophet himself (e.g., Isa 9:13).

The charge of failure to repent can comprise all or part of the accusation within a prophecy of punishment. In such a context it explains why Yahweh is in the process of inflicting the punishment that is described (Jer 15:5-9; 25:1-4) and thus serves as the basis for its announcement. The charge of failure to repent occasionally has an additional function. The inevitability of a punishment that is already unleashed, due to a prior failure to repent, may become the basis for a renewed call to repentance. The very recognition that a prophecy of punishment is being fulfilled may put the people in a position to be responsive, even in the process of suffering the punishment, and on this basis they can be exhorted to return and undertake whatever faithfulness may now require (e.g., Amos 4:12). The charge of failure to repent in Zeph 3:1-7 serves both of these functions in relation to its larger context.

The opening "woe" cry hints that the impact of the punishment described in 1:2-18 is already being felt, or is about to be felt, in Judah. In relation to this punishment 3:1-7 serves to explain and underscore the inevitability of its affecting Judah along with the other nations. Largely because of inadequate

231

leadership the people have not shared the prophetic perception of Yahweh's present purpose. They have thus not been able to recognize the disparity between their ways and the demands of Yahweh's justice and have not been able to reform their lives accordingly. They could not even discern Yahweh's purpose after the punishment began to affect the world situation in general, and now it will not be stopped from affecting Judah in particular.

The dual function of 3:1-7 is in accord with the preceding call to repentance (2:1-3), which is predicated on the possibility of a new future beyond the present crisis. 3:1-7 recalls past behavior in order to provide a counterexample of what is presently called for, now that Yahweh's punishment is underway. In relation to 2:1-3 this unit serves to reinforce the notion that, despite the failures of the past and despite the inevitability of suffering the consequences, there is still an opportunity for repentance. This section thus opens onto and provides the basis for the following exhortation to be open to what Yahweh is presently doing, and hence open to the new future that is becoming apparent within the course of events: "Therefore wait for me, says Yahweh."

Setting

The prophetic charge of failure to repent reflects the conventional practice of prophetic public address but in a particular context. This manner of speaking presupposes an audience that has previously rejected a prophetic analysis of their situation, particularly an analysis that finds portents of disaster in present social conditions. The prophet charges them with their past failures in order to intensify the urgency of their reconsideration, even if circumstances have not changed so as to make the analysis any more plausible, but particularly if circumstances have changed — as is the case here. The report of Jeremiah's temple sermon (Jer 7:1-34; cf. 26:1-19) affords perhaps the clearest example of this elemental component of prophetic speech in its typical setting (see particularly Jer 7:25-26).

Although this unit conforms to the convention of the prophetic charge of failure to repent, there is no way of telling whether it was ever actually spoken in public, or whether it is a literary adaptation of this convention (→ Book as a Whole, Setting). Moreover, because 3:1-7 forms part of a series of prophecies of punishment (2:5–3:7) describing Yahweh's treatment of Judah as a "woe"-filled development (3:3a) that parallels his "woe"-filled treatment of the nations (2:5a), it is difficult to determine whether this unit ever existed independently outside the literary context of this section (→ 2:1–3:13).

Intention

This passage reminds its Judahite addressees of their history of infidelity. Judah has sinned as its leaders have failed, and all have mistakenly disregarded the prophetic pronouncements regarding these problems. This infidelity stands in stark contrast with the fidelity that Yahweh has shown, to which the various manifestations of his presence in their midst all attest. This unit specifically identifies the international sphere as the arena in which Yahweh has long been trying to make his purpose plain, so that the addressees will more readily realize what the prophet is now saying about the relation between the fate of other nations and the fate of Yahweh's own people within the divine plan.

Bibliography

→ 2:1-3.

AWAIT THE DAY OF YAHWEH! 3:8-13

Structure

I. Exhortation to wait for Yahweh to act	3:8-10
A. Introductory adverb: therefore	
B. Command	3:8a
1. Wait for me!	3:8aα¹
2. Oracle formula: says Yahweh	3:8aα²
3. [Wait] for the day when I arise as a witness!	3:8aβ
C. Motivation	3:8b-10
1. Yahweh's decision to destroy the world order	3:8b
a. Yahweh's decision: to gather nations and pour out my anger	3:8bα
b. The effect of carrying out his decision: all the earth shall be consumed	3:8bβ
2. Yahweh's goal: to create a new world order	3:9-10
a. Yahweh's action: I will change the speech of the peoples to a pure speech	3:9a
b. The effects of this action	3:9b-10
1) Basic description: all will call on Yahweh's name and serve him with one accord	3:9b
2) Specific example: from beyond the rivers of Ethiopia my suppliants will bring me an offering	3:10
II. Description of what the Day of Yahweh portends for his people who repent	3:11-13
A. Basic statement	3:11a
1. Future event formula: on that day	3:11aα
2. The fate of the repentant: you shall not be put to shame because of your rebellious deeds	3:11aβ
B. Elaboration: Yahweh's transformation of his people	3:11b-13
1. Described in terms of what Yahweh will remove	3:11b
a. Yahweh's action: I shall remove the proud	3:11bα

b. Its effect: you shall not be haughty   3:11bβ
2. Described in terms of what Yahweh will leave   3:12-13
    a. Yahweh's action: I will leave a humble and
        lowly people   3:12a
    b. Its effects   3:12b-13
       1) Basic statement: they will take refuge
           in Yahweh, as a remnant of Israel that
           will do right and speak the truth   3:12b-13a
       2) Explication: they will pasture and lie
           down, and none will make them afraid   3:13b

The command to wait for Yahweh and the time when he will act (v. 8), the element that initiates and dominates this entire unit, is supported by a description of what this action will mean for the nations of the world in general (vv. 9-10) and for the people of Yahweh in particular (vv. 11-13). The addressees are not explicitly identified, but the grammatical connection of the plural imperative *hakkû* (*RSV* "wait") with the preceding verses by means of the adverb *lākēn* (*RSV* "therefore") shows that they are to be identified with those described in the previous unit, i.e., with those who have recognized that the charge of failure to repent in 3:1-7 applies to them. In v. 7 there is a change in the manner of referring to the inhabitants of Jerusalem, shifting from a third person feminine singular personification of the city to the third person plural. This unit picks up on this shift and turns to address the same group with a plural command, i.e., the potentially repentant people of Judah, represented by the city of Jerusalem and its leaders. Direct address continues in vv. 11-12a, returning to the feminine singular forms implying a personified city. In vv. 12b-13 there is a shift back to third person plural forms, insinuating that "they" who finally heed the command, and thus become part of the transformed remnant of Israel, will not necessarily include all of Yahweh's people, even though all are initially addressed.

The grammatical connection of this unit with 3:1-7 shows further that the initial command and its supporting elements together represent the outcome of the preceding combination of exhortation and prophecy of punishment. The attitude that this unit calls for — the attitude of openness to the possibility that Yahweh will bring something positive out of the present crisis for his people and the world in which they live — is what the foregoing exhortations and prophecies all finally come down to (→ 2:1–3:13, Structure). The sections of this unit that motivate or explicate the initial command thus consist of material relative to several basic ideas that have already been presented.

In vv. 8-10, which deal with the nations in general, v. 8b explicitly reiterates language from 1:2-3 and 1:18aβ describing the destruction of the earth. The same verse neatly summarizes the whole gist of ch. 2, i.e., that the Day of Yahweh is an expression of his anger against all the nations. In 3:9-10 there is also an extension of an idea that has thus far only been hinted at. V. 11 implies that Yahweh's punishment of the peoples, including his diminution of their gods, portends a new relationship between them and Yahweh. Although the precise meaning of v. 10 is somewhat obscure, vv. 9-10 clearly envision that

Yahweh's transformation of the world order will bring not just the possibility of a new existence for Yahweh's people, free of any interference from the other nations, but also the possibility of a new future for the others as well. In the process of this change the outcome of the Tower of Babel episode (Gen 11:1-9) will be reversed. The language of the peoples, which was subjected to confusion because they rebelled against God, will be restored to its primordial purity (Zeph 3:9a) so that they may recover their capacity for common understanding and cooperation in service to a common God, Yahweh (v. 9b; cf. Gen 4:16b). The dispersion that began at Babel extended "over the face of all the earth" (Gen 11:9b), from Shinar at one end to Ethiopia at the corresponding other end (→ Zeph 2:1–3:13, Structure). It will be countered by the return of scattered humanity "from beyond the rivers of Ethiopia" (3:10a). As participants in this process all peoples may become Yahweh's "suppliants" *('ătāray),* and within the context of all humanity's restoration Yahweh has made a particular provision for the restoration of his own people (Bennett, 699-700).

In vv. 11-13, which deal with Yahweh's people in particular, v. 11a summarizes the import of 2:1-3, 7, and 9b concerning the fate of the repentant, while 3:13b explicitly echoes the stipulation of 2:7b, that the remnant of Yahweh's people shall "pasture" *(r'h)* and "lie down" *(rbṣ)* in their land. The creation of a "humble and lowly" *('ānî wĕdāl)* remnant through the purgation of the "proud" *('allîzê ga'ăwātēk)* and "haughty" *(lĕgābhâ)* from Yahweh's "holy mountain" *(har qodšî)* recalls the announcement of punishment directed against the temple and court establishment in 1:4b and 1:8-9. The whole notion of the remnant is extended by referring to it as "Israel" (v. 13), indicating that the new existence of Yahweh's people will not be any mere reconstitution of the state of Judah but rather a re-creation in some new form of the ancient entity that predated the separation of the northern from the southern kingdom.

Genre

By combining elements of command and motivation, this unit shows itself to be (→) parenesis. Because it is also a speech of Yahweh, whose motivational sections assume the form of (→) prophecies of punishment (v. 8b) and salvation (vv. 9-13), this unit can be more specifically described as PROPHETIC EXHORTATION. As such, it serves to evoke in its addressees a particular attitude or frame of mind in which its prophecies seem sensible and bound to be fulfilled. Prophetic exhortation can serve this function in conjunction with either prophecies of punishment, as in (→) 1:7-10 and (→) 1:11-18, or prophecies of salvation (e.g., Isa 43:16-21; 51:1-3). In conjunction with a prophetic speech concerning repentance, as is the case here, prophetic exhortation may serve to heighten the addressees' receptivity toward those prophetic perceptions on which the necessity of repentance is predicated. Notable parallels include Amos 4:12b (in the context of 4:1–5:17), Jer 4:3-4 (in the context of 3:6–4:4), and Isa 44:21-22.

Setting

This text reflects the kind of situation in which the people's acceptance of a prophecy has to be cultivated. In this case the problem is not so much that the people have understood and then rejected what the prophet says, as happened to Jeremiah and others, but rather that they have found the message difficult to comprehend from the outset. The very idea of a destruction of the world order, including Judah, in order to make possible both a new world and a new Israel, apparently seems implausible. Prophetic exhortation has thus already been utilized, along with the initial announcement of punishment itself (→ 1:7-10 and 1:11-18); and various developments, both domestic (1:7b, 11b) and foreign (1:12; 3:6), have been identified as signs of the beginning of this world-transforming process. Whatever tentative assent the prophet may have gained now needs to be nurtured, and the addressees are thus urged to expect that the rest of the process will eventually unfold.

Although this unit conforms to one particular convention of prophetic speech, there is no way of telling whether it was ever actually spoken in public, or whether it is a literary adaptation of this convention (→ Book as a Whole, Setting). Moreover, because 3:8-13 is so tightly connected with 2:1–3:7, paralleling 2:1-3 with respect to the initial command(s) and elaborating on themes introduced in 2:5–3:7, it is difficult to determine whether this unit ever existed independently outside the literary context of this section (→ 2:1–3:13).

Intention

This prophetic exhortation takes its addressees further into the change of heart and behavior that has already been called for in 2:1-3 as it reinforces their expectation that the prophecy on which their conversion is predicated will eventually come to pass. This expectation is based on the recognition that Judah can have hope despite the prospect of widespread destruction, not only because the destruction entails the breakup of the international order that has oppressed them, but also because it entails the future possibility of a new and more just existence for all peoples. In the context of a new world order, which fosters greater unity among nations based on universal recognition of Yahweh, the past sins of Yahweh's people will no longer have a negative effect.

Bibliography

M. Oeming, "Gericht Gottes und Geschicke der Völker nach Zef 3,1-13," *TQ* 167 (1987) 289-300; H. Steck, "Zu Zef 3,9-10," *BZ* 34 (1990) 90-95.

Chapter 5

THE THIRD MAJOR SECTION
OF THE BOOK (3:14-20)
AND ITS INDIVIDUAL UNITS

REJOICE IN THE PROMISE OF SALVATION! 3:14-20

Text

Ball (*Rhetorical Study*, 188) reports finding more than thirty different translations for the difficult language of 3:18. In view of the extreme diversity among the ancient versions, they can offer little help. It is less conjectural to try to make sense of MT as it stands. This verse may be rendered as follows: "Those from the assembly who were sorrowful I have removed from you; they were a burden on her, a reproach" (cf. Ben Zvi, 252-54; and Berlin, *Zephaniah,* 145-47, who also attempt a literalistic rendering of MT with similar results; cf. also the translations of Watts, 184; and Sabottka, 135-36). With regard to the combination of a second person feminine singular form ("from you") and a third person feminine singular form ("on her"), see below.

In the immediate context this verse describes Yahweh's extrication from the cultic community of those with feelings opposed to the rejoicing that has just been urged on the "daughter of Zion"//"daughter of Jerusalem" (3:14-17), i.e., his extrication of the group that will not join in celebrating the new future that Yahweh is creating for his people (3:19-20). As a disruptive force in the community, they were a "burden," a "reproach" impeding Yahweh's intention to make his people "renowned" (3:20bα). In the larger context, Yahweh's removal of this group signals the punishment of Judah's leading offenders that was promised several times previously (1:8-9, 12-13; 3:11bα). Yahweh's action is here described specifically as a purge of the cult (i.e., as his removing dissident participants *mimmô'ēd,* "from the assembly"), thus tying it closely with the promise in 1:4-6 to remove from the Jerusalem temple cult all those practicing idolatrous rites. In this regard note the use here of the same verbal root *('sp)* that is used in 1:2 to describe Yahweh's punishment of the earth in general (*RSV* "sweep away"), which constitutes the context for his removal of Judah's idolaters in particular.

Stinespring has objected to the traditional translation of *bat-ṣîôn* and *bat yĕrûšālāim* as "daughter of Zion" and "daughter of Jerusalem," respectively, suggesting that *bat* ("daughter") in construct relation with a place-name is actually an appositional genitive that constitutes a feminine personification of the place (W. F. Stinespring, "No Daughter of Zion: A Study of the Appositional Genitive in Hebrew Grammar," *Encounter* 26 [1965] 133-41). He thus proposes that *bat-ṣîôn* and *bat yĕrûšālāim* be translated here as "maiden Zion" and "maiden Jerusalem" (pp. 136-37), and this view has been accepted without comment in several recent studies (e.g., Ball, 265; Roberts, 219; cf. Berlin's rendering: "Fair Zion"//"Fair Jerusalem," *Zephaniah,* 141), as well as in various modern English versions (e.g., *NJPS, NAB, NRSV*). Whatever merits Stinespring's argument may have in relation to other examples of such phrases, in relation to 3:14 it amounts to a misunderstanding of the figure.

There is not just a feminine personification of Jerusalem here, but a feminine personification of both the city's inhabitants and their descendants. It is Jerusalem "herself" (i.e., the present generation) who, as "the oppressing city" (3:1b), will experience Yahweh's punishment; it is her "daughter" (i.e., the next generation) who will form the "remnant of the *house* of Judah" (i.e., Judah's descendants, 2:7; cf. 2:9b) and be restored as the new Israel (3:13a). Thus a personification of the younger generation (i.e., the "daughter") is being urged in 3:14 to rejoice over the possibility that they will someday constitute the new Jerusalem, to whom the prospect of salvation will be even more fully pronounced (3:16).

The transgenerational dimension of the figure is further evident from the way in which 3:18 combines both second and third person feminine singular forms (see the translation proposed above). Although there is a shift at 3:18 from nonoracular to oracular prophetic speech, direct address of the same group continues. Yahweh speaks to the younger generation about their predecessors. He announces that he has removed the dissident group "from you" (i.e., the daughter) because they were a burden "on her" (i.e., the mother).

A similar figure is also used in the immediately preceding unit (3:8-13) to describe the restoration of the capacity for cooperative communication, lost in the attempt of humanity's primeval ancestors to build the Tower of Babel (3:9; → 2:1–3:13, Structure). Those from the earliest generations of the human race, whose efforts to build were divinely frustrated, are in 3:10 characterized by Yahweh as "those scattered by me" (*pûṣay; RSV* "my dispersed ones"; cf. the use of the same verb, *pwṣ,* in Gen 11:8-9). The latter generations of their descendants, who will witness the reversal of this process, are thus characterized as "the daughter *(bat)* of those scattered by me" (cf. Ball, 253, who sees this phrase in terms of the typological correspondence with Babel but still somewhat inconsistently rejects its transgenerational significance). In view of the way that the transgenerational denotations of *bat-ṣîôn//bat yĕrûšālāim* are reinforced by the overall context, it is doubtful that these phrases constitute appositional genitives, at least in this particular case. The traditional translation, "daughter of Zion"//"daughter of Jerusalem," should thus be retained here.

Structure

I. Elaborated call to rejoicing		3:14-17
A. Call to rejoicing		3:14-15
1. Call proper: threefold command		3:14
2. Motivation: the hopeful prospect that emerges from what Yahweh has already done		3:15
B. Elaboration: narrative description of how Yahweh's people will be encouraged by the anticipation of Yahweh's triumph		3:16-17
II. Description of the salvation that Yahweh is bringing about: speech of Yahweh		3:18-20
A. Speech proper		3:18-20bβ^1
1. What Yahweh has already done		3:18
2. What Yahweh will eventually do		3:19-20bβ^1
B. Speech report formula		3:20bβ^2

Despite the tendency of many commentators to make sharp divisions within this section, there are several indications of its formal coherence (Kapelrud, 38-39; Keller, 212-13; Ball, *Rhetorical Study,* 262-80; Sweeney, 403). In vv. 14-17 there is a point-for-point correspondence between vv. 14-15 and vv. 16-17 with respect to various aspects of both form and content (→ 3:14-17, Structure). Moreover, the same combination of motivated commands (vv. 14-15) with narration of things to come (vv. 16-17) is also found throughout ch. 1 (→ 1:2-18, Structure) and is thus consistent with the overall compositional style of the book as a whole. Just as vv. 14-17 are based on a progression from the already to the not yet, so are vv. 18-20. In vv. 14-17 there is a progression in the way the people are directed to respond to Yahweh, from "rejoicing" because of what he has already accomplished (vv. 14-15) to "not being afraid" because of what he will someday bring about (vv. 16-17). In vv. 18-20 there is a progression in the mode of divine activity itself, from the punishment of Judah's apostate leaders that Yahweh has already accomplished (v. 18; → Text) to the restoration of Judah's repentant remnant that he will someday bring about (vv. 19-20). Formal affinity between vv. 14-17 and vv. 18-20 is further evident in the combination of direct address in feminine singular (vv. 14aα, 14b, 18-19) and masculine plural (vv. 14bβ, 20) that characterizes both units.

The first unit of this section calls for a celebration (v. 14) because the beginning of a process of deliverance can already be discerned (v. 15a). It then goes on to describe the climax of rejoicing that will eventually be reached (vv. 16-17). This progression necessarily implies that the process of salvation, on which the climax of rejoicing is predicated, will eventually be completed over the course of a generation or so (→ Text). The speech of Yahweh in the second

239

unit (vv. 18-20) follows out this implication by further specifying what Yahweh has done to begin the process (v. 18) and then describing what this initiative shows about both the general goal of Yahweh's action (vv. 19bβ, 20b) and the specific measures he intends to take in realizing those goals (vv. 19abα, 20a).

Genre

Motivated by claims about the nature of Yahweh's actions and their consequences, commands are combined with narration of things to come. A speech of Yahweh serves to explicate this combination. This section is thus PROPHETIC EXHORTATION of the same sort as (→) 1:7-18. This genre functions here with regard to prophecy of salvation in much the same way that it functions there with regard to prophecy of punishment. The addressees are urged not only to realize that Yahweh has a certain intention toward them, but also that he has already begun taking steps to realize this intention.

This section may be compared with passages from other prophetic books, like Isa 54:1-10 and Joel 2:19b-3:5 (*RSV* 2:19b-32), where encouraging commands can also be found in combination with speeches of Yahweh describing the saving deeds that he has performed and will perform (Westermann, 270-71; Wolff, 57-70). This section also has two distinctive features of its own, however. First, the narrative description of things to come does not just recount what Yahweh will do, but rather quotes something that will be said to Jerusalem because of what he will have done (vv. 16-17). This unit is thus a prophecy not only about the future action of Yahweh but also about the future role of prophecy. The victory won by Yahweh will not obviate the need for prophetic discernment of his works and ways. Second, this text not only claims that the process of salvation has already been initiated by Yahweh, but also identifies its starting point with a particular event, namely, an excommunicatory purge of the Jerusalem cult (→ Text). This exhortation thus urges its addressees to apprehend salvation as it is evident in specific prophetically discerned historical signs.

Setting

As Westermann (pp. 270-71) and Wolff (pp. 60-61) have suggested, it is possible that prophetic exhortations concerning salvation were at home in complaint liturgies. Begrich's thesis of their derivation from priestly oracles of salvation, which were supposedly a definitive characteristic of this particular cultic setting, has been shown to be problematic (→ 3:18-20, Genre and Setting). It is nevertheless plausible, in view of such narrative descriptions as 2 Chr 20:14-17, and in view of the many ways in which a comparable text like Joel 2:19b-3:5 (*RSV* 2:19b-32) explicitly reflects a cultic context, that a complaint liturgy could in some instances provide a setting for the kind of prophetic exhortation found in this section.

240

Certain features of this particular example of the genre point in another direction, however. In view of this section's emphasis on the outcome of Yahweh's deliverance as an authentication of the prophetic role, and in view of its emphasis on the identification of a particular historical event as a portentous sign, we might think more in terms of a setting like the one in which Isaiah accosted King Ahaz (Isa 7:1-17). To be sure, there are some notable differences between the exhortation Isaiah is reported to have delivered on that occasion and the one in this text. Isaiah's commands are negative, and the speech of Yahweh that follows them describes salvation accordingly, in terms of what is guaranteed by Yahweh not to happen. The basic combination of commands plus a substantiating speech of Yahweh is nevertheless evident in both texts. In both cases the point of this parenetical combination is to get the addressees to realize that events do not actually mean what they seem. Moreover, in both cases this realization depends on the prophetic discernment of Yahweh's favorable intentions in an otherwise ordinary or ambiguous event that has already happened — whether a purge of the cult or a young woman's conception of a child. (As the *RSV* note to Isa 7:14 indicates, the form of the Hebrew verb for "conceive," *hārâ*, is normally to be translated in the past tense.)

Another clue to the setting of Zeph 3:14-20 comes from the initial commands of the call to rejoicing. They show that this exhortation is not addressed to an individual like Ahaz, but to the inhabitants of Jerusalem collectively personified as one of the city's "daughters" (→ Text). These commands reflect the conventions of a victory celebration (→ 3:14-17, Setting), thus suggesting an air of public festivity rather different from the tone of the confrontation between Isaiah and the king. The text thus reflects a situation in which a prophet would seek to evoke in the populace of Jerusalem a spirit of triumph, and to assure them that the prospect of deliverance was grounded in the reality of what was currently happening while also converting their perception of the kind of events that might be taken to indicate that deliverance was in progress.

Although this section of the book conforms to a convention of prophetic public speaking that might be styled apologetical, there is no way of telling whether it was actually spoken in public, or whether it is a literary adaptation of this convention (→ Book as a Whole, Setting).

Intention

This text aims to get its addressees to rejoice, realizing that within Yahweh's reaction against both his own unfaithful people and their enemies there lies a manifestation of his more basically favorable intentions toward Judah and all the nations. Yahweh's goal is to transform both his people and their world situation so that his people need no longer live in fear and so that his own joy will be complete. A purge of the Jerusalem cult thus appears to the prophetic eye to have a double meaning. On the one hand, it marks the beginning of Yahweh's reaction against his people and their leaders, as well as the beginning of his reaction against the surrounding enemy nations. On the other hand, it is also a sign of his intention to save those who take the prophetically discerned significance of this event to heart. He will eventually overcome the disintegrating impact of his people's sins and — in the process of dealing with the larger world situation — redefine their existence as his people.

Bibliography

C. Westermann, *Isaiah 40–66* (tr. D. M. G. Stalker; OTL; Philadelphia: Westminster, 1969); H. W. Wolff, *Joel and Amos* (tr. W. Janzen et al.; Hermeneia; Philadelphia: Fortress, 1977).

REJOICE IN EXPECTATION! 3:14-17

Structure

I. Call to rejoice because of what Yahweh has already accomplished	3:14-15
A. Call proper: threefold command	3:14
1. Sing aloud, O Daughter of Zion!	3:14aα
2. Shout, O Israel!	3:14aβ
3. Rejoice and exult with all your heart, O Daughter of Jerusalem!	3:14b
B. Reasons for rejoicing: threefold statement	3:15
1. What Yahweh has done	3:15a
a. He has taken away the judgments against you	3:15aα
b. He has cast out your enemies	3:15aβ
2. The position Yahweh has thereby assumed: he is in your midst as King of Israel	3:15bα
3. The future prospect that has consequently been established: you shall fear evil no more	3:15bβ
II. Elaboration in terms of future salvation	3:16-17
A. Narrative introduction	3:16aα
1. Future event formula: on that day	3:16aα¹
2. Speech report formula: it shall be said to Jerusalem	3:16aα²
B. Speech	3:16aβ-17
1. Twofold negative command	3:16aβb
a. Do not fear, O Zion!	3:16aβ
b. Let not your hands grow weak!	3:16b
2. Reasons to heed this command	3:17
a. The position Yahweh has assumed: he is in your midst as your God who gives victory	3:17a
b. How Yahweh will respond to Judah's deliverance: threefold statement	3:17b

1) He will rejoice over you with gladness   3:17bα[1]
2) He will renew you in his love   3:17bα[2]
3) He will exult over you with loud singing   3:17bβ

The structural elements of vv. 16-17 neatly mirror those of vv. 14-15 (cf. Renaud, 22). The statement in v. 15bβ that Judah will not have to fear evil any more parallels the command not to fear in v. 16aβb. The assertion in v. 15bα that Yahweh is "in your midst" as king of Israel parallels the assertion in v. 17a that he is "in your midst" as a victory-giving warrior. The threefold command to rejoice in v. 14 parallels the threefold description of Yahweh's rejoicing over his people in v. 17b. The hinge between these parallels, which determines the nature of their interrelationship, is the narrative introduction to vv. 16-17.

Such a connection emphasizes the similarities and differences between what can presently be said about the reality of the salvation promised by Yahweh (vv. 14-15) and what can eventually be said about it "on that day" (vv. 16-17). Because of something that has already begun to happen (v. 15a), deliverance is now so certain that Judah can be urged to rejoice at the prospect (v. 14). Then when the deliverance is finally completed, Yahweh himself will be said to join in the celebration (v. 17b). Yahweh is already manifest as king in Jerusalem's sacred institutions, by virtue of the victories he has won in the past (v. 15bα), but then he will be manifest as the divine warrior who has reconfirmed his kingship with a new victory (v. 17a). Judah can already discover, in a prophetically informed response to Yahweh's initiative, the prospect of freedom from fear (v. 15bβ), but then she can be more definitely assured of this hope (v. 16aβb). This unit is thus basically a call to rejoice in the deliverance that has already been prophesied (cf. 3:9-12) because it has actually begun to be realized.

The anomalous aspect of the mirror-image relationship between vv. 14-15 and 16-17 is v. 15a, which heads the threefold statement of the reasons for rejoicing. There is no counterpart in vv. 16-17 to the claim that Yahweh has removed his judgment against Judah and neutralized any threat from their foes. There is, however, a counterpart to such a claim in the following verses. The final unit of the book thus answers the lack of a correlative for v. 15a in this unit and establishes the connection by means of which these two units form the third and final section of the book (→ 3:14-20, Structure).

Genre

This unit combines imperative calls to rejoicing (v. 14) with motivating statements of the reason for doing so (v. 15), and this combination makes it very similar to a (→) hymn of praise. This similarity, together with the prominent motif of divine kingship, has led some scholars to classify it as an enthronement hymn (e.g., Gerleman, 62; Horst, 199-200; Elliger, 81; Kapelrud, 39-40), though not without objection from other scholars (e.g., Rudolph, 298). Against such a categorization, Crüsemann (pp. 55-65) has cogently observed that it fails to account for several distinctive features of this text and similar texts (e.g., Isa 12:6; 54:1; Lam 4:21; Zech 2:14; 9:9; cf. the negative inversions in Joel 2:21-24 and Hos 9:1). First, the calls to rejoicing in these texts are generally feminine singular imperatives addressed to a feminine personification of a people or city, whereas hymnic calls to praise are typically masculine plural imperatives addressed to the people or the congregation as a whole. Second, the motivations in these texts are also in the form of direct address to the feminine figure, whereas hymnic motivations typically consist of third person description or of description directly addressed to Yahweh using second person masculine singular forms. Third, unlike hymns of praise, these texts occur typically in association with prophecies whose theme is salvation. Crüsemann therefore proposes that such calls to rejoicing should be seen as a form of prophetic speech that functions somewhat like a prophecy of salvation.

In this particular case the call to rejoicing is not only associated with a prophecy of salvation in the larger context, i.e., in (→) vv. 18-20. Elements of such a prophecy have also been incorporated into the motivation of the call itself in v. 15. Yahweh's deliverance is grounded in a description of a previous action of his ("he has taken away the judgments against you, he has cast out your enemies") as well as a description of his attributes and status ("the king of Israel, Yahweh is in your midst"). The eventual outcome of Yahweh's deliverance is also described ("you shall fear evil no more"). The missing element is a description of the act of deliverance itself, which is supplied in the closely related following unit (→ 3:18-20, Genre).

Within this call to rejoicing there are also elements of other genres besides the prophecy of salvation. Both the call and its motivation (vv. 14-15) are elaborated by a narration of things to come (vv. 16-17), which results in an overall structure that is very similar to the structure of the exhortations in (→) 1:7-10 and 1:11-18. In relation to the preceding descriptions of salvation for Yahweh's people (2:7, 9b; 3:9-13) this unit functions much as the exhortations in 1:7-10 and 1:11-18 function in relation to the preceding prophecy of punishment (1:2-6). It induces the addressees to recognize in their present experience the embryonic signs of a future that is well on its way. In contrast with the exhortations in ch. 1, which follow the prophecy that they explicate, this unit precedes the prophecy that it explicates. After the addressees have been prepared to recognize the proleptic indications of Yahweh's ultimately favorable intentions toward them, the speech of Yahweh in 3:18-20 proceeds to identify what these favorable intentions are (v. 18) as it redescribes what the final outcome will be (vv. 19-20; cf. 3:9-13). This unit is thus a PROPHETIC CALL TO REJOICING that has the particular function of introducing a (→) prophetic exhortation concerning salvation.

Setting

Crüsemann has suggested that the prophetic call to rejoicing derived from the custom of addressing the female participants in fertility cults to elicit from each of them a joyful response to the promise of fecundity. It is perhaps plausible to adduce a fertility cult as the background for some of the imagery that is occasionally encountered in this form of speech (e.g., Isa 54:1; Joel 2:21-24), but as a general explanation of the genre's origins this proposed setting seems rather far-fetched. By describing Yahweh as a "victory-giving warrior" (v. 17a), this text explicitly identifies its rejoicing as a victory celebration. Moreover, the verbs that describe rejoicing in v. 14 and v. 17b can denote, among other things, the festivity of triumph (e.g., Ps 21:2 [*RSV* 1]; Ps 149), in which women customarily led the singing and dancing (e.g., Exod 15:20-21; Judg 11:34; 1 Sam 18:6-7). As participants in victory celebrations, the women of a people could be collectively described as their "daughters" (e.g., 2 Sam 1:20). The figure of the "daughter of Zion"//"daughter of Jerusalem" indicates that the call to rejoicing reflects the customary conventions of the victory celebration.

There are thus strong indications that this call to rejoicing was adapted from a kind of speech that was conventional in victory celebrations. Its addressees are collectively personified as a feminine participant in one of Jerusalem's triumphs, and the divine activity that constitutes the reason for rejoicing is characterized in terms of military success. Such a view of this text's setting would also explain the feminine singular direct address also found in similar texts (e.g., → Zech 9:9-10) that Crüsemann has identified as a basic element of their genre, differentiating their form from the otherwise very similar form of the hymn of praise.

It would also explain why the motivations of the calls to rejoicing in these texts typically remain in the second person feminine singular, in contrast with the motivations in hymns. (As noted above, in the motivations of hymns there is typically a change from the second person masculine plural of the calls to praise to either third person description of Yahweh or second person masculine singular direct address of Yahweh.) In prophetic calls to rejoicing the motivations typically remain in the second person feminine singular because this genre remains addressed entirely to human beings. It celebrates Yahweh, but is not directed to him. In hymns of praise, however, there is a shift away from the direct address of the congregation in the calls to praise when Yahweh's praiseworthy attributes are described. In accord with their cultic setting, hymns are meant for Yahweh as much as for the congregation. They are about Yahweh and are also directed either directly or indirectly to him.

Although this section of the book conforms to a manner of speaking that was typical of victory celebrations, which prophets adapted for their own purposes, there is no way of telling whether it was ever publicly spoken by a prophet, or whether it is a literary adaptation of this prophetic practice (→ Book as a Whole, Setting).

Intention

This unit aims to engender in its addressees an attitude of anticipatory joy, born of confidence that Yahweh is emerging victorious over all threats to the promised future of a repentant remnant of Judah. Yahweh has signaled the start of his efforts to change both the internal conditions that have caused his decision to punish his people and the external conditions that have caused the enmity of neighboring states and superpowers. The attitude engendered by this unit further includes a growing awareness of Yahweh's presence and a diminishing sense of the need to fear evil, as well as the expectation that the people's joy will eventually be complete through full participation in the divine joy of Yahweh when his victory is finally won.

Bibliography

F. Crüsemann, *Studien zur Formgeschichte von Hymnus und Danklied in Israel* (WMANT 32; Neukirchen-Vluyn: Neukirchener, 1969).

THE PROMISE OF SALVATION, 3:18-20

Structure

I. Speech of Yahweh	$3{:}18{-}20b\beta^1$
A. Description of what Yahweh has done: I have removed from you the apostates who were a reproach for Jerusalem	$3{:}18$
B. Description of what Yahweh will do	$3{:}19{-}20b\beta^1$
1. Stated in terms of his treatment of humanity in general	$3{:}19$
a. With respect to Judah's enemies	$3{:}19a$
1) Statement proper: I will deal with all your oppressors	$3{:}19a\alpha$
2) Future event formula: at that time	$3{:}19a\beta$
b. With respect to the disadvantaged	$3{:}19b$
1) Yahweh's actions	$3{:}19b\alpha$
a) The physically disabled: I will save the lame	$3{:}19b\alpha^1$
b) The socially marginal: I will gather the outcast	$3{:}19b\alpha^2$
2) Yahweh's goal: I will change their shame into praise and renown in all the earth	$3{:}19b\beta$
2. Stated in terms of Judah's salvation	$3{:}20ab\beta^1$
1) Yahweh's action	$3{:}20a$
a) Future event formula: at that time	$3{:}20a\alpha^1$
b) I will bring you home at the time when I gather you together	$3{:}20a\alpha^2\beta$
2) Yahweh's goal: I will make you renowned and praised among all the peoples of the earth when I restore your fortunes before your eyes	$3{:}20b\alpha\beta^1$
II. Speech report formula: says Yahweh	$3{:}20b\beta^2$

This unit emerges as an elaboration and extension of 3:15 above. Like the preceding unit, it begins with a description of what Yahweh has already done (v. 18), but then it continues with a specific description of the deliverance that he will eventually accomplish (vv. 19-20) in the process of reaching the outcome already described in vv. 15b-17 (→ 3:14-17, Structure). This outcome is further elaborated here in terms of the "renown" *(šēm)* that Yahweh eventually intends to establish, both for the disadvantaged in general (v. 19b) and for the restored repentant remnant of his people in particular (v. 20). In contrast with the preceding unit, however, this unit is a speech of Yahweh. Yahweh states that he has already eliminated the apostates (v. 18a; → 3:14-20, Text; cf. 1:4-6), whose infidelity has made Judah suffer reproach (v. 18b; cf. 2:8a, 10). The identification of this particular event as the initiation of Yahweh's deliverance leads to further specification of what he will now accomplish on his people's behalf. He is countering their oppressors (v. 19a), and this realization substantiates the expectation that he will fulfill his larger plan to rehabilitate all the disadvantaged, including the physically disabled and the socially marginal (v. 19b), and to restore the repentant remnant of Judah (v. 20).

Genre

Following Begrich, Westermann attempted to define the promise of salvation *(Heilzusage)* as the most prominent and quintessential representation of all prophecy concerning salvation. On the basis of examples in Isa 40–55 Westermann identified a particular combination of elements as characteristic of this genre: (1) an announcement of salvation, sometimes including a description of Yahweh's general goal as well as the particular act of deliverance that he intends to accomplish; (2) a grounding of this announcement in some attribute or prior act of Yahweh; (3) direct address; and (4) the formulaic assurance of salvation, "fear not!" ("Heilswort," 355-59). The last two of these elements were taken to indicate a more or less direct line of development between the examples in Isa 40–55 and the kind of salvation oracle that the priests at local sanctuaries once supposedly proclaimed to those who prayed for deliverance with psalms of (→) complaint, showing the promise of salvation to be a late adaptation of this old cultic custom (Begrich, "Das priesterliche Heilsorakel"). This thesis, which has long dominated the scholarly conception of prophecy concerning salvation, now appears to be problematic.

Conrad has shown that the prophecies of salvation in Isa 40–55 are not sufficiently uniform in their structure to constitute the kind of generic subclass that Begrich and Westermann have attempted to define ("The 'Fear Not' Oracles"). He has also shown that the priestly oracles in the Psalms do not have the kind of ideal structure that Begrich envisioned for them as responses to complaints ("Second Isaiah," 235-41), and that the "fear not!" formula is not particularly characteristic of such oracles but rather has a variety of uses in other contexts *(Fear Not, Warrior,* passim). Conrad's work has thus considerably reinforced the earlier argument of Raitt, who criticized

Begrich and Westermann for focusing too much on the peculiarities of Second Isaiah and generalizing too broadly on this rather circumscribed basis. Raitt maintained that the prophecy of salvation should not be conceived as having reached its culmination at such a late stage in the development of Israel's prophetic tradition and should not be conceived as having done so by adapting any conventional form of speech from the cult or elsewhere (Raitt, 128-73).

Westermann has thus more recently admitted that the promise of salvation *(Heilzusage)* is restricted to a few examples from Isaiah, and that its form is just one minor variation on a more broadly defined generic form whose development can be traced from Israel's beginnings *(Prophetic Oracles,* 11-42). Its most elemental manifestation is an announcement of salvation, describing some act of deliverance that Yahweh will perform or some state of well-being that Yahweh will bring about. The announcement of salvation can stand alone, but various elements may also be added, such as an explicit indication of its being partly or entirely an oracular speech of Yahweh or a grounding of Yahweh's capacity to accomplish salvation in some attribute or previous action of his. The form resulting from the addition of such elements may simply be called a (→) prophecy of salvation.

In this unit the description in vv. 19-20 of the salvation that Yahweh will accomplish is grounded in a description in v. 18 of what he has already done. This salvation is described not only in terms of such direct actions as the "gathering" *(qbṣ)* that Yahweh will perform in order to deliver his people but also in terms of the status that he will achieve for them — the status of a "name" *(šēm; RSV* "renown"). There is also oracular speech of Yahweh throughout the unit, although there is in v. 18 no speech report formula or other introductory indication of any prophetic intermediary. There is simply an abrupt transition to first person, without any explicit indication of Yahweh's being the speaker until the concluding speech report formula in v. 20bβ[2]. Despite the abruptness of this transition, continuity with the preceding unit is maintained by the emerging mirror-image structural correspondences between 3:14-17 and 3:18-20 (→ 3:14-17, Structure). Yahweh thus in effect interjects himself into the prophet's call to rejoicing, giving a direct point-for-point divine confirmation of the claims on which the call is predicated. This unit can be classified as a PROPHECY OF SALVATION, but one that is tightly integrated with the preceding unit into a (→) prophetic exhortation (→ 3:14-20, Genre).

Setting

Westermann followed Begrich in describing such prophecies of salvation as a late exilic prophetic adaptation of the preexilic priestly oracle of salvation, which originally had its setting in the liturgy of complaint ("Heilswort," 356-59). This concept of the setting depends largely on the assumption that the phrase "fear not!" was a formula characteristic of this priestly oracular form. In view of Conrad's critique (→ Genre) this assumption can no longer be sustained, and the setting of the prophecy of salvation must be sought in some other context.

The main evidence for prophecy of salvation in preexilic times comes from narrative accounts of oracular inquiries, particularly those made to determine the advisability of military actions. These accounts portray a king or other commander asking a prophet whether to launch an attack or mount a defense, and the prophet answering positively or negatively in terms of whether Yahweh would grant his people success (e.g., 1 Kgs 22:1-12; Jer 21:1-2; cf. Judg 1:1-2; 1 Sam 23:2-4; 2 Sam 5:19; see Long, 84-100; also Westermann, *Prophetic Oracles,* 21-35). An affirmative reply to such an inquiry might be given in the form of a (→) prophecy of punishment against a foreign nation, indirectly describing Yahweh's salvation of his people in terms of his defeating their enemies. An affirmative reply might also be given in the form of a speech of Yahweh directly describing his intention to give them victory over their enemies (e.g., 1 Sam 23:4b; Judg 1:2b).

Prophecies of salvation, of the sort represented by this unit, may have derived from this latter kind of prophetic speech. They may have emerged as unsolicited versions of the promises of victory that were in preexilic times often made in response to oracular inquiries concerning military matters. Given a wider application, this kind of speech could be used in the context of prophetic public oratory to express the idea that Yahweh would win for his people a kind of victory that might have little or nothing to do with the actual deployment of their armies (e.g., Jer 28:1-4).

Although this section of the book conforms to a convention of prophetic speech, there is no way of telling whether it was ever actually spoken in public, or whether it is a literary adaptation of this convention (→ Book as a Whole, Setting).

Intention

This unit announces what Yahweh has done to remove the cause of his negative judgment against his people and effect the neutralization of their enemies. It identifies an excommunicatory purge of the Jerusalem cult as the starting point in Yahweh's efforts to bring about his prophetically revealed intentions of destroying Judah's present civil order because it has led to such infidelity, as well as the present international order, because it has led the nations to oppress his people. This overall change, which has now gotten underway, will eventually result in a reversal of Judah's misfortune and a restoration of the scattered remnant of Yahweh's people, in the context of Yahweh's efforts to heal the hurts of all humanity.

Bibliography

J. Begrich, "Das priesterliche Heilsorakel," *ZAW* 52 (1934) 81-92; idem, *Studien zu Deuterojesaja* (1934; repr. TBü 20; Munich: Kaiser, 1963); E. W. Conrad, "The 'Fear

Not' Oracles in Second Isaiah," *VT* 34 (1984) 129-52; idem, *Fear Not Warrior: A Study of 'al tîrā' Pericopes in the Hebrew Scriptures* (BJS 75; Chico, Calif.: Scholars Press, 1985); idem, "Second Isaiah and the Priestly Oracle of Salvation," *ZAW* 93 (1981) 234-46; T. M. Raitt, *A Theology of Exile* (Philadelphia: Fortress, 1977); C. Westermann, "Das Heilswort bei Deuterojesaja," *EvT* 24 (1964) 355-73; idem, *Prophetic Oracles of Salvation in the Old Testament* (tr. K. Crim; Louisville: Westminster/John Knox, 1991); idem, "Sprache und Struktur der Prophetie Deuterojesajas," in *Forschung am Alten Testament* (TBü 24; Munich: Kaiser, 1964) 92-170.

HAGGAI

Bibliography

P. R. Ackroyd, *Exile and Restoration* (OTL; Philadelphia: Westminster, 1968) 153-70; idem, "Studies in the Book of Haggai," *JJS* 2 (1951) 163-76; 3 (1952) 1-13; L. Alonso Schökel and J. L. Sicre Diaz, *Profetas: Comentario,* vol. 2 (NBE; Madrid: Cristiandad, 1980); S. Amsler, *Aggée* (CAT 11c; Neuchâtel: Delachaux & Nestlé, 1981); W. A. M. Beuken, *Haggai–Sacharja 1–8* (SSN 10; Assen: Van Gorcum, 1967); T. Chary, *Aggée–Zacharie–Malachie* (SB; Paris: Gabalda, 1969); K. Elliger, *Das Buch der zwölf Kleinen Propheten,* vol. 2 (4th ed.; ATD 25/2; Göttingen: Vandenhoeck & Ruprecht, 1959); M. H. Floyd, "The Nature of the Narrative and the Evidence of Redaction in Haggai," *VT* 45 (1995) 470-90; F. Horst, "Haggai," in T. H. Robinson and Horst, *Die Zwölf Kleinen Propheten* (HAT 14; Tübingen: Mohr [Siebeck], 1938); K. Koch, "Haggais unreines Volk," *ZAW* 79 (1967) 52-66; E. W. March, "The Book of Haggai," *NIB* 7:707-32; R. Mason, "The Purpose of the 'Editorial Framework' of the Book of Haggai," *VT* 27 (1977) 413-21; C. L. Meyers and E. M. Meyers, *Haggai, Zechariah 1–8* (AB 25B; Garden City, N.Y.: Doubleday, 1987); H. G. Mitchell, "Haggai," in Mitchell, J. M. P. Smith, and J. A. Bewer, *A Critical and Exegetical Commentary on Haggai, Zechariah, Malachi and Jonah* (ICC; Edinburgh: T. & T. Clark, 1912); D. L. Petersen, *Haggai and Zechariah 1–8* (OTL; London: SCM, 1985); H. Graf Reventlow, *Die Propheten Haggai, Sacharja und Maleachi* (ATD 25/2; Göttingen: Vandenhoeck & Ruprecht, 1993); P. L. Redditt, *Haggai, Zechariah, Malachi* (NCB; Grand Rapids: Eerdmans, 1995); W. Rudolph, *Haggai, Sacharja 1–8, Sacharja 9–14, Maleachi* (KAT 13/4; Gütersloh: Gerd Mohn, 1976); R. L. Smith, *Micah–Malachi* (WBC 32; Waco: Word, 1984); H. W. Wolff, *Haggai: A Commentary* (tr. M. Kohl; Minneapolis: Augsburg, 1988).

THE BOOK AS A WHOLE

Structure

The book of Haggai is a narrative that consists of five explicitly dated episodes, in each of which the prophet is the central character: 1:1-12; 1:13-15a; 1:15b–2:9; 2:10-19; and 2:20-13 (the last two taking place on the same date). The question of whether 1:15b concludes 1:13-15a or introduces 2:1-9 has been much discussed. Here I follow the preponderance of critical opinion in favor of the latter position, but this is of little or no consequence for the analysis of the book's overall structure (see P. A. Verhoef, "Notes on the Dates in the Book of Haggai," in *Text and Context* [*Fest.* F. C. Fensham; ed. W. Classen; JSOTSup 48; Sheffield: JSOT Press, 1988] 262). The narrative recounts events that span a period of approximately four months during "the second year of Darius the king," i.e., Darius I of Persia, who reigned from about 521 to 485 BCE over the territory formerly occupied by the kingdom of Judah. The story thus unfolds against the background of Judah's previous destruction by the Babylonians and the exile of many of its subjects to Babylon in 586, as well as the overthrow of the Babylonians by the Persians and their authorization of the exiles' return to their homeland in 538. From its outset the story assumes the ongoing attempts of the returnees to redefine for Judah some new form of communal existence consistent with the relatively tolerant conditions imposed under Persian hegemony. The prophet is described as playing a key role in the restoration, as he brings the reconstruction of Yahweh's temple in Jerusalem through its most crucial phase. He thus helps to redefine Judah as a community based on its recognition of the Second Temple's centrality.

The narrative is not concerned with the restoration in its entirety, or even with the rebuilding of the temple as such, but only with certain events in which Haggai was directly involved. Other events are both assumed from the outset and mentioned in passing as the story unfolds. The overall background of the narrative action can be outlined by comparing the chronology of Haggai with the course of events described in the book of Ezra, particularly in Ezra 2:68–

3:13. This will not satisfy a modern historian's curiosity about the way the restoration actually came to pass, nor even help to resolve the vexed problem of
the chronology within Ezra-Nehemiah itself, but it will at least provide a plausible basis on which the gaps left in Haggai's account can be imaginatively
filled in (see S. Japhet, "'History' and 'Literature' in the Persian Period: The
Restoration of the Temple," in *Ah, Assyria . . .* [*Fest.* H. Tadmor; ed. M. Cogan
and I. Eph'al; ScrHier 33; Jerusalem: Magnes, 1991] 174-88).

The narrative in Haggai does not explicitly mention any earlier attempts
to rebuild the temple in the time of Cyrus, but neither does it presuppose that
the project promoted by Haggai is the first such attempt. Haggai may thus be
seen as a reinstigator of the work that began but foundered nearly two decades
earlier, and hence a promulgator of the project previously authorized by Cyrus
(Ezra 5:14-16; cf. Ezra 3:7). In the first episode (Hag 1:1-12) the issue is not
whether to rebuild the temple but whether now is the right time to do so (1:2-
3). In the fourth episode (2:10-19) the priests are imparting regulations concerning *běśar qōdeš* (*RSV* "holy flesh"), which seems to entail the operation of
the sacrificial cult. The narrative thus assumes from the start that both imperial
policy and local leadership are committed in principle to the temple's reconstruction, and that the altar has already been rebuilt so that at least some kinds
of sacrifices might be resumed within the sacred precinct of the temple site.
The work on the *bayit yhwh* ("house of Yahweh") itself, however, has not yet
commenced; and its foundation has not yet been "laid" *(ysd)*.

This is precisely the state of affairs described in Ezra 2:68–3:7 (assuming that *ysd* can mean repairing an old foundation as well as laying a new one,
and that the "founding" of the temple can mean the ritual dedication of work in
progress as well as the actual positioning of the first stones; see A. Gelston,
"Foundations of the Second Temple," *VT* 16 [1966] 232-35; also D. L.
Petersen, "Zerubbabel and Jerusalem Temple Reconstruction," *CBQ* 35 [1974]
366-72). According to the account in Ezra, some of the elders meet to raise
funds for the rebuilding project, and six months later a mass meeting is held to
celebrate the reconstruction of the altar and the resumption of sacrificial worship at the temple site. Work on the "house" itself, however, has not yet been
resumed, and the foundation has not yet been rededicated. From this starting
point the narrative of Haggai begins to unfold: "In the second year of Darius
the king, in the sixth month, on the first day of the month." Haggai begins trying to get the work on the temple edifice started (1:1a), and nearly a month
later it is finally begun "on the twenty-fourth day . . . in the sixth month"
(1:15a). In Ezra the same work is said to have begun about fourteen months after the initial meeting of the elders, and about eight months after the resumption of sacrifices on the new altar (Ezra 2:68; 3:1, 6, 8-9).

When the project has been underway for a couple of months, it seems to
many that the emerging structure does not measure up to their ideal memory of
the Solomonic temple. Because the foundation is rededicated in an atmosphere
charged with such disappointment, the celebration evokes expressions of grief
as well as joy (Ezra 3:10-13). Under these same conditions, and about the
same time (i.e., "in the second year of Darius the king, in the seventh month,
on the twenty-first day of the month"), Haggai intervenes to bolster the falter-

ing morale and encourage the continuation of the work (Hag 1:15b–2:9). Less than two months later, "on the twenty-fourth day of the ninth month," there has been considerable progress. From this vantage point Haggai urges the community to look back and compare the miserable conditions that existed before they started their work on the temple with the improved conditions that have begun to emerge since the rededication of its foundations (2:15-19) — an occasion to which Haggai refers retrospectively in 2:18 but does not otherwise describe (→ 2:10-19, Text and Structure). From the same point in time Haggai concludes with a glimpse of the hopeful future that the temple's restoration brings with it (2:20-23).

The five episodes are not all equally weighted in the scheme of the book as a whole. The first two episodes, 1:1-12 and 1:13-15a, have a close affinity because of their similar narrative pattern. Both begin with an oracular pronouncement of Haggai (1:1-11, 13) and conclude with a description of the various reactions to his speech (1:12, 14b). They are also connected by the way in which the second episode reports the community's eventual full compliance with the command given in the first episode, to begin rebuilding Yahweh's house (1:8, 14b). The last two episodes, 2:10-19 and 2:20-23, have a similarly close affinity because of their taking place on the same day (2:10, 20), and because the latter is explicitly identified as the sequel to the former (note šēnît [RSV "a second time"] in 2:20). The narrative thus progresses from the two closely bonded episodes with which it begins (1:1-12, 13-15a) to the two closely bonded episodes with which it concludes (2:10-19, 20-23), and the central episode in 1:15b–2:9 serves as the pivotal link between these two major sections of the book.

In the first two episodes (1:1-15a) the rebuilding of the temple is approached as a largely local and internal matter. The issue is defined in terms of the community's own socioeconomic viability, as Haggai asserts that their failure to be productive is rooted in their failure to take up this particular task. The community is initially motivated to begin the work in an attempt to reverse the misfortune that plagues their immediate living situation. The broader cosmic perspective that begins to open up in 1:15b–2:9 is only hinted at in 1:10-11, where the cause of the community's economic failure is identified with Yahweh's restriction of creation's capacity for productivity.

In the central episode (1:15b–2:9), after the work has been in progress for about a month, the rather unimpressive results bring to a head the issue of whether the effort will persist. In order to encourage its continuation the prophet broadens his argument to consider the larger significance of the project. The completion of the temple is not only an essential prerequisite for the socioeconomic welfare of this particular locality. It is also an integral part of Yahweh's grand design to reorder the whole world so that his people have a secure and prosperous place in it, as he did once before when he brought them out of Egypt and made them a nation in the land of Canaan. The project is thus a sign of his intention to reconfigure the interplay of both cosmic and international forces in order to create a new historical opportunity for Judah. The question of whether to complete the temple is thus a question of whether Judah will seize this historic opportunity to regain their integrity as a people in some new form.

In the two final episodes (2:10-23), which take place exactly three months after the work of rebuilding began, the issue is the momentum of the project's continuation. Yet another dimension is added to the argument for the work to proceed, in addition to the considerations of Judah's socioeconomic welfare that are presented in 1:1-15a and the considerations of Judah's world-historical status that are presented in 1:15b–2:9. Through dramatic interaction with the priests Haggai demonstrates the need for a fully restored cult that can effectively purify, and hence sanctify, the people of Judah in relation to Yahweh (2:10-14). The observation that they cannot yet offer anything fit for Yahweh (2:14) leads Haggai to observe further that now they do at least have something to offer him (2:15-19a). His initial claims regarding the project's beneficial effects on the local economy (1:1-15a) have already begun to be fulfilled. This provides a basis on which to expect the similar fulfillment of his additional claims regarding the project's beneficial effects on Judah's attainment of some well-defined sociopolitical status (1:15b–2:9; → 2:10-19, Structure). The book ends by opening up a vast new historical prospect for Judah, in which Judah regains some recognition among the kingdoms of the earth, and its governor Zerubbabel — by virtue of the instrumental role he has played in rebuilding the temple — becomes the new earthly representative of Yahweh's heavenly kingship over all creation. Such expectation makes the work on the temple all the more urgent, and thus provides an impetus for bringing it to completion.

Genre

Prophetic speech is prominent in Haggai, as it makes up most of the book; but it is not predominant. In every case this element is thoroughly incorporated into the narrative that runs through the book as whole, so that the speeches serve to develop the plot from beginning to end. Recent scholarship has generally supposed that the narrative is an editorial framework used by a redactor to present oracles once spoken by Haggai. Scholars have therefore attempted to separate the speeches from their context in the story, so that their message and form-critical classification can be considered apart from the editorial viewpoint expressed in the narration (e.g., Ackroyd, "Studies," 166-73; Beuken, 27-83 passim; Mason, "Editorial Framework"; Wolff, 17-18 and passim). In view of the extent to which prophetic speech forms an integral part of the narrative, however, it is doubtful whether Haggai's ipsissima verba or any traditions regarding them can be retrieved from their redactional representation.

Each of the book's three main sections (1:1-15a; 1:15b–2:9; 2:10-23) is narrated so as to create an ambiguous relationship between the narrator and the prophetic main character. In the first section the point at which the narrator leaves off and the prophet starts speaking is uncertain (→ 1:1-12, Structure). In the second section the narrator begins as if to report the public communication of a prophecy, but the prophecy subsequently assumes the form in which it would have been privately revealed to Haggai (→ 1:15b–2:9, Structure). In the third section the narrator conversely begins as if to report the private revelation of a prophecy to Haggai, but then suddenly shifts to reporting its public communication (→ 2:10-19, Structure). Various commentators have noted these incongruities, but they have generally regarded them as by-products of redaction rather than distinctive features of a particular type of narration. Two considerations make the latter alternative more probable, however.

First, if these incongruities were the result of enclosing collected oracles within a narrative "editorial framework," they would tend to occur at the juncture between the narrator's reporting and the prophet's direct discourse. This is not generally the case, however. Only in 1:15b–2:9 does the ambiguity in the relationship between prophet and narrator arise in such a context (i.e., at 2:2). In (→) 1:1-12 this ambiguity results from the mixed signals that appear in 1:2, within the narrative introduction (1:1-3). In (→) 2:10-19 it grows out of the change that suddenly interrupts the oracular speech at 2:12b, as a prospective description of what the prophet is to ask the priests shifts elliptically to a retrospective description of what he and they have said to each other in their dialogue. Thus in two out of three cases the incongruity seems to be a deliberate result of the way the narrative introduction itself is composed (1:1-12), or of the way the oracular material itself is presented (2:10-19), rather than as the result of redactionally combining these two supposedly disparate sorts of material.

Second, distinctive patterns of phraseology, which serve to develop the thematic progression of the book as whole, permeate both narration and prophetic speech alike. For example, Zerubbabel and Joshua are sometimes characterized in the same terms and sometimes characterized in different terms as the story unfolds (1:1, 12, 14; 2:2, 4, 21, 23; for details → 1:15b–2:9, Structure). Such variation creates a growing contrast between the role of Zerubbabel and the role of Joshua, so as to prepare for the qualitatively different position that is assigned to Zerubbabel at the climactic conclusion to the narrative, where he is finally described as Yahweh's chosen "servant" ('ebed) who represents him like a "signet ring" (ḥôtām). The key theme of Zerubbabel's status is thus developed by a pattern of phraseological similarities and differences that not only runs through the narrative sections (1:1, 12, 14) but also reaches into the core of a couple of oracles (2:2, 4, 21, 23). This suggests that both reporting narration and prophetic speech were largely fabricated in the same compositional process. (The characterization of the community is developed through a similar phraseological progression from "remnant" [šĕ'ērît] to "people of the land" ['am hā'āreṣ] to "nation" [gôy]; → 1:15b–2:9, Structure.)

The text of Haggai should thus be treated as an integral whole. The ambiguous relationship between the narrator and the prophetic main character, an ambiguity that generally characterizes all of its main sections, should also be regarded as an intentional device, not as the inadvertent by-product of providing Haggai's oracles with a redactional framework. The book of Haggai is a continuous series of episodes in which a prophetic speaker plays the central role, not a collection of prophetic speeches to which narrative annotations have been added. Form-critical analysis must therefore first ask what kind of narration this is (Petersen, 32-34), and only then might it also be appropriate to ask whether it represents the speeches of its main character in accord with any particular conventions of prophetic speech. The answers to these questions will not give the modern historian any direct access to any words that Haggai may have actually said, but they will provide some indication of whether this type of narration would tend to describe prophetic activity accurately and realistically.

In effect, such narration creates a "split personality" for both the narrator and the prophetic main character. Each speaks from a perspective that is shifting; and the two shifting perspectives are at some points convergent, but at other points divergent. This shows that a firm distinction is continually being drawn between the prophet's outlook on the events in which he was immediately involved and the narrator's somewhat different retrospective outlook on those same events; but it also shows that the boundary line between these two different outlooks is continually being blurred.

Even though writing of this sort precludes the recovery of any source materials on which it may have been based, it nevertheless seems to reflect a dependence on prior documentation. If everything in Haggai were made up from scratch, it is unlikely that its narration would be so prominently characterized by perspectives that are shifting in the way just described. This account of Haggai's activities is thus probably based on source materials of some sort, even though they have been recomposed to such an extent that they are no longer analyzable or recoverable as such. For this reason, and because the book is also obviously concerned with ordering events in a chronological and meaningful sequence, Haggai can be described as historiography (→ history).

At the same time, however, this type of narration aspires to do more than simply transmit the information gained from its sources. It is more than a report — more than even a highly interpretive report — of what Haggai once divined regarding Yahweh's involvement in key events of the restoration. The continual blurring of the author's and the prophet's perspectives reflects the author's close identification with Haggai, and thus betrays a prophetic self-consciousness on the author's part as well as a historiographical purpose. Such narration also serves to express what the author has divined through studying the records of Haggai's prophecies. By this means the author has gained new prophetic insight into the meaning of the restoration for the author's own time. By composing this narrative, the author has communicated these insights to an audience of readers. By studying the book of Haggai, its readers not only gain information about the prophet's role in the restoration but are also shown how to gain prophetic insight into the meaning of those same events for their own time.

Petersen has suggested that the book of Haggai belongs to a genre that is also represented by such texts as 2 Kgs 22–23, Jer 26 + 36, and Jer 37–41 (pp. 34-36), a genre identified by Lohfink as "the historical short account" (*historische Kurzgeschichte;* see N. Lohfink, "Die Gattung der 'Historischen Kurzgeschichte' in den letzten Jahren von Juda und in der Zeit des Babylonischen Exils," *ZAW* 90 [1978] 319-47). From Lohfink's analysis of these texts Petersen concludes that they have several things in common with the book of Haggai, including: (1) short prose narration; (2) focus on some important person(s); (3) historical purpose shown by sequencing events with time markers;

(4) several different scenes; (5) dates marking boundaries between scenes; (6) scenes of unequal length; and (7) an apologetic tendency. Petersen finds the last of these factors particularly important, and would therefore prefer to call the genre a "brief apologetic historical narrative." The comparison of Haggai with these other texts is a helpful first step toward identifying the genre of Haggai, but the resulting definition does not specifically capture two distinctive characteristics of the narration in this prophetic book.

First, although the proposed genre is called "historical," it is not defined in terms of any real distinction between history and fiction. This is evident from the fact that Lohfink envisions the category to include Ruth and Jonah, which are presumably fictional stories. The sequencing of episodes with time markers, in and of itself, does not necessarily mean that a narrative purports to be historical in any strict sense, i.e., that it is a historiographical composition based on an investigation of the past using the most direct sources of information available. It may mean only that some purely fictional events are imagined as happening at a real time and place. Haggai's narration is remarkable precisely because of the way it shows its reliance on source materials, but without slavishly excerpting them verbatim and wholesale. It is thus historical in a strict sense, i.e., historiographical, and in this regard may or may not be comparable with any of the other texts adduced by Lohfink.

Second, although the proposed genre definition takes account of Haggai's apologetic tendency, it does not reckon with the specifically prophetic nature of it. The narrative of Haggai resembles all historiography in having an interpretive bias. Unlike much historiography, however, it has an interpretive bias that is rooted in the prophetic self-consciousness of its author. As a historian, the author describes and interprets Haggai's claims about Yahweh's involvement in the restoration. As a prophet, the author also makes closely related yet different claims of his or her own about Yahweh's involvement in those same events. The unusual form of the narrative serves to express the author's own prophetic perceptions, while also representing them as symbiotically dependent on Haggai's prophetic perceptions. The book of Haggai is indeed historical apologetic ($\rightarrow$ Intention), but it is historical apologetic of a peculiarly mantic sort. Although the other texts adduced above are obviously prophetic narratives, in the sense that they are concerned with prophets and prophetic activity, they may or may not be comparable with Haggai in this regard.

The narration in the book of Haggai is historiography that purports to be revelatory, as it entails the mantic study of records documenting earlier prophetic revelations. The characteristic effect of such narration depends on its having a certain transparency in relation to its sources, through which their coloration can be glimpsed but their contours cannot be clearly discerned. The reader is thus drawn into a subtle oscillation between two shifting foci. At one point the focus is on the prophetic insights that Haggai is reported to have had, which have been validated in the way the events of his career turned out. Then, with scarcely a blink, the focus shifts to the prophetic insights that the author has derived from studying Haggai, which extend Haggai's perceptions of Yahweh's involvement in those events to show how he might also be involved in new situations. The genre of Haggai may simply be called PROPHETIC HIS-TORY, if this designation is understood as a technical term applying only to narration of the sort just described. Such history has a plot and must therefore progress through several interrelated episodes, but the length of the narrative or its individual episodes is not otherwise a factor in the definition of this genre.

In ancient historiography speeches tend to come more from the historian than from the speaker to whom they are attributed, at least with respect to their compositional form. This does not make the investigation of their genre irrelevant, however, because the author's historiographical purpose may be served by having a speaker make a particular kind of speech. It may thus be important to recognize the conventions that govern the speeches made by the main characters in order to understand the overall development of the narrative. This is particularly true in the case of Haggai because its plot is advanced primarily by means of the prophet's speeches. As I analyze each episode of Haggai below, I therefore give some consideration to the genre of the prophetic speech that it contains. This can provide only a description of the conventions governing the narrative's portrayal of Haggai, however, and not a description of the conventions governing the words that Haggai actually said.

Although the classification of Haggai as prophetic history precludes any pretense of direct access to either the source materials with which the author worked or the prophet's ipsissima verba, it nevertheless also provides a basis on which to assert that the book is probably a good paraphrase of Haggai's original message. In communicating to an audience with this genre, the plausibility of the author's insights depends on their being perceived as extensions of earlier prophetic insights, whose reliability is already recognized (Ackroyd, "Studies," 8). The narrative would therefore need to represent what Haggai said, and how he said it, with considerable verisimilitude, if not with detailed factual accuracy.

Setting

This kind of historiography would have been produced by persons with scribal training, who were also imbued with prophetic self-consciousness, working in the context of an institution where records of prophetic activity were preserved and studied. More specifically, this particular text shows careful reflection on the role of prophecy in the development of a new form of Jewish communal life following the restoration, emphasizing the function of prophecy as a source of information and advice for the regime of governor and high priest, while also analyzing the dynamics of such prophecy's popular effects. This text also shows an interest in the temple, not only as an institution with religious and theological significance, but also as an institution with a considerable social and economic impact on the community and its overall welfare. This range of interests implies a scribal group with some influence on the formulation of the policies that governed the postexilic community.

This group can be further characterized with respect to its attitudes toward contemporary international developments and its views on what can be learned from Judah's past. The reconstruction of the temple is described as the sign of a larger transformation in which Yahweh is redefining the world order, and thereby also redefining the sociopolitical form assumed by Judah. This amounts to a theological interpretation of the political process through which Darius I established his rule over the area by both suppressing widespread revolt among subject peoples and reorganizing the structures of local governance within the imperial administration (P. Briant, "Persian Empire," *ABD* 5:238-40). The chaotic events surrounding Darius's accession are viewed as a crisis holding great positive potential for Judah. They portend that the community's attainment of greater internal cohesion, through its organized efforts to restore and maintain the temple, will also result in a redefinition and clarification of Judah's somewhat uncertain political status. The nature of the new polity to be assumed by Judah is left altogether ambiguous, however, so that it might range anywhere from the restoration of complete national independence to formal recognition as a particular kind of provincial district within the empire. In any case Zerubbabel will lead this new Judah as the earthly human representative of Yahweh's rule over all creation, just as the Davidic kings once did, by serving as founder and patron of a second temple even more glorious than the first. The book of Haggai is thus characterized by a positive outlook on the favorable status that Judah might attain — and actually began to attain — under Darius (E. Stern, "The Persian Empire and the Political and Social History of Palestine in the Persian Period," in *The Cambridge History of Judaism*, vol. 1: *Introduction; the Persian Period* [ed. W. D. Davies and L. Finkelstein; Cambridge: Cambridge University Press, 1984] 70-87 passim).

The book of Haggai presents a somewhat eclectic view of what Judah can learn from its past. Beuken has argued that the book's scribal authors can be specifically identified with the group that produced the Chronicler's History, but Mason has shown that many of the traits claimed by Beuken to be distinctively Chronistic are generally characteristic of the Deuteronomistic History as well ("Purpose," 414-20). He thus proposes that the composition of Haggai should be more generally attributed to a scribal group functioning within the postexilic temple milieu (R. Mason, *Preaching the Tradition* [Cambridge: Cambridge University Press, 1990] 194-95). This exemplifies the difficulties that attend attempts to place Haggai squarely in any particular postexilic camp (e.g., P. Hanson, *The Dawn of Apocalyptic* [Philadelphia: Fortress, 1975] 175-76). The book appears rather to resemble various exilic and postexilic documents in some respects, and to differ from those same documents in other respects, so that its outlook can hardly be defined in any clearcut partisan terms. For example, Haggai shares the Deuteronomistic History's openness to the possibility that Yahweh's people can exist in a variety of sociopolitical forms, and not necessarily as an independent monarchy, as long as its leadership has prophetic legitimization and guidance. But at the same time Haggai also resembles the Chronicler's History in viewing the founding and maintenance of a temple with a royal pedigree as the primary institutional expression of such prophetically inspired leadership.

Haggai's narrative comes to an end "on the twenty-fourth day of the ninth month, in the second year of Darius" (2:10), while the work on the temple is still in progress. This makes the final months of 520 BCE the terminus a quo for the composition of the book, but it does not place any limitations on the terminus ad quem. If the book were written before the temple was finished, it could have served as propaganda for bringing the work to completion; but it could just as well have been written after the temple was finished, to show its institutional significance by recounting only the critical period in which the construction came to be resumed. In view of the possibility that the book was written rather soon after the events it describes, it is also possible that Haggai himself could have had something to do with its composition. The book contains no autobiographical reporting, however, in marked contrast with the book named for Haggai's contemporary, Zechariah, which is otherwise strikingly similar in style (→ Zech 1:7–6:15). This suggests that Haggai himself played no direct authorial role in composing the book that bears his name.

Intention

This text celebrates the instrumental role that Haggai briefly played in bringing the reconstruction of the Second Temple through a particularly critical phase, in which economic failure first threatened to keep the rebuilding plans of the returned exiles from being realized, and modest results later threatened to derail the project once the work was begun. Haggai's effectiveness is initially analyzed in terms of the way he directs his efforts primarily to the other religious and political leaders, who are in a position to determine community policy, while also attempting to influence popular attitude. This double-barreled approach unleashes the Spirit of Yahweh, which animates both the leaders and a sufficient number of people to engage the task.

As the story unfolds, Haggai's view, that the divine blessing of socioeconomic viability is contingent on the community's willingness to undertake the task, is validated in the short term by a resurgence in agricultural productivity. The narrative thus provides grounds for expecting that Haggai's view of the temple's larger significance will similarly be validated by the way things turn out in the long term. Readers are thus prompted to ask whether the events that have happened in the meantime, since the last episode recounted in the book, provide any confirmation of Haggai's view that the restoration of the temple under Zerubbabel is part of Yahweh's plan to restore his people's place among the nations.

Readers' responses may well vary, depending on their historical distance from the time of Haggai as well as their theological presuppositions. If Haggai was written before the rebuilding project was finished, those who read it in that context might be led to consider whether the world-historical transformation envisioned by Haggai was actually in progress, and whether they should align themselves with it by supporting the work's completion. Those who read the book in the wake of the temple's restoration might be led to consider whether its growing recognition as the central institution of the Jewish people, by those living both in the province of Judah itself and in the expatriate communities of the diaspora, might not be the fulfillment of what Haggai had prophesied. If so, should they not personally acknowledge the temple's centrality and give it their support? Modern readers might be led to consider whether contemporary experience holds anything analogous to the situation analyzed by Haggai, and whether Haggai's insights regarding God's involvement in the events of his own day might also be applicable to contemporary events. (For example, is God working through the disintegration of Christendom and the establishment of the modern state of Israel to re-create the institutional identities and sociopolitical forms in which the covenant people exist?) In any case readers of this prophetic history are meant to consider whether Haggai's revelatory insights, which were initially limited to his particular situation, can now be extended on the model provided by the book to cover new situations. This will finally depend on what readers think about God.

Chapter 2

THE INDIVIDUAL UNITS

THE LEADERS AND PEOPLE OF JUDAH HEED THE PROPHET'S CALL TO BEGIN REBUILDING THE TEMPLE, 1:1-12

Text

In 1:5b and 1:7b the *RSV*'s translation of *śîmû lĕbabkem 'al-darkêkem* as "consider how you have fared" captures part of what this phrase means, but the expression does not refer only to the present consequences of past behavior. This command could be more literally rendered as "take to heart your ways," which shows that it is basically a call to reflect on the causal relationship between the people's choices and their general welfare (Wolff, 30). In the context of the prophet's speech the addressees are thus being challenged by this phrase to imagine how a positive change on their part might eventually lead to some improvement in their situation, as well as to consider how their negative actions have brought them to their present predicament.

The community's initial response to the prophet is described in v. 12a with the phrase *šema' bĕ*. This can sometimes have the meaning that the *RSV* attributes to it, namely, "to obey." Here, however, it appears not to describe the people's actual compliance with the command of Yahweh in v. 8, since 1:13-14 indicates that it took further prophesying by Haggai and direct intervention by Yahweh in order to bring this about. In this context the expression instead indicates that everyone recognized the validity of the claims made by Haggai in 1:4-11, thus acknowledging him as an authentic mediator of divine revelation. They then became afraid (1:12b) because of all that this implied. In this instance it would therefore be better to say that "the people heeded" or the like, than to say that they actually "obeyed."

Structure

	(aa) On the land and its produce	1:11a
	(bb) On humans, animals, and work	1:11b
b. The community's response		1:12
1) The community in large part		1:12a
a) How they collectively responded: they heeded		1:12aα
b) Identification of constituents		1:12aβ
(1) The two leaders		1:12aβ¹
(a) Zerubbabel, son of Shealtiel		
(b) Joshua, son of Jehozadak, the high priest		
(2) All the remnant of the people		1:12aβ²
c) What they heeded		
(1) The voice of Yahweh		
(2) The words of the prophet		
d) Why they heeded: Yahweh commissioned it		1:12
2) The people as a whole: they were afraid at Yahweh's presence		1:12b

Most commentators delineate the initial unit of ch. 1 as 1:1-11 and the second as 1:12-15a, describing the former in terms of the prophet's speech and the latter in terms of the people's response. The main problem with this division is that 1:13 is just as much concerned with reporting the prophet's speech as 1:3-11, and can thus hardly be lumped under the rubric of the people's response. Moreover, the description of the people in 1:2b is ambiguous with respect to whether it is part of the prophet's speech; it can also be read as part of the narrative introduction to the prophet's speech (see below). The narrative description in ch. 1 is indeed marked by shifts from prophetic speech (1:3-11 and 1:13) to the people's reaction (1:12 and 1:14b), but in a more complex way than is suggested by the commonly accepted division of ch. 1 into 1:1-11 and 1:12-15a.

In ch. 1 a contrast is drawn between the effect of one prophecy that is primarily addressed to the two leaders of the community, Zerubbabel and Joshua (1:1-11), and the effect of another prophecy that is primarily addressed to the people themselves (1:13). The first prophecy is intended to reverse the prevailing popular attitude (1:2), but it has only limited success. A good part of the community, including both the leaders and "all the remnant (šĕ'ērît) of the people," are persuaded by Haggai's argument (1:12a); but the people as a whole are too afraid to act on it, even though they recognize in Haggai's words a true manifestation of Yahweh (1:12b; → Text). It takes another prophecy (1:13), combined with the animating inspiration of Yahweh himself (1:14a), to overcome the fear of the people as a whole, so that the two leaders and "all the remnant of the people" can finally take concerted action (1:14b).

The chapter thus falls into two closely interrelated units (1:1-12 and 1:13-15a) describing the initiation and the culmination of the process through which the community was convinced to change both its attitude and its behavior regarding the reconstruction of the Jerusalem temple (1:2b). The first episode (1:1-12) emphasizes the impact on the whole community of the prophet's dealing with the leaders, and the second episode (1:13-15a) in contrast emphasizes the impact of the prophet's dealing directly with the people. In both episodes, even though the people as a whole are addressed by the prophet, only a "remnant *(šĕ'ērît)* of the people" respond positively (1:12a, 14a). Each of these two units contains elements of the prophet's speech (1:4-11, 13) and the community's response (1:12, 14b) in addition to other elements. It is specifically noted that the whole process epitomized by these two episodes took a total of twenty-three days (1:1a, 15a).

The narration in 1:1-12 is characterized by the programmatic integration of two somewhat discrepant perspectives on the event that is reported. The narrator's perspective has a double focus. First it emphasizes the way in which Haggai's prophecy particularly affects Zerubbabel and Joshua (1:1b). Second, the positive but limited response made by these two leaders and "all the remnant of the people" is contrasted with the fearful reluctance of the people as a whole to become actively involved (1:12). The perspective that is reflected in the prophet's own speech, however, focuses on the community as a whole, without drawing any distinction between leaders and people, or any distinction between "the remnant" and the people as a whole. None of the ways in which the prophet describes his addressees in 1:4-11 pertains particularly to Zerubbabel and Joshua, as opposed to the people, or to one segment of the population rather than another.

These two perspectives are integrated by a somewhat unusual narrative device, which employs formulas typically used for reporting oracular prophetic speech in order to give voice to the narrator as well as the prophet. Other prophetic books begin with a prophetic word formula in the form of a relative clause, used as a (→) superscription: *dĕbar yhwh 'ăšer hāyâ 'el* ("the word of Yahweh that came to . . ."), i.e., Hos 1:1; Joel 1:1; Mic 1:1; Zeph 1:1. Haggai, however, joins Jonah and Zechariah in using basically the same formulaic elements, but not in a relative clause construction, to introduce narration: *hāyâ dĕbar yhwh 'el* ("the word of Yahweh came to . . ."). Haggai gives this a further distinctive twist by using the prepositional phrase *bĕyad* ("by the hand of . . .") instead of the preposition *'el* ("to"), thus emphasizing the agency rather than the receptivity of the prophet: "The word of Yahweh came by the hand of Haggai, the prophet" (1:1bα; cf. Jonah 1:1a; Zech 1:1b). It is significant that this particular version of the prophetic word formula is used to introduce both the narration of this episode as a whole (1:1bα) and the report of Haggai's prophetic speech (1:3), and it is likewise significant that the messenger formula, *kōh 'āmar yhwh ṣĕbā'ôt* ("thus says Yahweh of hosts"), is similarly used both to report the complication that the prophet's speech begins to resolve (1:2a) and to mark the beginning of the major sections in the prophet's speech (1:5a, 7a).

The effect of such a device is not only to show that the narrator's obviously tendential perspective is just as revelatory as Haggai's own, but also to assert that these two perspectives are virtually convergent, even as they differ. The narrator's recounting of this episode is just as much a part of the revelation that "came by the hand of Haggai the prophet" as the reported speech of the prophet himself. The nexus of the integration of these two perspectives is 1:2. With respect to the narrative action, this verse describes the complication that Haggai's prophesying serves to resolve. With respect to the prophetic discourse that is reported within the narrative, this verse also describes the statement of the popular position with which Haggai is in critical dialogue. It is not altogether clear whether the narrator is describing a condition that existed when Haggai appeared on the scene, or whether the prophet is summarily stating the position with which he is about to contend. In view of the introduction's overall style, this ambiguity appears to be by design.

Form-critical analysis has generally maintained that the speech in 1:4-11 is a composite made up of several short and originally different prophetic utterances, but no unanimity has been reached regarding either the number or the extent of the supposed component parts. Although recent commentators have tended to see a major division between 1:4-8 and 9-11 (e.g., Beuken, 185-202; Koch, 56-58; Steck), there is little agreement among them about the reasons for doing so (Whedbee, 185-87). It is difficult to see what rhetorical grounds there could be for either supposition. The two main sections of the speech, 1:4-6 and 7-11, are indicated by repetition of the same oracular directive urging the people to reflect on their behavior and its consequences (1:5, 7; → Text). The conceptual progression of the speech as a whole is revealed by the contrasting ways in which this same directive is elaborated in 1:6 and 8-11.

In 1:6 the result of the people's preoccupation with their own houses, at the expense of any attempt to restore Yahweh's house, is described in terms of a failure of human economic activity — failure of sowing to produce enough to eat and drink ($1:6a\alpha\beta^1$), failure of clothing to keep anyone warm ($1:6a\beta^2$), and failure of wages to retain their cumulative value (1:6b). In 1:8-11 the means of reversing this economic decline are explained, as its underlying cause is identified. The people should now undertake the rebuilding of the temple, precisely because their predicament is due to their neglect of this task (1:8-9). They have been unproductive not because of any lack of skill or effort on their part, but because of Yahweh ($1:9a\beta$). Since they have not acknowledged the creator by building him a temple, Yahweh has made heaven and earth incapable of engendering the fertility on which all economic productivity ultimately depends, and this has made life difficult for humans and animals alike (1:10-11).

The gist of the exhortation in 1:4-11 is thus somewhat paradoxical: Continued preoccupation with your own households will only keep you impoverished, but concern for Yahweh's house will address the root cause of your households' failure to prosper, and thus by implication make them economically viable. The command in 1:8, which requires a reversal of the situation described by the initial question in 1:4, becomes persuasive only when it is motivated by the explanatory combination of elements in 1:9-11, and sufficient grounds for it would not be evident from what is described in 1:6 alone (cf.

271

R. Mason, *Preaching the Tradition* [Cambridge: Cambridge University Press, 1990] 286-87, n. 6). The speech in 1:4-11 should therefore be treated not as a composite of prophetic utterances with a major division after v. 8 but as a single subunit of 1:1-12, which arrives at an implicitly negative answer to the question in 1:4 by giving in 1:7-11 an explanatory restatement of the problem that is initially called to the addressees' attention in 1:5-6. (Cf. Whedbee's similar treatment of the speech as an "organic unity" [pp. 188-89], although he retains a major break after v. 8.)

Genre

Form-critical analysis has tended to separate the "editorial framework" of this unit (1:1-2 + 12) from the prophetic speech (1:3-11) that is reported within it, and then to ask what kind of prophetic speech this is (e.g., Beuken, 27-37; Mason, "Purpose," 413-14). On the assumption that the speech is a composite made up of originally separate prophetic utterances, attempts have also been made to identify the various genres of its supposed component parts. In the immediately preceding discussion of this unit's (→) structure, I argued that the speech is probably not a composite because of the way in which it coheres rhetorically. This coherence makes the identification of any generic patterns within the subsections of the speech — such as admonition (e.g., Elliger, 86), futility curse (Beuken, 188), or question-answer schema (Whedbee, 189-92) — relatively unimportant, regardless of how clear-cut such patterns may or may not be. It is the genre of the speech in its entirety that matters most, but this question must also be approached in light of the way the speech relates to its narrative context.

I also observed above that this unit is structured precisely to blur but not to efface the different perspectives of the narrator and the prophet himself. This makes any attempt to strip away the narrative introduction and conclusion in order to deal primarily with the prophetic speech itself rather problematic. There is no seam at which one is self-evidently joined to the other, but only an ambiguous transitional link at 1:2 (cf. Beuken, 29-30). Form-critical analysis must therefore take as its starting point the fact that we have here a narrative in which a prophetic speech plays the central role, and not a prophetic speech that has been incidentally framed by narration. Only after dealing with the question of what kind of narrative this is would it then be appropriate to ask whether it purports to describe any particular kind of prophetic speech.

This text is above all a prophetic narrative, not only in the sense that it is obviously about a prophetic character engaged in typically prophetic activity, but also in the sense that the narrator's voice speaks with prophetic authority (→ Structure). Beyond this assertion of revelatory insight, the narrator's character is evident only in one minor but telling detail: The narrator knows the exact dates of the events that are recounted here (1:1). The narrator's voice thus betrays both a prophetic self-consciousness and a historical concern. Because the narrator's character is otherwise so largely undeveloped, apart from these two succinctly but still definitively signaled traits, no sharp distinction may be drawn between narrator and author. This text thus reflects an author who, like the narrator, functions in the dual role of both prophet and historian.

Because the insights expressed in the narration are presented as extensions of Haggai's prophetic insights, it is likely that the author relied on some traditional source of information about the prophecy that Haggai is here reported to have made. This does not necessarily mean, however, that material from this source was incorporated verbatim into the narrative, or that such source material is now directly recoverable through some sort of analysis (→ Book as a Whole, Genre). In its present form the prophecy has been integrally woven into this account of its impact on the community, and probably recomposed in the process, so that any attempt to recover an earlier form of it becomes extremely uncertain (contra Wolff, who confidently treats the speech as directly excerpted from the vignette memoir or "scene-sketch" [*Auftrittskizze*] of a disciple or friend [pp. 33-34]).

In identifying the genre of such a narrative one should note that 1:1-12 does not stand alone as an entirely separate episode. Although Haggai's prophecy in 1:3-11 is shown to be effective in 1:12, its full impact does not become evident until the end of (→) 1:13-15a. This unit is thus closely related to 1:13-15a in the composition of the (→) book as a whole, and constitutes part of a larger plot. As one episode in a sequence of similar episodes that together describe a course of events over a particular period of time, this narrative may be characterized as PROPHETIC HISTORY.

Given the limitations imposed by such a text on the historical investigation of Haggai's original words, 1:4-11 is perhaps best regarded as simply a reliable paraphrase, and thus an insecure basis on which to discern the genre of what the prophet actually said. One may nevertheless still raise the strictly literary question of whether the narrative employs any particular generic convention in its representation of this speech. The whole of 1:4-11 is structured to give an implicitly negative answer to the rhetorical question with which it begins: "Is it time for you to dwell in your paneled houses, while [Yahweh's] house lies in ruins?" The answer to this question serves to disabuse the audience of the popular attitude described in 1:2, which holds that "the time has not yet come to rebuild Yahweh's house." Regardless of whether the narrator or the prophet makes the statement in 1:2, the prophet takes issue with a position that is explicitly stated. One can therefore follow the lead of other scholars (e.g., Elliger, 86; Steck, 362-63; Whedbee, 187-89; R. L. Smith, 151-52; Mason, *Preaching*, 286, n. 6), although they have generally been concerned with a section ending in v. 8 rather than with Haggai's speech in its entirety, in seeing 1:2-11 as the narrative representation of a PROPHETIC DISPUTATION (cf. Isa 40:27-31; Jer 8:8-9; Ezek 11:14-21).

Setting

The setting of prophetic history in general is discussed above (→ Book as a Whole, Setting), but the setting of the genre of the speech remains to be considered. In this episode the narrative portrays Haggai attacking a widespread popular attitude with a particular kind of speech, a disputation. Although this portrayal limits the actual audience of the disputation to the leaders of the community, it notes that some of the people were also persuaded by the prophet's argument, along with the leaders. This seems to presuppose that Haggai's message was disseminated through the leaders acting in their capacity to determine public policy. There is little direct information about the setting of the prophetic disputation in general (Graffy, 118-24), but another example of this genre, Ezek 20:32-44, which is contained in an account of how "the elders of Israel came to inquire of Yahweh" through Ezekiel (Ezek 20:1-44), similarly attacks a popular attitude by targeting an audience of community leaders. The setting of the prophetic disputation should not be limited to this particular set of circumstances, but should rather be more broadly defined in terms of the prophet's general role as a public speaker who confronts both rulers and people to bring about changes in official policy or popular attitude (e.g., Isa 7:1-17; Jer 7:1-34; 26:1-6). The similarity between these two instances of the genre nevertheless suggests a more specific context, which might realistically be imagined as the kind of situation that could call forth a prophetic speech like the one described in 1:2-11.

Intention

This episode aims to show that the initiative of Haggai was singularly important and effective in the reinstigation of the temple rebuilding project, and it further aims to analyze how this initiative variously affected different sectors of the community. Although Haggai's economic and theological argument was persuasive for the leaders and a good number of the people, the risk of acting on it left the people as a whole apprehensive. Would the prosperity of the entire community really be increased, if everybody would only make the welfare of Yahweh's house a higher priority than the welfare of their own households? Even those who believed that Yahweh was the ruler of creation, and who thus acknowledged Haggai's claim that the blessings of economic prosperity were in some sense ultimately Yahweh's to give, might well not regard the prophet's argument as self-evidently true. Thus, by the end of this episode, favorable popular opinion has not yet reached the critical mass that would make it possible for the rebuilding actually to begin.

Bibliography

A. Graffy, *A Prophet Confronts His People: The Disputation Speech in the Prophets* (AnBib 104; Rome: Biblical Institute Press, 1984); D. F. Murray, "The Rhetoric of Disputation: Re-examination of a Prophetic Genre," *JSOT* 38 (1987) 95-121; O. H. Steck, "Zu Haggai 1:2-11," *ZAW* 83 (1971) 355-79; J. W. Whedbee, "A Question-Answer Schema in Haggai 1: The Form and Function of Haggai 1:9-11," in *Biblical and Near Eastern Studies* (*Fest.* W. S. LaSor; ed. G. A. Tuttle; Grand Rapids: Eerdmans, 1978) 184-94.

THE PEOPLE'S FEAR IS DISPELLED SO THAT MANY ARE INSPIRED TO COME AND REBUILD THE TEMPLE, 1:13-15a

Structure

I. Haggai's prophecy	1:13
A. Introduction: Haggai, Yahweh's messenger,	
spoke a message to the people . . .	1:13a
B. Speech of Yahweh	1:13b
1. Speech proper: I am with you	1:13bα
2. Oracle formula: says Yahweh	1:13bβ
II. Yahweh's action	1:14a
A. What he did: stirred up the spirit of many	
in the community	1:14aα
B. Identification of those inspired by Yahweh	1:14aβ
1. The two leaders	1:14aβ[1]
a. First leader	
1) Name: Zerubbabel	
2) Patronym: son of Shealtiel	
3) Title: governor of Judah	
b. Second leader	
1) Name: Joshua	
2) Patronym: son of Jehozadak	
3) Title: high priest	
2. All the remnant of the people	1:14aβ[2]
III. The response of those inspired by Yahweh	1:14b-15a
A. What they did: came and worked on the house	
of Yahweh of hosts	1:14b
B. When they did so: date citation	1:15a
1. Day: on the twenty-fourth (day) of the month	1:15aα
2. Month: in the sixth (month)	1:15aβ

This brief episode is closely related to its predecessor in (→) 1:1-12; it describes how the course of action urged by Haggai in 1:3-11 is finally undertaken. Like 1:1-12, this unit begins with a prophecy of Haggai (1:13; cf. 1:3-11) and concludes with the people's response (1:14b-15a; cf. 1:12). It differs from 1:1-12, however, by including between these two elements a report of divine intervention (1:14a). Direct action on Yahweh's part authenticates and actualizes Haggai's prophetic address.

The start of a new episode is marked by a shift in the terms with which Haggai is characterized. In 1:1-12 he is repeatedly described as a "prophet" (*nābî'*) through whom Yahweh's "word" (*dābār*) came (1:1bα, 3). Here (1:13a) he is described as Yahweh's "messenger" (*mal'āk*, which can also be translated "angel"), who speaks Yahweh's "message" (*mal'ăkût*). This latter terminology has somewhat broader connotations than the former. All prophets might be called "messengers of Yahweh" in some sense (e.g., 2 Chr 36:15-16;

cf. Isa 44:26; Mal 1:1; 3:1); but all "messengers of Yahweh" cannot be called prophets. The main function of a messenger is to be a sign of Yahweh's presence. This role can be played by an agent with more or less human capacities who, like a prophet, speaks a revelatory word of salvation or judgment (e.g., Gen 16:7-15; Judg 2:1-3). But it can also be played by a superhuman being who performs rather more supernatural feats, in addition to speaking a revelatory word (e.g., Judg 6:11-24; 13:2-20); or by heavenly beings whose appearance signals the divine presence (e.g., Gen 28:10-17); or even by certain natural elements that may on occasion become direct manifestations of their divine creator (e.g., Ps 104:4a).

As signs of Yahweh's presence, messengers often engender fear (e.g., Gen 28:17a; Judg 6:22); consequently, when Yahweh's intentions are positive, messengers also often have to reassure those to whom they appear with such formulaic phrases as "fear not!" (*'al tîrā'*, etc.; e.g., Gen 21:17b; Judg 6:23) and "Yahweh is [or 'I am'] with you" (*yhwh* [or *'ănî*] *'imměkā*, etc.; e.g., Judg 6:12; cf. Gen 28:15a). The characterization of Haggai as Yahweh's messenger thus pointedly introduces Haggai in a capacity that befits his sole action in this episode, which is to reassure the people that the divine presence manifest in his initial prophecy signals Yahweh's good intentions toward them, as it often has in the past. The previous episode describes how a significant part of the population recognized Haggai as an authentic medium of Yahweh's revelation (1:12a), thus engendering fear among the people as a whole (1:12b). In order to dispel their fear, Haggai simply states the message of Yahweh that conventionally serves this purpose: "I am with you" (1:13b; Petersen, 57-58; cf. H. D. Preuss, ". . . ich will mit dir sein!" *ZAW* 80 [1968] 139-73).

This word from Haggai does not result in the conversion of the whole populace to his point of view. It is still the case that only some of the people (i.e., "all the remnant") under the leadership of Zerubbabel and Joshua stand ready to carry out Haggai's directives. As the fear of this part of the community is dispelled, Yahweh motivates them by "stirring up" (*'wr*) their "spirit" (*rûaḥ*), thus enabling them finally to act on the prophetic claim that they have hitherto accepted only in principle (1:14). Although many commentators have maintained that 1:13 is an incidental aside (see those cited by Beuken, 37-38, n. 4), this brief speech of Haggai is a crucial element in the progression of the narrative, as it serves to move the work from potentiality to actuality, in compliance with 1:8. It takes a total of twenty-three days for this to come about (cf. 1:15a and 1:1a).

Genre

In this episode the narrator purports to know not only what was said by the prophet (1:13), how the community responded (1:14b), and when these things took place (1:15a), but also the nature of Yahweh's involvement in the course of events (1:14a). This knowledge of divine agency in the past is not presented as an insight of the prophet, based on his own immediate experience, but as an inference of the narrator, drawn in the process of reporting other facts more open to inspection. This betrays the author's prophetic consciousness even more clearly than the style of the narrative introduction in 1:1-3 (→ 1:1-12, Structure), showing that the author considers historiographical investigation in itself to be a potentially revelatory activity. This unit, viewed as the sequel to 1:1-12, is thus also to be characterized as PROPHETIC HISTORY (→ Book as a Whole; and 1:1-12, Genre).

Setting

→ Book as a Whole, Setting.

Intention

This text recounts the removal of the major obstacle that emerged as Haggai tried to get the temple-building project reinstigated, and it aims to analyze how this took place. In the wake of Haggai's effective argument, implying that this project would begin to reverse the economic failure with which Yahweh had plagued the community, the people were gripped by fear. This fear was overcome in two phases: Haggai prophesied again with words of encouragement addressed to the people as a whole, and Yahweh himself then strengthened the motivation of the project's supporters. As a result, there was no opposition from those who still did not support the project; and those who fully shared Haggai's view, led by Zerubbabel and Joshua, were enabled finally to act on their convictions.

YAHWEH COMMISSIONS HAGGAI TO ENCOURAGE THE CONTINUATION OF THE REBUILDING PROJECT, 1:15b–2:9

Structure

I. Introduction	1:15b–2:1
A. Date citation	1:15b–2:1a
1. Regnal year: in the second year of Darius the king	1:15b
2. Month: in the seventh (month)	2:1aα
3. Day: on the twenty-first (day) of the month	2:1aβ
B. Prophetic word formula: the word of Yahweh came by the hand of Haggai the prophet	2:1b
II. Haggai's prophecy that Yahweh will prosper the rebuilding project	2:1-9
A. Commission to prophesy	2:2
1. Command: speak!	2:2aα^1
2. Designation of addressees	2:2aα^{2}b

a. The leaders   2:2a$\alpha^2\beta$

  1) First leader   2:2aα^2

    a) Name: Zerubbabel

    b) Patronym: son of Shealtiel

    c) Title: governor of Judah

  2) Second leader   2:2aβ

    a) Name: Joshua

    b) Patronym: son of Jehozadak

    c) Title: high priest

b. All the remnant of the people   2:2b

B. Prophecy proper   2:3-9

  1. Rhetorical questions   2:3

    a. Concerning the former temple's glory:

      who of you that saw it is left?   2:3a

    b. Concerning the status of the present temple 2:3b

      1) How do you see it now?   2:3bα

      2) Is it not as nothing in your sight? 2:3bβ

  2. Exhortation to persevere   2:4-9

    a. Order to continue building   2:4-5a

      1) Commands   2:4a

        a) Commands of encouragement 2:4aα

          (1) To first addressee   2:4aα^1

            (a) Command proper

              α. Name: Zerubbabel

              β. Imperative: take courage!

            (b) Oracle formula: says Yahweh

          (2) To other addressees   2:4aα^2

            (a) Commands proper

              α. To a leader

                aa. Designation of addressee

                  α) Name: Joshua

                  β) Patronym: son of Jehozadak

                  γ) Title: high priest

                bb. Command: take courage!

              β. To the public

                aa. Designation of addressees:

                  all the people of the land

                bb. Command: take courage!

            (b) Oracle formula: says Yahweh

        b) Command to action: keep working! 2:4aβ

      2) Twofold motivation: *kî* clause   2:4b-5a

        a) First reason   2:4b-5aα

          (1) Basic statement: I am with you 2:4bα

          (2) Oracle formula: says Yahweh of hosts 2:4bβ

          (3) Expansion: according to the promise

              that I made to you when you

              came out of Egypt   2:5aα

A new episode is introduced with a date citation (1:15b–2:1a) indicating that twenty-five days have passed since the conclusion of the previous episode (1:15a). The main action is introduced in exactly the same terms as the main action of 1:1-12: "the word of Yahweh came by the hand of Haggai the prophet" (2:1b; cf. 1:1b, 3). The prophecy reported in this unit is basically a word of encouragement, similar to but much more elaborate than the prophecy reported in 1:13-15a. In contrast with 1:13b, however, which encourages the community to take up the project of temple rebuilding at a time when they are not yet involved in it, 2:2-9 encourages them to continue the work that they have already undertaken. In contrast with the narration in 1:1-12 and 1:13-15a, which reports both prophetic activity and the community's reaction, the narration in 1:15b–2:9 reports only the prophetic activity without describing any reaction.

There is again a discrepancy between the narrator's perspective and the prophet's (→ 1:1-12, Structure). From the narrator's viewpoint the prophecy represents a speech that has already taken place. This is indicated in 2:1b by the variation in the prophetic word formula, which specifies that the revelation of Yahweh was communicated *through* Haggai (i.e., *běyad ḥaggay,* "by the hand of Haggai"), rather than revealed *to* Haggai *('el ḥaggay).* From the speaker's viewpoint, however, the prophecy is a speech that has not yet taken place. This is indicated by the way in which 2:2-9 retains the form of a commission to deliver a message to the supporters of the temple project, without any explicit indication of whether the prophet actually carried out the command in 2:2.

Yahweh's directions regarding the delivery of the message (2:2) characterize some of the recipients in terms that are notably different from those in which Haggai is subsequently told to address them (2:4). In Yahweh's order to Haggai the two leaders are identified by name, patronym, and title (2:2a), and Haggai's popular supporters are identified as "all the remnant of the people" (2:2b). In the speech that Haggai is commanded to deliver, however, only Joshua is to be addressed in the same way that he is identified in the introduction, with the full complement of name, patronym, and title. Haggai is told to address Zerubbabel by name alone, without patronym or title, and his supporters are to be addressed as "all the people of the land" rather than as "all the remnant" (2:4a). These terminological variations are striking in view of the narrator's overall patterns of usage.

Joshua is invariably identified by name, patronym, and title wherever he is mentioned (1:1b, 12a, 14a; 2:2a, 4a). By contrast, Zerubbabel is only sometimes identified in this way (1:1b, 14a; 2:2a). In 1:12a his name and patronym are used without any title; and here in 2:4a there is only his name. This creates a difference between Zerubbabel and Joshua that foreshadows Zerubbabel's eventually being singled out as the recipient of a prophecy addressed specifically to him (→ 2:20-23), qualitatively distinguishing his status as governor from the high-priestly status of Joshua.

Haggai's supporters have until now been characterized as "all the remnant of the people" (1:12a, 14a; 2:2b), as opposed to "the people" in general (1:2, 13). It is thus a marked departure from precedent to address them here as "the people of the land." This shift similarly foreshadows the upcoming reference to a transformation in the nature of the body politic, as the "people" *('ām)* come to be characterized in 2:14a as a "nation" *(gôy).*

The phrase *'am hā'āreṣ* ("people of the land") can assume various connotations, depending on the context in which it is used (E. W. Nicholson, "The

Meaning of the Expression *'ām hā'āreṣ* in the Old Testament," *JSS* 10 [1965] 59-66). In Ezra 4:1-5, for example, it designates those who lived in the region of Judah prior to the return of the exiles from Babylon. They are "people of the land" because, in contrast with the *běnê haggôlâ* (*RSV* "returned exiles"), they have a relatively well-established place in "the land." Being excluded from participation in the temple rebuilding project, they come to oppose it and are thus also identified as *ṣārê yěhûdâ ûbinyāmin* (*RSV* "adversaries of Judah and Benjamin"). Here, however, it is just the opposite. It is not the opponents but the supporters of the project who belong to the group that comes to be called the "people of the land."

In the context of 1:15b–2:9 the phrase stands in contrast with the supporters' previous designation as "the remnant" *(šě'ērît),* a term indicating not only that they are the exiled survivors of the preexilic kingdom of Judah but also that they are the minority remaining faithful to the prophetically revealed word of Yahweh (G. F. Hasel, *The Remnant: The History of the Remnant Idea from Genesis to Isaiah* [2nd ed.; AUM 5; Berrien Springs, Mich.: Andrews University Press, 1974]). The shift in terminology indicates a social transformation that happens to this group in the course of the temple's reconstruction. The reestablishment of the sanctuary shows that the people in question are no longer a "remnant," i.e., no longer immigrants from Babylon and no longer consigned to a minority status because of their fidelity to the prophetically revealed will of Yahweh. With the restoration of the temple they instead become "people of the land," i.e., native members of a society in which those faithful to the prophetically revealed word of Yahweh are the dominant group. As part of the same process Yahweh is also transforming the world order, altering the balance of power among "all the nations" *(kol-haggôyim),* so that his faithful people can again take their place as a "nation" *(gôy)* on the world scene (2:6-9; cf. 2:14a; Petersen, 81-82; A. Cody, "When Is the Chosen People Called a Gôy?" *VT* 14 [1964] 1-6).

The message that Haggai is to deliver (2:3-9) is basically an exhortation designed to counter a decline in the morale of those involved in the rebuilding. They have sensed a disparity between the plain appearance of the emerging edifice and the glorious memory of its preexilic predecessor, and they have therefore become discouraged. The prophet reassures them that the present building is nevertheless as sure a sign of Yahweh's presence as any they have known before, since the pillar of cloud and fire that accompanied them in the exodus from Egypt, when they first embarked on their history as Yahweh's people (2:4-5a; cf. Exod 13:21). He also reassures them that its reconstruction is part of Yahweh's larger plan to reshape the world order, so as to secure for his people a peaceful and prosperous place among the nations (Hag 2:5a-7aα, 9b). As this plan is realized, lucrative international commerce will eventually bring so much prosperity that the new temple's splendor will rival and even exceed the splendor of the Solomonic sanctuary (2:7aβ-9a).

Genre

Form-critical analysis has generally assumed that the editorial framework in 2:1-2 can be stripped away, leaving in 2:3-9 a residue of traditional material that can then be subdivided into various types of oracular pronouncements (e.g., Beuken, 49-52; Koch, 58-59; Wolff, 59-60; cf. Mason, "Purpose," 413-14). This is problematic, however, in view of the extent to which the element of prophetic speech in 2:2-9 has been subsumed within the narrative action introduced by 2:1 and made an integral part of it. On the one hand, the discrepancy between the perspective of the narrator and the perspective of the prophetic speaker (→ Structure) suggests that the author was working with preexisting source materials documenting Haggai's prophetic activity (→ Book as a Whole, Genre). On the other hand, however, the recomposition of such source materials is also suggested by shifting terminology with which the recipients of the prophecy are characterized (→ Structure). This betrays an authorial touch that reaches right into the core of the prophetic speech, so as to incorporate it within the thematic and narrative progression of the book as a whole. This makes any attempt to separate oral prophetic speech from written editorial narration very dubious. Form-critical analysis must therefore start with the question of what kind of narrative this is, and then ask whether the narrator represents Haggai's words in accord with any particular genre of prophetic speech (→ Book as a Whole, Genre).

The narrative's genuinely historical concern is shown by the precision of the date citation and by the author's apparent reliance on records of Haggai's prophecies. A prophetic self-consciousness is also shown by the author's recomposition of this source material, not as a retrospective reinterpretation of what Haggai said but as a retrospective reinterpretation of what Haggai was commissioned by Yahweh to say. In making the narrator privy to Haggai's reception of revelation from Yahweh, the author virtually equates the revelatory insights that Haggai once claimed to communicate through his oracles with the revelatory insights that the author now claims to disclose through the narrative.

Although this episode differs from the preceding episodes (1:1-12, 13-15a) by not including any report of this prophecy's impact on the community, it becomes evident in the following episode (2:10-19) that Haggai was persuasive in urging the continuation of the work. In 2:18 it is indicated that the foundation was rededicated sometime during the interval of about two months that elapsed between the events described in 1:15b–2:9 and those described in 2:10-19 (→ 2:10-19, Structure). In relation to the context of the book as a whole, the effectiveness of this prophecy — in accord with the pattern set by the two previous units — is thus suggested. As one episode in a sequence of similar episodes that together describe a course of events over a particular period of time, this narrative may be characterized as PROPHETIC HISTORY.

Although it is probable that the author uses and sticks closely to the received record, because the plausibility of this kind of narrative depends on it, little can be said about the form in which Haggai himself may have reported his reception of this revelation, or even the form in which the author's sources reported it (contra Wolff's view [p. 72] that 2:3-9 is taken directly from a disciple's vignette memoir or "scene-sketch" [*Auftrittskizze*]). It is appropriate, however, to ask the literary question of whether the narration represents this intermediation in accord with any particular generic convention (→ Book as a Whole, Genre).

The speech itself (2:2-9) remains in form a REPORT OF A PROPHETIC REVELATION. Moreover, the revelation itself is of a particular sort, a COMMISSION TO PROPHESY. The body of the speech (2:3-9) is entirely subsumed under the command of Yahweh to Haggai (2:2), ordering him to make an oracular speech to designated addressees. Some scholars have treated 2:3-9 as a composite, made up of Haggai's originally separate oracular utterances; and on this basis different generic patterns — admonition, announcement of salvation, etc. — have been identified in various subsections of it (e.g., Beuken, 50-64; Koch, 58-59; Wolff, 72). Such analysis seems dubious not only because of the above-mentioned limitations imposed by the nature of the narrative on any historical investigation of this sort, but also because such an atomizing approach has not reached any measure of unanimity in its results. In any case, even if generic patterns are evident in various subsections of 2:3-9, it is more important to ask whether this speech in its entirety has been represented in the narration as a prophetic speech of any particular type.

According to Wolff, 2:3-9 begins as a disputation but does not finally take any shape that form criticism would recognize as self-contained discourse (p. 72). This observation is questionable on both counts. With regard to the former claim, a closer inspection shows that any similarity between the beginning of this subunit and the form of a disputation — like the one in 1:2-11 (→ 1:1-11, Genre) — is only superficial. At 2:4 the prophet does not actually begin to contend with the popular sentiment that he describes in his initial rhetorical questions in 2:3. On the contrary, his point of departure is to acknowledge the givenness of the common perception that the new temple indeed does not amount to much in comparison with its predecessor. This fact is not in question, but only the implication that might be drawn from it. This speech thus does not begin to do exactly what a (→) prophetic disputation typically begins to do, namely, to state an opinion with which the speaker disagrees and then take issue with it.

With regard to Wolff's latter claim, that the speech in 2:3-9 cannot be form-critically classified, several scholars have observed that it shows the same sort of rhetorical coherence as speeches attributed to various kinds of authoritative figures, including but not limited to prophets. There is disagreement, however, about how to characterize such speech.

McCarthy, following Lohfink, proposes that Haggai's speech can be generically identified as an "installation to office" (*Amtseinsetzung;* see esp. pp. 33-34; cf. Beuken's view that vv. 4-5 are of this genre, pp. 53-60). He defines this form partly in terms of the formulaic clustering of such imperatives as *ḥăzaq* (2:4a; *RSV* "take courage!") and *'al-tîrā'* (2:5b; *RSV* "fear not!"), which are evident in this pericope, as well as similar imperatives that typically appear with these elsewhere, such as *'ĕmāṣ* ("be resolute!") and *'al-tēḥāt* ("do not be discouraged!"). The form is more basically defined, however, in terms of certain essential structural elements that underlie such formulaic language, including: (1) the encouragement to perform some task, (2) a description of the task, and (3) the assurance of divine aid. Speeches with these characteristics are often used by someone in authority to commission subordinates to a new office, or to legitimate their succession to an already existing office (e.g., 1 Chr 28:10; 2 Chr 19:5-7; 32:6-8).

Conrad has called Haggai's speech a "royal war oracle" on much the same basis (see esp. pp. 72-75), emphasizing the primacy of the formula *'al-tîrā'* ("fear not!") as an identifying factor, and alternatively describing the basic structural elements in terms of (1) assurance (i.e., the "fear not" imperative with an optional object), (2) basis for assurance (i.e., a motive clause accompanying the imperative), and (3) directives to pursue or persist in some conflicted activity. Conrad maintains that speeches with these characteristics originated in military contexts and that their directives were backed by the kind of royal authority with which Yahweh would address kings, or with the kind of royal authority with which kings would address warriors (e.g., Josh 11:6; 2 Chr 20:15-17). Other uses of this form, particularly prophetic adaptations, generally carry the connotations of its having been derived from such a setting, and thus imply that the action urged on the audience is metaphorically conceived in terms of waging war against Yahweh's foes (e.g., Jer 42:9-11).

Mason's effective argument against McCarthy's position applies to Conrad's as well. He points out that speeches with this formulaic language and these basic structural elements occur in such a wide variety of contexts that they cannot in every case be said to serve any one particular function (*Preaching,* 24-25). Speeches of this sort thus do not necessarily indicate either an installation to office or an incitement to fight metaphorically against the "foe," although in some contexts they may do so. In this particular case the speech is not addressed to leaders who are about to assume some new office or duty, but to leaders who are already in office, and to the people as well. This speech does not inaugurate the performance of some new duty, but rather encourages perseverance in a task already undertaken. The main obstacle to the continuation of the work is not some external "foe" against which the community must metaphorically fight, but rather their own defeatist attitude. The genre thus cannot be aptly designated as either an installation to office or a royal war oracle, but must rather be conceived more broadly (cf. Mason's characterization of it as "encouragement for a task," *Preaching,* 123).

The prophecy that Yahweh commissions Haggai to proclaim has considerable rhetorical coherence. It takes the admittedly unimpressive appearance of the emerging temple structure as its point of departure (2:3). The rest (2:4-9) is mainly designed to argue that although it is indeed unimpressive, the partially rebuilt temple is nevertheless an effective sign of Yahweh's presence (2:4b-5a), and it marks the beginning of a historical transformation that will have an impressive outcome (2:6-9). There is thus no reason to lose heart (2:4a, 5b). The distinctive phraseology conjures up associations with several specific contexts in which such language would be equally appropriate, such as military operations and inaugural ceremonies; but this speech does not function in its own context as a similar speech might function in these specific contexts. With respect to its overall form, it is therefore best to characterize it simply as a PROPHETIC EXHORTATION (cf. R. L. Smith, 156).

Setting

The setting of the prophetic history genre is discussed above (→ Book as a Whole, Setting). This episode of prophetic history consists of a report of a commission to prophesy, a form that has a double function. Its secondary function is to communicate indirectly the message of a particular revelation (2:3-9), as it allows the reader to "overhear" what Yahweh imparts to the prophet. Its primary function, however, is to communicate directly that the prophet got both the message and the authority to deliver it straight from Yahweh himself (2:1b-2). The form thus presupposes a setting in which the prophet's authority is in question. Describing Haggai's exhortation to continue the project in this particular way suggests that the claims on which he based his attempt to reinstigate the rebuilding have become questionable. Although his efforts to get the work started were effective, nothing has yet happened to substantiate the notion that this will generate an economic turnaround. The authenticity of the prophetic message, that Yahweh wants the work to continue as part of his still operative plan to prosper his people, must therefore be reinforced.

The setting of prophetic exhortation itself can be described only in the most general terms, in the context of prophetic public oratory. In this particular case repeated references to "this house" (2:3, 7b, 9a; cf. "this place," 2:9b) suggest that Haggai is supposed to proclaim the message at the temple site on some public occasion. There was ample precedent for such an event, as prophets used to address the people about serious current issues at such gatherings (e.g., Jer 7:1-34; Amos 7:12-13; 1 Kgs 13:1-2). There is also some evidence for occasional assemblies at the ruins of the Jerusalem sanctuary during the exile (Jer 41:4-5), as well as for periodic assemblies there once the rebuilding resumed (Ezra 3:1-6). The situation into which 1:15b–2:9 projects the delivery of the speech in 2:3-9 is thus a realistic indication of the setting in which prophetic exhortations of this sort were typically made (→ Zeph 1:7-10; 1:11-18).

Intention

This unit advances both the narrative and the thematic progression of the book's whole story. An earlier episode (1:1-12) describes how Haggai helped to reinstigate the temple rebuilding project through a confrontational argument cast in negative terms: Despite all seemingly self-evident expectations to the contrary, the community could only reverse the economic decline with which Yahweh had plagued them by undertaking this work. The present episode (1:15b–2:9) goes on to describe how Haggai helped to maintain the project by a more amenable argument cast in more positive terms: The reconstruction of the temple is now the starting point and centerpiece in a process of cosmic transformation, through which Yahweh plans to provide for his people a secure and prosperous place among the nations.

In earlier episodes the fear of the whole population (1:12) had to be dispelled, so that the project's supporters could get the work started (1:13-15a). In this episode the fear of those who support the project must also be dispelled, so that they can now manage to keep the work going. In order for them to maintain their morale, they are urged to see themselves as participants in a recapitulation of the great world-transforming process, through which Yahweh brought his people out of slavery in Egypt, gave them land, and made them a nation (2:5aα; also note *'ôd* ["again"] in 2:6aβ). The restoration of the temple thus signals that Yahweh's people have once again been liberated from captivity, that they have once again assumed their place in the land (i.e., as *'am hā'āreṣ* ["people of the land"], 2:4bβ), and that they are once again on the way to becoming a nation (i.e., a *gôy* [2:14a] among the *gôyim* [2:7]).

Bibliography

E. W. Conrad, *Fear Not, Warrior: A Study of 'al tîrā' Pericopes in the Hebrew Scriptures* (BJS 75; Chico, Calif.: Scholars Press, 1985); N. Lohfink, "The Deuteronomistic Picture of the Transfer of Authority from Moses to Joshua," in *Theology of the Pentateuch* (tr. L. M. Maloney; Minneapolis: Fortress, 1994) 234-47; D. J. McCarthy, "An Installation Genre?" *JBL* 90 (1971) 31-41.

HAGGAI SHOWS THE NEED FOR FULL RESTORATION OF THE TEMPLE CULT, 2:10-19

Text

Translations of 2:15-19 vary widely. The structural analysis given below is based on the following rendering, which follows LXX rather than MT in two places. In v. 16a *mah-hĕyîtem* (*RSV* "how did you fare?") is preferred over MT *mihyôtām* ("since they were"), and in v. 19a *'ôd* ("again") is preferred over MT *'ad* (*RSV* "still").

(15) But now, from this day forward, take to heart how it was before stone was put upon stone in the temple of Yahweh: (16) How were you then? Someone would come to a grain heap for twenty measures, but there would be only ten; someone would come to the wine vat to draw out fifty measures, but in the press there would be only twenty. (17) I smote you and every work of your hands with scorching, mildew, and hail, but to no avail (?), says Yahweh. (18) From this day forward, from the twenty-fourth day of the ninth month, take to heart how it has been since the day when the foundation of Yahweh's temple was laid. Take it to heart! (19) Is there [not] still seed in the storehouse? Have not even the vine, the

fig, the pomegranate, and the olive tree again borne [fruit]? From this day on I will bless you.

This translation follows many of the linguistic options advocated by D. J. Clark ("Problems in Haggai 2.15-19," *BT* 34 [1983] 432-39). The temporal relations between the first two clauses in v. 18 are understood in accord with the proposal of A. Fernandez ("El Profeta Ageo 2,15-18 y la fundación del segundo templo," *Bib* 2 [1921] 206-15). Neither of the conclusions reached by these scholars regarding the chronology of the temple "founding" *(ysd)* is adopted here, however (→ Structure; also Book as a Whole, Structure). With regard to the syntax of v. 19, this translation follows Meyers and Meyers (*Haggai,* 48).

Structure

2) Response proper: yes	2:13bβ
3. Haggai's explication of the inquiry's outcome	2:14-19
a. Speech report formula: and Haggai answered and said . . .	2:14aα¹
b. Explication proper: speech of Yahweh	2:14aα²-19
1) Description of the people's overall situation in terms of ritual purity	2:14aα²b
a) Compound comparison	2:14aα²bα
(1) Initial statement: so it is with this people and this nation before me	2:14aα¹
(2) Oracle formula: says Yahweh	2:14aα²
(3) Subsequent statement: so it is with every work of their hands and whatever they offer there	2:14aβbα
b) Conclusion drawn from comparison: it is unclean	2:14bβ
2) Exhortation to consider how the situation has improved since rebuilding began	2:15-19
a) Call to consider conditions before rebuilding began	2:15-17bβ¹
(1) Command to consider the matter	2:15a
(a) Temporal modifier: now	2:15aα
(b) Imperative: take it to heart!	2:15aβ
(c) Temporal modifier: from this day forward	2:15aγ
(2) Matter to be considered	2:15b-17bβ¹
(a) Generally stated: how it was before stone was put upon stone . . .	2:15b
(b) Specifically stated	2:16-17bβ¹
α. Description of conditions then: dearth	2:16
β. Nature of Yahweh's involvement then: I smote you . . .	2:17abβ¹
b) Oracle formula: says Yahweh	2:17bβ²
c) Call to consider conditions since the foundation was laid	2:18-19
(1) Command to consider the matter	2:18abα
(a) Imperative: take it to heart!	2:18aα
(b) Temporal modifiers	2:18aβbα
α. From this day forward	2:18aβ
β. Date citation	2:18bα
aa. Day: from the twenty-fourth (day)	2:18bα¹
bb. Month: in the ninth (month)	2:18bα²

(2) General statement of the matter to be
considered: how it is now that the
foundation is rededicated   2:18bβ[1]

(3) Reiteration of the command to
consider the matter: take it to heart!   2:18bβ[2]

(4) Specific statement of the matter to
be considered   2:19

     a. Description of present conditions (rhetorical
questions): fertility and fruitfulness   2:19a

     b. The nature of Yahweh's involvement now:
from this day I will bless you   2:19b

Critics formerly tended to divide this unit in two, separating 2:10-14 from 2:15-19 and transposing the latter pericope to follow on 1:15a. This practice was based partly on a claim that 2:15-19 is more plausibly linked with ch. 1 than with 2:10-14 because of the close thematic similarity between 2:15-19 and 1:5-11. The transposition of 2:15-19 to follow on 1:15a was also based partly on a claim that the "people" and "nation" mentioned in 2:14 are foreigners rather than Haggai's own people, thus making it seem that 2:10-14 and 2:15-19 are concerned with different groups. Even among older commentators this view was not unanimous (e.g., Mitchell, 67-69), and recent studies increasingly tend to reject it (e.g., Koch, 60-66; May, 190-94; Alonso Schökel and Sicre Diaz, 1138-39; Rudolph, 44-53; Petersen, 74-85; Meyers and Meyers, 76-82; Hildebrand, 154-55; March, 727), although not without exception (e.g., Amsler, *Aggée*, 28-39; Wolff, 39-49). The following analysis of 2:10-19 generally supports the emerging consensus that 2:10-14 and 2:15-19 belong together, and seeks to provide further reasons for it.

The beginning of a new episode is indicated by the date citation with which this unit begins (2:10a). Three months and twenty-three days have elapsed since Haggai first began to urge the reinstigation of the temple rebuilding project (1:1a), and exactly three months have passed since the work on this project was begun (1:15a). Two months and three days have elapsed since the immediately preceding episode (1:15b–2:1a), in which Haggai encouraged the project's supporters not to mind the disappointingly unimpressive appearance of the emerging structure, and to continue with the work.

Two other temporal markers emerge in the prophet's concluding speech (2:14-19) that further serve to locate the date of this episode in relation to previous events. The people are exhorted to compare how poorly they fared "before stone was put upon stone" (2:15a) with how well they have fared "since the day when the foundation of Yahweh's temple was laid" (2:18bβ). The time when stone began to be put upon stone, i.e., when the work of the present attempt to rebuild first began, has previously been described (1:1-15a); but 2:18bβ is the first reference to the day when the foundation was laid. In accord with the course of events outlined above (→ Book as a Whole), these two events are not necessarily to be equated. The commencement of the work would of course move rather quickly to the laying of the foundation as the first major task to be accomplished, but the occasion on which the laying of the foundation was ceremonially celebrated might be at some other time.

In Ezra 3:10-13 the foundation ceremony is described as the time when those who remembered the First Temple expressed their disappointment over the emerging structure. Although the same motif of disappointment is prominent in Hag 1:15b–2:9, so that the events described in Ezra 3:10-13 and Hag 1:15b–2:9 might be generally envisioned as occurring around the same time (→ Book as a Whole, Structure), the occasion for the delivery of the speech in 1:15b–2:9 is not explicitly identified with the foundation ceremony. It therefore appears that the narrative of Haggai does not give any explicit account of this ceremony or assign any particular date to it, but rather assumes its celebration at some point during the interval of three months that separated the initiation of the work (1:13-15a) from the events described in the present episode (2:10-19), around the same time as the event described in 1:15b–2:9. The day of the foundation ceremony is identified in 2:18bβ as a decisive turning point, at which Yahweh's reversal of his people's fortunes became manifest. This is a realization born of hindsight, however, that becomes apparent only from the subsequent vantage point of "this day," i.e., "the twenty-fourth day of the ninth month" (2:18abα). It is now time for the community to take stock of how the work on the temple has progressed and how it has changed their overall situation, in view of their having passed such a turning point as the foundation ceremony and in view of all that Haggai has previously prophesied.

To this end Haggai undertakes a prophetic symbolic action. He is commissioned by Yahweh to ask the priests for a ruling (š'l tôrâ; RSV "decide this question") on an issue of cultic purity (2:11-12a). In carrying out this command (2:12b), Haggai also elicits from the priests their answer to a similar question (2:13). This is the kind of counsel that priests are typically called on to give in the ordinary course of things (J. Begrich, "Die priesterliche Tora," in Werden und Wesen des Alten Testaments [BZAW 66; ed. P. Volz, F. Stummer, and J. Hempel; Berlin: Töpelmann, 1936] 63-88). In this particular case, however, the symbolic nature of the request is evident from the way in which the prophet does not pursue the priestly ruling as an end in itself, but rather uses it as the basis for an analogy (2:14) describing the general condition of the people's relationship to Yahweh (Horst, 202). There is no explicit indication that Haggai made his encounter with the priests into a public spectacle, but the way in which he finally turns to address the people collectively (2:14-19) implies the presence of at least some additional observers. The request for a priestly ruling provides the prophet with a point of departure from which to address the people in Yahweh's name. On the basis of certain well-established principles of cultic purity, which have now been dramatically reiterated, the prophet can state where they presently stand in the light of all that has thus far been accomplished (2:15-19).

The narration of this episode shows a shift in perspective at 2:12b (Wolff, 88-89). Up to this point the narrator describes the prophetic symbolic action prospectively, in terms of Yahweh's command concerning what the prophet is to do. At 2:12b, however, the narrator begins to describe the same event retrospectively, in terms of how the priests responded to the prophet as he complied with Yahweh's command. The initially prospective viewpoint is reinforced by the way in which the introductory prophetic word formula in 2:10b departs from the phraseological variation that has characterized its usage until now. Here the narrative does not begin by saying that the word of Yahweh was communicated *through* Haggai (i.e., *běyad haggay*), as in previous episodes (1:1b, 3; 2:1b), thus implying that the prophetic activity in question has already been performed. Here it instead begins by saying that the word of Yahweh was revealed *to* Haggai (*'el-haggay*), in accord with the more usual phraseology elsewhere (→ 1:1-12, Structure), thus implying that the prophet has received a revelation regarding some activity yet to be performed. (The *RSV* does not catch this distinction, as it here translates *'el-haggay* as "by Haggai," just as it translated *běyad haggay* in 1:1b, 3, and 2:1b.) Despite this strong insistence on introducing the prophet's symbolic action from a prospective viewpoint, however, the narration soon shifts in 2:12b to a retrospective account of how Haggai's encounter with the priests turned out.

This is similar to, but precisely the reverse of, the previous episode's shift in perspective. In (→) 1:15b–2:9 the narration is begun from the retrospective viewpoint of revelation communicated (1:15b–2:1), and is then continued from the prospective viewpoint of revelation received (2:2-9). This has the effect of transferring the reader from the relatively objective realm of observable events to the relatively subjective realm of the prophet's self-awareness. Here the reverse shift has the reverse effect of transferring the reader from the relatively subjective realm of the prophet's self-awareness to the relatively objective realm of observable events. Such transference is in keeping with the present episode's concluding emphasis on the claim that Haggai's previous prophecies have manifestly begun to be fulfilled, so that a bold new historical prospect is opened up (2:15-19).

In carrying out Yahweh's command Haggai asks the priests two questions that seem to presuppose the resumption of at least some cultic activity on the temple site (Koch, 61; Petersen, 84-85), one concerning the holiness of sacrificial meat and the other concerning the impurity arising from contact with a corpse or some other impure thing (*těmē'-nepeš*, 2:12-13). Although the work of rebuilding the temple is not yet complete, the nature of the narrative action nevertheless suggests that the priests are back in business. In the implied background against which this episode takes place the sacrificial cult is thus again functioning, though somewhat defectively. This is consistent with the account in Ezra 2:68–3:13, according to which the altar was rebuilt even before the foundation was relaid, so that at least some kinds of sacrificial rites could be observed pending the completion of the building and the further restoration of the cult in its entirety.

Haggai first asks whether contact with something that has touched a holy object can make other objects holy, to which the answer is negative (2:12). He next asks whether contact with someone who has touched something impure can make other objects impure, to which the answer is positive (2:13). Haggai then draws an analogy, describing the present status of the people's relationship with Yahweh in terms of the priests' statements regarding holiness and impurity (2:14).

Through the restoration of the cult that is now in progress, the "people" (*'ām*) are well on their way to becoming a "nation" *(gôy)* once again, in accord with Yahweh's promise (→ 1:15b–2:9, Structure). There is more to the matter of restoration, however, than the socioeconomic and political aspects on which Haggai has focused until now. These are closely related to, but nevertheless distinct from, the specifically religious and cultic aspects of the relationship between Yahweh and his people, to which the prophet now turns. The full restoration of this relationship requires attention to questions of holiness and purity as well.

Some have proposed that although Zechariah's question concerns ritual purity, the analogy drawn from the answer makes a point concerning ethical purity (e.g., May, 194-95; Hildebrand, 163-64). This is to introduce a distinction that is foreign to this text, however. The whole thrust of the book up to this point has been to describe how the restoration of the temple will benefit the community, and this unit continues in the same vein by showing that full restoration of the sacrificial cult, which was operative even before Zerubbabel reinstigated the work on the temple building, remains defective without the completion of this work. As (→) Zech 7:1–8:23 shows, the prophecy of this period was quite capable of distinguishing between cultic propriety and ethical integrity, and of recognizing that the former does not necessarily result in the latter, but Haggai is not concerned with making a point of this kind here.

Through the people's participation in the partially restored cult they came into contact with things that touch on holiness — especially the holiness that emanates from Yahweh's own presence (*lĕpānay* [*RSV* "before me"]; cf. *'ănî 'ittĕkem* [*RSV* "I am with you"], 1:13b; 2:4bα). In the sacred precinct surrounding the rebuilt altar they offered the regular round of *'ōlôt* (*RSV* "burnt offerings"), as well as occasional *nĕdābôt* (*RSV* "freewill offerings"), and they celebrated such festivals as the Feast of Booths (Ezra 3:3b-5); but for whatever reason they seem not to have offered the *ḥaṭṭō't* (*RSV* "sin offerings"; Lev 4:5-13) that were often a necessary part of atoning for impurity (e.g., Lev 12:1-8; 15:1-32), as well as the central feature of the ritual for the Day of Atonement (Lev 16). From Haggai's viewpoint the resumption of some kinds of sacrifices may well have been a step in the right direction, but a cult without the means of atonement was inadequate (→ Zech 3:1-10).

As the priests' answer to his first question indicates, the recognition of a holy place cannot in itself make the people holy. Profane things cannot be sanctified, if they are also impure to begin with. A cult that is only partially restored thus cannot fulfill its function of sanctification because of the principle stated in the priests' answer to Haggai's second question, that impurity begets impurity. The problem is that the people are impure to begin with, hence "all the work of their hands" is impure, and thus whatever they bring to offer in the partially restored sanctuary is impure (Petersen, 84-85; Reventlow, 26-27; March, 727). Full restoration of the cult is necessary, so that the people can have not only a holy place but also an adequate means of atoning for their impurity. They may then present pure offerings, and the cult can begin to fulfill its function of purification and sanctification.

In conclusion the prophet attests to Yahweh's desire for this eventuality with reference not to things that will someday be accomplished but to things that have already been achieved (2:15-19). Yahweh's intention, to restore to his people the cultic means of purifying and sanctifying both themselves and "the work of their hands," is evident from the extent to which he has already prospered "the work of their hands." This particular moment in time, "the twenty-fourth day of the ninth month," affords a vantage point from which to see that the people's support of the rebuilding project has indeed led to increased prosperity in only a very short time, as was implied in Haggai's analysis of the reasons for their earlier economic failure. Yahweh's promise of socioeconomic blessings is already being fulfilled, thus engendering confidence in his intentions to bless the project in other ways as well. The prophet seeks to foster this kind of confidence in the people, so that the work will "from this day forward" gain the momentum necessary to ensure its completion.

Genre

There has hardly been any form-critical analysis of 2:10-19 as such. Many have assumed that removal of the editorial introduction in 2:10 leaves an earlier report of Haggai's prophetic activity more or less intact, and that the prophetic speech in 2:15-19 is not an integral part of this unit. With regard to the latter assumption, Koch has stood virtually alone in arguing on specifically form-critical grounds that 2:15-19 is an appropriate conclusion to Haggai's foregoing dialogue with the priests: The dialogue shows, by way of analogy, that the people are inevitably impure; and the prophecy in 2:15-19 elaborates on the analogy by proclaiming Yahweh's intention to deliver them from this unfavorable condition (Koch, 60-66). The structure analysis above generally concurs with Koch's argument that form-critical analysis must reckon with 2:15-19 as an integral part of this unit. But what about the editorial introduction in 2:10?

Although the author probably based the composition of this episode on an earlier story about Haggai, the remains of this earlier story cannot now be neatly separated from the author's subsequent editorial work. The perspective of the introduction in 2:10 is not distinct from the perspective of the story that begins to unfold from 2:11. On the contrary, the commission in 2:11-12a, on which the rest of the story is necessarily predicated, is described from exactly the same prospective viewpoint as the introduction in 2:10 (→ Structure). There is thus no clear separation of the author's introductory editorial comment from the story. There is only an elliptical transition within the story itself, as the prophet's action is first described in terms of his being told what to do, and is then suddenly described in terms of his having done as he was told (2:12). This combination of two disparate perspectives in the same narrative suggests reliance on a source with a perspective different from the author's; but a transition of this kind at this juncture in the narrative also indicates an artful sort of recomposition that makes any attempt to sift out the original source material rather dubious.

Such recomposition is also evident from the way in which the prophet's

293

speech in 2:14-19 makes cross-references and allusions to parts of previous episodes, so that this episode can advance the thematic and narrative development of the book as a whole. For example, 2:15-17 echoes and explicitly refers back to the prophet's description in 1:5-11 of the economic crisis prior to the rebuilding. Also, as previously mentioned, the use of the term "nation" *(gôy)* in 2:14 resonates with Yahweh's promise in 2:6-7 to secure his people's status among "all the nations" *(kol-haggôyim; →* 1:15b–2:9, Structure). The blessing of agricultural fertility described in 2:19a expressly reverses the punishment of agricultural infertility described in 1:6a and 1:10-11, and begins to fulfill the promise of prosperity expressed in 2:9b. Such textual features show that this unit has been shaped to fit the place it now holds in the book as a whole.

In view of these considerations, form-critical analysis must reckon with 2:10-19 in its entirety, and must first ask what kind of narrative this is. It may then be appropriate to ask in addition whether the writer has composed this narrative in accord with any traditional manner of recounting the exploits of prophets.

Like the preceding units, this unit shows the author's dual concern with both historical accuracy and revelatory insight. The narrative purports not only to give a factual account of all that Haggai did and said on this occasion, but also to communicate the author's insight that the prophet was acting in accord with divinely revealed instructions. (This insight is articulated here from the author's viewpoint, even if it did not originate with the author.) A historiographical purpose is obviously evident in the precise chronology that informs both the introduction (2:10) and the concluding prophetic speech (2:14-19), and a historiographical method also seems evident in the author's apparent unwillingness to efface all traces of earlier source material. History and prophecy meet in the apologetic claim, recounted in 2:18-19, that the course of events is beginning to unfold in fulfillment of Haggai's previous prophecies. These traits show that this episode is basically similar to its predecessors, and as part of this series it belongs to the genre of PROPHETIC HISTORY.

Writing as a historian, the author nevertheless presents this episode in accord with a set of popular conventions for reporting prophetic activity, probably following the precedent set by the source on which the present account depends. The narrative retains the basic elements of a divine command to perform a symbolic action, a report of compliance with the command, and an oracular interpretation of the symbolic action's significance. Thus it can also be classed as a REPORT OF A PROPHETIC SYMBOLIC ACTION (Fohrer, 15-19; cf. Amsler, *Aggée,* 36; Wolff, 89; Reventlow, 25-26; → Zech 6:9-15).

Hildebrand identifies the speech of Haggai in vv. 15-19, explicating the analogy drawn from the priests' reply to his question (v. 14), as a prophecy of salvation (p. 160). As Koch points out, this subunit shows a thematic progression from impurity and infertility to purity and fertility, based on Yahweh's intention to deliver his people from the former state, and thus can hardly be characterized as a prophecy of judgment (pp. 63-64). It does not follow, however, that the overall form of the speech is adequately grasped by conversely calling it a prophecy of salvation. Both the part of the speech describing the present prospect of being blessed with plenty (v. 19) and the part of the speech describing the previously existing condition of being cursed with want (vv. 15b-17) are formally subordinated to the commands to consider what is implied in the incipient change from the latter to the former (vv. 15a, 18). The speech itself is thus better characterized as a PROPHETIC EXHORTATION.

Setting

The setting of the prophetic history genre is discussed above (→ Book as a Whole, Setting). This particular episode of prophetic history is narrated in accord with a set of conventions that characterize a report of a prophetic symbolic action (→ Genre). Such stories were circulated by prophets themselves (e.g., Hos 3:1-5) as well as by their supporters (cf. Hos 1:2-11), not only to spread the word about the dramatic acts that prophets would sometimes conspicuously perform and to explain their meaning, but also to show that these acts were imbued by Yahweh with the revelatory significance that the prophets claimed for them (Fohrer, 108-18). This genre generally reflects a setting in which the popular reaction to the prophets' "guerrilla theater" was ambivalent, so that it could be regarded as either a forceful gesture or an empty antic, depending on whether it managed to establish any credibility (e.g., Jer 27–28). This type of report serves to give prophetic symbolic action favorable publicity, and thus to bolster its credibility as a portentous omen of its stated significance.

The action undertaken by Haggai is not particularly bizarre, as is often the case with the actions undertaken by other prophets (e.g., Isa 20:1-6; Jer 13:1-11; Ezek 4:1–5:12), and the report thus does not have to defend the very plausibility of what Haggai did. Here the genre serves to affirm that the point of this rather ordinary action is more than it may at first seem, i.e., more than merely the moral expressed in the analogy drawn by Haggai regarding the people's impurity. The outcome of the inquiry, as interpreted by Haggai, is also an epiphanic disclosure of where they presently stand in relation to Yahweh's grand design for the restoration.

Intention

This unit continues and complicates the story of Haggai, portraying him as singularly effective in the continuation of the temple rebuilding project. More specifically, this episode shows how he helped the community to see that the project had passed a critical turning point, how he demonstrated another compelling reason for them to continue with the project, and how he identified the ground for their hope in its final completion.

In previous episodes Haggai emphasized the necessity of restoring the temple, in order for Judah to regain its socioeconomic viability on the local level. Now that some kinds of sacrifices have been reinstituted, and now that the foundation has been relaid, this aspect of the restoration process is well underway — as the prospect of a good harvest proves. There is more to the matter than just setting apart a holy place and reaching a certain level of organizational capability, however, although both of these things are of basic importance. It is also crucial for the temple building to be completed, so that the cult can become fully functional as a means of both purification and sanctification. This is necessary for the full realization of Yahweh's promise that Judah will gain a secure and prosperous position in the new world order now emerging. There are already tangible signs of improvement in the local situation, as a result of the work done thus far. These signs provide the motivation for the people to complete the work, and thus enter into the role that Yahweh is creating for them on the world scene.

Bibliography

S. Amsler, *Les actes des prophètes* (Essais bibliques 9; Geneva: Labor et Fides, 1985); idem, "Les prophètes et la communication par les actes," in *Werden und Wirken des Alten Testament* (*Fest.* C. Westermann; ed. R. Albertz et al.; Göttingen: Vandenhoeck & Ruprecht; Neukirchen-Vluyn: Neukirchener, 1980) 194-201; G. Fohrer, *Die symbolischen Handlungen der Propheten* (2nd ed.; ATANT 54; Zurich: Zwingli, 1968); D. R. Hildebrand, "Temple Ritual: A Paradigm for Moral Holiness in Haggai II 10-19," *VT* 39 (1989) 154-68; H. G. May, "'This People' and 'This Nation' in Haggai," *VT* 18 (1968) 190-97; E. M. Meyers, "The Use of *tôrâ* in Haggai 2:11 and the Role of the Prophet in the Restoration Community," in *The Word of the Lord Shall Go Forth* (*Fest.* D. N. Freedman; ed. C. L. Meyers and M. O'Connor; Winona Lake, Ind.: Eisenbrauns for the American Schools of Oriental Research, 1983) 69-76.

YAHWEH COMMISSIONS HAGGAI TO ANNOUNCE TO ZERUBBABEL HIS ELECTION TO RULE JUDAH IN A NEW WORLD ORDER, 2:20-23

Structure

The prophetic word formula (2:20a) indicates a new action and thus marks the beginning of a new episode. A close relationship between this episode and its immediate predecessor (2:10-19) is shown by the formula's inclusion of the term *šēnît* (*RSV* "a second time"), and by the way in which the date citation in 2:20b partially reiterates the calendrical information given in 2:10a, thus indicating that both this episode and the preceding one take place on the same day. The version of the prophetic word formula in 2:20a also follows the phraseological precedent set by 2:10b, in contrast with the version that invariably appears in all previous instances (1:1b, 3; 2:1b), in saying that the word of Yahweh came *'el-ḥaggay* ("to Haggai") rather than *beyyad ḥaggay* ("by the hand of Haggai"; → 2:10-19, Structure). This, too, reinforces the status of 2:20-23 as a sequel to 2:10-19.

Unlike the action of any previous episode, the action of this episode is narrated entirely from one and the same prospective viewpoint. The introduction (2:20) describes Haggai's reception of a revelation from Yahweh, and the revelation itself remains in the form of a commission to proclaim a message to Zerubbabel (2:21a). There is nothing narrated from a retrospective viewpoint to indicate whether Haggai actually proclaimed the message to Zerubbabel in accord with Yahweh's command. A prophetic self-consciousness is indicated by the way in which the narrator presumes to have direct knowledge of Haggai's divinely inspired perceptions.

Zerubbabel's being singled out as the recipient of a particular promise of Yahweh has been foreshadowed by the distinctive variation in the terms with which he is identified (→ 1:15b–2:9, Structure). Here he is again designated by his title, "governor of Judah" (2:21a; cf. 1:1b, 14a; 2:2a), a term that is previously omitted twice (1:12a; 2:4a); and here he is also directly addressed by his patronym, "son of Shealtiel" (2:23a; cf. 1:1b, 12a, 14a; 2:2a), a term previously omitted only once (2:4a). The special status conferred on Zerubbabel by this prophecy, as Yahweh's "servant" (*'ebed*) resembling his "signet ring" (*ḥôtām*), seems to make his role qualitatively different from the role of Joshua or any other leader. The marked reiteration of Zerubbabel's title and patronym at this climactic point also seems to indicate, however, that Yahweh's election of Zerubbabel involves investing the office of governor with deeper significance, rather than assigning Zerubbabel to some other role (Petersen, 105-6; also R. T. Siebeneck, "The Messianism of Aggeus and Proto-Zacharias," *CBQ* 19 [1957] 316-28).

The reference to Yahweh's "shaking the heavens and the earth" (2:21) links this promise to Zerubbabel with Yahweh's previous promise concerning the glorification of the temple (2:6-9), where the same phrase is used to describe the cosmic context of the transformation that Yahweh is bringing about. Zerubbabel's election is thus part and parcel of the process by which the temple is being restored, but Zerubbabel's assumption of his rightful status requires a change somewhat more drastic than what is required for the temple to assume its rightful status. On the international scene the glorification of the temple entails only the "shaking of the nations," i.e., a redistribution of the international balance of power among the existing empires, so that Judah can benefit from interstate commerce (2:7). The election of Zerubbabel entails, however, the "overthrow" *(hpk)* and "destruction" *(šmd)* of the nations' dominions and armies (2:22), i.e., the creation of a new world order.

As the international macrocosm is transformed through the conflict of imperial powers, the microcosm of Judah is transformed through the restoration of the temple. In this context of a world transformed, acting in his capacity as governor of Judah, Zerubbabel can represent the royal dignity of Yahweh. He can be the earthly sign of Yahweh's heavenly kingship over all creation, just as a signet ring can represent the person, nobility, and power of its unseen owner.

Genre

As is generally the case with most other units of Haggai, the form-critical analysis of this unit has attempted first to remove the "editorial framework" in 2:20, and then to treat the oracular material in 2:21-23 as a composite of originally separate prophetic utterances, each based on a different generic convention (e.g., Beuken, 78-83; Wolff, 98-99; cf. Mason, "Purpose," 413-14). In 2:20-23 such an attempt to distinguish the written editorial introduction from the originally oral oracular source is not altogether mooted, as it is in previous units, by the interplay of discrepant narrative perspectives. There are nevertheless several other signs of authorial recomposition within the prophet's speech in 2:21-23. These show that the oracular material in this unit has become such an integral part of the overall narrative that making any clear-cut distinction between the editorial introduction and the original words of the prophet is problematic here as well.

For example, the distinctive pattern of variation in the terms by which Zerubbabel is identified (→ Structure; also 1:15b–2:9, Structure) pervades material that is generally reckoned part of the editorial framework (1:1b, 3, 12, 14), but it also reaches into the heart of the oracular material both here (2:21a, 23a) and elsewhere (2:2, 4a). In 2:21b-22 the scenario of Yahweh's action is described in much the same way as the scenario in 2:6-7, not only with respect to their general features but also with respect to specific terminology on both the cosmic plane (e.g., "shake the heavens and the earth") and the international plane (e.g., "nations"). The close correlation of the prophetic speech in this episode with the prophetic speech in a previous episode, as they relate in this one aspect of their material content, serves to advance the narrative and thematic progression of the book as a whole (→ Structure).

Such textual features do not by any means preclude the possibility that the author of this unit used sources based ultimately on preexisting tradition, into which discrete prophetic utterances were previously gathered by the prophet's disciples or colleagues to make a vignette memoir or "scene-sketch" (Wolff, 98-99). But they do suggest that even if such source material was used, the author was also concerned to do more than just encase it in an "editorial framework." The oracular material has become thoroughly incorporated into the narrative of the book as a whole, contributing to its coherent development from beginning to end. Thus even in the case of this unit, where the problem of making a redaction-source distinction initially seems not as acute as in previous units, form-critical analysis must first ask what kind of narrative this is. Only then is it appropriate to ask whether the narrative unfolds, and whether it represents the speech of its prophetic main character, in accord with any other particular set of generic conventions.

By the way in which this unit is appended to its predecessor in the introduction (2:20), and by the way in which the theme of Judah's place among the nations reaches its climax in Yahweh's promise to Zerubbabel (2:21-23), this episode is shown to be the last in a series of similar episodes that together span a particular period of time. It is thus the conclusion to a PROPHETIC HISTORY.

This historiographical narrative limits itself to the description of a message the prophet received from Yahweh, and says nothing about whether the prophet proclaimed the message (→ Structure). It thus follows the conventions that characterize a REPORT OF A PROPHETIC REVELATION. The revelation that is contained in this report (2:21-23) consists entirely of a speech (2:21b-23) that the prophet is commanded to proclaim to a particular person (2:21a). The revelation itself thus takes a conventional form, the form of a COMMISSION TO PROPHESY. The speech that the prophet is commanded to proclaim is addressed to a political leader, legitimating the leader's status as Yahweh's representative. In preexilic times an oracle of this general sort appears to have been proclaimed by prophets in order to give divine sanction for kings on their accession (e.g., 1 Sam 10:1; 2 Sam 7:5-16; cf. Pss 89:20-38 [*RSV* 19-37]; 132:11-12; also 2 Kgs 9:6-10a; cf. Pss 2:7-9; 110:4), but such prophecies are not well enough attested to define them as a particular genre. The prophecy addressed to Zerubbabel generally reechoes the formulaic language that had traditionally described Yahweh's election of the Davidic dynasty and the status of the Davidic king as his vice-regent (J. E. Tollington, *Tradition and Innovation in Haggai and Zechariah 1–8* [JSOTSup 150; Sheffield: JSOT Press, 1993] 131-44), and some sort of parallel is clearly being drawn between the authority that is being given to the Davidide, Zerubbabel, and the election of preexilic kings. This seems more a matter of allusive phraseology, however, than the imitation of any particularly royal oracular form.

The speech that Haggai is ordered to give is thus a traditional sort of PRO-PHETIC PROMISE (Elliger, 97).

Setting

The setting of prophetic history is discussed above (→ Book as a Whole, Setting), as is the setting of this particular kind of revelation report, i.e., a commission to prophesy (→ 1:15b–2:9, Setting). Divine promises of the sort found in this unit were typically made in public or in private on the occasion of a king's accession, and prophets also generally made such promises during the consultations in which they advised kings (e.g., 2 Sam 7:4-16; 12:13; 2 Kgs 22:18-20a; cf. 1 Chr 22:9-10; 28:6-7). This suggests that Haggai is cast in an analogous advisory role, particularly in relation to Zerubbabel here, but also more generally in relation to Joshua and the leadership as a whole.

Intention

This episode brings the book to a climactic conclusion by showing that the prospect of the temple's completion brings with it new historical possibilities for Judah under Zerubbabel. As the work of rebuilding continues, Yahweh is in the process of reconfiguring the powers that be. The return of agricultural fertility gives tangible evidence of the changes that he has thus far made with regard to cosmic forces, and also attests to his initiation of similar changes with regard to international political forces. In the course of these changes Judah can hope to attain a more stable political identity (even if this results only in the clarification of their status as some kind of imperial province; → Book as a Whole, Intention). With a well-defined polity centered around the institution of the restored royal temple, Zerubbabel's governorship can signify something similar to what the Davidic monarchy once signified: the cosmic kingship that Yahweh exercises as creator of heaven and earth.

ZECHARIAH

The book of Zechariah is discussed in six sections, the first dealing with the book as a whole, and the others dealing with the book's five major individual units: 1:1-6, 1:7–6:15, 7:1–8:23, 9:1–11:17, and 12:1–14:21. Scholarly works pertaining to two or more of these sections are listed immediately below. Works that are relevant only to one of the book's major sections, or to a particular unit within a section, are listed after the discussion of that section or unit.

Bibliography

L. Alonso Schökel and J. L. Sicre Diaz, *Profetas: Comentario,* vol. 2 (NBE; Madrid: Cristiandad, 1980); S. Amsler, "Zacharie 1–8," in Amsler, A. Lacoque, and R. Vuilleumier, *Aggée, Zacharie, Malachie* (CAT 11c; Neuchâtel: Delachaux & Niestlé, 1981); J. G. Baldwin, *Haggai, Zechariah, Malachi* (TOTC; London: Tyndale, 1972); W. A. M. Beuken, *Haggai–Sacharja 1–8* (SSN 10; Assen: Van Gorcum, 1967); M. Bič, *Das Buch Sacharja* (Berlin: Evangelische Verlagsanstalt, 1962); M. Butterworth, *Structure and the Book of Zechariah* (JSOTSup 130; Sheffield: JSOT Press, 1992); T. Chary, *Aggée, Zacharie, Malachie* (SB; Paris: Gabalda, 1969); B. S. Childs, *Introduction to the Old Testament as Scripture* (Philadelphia: Fortress, 1979) 472-87; M. Delcor, "Les sources du Deutéro-Zacharie et ses procédés d'emprunt," *RB* 59 (1952) 385-411; K. Elliger, *Das Buch der zwölf Kleinen Propheten,* vol. 2 (4th ed.; ATD 25/2; Göttingen: Vandenhoeck & Ruprecht, 1959); R. Hanhart, *Sacharja* (BKAT XIV/7, fasc. 1 and 2; Neukirchen-Vluyn: Neukirchener, 1990-91); P. Hanson, *The Dawn of Apocalyptic* (Philadelphia: Fortress, 1975); F. Horst, "Sacharja," in T. H. Robinson and Horst, *Die Zwölf Kleinen Propheten* (HAT 14; Tübingen: Mohr [Siebeck], 1938); R. Jones, *Haggai, Zechariah, and Malachi* (TBC; London: SCM, 1962); M. G. Kline, "The Structure of the Book of Zechariah," *JETS* 34 (1991) 179-93; A. Lacocque, "Zacharie 9–14," in S. Amsler, A. Lacocque, and R. Vuilleumier, *Aggée, Zacharie, Malachie* (CAT 11c; Neuchâtel: Delachaux & Niestlé, 1981); P. Lamarche, *Zacharie IX–XIV* (EBib; Paris: Gabalda, 1961); K. Larkin, *The Eschatology of Second Zechariah* (CBET 6; Kampen: Pharos, 1994); R. Mason, *The Books of Haggai, Zechariah, and Malachi*

(CBC; Cambridge: Cambridge University Press, 1977); idem, *Preaching the Tradition* (Cambridge: Cambridge University Press, 1990); idem, "The Relation of Zech. 9–14 to Proto-Zechariah," *ZAW* 88 (1976) 227-39; idem, "Some Echoes of the Preaching in the Second Temple? Tradition Elements in Zechariah 1–8," *ZAW* 96 (1984) 221-35; idem, "Some Examples of Inner Biblical Exegesis in Zechariah 9–14," *StEv* 7 (TU 126; Berlin: Akademie, 1982) 343-54; C. L. Meyers and E. M. Meyers, *Haggai, Zechariah 1–8* (AB 25B; Garden City, N.Y.: Doubleday, 1987); idem, *Zechariah 9–14* (AB 25C; New York: Doubleday, 1993); H. G. Mitchell, "Zechariah," in Mitchell, J. M. P. Smith, and J. A. Bewer, *A Critical and Exegetical Commentary on Haggai, Zechariah, Malachi and Jonah* (ICC; Edinburgh: T. & T. Clark, 1912); B. C. Ollenburger, "The Book of Zechariah," *NIB* 7:735-840; B. Otzen, *Studien über Deuterosacharja* (AThD 6; Copenhagen: Prostant Apud Monksgaard, 1964); R. E. Person, *Second Zechariah and the Deuteronomic School* (JSOTSup 167; Sheffield: JSOT Press, 1993); D. L. Petersen, *Haggai and Zechariah 1–8* (OTL; Philadelphia: Westminster, 1984); idem, *Zechariah 9–14 and Malachi* (OTL; Louisville: Westminster/John Knox, 1995); A. Petitjean, *Les Oracles du Proto-Zacharie* (Paris: Gabalda, 1969); S. L. Portnoy and D. L. Petersen, "Biblical Texts and Statistical Analysis: Zechariah and Beyond," *JBL* 103 (1984) 11-21; P. L. Redditt, *Haggai, Zechariah, Malachi* (NCB; Grand Rapids: Eerdmans, 1995); idem, "Israel's Shepherds: Hope and Pessimism in Zechariah 9–14," *CBQ* 51 (1989) 631-42; H. Graf Reventlow, *Die Propheten Haggai, Sacharja und Maleachi* (ATD 25/2; Göttingen: Vandenhoeck & Ruprecht, 1993); W. Rudolph, *Haggai, Sacharja 1–8, Sacharja 9–14, Maleachi* (KAT 13/4; Gütersloh: Gerd Mohn, 1976); M. Sæbø, *Sacharja 9–14* (WMANT 34; Neukirchen-Vluyn: Neukirchener, 1969); idem, "Die deuterosacharjanische Frage: Eine forschungsgeschichtliche Studie," *ST* 23 (1969) 114-40; R. L. Smith, *Micah–Malachi* (WBC 32; Waco: Word, 1984); R. Weis, "A Definition of the Genre *Maśśā'* in the Hebrew Bible" (Diss., Claremont Graduate School, 1986); I. Willi-Plein, *Prophetie am Ende* (BBB 42; Cologne: Peter Hanstein, 1974).

Chapter 1

THE BOOK AS A WHOLE

Structure

It is widely acknowledged that the book of Zechariah consists of five main sections. First comes an introduction (1:1-6), followed by two sections that similarly begin with an identification of the prophet and a date citation (1:7–6:15; 7:1–8:23). Then come two more sections (9:1–11:17; 12:1–14:21), each of which is entitled a *maśśā'* (*RSV* "oracle"). There is considerable disagreement, however, with regard to how these sections are interrelated. It has long been noted that the style of the first three differs markedly from the style of the last two. The major divisions and the individual units in chs. 1–8 are rather clearly delineated in terms of both form and content, and the basic principles of their organization seem fairly obvious. By contrast the composition of chs. 9–14 seems less coherent and rather loosely organized. This suggests that chs. 9–11 and chs. 12–14 may stem from a common author; and it raises the question of whether the former part of the book, which contains material explicitly attributed to Zechariah (i.e., chs. 1–8), might not be more directly connected with this prophet than the latter part of the book, which does not have any such attribution (i.e., chs. 9–14).

Scholarly opinion on this question has shifted and diverged. Those who first investigated the matter in the eighteenth and nineteenth centuries, using the diachronic methods that were then rather recently developed, tended to conclude that the prophecies in chs. 9–11 and 12–14 were largely composed by some anonymous author(s) before the time when Zechariah is said to have prophesied in chs. 1–8, i.e., prior to the advent of the Persians in the late sixth century BCE. This kind of position is still held by some (most notably Otzen), but in this century a majority have come to believe that the prophecies in the last two sections of the book were anonymously composed somewhat later than the time of Zechariah. Beyond this, however, there has been little agreement with regard to whether the prophecies in "Deutero-Zechariah" (i.e., chs. 9–14) form one or more distinct works, when they were composed, and how they came to be associated with the prophecies explicitly attributed to Zechariah in chs. 1–8. The material in chs. 9–14 has thus been assigned widely varying dates, ranging from the late sixth to the second century (Otzen, 17-36; Sæbø, "Die deutero-Sacharjanische Frage," 118-32).

Because of the inability of historical-critical scholarship to reach any consensus on these matters, the quest for a historical explanation of how chs. 9–14 came to be composed and joined to chs. 1–8 has become less urgent, and in some quarters has even been abandoned. Recent studies continue to treat chs. 1–8 in close relation to events of the early Persian period, but chs. 9–14 are instead mined for repeated words and phrases (Butterworth), rhetorical patterns (Lamarche and Baldwin), various kinds of allusions to other biblical texts (Delcor, Mason, Person, and Larkin), and mythic motifs (Hanson), to see if this search can provide any information about what kind of text this is, how it is organized, and why it was appended to chs. 1–8. Once the language of the text has been described through this kind of analysis, there may be a basis on which to venture some generalizations about who would use such language and what their circumstances would be: anti-hierocracy visionaries from the end of the sixth to the middle of the fifth century (Hanson, 281-401; cf. Lacocque, 139-44), or members of the Deuteronomic scribal school in the early postexilic period (Person, 146-49, 161-68), or late-fourth- or early-third-century sectarian reinterpreters of the earlier prophets (Mason, *Haggai,* 80), etc.

This tendency of recent scholarship, to grant priority to synchronic over diachronic concerns, is taken to its logical extreme in Childs's assertion that a historical explanation of Zechariah's overall form has proved difficult precisely because it is both inappropriate and impossible (pp. 481-86). It is only necessary to see how the various sections of the book are mutually affected by their present configuration, because they have assumed this configuration through a canonical rather than a redactional process. Childs believes that, unlike a redactional process, which is in principle subject to historical investigation but in practice often eludes it, a canonical process is not open to historical inquiry. Because of the way biblical documents were finally shaped, they now refer more to the timeless truths manifest in them than to the historical conditions under which such truths were originally apprehended. In the case of Zechariah such shaping was achieved by the addition of the historically vague material in chs. 9–14 to the more historically specific material in chs. 1–8, thus generalizing the historical changes mentioned by the latter into "a more mature and developed testimony to the ultimate hope of the nations" (p. 486). Childs argues that because this process was canonical in his particular sense of the term, one cannot peer into it.

The fascination of recent scholarship with the language, rhetoric, and intertextual allusions of chs. 9–14, and its concomitant concern with identifying the thematic rather than the historical connections between this material and chs. 1–8, have produced useful information and insights. Such synchronic approaches have avoided many of the liabilities of the older diachronic approaches, but it is evident that the synchronic approaches have similar liabilities of their own. The results are certainly no less divergent. Butterworth's survey of the various descriptions of Zechariah's structure makes one wonder whether the scholars that produced them were all reading the same text. Childs's view of the canonical shape of Zechariah as a juxtaposition of texts with no direct literary dependence on one another (p. 481) stands diametrically opposed to Kline's view of its canonical shape as the product of a single author's original master plan for the whole work (pp. 192-93). On the basis of a predominantly synchronic approach to the final form of Zechariah as a whole, conclusions apparently run in all directions — just as they do on the basis of a predominantly diachronic approach.

As Mason has aptly noted (*Haggai,* 81), Zechariah does more than most texts to foster humility in its interpreters. Because so many of its problems have proved to be intractable, proposals regarding their solution can only be rather tentative. Any attempt at interpretation must nevertheless stake some claim regarding the approach that seems most promising, and so I have sought to avoid the by now apparent limitations of either a purely diachronic or a purely synchronic approach. The final form of the text is thus the primary object of investigation, but this investigation is guided by the historical consideration of whether the final form follows any identifiable conventions or genres of ancient literature. Questions of date and authorship are entertained, but only to the extent that the identification of the literary genre provides some basis on which to do so.

The form of the book as a whole is its canonical form only in the sense that this is the form in which it has assumed its place in the various canons of Holy Scripture. It does not necessarily follow that the process through which Zechariah finally took literary shape and the process through which it received its canonical status were one and the same. It is certainly possible that the growth of a corpus of prophetic literature, as a collection of documents that were thought to be singularly authoritative, could have influenced the composition of the documents being added to that corpus. But one cannot therefore assume a priori, as Childs has, that canonization would inevitably influence composition or that it would inevitably do so in a particular way. The effects of the canonical process must be demonstrated by showing that the composition has a form best explained in terms of canonization's influence, and not just asserted by claiming that the composition has an unexplainable form. The following description of Zechariah as a whole does not go into the question of whether it took its present shape for reasons relating to the development of the canon, but some aspects of the discussion are obviously relevant to this larger concern.

The entire book is explicitly related to revelations received by the prophet Zechariah early in the reign of the Persian emperor Darius I. This does not mean that contents of the entire book are said to be revelations received by Zechariah during this time. Indeed, only the prophecies in chs. 1–8 are identified as such. The prophecies in chs. 9–14 have headings that in contrast do not attribute them either to Zechariah or to anyone else in particular. The book's two final sections thus record the revelations and activities of some anonymous prophetic figure(s). Chs. 9–11 and 12–14 are nevertheless related to the preceding prophecies of Zechariah by virtue of their title, and because they provide a concrete illustration of what the introduction (1:1-6) says about the way authentic prophecies have an effect above and beyond the generation to which they were originally addressed, and thus continue to speak to later generations that live under very different historical conditions.

Zech 9–11 and 12–14 are each given the title of a *maśśā'*, a term that in this case means something like "a reinterpretation of a previous revelation" (cf. Weis, 269-70). Such a heading indicates that these two sections purport to restate Zechariah's message to the people of his own time, as this message is recorded in chs. 1–8, for the people of a later time (→ 9:1–11:17, Genre; 12:1–14:21, Genre). This terminology is substantiated both formally and materially by the way in which the two final sections are related to the preceding sections in chs. 1–8.

As the introduction in 1:1-6 programmatically defines the capacity of prophecy to outlive the generation to which it was originally addressed, it describes this historical process in terms of three variable elements: the prophetic disclosure of Yahweh's purpose, the extent to which his people recognize and respond to this disclosure, and the international conditions of the world situation. These can interact in various ways. Yahweh's unfavorable intentions toward his people may be expressed through a hostile world situation, but because of their appropriate response to the prophetic word, his intentions toward them may turn favorable and become expressed through a friendlier world situation. Conversely, Yahweh may be fostering an international situation that will be advantageous for his people, but their failure to recognize the prophetic claims to this effect may foreclose the possibility of Yahweh's purpose being fully realized, etc.

With respect to the message of Zechariah recorded in chs. 1–8, its continuity with the general message of the preexilic prophets is conceived in terms of such a historical process, even though its content is substantially different. The disclosure of the preexilic prophets, that Yahweh would use the world situation to destroy his people if they did not repent, was rejected for generation after generation; but it was finally recognized as authentic, and the people at last responded appropriately with repentance. Conceived in such terms, the efficacy that preexilic prophecy demonstrated over time provides the kind of basis on which Zechariah can now disclose that Yahweh's intentions have changed, and that he is now using the world situation to bring

306

about the restoration of his people, if they will only respond appropriately (→ 1:1-6).

With respect to the message of chs. 9–14, its essential continuity with the message of Zechariah in chs. 1–8 is similarly conceived in terms of such a historical process despite some substantial differences. In this case Yahweh's intentions have remained basically the same, but because of a change in the world situation and a less than appropriate response from some of his people, he first decides to modify his intentions (→ 9:1–11:17), and then to call for a different sort of response as he radically transforms the world situation in accord with his original purpose (→ 12:1–14:21). Throughout the book of Zechariah Yahweh remains firmly resolved to restore his people, but the actualization of this purpose takes different forms in different historical circumstances. Under the conditions of the *Pax Persica* in the reign of Darius I that constitute the immediate historical background of chs. 1–8, restoration involves such things as the ongoing return of the Babylonian exiles to Jerusalem and the rebuilding of the temple. Under the drastically changed conditions that constitute the historical background of chs. 9–14, as Jerusalem's initially secure status becomes threatened by both the faithlessness of Judah's leaders and continual enemy attacks, restoration involves such things as a political reorganization that will improve the city's governance and defenses, and even the creation of a new world free from international conflict.

In describing how the prophecy of one generation can also speak to later generations, 1:1-6 also describes two things each generation needs to know for themselves that can be learned by reflecting on the prophecies once addressed to their forebears: (1) how Yahweh is now involved in their common life, and (2) how they are to respond (→ 1:1-6, Structure). These two elements constitute the basic organizing principle for the structure of the book as a whole. They are combined somewhat differently in the two main parts of the book, however. With respect to 1:7–6:15 and 7:1–8:23, the former focuses on how Yahweh is involved in the common life of his people, and the latter focuses on how they are to respond. 1:7–6:15 persuasively describes Zechariah's claim that Yahweh's intention to restore and bless his people will be realized through the completion of the temple rebuilding project. 7:1–8:23 is designed to deepen the people's understanding of the kind of response that is appropriate to this divine initiative, so that it is a question not just of whether Yahweh is worshiped properly but also of whether their whole life shows true commitment to the ideals represented by such worship. (This does not mean that 1:7–6:15 says nothing about responding to Yahweh, or that 7:1–8:23 says nothing about his involvement in contemporary affairs, but only that these two sections are complementarily related by the way each respectively focuses on one of these two elements.)

With regard to 9:1–11:17 and 12:1–14:21, the same combination of elements is again the basic organizing principle, rather than hope undercut by pessimism (e.g., Redditt, "Israel's Shepherds"), but their overall interplay differs somewhat. These two sections are not designed so that one focuses on Yahweh's involvement and the other on the people's response. Rather, each section is designed to combine a description of what Yahweh is doing with di-

307

rections regarding an appropriate response. In 9:1–11:17 this combination of elements is developed in a relatively complex way, as various aspects of Yahweh's activity call for varying responses, and the nature of Yahweh's involvement also changes in reaction to his people's response. In 12:1–14:21 the development of these same two basic elements is less complex but more subtle, as they are related through narration continually describing the interaction between Yahweh and the people, but primarily emphasizing the kind of response they are to make when he precipitates the crisis through which the world will be radically transformed.

Zech 1:1-6 is thus the introduction not just to the rest of chs. 1–8 but to the entire book. Together 1:7–6:15 and 7:1–8:23 constitute a specific illustration of the general principles outlined in 1:1-6, as they apply to the relationship between Zechariah and his predecessors in an earlier time. 9:1–11:17 and 12:1–14:21 each constitutes a specific illustration of the same general principles as they apply to the relationship between Zechariah and his successors in a later time. 9:1–11:17 is an elaboration on all that is contained in 1:7–8:23. 12:1–14:21 is similarly an elaboration on all that is contained in 1:7–8:23, but one that also presupposes and extends 9:1–11:17. It thus appears that 9:1–11:17 is a restatement of Zechariah's insights regarding the establishment of Persian hegemony, occasioned by the occurrence of the similarly epoch-making establishment of a new and different hegemony. 12:1–14:21 is a further restatement of Zechariah's insights regarding the Persian dispensation, occasioned by this subsequent dispensation's taking a decisive turn for the worse (→ Setting).

Genre

The book as a whole has a well-defined compositional form, but it is generically diverse at every level. Both 1:7–6:15 and 7:1–8:23 have the form of a (→) report of a prophetic revelation, but each consists of different generic components. (→) Prophetic vision reports are the predominant form in 1:7–6:15, but they are combined with a (→) prophetic exhortation (2:10-17 [*RSV* 6-13]) and a (→) report of a prophetic symbolic action (6:9-15). 7:1–8:23 is basically a (→) report of an oracular inquiry, but it is expanded with additional materials of a generically different sort. Both 9:1–11:17 and 12:1–14:21 have the form of a (→) *maśśā'*, but each consists of somewhat different generic components. 9:1–11:17 combines a (→) prophecy of punishment against foreign nations (9:1-8) with various sorts of directives (9:9–11:3) and a report of a (→) prophetic symbolic action (11:4-17), whereas 12:1–14:21 combines a (→) prophecy of punishment against foreign nations (12:1–13:6) with (→) prophecies of salvation (13:7–14:21).

Such diversity in the component parts of a work does not necessarily mean that the work as a whole has no genre of its own, or that its pieces form only an anthology or collection. For example, *Canterbury Tales* and *The Decameron* are works of a definite literary type, despite the great diversity of the tales from which they are made. These works are not just anthologies or collections of tales, because in each case the telling of the tales is reported in accord with the integrative concept narrated in the author's introduction. Although the analogy is not a precise one, Zechariah is similarly a work of a particular type, not just a collection of redactional pieces, because its prophecies are presented in accord with the integrative concept spelled out in the introduction. The work as a whole thus fits loosely into the same generic category as 1:1-6, because it ascribes to Zechariah and his anonymous successors the same kind of relationship that 1:1-6 ascribes to Zechariah and his anonymous predecessors. It may thus be characterized as a PROPHETIC HISTORICAL EXEMPLUM (→ 1:1-6, Genre).

Setting

The production of this kind of text presupposes the existence of a scribal school where records of prophetic activity were kept and studied. The work of such groups might include the editing of a prophet's records into a single document, the recomposition of traditional materials into new forms of prophecy, and the composition of altogether new prophecies based on traditional models. Such documents were usually named for the prophet on whose records they were based, rather than for the scribe who wrote them. The work of the scribes was thus understood to be a restatement of what had been learned from their study of a particular prophet.

It is often assumed that such schools would have emerged only as great prophetic figures began to disappear, but this is not necessarily the case. It is more likely that prophecy coexisted with scribal schools well before the exile, as one of their objects of study. Otherwise, how would prophetic records have ever been preserved in the first place? How else would some considered judgment have been reached as to whether some prophets were greater than others? How else would the recognition of a prophet's greatness have been expressed through the production of a document named after him, restating his insights in a form that future generations could study and learn from?

Some say that all or part of Zechariah has a cultic setting, but what this means is not always clear. With respect to chs. 1–8, some of the visionary prophecies in 1:7–6:15 describe a scene that includes some part of the temple precincts (e.g., 3:1-10; 4:1-14), but it does not necessarily follow that the prophet was actually located there when such a scene was either imagined or communicated (as R. L. Smith, for example, seems to suppose by designating "the temple area" as the setting of the vision reports [pp. 185-215, passim]; cf. Halpern's view of the vision cycle in [→] 1:7–6:15 as a "reverie" recited at the celebration of the Second Temple's foundation). There is no evidence that visions were routinely received or reported, or that vision cycles were recited, during the conduct of any regularly celebrated public rite (→ 1:8-17, Setting). The revelation reported in 7:1–8:23 takes the form of an extended reply to an oracular inquiry concerning certain cultic practices, but such replies were usually not performed liturgically (→ Hab 2:1-5, Setting). Several scholars (e.g., Beuken, Mason) have rightly emphasized the sermonlike rhetoric at various points in the text, particularly in 7:1–8:23, but no part of the book in its present form shows any signs of actually having been preached as a sermon during worship.

With respect to chs. 9–14, a cultic setting has sometimes been invoked as the most likely context for the complex of mythic motifs that permeates this part of the book. Because these motifs come from the myth of Yahweh's cosmogonic combat with a sea monster, a story that was supposedly rehearsed or dramatized as part of the New Year celebration, their presence has been taken to indicate that all or part of chs. 9–14 were formed from material with some similar but derivative cultic use (e.g., Otzen, 135-42). Some reconstructions of the New Year Festival also feature the ritual humiliation of the king, and this has similarly been seen as an appropriate context for the prophecies invoking Yahweh's punishment of the "shepherd" in 11:17 and 13:7, as well as for the vague reference in 12:10 to the people's mourning for someone they have wounded (e.g., R. L. Smith, 277, 283). Every point of this argument is highly questionable. On the one hand, any reconstruction of an Israelite New Year Festival is shaky, and the inclusion of the king's ritual humiliation in any such hypothesis is shakier still. On the other hand, it is unlikely that the references to either the "shepherd" (11:17; 13:7) or the wounded one (12:10) have any overtly royal connotations (→ 11:4-17; 12:9–13:1; 13:7-9). Along these lines one might argue on firmer ground that, because chs. 9–14 contain mythic motifs also found in the cultic poetry of the psalms, they resemble various cultic expressions in content. This is perhaps why Mason seems to compare chs. 9–14 with the Psalter, as he calls this part of Zechariah an "eschatological 'hymn-book'" (*Haggai*, 81). With respect to form, however, the individual units of chs. 9–14 have little in common with individual psalms (although in a few cases there are some superficial phraseological similarities); and on the whole chs. 9–14 have even less in common with the Psalter. This shows that chs. 9–14 did not have the same kind of cultic usage as the psalms or the Psalter.

The book of Zechariah assumed a kind of cultic function, as it eventually became a scriptural source from which *haptārôt* were selected for reading in synagogue worship, complementing the lesson from the Torah with a lesson from the Prophets. It is doubtful, however, that this practice was established by the time Zechariah reached its final form (C. Parrot, "The Reading of the Bible in the Ancient Synagogue," in *Mikra: Text, Translation, Reading, and Interpretation of the Hebrew Bible in Ancient Judaism and Early Christianity* [ed. M. J. Mulder; Assen: Van Gorcum; Philadelphia: Fortress, 1988] 153-54), and thus unlikely that any part of the book was composed for this particular purpose. In sum, Zechariah is a cultic text in the sense that it focuses on matters relating to the place and conduct of worship, and in the sense that it sometimes describes Yahweh in terms like those used in hymns and public prayer. This may well be due to an ongoing institutional affiliation of some kind between the priests that administered the restored sanctuary and the scribal group that first produced chs. 1–8 and then added chs. 9–11 and 12–14 at a later date. The book of Zechariah has many cultic associations of various sorts, but its compositional form was not designed for any particular ritual use. It thus does not have a cultic setting, strictly speaking.

Because the literary form of Zechariah is defined in terms of relating this prophet's insights to a later era, the description of its setting inevitably takes on a historical as well as a sociological dimension. We must reckon not only with scribal activity, but also with its effects over a particular span of time. The autobiographical reporting in both 1:7–6:15 and 7:1–8:23 indicates that the raw materials for these sections came largely from Zechariah himself, suggesting that he may have deposited the records of revelations received at various times with the scribes who studied them, and that he may even have been a member of their group. The third person reporting in the editorial introductions to these sections (1:7; 7:1) appears to indicate subsequent redactional activity on the part of someone other than Zechariah; and the overall stylistic consistency that permeates these two sections, as well as the introduction in 1:1-6, suggests that chs. 1–8 assumed their present form as a result of the same redactional activity. Since the editorial introduction to chs. 7–8 dates the revelation reported in that section to the ninth month in the fourth year of Darius's reign, chs. 1–8 would necessarily have been composed sometime afterward, i.e., sometime after November-December 518 BCE.

The editorial introductions in chs. 1–8 give rather precise dates, subsuming all the prophecies in this part of Zechariah under the rubric of revelations received at specific times during the second and fourth years of Darius's reign. In view of such chronological precision, the general lack of further information about the events of these years and how they occasioned these revelations is somewhat surprising. Only one reference directly relates the revelations of Zechariah to a particular major development. Zech 4:9 indicates that the temple rebuilding project under the direction of Zerubbabel has advanced far enough to celebrate the foundation ritual, but that the temple itself remains incomplete. The redactor of chs. 1–8 seems to presuppose the audience's familiarity with the early Persian period, and to assume that the dates cited in 1:1, 1:7, and 7:1, the naming of Zerubbabel and Joshua as contemporary figures, and the cursory reference in 4:9 to the temple's unfinished condition will provide the reader with enough information to locate Zechariah's revelations within the course of events. This suggests that chs. 1–8 were finished relatively soon after the time they describe, when the details of the exiles' return from Babylon to Judah and the ensuing restoration of Jerusalem were still part of the people's living memory.

If it were not for the information provided by outside sources, primarily in the books of Haggai and Ezra, modern readers would have no way of filling in the background against which the revelations in chs. 1–8 take place. The problem of reconciling the various disparate data from these sources in order to devise a workable chronology of the restoration is notoriously difficult. Here I make no attempt to solve this problem. My aim is simply to provide a few relatively fixed points of reference that are helpful for understanding certain aspects of the description within chs. 1–8, as well as the process by which this part of the book was produced.

Two developments are particularly important in the historical background of chs. 1–8. First, the work of rebuilding the Jerusalem temple was reinstigated shortly before the date of the first revelation in 1:1-6. An unsuccessful attempt had been made nearly two decades earlier, when exiles from Babylon first began to return in the time of Cyrus (Ezra 5:14-16; cf. 3:7). The project was revived in the reign of Darius, when Joshua was high priest and Zerubbabel was governor, with the support of the prophets Haggai and Zechariah. Work on the building was begun again in the sixth month of Darius's second year (Hag 1:15a). About a month later the foundation was rededicated; but around the same time morale began to falter, as it became apparent that the emerging structure would be decidedly inferior to its predecessor (Ezra 3:10-13; cf. Hag 1:15b–2:9). In the eighth and eleventh months of that same year Zechariah is reported to have received revelations, whose focal point was the issue of whether this project would reach completion (→ Zech 1:7–6:15; 7:1–8:23). This issue remains unresolved within the overall time frame of chs. 1–8, which extends only to the fourth year of Darius's reign (7:1). The temple was not finished until Darius's sixth year (Ezra 6:14-16).

Another important development was the resumption of sacrificial worship on the site of Jerusalem's sacred precincts several months before the work on the temple itself was reinstigated (Ezra 3:1-6). This would not have amounted to a full restoration of the sacrificial cult because it seems that certain kinds of sacrifices — particularly those concerned with sin, guilt, and atonement — were not resumed until the sanctuary was completely rebuilt (Ezra 3:4-5; cf. Lev 4:1–6:7; 16:1-34). Parts of Zech 1:7–6:15 presuppose this development to some extent (e.g., → 3:1-10); but 7:1–8:23 is entirely dependent on it, since this whole section is an extension of a response to an oracular inquiry concerning cultic questions (7:3-6) of a sort that would hardly have arisen without the resumption of some kind of worship in Jerusalem. The revelation in 7:1–8:23 is dated to the fourth year of Darius's reign, more than two years after the altar's reconstruction enabled some kinds of sacrifice to be performed again, but more than two years before the temple itself was finished.

The reader of chs. 1–8 can therefore imagine that Zechariah had already been a prophet for a long while when he received a revelation in the second year of Darius's reign — long enough to have addressed the parents of the generation that mainly made up his audience at that time (1:2-3; → 1:1-6, Text). In this capacity he gave support and leadership to the efforts of the Babylonian exiles to return to Judah and restore Jerusalem. Shortly after the beginning of Darius's reign those efforts entered a critical phase as the altar of the Jerusalem sanctuary was reconstructed, the cult was partly put back in operation, and the work of rebuilding the temple was reinstigated. The project of cultic restoration got off to a good start, but during its second year the momentum slowed. A year or two into this slump, the records of the prophecies made by Zechariah concerning various earlier aspects of the return and restoration were reviewed to see what they portended regarding the ongoing viability and completion of the project. As a result of such study the significance of the temple, as part of a larger historical process with cosmic implications, was reaffirmed by editing the most pertinent prophecies of Zechariah into a document consisting of chs. 1–8.

Because chs. 1–8 describe the prospect of the temple's completion and the cult's full restoration so compellingly as a central necessity in both the people's common life and the overall scheme of things, it seems likely that they were composed sometime between the terminus a quo in the fourth year of Darius's reign (7:1) and the eventual completion of the temple in the sixth year (i.e., ca. 518-516 BCE). In this context the document would have served to gain support for the project. It is also conceivable, however, that chs. 1–8 were composed sometime after the temple's completion, so as to reconsider the fully functioning institution from the standpoint of a moment when its reestablishment seemed doubtful. In this context the document would have served to explain the temple's significance by representing a critical turning point in the process of its restoration. Even if chs. 1–8 were written after the temple's completion, the presupposition of a readership generally familiar with the first few years of Darius's reign makes it difficult to suppose that this document was written much later than the turn of the century.

Many scholars have reached similar conclusions regarding chs. 1–8, but the composition and dating of chs. 9–14 are much more controversial. Some would contest the division of chs. 9–14 into two sections, 9–11 and 12–14, in which case the process of composition could not be conceived in terms of how these two sections were added. For example, Otzen and Sæbø see chs. 9–14 as the accumulation of four sections (chs. 9–10, 11, 12–13, 14), although they disagree about the respective dates of these sections. Redditt (*Haggai*, 102-3; "Israel's Shepherds," 636) argues that chs. 9–14 grew outward from a central core that included material from ch. 11. Lamarche (pp. 131-33) treats chs. 9–14 as a single entity. Other scholars would recognize a fundamental literary break between chs. 9–11 and 12–14, but would not necessarily agree in seeing the latter as a historical sequel to the former (e.g., Butterworth, 72-79; Person, 24; Meyers and Meyers, *Zechariah 9–14*, 32-35; Larkin, 42-52).

When one considers the date and authorship of chs. 9–14 from the standpoint of literary form, the identification of chs. 9–11 and 12–14 as examples of the *maśśā'* genre has a direct bearing on the way these issues are raised. Because this genre serves to restate revelations concerning the events of a particular time in terms applicable to the events of another time, chs. 9–11 and 12–14 can be described as additions to chs. 1–8 that have used Zechariah's views of early Persian developments as the basis on which to understand Yahweh's involvement in later developments. The scribes who wrote chs. 9–11 and 12–14 have discerned in their own day the same pattern of divine activity that Zechariah discerned in his day, which they have learned to recognize through their study of chs. 1–8.

Zech 12–14 is a *maśśā'* in a double sense, because it reapplies the revelations of Zechariah in chs. 1–8 to another time, as it also reapplies the prophetic insights expressed in chs. 1–9 to changed conditions. For example, one of the themes expressed in chs. 1–8 that figures prominently as a pattern of divine activity in chs. 9–11 is that Yahweh's goal of restoring Judah is two-pronged: Through the Persians he is creating a world situation in which the international conditions are favorable, and at the same time he is also providing the kind of local leadership that can take advantage of this situation and make it work for Judah's benefit. Chs. 9–11 restate a variation on this theme in terms of the different conditions in a later time, and chs. 12–14

313

restate a further variation on this same theme in view of one major change in those later conditions.

In reapplying this theme to the conditions of another time, chs. 9–11 describe a situation in which Yahweh is again creating a favorable international situation, which is threatening only in ways that Judah can well withstand. The real threat comes from bad local leadership, which exploits the international situation to their own advantage rather than for the people's benefit. In accord with the pattern, Yahweh is again trying to provide the right kind of leadership, which now involves purging those in authority. A prophecy pitting Yahweh's "sword" against a "shepherd" leader comes at the end of this section (11:17), where it describes the impending crisis caused by Judah's failure to deal with this leadership problem.

The variation on this same theme in chs. 12–14 is occasioned by one major change: The world situation is no longer favorable, and international conflict now threatens Judah's existence. Yahweh's efforts on the international scene are thus mainly devoted to strengthening Judah's capability to defend themselves, and his attempts to provide them with good leadership are combined in the same process. The attacks of foreign enemies foment the emergence of a new form of leadership that enables Judah to withstand continual assault but whose other ramifications are not altogether beneficial. Thus neither aspect of Yahweh's two-pronged goal can be fully realized under this particular change. At best Judah can maintain its existence in the face of continual attacks and attain a type of governance whose effectiveness is measured solely in terms of mobilizing them for self-defense. Another prophecy pitting Yahweh's "sword" against a "shepherd" leader comes at the middle of this section (13:7-9), where it signals Yahweh's decision to let this new form of leadership fail and to let Jerusalem be defeated, so as to begin the cataclysmic process of transforming the whole creation. Only by such radical means can his people be delivered from both the chronic problem of bad leadership and the continual threat of enemy attack.

Chapters 12–14 can thus be described as an addition not only to chs. 1–8 but also to chs. 9–11. Chs. 12–14 elaborate on the same pattern of divine action that chs. 9–11 have derived from chs. 1–8; and they elaborate on this pattern in much the same way that chs. 9–11 do, by showing how Yahweh's good intentions to restore his people can be thwarted through the interaction of such other historical variables as the international situation and the quality of their response to his initiatives. In these ways chs. 12–14 do the same things vis-à-vis chs. 1–8 that chs. 9–11 do, and in this sense they are — like chs. 9–11 — an addition to chs. 1–8. At the same time chs. 12–14 also go beyond chs. 9–11, as they restate the problem of Yahweh's present purpose being frustrated even more acutely, and then go on to describe the radical solution to this problem. In this sense chs. 12–14 are also an addition to chs. 9–11 (cf. the similar conclusion that Portnoy and Petersen have reached by very different means).

The literary history of the book of Zechariah thus extends from the composition of chs. 1–8 sometime in the late sixth century to include the subsequent addition of chs. 9–11 at a time that initially seemed to promise as much improvement in Judah's status as the coming of the Persians, if Judah's local leadership could only seize the opportunity. Chs. 12–14 were added shortly thereafter, when it became apparent that this new era would instead be characterized by international conflict that threatened to destroy Judah, no matter what form of more effective leadership emerged to meet the challenge of foreign hostility. These additions were produced by scribes who studied chs. 1–8 and thus learned from Zechariah's description of Yahweh's involvement in the early Persian era to recognize a similar pattern of divine activity in the events of their own time. In order to express this recognition, they first compiled from their records various other prophecies that were either traditionally associated with Zechariah or judged to be compatible with his views. They then edited and augmented these materials to produce chs. 9–11 and 12–14 in their present form, as additions to the prophecies of Zechariah himself.

Building on the work of Delcor and Mason, other scholars have recently emphasized the importance of such reinterpretive scribal activity as a factor in the creation of chs. 9–14 (e.g., Person, Larkin; cf. Meyers and Meyers, *Zechariah 9–14,* 35-45). Person's analysis is unfortunately marred by an untenably sharp distinction between a prophet and a redactor (pp. 32-37) that fails to recognize that scribal activity may also be divinatory and hence prophetic. He argues that chs. 9–14 are a fifth-century Deuteronomistic reinterpretation of chs. 1–8 (p. 139), but this entails a concept of reinterpretation as little more than the reuse of catchwords and imagery. The language of chs. 9–14 may well be Deuteronomistic in this sense, but the dating of chs. 9–11 and 12–14 cannot therefore be reduced to a question of who might have reused such language and when they might have done so. Anyone steeped in the study of Deuteronomistic texts might well reuse such language at any time after those texts were composed.

Larkin's concept of reinterpretation as a scribal activity that is also truly prophetic (i.e., "mantological wisdom"; pp. 27-39) is more adequate theoretically. In practice, however, her analysis does not show that prophetic texts actually had any substantial impact on their scribal reinterpreters (→ 9:1–11:17, Genre; 12:1–14:21, Genre). In the end it again seems largely a matter of wordplay. Larkin is not particularly concerned with the dating of chs. 9–14, but rather with the issue of their eschatological and apocalyptic nature. She nevertheless conceives eschatological and apocalyptic texts as the products of mantological learning that seeks to engage history rather than to reject it. Precisely for this reason her work pointedly begs the historical question. What did mantic scribes learn from studying older prophetic texts, if not to see Yahweh similarly at work in their own day? In order for us to grasp what they discerned in this regard, must we then not have at least some rough idea of the time and conditions under which they lived?

A complete description of the setting of this book thus entails a consideration of the historical context in which the prophetic insights of 9:1–11:17 and 12:1–14:21 were most plausibly expressed. There seems to be a recent trend in favor of dating these texts to the Persian period, around the fifth or even the late sixth century (e.g., Hanson, 280-401; Lacocque, 139-44; Person, 139-75; Meyers and Meyers, *Zechariah 9–14,* 26-29; Petersen, *Zechariah 9–14,* 4-5). It is more likely, however, that they were composed in the early Hellenistic period during the final decades of the fourth century (ca. 330-300 BCE), for reasons that are given below (→ 9:1–11:17, Setting; 12:1–14:21, Setting). The book as a whole thus draws an extended analogy between Yahweh's activity in the first few decades of the Persian period and Yahweh's activity in the first few decades of the Hellenistic period.

Intention

When the coming of the Greeks is viewed through the lens of Zechariah's prophetic perceptions regarding the coming of the Persians, the focus is initially on the way in which the Jewish community's internal situation in the former era corresponds with its internal situation in the latter era. As long as Greek hegemony appears to create conditions favorable to the security of Yahweh's sanctuary in Jerusalem and the general welfare of the Jewish community, the issue is whether the people are motivated to seize this historical opportunity to define and hold their place as a minority group within the empire's new ethnic mix, as the returned exiles finally managed to do in the Persian setting. In order to accomplish this, it is crucial for them to have leaders that live up to the precedent set by Zerubbabel and Joshua. Aided by the insight of Yahweh's prophets, these two perceived what was concretely necessary in order for the community to represent the reign of God in their historical context, and they effectively led the community through times of crisis toward this goal. When bad leadership fails to follow this precedent, it jeopardizes not only the internal cohesion of the community but also the favorability of their external circumstances.

When external circumstances take a turn for the worse, so that Greek hegemony becomes a threat to the very existence of the Jewish community, focusing on the same point of internal leadership brings a somewhat different issue into view. The question is now whether the various factions within the community that have been exacerbated by bad local leadership can unify and reorganize themselves to insure the whole community's survival. In light of the correspondence drawn between this threatening situation and the experience of the returned exiles, this question takes on a theological dimension. Can Yahweh's people adapt to the changing world situation in a way that does not also compromise their capacity to represent God's reign? As the returnees of the Persian era soon discovered, forms of community life that had grown up under the extenuating conditions of exile and had seemed appropriate as means of insuring the community's survival under those conditions subsequently turned out to be distorted in other fundamental respects. Reflection on this past experience shows that the community may succeed in maintaining itself, but at the cost of its reason for being, as its capacity to represent the kingdom of God becomes impaired. Those who have experienced the Greek threat to their existence are thus challenged to realize that, although it is important for them to have the kind of social organization that will enable them to defend themselves, this is not the ultimate consideration.

The returnees had to let their exilic form of communal life disintegrate, for although it had been effective for their survival, it was deficient in other respects. In the process of letting it go, they discovered a new world of better possibilities in the restoration. In the light of this precedent, it appears that the form of communal life developed in the face of the Greek threat will likewise have to disintegrate because it is similarly deficient. Through this catastrophe, however, those who are left can also discover the better possibilities of the new world Yahweh is already creating. Under the radically transformed conditions of this new creation, such conflicts will no longer impair the capacity of Yahweh's people to represent the kingdom of God.

By thus tracing the way in which this text expanded the horizon of its readers in the early Hellenistic period, modern readers learn how it can similarly expand their horizons. When God's people are threatened by hostility from the world at large, their survival in some recognizable form is certainly important, and the hand of God can be seen at work in the new forms of communal life and leadership that are developed in reaction to this threatening situation. When survival rather than fidelity becomes the ultimate consideration, however, these forms of communal life may become distorted in ways that impair their capacity to represent the kingdom of God. The point is not for the covenant community to survive at all costs in any particular form. It is rather to realize that in the struggle to survive there comes a time when the community can only let its past mode of existence go and trust the capacity of the Creator to bring new realities into being.

Chapter 2

THE FIRST MAJOR SECTION
OF THE BOOK (1:1-6)

REPORT OF A PROPHETIC REVELATION INTRODUCING THE BOOK OF THE PROPHET ZECHARIAH, 1:1-6

Text

In v. 3 the *RSV* treats *wĕ'āmartā* as a consecutive perfect, giving it the sense of a command: "Therefore say to them. . . ." Despite the apparent consensus of ancient versions and modern commentators, which the *RSV* translation reflects, there is no compelling reason to take this verb as anything but a description of habitual or repeated past action.

On the purely grammatical level it would be necessary for this form to stand in sequential relationship to an imperfect or a command of some sort, in order for it to be a consecutive perfect. Here, however, it stands in sequential relationship to the perfect verb *qāṣap* ("he was angry") in v. 2. Van der Woude argues (p. 164) that *wĕ'āmartā* is here analogous to other cases of a consecutive perfect used independently to introduce a command or wish, apparently without any sequential relationship to an imperfect or another command. This usage is very poorly attested, however (see GKC §112aa), and most of the examples cited have an imperfect or a command somewhere in the surrounding context, on which the allegedly independent consecutive perfect instead seems to be loosely dependent. (In 1 Sam 6:5, e.g., *waʿăśîtem* [*RSV* "you must make"] is related to the imperfect *yāqēl* [*RSV* "lighten"] that follows rather than precedes it, since neither any verb nor any independent clause precedes it in the direct discourse of which it forms an integral part. Similarly, in 1 Kgs 2:6 *wĕʿāśîtā* [*RSV* "act!"] is related to the following negative imperfect directive *wĕlō'-tôrēd* [*RSV* "do not let . . . go down"].)

Here *wĕ'āmartā* is clearly coordinated with *qāṣap* not only by the norms of verbal syntax but also by the relationship between the prepositional phrases in their respective clauses. The antecedent for the pronominal suffix in the

318

phrase *'ălêhem* ("to them") is the object in the phrase *'al-'ăbôtêkem (RSV* "your fathers"), thus showing that the group against whom Yahweh's anger was directed and the group to whom the prophet spoke are semantically one and the same.

On the level of phraseology some have argued that *wĕ'āmartā* is the formulaic complement of a once foregoing command that has now dropped out of the text, whether some form of *qr'* ("cry"; so K. Budde, "Zum Text der drei letzten Propheten," *ZAW* 26 [1906] 5), or *dbr* ("speak"; so Mitchell, 110), or *hlk* ("go"; so Horst, 216). In sequential relationship with such a command, the perfect form with which v. 3 commences could also be understood as a command. Such proposals obviously have the liability of arguing from silence since there is no evidence of any such hypothetically original text. They also presuppose that the action described by the verb is Yahweh's commissioning the prophet to speak on his behalf (cf. Mason, *Haggai,* 32-34), but this proves not to be tenable in view of how this introductory section develops (→ Structure).

Along similar lines some have also argued (e.g., Petitjean, 8-13) that *wĕ'āmartā* is a standard complement of the prophetic word formula in v. 1 (i.e., *hāyâ dĕbar yhwh 'el . . . ,* "the word of Yahweh came to . . ."). Among the many examples cited, however, whether in the first person form (*'ēlay,* "to me") or the third person form that we have here, there is none in which a *waw*-plus-perfect form like *wĕ'āmartā* occurs out of sequence with a preceding imperfect or command. The data thus do not really support the claim for which they are adduced, but rather underscore that there is no distinctive formulaic usage that governs the connection between v. 2 and v. 3. It is thus best to understand *wĕ'āmartā* as a perfect coordinated with another preceding perfect in order to indicate ongoing or habitual past action (see GKC §112h and the examples cited there). 1:2-3 should thus be translated: "Yahweh was very angry with your forebears, and you [repeatedly] said to them. . . ."

Structure

I. Narrative introduction	1:1
A. Date citation	1:1a
1. Month: the eighth	1:1aα
2. Regnal year: the second of Darius	1:1aβ
B. Prophetic word formula	1:1b
1. Formula proper: the word of Yahweh came to Zechariah	1:1bα
2. Expansions	1:1bβ
a. Two-generation patronymic genealogy	1:1bβ¹
1) First generation: son of Berechiah	
2) Second generation: son of Iddo	
b. Specification of role: the prophet	1:1bβ²
3. Direct discourse marker: *lē'mōr* ("saying . . .")	1:1bβ³
II. Main body: speech of Yahweh	1:2-6

A. Account of distant past generations' refusal to heed
Yahweh's prophets — 1:2-4bα
  1. Introductory description of the general situation:
Yahweh was angry with your forebears — 1:2
  2. The prophetic reaction (addressed directly
to Zechariah) — 1:3-4bα
    a. Speech report formula: and so you said
to them . . . — 1:3aα^1
    b. Prophetic injunction to past generations:
speech of Yahweh — 1:3aα^{2}β-4bα
      1) Messenger formula: thus says Yahweh
of hosts — 1:3aα^2
      2) Speech proper — 1:3aβ-4a
        a) Call to repentance — 1:3aβb
          (1) Call proper — 1:3aβ
            (a) Command: return to me! — 1:3aβ^1
            (b) Oracle formula: says Yahweh
of hosts — 1:3aβ^2
          (2) Result of heeding the call — 1:3b
            (a) Description of result:
I will return to you — 1:3bα
            (b) Speech report formula:
says Yahweh of hosts — 1:3bβ
        b) Admonition: speech of Yahweh — 1:4ab
          (1) Admonition proper — 1:4abα
            (a) Negative command: do not be
like your forebears! — 1:4aα^1
            (b) Expansion: characterization
of the forebears — 1:4aα^{2}bα
              α. How they were treated by
previous prophets — 1:4aα^{2}β
                aa. What those prophets did:
cried out . . . — 1:4aα^2
                bb. What those prophets said — 1:4aβ
                  α) Messenger formula — 1:4aβ^1
                  β) Call to repent — 1:4aβ^2
              β. How they responded:
they did not heed — 1:4bα
          (2) Oracle formula: says Yahweh — 1:4bβ
C. Consideration of whether more recent past generations
have learned to heed the prophets — 1:5-6
  1. Introductory pair of positive rhetorical questions
concerning past generations — 1:5
    a. First question — 1:5a
      1) Subject: the forebears — 1:5aα
      2) Question proper: where are they? — 1:5aβ
    b. Second question — 1:5b

1) Subject: the prophets	1:5bα
2) Question proper: do they live forever?	1:5bβ
2. Concluding negative rhetorical question concerning eventual change	1:6
a. Subject: the words and statutes that Yahweh commanded the prophets	1:6aα
b. Question proper	1:6aβb
1) Main clause: did they not overtake the forebears?	1:6aβ
2) Compound clause of result	1:6b
a) First result: so that they repented	1:6bα
b) Second result: so that they acknowledged Yahweh to have his purpose	1:6bβ

The initial verse of this opening section resembles the introductions to the next two major sections of the book (1:7; 7:1), as well as the introductions to the various sections of Haggai (1:1; 2:1; 2:10; cf. 2:20). The basic elements that they all have in common are (1) a date citation consisting of the regnal year of the Persian emperor Darius and the month, which is sometimes named as well as enumerated; and (2) the use of the prophetic word formula to initiate the reporting narration of the section as a whole. Of all these introductions, only Zech 1:1 fails to enumerate the day of the month. Other elements are somewhat more variable. The patronymic genealogy occurs only here and in Zech 1:7. The main character is identified as *hannābî'* ("the prophet") in Zech 1:1, 7 and Hag 1:1; 2:1, 10; but not in Zech 7:1 or Hag 2:20. Darius is explicitly identified as *hammelek* ("the king") in Zech 7:1 and Hag 1:1; 2:1; but not in Zech 1:1, 7 or Hag 2:10, 20.

The basic function of such introductions is to relate the words and deeds of the prophet to the course of world events in general, and more specifically to the time when Persian hegemony over the ancient Near East was firmly established under Darius I. The stylistic variations serve to nuance the basic function of each introduction in relation to the contents of the section into which it leads. In this case the failure to cite a particular day suggests that the following revelation came to Zechariah gradually, over an extended period of time rather than on a specific occasion, but this becomes apparent only as the text unfolds to show the relative precision with which other revelations can be dated. From the explicit inclusion of the epithet *hannābî'* ("the prophet") and from the inclusion of the genealogy, it is more immediately evident that the emphasis is on the prophetic role and on Zechariah's descent from two representatives of the past generations with whom the revelation is initially concerned.

The syntax of the epithet *hannābî'* ("the prophet") is grammatically ambiguous, so that one cannot tell whether it stands in apposition to the first name (i.e., Zechariah) or the last name (i.e., Iddo) in the genealogy. Is Zechariah being characterized as a prophet with a particular descent, or as someone with a particularly prophetic descent? The matter is complicated by the fact that the same Zechariah is elsewhere identified as the son, not the grandson, of someone named Iddo (Ezra 5:1; 6:14), and by the fact that someone named Zechariah is elsewhere said to belong, by virtue of having a father named Iddo, to a priestly rather than a prophetic family (Neh 12:16). The descent itself is thus in question, as well as the precise nature of its bearing on Zechariah's prophetic status.

Regardless of how the details of Zechariah's paternity are finally to be sorted out, the reader heads into the main body of this section knowing that Zechariah's prophetic role has some kind of transgenerational dimension. This somewhat vague initial impression takes a more definite shape as the unit unfolds to show how the significance of the prophetic message to past generations is affected by the cumulative historical experience of Yahweh's people. The unit narrates just one action, the prophet's reception of a revelation. The revelation is directly quoted as a speech of Yahweh, and this speech takes the form of a story. The story is told as if it were addressed not only to Zechariah as the recipient of the revelation (note the second person singular verb with which v. 3 begins), but also to the people in Zechariah's audience (as indicated by various second person plural forms on various levels of discourse). In effect, Zechariah's audience is allowed to overhear Yahweh telling him a story that is also intended for them.

The story begins by recalling for the audience how angry Yahweh was with their "forebears" (*ʾăbôtêkem; RSV* "fathers"). This retrospective appears initially to be limited to their parents' generation, because the story continues in v. 3 with a description of how Zechariah himself used to remonstrate with such "forebears" on Yahweh's behalf, urging them to "return." As this call to repentance is elaborated in v. 4, however, this perspective on the past is broadened to include not only what Zechariah has said to the older generation, some of whom are still alive, but also what the "former prophets" said to all previous generations. The whole history of Yahweh's people thus becomes characterized by the way in which each generation was in turn exhorted by the prophets not to be like their predecessors, and by the way in which each successive generation failed to heed this warning.

The story's complication and conclusion are expressed in a set of rhetorical questions. The pair of positively formulated questions in v. 5 raises the issue of the eventual fate of the past generations, and of the prophets who confronted them. Both are obviously dead and gone, but the ensuing negatively formulated question in v. 6 points out that the prophets' insights into Yahweh's purposes have outlived their own time. The ongoing applicability of these insights has become evident as the consequences of the people's rejection finally caught up with them. Relatively recent past generations have come to realize the truth of the prophets' message by suffering the tragic consequences of their ancestors' willful disobedience. The conclusion suggests that the people's character may possibly change. When the historical crisis experienced by recent past generations is seen in the light of the prophetic tradition represented by Zechariah, there is some motivation for them not to be like their forebears.

The text's audience overhears Yahweh telling Zechariah a very brief story, but one whose rhetorical accomplishments are nevertheless considerable. The narrative initially focuses the audience's attention rather narrowly on their parents' generation and Zechariah's repeated attempts to reach them, and then deftly expands this focus to encompass the entire history of the prophets' repeated attempts to reach all past generations. This broad perspective is then likewise deftly narrowed again as this history is succinctly brought up to date, focusing finally on Zechariah and the present generation of the audience themselves. If the audience has learned the lesson of the past, they will not only heed what this prophet is telling them about Yahweh's purposes. They will also have learned the need for continual repentance, and thus be prepared to hear a prophetic message that tacitly assumes this to be the basis for any relationship with Yahweh, and goes on to deal with other concerns. Precisely because of the way Zechariah stands in continuity with the entire prophetic tradition, the message he brings them at this historical juncture can take a new and different turn.

Genre

Some have seen 1:1 as a (→) superscription (e.g., Horst, 216; Jones, 54), but Rudolph rightly points out that this is not the case (p. 67). Although it shares with some superscriptions the technical terminology of the (→) prophetic word formula, v. 1 has the syntax of a complete sentence, whereas superscriptions take the form of an incomplete sentence (Tucker, 57-61). Unlike superscriptions, which simply head whatever they introduce, v. 1 both narrates and grammatically governs with *lē'mōr* (*RSV* "saying") the ensuing "word of Yahweh." The first verse is thus an integral part of the narrative in 1:1-6 that in its entirety constitutes a REPORT OF A PROPHETIC REVELATION.

The revelation itself (vv. 2-6) is structurally complex. Many commentators have rightly identified a strong sermonic tendency in this unit's calls to repentance, rhetorical questions, and historical retrospectives (e.g., Beuken, 88-103; Mason, "Some Echoes," 226-29; idem, *Preaching,* 198-205). The question is whether these various elements finally cohere in the form of a sermon or the like. Some have argued that this mixture of things is form-critically unclassifiable (e.g., Elliger, 100-102; Rudolph, 67-71; Petersen, who labels it a "pastiche" [*Haggai,* 135]), but the compositional structure has a basically narrative form. This fact is perhaps obscured by the somewhat unusual way in which the plot is developed in vv. 5-6 by means of rhetorical questions, but this is clearly shown to be their function by the way the last question in v. 6a leads into the "happy ending" of v. 6b. It is thus better to describe the revelation in vv. 2-6 as a kind of narrative rather than a kind of sermon (cf. Petersen, *Haggai,* 135-36, n. 19). This does not preclude the possibility that such a narrative may have some homiletical function, nor does it imply that preaching cannot include the telling of stories. It is rather to acknowledge that sermons do not by definition assume a predominantly narrative form, as this text does. This unit's generic classification should reckon with this fact.

The brief story in vv. 2-6 is designed to get its audience to think theologically about the past. It retells their history from the standpoint of Yahweh's involvement with past generations through his prophetic messengers, in such a way that they are compelled to consider how Yahweh might be involved with their own generation, and to reassess their attitude toward the prophetic message that Zechariah now brings them. The narrative is therefore a PROPHETIC HISTORICAL EXEMPLUM (→ Nah 1:2–2:11 [*RSV* 1:2–2:10], Genre; cf. Deut 32; Ps 78).

This unit is on the whole a report about Zechariah, not a report by Zechariah. It describes him as having from the outset a general awareness of his role as a transitional figure in the prophetic tradition. Zechariah certainly could have conducted his career with some such sense of his mission, but the text's well-developed view of his place among the prophets probably results from a retrospective reconsideration of all that he did.

Setting

This genre reflects a setting characterized by intense scholarly reflection on the meaning of the past, and by efforts to influence the climate of public opinion with the fruits of such reflection. The form implies an ancient "think tank," where prophetic traditions were scrutinized to determine their bearing on current affairs, and community leaders were lobbied to formulate and win support for policies in accord with the results. To exercise such prophetic influence was one function of the scribal establishment in both pre- and postexilic times.

In this particular case the relationship between Zechariah and the tradition of preexilic prophecy is the object of reflection. Zechariah's message of Yahweh's favor obviously differs from the messages of the preexilic prophets, which seem from a postexilic perspective to have mostly been warnings of judgment and calls to repentance. Despite this difference a certain continuity is perceived to exist, which makes Zechariah's message seem as urgent now as the message of the preexilic prophets was in its own time. Zechariah's prophetic insights should therefore inform the policies by which the postexilic Jewish community is shaped and governed.

Such a studied conclusion regarding Zechariah's overall significance could scarcely have been reached before the rededication of the Second Temple (ca. 515), in whose reconstruction Zechariah was instrumental. As this institution became definitive for the identity of postexilic Judaism, some scribal group with political influence sought to show that Zechariah's view of its significance should become normative. Because this group attempted to discern the implications of Zechariah's message by putting him in such broad historical perspective, it is unlikely that the prophet himself was included — although it is certainly not impossible for Zechariah to have been involved in such a retrospective assessment of his own career.

Intention

This unit introduces the entire book by showing that Zechariah takes up where "the former prophets" leave off, and that under the radically changed conditions of the restoration he continues to challenge Yahweh's people in basically the same way. Zechariah stands in relation to the generation of the audience's parents as the whole prophetic tradition stands in relation to all past generations. He thus represents the culmination of the repeated call to repentance — a call that the parents' generation has finally learned to heed because of the exile. This puts Zechariah in a different relation to the present generation of the audience. For them he represents a turning point in a double sense. First, if they learn from their forebears not to ignore the need to "return" to Yahweh, they will not have to endure the same kind of hardship. Second, if they learn this lesson, their relationship with Yahweh can become characterized by restoration and divine favor, rather than by destruction and divine wrath.

Although Zechariah's prophecies mark his addressees' entrance into a new historical era, with conditions that are somewhat different from those of their parents' generation, the issue of how to discern Yahweh's involvement is basically the same as before. The problem is first to know what Yahweh's purpose is, and then to recognize what constitutes an appropriate response. It is the prophets who have both the capacity to grasp and the duty to proclaim such things. The new generation will hear from Zechariah a somewhat novel view of Yahweh's purpose and how they should respond. Their failure to heed these prophetic insights would be as tragic in its own way as the consequences of their forebears' failure to heed the former prophets' calls to repentance.

By showing that Zechariah's prophecies are formally the same as those of his predecessors, despite the material differences that arise from new historical conditions, this unit creates a model for extending the application of Zechariah's prophecies. The last two sections of the book (9:1-11:17 and 12:1-14:21) are appended to the first two sections (1:7-6:15 and 7:1-8:23) on the assumption that Zechariah's prophecies are formally applicable to later times, despite the material differences that arise from new historical conditions (→ Book as a Whole). Just as the former prophets' message of judgment and divine wrath provided Zechariah with the theological ground on which he could, in an era of change, somewhat paradoxically reverse their message in their name, Zechariah's message of restoration and divine favor (1:7-8:23) also provided later reinterpreters with the theological ground on which they could, in a new and different era, somewhat paradoxically reverse his message in his name (9:1-14:21).

Bibliography

G. Tucker "Prophetic Superscriptions and the Growth of a Canon," in *Canon and Authority* (ed. G. W. Coats and B. O. Long; Philadelphia: Fortress, 1977) 56-70; A. S. van der Woude, "Seid nicht wie eure Väter! Bemerkungen zu Sacharja 1:5 und seinem Kontext," in *Prophecy* (*Fest.* G. Fohrer; ed. J. A. Emerton; BZAW 150; Berlin: de Gruyter, 1980) 163-73.

Chapter 3

THE SECOND MAJOR SECTION
OF THE BOOK (1:7–6:15)
AND ITS INDIVIDUAL UNITS

REPORT OF A PROPHETIC REVELATION CONCERNING
THE COMPLETION OF ZERUBBABEL'S TEMPLE
REBUILDING PROJECT, 1:7–6:15

Structure

I. Narrative introduction	1:7
A. Date citation	1:7a
B. Prophetic word formula	1:7bαβ[1]
C. Direct discourse marker *(lē'mōr)*	1:7bβ[2]
II. Main body: revelation concerning the restoration of	
Jerusalem and the temple	1:8–6:15
A. First episode	1:8–3:10
1. Narration begun: series of three night	
vision reports	1:8–2:9 *(RSV* 1:8–2:5)
a. First vision: heavenly horsemen on	
earth patrol	1:8-17
b. Second vision: four horns cast down by	
four artisans	2:1-4
c. Third vision: a man going to measure Jerusalem	2:5-9
2. Narration interrupted: exhortation urging	
response to Yahweh's initiative	2:10-17 *(RSV* 6-13)
a. Addressed to the exiles: leave	
Babylon and return to Jerusalem	2:10-16
b. Addressed to "all flesh": silence!	2:17
3. Narration resumed (concluding fourth vision):	
Joshua commissioned in the heavenly council	3:1-10

B. Second episode	4:1–6:15
1. Series of four night vision reports in two scenes	4:1–6:8
a. First scene	4:1–5:4
1) Narrative introduction	4:1
2) Pair of visions	4:2–5:4
a) Fifth vision: the lampstand	4:2-14
(1) Vision report proper	4:2-7
(a) Narration begun	4:2-6aα
(b) Narration interrupted: nonvisionary oracle	4:6bβ-7
(2) Aside: report of nonvisionary revelation	4:8-10a
(a) Introductory prophetic word formula	4:8
(b) Oracle proper	4:9-10a
(3) Return to vision report proper: narration resumed	4:10b-14
b) Sixth vision: a flying scroll	5:1-4
b. Second scene	5:5–6:8
1) Narrative introduction	5:5
2) Pair of visions	5:6–6:8
a) Seventh vision: an ephah	5:6-11
b) Eighth vision: chariots of Yahweh	6:1-8
2. Concluding report of nonvisionary revelation: symbolic action involving crowns	6:9-15
a) Introductory prophetic word formula	6:9
b) Revelation proper	6:10-15

The structure of 1:7–6:15 as such has hardly been addressed. Scholarly attention has focused instead on a so-called cycle of visions that can supposedly be reconstructed by removing the oracular material from the strictly visionary material in the vision reports themselves (i.e., 1:14-17; 3:8-10; 4:6aβ-10a) and by disregarding the oracular units that contain no visionary elements (i.e., 2:10-17 [*RSV* 6-13]; 6:9-15). Sometimes the fourth vision is also omitted because its form seems somewhat anomalous in comparison with the others (→ 3:1-15, Structure), leaving an "original" set of visions that ideally numbers seven (e.g., Jeremias, 201-23; although Meyers and Meyers assert that 3:1-15 is "essential in form and meaning to the sequence," they nevertheless remain fixed on the same original ideal form, as they describe the resulting cycle in terms of a "7 + 1" structural pattern [*Haggai,* lvii-lviii]). By means of such excision and rearrangement the analysis of this section's structure has generally been reduced to a question of the symmetries among the seven or eight visions that remain.

Visions can supposedly be paired on the basis of corresponding traits, thus revealing a symmetry that defines the structure of the vision cycle. There is little agreement, however, on the nature of these correspondences. According to Baldwin (pp. 80-81) and Ollenburger (pp. 736-37), the arrangement of the visions creates a thematic chiasm. Seybold (pp. 107-8) holds that there is a pattern of similarities and differences among the kinds of symbolic figures that are visualized. In Halpern's view (pp. 79-89) the arrangement is based on the successive phases of a myth-ritual complex, in which various aspects of ancient Near Eastern temple foundation ceremonies are correlated with various episodes from the myth of cosmogonic creation through a god's combat with chaos. According to Meyers and Meyers (*Haggai,* lv-lvii) it is based on a combination of factors, including a common theme or subject matter (e.g., the horses in both 1:8-17 and 6:1-8), common stylistic features (e.g., the two-part structure of both 2:1-4 [*RSV* 1:18-21] and 5:5-11), common formulaic language (e.g., the same variations on the vision report formula), and common purview (whether the scope of the vision is universal or local, etc.).

Despite these rather different understandings of what constitutes the basis for the vision cycle, scholars generally agree that some such structure dominates 1:7–6:15 as a whole, and that all or some of the nonvisionary material has been secondarily added to it. This remains the basic presupposition of even the more recent attempts to see the visionary and the oracular materials in some sort of complementary relationship (e.g., Meyers and Meyers, *Haggai,* lix; Petersen, *Haggai,* 20-22; Ollenburger, 737-38). This section of the book has thus generally been read in terms of the thematic progression represented by the sequence of visions alone (following Galling, 33-36), whether this is described as a multifaceted message of salvation addressed to the recently resettled restoration community (e.g., Mason, *Haggai,* 29-31), a recapitulation of the divine warrior myth (e.g., Halpern, 189), or a theological rationale for the program of restoration advocated by the prophet (e.g., Petersen, *Haggai,* 116-19). The only significant dissent from this approach comes from Beuken (pp. 115-18), who argues that a parenetical framework reflecting postexilic preaching practice (i.e., 2:6-13 and 6:15; cf. 1:3-4) has come to dominate the vision cycle. He thus views this section as a report based on preaching informed by the concerns of the Chronicler's circle, such as the messianic significance of the restored temple.

The view that 1:7–6:15 is structured as a vision cycle, to which other oracular material has been secondarily added, is problematic regardless of whether the visions or the parenetic sections are finally regarded as dominant. First, there is no reason for arbitrarily excising the oracular material from the vision reports. The vision report genre typically contains some explication of the symbolic figures that are visualized by prophetic recipients of visions, and this explication frequently takes the form of oracular speech (e.g., Amos 8:1-3; 9:1-4; Jer 1:11-16; 24:1-10; Ezek 37:1-14, etc.; → Zech 1:8-17, Genre). There is thus no a priori basis on which to suppose that 1:14-17 did not originally belong with 1:8-13, or that 3:8-10 did not originally belong with 3:1-7. In the case of 4:1-14 there is some ostensible reason to suppose that vv. 6aβ-10 have been inserted into the surrounding vision, but this is because of their obviously intrusive position in relation to their context, not because of some arbitrary presupposition about the incompatibility of visionary and oracular material.

Second, the types of correspondences between the visions that have generally been taken to indicate their symmetrical arrangement into a cycle also serve as the basis on which the purely oracular units are connected with the vision reports. In several cases such correspondences create links between the visionary and nonvisionary material that are just as pronounced as the links between the visions themselves. For example, although the first vision (1:8-17) and the final vision (6:1-8) have in common the motif of the heavenly horses, the final vision has similar motifs in common with the prophetic exhortation in 2:10-17 (*RSV* 6-13), namely, the four winds of heaven (2:10b; 6:5) and the "land of the north" (2:10a; 6:8). The first and last visions similarly have in common the narrative theme of "patrolling the earth" (1:10-11; 6:7), but the fourth vision (3:1-10) and the final unit (6:9-15) also have in common the narrative theme of investing Joshua, the high priest, with certain symbolic objects. The fifth vision (4:1-14) and the final unit are likewise linked by their description of objects that will occupy a prominent place in the rebuilt temple (i.e., the golden lampstand and the crown[s] made of silver and gold). The phenomenon of correspondence in motifs and narrative themes thus pertains to this whole section of the book, including the nonvisionary material, and not just to the visions. It serves as a means of interrelating all the units of this section with one another, visionary and nonvisionary units alike, and not as the basis on which the visions alone are shown to be interrelated in a cycle.

The vision cycle hypothesis is thus untenable. From this conclusion it follows not only that 2:10-17 and 6:9-15 are to be seen as units that are just as important as the visions with respect to the overall structure of this section as a whole, but also that symmetricality is not necessarily the principle by which the vision reports themselves are interrelated with one another. The various kinds of correspondences between pairs of visions, in terms of which their symmetrical arrangement has generally been defined, are indeed evident and operative. But the importance of these particular links between these particular units is relativized by the recognition that they are only part of larger web of correspondences that also link various units to one another in all sorts of ways. (Note, for example, the way in which the narrative theme of "going forth" [yṣ'] links the sixth [5:1-4], seventh [5:5-11], and eighth [6:1-8] visions. The curse [5:3-4], the ephah [5:5-6], the winged women [5:9] and the interpreter angel himself [5:1] all "go forth," as do the chariots of the heavenly hosts [6:1, 5-7].)

The compositional structure of 1:7–6:15 becomes evident when one examines in detail its pattern of introducing each unit, including each subunit of the two-part vision reports, particularly with respect to its use of formulaic language. The introduction to this section as a whole (1:7) is distinguished from the main body (1:8–6:15) by its use of third person narration and its lack of oracular speech. The main body in contrast uses first person forms throughout, and in each unit there is some oracular speech. The constituent units and subunits are introduced as follows:

1:8-17	I saw in the night. . . .
2:1-4	And I lifted my eyes and saw. . . .
2:5-9	And I lifted my eyes and saw. . . . And Yahweh showed me. . . .
2:10-17	Alas! Alas! Flee! . . . says Yahweh.
3:1-10	And he showed me. . . .

4:1-17   And the angel . . . came again and waked me . . . and said
          to me, "What do you see?" And I said, "I see. . . ." And he
          said to me, "This is the word of Yahweh to Zerubbabel. .
          . ." And the word of Yahweh came to me. . . .
5:1-4   And again I lifted my eyes and saw. . . .
5:5-11   Then the angel came forward and said to me, "Lift your
          eyes and see." . . . And I lifted my eyes and saw. . . .
6:1-8   And again I lifted my eyes and saw. . . .
6:9-15   And the word of Yahweh came to me. . . .

From these data showing the skeleton of 1:8–6:15, it is evident that the main
body of this section of the book is fundamentally a narrative in two episodes.
At the beginning of each episode stands the most basic variant of the vision report formula, using r'h ("see") in its qal perfect form (1:8; 4:2; → 1:8-17,
Genre). Each episode consists mainly of a series of vision reports, whose continuity within the episode is indicated not only by the recurrence of r'h in its
waw-consecutive qal imperfect form (2:1, 5; 5:1, 9; 6:1), but also by the complementary use of the idiomatic phrase "to lift the eyes" (ns' 'ynym), indicating
a shift in the field of perception (2:1, 5; 5:1, 5, 9; 6:1). The patterned use of
formulaic language relating to visionary experience, as it has been considered
thus far, shows that 1:8–6:15 falls into two episodes, the first of which begins
with a series of three vision reports (1:8–2:9), and the second of which begins
with a series of four vision reports (4:1–6:8).

    This outline of the structure can be further filled in by considering some
additional aspects of the narrative's description, such as the circumstances under which the prophet receives these revelations and the actions of the other
main character, the angelic interpreter. In 1:8 it is reported that Zechariah saw
something "at night" (hallaylâ). With this one quick stroke the scene is set for
the prophet's reception of the first series of visions (1:8–2:9), throughout
which the angelic interpreter figures prominently. The continuity is suddenly
interrupted at 2:10, however, by the occurrence of a prophecy that is not in the
form of a vision report. The narrative representation of the prophet's seeing in
the dark is at this point abandoned altogether, and the character of the angelic
interpreter — whose role has so far been defined exclusively in relation to this
perceptual phenomenon — thus disappears. Although 3:1 indicates a return to
the prophet's reception of visionary revelation, there is no indication that his
situation has reverted to the conditions under which the episode began. This
vision differs in several ways from the three in the preceding series (→ 3:1-10,
Structure), but it is particularly distinctive with respect to its representation of
the divine council. There is no explicit indication that this heavenly scene is
perceived in the darkness of night, and the angelic interpreter remains absent
or at least anonymous. (There are angelic figures in 3:1-10, but the epithet
haddōbēr bî [RSV "who spoke with me"] with which the interpreter is repeatedly and distinctively characterized in the preceding visions is not applied to
any of them.)

    Although the narrative abandons the representation of night visions with
the angelic interpreter in 2:10-17, and although the representation of visionary

330

phenomena is only partially resumed in 3:1-10, it is evident from the introduction in 3:1 that both 2:10-17 and 3:1-10 belong together with 1:8–2:9 in a single episode (cf. Joubert). The fourth vision report begins with a *waw*-consecutive hiphil imperfect form of *rʾh* ("see"), whose subject is not explicitly identified (lit. "he made me see"; *RSV* "he showed me"). According to formulaic usage Yahweh is generally the subject of such a verb (e.g., Amos 7:1, 4, 7; 8:1; Jer 24:1), but without any explicit indication of this fact the reader is left with a blank to fill in. This creates a link between 3:1-10 and the preceding material, for the reader can only fill in this blank by considering the precedents within the foregoing part of the book for this sort of narrative description.

Numerous explicit references to Yahweh in the immediately preceding unit suggest that he may be the subject of the initial verb in 3:1. (The divine name is reiterated nine times in 2:10-17.) However, two previous examples of the hiphil vision report formula (1:9b; 2:3) make this matter more ambiguous. In 2:3 Yahweh is explicitly identified as the subject, but in 1:9b the angelic interpreter is the subject. In the final analysis the hiphil verb in 3:1 resembles the one in 2:3 more than the one in 1:9b, because the first two are both third person forms spoken by the prophet, but the last is a first person form spoken by the angelic interpreter. Yahweh is thus probably the subject of *wayyarēnî* in 3:1. In any case, 3:1-10 is integrally linked with other parts of the first episode by the way it begins, as it describes the action of a character whose identity can be ascertained only by reconsidering how the story has thus far been told.

In sum, the first episode of the narrative in 1:8–6:15 begins with a series of three vision reports (1:8–2:9), all of which represent symbolic figures visualized by the prophet in the dark of night, requiring the explanation of an angelic interpreter. This action is suddenly interrupted by a prophetic exhortation (2:10-17). At this point the nighttime conditions become more or less irrelevant, and the angelic interpreter disappears, as the first person voice shifts from recounting the reception of revelation to rehearsing its proclamation (note the direct address and parenetical forms; → 2:10-17, Structure). In 3:1-10 the prophetic voice returns to recounting the reception of visionary revelation, but not necessarily back to night visions. The close relationship between this heavenly council scene and the foregoing prophecies is nevertheless evident from the fact that its introduction proceeds on the basis of what has been formerly expressed in both the preceding exhortation (2:10-17) and the preceding series of night visions (1:8–2:9).

A second episode begins to unfold at 4:1, as both the angelic interpreter's return (*wayyāšāb;* *RSV* "[he] came again") and the resumption of the night vision phenomenon are explicitly indicated. With regard to the latter, it is not reiterated here that the prophet saw something "at night" (1:8). A similar idea is instead expressed through a metaphorical comparison of the prophet's being primed to receive revelation with someone's being roused from sleep. Since one usually sleeps at night, being roused from sleep to see something is tantamount to seeing it in the dark.

Unlike the first episode, in which the prophet is the main character and the angelic interpreter plays only a supporting role, the second episode features the angelic interpreter as a main character on a par with the prophet. In

1:8–3:10 every segment of the narrative is initiated by the action of the prophet, or by Yahweh's action impinging directly on the prophet (1:20; 3:1a); the angelic interpreter only reacts, mostly with words but sometimes also with movement (e.g., 2:7a). In 4:1–6:15, however, the action of the angelic interpreter is as prominent and proactive as the action of the prophet. In the four-vision series (4:1–5:11) they alternately take the lead, thus marking its division into two subunits (4:1–5:4; 5:5–6:8) in which the angel first elicits the vision seen by the prophet (4:1-14; 5:5-11) and the prophet subsequently sees another vision on his own (5:1-4; 6:1-8).

There is another indication that 4:1–6:15 is related to 1:8–3:10 as a second episode. It is not only stated in 4:1 that the angelic interpreter has "returned" *(wayyāšāb)*. It is also explicitly stated in 5:1 and 6:1, with the same verb *(wā'āšûb)*, that the prophet is "again" having visionary experiences. This makes 5:1-4 the sequel to 4:1-14, and 6:1-8 the sequel to 5:5-11, but it also makes the visions in 4:1–6:8 collectively the sequel to those in 1:8–3:10. When the prophet is said in 5:1 to have "seen" *(r'h)* something "again" *(šwb)*, this is in reference to 4:1-14, where he has previously "seen" something (4:2). But when it is also said in 5:1 that "lifting his eyes" *(nś' 'ynym)* is something that he has done "again" *(šwb)*, this cannot be in reference to 4:1-14, for he has not "lifted his eyes" in this unit of the narrative. It can only refer back to the previous descriptions of this same action in 2:1 and 2:5.

Just as the continuity of the first episode (1:8–3:10) is interrupted by a prophecy that is not wholly integrated into the narrative (2:10-17), the continuity of the second episode is similarly interrupted by the intrusion of the prophecies in 4:6aβ-10a. In the former case the prophetic exhortation in 2:10-17 breaks the narrative link between two units of the episode (i.e., between 2:5-9 and 3:1-10), thus marking the end of the series of three vision reports in 1:8–2:9 and setting the vision report in 3:1-10 apart from these three others. In the latter case, however, the two prophecies in 4:6aβ-10a break the narrative within a single unit, as they are plunged into the midst of the dialogue within 4:1-6aα + 10b-14.

Moreover, each of these two intrusive prophecies, 4:6aβ-7 and 4:8-10a, is related to the narration that contains them in a different way. The first (4:6aβ-7) is inserted within the dialogue between the prophet and the angelic interpreter, so that it becomes the first part of the angel's twofold reply to the prophet in 4:6a-7 + 10b: "Then he said to me, 'This is the word of Yahweh to Zerubbabel. . . . [And] these seven are the eyes of Yahweh. . . .'" This is somewhat disruptive, but it remains within the structure of the direct discourse, and it does not break the continuity of the narrative altogether. In contrast, the second prophecy (4:8-10a) has its own narrative introduction (4:8), which parallels the introduction to the narrative that contains it (4:1-2aα[1]), and thus constitutes an aside on the part of the narrator. Unlike the first (4:6aβ-7), this second prophecy (4:8-10a) does not form part of the dialogue between the angelic interpreter and the prophet (→ 4:1-14, Structure).

The relationship between 6:9-15 and the preceding series of visions in 4:1–6:8 is in some respects comparable to the relationship between 2:10-17 and the preceding series of visions in 1:8–2:9, but in other respects comparable to the relationship between 3:1-10 and 1:8–2:9. Like 2:10-17, 6:9-15 marks the end of the night visions and the onset of a different sort of prophetic revelation that does not require the angel's explanation. Like 2:10-17, 6:9-15 also concludes with the same hortatory description of the prophet's public authentication as Yahweh's intermediary: "You will know that Yahweh of hosts has sent me to you" (2:15b; cf. 6:15b). Like 3:1-10, however, 6:9-15 is introduced so as to maintain some continuity with the preceding series of vision reports. Just as the narrative continuity of 3:1-10 with 1:8–2:9 is reinforced by introducing 3:1-10 with the same hiphil vision report formula that is previously used to introduce a subunit of 2:1-4, the narrative continuity of 6:9-15 with 4:1–6:8 is also reinforced by introducing 6:9-15 with the same prophetic word formula that is previously used to introduce a subunit of 4:1-14 (cf. 4:8; 6:9).

In sum, the narrative in 1:8–6:15 has a second episode that begins with a series of four vision reports (4:1–6:9), all of which represent symbolic figures visualized by the prophet in a state of nocturnal heightened awareness induced by the angelic interpreter (4:1-2). The character of the angelic interpreter is generally more important in the second episode than in the first, as he takes a more directive role in the process of prophetic revelation. In 6:9-15 the narrative continues to recount the reception of revelation, but in a nonvisionary mode. The connection between 6:9-15 and the foregoing visions is evident from the fact that it is introduced like a prophecy that is previously cited in the narrator's aside within the first vision (4:8-10a). The dual function of 6:9-15, as the conclusion not only to the second episode but also to the two episodes of this section as a whole, is evident from the fact that it reechoes in 6:15 much the same parenetical note that is sounded in 2:10-17.

The units within each of this section's two episodes are arranged so as to form contrasting patterns with respect to their cosmic perspective. The description in each unit somehow encompasses the relationship between heaven and earth. The heavenly realm is where Yahweh lives and the place from which he deploys in quasi-military fashion the forces that affect developments on earth. The earthly realm is where humanity lives, where the nations vie for dominance, and where the restoration of Judah is being attempted. The relationship between these two realms of the cosmos is represented in a variety of ways, sometimes emphasizing a relatively heavenly perspective and sometimes a relatively earthly one. In either case it is generally assumed that heavenly developments have their earthly correlatives, and vice versa. The earthly correlatives of heavenly developments can be described in terms of their worldwide effects or in terms of their local effects, or in terms of both.

The cosmic perspective of the units in 1:8–6:15 can be schematized as follows:

First episode
1:8-17　　The angelic hosts are located at the juncture between heaven and earth, and are described in terms of their influence on "all the earth" in general, and on Judah and Jerusalem in particular.
2:1-4　　 The earthly manifestations of heavenly forces are described

in terms of their influence on the international order as this affects Judah.

2:5-9   A human being in an earthly location is described in terms of the influence of a heavenly being on his actions.

2:10-17 Yahweh's influence on international developments is described in terms of his deploying "the four winds of heaven," and his influence on "all flesh" in terms of what he does in his heavenly "dwelling place."

3:1-10   Actions taken by divine beings in the heavenly council with respect to a human being, the high priest Joshua, are described in terms of their effect on the cultic life of Judah.

Second episode

4:1-14   The symbolic tableau in the Jerusalem temple is described in terms of the heavenly reality that it sacramentally represents.

5:1-4   The supramundane capabilities of a Torah scroll are described in terms of a divine agency that enforces covenant norms over "all the earth."

5:5-11   The pretensions of an idolatrous cult object to rise above its earthbound nature, and thus become a manifestation of a heavenly reality, are parodied.

6:1-8   The angelic hosts are located at the juncture between heaven and earth, and are described in terms of their influence on world affairs along the earth's north-south axis.

6:9-15   Actions taken by human beings involving a symbolic object, and their subsequent enshrinement of that object in the Jerusalem temple, are described in terms of what they signify regarding the earthly representation of Yahweh's heavenly kingship.

From this brief description of each unit one can see that the cosmic perspective in the first episode descends from the juncture of heaven and earth (1:8-17) down to earth (2:5-9), and then rises back upward (2:10-17) all the way into heaven itself (3:1-10). The progression in the second episode conversely begins on earth (4:1-14), rises gradually (5:1-11) up to the juncture of heaven and earth (6:1-8), and then abruptly descends back down to earth again (6:9-15). (Ollenburger's view of how cosmic scope figures in the structure of 1:7–6:15 [pp. 736-37, 748] differs largely from mine because he fails to take 2:7-14 and 6:9-15 into account.) In view of these contrasting patterns, the first episode appears to be emphasizing that certain earthly developments are due to Yahweh's heavenly initiative, whereas the second episode appears to be conversely emphasizing that heavenly realities are effectively manifest in certain earthly developments — although in both cases the correspondences between heaven and earth are but two sides of the same coin.

Both episodes are concerned with the return of the Jewish exiles to Jerusalem and the rebuilding of the temple, events that are seen as earthly developments with heavenly correlatives. The first episode, however, focuses primarily on the return of the exiles. There is one reference to temple rebuilding in 1:16, which makes clear that this is a fundamental goal of the return; but the theme of temple rebuilding is not picked up again until the second episode, where it is emphasized at key points (4:6b-10a; 6:13, 15; cf. 5:11). The individual units of the first episode touch on various aspects of the return: the dramatic international changes that made it possible (2:1-4, 12-13; 1:14b-16a); the construction involved in the resettlement of the ruined city's site (1:16b; 2:5-9); and the socioeconomic revitalization of the city and the surrounding region (1:17aβ; 2:8b; 3:10; cf. 2:13aβ). In 3:1-10 concern is also expressed for the recovery of cultic practices that are legitimate, in the sense that the threat of impurity has been removed (3:3-5a), so that guilt can be duly expiated (3:9bβ). Although the recovery of legitimate sacrifices certainly implies the eventual completion of the temple, the resumption of sacrifice was an issue quite apart from the reconstruction of the building since sacrificial worship was resumed in the sacred precincts before the reconstruction of the building itself was undertaken (Ezra 3:1-6), just as sacrifice to Yahweh was already practiced at Jerusalem under David even before the First Temple was completed under Solomon (2 Sam 6:17-18; 1 Chr 21:18–22:1).

Although the units of the first episode converge thematically in their emphasis on return as opposed to temple rebuilding, their temporal perspectives are diverse. Zech 2:1-4 and 2:10-17 generally reflect the time when the international changes were in progress, changes that made it possible for the dispersion of the exiles to be reversed and for Jewish emigration from Babylon to get underway. 1:8-17 reflects a time after some had returned but when the work of reconstructing the city had scarcely begun. Both 2:5-9 and 3:1-10 reflect a time after some progress in the work of resettlement had been made, when the returnees began to be faced with such issues as whether the city would need a new wall to be viable, and whether the ritual impurity endemic to the exile would impair the legitimacy of the priests and hence the efficacy of their newly resumed sacrifices.

The second episode focuses more on the rebuilding of the temple than on the return of the exiles. One of its units (6:1-8) concerns Yahweh's creation of an impetus to return through his reorientation of the cosmic balance of power toward Jerusalem. The other units, however, all touch on various aspects of the temple rebuilding project itself. Two (4:1-14 and 6:8-15) overtly concern Zerubbabel's leadership of the project, and the problem of redefining the temple's status as a royal sanctuary despite Judah's present lack of a king. Two others (5:1-4 and 5:5-11) concern the effects of such a redefinition on the Jewish community at large, many members of which remain in the dispersion. Together with those now in Judah, they will form a worldwide covenant community centered around the temple and maintained through scriptural instruction in the norms of the covenant relationship (5:1-4), rather than through the establishment of any rival sanctuaries elsewhere (5:5-11). Although 6:1-8 does not explicitly refer to either the issue of the rebuilt temple's royal status or the issue of Jerusalem as the sole central sanctuary, it complements the concerns of the other units in the second episode by affirming that Yahweh's Spirit is operative in the dispersion in such a way as to orient the dispersed community toward Jerusalem.

Although the units of the second episode converge thematically, they are nearly as diverse in their temporal perspectives as the units of the first episode. 6:1-8 reflects the creation of the new world order under the Persians, established initially by Cyrus and later consolidated by Darius, that made the restoration of Judah possible. 6:9-15 reflects the time when support was being recruited and funds were being raised from those who had recently returned, so that the rebuilding project could be inaugurated (cf. Ezra 2:68-69). Zech 4:1-14 reflects a time during the rebuilding when the completion of the project seemed in doubt. Neither 5:1-4 nor 5:5-11 directly reflects any particular turn of events, but they counter opposition to the ideals of the restoration embodied in the temple rebuilding project of Zerubbabel and Joshua. They thus probably emerged around the time this project was being planned and started.

The units of each episode thus converge in their thematic concerns and diverge in their temporal perspectives, as they move through an orderly progression in their cosmic perspectives. One other important aspect of each episode's structure remains to be discussed in order to describe the overall effect of 1:8–6:15. The hortatory elements play an important role in this section as a whole. In the first episode the importance of the hortatory element is indicated not only by the singular presence of an entire unit of parenetical material (2:10-17), but also by the striking way in which this unit interrupts the well-defined narrative sequence linking the three preceding units (1:8–2:9) with the following unit (3:1-10). In the second episode the importance of the hortatory element is less immediately evident because it forms only a subsidiary part (6:15aβb) of a larger unit (6:9-15) and because its parenetical effect is expressed indirectly through a conditional clause (6:15b) rather than directly through imperatives (cf. 2:10-11, 14). Nevertheless a strong linkage between 2:10-17 and 6:15aβb is created by the verbatim repetition in the latter verse of a phrase that occurs twice in the former unit: "and you will know that Yahweh of hosts sent me to you" (2:13b, 15b).

This linkage constitutes the dominant note in the chord with which this section as a whole concludes. (Beuken [pp. 115-18] is thus right to call attention to the importance of the parenetical elements in the composition of 1:7–6:15, although his suggestion that they were once the structurally dominant link between 1:2-6 and 1:8–6:15 at an earlier stage of traditio-historical development is perhaps not the best way of accounting for their present function.) Moreover, a nearly verbatim variation on the same refrain (4:9b) also appears in one of the prophecies (4:8-10a) that interrupt the dialogue in the fifth vision (4:1-14). By virtue of this refrain the major interruption in the narrative continuity of the first episode (2:10-17) is linked with the major interruption in the narrative continuity of the second episode (4:8-10a), and both are in turn linked with the reversion to direct address at the conclusion to this entire section. The function of the hortatory elements in both episodes and the function of the narrator's aside in 4:8-10a are thus explicitly interrelated by virtue of the way they all feature the motif of the prophet's authentication through the outcome of events.

The relationship between the hortatory elements and this motif becomes evident when one considers the relationship of the introduction (1:7) and the main body (1:8–6:15) of this section. Although the two-episode narrative orders its prophecies in terms of cosmic rather than temporal perspective, the compositional form of 1:7–6:15 puts them collectively under a single overarching temporal perspective. The time indicated in 1:7, i.e., "the eleventh month in the second year of Darius," would be some twenty years after the first groups of returning exiles had managed to resettle Jerusalem under the leadership of Sheshbazzar, but had not succeeded in their efforts to rebuild the temple (Ezra 5:13-15). It would also be some months after attempts to reinstigate the rebuilding project had been launched under the leadership of Zerubbabel (Hag 1:1-15a).

From the temporal perspective of this section as a whole the individual prophecies concerned with various aspects of the exiles' return (primarily those in 1:8–3:10) would have already been fulfilled, and the authenticity of the prophet who foretold such things would have thereby been established. From this same temporal perspective the individual prophecies concerned with various aspects of temple building (primarily those in 4:1–6:15) would remain to be fulfilled, and the authenticity of the prophet who foretold such things would remain to be established. The fulfillment of the prophecies regarding the return would provide a basis for supposing that those regarding the rebuilding of the temple would likewise be fulfilled. The prophet's perception of how the powers of heaven and earth were correlated to bring about the return would have been validated, and this would validate his perception of how those same powers were currently being correlated in order to bring about the completion of the temple.

The juxtaposition of already-fulfilled prophecy concerning the return with yet-to-be-fulfilled prophecy concerning the restored temple is characteristic not only of the relationship between the first and second episodes of this section but also of the hortatory sections themselves. When one considers 2:10-17 in isolation, both the new phase in Judah's political existence represented by the return to Jerusalem (2:10-13) and the new phase in Judah's relationship with Yahweh represented by the restoration of the temple sanctuary (2:14-16) are prospective developments, predicated only on the prophet's claim that Yahweh is prepared to take action that is cosmic in scope (2:17). When this same unit is considered in relation to the time frame of this section as a whole, however, the international changes envisioned in 2:11-13a have been more or less realized, and their prediction has thus been authenticated (2:13b). The restoration of a newly redefined relationship between Yahweh and his people, in which Yahweh's presence will be sacramentally manifest (2:15a, 16) remains to be realized, however, and the prophetic perception of this possibility remains open to question (2:15b). It is the fulfillment of the part of this prophecy concerning the return that provides a pragmatic warrant for accepting the part of this prophecy concerning the temple's reconstruction.

When one similarly considers 6:9-15 in isolation, it seems to presuppose the return of at least some exiles, and it is ambiguous with regard to whether Zerubbabel's program of rebuilding has yet been inaugurated (→ 6:9-15,

337

Structure). The question seems to be whether the goal of the return is the rebuilding of the temple (6:15aα), and whether the returned exiles share the prophet's perception of what is at stake in this project (6:15b). When this same unit is considered in relation to the time frame of this section as a whole, however, the ambiguity has been resolved. The rebuilding has begun, and the question now seems to be whether it will be completed (4:9). In this context the hortatory section of the unit (6:15aβb) serves to signal that one of the consequences of the prophetic symbolic action commissioned in 6:9-13 has indeed begun to materialize: the returnees have begun to collaborate in the rebuilding effort (6:15aα). This authentication of one part of what was foretold concerning the outcome of that symbolic action provides the basis for granting credence to the other part of what was foretold, namely, that the crown(s) involved in the symbolic action will eventually be placed in the restored temple (6:14). Credence in both aspects of the symbolic action's portended outcome would in turn foster identification with and acceptance of the entire rebuilding project, based on the prophet's perception of its theological significance (6:15b).

With respect to the interpretive problem posed by the two prophecies in 4:6aβ-7 and 4:8-10a, whose intrusiveness has usually led them to be read in separation from their present context, it is noteworthy that they may be compared with the hortatory parts of this section in three respects. First, the interrelationship of these two prophecies is defined in terms of precisely the same juxtaposition of the already fulfilled and the still unfulfilled that characterizes the hortatory passages. The former (4:6aβ-7) foretells Zerubbabel's overcoming great opposition and gaining popular acclaim, through the use of divinely inspired persuasion rather than force, in order to lay the ceremonial "prime stone" (hā'eben hārō'šâ; RSV "top stone"), and thus reconsecrate the temple rebuilding project (→ 4:1-14). From the temporal perspective of this section as a whole (1:7) this prophecy would have already been fulfilled. The latter (4:8-10a) foretells the completion of this project by the same person that began it, Zerubbabel. From the temporal perspective of this section as a whole this prophecy would still be unfulfilled.

Second, this juxtaposition of already fulfilled and still unfulfilled prophecy serves precisely the same purpose here that it serves in the hortatory passages. The fulfillment of one prophecy becomes the basis on which the fulfillment of the other can be expected. In this case the motif of the prophet's authentication through the outcome of events (4:9b) did not originally increase the persuasiveness of 4:9-10a by calling public attention to 4:6bβ-7. It only promised some unidentified individual that the prophet would be vindicated by the fulfillment of 4:9-10a itself (note the second person masculine singular form wĕyāda'tā ["you will know"] in v. 8b). In the present context, however, it has been readdressed to the audience of this text (note the second person plural suffix on the preposition 'ălêkem ["to you"]), in combination with 4:6aβ-7, so that each one of the addressees is now led to suppose that the prophecy in 4:9-10a will be fulfilled precisely because the one in 4:6aβ-7 has been.

Third, the relation of these two prophecies to the narration that surrounds them is precisely parallel to the relation of the two units containing hortatory material to the narration that surrounds them. Just as 2:10-17 interrupts the narration of 1:8–3:10 but nevertheless remains contained within it, 4:6aβ-7 also interrupts the narrated dialogue of 4:1-14 but nevertheless remains contained within it (see above). Just as 6:9-15 breaks off from the narration of visionary experience and instead describes the reception of revelation with the prophetic word formula (6:9), 4:8-10a also breaks off from the narration of visionary experience and instead describes the reception of revelation with the prophetic word formula (4:8). Both the concluding report in 6:9-15 and the aside in 4:8-10a envision the prospect of the temple's eventual completion.

The prophecies in 4:6aβ-7 and 4:8-10a are obviously insertions in some sense, but in view of their functional affinities with the hortatory materials in 2:10-17 and 6:9-15, it is apparent that their juxtaposition in their present context is stylistically consistent with the way in which 2:10-17 and 6:9-15 have been combined with the eight vision reports in the overall makeup of 1:7–6:15. (Such observations as Halpern's, that 4:6aβ-10a creates an "unparalleled" and "stylistically intolerable" interruption [p. 189], are thus quite mistaken.) The intrusiveness of these two subunits is rhetorically functional, as their juxtaposition defines the issue that the compositional structure of 1:7–6:15 is designed to resolve. Scholars commonly suppose that the vision cycle existed first, and that 4:6aβ-7 and 4:8-10a were subsequently inserted into it, but it appears that the "cycle" was configured from preexisting records of revelation to provide a context for these two oracles. Redditt (p. 42) even proposes that 4:6aβ-7 and 4:8-10a, along with 3:1-10, were redactional pieces made up as reinterpretive additions to the vision reports. Just the reverse is more likely, however. The vision of the lampstand was probably formulated in order to link these three previously existing prophecies in a reinterpretive narrative context (→ 4:1-14, Structure).

Genre

This section of the book is a redactional composite that is generically heterogeneous. It combines prophetic vision reports, reports of other nonvisionary kinds of revelation (4:8-10a; 6:9-15), and prophecies of a parenetical or similarly hortatory sort (2:10-17; 4:6aβ-7). Despite this heterogeneity nearly all the individual units resemble the introduction (1:7) in emphasizing the reception of revelation rather than its communication. Only 2:10-17 and 4:6aβ-7 conversely emphasize the communication of revelation, and both are formally and thematically incorporated into the surrounding narration of revelation's reception (→ Structure).

Several scholars have described this section as apocalyptic literature, focusing on three of its distinctive features: (1) the predominance of the visions, (2) their description of divine activity from a heavenly perspective, and (3) the essential role played by the angelic interpreter in explaining the earthly implications of Yahweh's heavenly initiatives (e.g., Amsler, "Zacharie et l'origine," 227-29; Gese, 24-41). Zech 1:7–6:15 is indeed comparable in these respects with other texts that are commonly recognized as apocalyptic, but several qualifications are in order. A careful distinction needs to be made between texts that show some of the features commonly associated with apocalyptic literature, and are hence to some extent apocalyptic in a general sense, and texts that more specifically have the literary form of an apocalypse. Because this section resembles apocalypses in several very basic ways, it may fairly be called apocalyptic in a general sense, regardless of just how one chooses to delineate the development of apocalyptic from prophecy. It may therefore be seen as a step in the evolution of apocalyptic (North). It is questionable, however, whether 1:7–6:15 can be classified as an apocalypse with respect to its overall literary form (→ 12:1–14:21, Genre).

Such classification has been based exclusively on the visions, at the expense of the other nonvisionary prophecies that are also an integral part of this section. It actually identifies the genre of the so-called vision cycle that supposedly constituted the original form of this section, rather than the genre of the text as we now have it (e.g., Gese, 24-41). Since the hypothesis of the vision cycle is untenable (→ Structure), the question of its genre is moot; but one may still ask whether the present text has the form of an apocalypse. In reply it must be noted that although this section is made up mostly of vision reports, the structure in its overall narrative does not in the final analysis take the form of a vision report, nor does the structure of either one of its two main episodes (1:7–3:10; 4:1–6:15). This is the main reason for not identifying it as an apocalypse (→ 12:1–14:21, Genre).

The issue may also depend to some extent on the complicated question of whether 1:7–6:15 describes Yahweh eschatologically (Knibb, 175). Although most scholars regard eschatological description as a definitive feature of apocalypses, this view is by no means unanimous (e.g., C. Rowland, *The Open Heaven* [New York: Crossroad, 1982] 23-48); and even among those who hold the majority view there is no commonly accepted definition of eschatology (Larkin, 9-27). In any case the description in 1:7–6:15 is clearly not eschatological in the root sense of the word. That is, it does not portray the end of the world or of human history, but rather describes the coming of the Persians as a development in which a divinely initiated turning point in world history is manifest. In this context Yahweh is creating a new world order conducive to the Jewish exiles' reestablishment of a geopolitical base in their former homeland, the centerpiece of which is the restored royal sanctuary in Jerusalem. Every aspect of this earthly historical process has its supramundane heavenly correlative, but nothing is ever portrayed from a wholly otherworldly perspective (→ Structure). Whether or not one wishes to call such description eschatological, it is rather more earthbound than the description in apocalypses generally tends to be. Only in 3:1-10 does this section describe anything from a primarily heavenly perspective, as apocalypses often do, and in this one case the scene of the heavenly council is envisioned in accord with well-established prophetic precedents (e.g., Isa 6:1-13; 1 Kgs 22:19-23). For this reason also, Zech 1:7–6:15 should probably not be identified as an apocalypse.

Because this section appears to be a redactional composite, which reinterprets previously existing prophecies by arranging and connecting them in a particular sequence, Fishbane has described chs. 1–6 as a "mantological anthology," comparing this part of Zechariah with such texts as Amos 7–8 and Dan 7–12 (M. Fishbane, *Biblical Interpretation in Ancient Israel* [Oxford: Clarendon, 1985] 520-21). This designation rightly emphasizes that the redaction of this text was both a scribal literary activity and a profoundly prophetic activity, in which Yahweh's ongoing involvement in human affairs was divined through the process of studying and recomposing mantic texts. The redaction of Zech 1:7–6:15 is thus aptly characterized as mantological, but its classification as an anthology is problematic. Here once again attention has been focused on the visions at the expense of the nonvisionary material, so that chs. 1–6 have been compared with Amos 7–8 and Dan 7–12 on the assumption that they are all primarily collections of visions, in which other kinds of prophecies might be secondarily or incidentally included. An anthology is a serially arranged selection of texts that are in some way representative of various authors, genres, periods, etc. Despite the fact that the texts Fishbane adduces have several visions in common, they have quite different overall structures, none of which exactly fits the description of an anthology. With respect to the text in question here, this designation hardly does justice to the way in which various kinds of prophecies have been sequenced and synthesized in a complex narrative form (→ Structure).

Although the materials from which this section was composed are diverse, and although the narrative into which they have been incorporated is complex, the whole is subsumed under the rubric of a relatively common and readily recognizable generic convention, which is indicated by the use of the (→) prophetic word formula in the introduction (1:7). If one keeps in mind that it is a redactional composite of a mantological sort, and that it has some apocalyptic traits, this section remains basically a narrative about the reception of a revelation. It can thus be generically classified as a REPORT OF A PROPHETIC REVELATION.

Setting

From a psychological standpoint it is possible that a narrative such as this might recount autobiographically the extraordinary experiences of a single night (as Petersen [*Haggai*, 111-12] has most recently observed), whether or not visionary elements are to be associated with dream-state phenomena (→ 1:8-17, Structure). From the standpoint of literary form, however, several considerations argue against this possibility here and make it difficult to assume that this is what the narration of 1:7–6:15 purports to represent.

First, the various individual prophecies have disparate temporal perspectives (→ Structure). If they were all initially revealed on the date that is cited in 1:7, then a good many of them would have to have been not only conceived as *vaticinia ex eventu* but also openly presented as such. This cannot be ruled out a priori, but it is not consistent with what is generally known about such prophecy after the fact. It is more typical to tell of a seer who lived long ago and foresaw things that eventually came to pass (e.g., Dan 8), than to tell of a seer who at a certain point in time "foresaw" things that had even then already taken place. In order to show that Zech 1:7–6:15 recounts what actually transpired in a single night, one would have to document some comparable use of the *vaticinium ex eventu* and explain what purpose it could serve.

Second, although the narrative structure of this whole section is basically defined in terms of a series of night visions, it is also defined in terms of interruptions within and deviations from this pattern (→ Structure). Such interruptions and deviations would probably not be characteristic of a narrative designed simply to recount what a prophet envisioned in the course of one night.

Third, the most telling consideration is the overt distinction that is drawn between the third person biographical perspective from which the introduction in 1:7 is framed and the first person autobiographical perspective from which the individual prophecies are framed (only 4:6aβ-7 has no explicit first person markers). By characterizing the narrator of this whole section as someone other than the prophet himself, the introduction assumes a rhetorical stance toward the revelatory experiences reported in 1:8–6:15 that differs from the rhetorical stance assumed in the individual units themselves. Throughout this section someone other than the prophet is telling the audience what the prophet has reported concerning his own revelatory experiences. It is from the less directly involved perspective of this other narrator, not from the more directly involved perspective of the prophetic recipient of the revelations, that they hang together collectively and constitute a single revelation that pertains to one particular point in time.

In other words, the shape of this section as a whole derives neither from the phenomenal characteristics of the revelatory experiences that are communicated through it nor from the way these revelatory experiences may have been ordered in the reporting activity through which they were initially communicated by the prophet himself. It derives instead from a process of subsequent reflection on the products of this reporting activity, through which it was discerned that the prophecies in 1:8–6:15 had some collective revelatory significance for the situation in which the community of returned exiles found itself on a particular day late in the second year of Darius's reign.

In view of these considerations it is probable not only that the composition of 1:7–6:15 was the result of redactional activity, through which prophecies originating over the course of several years were reworked into their present form. It is also probable that this is what such a form would have conventionally signaled to its audience. The shift in narrative viewpoint at the transition from the introduction (1:7) to the main body (1:8–6:15) clearly attributes the realization, which these prophecies relate as a single revelation to the date cited in the introduction, to someone who has studied them rather than to the prophet himself. The prophetic insight that has shaped this section as a whole thus belongs to the redactor, and this insight constitutes a revelation "to Zechariah" in the sense that it derives from Zechariah's reports of revelations he has received.

Zechariah was no doubt still alive in the second year of Darius's reign, and he continued to prophesy for several more years. It is thus perhaps possible that the introduction is a fictive device used by Zechariah himself to distinguish his retrospective insights concerning the cumulative significance of his own earlier prophecies from the views he once expressed in the prophecies themselves. It is also possible that such insights could have been reached and articulated by someone else, even during the prophet's own lifetime. Moreover, it is by no means necessary to suppose that the redactional production of 1:7–6:15 was contemporary with the date in 1:7. This section could also have been composed considerably later, in which case the redactor would be retrospectively locating a time in the prophet's career when several of his previous prophecies concerning return and rebuilding would have come decisively to a head. In any case, the form of 1:7–6:15 reflects the setting of a scribal group to which Zechariah himself may or may not have belonged. In such a group records of Zechariah's prophecies would have been preserved to be read and interpreted in view of the changing historical situation, so that they might eventually be redacted into a form that expressed the prophetic insights reached through this process of study and reflection.

Intention

The aim of this section is to relate the audience to a particular point in Zechariah's career when the completion of the temple-rebuilding project already begun by Zerubbabel, to which Zechariah had given his support, was threatened. Readers are meant to see this project as an integral part of a larger historical process that has been decisively shaped by Yahweh's redirection of cosmic forces within his heavenly realm. They can then recognize that thus far the prophet has accurately discerned the influence of Yahweh's heavenly initiatives on earthly developments, so that events from the initial return of the exiles years earlier to the reinstigation of the temple project under Zerubbabel have unfolded in accord with the divine goal. Readers are then confronted with the issue of whether they will be guided by the prophet's discernment of the heavenly developments that are impelling the project toward its completion. They are induced to do so by a figurative sketch of what the temple's completion would mean for the worldwide Jewish community under the conditions of the new emerging world order. Those who accept this prophetic vision of the destiny intended by Yahweh for Jerusalem, and who therefore give their support to the temple being rebuilt by Zerubbabel, will find the vision validated and their faith confirmed by the outcome.

For readers contemporary with the events described in this section of Zechariah, who lived when Zerubbabel's work was started but not yet finished, this text would have functioned as an inducement to support the temple project. For audiences of a later period this text would constitute a review of Zechariah's prophecies, seen in the light of the time when the issue of his credibility regarding the restoration's goals came decisively to a head. Those who read this text in the wake of the temple's completion are imaginatively put back into the circumstances that made this eventuality seem remote, and thus enabled to recapitulate the process of its being foretold and coming to pass. They can thus understand the Second Temple's significance in terms of Zechariah's view of why the old royal sanctuary needed to be rebuilt.

Bibliography

S. Amsler, "Zacharie et l'origine de l'apocalyptique," in *Congress Volume: Uppsala, 1971* (VTSup 22; Leiden: Brill, 1971) 227-31; K.-M. Beyse, *Serubbabel und die Königserwartungen der Propheten Haggai und Sacharja* (AzT 48; Stuttgart: Calwer, 1972); M. Bič, *Die Nachtgesichte des Sacharja* (BibS [N] 42; Neukirchen-Vluyn: Neukirchener, 1964); M. Floyd, "Cosmos and History in Zechariah's View of the Restoration (Zech 1:7–6:15)," in *Problems in Biblical Theology (Fest.* R. Knierim; ed. H. T. C. Sun and K. L. Eades; Grand Rapids: Eerdmans, 1997) 125-44; K. Galling, "Die Exilwende in der Sicht das Propheten Sacharja," *VT* 2 (1952) 18-36; H. Gese, "Anfang und Ende der Apokalyptik, dargestellt am Sacharjabuch," *ZTK* 70 (1973) 20-49; B. Halpern, "The Ritual Background of Zechariah's Temple Song," *CBQ* 40 (1978) 167-90; C. Jeremias, *Die Nachtgesichte des Sacharja* (FRLANT 117; Göttingen: Vandenhoeck & Ruprecht, 1977); W. H. Joubert, "The Determination of the Contents of Zechariah 1:7–2:17 through a Structural Analysis," in *Aspects of the Exegetical Process (OTWSA* 20-21; ed. W. C. van Wyk; Hercules, South Africa: NHW Press, 1977-78) 66-82; M. A. Knibb, "Prophecy and the Emergence of the Jewish Apocalypses," in *Israel's Prophetic Tradition (Fest.* P. R. Ackroyd; ed. R. Coggins, A. Phillips, and M. A. Knibb; Cambridge: Cambridge University Press, 1982) 155-80; R. North, "Prophecy to Apocalyptic via Zechariah," in *Congress Volume: Uppsala, 1971* (VTSup 22; Leiden: Brill, 1972) 47-71; D. L. Petersen, "Zechariah's Visions: A Theological Perspective," *VT* 34 (1984) 195-206; P. L. Redditt, "Zerubbabel, Joshua, and the Night Visions," *CBQ* 54 (1992) 249-59; L. Rignell, *Die Nachtgesichte des Sacharja* (Lund: Gleerup, 1950); J. W. Rothstein, *Die Nachtgesichte des Sacharja* (BWAT 8; Leipzig: Hinrichs, 1910); H.-G. Schöttler, *Gott inmitten seines Volkes* (TTS 43; Trier: Paulinus, 1987); K. Seybold, *Bilder zum Tempelbau* (SBS 70; Stuttgart: Katholisches Bibelwerk, 1974); idem, "Die Bildmotive in den Visionen des Propheten Sacharja," in *Studies on Prophecy* (VTSup 26; Leiden: Brill, 1974) 92-110; A. S. van der Woude, "Serubbabel und die messianischen Erwartungen des Propheten Sacharja," *ZAW* 100 (1988 Supplement) 138-56.

INTRODUCTION TO A REPORT OF A PROPHETIC REVELATION, 1:7

Text

The concluding direct discourse marker *(lē'mōr)* has a dual function. It connects 1:7 to the main body of this section as a whole (1:8–6:15), and it also leads from 1:7 into the first unit of this section (1:8-17). With respect to the former aspect of its function it indicates that the narrator regards all of 1:8–6:15 as, in effect, a "speech of Yahweh" addressed to Zechariah; and with respect to the latter aspect of its function it also indicates that Zechariah's report of what Yahweh "said" to him in 1:8-17 is in effect a speech of Yahweh addressed to the prophet's audience. The *RSV* translation of *lē'mōr* ("and Zechariah said . . .") attempts to capture the latter aspect of this dual function, but in a way that completely obscures the former aspect.

Structure

I. Date citation	1:7a
A. Day: the twenty-fourth	1:7aα^1
B. Month	1:7aα^2
1. Enumerated: the eleventh	
2. Named: Shebat	
C. Regnal year: the second of Darius	1:7aβ
II. Prophetic word formula	1:7b
A. Formula proper: the word of Yahweh came to Zechariah	1:7bα
B. Expansions	1:7bβ
1. Two-generation patronymic genealogy	1:7bβ^1
a. First generation: son of Berechiah	
b. Second generation: son of Iddo	
2. Specification of role: the prophet	1:7bβ^2
C. Direct discourse marker: *lēʾmōr* ("saying")	1:7bγ

The initial verse of 1:7–6:15 resembles the initial verse of the book's introductory section (1:1-6) and the initial verse of the book's following section (7:1–8:23), as well as the initial verses of Haggai's main sections (1:1; 2:1, 10; cf. 2:20). The basic elements that they all have in common are (1) a date citation consisting of the regnal year of the Persian emperor Darius and the month, which is sometimes named as well as enumerated; and (2) the use of the prophetic word formula to initiate the reporting narration of the section as a whole. Other elements are somewhat more variable. In this case the distinctive features include the specific identification of Darius's second year as the month of Shebat and a reiteration of the brief genealogy previously listed in 1:1b, along with the epithet *hannābîʾ* ("the prophet"), which here holds the same syntactically ambiguous position that it holds in 1:1b (→ 1:1-6, Structure).

In relation to its predecessor (1:1) this introductory verse moves the action ahead three months and gets rather more specific about the point in time when the revelation was received, as it also reiterates all the information with which Zechariah was initially characterized. In so doing it continues the previous introduction's emphasis on the transgenerational dimension of Zechariah's prophetic role, but also moves from the introductory section's broad generalities about Zechariah's continuity with the prophetic tradition of past generations to the specifics of his message for the present generation (→ 1:1-6, Structure). Beyond helping to provide such added specificity this particular date, "the twenty-fourth day of the eleventh month, i.e., the month of Shebat," was exactly five months after the work of rebuilding the temple began (Hag 1:15a), and exactly two months after Haggai performed a prophetic symbolic action in which he exhorted the people to consider what had happened since they celebrated the refoundation ceremony (Hag 2:10; cf. 2:18). The revelation in 1:8–6:15 is thus temporally located some months into the project, and a couple of months after the important event of the refoundation ceremony, but before the work was finished. The introductory information in 1:7 sets the scene for developing one of this section's main themes, the question of whether the task will ever be finished (→ 1:7–6:15, Structure).

Genre

Such verses are sometimes loosely called headings because they obviously resemble in some ways the superscriptions of other prophetic books; and they are sometimes called introductory formulas because they consist of formulaic elements. In this case the (→) prophetic word formula and date citation are here combined so as to initiate reporting narration. This usage stands in contrast with the way in which the prophetic word formula is typically used in prophetic superscriptions, so that it is not integrally connected with whatever it introduces (Tucker, 57-58). The formulaic components of 1:7 are thus not combined into a generically independent sort of heading, like a (→) prophetic superscription. This verse is rather an integral part of the REPORT OF A PROPHETIC REVELATION, which it serves to introduce.

Setting

→ 1:7–6:15, Setting.

Intention

This introduction sends readers into the immediately following report of the revelations received by Zechariah with a particular orientation. They are to view the action from the standpoint of an authoritative narrator, who retrospectively perceives that these revelations collectively have some bearing on the progress of the temple's reconstruction as of this particular date.

Bibliography

G. Tucker, "Prophetic Superscriptions and the Growth of a Canon," in *Canon and Authority* (ed. G. W. Coats and B. O. Long; Philadelphia: Fortress, 1977) 56-70.

ZECHARIAH IS COMMISSIONED TO REVEAL YAHWEH'S CREATION OF A NEW WORLD ORDER CONDUCIVE TO THE RESTORATION OF JUDAH AND JERUSALEM, 1:8-17

Text

In v. 8a the *RSV* translates the phrase *bammĕṣūlâ* as "in the glen." The root of the noun *mĕṣūlâ* is uncertain. It could derive from *ṣll*, in which case it might indicate a "shadowy" place (so Meyers and Meyers, *Haggai,* 110-11); or it could derive from *ṣwl*, in which case it might indicate a "deep" place or "depression" (on which the *RSV* is presumably based). In any case it describes some feature of the scene, which lies at the juncture between earth (where myrtle trees grow [v. 8a] and from which the angelic horse patrol has just returned [vv. 10-11]) and heaven (where Yahweh can be directly addressed [v. 12]). From such a vantage point the very structure of the cosmos lies exposed. In view of this context the derivation of *mĕṣūlâ* is perhaps better understood in terms of the latter alternative (so Chary, 57; Petersen, *Haggai,* 137; Ollenburger, 750), which would make it a reference to the primordial depths (cf. substantives also derived from *ṣwl* with a similar meaning in Exod 15:5; Isa 44:27; Jonah 2:4; Mic 7:19; Zech 10:11; Pss 68:23 [*RSV* 22]; 69:3, 16 [*RSV* 2, 15]; 88:7 [*RSV* 6]; 107:24; Neh 9:11). The figures on this scene are not actually "in" the primordial depths but are rather "standing" on their verge. The phrase *bammĕṣūlâ* thus might be rendered "by the abyss."

Structure

I. Introductory vision report formula	1:8aα^1
A. Main verb: I saw . . . *(rā'îtî)*	
B. Temporal modifier: in the night *(hallaylâ)*	
II. Vision proper	1:8aα^2-17
A. Coordinating interjection: and behold! *(wĕhinnēh)*	1:8aα^2
B. Description of the vision	1:8aβ-17
1. Scene	1:8aβb
a. Central figure: a man	1:8aβ
1) His characteristic pose: mounted on a red horse	1:8aβ^1
2) Their situation: standing among the trees in the glen	1:8aβ^2
b. Background figures: mounts of other colors behind him	1:8b
2. Dialogue	1:9-17
a. Concerning the horsemen and the completion of their mission	1:9-10
1) Prophet's question to the angelic interpreter	1:9a
a) Introduction: I said	1:9aα

b) Question proper: what are they?   1:9aβ

2) Angelic interpreter's reply to the prophet   1:9b

    a) Introduction: the angel who talked with
me said . . .   1:9bα

    b) Reply proper: I will show you   1:9bβ

3) The chief horseman's answer to the
prophet's question   1:10

    a) Introduction: the man standing among
the trees answered and said . . .   1:10a

    b) Answer proper: they are Yahweh's
earth patrol   1:10b

4) The horsemen's report to their chief   1:11

    a) Introduction: they answered the angel
of Yahweh standing among the trees
and said . . .   1:11aαβ¹

    b) Report proper: we have patrolled . . .
and all the earth remains at rest   1:11aβ²b

b. Concerning the prophet and the destiny
of Jerusalem   1:12-17

1) The chief horseman's complaint
to Yahweh   1:12

    a) Introduction: the angel of Yahweh
responded and said . . .   1:12aα¹

    b) Complaint proper: how long, O Lord?   1:12aα²b

2) Yahweh's reaction: gracious and comforting
words to the angelic interpreter   1:13

3) Angelic interpreter's speech to the prophet:
commission to prophesy   1:14-17

    a) Introduction: the angel who talked with
me said to me . . .   1:14aα

    b) Speech proper   1:14aβ-17

      (1) Commission to proclaim Yahweh's
plan of rebuilding the temple
in Jerusalem   1:14aβ-16

      (a) Commission formula: cry!
(qĕrāʾ lēʾmōr)   1:14aβ¹

      (b) Speech of Yahweh to
be proclaimed   1:14aβ²-16

        α. First part: Zion and
the nations   1:14aβ²-15

        aa. Messenger formula:
thus says Yahweh . . .   1:14aβ²

        bb. Speech proper   1:14b-15

          α) Yahweh's zeal for
Zion and Jerusalem   1:14b

          β) Yahweh's anger toward
the nations   1:15

β. Second part: Jerusalem itself   1:16
  aa. Introduction   1:16aα¹
    α) Therefore . . .
    β) Messenger formula:
      thus says Yahweh . . .
  bb. Speech proper   1:16aα²b
    α) What Yahweh has
      already done: I have
      returned with
      compassion   1:16aα²
    β) What will eventually
      result   1:16aβb
      aa) The temple will
        be rebuilt   1:16aβ¹
      bb) Oracle formula   1:16aβ²
      cc) Measurable progress
        will be made   1:16b
  2) Commission to proclaim the reelection
    of Jerusalem   1:17
    a) Reiterated commission formula:
      cry again! (*'ôd qĕrā' lē'mōr*)   1:17aα¹
    b) Speech of Yahweh to be proclaimed   1:17aα²b
      (1) Messenger formula: thus says
        Yahweh . . .   1:17aα²
      (2) Speech proper   1:17aβb
        (a) Promise for the cities of Judah
          in general: prosperity again   1:17aβ
        (b) Promise for Zion and Jerusalem
          in particular   1:17b
          α. For Zion: Yahweh will
            comfort again   1:17bα
          β. For Jerusalem: Yahweh
            will choose again   1:17bβ

The qal form of the verb *r'h* with which this vision report begins (*rā'îtî*, "I saw") does not necessarily indicate anything other than normal visual perception. The qualifying term *hallaylâ* (*RSV* "in the night," or, perhaps better, "last night"; see Meyers and Meyers, *Haggai*, 109-10, 126) suggests, however, that something unusual may be afoot, since the darkness of night is not normally the condition most conducive to sharpness of sight. Likewise there is at first nothing particularly extraordinary about the scene that is conjured up: a man mounted on a red horse positioned among a group of trees. The qualifying phrase *'ăšer bammĕṣūlâ* ("which is by the abyss"; → Text) suggests, however, that this is no ordinary earthly setting but rather a place of cosmic significance. The background presence of an undetermined number of other mounted personnel is impressionistically implied by the mere mention of their variously colored horses at the close of v. 8. Neither the identity of

349

these riders nor the nature of their location is spelled out any further, but both of these matters are somewhat clarified as the account of the vision unfolds.

The agent of clarification is an angelic being whose interposition between the prophet and the various figures within the scene is not apparent until the prophet asks him what they are (v. 9a). Both the tag line that is applied to this angelic being (*hammal'āk haddōbēr bî,* "the angel who explains things to me") and the nature of his reply to the prophet (*'ar'ekkā; RSV* "I will show you") show his role, which is to provide paranormal guidance for the prophet's understanding of his visionary experience (v. 9b). The angelic interpreter thus directs the prophet into the scene itself, where the head horseman explains to him what this group of riders are and what they have been doing. They are Yahweh's cosmic security and intelligence forces who have been sent by him to patrol the earth. Having accomplished their mission, they now report back that "all the earth remains at rest" (v. 11b).

Critics have questioned who the recipient of this report is (D. J. Clark, "The Case of the Vanishing Angel," *BT* 33 [1982] 213-18). He is identified as "the angel of Yahweh standing among the myrtle trees" (v. 11a). Thus far the phrase "standing among the myrtle trees" has twice been applied only to the head horseman, who in both cases is also explicitly said to be a "man" (*'îš*), and the term "angel" has been applied only to the angelic interpreter (v. 9bα). Some have identified the recipient of the report with the head horseman by virtue of their common positioning, and others have identified him with the angelic interpreter by virtue of their common angelic nature.

If the head horseman is the recipient, it follows that v. 11 describes the report of the whole troop to their superior, and that v. 12 then describes the recommendation (as it were) brought back by the head horseman to their commander-in-chief, Yahweh himself, who initially ordered the reconnaissance patrol. By describing the role of the head horseman in this way the narrator would be saving until now the additional bit of information that this "man," and by implication the whole troop as well, all belong to the category of angelic beings. (Angels can appear in human form, e.g., Josh 5:13-15; Judg 13:9b-11.) If the angelic interpreter is also "the angel of Yahweh" mentioned in vv. 11-12, however, it follows that he has abandoned his role as an intermediary between the scene and the prophet, and has assumed the same location as the head horseman within the scene ("standing among the myrtle trees") in order to serve as an intermediary between the mounted patrol and Yahweh when they return from their mission.

This ambiguity seems not to be conclusively resolvable. If Yahweh himself sent the patrol out (v. 10b), however, why would there need to be any intermediary between him and them when they return? In such sparsely descriptive narration it seems unlikely that a phrase reiterated in association with one character, so as to become virtually an identifying epithet, would then suddenly be shifted to another character. Such considerations make it somewhat more probable that "the angel standing among the myrtle trees" is the head horseman, acting here as the one to whom Yahweh has delegated the command of this angelic host. In this capacity he receives their report (v. 11) and then addresses Yahweh concerning its implications for a change in the divine policy toward Judah and Jerusalem (v. 12).

In any case the report itself, that "all the earth remains at rest," is not relayed directly to Yahweh. He is addressed in v. 12 as if he has been present all along, so as to overhear all that has been said. Through a reproachful complaint Yahweh is asked, in effect, whether the peacefulness of the earth does not signal that it is now time for a change. Yahweh's relationship between Jerusalem and Judah has lately been characterized by a lack of compassion (*rḥm;* *RSV* "mercy") and by anger (*z'm; RSV* "indignation") on his part, but this has now gone on long enough to have reached a critical turning point (i.e., "seventy years"). The world situation is propitious, and the time is right for something different.

Yahweh signals his intention to initiate a new era in his subsequent speech to the angelic interpreter (v. 13). The substance of his message is first described only in the most general way, as "good" and "compassionate" (*rḥm;* *RSV* "comforting"), but in view of the broadly negative terms in which the recent past has been described, these broadly positive terms are sufficient to indicate a decisive change on Yahweh's part. Yahweh's design emerges in greater detail as the angelic interpreter relays to the prophet the words of Yahweh that define the key role he is to play in realizing the divine plan (vv. 14-17). It will be the prophet's role both to mark the beginning of this new era in the unfolding course of events and to interpret its theological significance. The event that manifests the new age is the restoration of the Jerusalem temple within the context of the ongoing return of the exiles to resettle and rebuild the city as a whole (v. 16aβb).

This historical process is evidence of an underlying reversal in Judah's relationship with Yahweh vis-à-vis the other nations of the world. When Yahweh was more angry with his own people than he was with the rest, he would let enemies dominate Judah as a means of expressing his anger. But the foreign rulers outdid themselves in oppressing Judah and made their domination harder than was necessary to convey Yahweh's wrath. Yahweh has thus become jealous for his own people, and he is now more angry with those who oppressed Judah than he is with Judah (vv. 14b-15). This turnabout is shown partly in the new world order inaugurated by the Persians, in which Judah's former dominators have become the dominated, and partly in the new construction envisioned for Jerusalem, where Yahweh has now shown his compassion once again (v. 16aα). The prophet is to emphasize further that the rebuilding of Jerusalem also portends the recovery of the socioeconomic stability that Judah once enjoyed (v. 17aβ), as well as the renewal of Judah's divinely elected status (v. 17b).

The realm that the prophet has entered through this vision lies beyond the ordinary earthly human realm, but it does not lie completely within heaven itself. He has entered the zone of the juncture between heaven and earth, where the activities of angelic beings represent the impinging of heavenly developments on earthly ones. Yahweh has direct access to and direct control over this realm. He ordains the movements of the angels within it, and from it he deploys angels to affect earthly events somewhat more indirectly. The prophet has been allowed to view the very nexus of this cosmic connection (here "by the abyss," v. 8a; → Text), and thus to understand the interplay among the larger forces that obviously affect human life but whose significance is difficult for human minds to grasp. From this vantage point he is able to perceive the meaning of the current world situation for Judah in the light of Yahweh's intentions for his people.

Genre

Various typologies have been proposed for texts describing prophetic visions, based on such factors as the kinds of religious experience from which visionary language might result, the static or dynamic positioning of the main figures within the scene, the kinds of visual images involved, the presence or absence of divine beings, the relationship between things seen and things said or heard, the use or disuse of question-and-answer interaction between the prophet and a divine being, etc. (see the reviews of proposals in Long, 353-55; and Niditch, 1-12). Such typologies have resulted in artificial distinctions that seem arbitrary and that finally break down when actually confronted with the heterogeneity of the texts themselves. (Amsler ["La parole visionnaire," 359-61] identifies twenty-two texts that can be categorized as vision reports: Amos 7:1-3, 4-6, 7-9; 8:1-3; 9:1-4; Isa 6:1-11; Jer 1:11-12, 13-16; 24:1-10; 38:21-22; Ezek 1-3; 8-10 + 11:22-25; 37:1-14; 40-48; and the eight visions of Zech 1-6 [→ 1:7–6:15, Structure].) The phenomenon seems to require descriptive categories that are analytically less ambitious and substantially more comprehensive.

One feature that generally characterizes all such texts is the use of terms denoting visual perception, almost always including some form of the verb *r'h* ("see") to introduce the narration of the vision from a first person point of view. (The only exception is Ezek 37:1-14; and Ezek 40:2 uses a nominal rather than a verbal form of the root *r'h*, i.e., *mar'ôt* ["visions"].) This terminology is formulaic, but it can take various forms. Most often there is simply either the perfect form *rā'îtî* ("I saw") or, if the act of visual perception is coordinated with some other verbal action in the narration, the *waw*-consecutive imperfect form *wāyyēr'eh* ("and I saw"). The hiphil can also be used to describe the prophet's sense of a divinely authored perception, e.g., *hir'anî* ("he [i.e., Yahweh] showed me") in Amos 7:1, 4, 7; 8:1. Such terminology can be used in conjunction with other formulaic expressions such as date citations of various sorts (e.g., Ezek 8:1-2; Isa 6:1); the idiomatic phrase "to lift the eyes" (*nṣ' 'ynym;* e.g., Zech 2:1 [*RSV* 1:18]; 2:5 [*RSV* 1]; etc.); and the formulaic description of possession that is characteristic of Ezekiel: "the hand of Yahweh was upon me" (e.g., Ezek 8:1). In two of Jeremiah's visions the prophetic word formula ("the word of Yahweh came to me") first introduces the narration, and *r'h* then appears in the immediately following question-and-answer exchange between Yahweh and the prophet: ". . . 'what do you see?' And I said, 'I see . . .'" (Jer 1:11, 13). In every case the formulaic use of *r'h* indicates that the prophet has perceived something, and that this is being reported from a first person perspective. The interjection *hinnēh* ("behold") often serves as a transitional link between the formulaically reported fact of the prophet's having seen something and the description of the vision's content.

This formulaic use of *r'h,* in and of itself, does not constitute any technical terminology for the description of prophetic visionary phenomena. Any persons seeing something very ordinary, and doing so in a quite normal way, might well report their observations in just the same terms. It is the extraordinary nature of what is seen that defines prophetic vision reports as such. In every case there is some indication that the figures appearing on the field of perception, whether or not they are to any extent bizarre, have some revelatory significance. This revelatory significance is often obvious because the figures within the scene are superhuman beings, or because the scene itself is heavenly or supramundane. But even the most ordinary objects of human daily life, such as a basket of fruit (Amos 8:1-2) or a boiling pot (Jer 1:13), can take on a revelatory significance when Yahweh himself shows them to the prophet or speaks to the prophet about them, or when — as in the case of several visions from Zechariah — an angelic being appears to interpret them. The potential for revelatory significance can thus be signaled in a variety of ways, but in every case there is some indication that the things seen show something about Yahweh's involvement in human affairs.

Following the description of what the prophet has seen, the narrative of a vision report is typically developed so as to elucidate its meaning. Sometimes there is simply an abrupt transition from the verbal image to a direct statement of what it portends. This statement may be an oracular speech of Yahweh (e.g., Amos 9:1-4), but it need not take that form (e.g., Jer 38:21-22). Generally, however, the narrative development entails dialogue between the prophet and Yahweh, or between the prophet and some other heavenly being, which may or may not be cast in the form of questions and answers. When there are questions and answers, Yahweh or his angelic representative sometimes questions the prophet (e.g., Jer 1:13; Ezek 37:3), and the prophet sometimes questions Yahweh or his angelic representative (e.g., Zech 1:9). In some cases the meaning of the symbolic image is explicitly stated in the course of the dialogue (e.g., Jer 1:11-12), but in most cases it emerges implicitly from the way in which the narrative unfolds. The narrative action may consist only of dialogue (as in this case, Zech 1:8-17), but it may also include other kinds of activity along with dialogue (e.g., Zech 2:5-9 [*RSV* 1-5]). Often the narrative involves or culminates in a summary statement of the revelation in the form of an oracular speech of Yahweh (e.g., Isa 6:1-11), but the dialogue may also remain on the level of conversational exchange without necessarily leading to such overt pronouncements concerning Yahweh's intentions (e.g., Zech 5:5-11). In any case, it is the prophet's assessment of Yahweh's intentions, whether these are expressed explicitly or implicitly, that the vision report serves to communicate.

Hanhart would like to designate vision reports with an angelic interpreter as apocalyptic visions (pp. 48-50). This designation is appropriate if it serves to indicate only that such vision reports contain a motif that is common in other apocalyptic texts and are thus apocalyptic in a general sense. By virtue of this feature these texts do not necessarily constitute a genre of their own, however, or even a formally distinct subtype of the prophetic vision report. They do not on this account have the form of an apocalypse (→ 12:1–14:21, Genre).

The present text (1:8-17) has all the basic hallmarks of a PROPHETIC VISION REPORT. It commences with the most basic form of the vision report formula, the first person qal perfect form of *r'h* ("I saw") plus the transitional interjection *hinnēh* ("behold"). There are three indications that the scene has revelatory significance. First, in the vision report formula itself the qualifying noun phrase *hallaylâ* (lit. "the night") is used adverbially to modify the main verb. This has raised questions regarding the relationship between visionary phenomena and dreams (→ Setting), but on its face this phrase simply indicates that the prophet's visualization occurs sometime during the night, i.e., when it is dark. Ordinary visual perception requires light, and things that are visible in the dark thus have some extraordinary significance. Second, the location of the central figure "by the abyss" (v. 8a; → Text), together with the nature of the action that subsequently takes place, indicates that the scene is supramundane. Third, the presence of the angelic interpreter, whom the prophet immediately recognizes as such (v. 9), indicates that there is some divine message to be communicated (*mal'āk,* which the *RSV* renders "angel," means literally "messenger"). The action that ensues consists entirely of dialogue — although in the course of the dialogue other action, such as the reconnoitering of the earth by the angelic mounted patrol (v. 11), is reported. The dialogue is prompted by the prophet's questioning of the angelic interpreter, but it extends to include the leader of the angelic patrol (v. 11) and Yahweh himself (vv. 12-13), each addressing another in turn. The dialogue culminates in an oracular pronouncement of Yahweh, communicated to the prophet through the intermediation of the angelic interpreter. The oracle elucidates the meaning of the scene by disclosing that, in view of what the angelic host has reported about conditions on earth, it is now time for the prophet to embark on the mission of communicating Yahweh's new plans for his people.

Setting

The citation of a particular date (1:7a) in the introduction (1:7) to this whole section of the book (1:7–6:15), combined with the adverbial use of *hallaylâ* (*RSV* "in the night") in the formulaic introduction (1:8aα[1]) to this particular vision report (1:8-17), has suggested to some scholars that all eight of Zechariah's visions are being recounted within the time frame of a single night (→ 1:7–6:15, Structure). This has raised questions regarding the possibility of a relationship between these vision reports and dream phenomena. Many scholars suppose that the reports are somehow rooted in dream experiences, and some have also recently argued that the form of such reports reflects the practice of dream interpretation (so Niditch, Hanhart; see below).

As Amsler has emphasized ("La parole visionnaire," 361-62), the conventional terms in which prophetic visions are described afford virtually no information about the kinds of religious experience from which they may have originated. But one small piece of evidence in Zech 4:1 has some bearing on the matter in this particular case. This verse describes the inception of visionary experience in terms of the prophet's being roused by the angelic interpreter, in a manner that is comparable to being awakened from sleep. Since one goes to sleep, rather than wakes up, in order to dream, "awakening" is hardly the metaphor that one would choose to describe a revelatory experience that is imparted through a dream (unless, perhaps, there were some contextual indication of an ironic inversion of descriptive terms, which is not the case here). Such language points instead to a state of altered consciousness that stands in relation to the normal waking state much as the normal waking state stands in relation to sleep, i.e., a state of heightened awareness. In sum, there is hardly any evidence regarding the nature of the experience in which vision reports are rooted, but the one clue that we do have does not suggest thinking in terms of a dream state. It rather suggests the kind of trance in which certain powers of perception, particularly the capacity for inner visualization, are markedly enhanced.

Niditch (pp. 18-19) and Hanhart (pp. 47-48) regard the question-and-answer exchange that characterizes many accounts of symbolic visions as indicative of a close relationship between prophetic vision reports and the ancient mantic art of dream interpretation. There do appear to be some similarities between vision reports and the forms of expression associated with dream interpretation. In particular, dream reports sometimes use much the same formulaic terminology as vision reports to describe the perception of symbolic images (e.g., Dan 4:6-14 [*RSV* 10-18] begins with the Aramaic equivalent of the vision report formula discussed above). This linkage of dream interpretation and prophetic vision reports on the basis of the question-and-answer motif is problematic, however, in several respects.

First, in some prophetic vision reports this motif does not appear at all (e.g., Jer 38:21-23; Zech 3:1-10). Moreover, the narrative descriptions of dream interpretation do not generally portray the procedure as involving any question-and-answer exchange between the dreamer and the interpreter concerning the meaning of the dream itself (e.g., Gen 40:1-19; 41:1-36; Dan 4:1-24 [*RSV* 4-27]). In the very act of bringing the dream to an interpreter there is probably some implicit questioning on the part of the dreamer with regard to its meaning, and likewise in the very act of the interpreter's hearing the dream report there is probably some implicit questioning on the part of the interpreter with regard to the contents of the dream. But the fact that both sorts of inquiry can be conventionally described in accounts of dream-interpretation procedures, without using any explicit direct question-and-answer exchange between the dreamer and the interpreter, suggests that such exchange is not as definitive a factor in the process as Niditch and Hanhart suppose. If dream interpretation need not involve any question-and-answer exchanges, and if there can be prophetic vision reports that lack such an exchange altogether, any linkage of the two phenomena on the basis of this alleged commonality becomes rather weak.

Moreover, there is a fundamental difference between dream interpretation and visionary prophecy that finally makes their comparison untenable. In the process of dream interpretation one person is interpreting the experience of another person. The dreamer tells the dream to the interpreter, and the interpreter then tells the meaning to the dreamer. The report of the dream and the explanation of its meaning are thus expressed in two different and separate forms, each of which is spoken by one of the two different persons involved. In the practice of visionary prophecy, however, one person is interpreting his or her own experience. The prophet tells both the vision and the interpretation to the audience. As we have seen, the interpretation may not involve the prophet's interaction with anyone else at all. Even when there is a question-and-answer exchange of some kind, whether between the prophet and Yahweh or between the prophet and an angelic interpreter, these are characters within the vision. Neither Yahweh nor the angelic interpreter is another "person" analogous to the dream interpreter, to whom the prophet would be bringing the vision for an explanation. Rather, both are characters in the prophet's own internal dialogue, which serve to dramatize his or her own reflections on the meaning of the visualization. The vision report is therefore a single textual unit in which elements of visual description and interpretive explication are integrated in one and the same compositional form.

It is thus necessary to distinguish between such forms as the (→) dream report and the (→) dream interpretation speech on the one hand and the (→) prophetic vision report on the other hand, as well as to distinguish between the two different kinds of mantic activity in which these forms of expression had their respective settings. Dream reports and dream interpretation speeches emerged from a divinatory procedure in which one person brought a dream experience to be analyzed and interpreted by another person. Prophetic vision reports emerged from a divinatory procedure in which one person communicated preternatural insights based on what had been discerned in the prophet's own mind's eye, perhaps while in a trance state. Such a distinction is presupposed in the story of Daniel's interpretation of Nebuchadnezzar's dream (Dan 2). The king commands his diviners to interpret a dream, which he refuses to tell them. Their reply, to the effect that interpretation under such conditions is humanly impossible (2:2-11), shows that dream interpretation did not conventionally involve both visualization and interpretation on the diviner's part. Modeling a different type of prophetic inspiration, Daniel is able both to discern what the king saw in his dream and to disclose the meaning, thus combining these two elements in a single speech (2:26-45). The distinction between the forms of expression pertaining to dream interpretation and the form of the prophetic vision report begins to blur only when both are appropriated for a derivative use in a different setting. The dream report gets subsumed into the prophetic vision report, as an alternative convention for describing symbolic images with revelatory significance, when the prophetic vision report itself is developed by those who produced apocalypses into one of the central features of that genre (e.g., → Dan 7; Zech 12:1–14:21, Genre). Although we have no direct information on the matter, it is certainly plausible that in Zechariah's time both the distinctively different mantic activities of dream interpretation and visionary prophecy were practiced by the same prophetic groups. Even if these two forms of divination had a common setting in this sense, however, nothing suggests that the prophetic vision report was closely related to dream interpretation in any other way.

Building on Long's observation that vision reports were sometimes given in reply to oracular inquiries (p. 365), we can be somewhat more specific about the kind of divinatory procedure in which visionary prophecy played a major role. An oracular inquiry was an attempt by a prophet to discern Yahweh's will with regard to a particular set of circumstances or a pressing problem. Both the terminology and the motivation for such inquiries were variable. A king might "inquire" *(drš)* concerning the prospect of military victory (1 Kgs 22:5); and the elders of the exile community might likewise "inquire" about their general welfare (Ezek 20:1). One might also "entreat the face" *(ḥlh 'et-pĕnê)* of Yahweh (Zech 7:2; *RSV* "entreat the favor") regarding a cultic custom, or simply "ask" *(š'l;* Jer 38:14b) or "pray" to Yahweh (hithpael of *pll;* Jer 42:2-4) through a prophet. Sometimes a prophet might undertake an oracular inquiry on her or his own initiative, in which case there was apparently some preparation involved. Such preparation could be described in terms of sentinel imagery: "I will station myself on the tower, and look to see *(lir'ôt)* what [Yahweh] will say to me" (Hab 2:1). It might then take some time for the revelatory response to come — ten days in one case (Jer 42:7). Sometimes this revelation might assume the form of a vision (e.g., 1 Kgs 22:19-23; Jer 38:21-22), but other times not (e.g., Jer 42:7-22; Ezek 20:2-44); and sometimes it might be a "vision" in only a figurative sense (i.e., a *ḥāzôn,* as in [→] Hab 2:1-5). Visionary experience thus appears to be a state of consciousness that prophets sometimes attained in the course of oracular inquiries, and vision reports were therefore one of the ways in which they sometimes answered such inquiries.

Although Zechariah once entertained and responded to a request for an oracular inquiry (Zech 7:2-7), he did not respond on that occasion with a vision report (→ 7:1–8:23, Structure); and although there are eight vision reports in 1:7–6:15, there is no explicit indication that any of them was prompted by such a request. Since Zechariah is known to have engaged in this divinatory practice, it is plausible to suppose that the eight vision reports may have been the result of oracular inquiries. Lacking any direct information regarding a request, however, we can only surmise that they resulted from the kind of oracular inquiry that prophets might undertake on their own initiative.

This particular vision report reflects a historical situation in which there was peace and stability on the international level (v. 11b); but on the local level the rebuilding of the temple remained unrealized, and Jerusalem was not yet repopulated enough to become economically viable (vv. 16-17). The quietness of the world order is given a positive theological significance and is taken to be a sign of Yahweh's decisive change of heart toward Judah, as well as a concrete indication of Judah's presently propitious prospects despite the difficulties encountered by the returned exiles. Some have seen in v. 15 an expression of anti-Persian sentiment, but in view of the fact that the new world order so favorable to Judah has been created precisely by the Persians, this interpretation seems unlikely. It is more likely that the "complacent nations" with whom Yahweh is angry (*haggôyim haššaʾănannîm; RSV* "nations that are at ease") are Judah's former enemies, and that their present defeat and domination by the Persians are concrete indications of Yahweh's turning in anger on these former enemies. They previously "assisted" Yahweh (*'ozrû; RSV* "furthered") in bringing about the "disaster" *(rā'â)* through which he showed his unmerciful anger toward Judah, but in the total reversal that Yahweh is bringing about the Persians now play an analogously ancillary role in giving Judah the historical opportunity through which Yahweh shows his compassionate favor toward his people.

This unit could conceivably be dated as early as the time of Cyrus (ca. 535), when the Persians first took firm control of the international situation and the return was just getting underway (Ezra 1–2; Mitchell, 121-23). V. 16a, however, seems to imply that there is some sign of Yahweh's having "returned" *(šwb)* to Jerusalem, which suggests that there is already some cultic manifestation of his presence there. This suggests a later date, after the upheavals following the death of Cyrus's son Cambyses, in the context of the international equilibrium reestablished during the reign of Darius (ca. 520). By this time the restoration of the cult seems to have gotten as far as the erection of an altar and the resumption of sacrifice within the sacred precincts, but the work of rebuilding the temple itself was not yet finished (Ezra 3:2-6).

Intention

A prophetic vision report resembles (→) a report of a prophetic revelation in emphasizing the reception of revelation rather than its communication to some audience (Amsler, "La parole visionnaire," 361-62). For example, prophecies introduced with the messenger formula ("thus says Yahweh") claim to be reporting something that was revealed to prophetic intermediaries by Yahweh, but in a way that foregrounds the delivery rather than the dispatch of the revelatory message. In contrast the vision report, like all reports of revelation generally, describes the point at which prophets become aware of having a revelation to deliver. They impressionistically communicate not only the imaginary form in which the revelation first dawned on the prophetic consciousness but also the reflective process through which the prophets came to grasp the full significance of such experiences. A vision report portrays the prophet's response to his or her own revelatory experience, and thus provides its audience with a model of how to respond to the prophet. The prophet apprehends a visualization and subsequently interacts with it, so as to grasp it more profoundly. The audience is meant to do likewise with their initial apprehension of the prophet's report.

This audience response is informed in two ways by the description of the visual symbol that is a conventional part of the vision report. First, the symbol works its way into the audience's imagination, as well as into their thought. They cannot actually share the prophet's experience, but they can catch and hold in their own mind's eye some representation of what the prophet has "seen," so that their reflection on the prophetic message comes to be shaped by this visual symbol. Second, the description also invites them to seek in the observable reality of their own lives some intuitive, visible sign corroborating the prophet's assessment of Yahweh's involvement in their situation. It invites them to reconsider how they "see" themselves, and thus how they act, in relation to their circumstances.

In this particular example of the genre the prophet envisions an angelic host that has returned from earthly maneuvers to report that a stable world order now reigns. Through the prophet's interaction with the figures in the scene he comes to realize that the normally invisible cosmic forces deployed by Yahweh have influenced the world situation, so that it now stands at a decisive turning point. Yahweh has removed Judah's enemies from their previous position of dominance, thus altering the form in which he previously expressed his anger, and has created an international context through which he can instead show favor toward his people. The prophet comes to realize further that his role is to show that the condition of exile has now come to an end, theologically speaking, and that the new historical opportunities brought about by the Persians signify Yahweh's intentions to renew a positive relationship with his people. As the audience watches the prophet come to this realization, they are invited to see whether the current world situation does not also seem to them to be remarkably propitious for the restoration of Judah, and whether the rebuilding of the temple in such a context might not signify both the renewed theophanic significance of Jerusalem and the prospect of economic viability for the community created by the returning exiles.

Bibliography

S. Amsler, "La parole visionnaire des prophètes," *VT* 31 (1981) 359-63; F. Horst, "Die Visionsschilderungen des alttestamentlichen Propheten," *EvT* 20 (1960) 193-205; J. Lindblom, *Prophecy in Ancient Israel* (Philadelphia: Fortress, 1967) 122-48; B. O. Long, "Reports of Visions among the Prophets," *JBL* 95 (1976) 353-65; S. Niditch, *The Symbolic Vision in Biblical Tradition* (HSM 30; Chico, Calif.: Scholars Press, 1980); M. Sister, "Die Typen der prophetischen Visionen in der Bibel," *MGWJT* 78 (1934) 399-430.

ZECHARIAH ENVISIONS YAHWEH'S INVOLVEMENT IN THE PACIFICATION OF HIS PEOPLE'S ENEMIES, 2:1-4 (*RSV* 1:18-21)

Structure

I. First act	2:1-2
A. Introductory vision report formula	2:1a
1. Expressed in terms of movement: I lifted my eyes	2:1aα
2. Expressed in terms of perception: I saw *(wā'ēre')*	2:1aβ
B. Vision proper	2:1b-2
1. Coordinating interjection: and behold! *(wĕhinnēh)*	2:1bα

The narration first indicates, by means of the idiomatic expression *nś' 'ynym* ("to lift the eyes"), that the prophet's field of perception has shifted to behold something new. The angelic host standing "by the abyss" has disappeared, and four horns have come into view. No details are given as to whether these are the horns of some animal, whether they are attached to anything, etc. Nor is there any information regarding the background against which they appear. The vision report is basically structured as a contrast between this stark and minimally described scenario that the prophet himself sees (2:1-2) and the four additional figures that Yahweh subsequently "shows" him (2:3-4; note the hiphil form of *r'h* in v. 3aα). Yahweh brings onto the field of vision four *ḥārāšîm* or "artisans" (*RSV* "smiths"), i.e., persons who have whatever technical ability is necessary to work with whatever material the horns are made of.

In response to the prophet's question about the horns (v. 2a), the angelic interpreter identifies them as symbols of the various powers that have attempted to destroy the national identity of Yahweh's people by dispersing the population of both the northern and the southern kingdoms (v. 2b). In response to the prophet's question about the artisans (2:4a), they are identified as forces that have come to "terrify" (hiphil of *ḥrd*) and to "cast down" *(ydh)* the nations that scattered Judah (v. 4bβ). A contrast is thus drawn between two kinds of imperial powers: those represented by the horns, which have often appeared throughout Israel's history and have maintained control by such dehumanizing policies as mass deportation ("so that none held head high," v. 4bα^2); and those represented by the artisans, which have more recently appeared and have been shown by Yahweh to be capable of ruling in a somewhat more humane and creative way.

This historical development holds within itself a certain transformative potential that is brought out in the answer to the prophet's second question, "What are they coming to do?" (v. 4a). The artisans are said to represent the advent of forces with the power to pacify the imperialistic "scatterers." Such an advent implies that the world is being ordered differently, so that Judah can now resume some new place among the nations, and the threat of dispersion no longer poses a threat to their identity as the people of Yahweh.

Genre

This unit shows the definitive traits that characterize a PROPHETIC VISION RE-PORT (→ 1:8-17, Genre). Each of its two acts, 2:1-2 and 2:3-4, is introduced by a type of vision report formula. The revelatory significance of the scene is initially indicated by the prophet's questioning of the angelic interpreter (v. 2a), but it is further underscored by the hiphil form of the vision report formula in v. 3: "Yahweh showed me. . . ." The meaning of the symbolic images is elucidated entirely through dialogue, first in a question-and-answer exchange between the prophet and the angelic interpreter regarding the significance of the horns, and then through another question-and-answer exchange regarding the significance of the artisans' effect on the horns. (It is not clear whether the second exchange is between Yahweh and the prophet, or between the angelic interpreter and the prophet.)

Setting

This vision was probably reported by the prophet in the course of an oracular inquiry undertaken on his own initiative (→ 1:8-17, Setting). Its sharp contrast between imperial powers that "scatter" and those that rule more creatively reflects the establishment of Persian hegemony over the region extending from Babylon to Judah. The oracular inquiry was probably prompted by the prophet's desire to discern whether Yahweh's purpose for Judah was to any extent manifest in this recent development, and the reply is decidedly affirmative. The possibility of a new future for Judah, and perhaps for Israel as a whole, lies within this political innovation.

Intention

The prophet is here portrayed in the process of realizing the potential that Persian rule holds for Judah. This new kind of imperium threatens to terrify and overthrow all those with any vested interests in the exilic status quo. The audience is thus challenged to examine where their vested interests lie, and to consider whether they should not align themselves with the political possibilities afforded by the new world order. Their thoughts along these lines are informed by the imaginative visual imagery, which emphasizes that the new rulers have the same kind of superiority over the old rulers that skilled artisans have over the materials and objects on which they work.

Bibliography

R. M. Good, "Zechariah's Second Night Vision (Zech 2:1-4)," *Bib* 63 (1982) 56-59.

ZECHARIAH ENVISIONS YAHWEH PROVIDING THE RESTORATION OF JERUSALEM WITH PROTECTION AND PROSPERITY, 2:5-9 (*RSV* 1-5)

Structure

I. Introductory vision report formula	2:5aα
A. Expressed in terms of movement: I lifted my eyes	2:5aα¹
B. Expressed in terms of perception: I saw *(wā'ēre')*	2:5aα²
II. Vision proper	2:5aβ-9
A. First act	2:5aβ-6
1. Coordinating interjection: and behold! *(wĕhinnēh)*	2:5aβ¹
2. Description	2:5aβ²-9
a. Scene	2:5aβ²b
1) Central figure: a man	2:5aβ²
2) Characteristic pose: a measuring line in his hand	2:5b
b. Action	2:6-9
1) Dialogue between the prophet and the man	2:6
a) Prophet's question	2:6a
(1) Introduction: I said . . .	2:6aα¹
(2) Question proper: where are you going?	2:6aα²β
b) Man's reply	2:6b
(1) Introduction: he said to me . . .	2:6bα¹
(2) Reply proper: to measure Jerusalem	2:6bα²β
B. Second act	2:7-9
1. Coordinating interjection: and behold! *(wĕhinnēh)*	2:7aα¹

2. Description $2:7a\alpha^2$-9

  a. Interaction involving the angelic interpreter
     and another angel $2:7a\alpha^2b$

    1) Angelic interpreter's action:
      he came forward $2:7a\alpha^2\beta$

    2) Other angel's reaction: he came forward
      to meet him   2:7b

  b. Speech of angelic interpreter to the other angel   2:8-9

    1) Introduction: he said to him . . . $2:8a\alpha^1$

    2) Speech proper $2:8a\alpha^2$-9

      a) Commission to carry a message $2:8a\alpha^2\beta$

        (1) Double command: run and say! $2:8a\alpha^2$

        (2) Designation of the recipient:
          that young man $2:8a\beta^1$

        (3) Direct discourse marker *(lē'mōr)* $2:8a\beta^2$

      b) Message proper   2:8b-9

        (1) Basic statement concerning a future
          of peace and plenty for Jerusalem   2:8b

        (2) Rationale in terms of Yahweh's relation
          to the city: speech of Yahweh   2:9

          (a) Introduction: I will be for her . . . $2:9a\alpha^1$

          (b) Oracle formula: says Yahweh $2:9a\alpha^2$

          (c) Conclusion $2:9a\beta b$

            α. With respect to the city's
              exterior: wall of fire $2:9a\beta$

            β. With respect to the city's
              interior: glory   2:9b

The narration of the third vision begins with the idiom *nś' 'ynym* ("to lift the eyes"), which shows that the prophet's field of perception has shifted to behold something new. The prophet sees "a man" (*'îš;* cf. 1:8) holding a measuring line, with whom he converses directly, without the intermediation of the angelic interpreter (2:5-6). The prophet questions the man concerning the nature of his errand, which is to take Jerusalem's measurements. The angelic interpreter then intervenes, only to be intercepted by another angelic figure who entrusts him with an urgent message (2:7-9). Although the function of the message is to clarify the significance of the scene for the prophet, there is some ambiguity as to whether he is the one intended to receive it. The recipient is designated as *hanna'ar hallāz* (*RSV* "that young man"), which could conceivably refer to either the prophet or the man with the measuring line. Since Zechariah has previously been characterized as old enough to have addressed the parents of the present generation (1:2), this phrase probably refers to the surveyor. In any case the message explicates the theological significance of the fact that is represented in the first part of the vision, namely, that the restoration of Jerusalem has made measurable progress.

The imagery of the measuring line harks back to 1:16b, where the prophet is commissioned to prophesy that "the measuring line (*qāw[h]*) shall be stretched out over Jerusalem." This is somewhat different from the kind of "measuring line" *(ḥebel middâ)* mentioned here. The former is typically used in the construction or demolition of buildings not only to indicate their dimensions but also to justify corners, level walls, etc. (e.g., Isa 44:13). The latter is typically used to mark off or subdivide a given area, or to survey parcels of land (e.g., Amos 7:17; Petersen, *Haggai,* 167-68). These contrasting connotations serve to emphasize that the rebuilding of new edifices, which would involve the use of a *qaw(h),* has now become extensive enough to entail the use of a *ḥebel middâ.* The third vision thus signals that the prophecy of the first vision (1:14b-17) has begun to be fulfilled.

The prophecy of the first vision involved more than mere physical reconstruction, however. It also held out the prospect of restored economic prosperity and of Jerusalem's return to the status of Yahweh's "chosen" *(bḥr)* dwelling place (1:17). The second part of the third vision (2:7-9) speaks to these concerns. Judah's elect status implies its inviolability (e.g., Pss 46:5-8 [*RSV* 4-7]; 48:2-9 [*RSV* 1-8]; etc.), and such inviolability implies the protection of a city wall. The urgent message conveyed by the angelic interpreter to the other angel explains, however, that Jerusalem's walls need not be rebuilt in order for the city to protect itself and sustain itself economically. According to the old international order a central city had to be fortified in order to become the repository of the surrounding region's surplus production. According to the new international order (2:1-4), however, Jerusalem does not need fortifications in order to assume this role. Jerusalem can regain its status as the prosperous capital, bursting with "a multitude of people and cattle," even though it resembles its dependent villages in being without a wall (2:8b).

The measurable progress that Jerusalem's restoration has thus far made is finally given a theological interpretation that encourages its continuation. From the providential fact that such progress has been made even without a wall, it is evident that Yahweh has protected Jerusalem's restoration, and that he will continue to do so (2:9a). His continued protection also entails, however, that his "glory" *(kābôd)* should have some concrete representation in the city (2:9b). This involves the completion of the temple as the basis for Judah's restored socioeconomic viability and prosperity.

Genre

This unit begins with vision report formulas (2:5aα) and describes a scene with revelatory significance. It is therefore a PROPHETIC VISION REPORT (→ 1:8-17, Genre). The revelatory nature of the visual symbols is shown not by the initial exchange between the prophet and the man with the measuring line (2:2), but by the subsequent interaction between the angelic interpreter and the other angel (2:7-9). The message that the angelic interpreter is commissioned to deliver (2:8b-9), the delivery of which is not actually narrated, explains the meaning of what the man with the measuring line is up to. The very fact of Jerusalem's measurability, despite its lack of fortifications, signifies Yahweh's intention to prosper and protect the restoration of the city.

Setting

This text reflects historical circumstances midway through the restoration of Jerusalem, after the first returnees had begun the rebuilding and resettlement of the city, but before any stability had been attained and before the temple itself was completed. This vision was probably reported by the prophet in the course of an oracular inquiry undertaken on his own initiative (→ 1:8-17, Setting), through which he sought to discern the significance of this state of affairs.

Intention

This report shows the prophet developing a positive attitude toward the slow progress of the restoration because of the way he perceives Yahweh to be involved in the process. The audience is thereby challenged to reexamine any presuppositions that might lead them to view such slow progress negatively, whether these be suppositions regarding Yahweh's disposition or presuppositions regarding the realities of the international situation. The very fact that some headway has been made without having to refortify the city is proof of Yahweh's intention to be compassionate rather than angry toward his people (1:13-17) and proof of his ushering in a new international order (2:1-4). Judah can now secure a place among the nations, with Jerusalem as its capital, without any heavy system of defense. The assurance of Yahweh's providence is imaginatively reinforced by the symbol of the surveyor heading for Jerusalem, whose repopulation and urban redevelopment have now become extensive enough to require his services, and by the association of this vitality with the imagery of the divine light, which breaks forth as both an outer protective burning fire and an inner glorious theophanic radiance.

THE EXILES ARE URGED TO SEE THEIR RETURN AS PART OF A WORLDWIDE PROCESS INITIATED BY YAHWEH, AND TO ACT ACCORDINGLY, 2:10-17 (RSV 6-13)

Text

The *RSV* translates the command at the beginning of v. 11 (*RSV* v. 7) as "Escape to Zion," but it would be better rendered as "Escape, O Zion." Also, v. 12 is better translated as follows: "For Yahweh of hosts has said so. He sent me after glory to the nations that plundered you; for whoever touches you touches the apple of his eye." For an example of 'aḥar ("after") used in this way, see 2 Chr 25:27.

365

Structure

The focus of this exhortation is obviously on the Babylonian exiles, but the prophet's appeal to them encompasses the changing overall world situation. The Persians have turned their conquest of Babylon to Judah's benefit by authorizing and financing the exiles' return to Jerusalem and their restoration of the temple. The plunderers are in this sense now becoming the plundered (2:12-13). Moreover, the kind of international order established by the Persians is also transforming the basis on which the identity of Yahweh's people is defined. In regaining their homeland the exiles are not reverting to the preexilic status quo, according to which the covenant relationship was embodied in an independent national state. They are instead creating a new kind of religious community in which national citizenship no longer constitutes the basis for their relationship with Yahweh. In view of this development the conversion of the Gentiles and their membership in the covenant community now becomes a distinct possibility (2:15a). The worldwide scope of the exhortation is evident not only in the way it addresses the exiles on the basis of these two changes (2:10-16), but also in its brief climactic conclusion with an appeal addressed to "all flesh" (2:17). All are urged to join in acknowledging Yahweh as the author of this transformative process, which culminates in the restoration of the Jerusalem temple as the earthly representation of his heavenly dwelling place.

The main part of the exhortation, addressed specifically to the exiles, falls into two complementary sections. The first (2:10-13) is characterized by a mood of sorrow (hôy [*RSV* "ho!"], vv. 10-11), as it views the departure from Babylon in terms of a disastrous upheaval through which the equilibrium of the world order is being restored. The second (2:14-16) is contrastingly characterized by a mood of festive celebration ("sing and rejoice!" v. 14a), as it describes the return to Jerusalem in terms of a restored relationship between Yahweh and his people.

The appeal to leave Babylon (2:10-11) is permeated with allusions to dislocation. Babylon itself is described in mythic terms as 'ereṣ ṣāpôn ("land of the north"), i.e., the locus of cosmic disruption (cf., e.g., Jer 1:14; 4:6b, 23-27; 6:16b; Petersen, *Haggai,* 174-75; also B. S. Childs, "The Enemy from the North and the Chaos Tradition," *JBL* 78 [1959] 187-98). The command to "flee!" *(nws)* is motivated by the clause: "for I have spread you abroad as the four winds of heaven" (v. 10). In other words, the exile to Babylon was like a storm in which the four winds were blown from their respective quarters of heaven to other quarters. The command to "escape!" *(mlṭ)* is addressed to the exiles personified as "Zion . . . who dwells with the daughter of Babylon," as if the very terrain of the earth had become so convoluted as to superimpose one place on the other. By couching its directives in such imagery the appeal implies that the exiles' return to Jerusalem constitutes a movement away from the place from which the forces of chaos emerge back to the place from which the forces of stability emanate. It thus signifies the correction of a great cosmic aberration, like the return of the four winds to their respective quarters of heaven once the storm has blown over.

Yahweh has decreed that now is the time for such an earth-shaking reversal (v. 12aα; cf. v. 13a). He has thus sent the prophet on a mission involving Judah's recovery of some tangible recompense for the wrongs suffered at the hands of their enemies during their existence as a nation (v. 12aβ; → Text). Yahweh is not taking this course of action because Judah has now done something to deserve a better fate, but simply because the past attacks on Judah's national integrity were also to some extent attacks on Yahweh himself (v. 12b). He is now reasserting his own integrity, which is manifest in the just equilibrium of the world order (v. 13aα). As this equilibrium is restored, Judah will experience a reversal in its status, from being the victim of imperial prerogatives to being a partaker in those prerogatives (v. 13aβ). This reversal will tangibly authenticate the prophet's theological interpretation of current international developments (v. 13b).

In the appeal to celebrate the restoration of Jerusalem (vv. 14-16), the exiles are urged to recognize that the covenant relationship is being redefined in the process. The sign of Yahweh's renewed presence in Jerusalem, which authenticates the prophet's interpretation of the restoration as an act of cosmic significance, is the new possibility of the Gentiles' inclusion among the people of Yahweh (vv. 14b-15). On this development both the reconstitution of Judah as Yahweh's inherited portion and the reelection of Jerusalem as Yahweh's divinely protected dwelling place are singularly predicated (v. 16).

Genre

This unit is structured on the basis of a series of commands: "flee!" (v. 10aα²); "escape!" (v. 11aβ); "sing and rejoice!" (v. 14aα); and "silence!" (which is not an imperative but is nevertheless a command; v. 17aα¹). All of these commands have motivations based on prophetic claims about Yahweh, and the motivations of all but the last command contain oracular speech of Yahweh. The things that the prophet urges on his audience are all predicated on the realization that Yahweh brought about the exile through the plundering of Judah by its conquerors and through the scattering of Judah among the nations (vv. 10b, 12aβ). If he was once capable of doing such a thing, he is now capable of reversing the process to bring about something new. The plunderers are thus becoming the plundered (v. 13a), the exiles are coming home (vv. 10-11), Yahweh is returning to dwell with his people in their land (vv. 14b, 15bα, 16b), and he is reelecting Jerusalem as his chosen dwelling place (vv. 16b, 17b) in order to create a covenant community made up of people from many nations (v. 15a).

Those who recognize the cogency of the prophet's insights into what is currently happening, and who thus commit themselves to participate in this historical process, will find that both the prophet's claims and their commitment are confirmed by the outcome (vv. 13b, 15bβ). Such (→) parenesis, predicated on pragmatically self-authenticating revelation, belongs to the generic category of PROPHETIC EXHORTATION.

Setting

This genre generally reflects the prophetic convention of public address. Most of this speech is explicitly directed to the exiles living in Babylon, but in the broader context of an appeal to "all flesh" (v. 17). The rhetorical situation is thus comparable to the arena in which hymnic calls to praise are addressed to "all nations" (e.g., Ps 117:1) or "all the earth" (e.g., Ps 66:1). It would be absurd to suppose that such language indicates that the speaker is actually in a position to address the whole world face-to-face. It indicates rather that the rhetorical context is conceived in terms of a microcosm. The prophet is thus not necessarily in Babylon itself. He could just as well be in Jerusalem speaking to a group of returned exiles in terms that extend to encompass their fellows still scattered to the ends of the earth. In such a setting the speech would serve to inform the attitude of the audience regarding the theological significance and larger implications of their previous decision to come back to Jerusalem. Through the contacts of the returnees with those still in Babylon, the speech would also encourage further emigration to Judah.

Intention

This speech imparts to those who have returned to Jerusalem, and to those who are considering such a move, a sense of participating in a great cosmic drama. On the international level this drama entails restoring the equilibrium of the world order under a new imperial regime, and on the local level it entails restoring the city and sanctuary that constitute the sign of Yahweh's agency in the world at large. The outcome of this drama holds great promise not only for the Jews but for all humanity. The renovation of Zion is thus a compelling development whose joyful prospects far outweigh the upheaval that undeniably accompanies any abandonment of the status quo, thus overcoming the sense of loss that threatens to keep the exiles in Babylon and to undermine the morale of those who have recently returned.

ZECHARIAH ENVISIONS THE PURIFICATION OF JOSHUA, SO THAT HE CAN SERVE AS HEAD OF THE RESTORED TEMPLE CULT, 3:1-10

Text

The *RSV* translation of *haśśāṭān* as "Satan" (vv. 1-2) is problematic, as this term means something more like "the accuser" here (→ Structure).

The ancient versions are virtually unanimous in attesting a third person form of the verb *'mr, wayyō'mer* ("and he said") in v. 5aα[1], instead of the MT's first person form, *wā'ōmar* (*RSV* "and I said"), which would make the angel of Yahweh the subject of the verb rather than the prophet. On the one hand the angel's commanding that Joshua be given a clean turban would be consistent with his earlier command that Joshua's dirty clothing be removed (v. 4a), and consistent with his previous declaration that he will be the one to reclothe Joshua (v. 4b). On the other hand it is the prophet's characteristic role here to bring about the divine legitimation of Joshua as the high priest. It would therefore be appropriate for the prophet, as a delegate of the divine council, to take a leading part in the ritual of purification by ordering a clean turban for Joshua.

I follow the MT (and *RSV*) here, but the choice is not conclusive. (See further N. L. A. Tidwell, "*wā'ōmer* [Zech 3:5] and the Genre of Zechariah's Fourth Vision," *JBL* 94 [1975] 343-55.)

Structure

3) Statement describing what he is about to do
for Joshua: I am clothing you with rich apparel 3:4bβ^2

3. Speech of the prophet directing background
figures to act   3:5a

    a. Introduction: I said . . .   3:5aα^1

    b. Speech proper: let them put a clean turban
on his head   3:5aα^{2}β

4. Compliance of background figures with the
prophet's directive   3:5bαβ^1

    a. They put a clean turban on Joshua's head   3:5bα

    b. They clothed him with garments   3:5bβ^1

III. Third act: Joshua's commission to head the restored
temple cult   3:5bβ^2-10

A. Introductory description of the scene   3:5bβ

    1. Central figure: the angel of Yahweh   3:5bβ^1

    2. His position: standing by   3:5bβ^2

B. Action: an oracular word of Yahweh spoken by the
angel to Joshua   3:6-10

    1. Introduction: the angel of Yahweh enjoined
Joshua . . .   3:6

    2. Speech proper   3:7-10

        a. Messenger formula: thus says Yahweh
of hosts . . .   3:7aα^1

        b. Oracular word of Yahweh   3:7aα^2-10

           1) Concerning Joshua's status   3:7aα^{2}b

               a) Conditions of legitimate high-priestly
service   3:7aα^2

                  (1) First condition: if you walk in
my ways . . .

                  (2) Second condition: if you keep
my charge . . .

               b) High-priestly prerogatives   3:7aβb

                  (1) Authority over the temple cult:
you shall rule my house and
have charge of my courts   3:7aβ

                  (2) Entrance into the heavenly council:
I will give you the right of access
among those standing here   3:7b

           2) Concerning events that will confirm
Joshua's legitimacy   3:8-10

               a) Call to attention   3:8a

                  (1) Command: hear now!   3:8aα^1

                  (2) Addressees   3:8aα^{2}β

                     (a) Initial designation of primary
addressee: Joshua the high priest   3:8aα^2

                     (b) Subsequent designation of other
addressees   3:8aβ

α. Their inclusion: you and your
friends who sit before you   3:8aβ[1]
β. Motivation for their inclusion:
they are men of good omen   3:8aβ[2]
b) Announcement of confirmative
sign-events   3:8b-10
(1) The divine initiative   3:8b-9bα
(a) Actions undertaken by Yahweh   3:8b-9bα[1]
α. Designation of a
complementary position of
leadership: I will bring my
servant the Branch   3:8b
β. Provision of a ritual stone:
I will engrave an inscription
on the stone and put it
before Joshua   3:9abα[1]
(b) Oracle formula: says Yahweh
of hosts   3:9bα[2]
(2) Result of divine initiative   3:9bβ-10
(a) Yahweh's accomplishment   3:9bβ
α. His deed: I will remove the
guilt of this land   3:9bβ[1]
β. Temporal indication: in one day   3:9bβ[2]
(b) Consequences for the people   3:10
α. Introduction   3:10aα
aa. Temporal indication:
in that day   3:10aα[2]
bb. Oracle formula: says
Yahweh of hosts   3:10aα[2]
β. Description of general
conditions: you will each
invite your neighbor under
your vine and fig tree   3:10aβb

This unit opens with the formulaic term *wayyar'ēnî* (*RSV* "he showed me"; lit. "he caused me to see"). The antecedent of the pronominal subject is presumably Yahweh, but the reference is not altogether clear since both Yahweh and the angelic interpreter have previously "shown" the prophet something (1:9b; 2:3 [*RSV* 1:20]). In the foregoing exhortation (2:10-17 [*RSV* 6-13]) the prophet's appeal to return to Jerusalem is based on two briefly recounted actions of Yahweh: he previously dispersed the exiles (2:10b), and he now has sent his prophet on a mission to reverse this process (2:12a). The narration thus commences at 3:1 with the implication that Yahweh is generally the main agent (→ 1:7–6:15, Structure).

This vision report differs from its three predecessors (1:8-17; 2:1-4 [*RSV* 1:18-21]; 2:5-9 [*RSV* 1-5]) in several notable respects. First, the angelic interpreter is not explicitly identified as playing any part in what happens here. After disappearing from the scene at 2:10, he does not reappear until he returns and rouses the prophet in the next episode (4:1). Second, the main subject of the vision is a historically identifiable person, Joshua the high priest (Hag 1:1; Ezra 3:2-9; 5:2; Sir 49:12; etc.), rather than an angelic being or some purely symbolic figure. Third, the import of the visualization is not indicated through any question-and-answer process involving either the prophet or any of the other various characters within the vision. Its significance is instead made evident in the progression of the narrative action through three distinct phases or acts (vv. 1-2, 3-5a, 5b-10), and particularly in the oracle that brings the narration to its close (vv. 7-10).

These differences mark a thematic turning point in the first episode of this section of Zechariah (→ 1:7–6:15, Structure). The three preceding vision reports (1:8–2:9 [RSV 1:8–2:5]), as well as the intervening exhortation (2:10-17 [RSV 6-13]), are focused on the theme of the exiles' return to resettle and rebuild Jerusalem. Here the focus shifts to the somewhat more narrow concern of reconstituting the temple cult itself, beginning with the important issue of the purification of its priestly personnel.

The first act (3:1-2) begins in medias res. The scene includes Joshua, the angelic śāṭān, and Yahweh himself. There is only one indication of what is going on: the purpose clause that is included in the description of the śāṭān's position (v. 1b). He stands at Joshua's right hand "to accuse him" (lĕśiṭnô). This shows that the śāṭān is here functioning as the adversarial angelic being that prosecutes cases before the tribunal of the heavenly council (cf. Job 1:6; 2:1), rather than the malevolent prince of demons that "Satan" subsequently became. It also shows that a trial of some sort is in process. The śāṭān has apparently accused Joshua of something; but Yahweh, the judge, dismisses the charge on the grounds that Joshua is metaphorically comparable to "a brand plucked from the fire" (Zech 3:2b). In the course of Joshua's acquittal Yahweh identifies himself as "the one who has chosen Jerusalem" (v. 2aβ). The metaphor thus assumes its significance in relation to Yahweh's past actions and present intentions vis-à-vis Jerusalem. The fire represents the destruction that Yahweh brought on the city and his sanctuary there. Joshua is comparable to a burned stick from that fire in the sense that he, as a legitimate descendant of the Jerusalem priesthood, is one of the few remaining traces of the cult that was destroyed. This status becomes the ground for dismissing the śāṭān's charges because it qualifies Joshua to become Yahweh's chief agent in reestablishing his sanctuary, and thus restoring Jerusalem to its former "chosen" (bḥr) status.

In the second act (3:3-5a) it becomes apparent that the śāṭān had accused Joshua of a particular impediment to his playing this role, namely, impurity. Having dismissed the charge, Yahweh declares Joshua pure, as other participants in the court's proceedings (including the prophet? → Text) help to divest him of his dirty clothing and dress him in clean garments that are indicative of his cultic purity. (Cf. the similar pattern of narrative action in Isa 6, where Yahweh's reaching a judgment in the heavenly council leads to the purification of the prophet, also accompanied by an outward symbolic sign [vv. 6-7].)

In the third act (Zech 3:5b-10) the vision report reaches its climax, as an angel of Yahweh delivers an oracular message to Joshua, confirming his prerogatives as high priest. On the condition that he remain loyal to Yahweh, Joshua will be in charge of the newly rebuilt temple. He will thus be privy to the deliberations of the heavenly court, of which the temple is the earthly representation (v. 7; *mahlĕkîm* may indicate rather more indirect participation in these deliberations than *RSV* "right of access" would indicate; see VanderKam, 559-60). Moreover, Yahweh will provide signs that serve to authenticate Joshua's legitimacy in the eyes of his associates — men who know a "good omen" *(môpēt)* when they see one (v. 8aβ[2]; Harrelson, 117). He will designate someone to serve in a complementary leadership role (v. 8b), a "servant" *('ebed)* of Yahweh metaphorically characterized as a *ṣemaḥ* ("branch"). Yahweh will also provide Joshua with a divinely inscribed, seven-faceted stone, which is apparently to be used in rituals of atonement (v. 9; cf. the similarly inscribed "fourteen-eyed" stones of the high priest's regalia described in Exod 28:5-30; VanderKam, 567-69). With Joshua properly installed, and with the cult thus legitimately administered, Judah can atone for its sins, so that peace and prosperity will eventually prevail (Zech 3:9b-10).

The reference in v. 8b to a figure called a "branch" has been much discussed with respect to whether it designates Zerubbabel and whether it makes him messianic in any specific sense. In this regard it should be noted that the historical identity of this figure is only gradually revealed as this whole section of the book unfolds. Here the very concept of such a figure is simply introduced in terms of his function as a portentous legitimizer of Joshua's high-priestly role, to whom this function is being assigned by Yahweh himself (not by Joshua, contra Harrelson, 120). It should also be noted that the term *ṣemaḥ* has only very loose messianic connotations (contra J. G. Baldwin, "Ṣemaḥ as a Technical Term in the Prophets," *VT* 14 [1964] 93-97), as it metaphorically describes someone's "growth" into a leadership role that is somehow analogous to David's (Jer 23:5; 33:15; cf. Isa 4:2a; Ps 132:17a), and not a direct descendant of David's royal line. (This stands in marked contrast with the term *nēṣer* in Isa 11:1, which does indicate direct descent with similar imagery and is often also translated as "branch.")

In v. 8 Yahweh promises Joshua that the action of the heavenly council, allowing Joshua to serve as a properly pure high priest, will receive a certain kind of earthly attestation. Someone whose authority is widely recognized will assume the divinely delegated task of confirming Joshua's high-priestly authority. Here the designation of someone branchlike is not an end in itself but an integral part of the process through which Yahweh shows Joshua to be the legitimate high priest (vv. 7-9) and thus provides his people with an efficacious means of atoning for their sins once again (v. 9bβ). The statement that Yahweh will "bring forth" *(mēbî')* someone to do this does not necessarily imply that this person is not yet on the scene (contra VanderKam, 561; Harrelson, 120-21), but only that he has not yet fully assumed the specifically branchlike aspect of his role, by virtue of which he will provide Joshua with such legitimation.

The historical identity of this person, as well as the precise sense in which he is Davidic, is yet to be disclosed. He is subsequently identified as Zerubbabel, since he is explicitly named as temple builder in 4:9, and the role of branch is also explicitly defined in terms of temple building in 6:12-13 (→

4:1-14, Structure; 6:9-15, Structure). Zerubbabel thus "branches" into a role like that of a Davidic king by becoming the builder and chief patron of the sanctuary that will eventually include the temple, and in this capacity he grants official recognition to the priests (1 Chr 23–24).

Genre

The revelatory significance of this vision is indicated by the particular form of the introductory vision report formula (the hiphil of r'h, "he showed me," with Yahweh as the implied subject), as well as by the fact that the scene is a heavenly one. Yahweh is the author of the vision, and he himself is present in it as judge of the heavenly court. The central figure is, however, a human being: Joshua the high priest. The meaning of the vision thus generally concerns the relationship of the earthly high priest to the heavenly council. It deals with the question of whether and how the high priest can serve as the heavenly council's earthly representative. In order to serve as high priest and thus effect the purification and atonement of the community, Joshua himself must first be pure. In order to be the human representative of Yahweh's divine kingship, he must moreover be somehow associated with human kingship.

These issues are first dealt with in terms of actions taken by the council on the heavenly plane alone (vv. 3-5a), and then in terms of corresponding developments on the earthly plane, through which the implications of the divine council's actions become humanly manifest (vv. 5b-10). The special status that the divine council has conferred on Joshua (vv. 3-5a) will become evident to the corresponding earthly council of Joshua's advisers (i.e., the "colleagues" [rē'îm; RSV "friends"] with whom he "sits" [v. 8a]), and will be manifest in the self-authenticating way that he administers the temple cult (vv. 5b-10). In cooperation with Yahweh's kingly branchlike servant, Joshua will use the sacramental tokens of his office efficaciously in making atonement for the people's sins.

The meaning of what the prophet sees in this vision is thus elucidated in a way that does not entail a progressive clarification or deepening of the prophet's understanding. 3:1-10 is in this respect somewhat different from the preceding visions, in which the prophet comes to understand the visualization through question-and-answer interchange. Here the prophet knows from the start what is going on, and — if the MT of v. 5a is correct (→ Text) — he also participates in the affairs of the divine council as a human being who already enjoys the same privilege of access that comes to be granted to Joshua (v. 7b). Although 3:1-10 differs notably in this respect from the general pattern, it can nevertheless be categorized as a PROPHETIC VISION REPORT (→ 1:8-17, Genre).

Setting

As the returned exiles undertook the restoration of the cult, an altar was constructed in the sacred precincts so that some types of sacrifices could be resumed even before the reconstruction of the temple itself was begun (Ezra 3:1-7; cf. Hag 1:1-15a). Questions concerning the qualifications of the priestly personnel would thus have emerged quite apart from the issue of the temple's completion. Some could not prove their descent from priestly families, and it appears that in such cases the question of legitimacy was decided through a divinatory procedure (Ezra 2:61-63). Even those whose genealogy was never in doubt would have been unable to maintain their priestly purity under the conditions of the exile, and this was especially problematic in the restoration of the cult. With no legitimate cultic means of first atoning for the sins of the priests, the priests could provide no legitimate cultic means of atoning for the people's sins (Lev 9:7-21).

This text seems to presuppose that Joshua's inability to maintain his own priestly purity under the conditions of exile would in effect disqualify the reconstituted cult as a legitimate means of the people's atonement. In view of the fact that other questions of priestly legitimacy were handled through divinatory procedures, it seems plausible to suppose that this one was handled similarly. This vision thus was probably reported in the course of an oracular inquiry undertaken by the prophet on his own initiative (→ 1:8-17, Setting) in an attempt to discern whether or not the sacrificial cult, over which Joshua was beginning to preside, was efficacious. The reply affirmed that, in view of the extenuating circumstances, Yahweh himself had purified Joshua and thus legitimated the newly restored cult — to the extent that it was functional without the temple yet being rebuilt — by a special divine decree.

Intention

Vision reports, like reports of revelation in general, often make the prophet into a model of how the audience is to understand their revelations. This particular example of the genre, however, emphasizes the prophet's privileged position in relation to Yahweh rather than his commonality with the audience. His immediate recognition of the scene (and perhaps his knowing participation in it as well; → Text) underscores his unique role as a human being privy to the deliberations of the heavenly council. The prophet thus claims to be uniquely qualified to determine Joshua's qualifications for his position. This claim is not altogether arbitrary because it is subjected to the pragmatic test of whether Joshua's administration of the cult proves efficacious and beneficial for the community in the long run. The audience is invited to imagine the transformative and purificatory effect of Joshua's cultic leadership in terms of his being divested of his dirty rags and reclothed in clean and splendid robes.

Bibliography

W. Harrelson, "The Trial of the High Priest Joshua: Zechariah 3," *ErIs* 16 (1982) 116-24; J. C. VanderKam, "Joshua the High Priest and the Interpretation of Zechariah 3," *CBQ* 53 (1991) 553-70.

ZECHARIAH ENVISIONS THE LAMPSTAND, SET IN THE TEMPLE BUILT BY ZERUBBABEL, AS THE EARTHLY REPRESENTATION OF YAHWEH'S HEAVENLY DWELLING, 4:1-14

Structure

I. Introductory preliminaries to a vision	4:1-2bα^1
A. Action of the angelic interpreter	4:1
1. He returns	4:1a
2. He rouses the prophet: described metaphorically	
in terms of awakening	4:1b
B. Dialogue between the angelic interpreter and the	
prophet	4:2abα^1
1. Angelic interpreter's question to the prophet	4:2a
a. Introduction: he said to me . . .	4:2aα
b. Question proper: what do you see?	4:2aβ
2. Prophet's reply	4:2bα^1
a. Introduction: I said . . .	
b. Reply proper (vision report formula):	
I see *(rāʾîtî)* . . .	
II. Vision proper	4:2bα^2-14
A. Coordinating interjection: and behold! *(wĕhinnēh)*	4:2bα^2
B. Description of the vision	4:2bα^2-14
1. Scene	4:2bα^2-3
a. Central figure: a golden lampstand with	
seven lights, etc.	4:2bα^{2}β
b. Peripheral figures: two olive trees, one on	
the right and the other on the left	4:3
2. Action: dialogue between the prophet and the	
angelic interpreter	4:4-14
a. Exchange establishing the prophet's need of	
an explanation	4:4-5
1) Prophet's initial question to angelic interpreter	4:4
a) Introduction: and I responded and said . . .	4:4a
b) Question proper: what are these, my lord?	4:4b
2) Angelic interpreter's question in return	4:5a
a) Introduction: he responded and said	
to me . . .	4:5aα
b) Question proper: do you not know	
what these are?	4:5aβ
3) Prophet's reply to angelic interpreter	4:5b
a) Introduction: and I said . . .	4:5bα
b) Reply proper: no, my lord	4:5bβ
b. Angelic interpreter's explanation of	
the lampstand	4:6-10
1) Beginning of explanation	4:6-7

       a) Introduction: he answered and said
          to me . . .   4:6aα

       b) Digression concerning the role of
          Zerubbabel in the temple's
          reconstruction   4:6aβ-7

          (1) Introduction: this is the word of
             Yahweh concerning Zerubbabel   4:6aβ

          (2) Speech of Yahweh   4:6b-7

             (a) Basic statement: not by might,
                nor by power, but by my Spirit   4:6bα

             (b) Speech report formula: says
                Yahweh of hosts   4:6bβ

             (c) Elaboration: Zerubbabel shall over-
                come a mountain of obstacles to
                celebrate the temple's refoundation
                and win popular acclaim   4:7

   2) Interruption of explanation: narrator's aside
     to the audience   4:8-10a

       a) Introductory prophetic word formula:
          the word of Yahweh came to me saying . . .   4:8

       b) Prophecy concerning the completion
          of the temple by Zerubbabel   4:9-10a

          (1) The event that will come to pass: as
             Zerubbabel began the work of
             rebuilding, he will also finish it   4:9a

          (2) Its effect   4:9b-10a

             (a) With respect to the prophet's
                recognition: you will know that
                Yahweh sent me to you   4:9b

             (b) With respect to a change in popular
                attitude toward the rebuilding project:
                those who despised the day of
                small things will rejoice . . .   4:10a

   3) Resumption of explanation   4:10b

       a) Significance of the lampstand's seven
          lights: they are the eyes of Yahweh   4:10bα

       b) Their function: they range through
          the whole earth   4:10bβ

c. Exchange leading to explanation of the two
   olive trees   4:11-14

   1) Prophet's questions to the angelic interpreter 4:11-12

       a) Initial question   4:11

          (1) Introduction: I responded and said
             to him . . .   4:11a

          (2) Question proper: what are these two
             olive trees?   4:11b

       b) Subsequent question   4:12

(1) Introduction: I responded a second time and said to him . . .	4:12a
(2) Question proper: what are these two conduits (?) extending from the olive trees?	4:12b
2) Angelic interpreter's question in return	4:13a
a) Introduction: he said to me . . .	4:13aα
b) Question proper: do you not know what these are?	4:13aβ
3) Prophet's reply to angelic interpreter	4:13b
a) Introduction: I said . . .	4:13bα
b) Reply proper: no, my lord	4:13bβ
d. Angelic interpreter's explanation of the two olive trees	4:14
1) Introduction: he said . . .	4:14aα[1]
2) Explanation proper	4:14aα[2]b
a) With respect to the two olive trees themselves: they are "the two sons of oil" (*RSV* "the two anointed")	4:14aα[2]β
b) With respect to their position flanking the lampstand: they stand beside the Lord of all the earth	4:14b

The angelic interpreter, who has been offstage (as it were) during both the previous exhortation (2:10-17 [*RSV* 6-13]) and the fourth vision (3:1-10), reappears here to prepare the prophet for resuming night visions (→ 1:7–6:15, Structure). The prophet has previously volunteered descriptions of the things he saw, and the angelic interpreter's role has mostly been limited to answering the prophet's questions. Here, however, the angelic interpreter takes the lead in eliciting from the prophet a description of what he has seen (v. 2a); and when the prophet questions the angelic interpreter, the angelic interpreter questions him in return before giving an answer. By posing the ironic counterquestion, "Don't you know?" (vv. 5b, 13a) — which is tantamount to exclaiming, "You don't know!" — the prophet's dependence on the angelic interpreter's knowledge is underscored. This dependence stands in marked contrast to the immediately preceding vision (→ 3:1-10), where the prophet knowingly observes and perhaps even participates in the proceedings of the heavenly council without the need of any such intermediary. This contrast turns out to be significant for understanding why the structure of 4:1-14 unfolds so strangely (see below).

The prophet sees a golden lampstand flanked by two olive trees, one on its left and the other on its right. The details of the lampstand's design (v. 2b) are rather obscure (Meyers and Meyers, *Haggai,* 229-38), but the lampstand definitely has seven burning lights. The initial exchange between the prophet and the angelic interpreter regarding the meaning of these figures (vv. 4-5) provides the occasion for a double digression, as the latter begins his explanation (vv. 6-10). Two oracles, 4:6aβ-7 and 4:8-10a, intervene between the narrative introduction to the angelic interpreter's speech in v. 6aα and the point at which he finally manages to explain that the lamps represent the "eyes of Yahweh" (v. 10b). The dialogue then finally leads him to explain also that the olive trees represent "the two sons of oil" (v. 14; *RSV* "the two anointed").

The two oracles in 4:6aβ-10a are obviously intrusive, and most commentators thus identify them as textual insertions to be treated apart from the vision itself. These two prophecies may well have originated in some context other than the one in which they now stand. It does not necessarily follow, however, that they should be read as texts independent from the vision report, or as texts independent from one another.

In this regard it is important to note that these two oracles are worked into the vision report in quite different ways. The first one (vv. 6aβ-7) has been incorporated into the angelic interpreter's reply to the prophet's first question concerning the significance of the scene: "Then he said to me, 'This is the word of Yahweh to Zerubbabel . . . [and] these are the eyes of Yahweh. . . .'" The oracle addressed to Zerubbabel is thus formally an integral part of the dialogue within the narrative, even if its content does not connect very smoothly with the material that immediately precedes it. It is part of what the prophet learns from the angelic interpreter as the story unfolds.

The second oracle (vv. 8-10a) is introduced so as to interrupt the angelic interpreter's explanation altogether, as the narrator abandons the report of the vision and addresses the audience directly with a different nonvisionary revelation that came to him on some other unspecified occasion. This is to say, in effect, that the prophet has found out something through this visionary experience (4:1-7 + 10b-14) that corroborates an oracular pronouncement made earlier under other circumstances (4:8-10a). The inclusion of the first oracle within the narrative provides the point of departure for intruding the thematically similar second oracle as a narrator's aside. They should thus not be treated as anomalous glosses but read as integral parts of 4:1-14 (→ 1:7–6:15, Structure).

The first of these digressions (vv. 6aβ-7) forms the angelic interpreter's prelude to his explanation of the lampstand's meaning (v. 10b). The angelic interpreter recounts an oracle encouraging Zerubbabel to overcome all obstacles to the reinstigation of the temple building project (vv. 6b-7). This oracle first emphasizes that Yahweh's Spirit, rather than conventional might, will empower Zerubbabel (v. 6b). The obstacles are then directly addressed in an apostrophe, collectively describing them in metaphorical terms as a great mountain that Zerubbabel will level (v. 7a). In conclusion the oracle describes Zerubbabel's performance of a ritual act celebrating the temple's refoundation (A. Laato, "Zechariah 4, 6b-10a and the Akkadian Royal Building Inscriptions," *ZAW* 106 [1994] 53-69; following R. Ellis, *Foundation Deposits in Ancient Mesopotamia* [New Haven: Yale University Press, 1968]), thus winning much popular acclaim (v. 7b).

By describing Zerubbabel's successful initiation of the project in terms of leveling a mountain and celebrating an impressive public ceremony, the text implies that he will encounter obstacles of both a material and an attitudinal sort. This descriptive phraseology reflects his having to contend both externally with opposition from the surrounding authorities (e.g., Ezra 5) and internally with a lack of motivation on the part of the returned exiles (e.g., Hag 1:1-15a). Having no military force with which to oppose outside enemies, nor any means of coercing his own community to shed their complacency, Zerubbabel will have to rely on the spiritual empowerment of Yahweh to make him diplomatically effective in disarming the opposition, as well as theologically persuasive in dispelling the community's low morale (cf. Hag 1:14).

The second digression (vv. 8-10a) is an aside of the prophetic narrator to his audience and thus not formally part of what goes on in the vision. The narration of the angelic interpreter's explanation (vv. 6-10) is interrupted in order for the prophet to tell the audience that he has received from Yahweh another oracle dealing with much the same subject. This interruption is signaled by the prophetic word formula in its first person, complete-clause form ("the word of Yahweh came to me," v. 8), which indicates that the prophet is here speaking for himself rather than continuing to narrate the speech of the angelic interpreter. The oracle begins with a prediction that Zerubbabel will effectively complete the rebuilding of the temple, just as he has effectively launched the work (v. 9a). This achievement will authenticate what the prophet has been saying to the people about Yahweh's intentions for the restoration (v. 9b), and thus bring about a change in popular opinion. The sense of failure that was rooted in the project's inauspicious beginnings will give way to joy at the sight of Zerubbabel presiding over the temple's rededication (v. 10a).

After this interruption the angelic interpreter resumes his explanation of the lampstand, finally giving a direct answer to the prophet's question (v. 10b). The interpreter angel explains that the lampstand's seven lights represent "the eyes of Yahweh that range over the whole earth." The lampstand is thus identified as the sacramental representation of Yahweh's influential involvement in human affairs (A. L. Oppenheim, "'The Eyes of the Lord,'" *JAOS* 88 [1968] 173-74; cf. Ps 113:5-6).

The prophet asks twice about the olive trees, first in general terms (v. 11), then again more specifically in terms of the relationship between the branches of the trees and some hitherto unmentioned conduits (v. 12). The technicalities of this apparatus are unclear, but the main point seems to be that there is a close relationship between what the lampstand signifies and what the olive trees signify, by virtue of the fact that the olive trees supply the oil that is burned in the lamps (Meyers and Meyers, *Haggai*, 255-59). After countering the prophet's questions with a question of his own (v. 13), the angelic interpreter explains that the trees represent the two *běnê hayyişhār* (lit. "sons of oil"; *RSV* "anointed [ones]"; v. 14a). This allusive language figuratively identifies the olive trees with two human beings, who are thereby characterized as having a similar function, namely, providing the lampstand with oil. In view of the fact that the lampstand is to be the chief sacramental sign of Yahweh's presence (v. 10b), as was the ark in preexilic times, this would be one of the cult's most important administrative tasks. The two persons represented by the olive trees are thus the two leaders who bear the chief responsibility for the maintenance and operation of the temple cult.

The identity of these two persons, the nature of their joint authority, and the question of whether the vision imputes to them any kind of "messianic" status are issues much discussed. Scholarly interest has focused on the semantic connotations of the phrase *běnê hayyiṣhār* (v. 14a), and on whether it implies anything specifically concerning the anointing that is definitively characteristic of a messianic role (note *RSV* "the anointed [ones]"). It is by now evident, however, that these issues cannot be resolved on philological grounds alone. It may thus prove fruitful to consider them in the light of the overall literary context.

In this regard it is significant that the visions in 3:1-10 and 4:1-14 are related in a particular way. The scene in 3:1-10 is the court of Yahweh's heavenly dwelling place, and the scene in 4:1-14 is the corresponding court of Yahweh's earthly dwelling place (i.e., the temple). The temple is evidently the earthly representation of the heavenly throne room because Joshua gains access to the heavenly council by virtue of his earthly role as high priest in charge of the temple (3:7). The role of the two "sons of oil" is thus defined not only in terms of how they are metaphorically similar to the olive trees on the earthly plane described in 4:1-14, but also in terms of what they correspond to on the heavenly plane described in 3:1-10.

In this light it is hardly coincidental that the two "sons of oil" are in 4:14b characterized by the same descriptive term that is repeatedly applied, virtually as an epithet, to all members of the heavenly council in 3:1-10. Each of the figures on the heavenly scene, except the central figure of Yahweh himself, is introduced as a "bystander" *('ōmēd):* Joshua in vv. 1aβ and 3b, the *śāṭān* in v. 1b, various background figures in v. 4aα, and the angel of Yahweh in v. 5bβ (Meyers and Meyers, *Haggai,* 182-83). When Yahweh gives Joshua the right of access to the heavenly council (v. 7b), he describes its membership collectively as "these bystanders" *(hā'ōmědîm hā'ēlleh).* Just as these figures are all "bystanders" in relation to the king of heaven, the two "sons of oil" are "bystanders" in relation to "the Lord of all the earth" *(hā'ōmědîm 'al-'ădôn kol-hā'āreṣ,* v. 14). The status of these two leaders thus corresponds in earthly human terms to the role played by the attendants surrounding Yahweh's heavenly throne, and they are in this sense characterized as the earthly human representatives of Yahweh's divine kingship over all creation (Rudolph, 107; Petersen, *Haggai,* 232).

Within the context of 3:1–4:14 two persons are explicitly identified as having the kind of responsibility for the temple that is imputed to the two "sons of oil." Joshua is to "rule" *(dyn)* over Yahweh's house (3:7aβ), and Zerubbabel is the temple's builder and hence its chief patron (4:6aβ-10a). Since they are the human representatives of Yahweh's kingliness, the roles of Joshua and Zerubbabel are somewhat regal, and their status may thus perhaps be described as "messianic" in some sense. Because the temple was the central institution of the restored province of Judah, their joint responsibility for its operation and maintenance may perhaps be described as a "diarchy" of some sort. Certain descriptive features of the narrative in 3:1-10 and 4:1-14, however, impose important qualifications on the use of such terminology in relation to these particular texts.

First, Joshua and Zerubbabel do not represent Yahweh's sovereignty in just the same way that the preexilic kings did. Davidic monarchs were conceived as playing an earthly role that corresponded to the heavenly role of Yahweh himself, but Joshua and Zerubbabel are here cast in an earthly role corresponding to the role of Yahweh's heavenly attendants. It is rather the lampstand that occupies the central position on the earthly plane, which is analogous to the central position of Yahweh seated on his heavenly throne. The institution of the temple itself is thus conceived as a representation of what the monarchy used to signify, not the two leaders. It is only by virtue of their association with the temple that Joshua and Zerubbabel share in the representation of Yahweh's divine kingship.

Second, although Joshua and Zerubbabel are jointly responsible for the temple, and although both their respective roles are necessary for it to function, the office held by Joshua and the office held by Zerubbabel are not equally important with respect to the symbolic correspondence between the temple and Yahweh's heavenly dwelling place. As high priest, Joshua, not Zerubbabel, is the one who connects the earthly human realm with the divine heavenly realm. Zerubbabel's authority gains its sacramental significance primarily from the way in which it serves to confirm the authority of the high priest; and this complementary role, rather than his completely unmentioned Davidic ancestry or status as governor, is what entitles him to bear the epithet of ṣemaḥ ("branch," 3:8b; → 6:9-15). The temple with the high priest at its head, conceived as a reincarnation of the old royal sanctuary, thus serves as surrogate for the Davidic monarchy, and not the office held by Zerubbabel.

With regard to the overall compositional form of this unit, it is reasonable to suppose that 4:6aβ-7 and 4:8-10a were once independent of the vision report that now contains them. In view of the integral part these two oracles play in establishing the symbolic and thematic correspondences between 3:1-10 and 4:1-14, however, it is questionable whether the vision report itself ever existed without them. If the oracles are simply excised, there initially seems to be perfect continuity between the narrative introduction to the angelic interpreter's explanation (v. 6aα) and his statement concerning the significance of the lampstand's seven lights (v. 10b). On closer examination, however, the vision report thus reconstructed is deficient in several respects. First, without the oracles there is no explicit reference to the temple, and thus no indication that the scene has anything particularly to do with the sanctuary. Likewise, without the explicit references to Zerubbabel there is no basis on which to suppose that the two "sons of oil" in v. 14 have anything to do with official leadership. This phrase is in itself sufficiently ambiguous to include many other possibilities (Petersen, *Haggai*, 230-32). Most interpretations of 4:1-6aα + 10b-14 impute to the vision a significance that is possible only in view of what is connoted by the inclusion of 4:6aβ-10a, and it is difficult to imagine what sense the former might make without the latter.

Another distinctive feature of the text that may have some bearing on this matter is the reiterated motif of the angelic interpreter's counterquestions (vv. 5a, 13a) mentioned above. Such back talk from the angelic interpreter is unique to this vision report, as is the disruption of the dialogue by the insertion of oracles, and there may thus be some connection between these two unusual devices. When the prophet is asked by the angelic interpreter, "Do you not know what these are?" and is thereby brought to confess that he does not know, the prophet's lack of knowledge is not only emphasized. The counterquestion also expresses the angelic interpreter's surprise at the prophet's lack of knowledge, and thus suggests that there is some basis on which he could have known, or should have known, what the vision is all about. This suggestion in turn implies some previously existing revelation concerning both the temple, as the earthly representation of Yahweh's heavenly dwelling, and the status of Joshua and Zerubbabel, as the chief attendants of his earthly court. The visualization of the lampstand with the olive trees, together with the accompanying explanatory dialogue, thus serves to recontextualize more graphically the revelation that has already been imparted in earlier prophecies.

In other words, the narrative in 4:1-6aα + 10b-14 appears to have been composed as a means of bringing the different sorts of prophecies now found in 3:1-10, 4:6aβ-7, and 4:8-10a into relationship with one another, so as to sharpen the focus of their common import in a manner consistent with the overall design of (→) 1:7–6:15 as a whole. As a redactional device of this sort the narrative plays on the capacity of the vision report to make the prophet into a model of how the audience comes to understand the meaning of the revelation it conveys (→ 1:8-17, Intention). The narrative's structure not only exploits this capacity in showing the prophet as the recipient of the angelic interpreter's instruction concerning the revelatory significance of what is envisioned. It also carries this convention to an extreme with the motif of the angelic interpreter's counterquestions, thus showing the prophet as one who stands in need of reeducation concerning the full implications of what he himself has previously prophesied. By reading 4:1-14 in its present form and context, the audience is brought by the vision recounted therein to reconsider the full implications of 4:6aβ-7 in relation to 4:8-10a, in the light of the immediately preceding prophecy in 3:1-10.

Genre

This unit bears all the hallmarks of a PROPHETIC VISION REPORT. The introduction (vv. 1-2bα[1]) is unusually complex, but it basically amounts to an extended variation on the vision report formula. There is no difference in principle between all that is described concerning the angelic interpreter's priming the prophet to receive the vision, by "waking" him and questioning him, and what is implied in the hiphil form of the vision report formula (i.e. "he showed me"; e.g., 2:4 [*RSV* 1:20]; 3:1; cf. 1:9b). Formulaic terminology based on *r'h* appears in the interpreter angel's initial question, "What do you see?" *(rō'eh)*, as well as in the prophet's reply, "I see . . ." *(rā'îtî)*. The revelatory significance of the figures in the scene is signaled by the fact that an angelic being enables the prophet to envision it, and this significance is spelled out largely through dialogue, as is also the case in other examples of vision reports.

The incorporation of extraneous oracular material into the narrative is not typical of the genre, however. This phenomenon shows that a conventional form is here being used in an unconventional way. This example of the vision report does not simply interpret the symbolic imagery of the temple sanctuary's most prominent furnishings. It does this in a way that also reinterprets other prophecies concerning Joshua's role as high priest and Zerubbabel's role as temple builder. This is therefore a prophetic vision report that has been adapted to the purpose of mantic reinterpretation (see M. Fishbane, *Biblical Interpretation in Ancient Israel* [Oxford: Clarendon, 1958] 458-99).

Setting

This adaptation of the genre presupposes a situation in which the meaningfulness of the prophecies in 4:6aβ-7 and 4:8-10a has come into question, and an oracular inquiry is used to determine whether and how they are still applicable. The vision report is the form in which the outcome of the inquiry is expressed (→ 1:8-17, Setting). The way these prophecies are restated and juxtaposed gives some indication of the circumstances that led them to be thus reconsidered. The prediction in 4:6aβ-7 that Zerubbabel will overcome all obstacles to the resumption of the rebuilding, as well as the prediction in 4:8-10a that he will bring the project to its completion, are both linked with the emergence of a positive popular attitude toward his efforts (vv. 7b, 10b). The latter prophecy presupposes the fulfillment of the former, as it explicitly states that Zerubbabel has indeed gotten the project started (v. 9aα). He has therefore overcome the "mountain" of obstacles described in v. 7a, which presumably includes his overcoming any popular indifference or rejection that might have prevented him from beginning the work. The question posed by the juxtaposition of these two prophecies is whether the rebuilding will maintain sufficient popularity for it to be finished, as the second oracle predicts.

This question is rooted in doubts about the theological significance of Zerubbabel's role. The problem lies in the fact that it is anomalous for someone who is not a king to play the part of temple builder. There is an inner contradiction in what Zerubbabel is attempting because a sanctuary without a royal patron could hardly serve its proper purpose, which is to represent the divine cosmic kingship (see, e.g., A. Kapelrud, "Temple Building: A Task for Gods and Men," *Or* 32 [1962] 56-62). The vision report in 4:1-14 is designed to address this problem. As the sequel to 3:1-10 it shows how the still-to-be-completed Jerusalem temple, administered only by the high priest Joshua with Zerubbabel's cooperation, can nevertheless constitute a complete earthly representation of Yahweh's heavenly dwelling place, and thus be a manifestation of Yahweh's kingship over all creation (→ Structure). As 4:6aβ-7 and 4:8-10a are reread in the light of what the lampstand symbolizes, their ongoing applicability is made apparent, and the previous fulfillment of the former becomes the warrant for expecting the eventual fulfillment of the latter.

Intention

This report portrays the prophet discovering in a vision the underlying reason why two of his previous prophecies remain valid. The audience is thereby challenged to reexamine any of their presuppositions that might lead them to discount these same prophecies, and to reconsider their meaningfulness in the light of the vision. By the prophet's description of what he has seen (vv. 1-3) the audience is led to imagine the completed inner sanctuary of the temple, and to focus on the tree-flanked golden lampstand that will become its symbolic centerpiece. With minds informed by this image, they are invited by the explanatory dialogue (vv. 4-14) to acknowledge the potential of such a sanctuary, under the joint leadership of Joshua and Zerubbabel, to represent the reality of Yahweh's kingly rule. If they will view Zerubbabel's efforts in this light, they will come to understand why his program of temple reconstruction deserves their full support.

ZECHARIAH ENVISIONS A FLYING SCROLL EXTENDING THE COVENANT OVER ALL THE EARTH, 5:1-4

Text

The phrase *kol-hā'āreṣ* in v. 3a, which the *RSV* translates as "the whole land," is in this context better understood to mean "the whole earth" (→ Structure).

The verb *niqqâ*, which occurs twice in v. 3b, is an ordinary perfect. It should therefore be translated with some English past tense, "[he] has gone unpunished" or the like, rather than with the English future tense used by the *RSV* ("[he] shall be cut off"). The perfect form *hôṣē'tîhā* in v. 4a should likewise be translated in the past, as "I have sent it forth," rather than in the future (*RSV* "I will send it forth").

Structure

I. Introductory vision report formula	5:1abα[1]
A. Verb indicating repeated action: I again . . . *(wā'āšûb)*	5:1aα
B. Description in terms of movement: I lifted my eyes	5:1aβ
C. Description in terms of perception: I saw *(wā'ēre')*	5:1bα[1]
II. Vision proper	5:1bα[2]-4
A. Coordinating interjection: and behold! *(wĕhinnēh)*	5:1bα[2]
B. Description	5:1bβ-4
1. Scene: a flying scroll	5:1bβ
2. Dialogue	5:2-4
a. Angelic interpreter's question to the prophet	5:2a
1) Introduction: he said to me . . .	5:2aα
2) Question proper: what do you see?	5:2aβ

b. Prophet's reply to the angelic interpreter — 5:2b
1) Introduction: and I said . . . — 5:2bα^1
2) Reply proper — 5:2bα^{2}β
a) Basic statement: I see a flying scroll — 5:2bα^2
b) Elaboration: its dimensions — 5:2bβ
(1) Its length: twenty cubits — 5:2bβ^1
(2) Its breadth: ten cubits — 5:2bβ^2
c. Angelic interpreter's explanation of the visualization — 5:3-4
1) Introduction: he said to me . . . — 5:3aα^1
2) Explanation proper — 5:3aα^2-4
a) Basic statement — 5:3aα^{2}βb
(1) Significance of the image — 5:3aα^{2}β
(a) With respect to the scroll itself: this is the covenant curse — 5:3aα^2
(b) With respect to its flight: it extends over the whole earth — 5:3aβ
(2) Two-part rationale for the scroll's worldwide movement: a *kî* clause — 5:3b
(a) First part: everyone who steals has gone unpunished — 5:3bα
(b) Second part: everyone who swears falsely has gone unpunished — 5:3bβ
b) Elaboration: speech of Yahweh — 5:4
(1) Identification of Yahweh as the curse's commissioner — 5:4aα
(a) Speech proper: I have sent it forth — 5:4aα^1
(b) Oracle formula: says Yahweh of hosts — 5:4aα^2
(2) Threefold description of the curse's effect on an offender's house: speech of Yahweh resumed — 5:4aβb
(a) It enters the house — 5:4aβ
α. The house of the thief — 5:4aβ^1
β. The house of the one who swears falsely by my name — 5:4aβ^2
(b) It abides in the house — 5:4bα
(c) It destroys the house — 5:4bβ
α. The house in general — 5:4bβ^1
β. Its constituent materials in particular — 5:4bβ^2
aa. Its timbers
bb. Its stones

The idiomatic expression "to lift the eyes" indicates that the scene has shifted, and the verb *'āšûb* indicates that this change of scene is happening "again." The same kind of shift, which has previously marked the transition from the first to the second vision (i.e., from 1:8-17 to 2:1-4 [*RSV* 1:18-21]) and the transition from the second to the third vision (i.e., from 2:1-4 to 2:5-9 [*RSV* 1-5]), is now recurring. In the first episode (1:8–3:10) this idiom is used to show that the second and third visions form a series of visions starting from the first. Here in the second episode (4:1–6:15) the same idiom shows that the present vision and its successors (5:5-11; 6:1-8), all of which also begin with "lifting the eyes," likewise form a series starting from the immediately preceding vision of the lampstand (4:1-14; → 1:7–6:15, Structure).

Grouped together in a series, the succeeding visions develop ideas that are introduced by the initial vision. In the first episode both the vision of the four horns (2:1-4) and the vision of the man with the measuring line (2:5-9) elaborate in various ways on the previous vision's central theme of "all the earth at rest" (1:11), showing how that condition is established and what it implies for the progress of the restoration. In the second episode this vision and its two successors (5:5-11; 6:1-8) likewise elaborate in various ways on the previous vision's central theme of a community gathered around a royal sanctuary rather than a king (→ 4:1-14, Structure). The vision of the scroll explores the nature of the relationship that binds such a community together.

This scroll is a document of rather extraordinary capacities and dimensions, which give to its rather ordinary contents an impact larger than life. As the scroll flies far and wide, the angelic interpreter describes its function in terms of a "curse," placed by Yahweh on hitherto unpunished disobedient persons, which has the power to eradicate their "houses." The disobedient are epitomized as violators of the elementary prohibitions against stealing and taking Yahweh's name in vain. These prohibitions are representative of the two fundamental aspects of the covenant law (which later came to be described in terms of the Decalogue's "two tables"), rules concerning the community's obligations to God (e.g., "you shall not swear falsely by my name," Lev 19:12) and rules concerning the community's obligations to their neighbors (e.g., "you shall not steal," Exod 20:15).

The flying scroll thus indicates the form the covenant relationship must now take and the broader extent that it will now have in view of Judah's new polity. Because the dispersion is an ongoing reality despite the return of many exiles from Babylon, the restored Jerusalem sanctuary will be the focal point of a social identity that transcends Judah's territorial bounds. The covenant community can no longer be identified primarily in terms of Judah's body politic, and the force of the covenant law can no longer be measured in terms of Judah's civil jurisdiction. The covenant community can now be identified as the group that adheres to a documentary expression of the covenant ideals, whose character is shaped through an educational process of instruction based on such a document (i.e., *tôrâ*). The force of the covenant law can now be measured by how effectively the community's households are destroyed as a result of their failure to observe its rules.

The vision of the flying scroll is related to the vision of the lampstand as the other side of the same coin. As the temple in Jerusalem is restored in accord with the concept represented by the lampstand, a covenant community will form around it, of the sort that is represented by the scroll. This community will look to Judah and the Jerusalem temple as its home base, but extend through a network of extraterritorial familial relationships to encompass the whole world, maintaining itself through the study of its traditional ideals in documentary form.

Genre

In the beginning of this unit extensive use is made of the vision report formula's distinctive terminology, as forms of r'h ("see") occur not only in the prophet's initial statement (wā'er'eh, v. 1bα[1]), but also in the angelic interpreter's immediately ensuing question (rō'eh, v. 2aβ) and in the prophet's reply (rō'eh again, v. 2bα[2]). The revelatory significance of the visualization is indicated by the supernatural performance of the scroll and by the fact that an angelic being explains its significance — although here this significance is disclosed not through dialogue that elicits an explanation but simply through a direct statement by the angelic interpreter (vv. 3-4), culminating in an oracular speech of Yahweh (v. 4). This unit thus has the definitive characteristics of a PROPHETIC VISION REPORT (→ 1:8-17, Genre).

Setting

This vision report was probably the result of an oracular inquiry, undertaken by the prophet on his own initiative (→ 1:8-17, Setting) in an attempt to understand the failure of many exiles to return to Jerusalem. As a result of this inquiry he comes to understand how the covenant relationship can embrace both those who returned and those who remained in the dispersion.

Intention

Once again the audience sees the prophet in the process of coming to understand what he has seen, but in this case he is a relatively passive participant in the process. The angelic interpreter takes the initiative, questioning and instructing the prophet without waiting for him to express any questions of his own. The significance of the scroll is thus not something that the prophet has to eke out, nor an issue that he has to wrestle with, but a realization that proceeds rather directly from his understanding of the lampstand's significance. If the audience similarly understands the temple as it is conceived in 4:1-14, they will also immediately recognize what this understanding implies for the nature of the covenant relationship. It can be primarily defined no longer in geopolitical terms but in terms of factors suggested by this vision's striking image of a great Torah scroll that fills the sky and deconstructs various houses below.

ZECHARIAH ENVISIONS A MOVING CONTAINER THAT HOLDS NO PROMISE FOR TEMPLE BUILDING IN THE DISPERSION, 5:5-11

Text

Read v. 6bβ² according to the MT as "this is their eye over all the earth," rather than with the *RSV* according to the LXX as "this is their iniquity in all the land" (→ Structure).

Structure

b. Angelic interpreter's reaction 5:8
  1) Speech to the prophet explaining what the
    woman represents 5:8aα
    a) Introduction: he said . . . 5:8aα^1
    b) Speech proper: this is wickedness 5:8aα^2
  2) Action taken 5:8aβb
    a) With respect to the woman: he thrust
      her back inside the ephah 5:8aβ
    b) With respect to the lead lid: he weighs
      down the mouth of the ephah with it 5:8b
II. Second act 5:9-11
  A. Introductory vision report formula 5:9aα^1
    1. Expressed in terms of movement: I lifted my eyes
    2. Expressed in terms of perception: I saw *(wā'ēreh)*
  B. Vision proper: further developments on the
    same scene 5:9aα^2-11
    1. Coordinating interjection: and behold!
      (wĕhinnēh) 5:9aα^2
    2. Action involving additional figures 5:9aβ-11
      a. The ephah's transportation 5:9aβb
        1) Description of additional figures:
          two women 5:9aβ
          a) Their emergence 5:9aβ^1
          b) Their appearance 5:9aβ^2
            (1) Wind in their wings
            (2) Wings like a stork's
        2) Their main action: they lift the ephah up
          between heaven and earth 5:9b
      b. Dialogue 5:10-11
        1) Prophet's question to the angelic interpreter 5:10
          a) Introduction: I said to the angel who
            talked with me . . . 5:10a
          b) Question proper: where are they taking
            the ephah? 5:10b
        2) Angelic interpreter's reply to the prophet 5:11
          a) Introduction: he said to me . . . 5:11aα
          b) Reply proper 5:11aβb
            (1) What the two women will do with
              the ephah: build a house for it 5:11aβ
            (2) What will happen to it there: it will
              be firmly set on its base 5:11b

In the two previous visions the angelic interpreter has elicited from the prophet a description of what he has visualized (4:2a; 5:2a), but here the angelic interpreter's involvement is even more assertive. He commands the prophet to shift his gaze from the scroll to another object (v. 5a) and identifies the new object of attention by its mode of action: "See what this is that goes forth *(hayyôṣē't)*" (v. 5b). This is the same verb that is prominent in the preceding vision's description of the scroll: it "goes forth *(hayyôṣē't)* over the face of the whole earth" (5:3a) because Yahweh has "sent it forth *(hôṣē'tîhā)*" (5:4a). The introduction to 5:5-11 thus emphasizes the kind of action that is taking place, even before there is any identification of what the prophet has seen, and that this is the same kind of action that characterizes the scroll. Even when the object comes to be identified as an ephah (a container holding a standard measure of volume, something like a bushel), it is explicitly characterized again as "the ephah that goes forth *(hayyôṣē't)*." The ephah thus plays a role that is in some sense parallel to the role of the scroll.

At a point of transition that is crucial for the introduction, as the angelic interpreter moves from identifying the object to his explanation of what it represents (v. 6b), there is a text-critical problem. The MT reads *'ênām,* "their eye," but the LXX reads "their iniquity," reflecting the orthographically similar Hebrew form, *'āwōnām.* Most commentators favor the latter reading (as does the *RSV*), but in view of the tendency of the introduction to allude thematically to preceding material, this is not such an obvious choice. The qualifying phrase that fills out the angelic interpreter's explanation, *běkol-hā'āreṣ* ("over all the earth"), constitutes another leitmotif that, like the verb *yṣ'* ("go forth"), also establishes thematic connections. The repetition of this phrase reaches back not only to the scroll that goes forth "over the face of all the earth" (5:3a), but also further back to the lampstand in 4:1-14, whose lights represent the range of Yahweh's eyes "over all the earth" (4:10b). The action of the ephah and the scroll is thus coextensive with the scrutiny of Yahweh's eyes. This commonality suggests that the role of the ephah is also in some sense parallel to the role of the lampstand. Indeed, it is the ephah's destiny to become a symbolic cult object, installed as an object of veneration within a temple, just like the lampstand (v. 11). Since the lights of the lampstand are symbols of Yahweh's eyes, the possibility that the ephah also represents some kind of divine "eye" cannot be readily dismissed (Ollenburger, 778).

This whole question is further complicated by the absence within the unit itself of any clear-cut antecedent for the third person masculine plural pronominal suffix in v. 6b. Who are "they," i.e., the ones to whom this "eye" or this "iniquity" pertains? Most commentators think that this suffix refers to the people of Judah, but there is no indication within the pericope itself that this is the case. This opinion rests on an approach that attempts to relate this individual unit directly to some supposed historical context, without first taking the surrounding literary context into account. In view of the explicit connections drawn by the introduction between this vision and its predecessors, however, it would seem more sensible to look there first for some sign of who "they" are.

If one follows the normal rules of Hebrew grammar, the antecedents to this pronoun would be the nearest preceding substantives agreeing with it in gender and number. These criteria are met by the two substantives that are repeatedly paired in 5:3-4, the thief who steals *(haggōnēb/haggannāb)* and the perjurer *(hannišbā')* who swears falsely by Yahweh's name (Bič, *Nachtgesichte,* 56). "They" are thus the transgressors of the covenant, against whom the Torah scroll moves so forcefully. In view of this vision's relationship with the two immediately preceding visions, the angelic interpreter's explanation of the ephah should be understood as "their eye over all the earth," i.e., the equivalent of what is represented by the lampstand for those who do not share the concept of the covenant community represented by the scroll (Ollenburger, 780).

The equivalence is ironic, however. The lampstand represents for its adherents the independent global perspective of Yahweh himself, a perspective that is higher and broader than their own. The ephah is contrastingly said to be for its adherents nothing more than the reification of their own perspective ("*their* eye"), which could hardly attain the global scope to which it aspires. Further differences between the ephah and the preceding visualized objects are drawn out by the continuing description of the latter in vv. 7-8. The tableau of the lampstand includes golden containers overflowing with oil. The ephah is similarly a container that would normally hold agriculturally grown staples, such as grains and cereal foods, but in this case it holds only "wickedness." The scroll is out of all proportion to its contents, too big for anyone really to read the covenant law from it; its size magnifies the impact of its message. The ephah is similarly out of all proportion to its contents, too small actually to hold a woman; its size diminishes the impressiveness of her figure. As a cultic alternative to what the lampstand represents, preferred by those with a concept of community different from what the scroll represents, the ephah holds no promise of anything beneficial.

The second part of the vision (vv. 9-11), introduced by its own vision report formula (v. 9aα^1), further extends this negative comparison. The lampstand is flanked by the two olive trees, representing the two "sons of oil," whose ample productiveness connotes a right relationship with the created order. The ephah is flanked by the two women, whose anomalous storklike wings connote a perversion of the created order. The scroll can fly on its own because Yahweh has empowered it to do so, but the ephah requires the aid of the women to become airborne, and because of its weight it can scarcely get off the ground. The lampstand is going to have a temple built for it by Zerubbabel in Jerusalem, but the ephah is going to have a temple built for it by the two women in Shinar, i.e., Babylon (Gen 10:10).

By means of these similarities and differences the ephah is portrayed as the antithesis of all that the two preceding visions stand for. This vision satirizes the views of those who would build temples in the dispersion rather than rally around a central sanctuary in Jerusalem, those who favor an anthropomorphic cult image over a nondescript cult image like the lampstand, and those who would continue to revere a goddess rather than worship Yahweh alone (M. Smith, *Palestinian Parties and Politics That Shaped the Old Testament* [New York and London: Columbia University Press, 1971] 90-91). It mocks any concept of covenant community based on such cultic alternatives rather than on torah, by suggesting that these cults will actually result in just the opposite of what they intend. They will lead not to community but only to Shinar, i.e., the land of assimilative "scattering" (Gen 11:1-9).

Genre

Formulaic terms based on the verb *r'h* ("see"), together with the idiomatic expression *nś' 'ynym* ("lift the eyes"), are used in the introduction to both acts of this unit (vv. 5bα^{2}β, 9aα^1). The revelatory significance of the scene is indicated by the fact that the angelic interpreter commands the prophet to see it. The paranormal effect is heightened by the incongruence between the relatively small size of the ephah and the relatively large size of the woman said to be seated inside, and by the strange appearance of the stork-winged women. The significance of the vision is elucidated through explanatory statements of the angelic interpreter that result from both dialogue with the prophet (vv. 6b, 11) and interaction with the object visualized (v. 8aα). In each of its two acts this unit shows the basic pattern of the PROPHETIC VISION REPORT (→ 1:8-17, Genre).

Setting

This unit reflects attempts to set up Jewish temple cults in the dispersion, which cults involved the image of a goddess as well as the worship of Yahweh. There is no definite evidence of any such attempt among the Jews of Babylon (but see the possibility suggested by A. Lods, *The Prophets and the Rise of Judaism* [tr. S. H. Hooke; London: Routledge and Kegan Paul, 1937] 218). Here the toponym "Shinar" does not refer literally to just this place, however. It alludes mythically to the dispersion as a condition characterized by the threat of assimilation, and the vision's concluding reference to the building of a temple in Shinar is thus a description of a general tendency among the Jews of the dispersion, rather than a reference to the establishment of a particular sanctuary in Babylon. Jews in Egypt are known to have practiced such a cult in the immediate aftermath of the exile, as they took the worship of "the queen of heaven" with them when they left Jerusalem (Jer 44), and the Jews of Elephantine were perhaps involved in something similar later on in the Second Temple period (see A. Cowley, *Aramaic Papyri of the Fifth Century* B.C. [1923; repr. Osnabrück: Zeller, 1967] xviii-xxviii).

This vision demeans the exportation of this type of cult, in continuation with its popularity in Judah during preexilic times, as a basis for the formation of Jewish local communities in the dispersion. It satirizes this tendency from the viewpoint that proved to be the dominant influence on the restoration, which made Jerusalem the only place to build a temple for sacrifice; it proscribed any direct iconographic representation of deity; and it anathematized the worship of any god but Yahweh. According to this viewpoint the study of torah in documentary form would take the place of temple cult and sacrifice as the basic form of religious practice everywhere outside Jerusalem. Only this combination of a centralized temple cult in Jerusalem and devotion to torah elsewhere would enable the Jews to preserve their identity as a distinctive minority within the cosmopolitan culture in which they came to live throughout the empire.

As a leading proponent of rebuilding the Jerusalem temple, Zechariah was a representative of this "Yahweh alone" viewpoint. He probably reported this vision in the course of an oracular inquiry undertaken on his own initiative (→ 1:7-18, Setting) to discern the status of the rival form of postexilic Judaism that is so ironically portrayed in this text. From the prophet's standpoint this alternative form of Jewish cultic life lacked legitimacy and integrity.

Intention

In this text the prophet models for the audience the process of becoming disillusioned with the alternative form of Judaism represented by the ephah, in order that they might do likewise (→ 1:8-17, Intention). Although the mode of description is satirical, this alternative is treated as a serious rival to the program of restoration in which Zechariah was involved. It appears initially to be a movement with impressive momentum (vv. 5bβ-6bα), but the prophet comes to see it fall short in an attempt to mediate heaven and earth (v. 9b) because it is based on a human rather than a divine perspective (v. 6bβ). The attractiveness of this type of cult is genuine, but it is finally shown to have no basis in reality.

This rhetorical strategy is reinforced by symbolism suggesting that there are contradictions between what this alternative form of Judaism stands for and what it actually embodies. First there is the symbol of the ephah itself, which should ideally contain a full measure of good things but is notorious for not holding as much as it should (Deut 25:15; Amos 8:5; Prov 20:10; Lev 19:36; Ezek 45:10; Mic 6:11), and here holds only bad things. Then there are the feminine figures, including the woman seated within the ephah and the two other women who come to transport it. They are collectively described with the theophanic imagery pertaining to a goddess (Jeremias, 198-200). The woman in the ephah is carried "enthroned" (yôšebet [RSV "sitting"], v. 7b) across the sky by the winged women, in just the same way that Yahweh is flown through the heavens on his chariot-throne by winged cherubim (e.g., Ezek 1:4-15; Ps 18:11 [RSV 10]). In comparison the "theophany" of the ephah seems ridiculous, however. Yahweh's massive chariot can soar with ease, but the relatively compact ephah is weighted down to the point of being virtually earthbound. Attendants with storklike wings seem graceless in contrast with the impressive figure cut by the cherubim (D. N. Freedman and M. P. O'Connor, "kĕrûb," TDOT 7:314-19). All in all, the aspirations of this figure to rival the Jerusalem temple in representing the divine royal rule of heaven seem quite "containable."

Bibliography

M. Bič, *Die Nachtgesichte des Sacharja* (BibS [N] 42; Neukirchen-Vluyn: Neukirchener, 1964); M. H. Floyd, "The Evil in the Ephah: Reading Zechariah 5:5-11 in Its Literary Context," *CBQ* 58 (1996) 51-68; C. Jeremias, *Die Nachtgesichte des Sacharja* (FRLANT 117; Göttingen: Vandenhoeck & Ruprecht, 1977).

ZECHARIAH ENVISIONS YAHWEH REVERSING THE THREAT OF ASSIMILATION POSED BY THE DISPERSION, 6:1-8

Text

The structure analysis below is based on the following translation of v. 3b and vv. 5b-8:

> (3b) and the fourth chariot had dappled horses — strong ones they were! . . . (5b) These are the four winds of heaven that go forth from their post beside the Lord of the whole earth, (6) one of which has the black horses now heading north to Zaphon. The white ones have gone out after them, but the dappled ones have headed south to Teman. (7) These strong ones came forward and asked to go patrol the earth. And he said, "Yes, go patrol the earth," and they did so. (8) Then he cried out to me and said to me, "See, those heading north to Zaphon have given vent to my spirit/wind in the northland!"

The phrase *nwḥ* (hiphil) *'et-rûḥî* in v. 8bβ is understood here on the basis of the closest parallel to such usage, i.e., the phrase *nwḥ* (hiphil) *ḥēmâ* (Ezek 5:13; 16:42; 24:13; 21:22). The sense of the expression must be governed by the overall context, however, and hence it is not Yahweh's anger that is "vented" here but rather his creative influence *(rûaḥ)*.

Structure

I. Introductory vision report formula	6:1aα
A. Verb indicating repeated action: I again . . . *(wā'āšûb)*	
B. Description in terms of movement: I lifted my eyes	
C. Description in terms of perception: I saw *(wā'er'eh)*	
II. Vision proper	6:1aβ-8
A. Coordinating interjection: and behold! *(wĕhinnēh)*	6:1aβ^1
B. Description	6:1aβ^2-8
1. Scene	6:1aβ^2-3
a. Basic features	6:1aβ^2
1) Central figures: four chariots	
2) Their situation: coming out from between two mountains	
b. Elaboration: additional information	6:1b-3
1) With respect to the mountains: they were mountains of bronze	6:1b
2) With respect to the chariots: their horses	6:2-3
a) Coloring of each chariot's horses	6:2-3bβ^1
(1) First chariot: red	6:2a
(2) Second chariot: black	6:2b
(3) Third chariot: white	6:3a

The final change of scene in the second episode's series of four visions (4:1–6:8) is indicated by a reiteration of the idiomatic phrase "to lift the eyes," and the prophet sees four horse-drawn chariots emerging from between two mountains of bronze (v. 1). This section of the book (→ 1:7–6:15, Structure) is thus brought back full circle to a visionary scene much like the one with which it began, which also features horses (1:8-17). A basis for further comparison is established by the way the narration begins here, describing the different colors of the horses, and thus alluding to the different colors of the horses described in the first vision. As this unit unfolds, however, significant differences between it and the first vision also become apparent.

In the first vision the horses are mounts ridden by angelic beings in human form (1:8), and the focus is on the riders rather than on the horses themselves. Here, however, the focus is on chariots pulled by horses (6:1bα), and there is no mention at all of either riders or drivers — although the latter are of course inevitably implied by such imagery. In the first vision the angelic horse patrol is "standing by the abyss" (1:8aβ; → 1:8-17, Text), but here the horse-drawn chariots are in motion, emerging from between two bronze mountains. Both visions have groups of red and white horses in common, but they differ with respect to the colors of the other horses (in both the MT and LXX), and also with respect to how many other groups of horses there are (the MT has only one other group in 1:8, but two other groups in 6:2-3; the LXX has two other groups in both cases). In the first vision the differences in color do not correspond to any differences in action, as the angelic cavalry is assembled in one group to give a report of their mission (1:10b-11). Here, however, the colors serve to separate the chariot corps into four divisions, some of which are going in one direction and some in another.

The basic similarity between the first vision and the eighth indicates that both cases involve heavenly hosts. The differences, however, also indicate that in these two visions the respective roles of the heavenly host are not quite the same. In the first vision they were sent "to patrol the earth" (*lĕhithallēk bā'āreṣ,* 1:10b), and they have returned to report that "the earth remains at rest" (1:11), thus confirming that there is an international situation conducive to the restoration. The prophet now sees similar forces deployed on a different but closely related mission (vv. 5-6), and then sent on another reconnoitering patrol (*lĕhithallēk bā'āreṣ,* v. 7), like the one from which they have just returned in 1:8-17. Their capacity to influence world affairs is suggested by twice characterizing them as "strong ones" (*'ămuṣṣîm*), as they are involved in both phases of their action (vv. 3bβ², 7aα¹). In his reply to the prophet the angelic interpreter describes what is being accomplished by means of their strength (vv. 5-8).

The four divisions of the heavenly chariot corps are metaphorically identified with the four winds of heaven. Like the winds, they are invisible forces at work in the world whose effects are nevertheless materially evident. They emanate from their assigned post beside the throne of Yahweh (v. 5bβ). As chariots, they reflect the cosmic power of Yahweh, who can be described as a charioteer emerging victorious over the forces of chaos (e.g., Hab 3:8-15; imagery similarly involving the emanation of the winds as chariots from Yahweh's heavenly throne is found in Ps 104:3-4a). The movements of the angelic chariotry in heaven become manifest on earth as the windlike forces that blow various changes into being.

Some commentators have questioned the way in which the MT describes only three chariots in motion during the first phase of their action (vv. 5-6) and have claimed on the basis of the LXX that all four are initially involved in movement toward the four corners of the world. But this reading requires reconstructing a hypothetical original text that accords with neither the MT nor the LXX in their present form. According to both the MT and LXX, only three chariots are involved in the first phase of the action, and the fourth does not become involved until the second phase (v. 7); and in neither version is the first phase of the chariots' movement directed toward all four corners of the world. If one follows the MT, two chariots head north while one heads south (v. 6); and then all four chariots, collectively designated once again as "the strong ones," come and request Yahweh's permission to go patrol the earth (v. 7a; cf. v. 3bβ^2). If one follows the LXX, two chariots head north while one heads south; and then the fourth chariot alone comes and requests Yahweh's permission to go on patrol. Either way, the initial movement of the chariots is only along the north-south axis of the world, not along the east-west axis as well (Reventlow, "Tradition," 186-88).

Both the northern and southern compass points are designated by toponyms associated with holy mountains that serve to identify the two bronze mountains mentioned in the initial description of the scene. The two locations, from between which the chariots first emerge (v. 1aβ) and toward which they are moving (v. 6), are Zaphon and Teman. Both names serve as directional markers indicating the lay of the land from a Judeocentric perspective. In relation to Jerusalem, Mt. Zaphon lies along the Syrian coast and thus designates the north, while Teman lies toward Edom and thus designates the south. Both sites are also associated with mythic descriptions of deeds done by gods. Mt. Zaphon is sacred to Baal, who sustains earthly life through his struggles to tame chaos (represented by the god Yam) and overcome death (represented by the god Mot). In Israel's mythic topography this name thus applies to the place from which chaos breaks out, and it is associated in prophetic imagery with "the enemy from the north" that threatens to destroy Israel and Judah (e.g., Isa 14:31; 41:25; Jer 1:14; 6:22; cf. Ps 48:2-3 [*RSV* 1-2], where the same term is used with more positive connotations). Teman is the region identified with the mountain sacred to Yahweh, the regions also variously identified with Mt. Paran and Mt. Sinai. From his sanctuary there, Yahweh marches forth as a victorious warrior and charioteer to defend his people (e.g., Deut 33:2; Hab 3:3; Ps 68:8-9 [*RSV* 7-8]). This name indicates the place from which Yahweh launches heroic historical initiatives on Judah's behalf.

As the action unfolds against this backdrop, it becomes apparent that the action has returned to the juncture between heaven and earth (→ 1:7-18, Structure). Although earthly mountains set the scene, they do so in terms of their associations with the heavenly actions of gods, and from such a perspective one can see the correlation between earthly and heavenly actions. From this cosmically intermediate point one can quickly reach the earthly plane itself, and yet also have direct access to Yahweh on his heavenly throne (vv. 5, 7). The movement of the heavenly chariots along a north-south axis, between Zaphon and Teman, thus represents the reactualization of a mythic pattern of divine action, according to which Yahweh marches forth to quell whatever chaotic forces may threaten to overwhelm his people and disturb the cosmic order.

This mythic pattern is linked by the larger literary context with a specific historical situation (Reventlow, "Tradition," 188-90). In (→) 2:10-17 (*RSV* 6-13) the "land of the north" (*'ereṣ ṣāpôn*) is explicitly identified as Babylon (2:10-11). By the time of the restoration Babylon was no longer the source of chaos in any military sense, and the first two visions (1:8–2:4) portray Yahweh's deploying his forces through the Persians in order to bring the exile to an end. Even after the Persians authorized the return to Jerusalem, however, the ongoing reality of the dispersion meant that Babylon continued to embody the threat of assimilation. In this sense the "Babylonian exile" came to symbolize the antithesis of the restoration long after the imposition of exile by the Babylonians ceased to be a political fact. The movement of the heavenly hosts in this vision thus represents Yahweh's attempts to counter the cultural forces of chaos in the dispersion. Just as he once used the four winds to scatter his people into exile (2:10), he is now using the four winds to prevent them from being assimilated. Along a vector extending from the southern source of Yahweh's great defensive initiatives on his people's behalf, and running right through the center point of Jerusalem, Yahweh is bringing pressure to bear on the northern source of the confusion that threatens the restoration's success.

After initiating this action above, the angelic chariot forces ask Yahweh for permission to go and see how their actions are affecting earthly affairs (v. 7). (According to the LXX the fourth chariot does this, while the other three are presumably still engaged in their north-south movement; according to the MT the first three chariots leave their north-south movement and join the fourth, collectively making up "the strong ones" [v. 7aα], to ask Yahweh's permission.) Yahweh grants their request and they go to patrol the earth. Before they return with their report, the angelic interpreter concludes with an oracular speech of Yahweh (v. 8), directing the prophet's attention to what is being accomplished at the earthly pressure point. The force of the chariot moving northward has caused Yahweh's creative influence (*rûaḥ*, "spirit/wind") to be exerted there (*nwḥ* hiphil; → Text). By means of this divine impetus the dispersion has been brought into line with the other forces moving along the world axis, and thus brought into a dynamic relationship with Jerusalem and the mythic southern site of Israel's primeval origins.

Genre

The introduction uses terminology and idiomatic expressions associated with the vision report formula (→ 1:8-17, Genre). The revelatory significance of the scene is suggested by initially describing the two mountains as "mountains of bronze" (v. 1b), which suggests mythic topography even before this suggestion is subsequently confirmed by making the names of the mountains explicit (v. 6). The narrative elucidates the meaning of the scene through a combination of action and dialogue. Some action is reported through dialogue (e.g., the movement of chariots in vv. 5-6), and some is narrated directly (the movement of the chariots in v. 7b). The dialogue includes a question-and-answer exchange between the prophet and the angelic interpreter (vv. 4-6), as well as a command issued by a heavenly being (presumably Yahweh) to "go patrol the earth" (v. 7aβ). It culminates in an oracular speech of Yahweh (v. 8), addressed directly to the prophet, commanding him to "see!" the summary description of the scene's meaning (*rĕ'ēh; RSV* "behold!"; cf. 5:5bα). These details of the narrative development constitute minor variations, of the sort that are also evident in the preceding visions of this section, on the basic generic form of the PROPHETIC VISION REPORT (→ 1:8-17, Genre).

Setting

In order for the restoration to succeed, it was necessary not only for exiles to return in sufficient numbers but also for the symbolic center of gravity to shift from Babylon to Jerusalem, so that even those who remained in the dispersion would look to Jerusalem for leadership, just as those who remained in Judah had once looked to Babylon for leadership (e.g., Jer 24). In theological terms the question was — given that Yahweh had creatively reshaped the world situation so that the restoration could begin to take place — whether he would continue to influence the world situation so as to keep the process going. This vision was probably reported in the course of an oracular inquiry undertaken by the prophet on his own initiative (→ 1:7-18, Setting), in an attempt to address this issue. The reply affirmed that Yahweh was reversing the tendency of the Jewish community to center on Babylon and shifting their attention back toward the land of Judah.

Intention

In this text the audience sees the prophet come to realize that the historical process of restoration involves not only a change in location for those who return to Jerusalem but also a change in worldview for those who remain in the dispersion. It is important for them to focus their identity on what is happening in Judah, in order to reverse the tendency to assimilation that threatens them elsewhere. Yahweh is making the world situation conducive for them to do so, and they are invited to imagine Yahweh's creativity in terms of symbols that are both meteorological and military. The maneuvers of the heavenly hosts are invisible to the human eye, but their powerful influence as agents of Yahweh's creative spirit is nevertheless manifest in the winds of change that are blowing toward Judah.

Bibliography

H. Graf Reventlow, "Tradition und Aktualisierung in Sacharjas siebentem Nacht-gesicht: Sach 6,1-8," in *Alttestamentliche Glaube und biblische Theologie* (*Fest.* H. D. Preuss; ed. J. Hausmann and H.-J. Zobel; Stuttgart: Kohlhammer, 1992) 180-90.

ZECHARIAH SHOWS THAT ZERUBBABEL'S ROYAL AUTHORITY DERIVES FROM THE TEMPLE'S ROYAL STATUS, 6:9-15

Text

In v. 11 the plural form *'ăṭārôt* ("crowns") is much better attested than the singular variant followed by the *RSV*. In v. 14, however, the combination of a defective spelling of the same word with a singular verb suggests that there the original reading may have well been the orthographically similar singular form *'ăṭeret* (so *BHS*). The discussion below assumes that more than one crown is involved, but it is not necessary to resolve this text-critical problem in order to grasp the significance of the command that is enjoined on the prophet and hence the overall significance of the action (→ Structure).

In v. 14b it would be better to translate *zikrôn* as something like "a memorial" (*RSV* "reminder"). The person named Heldai in v. 10a is in v. 14b alternatively called *ḥelem,* and the person named Josiah in v. 10b is likewise alternatively called *ḥen* (Meyers and Meyers, *Haggai,* 340-43). The *RSV*'s retention of "Heldai" and "Josiah" in v. 14b suffices for all practical purposes, but this translation does not allow the text to suggest any of the connotations that these alternative designations might have. For example, they might be terms for official positions in the temple or provincial court (see A. Demsky, "The Temple Steward Josiah ben Zephaniah," *IEJ* 31 [1981] 100-102), and thus might connote that these two men will have assumed such positions by the time the crowns are placed in the temple.

Structure

I. Introductory prophetic word formula: and the word
   of Yahweh came to me, saying . . .   6:9
II. Revelation concerning the source of Zerubbabel's
   royal authority   6:10-15
   A. Directive concerning performance of a symbolic act   6:10-14
      1. Preparing for the symbolic act: the making
         of crowns   6:10-11a
         a. Order to acquire the necessary materials   6:10-11aα
            1) Basic command (initially stated with
               object unspecified): take!   6:10aα^1

2) Identification of donors — 6:10aα²β
  a) Heldai — 6:10aα²
  b) Tobijah — 6:10aβ¹
  c) Jedaiah — 6:10aβ²
3) Supplementary command concerning acquisition of materials — 6:10bα-β¹
  a) Stated initially with respect to time: go the same day — 6:10bα
  b) Restated subsequently with respect to location: go to the house of Josiah the son of Zephaniah — 6:10bβ¹
4) Elaboration of the status of all four persons thus far involved: they have returned from Babylon — 6:10bβ²
5) Basic command (subsequently restated with object specified): take silver and gold! — 6:11aα
 b. Command to make the crowns — 6:11aβ
2. Performing the symbolic act: what to do with the crowns — 6:11b-13
 a. Command to put crowns on the head of Joshua son of Jehozadak — 6:11b
 b. Order to address a speech of Yahweh to the high priest — 6:12-13
  1) Command: speak to him, saying . . . — 6:12aα
  2) Speech of Yahweh — 6:12aβ-13
   a) Introductory messenger formula: thus says Yahweh of hosts . . . — 6:12aβ
   b) Speech proper — 6:12b-13
    (1) Concerning another position of leadership besides Joshua's — 6:12b-13a
     (a) Basic statement announcing the designation of this position: behold a man whose name is Branch — 6:12bα
     (b) Elaboration — 6:12bβ-13a
      α. His status in general: he shall flourish in his own right — 6:12bβ¹
      β. His function: he shall build the temple — 6:12bβ²
      γ. Reiteration of his function: he shall build the temple — 6:13aα
      δ. His status in particular: he will have royal authority — 6:13aβ
    (2) Concerning Joshua's own priestly leadership role — 6:13b
     (a) His complementary status: beside the throne — 6:13bα

The prophet here reports his reception not of a revelatory vision but of a revelatory word (v. 9). The report has two parts. In the first part Zechariah describes the directions Yahweh gave him concerning the performance of a symbolic act (vv. 10-14). In the second part the prophet describes the effects of the act's performance, so as to elicit the audience's faith in him and the message communicated by this means (v. 15). The preparations for the symbolic act are given in some detail (vv. 10-11a). The prophet is to make crowns (or perhaps only one crown; → Text) out of gold and silver donated by three recently returned exiles, who are explicitly named; and he is to perform this task in the house of a particular person, who is also explicitly named. He is then to put the crown(s) on the head of Joshua the high priest (v. 11b), as he conveys to Joshua a message from Yahweh (vv. 12-13). The oracle delivered to Joshua promises that someone like "a branch" (ṣemaḥ) will rebuild the temple (vv. 12aβ²-13aα), and the outcome of the symbolic act is thus described in terms of this eventuality. Once the temple is finished, the crowns will be placed there to commemorate the example of those who helped to make them (v. 14), some of whom may by then have assumed official positions on the temple staff (→ Text). In the meantime the act will generate additional support for rebuilding the temple, inducing "those who are far off" to come — like those whose example is commemorated by the crowns — and support the work of rebuilding (v. 15aα). In conclusion the report's audience is advised that, if they trust in what the act is said by Zechariah to portend, they will find their faith in him confirmed by the project's growing momentum and progress (v. 15aβb).

Although there is some uncertainty about the number of crowns that are involved (→ Text), Yahweh definitely commands the crowning of just one person (v. 11b). Although Joshua is the person to be crowned, the accompanying oracle describes this act's significance largely in terms of another person and his role (vv. 12b-13). The crowning of Joshua shows something about the status and function of the "branch"-like person charged with building the temple, and something about the relationship of this person's role to Joshua's high priesthood. In view of the fact that Zerubbabel has previously been identified as the builder of the temple (4:9), he must be the one like a "branch," whose role is defined by the prophet's dramatic act. In view of the fact that the same "branch"-like role has figured in one of the preceding prophecies, the state-

405

ments about it here should be read in the light of what is said there. In (→) 3:1-10 Joshua's authority as high priest is legitimated by Yahweh's bringing forth someone "branch"-like to confirm it (3:8), and here Zerubbabel's assumption of this "branch"-like role is conversely confirmed by Yahweh's mandating a kind of cooperative interdependence between him and the high priest (v. 13b).

The prophet's act is obviously a symbolic one. It should also be noted, however, that it is symbolic action of a particular sort, based on the virtually paradoxical premise that something done to Joshua can be a telling sign of Zerubbabel's status. Such crowning cannot be symbolic in the rather direct sense that has often been supposed, i.e., it cannot be a ceremony marking either Joshua's or Zerubbabel's assumption of their respective offices. Yahweh's instructions refer to Joshua as the high priest (v. 11b), presupposing that he has already been invested with this office. By means of the crowning Zerubbabel is assigned some distinctively royal prerogatives, such as "ruling on his throne" (v. 13aβ); but the prophet's action hardly constitutes any sort of coronation for Zerubbabel, since he is not the one who is actually crowned. If any challenge to Persian rule were intended, or if any attempt to restore the monarchy were implied, this could hardly have been signified in such an oblique way (cf. Elisha's rather more forthright instigation of the rebellion against Joram by the anointing of Jehu, 2 Kgs 9:1-10).

The crowning is a prophetic symbolic action that combines a dramatic gesture with the delivery of a prophetic oracle. It thereby shows that certain aspects of the present political arrangement have an underlying theological significance. Although Zerubbabel is not actually a king, he can nevertheless play a kinglike role, at least as far as Yahweh is concerned. Elsewhere he is said to hold the office of provincial "governor" (*paḥat;* Hag 1:1b, 14a; 2:2a, 21a), and in this capacity he presumably exercises some kind of civil jurisdiction, but here this civil role goes completely unmentioned. Elsewhere he is also said to be of Davidic descent (1 Chr 3:19), but here his ancestry likewise goes completely unmentioned. This text emphasizes instead that he enjoys a quasi-royal status only by virtue of his function as temple builder (note the repetition in vv. 12bβ²-13aα). Precisely because his royal status depends on his association with the temple, he is thereby brought into a complementary relationship with the high priest in charge of the cult.

The nature of this complementary relationship is spelled out in the conclusion of Yahweh's message to Joshua (vv. 12b-13). First and foremost, in assuming the "branch"-like role of temple builder, Zerubbabel is exercising political authority that he enjoys in his own right. He literally "branches out from his own position" (*mittaḥtāyw yiṣmāḥ;* RSV "shall grow up in his place") to build the temple (vv. 12bβ²-13bα), and thereby invests his rule with royal dignity (v. 13aβ). From this exercise of his political authority a relationship with the priesthood follows inevitably, but this relationship is described somewhat ambiguously (v. 13bα). The phrase *'al-kis'ô* might indicate that the priest has a position "by [Zerubbabel's] throne" (so *RSV*), and the LXX similarly indicates that the priest is "at his right hand." Or this phrase might indicate that the priest is seated "on his own throne." In any case the priest shares the dais with Zerubbabel so as to indicate the political subordination of the priestly role to

Zerubbabel's civil authority. Zerubbabel "bears royal honor" *(yiśśā' hôd)* and "rules" *(ûmāšal)* from his throne (v. 13aβ) in a way that the priest does not, even if the priest has "a throne of his own" (cf. 1 Kgs 2:19). At the same time, however, Zerubbabel's royal dignity is contingent on his governing in accord with priestly counsel (v. 13bβ) because the priestly role is more theologically fundamental (→ 3:1-10, Structure; 4:1-14, Structure).

Because the oracle in vv. 12b-13 is concerned with defining the interrelationship between Zerubbabel's "branch"-like status and his function as temple builder, rather than with marking his assumption of either this status or this function, it is difficult to determine whether Zechariah's reception of this revelation occurred before or after the start of Zerubbabel's rebuilding project. The verbs describing his building activity, one a *waw*-consecutive perfect (*ûbānâ*, v. 12bβ²) and the other an imperfect (*yibneh*, v. 13aα), are ambiguous in this regard. They might well be translated with the English future tense ("he will build"; so *RSV*), in which case Zerubbabel might not yet have taken up this task; but they might just as well be translated with the English present progressive tense ("he is building"), in which case Zerubbabel would have already managed to get the work going. The oracle serves to define the implications of his responsibility for this project, whether or not he has yet begun it; and in any case the work remains to be finished. The symbolic act of the prophet points toward the completion of the temple, showing what it means for Judah's chief civil administrator to take the lead in restoring this particular institution.

Under the Persians Judah cannot aspire to be a kingdom in the ordinary sense, but Judah can nevertheless aspire to be *like* a kingdom in the theological sense, i.e., to be the earthly representation of Yahweh's heavenly rule. It is possible for Judah to assume this role because the restored temple is a royal temple, and hence Yahweh's designated surrogate for the Davidic monarchy. Royal status is indicated here by pointedly referring to the edifice with the word *hêkal* (vv. 12bβ-13aα, 14b), which can also denote the palace of a king, and thus abandoning the previously used term *bayit* (lit. "house"; 1:16; 4:9a).

The same idea is suggested by the fact that neither Joshua nor Zerubbabel will ultimately keep the crowns. They will be placed in the temple (v. 14), where they will presumably be displayed if they are to fulfill their memorializing function. The ongoing presence of the crowns in the temple would be a *zikrôn* (→ Text) not only in the sense that they would commemorate the example of their benefactors, but also in the sense that they would commemorate the performance of the prophetic act defining the significance of the institution. The crowns would thus be included among the symbolic objects with which the temple was furnished, subsidiary to the central position occupied by the tableau of the lampstand flanked by olive trees. Like the lampstand, the crowns would signify that the temple is the real seat of royal authority (→ 4:1-14).

Zechariah thus crowns the high priest Joshua in order to show that Zerubbabel's kingliness is not simply a matter of whatever civil jurisdiction he may exercise. On the contrary, his civil jurisdiction becomes kingly only by virtue of his association with the royal temple. Judah's restoration therefore requires more than merely gaining some measure of political recognition under a

407

governor. The rebuilding of the temple is even more essential, and this requires both the continuing return of those who are still in the dispersion and the continued support of those who have already returned, as well as Zerubbabel's leadership.

This report recounts only the prophet's commission to perform the symbolic act of crowning Joshua. It does not explicitly say anything about whether he should do this in public, or whether he did as he was told. The report nevertheless concludes in a way that implies both the prophet's compliance with Yahweh's command and his subsequent efforts to publicize this fact. In vv. 12-15 there is a gradual but noticeable transition from the message Yahweh is telling the prophet to the message the prophet is telling his audience, and this transition has two major aspects: (1) a shift in the temporal frame of reference, from a prospective to a retrospective outlook on the performance of the symbolic act; and (2) a concomitant shift in rhetorical stance, from the prophet's relatively matter-of-fact description of the crowning itself to his rather more urgent parenetical engagement with all those affected by what it portends.

In vv. 12-13 the prophet is clearly reporting what Yahweh told him to tell Joshua. In v. 14 the report presumably continues with Yahweh's telling Joshua what he or someone is finally to do with the crowns, as part of the directive given to him concerning the performance of the symbolic act. The continuity is not altogether clear, however. Because Joshua is not directly addressed in v. 14, the prophet could at this point be abandoning the report of what Yahweh commissioned him to tell Joshua, and could simply be telling his audience where the crowns will end up. (Note the *RSV*'s rather confusing use of quotation marks and paragraphing at this point.) In v. 15aα the description clearly moves beyond the directions for the symbolic act itself to a description of the effect the act will have on the larger course of events, but the same ambiguity continues with respect to whether the prophet is still speaking for Yahweh or beginning to speak for himself. Only in v. 15aβb is the ambiguity regarding the speaker finally resolved, as the prophet addresses himself directly to his audience, describing how the effect of the act will determine their perception of him.

The concluding emphasis on what the audience will "know" about the prophet (v. 15aβ), as a result of what will follow from the act, implies that the prophet has indeed done what Yahweh told him. The question is not whether the prophet will heed Yahweh in performing the act, but whether the people will heed what Yahweh is telling them through the prophet's having done so (v. 15b). The prophetic narrator is therefore speaking of something he has already done, and telling how he was inspired to do it, so that the audience will assent to his claims of what this act portends for them. Whether the act was initially performed in public or in private, this report would have made it known to a circle far wider than those who initially witnessed it.

Genre

As this unit contains a commission to perform a symbolic act, an indication of the prophet's compliance, and an oracular explanation of the act's significance, it is formally a REPORT OF A PROPHETIC SYMBOLIC ACTION (Fohrer, *Die symbolischen Handlungen,* 15-19; cf. Isa 20:1-6; Jer 19:1-15; Hos 1:2-11, etc.). It is somewhat unusual for this kind of report to conclude with a direct address of the audience, but here this device simply serves to extend and emphasize the expression of a concern that is innate to the genre: to elicit the audience's confidence in the revelatory significance of the symbolic act.

Setting

This text presupposes a situation beset by doubts about the theological significance of Judah's civil status under the Persians. It affirms on the one hand that Yahweh's relationship with his people could be historically embodied in Judah's becoming recognized as some kind of official entity within the empire; but it also affirms on the other hand that this in itself will not make Judah the sign of Yahweh's kingly rule over all creation. Only the restoration of Jerusalem's temple, as a reincarnation of the royal sanctuary established by David and Solomon, can provide the basis on which Judah could assume this significance. Zechariah's symbolic action, and the subsequent publicizing of it by means of this report, helped to create a theologically informed consensus about the direction in which the restoration should go.

Intention

The narration of this text is meant to provide an interpretive context from which Zechariah's symbolic act can speak for itself. Within this context the act discloses that Zerubbabel, as an imperial authority of whatever sort, cannot represent the kingdom of heaven until the temple is rebuilt. Assuming the power of the prophetic sign to engender what it represents, the report invites its audience to participate in realizing the future to which the sign points. If they will act in accord with the claim made by the sign, that only the royal temple can give this sacramental significance to Judah and its leadership, their assent will cause events to unfold in a way that confirms their faith.

Bibliography

S. Amsler, *Les actes des prophètes* (Essais bibliques 9; Geneva: Labor et Fides, 1985); idem, "Les prophètes et la communication par les actes," in *Werden und Wirken des Alten Testaments* (*Fest.* C. Westermann; ed. R. Albertz et al.; Göttingen: Vandenhoeck & Ruprecht: Neukirchen-Vluyn: Neukirchener, 1980) 194-201; G. Fohrer, "Die Gattung der Berichte über symbolische Handlungen der Propheten," *Studien zur alt-*

testamentlichen Prophetie (1949-1965) (BZAW 99; Berlin: Töpelmann, 1967) 92-112; idem, *Die symbolischen Handlungen der Propheten* (2nd ed.; ATANT 54; Zurich: Zwingli, 1968); G. Wallis, "Erwägungen zu Sacharja VI 9-15," in *Congress Volume: Uppsala, 1971* (VTSup 22; Leiden: Brill, 1972) 232-37.

Chapter 4

THE THIRD MAJOR SECTION
OF THE BOOK (7:1–8:23)
AND ITS INDIVIDUAL UNITS

REPORT OF AN ORACULAR INQUIRY CONCERNING
THE EFFECTS OF TEMPLE RESTORATION, 7:1–8:23

Structure

This section coheres around a story about an oracular inquiry. The people of Bethel send a delegation to Jerusalem, where the project of rebuilding the temple has begun but is not yet finished, to find out what this development portends for their customary fast commemorating the destruction of the temple (7:2-3). They are to inquire of Yahweh through the priests and prophets who are involved in the restoration. The narrative reports neither the arrival of the delegation in Jerusalem nor any arrangements they may have made for the conduct of the inquiry, but proceeds immediately to the revelation that Zechariah received in response to their intended request (7:4–8:23). This revelation eventually provides them with a direct answer to their question (8:18-19), but only after the prophet has digressed at some length (7:4–8:17).

This digression serves to explain the underlying meaning of the answer they finally receive. They ask only about the fast commemorating the destruction of the temple, but the digression begins with several counterquestions about the intention with which this and another similar fast have been observed all during the exile (7:5-6). These counterquestions begin to broaden the subject, so that by the time the answer is finally given, it has come to include a total of four fasts commemorating various aspects of Judah's overthrow (7:19). The delegation from Bethel is thus given to understand not only why they should discontinue the fast they initially asked about, but also why they should change all such fasts into feasts. The point is not just that the temple's restoration will make the observance of its destruction anomalous, but also that the temple's restoration signals the beginning of a whole new era in which all the causes and consequences of the exile are being decisively reversed.

The larger issue raised by the prophet's counterquestions is whether their fasting has really been a sign of their desire to serve Yahweh in an all-consuming and hence more than merely liturgical fashion, or whether it has simply been a symptom of their self-interest in maintaining the status quo (7:5-6). The prophet puts his attempt to raise this issue in historical perspective by asking further whether this is not precisely the kind of issue that the preexilic prophets used to raise in their day (7:7).

The way is thus prepared for an exhortation urging obedience to the kinds of noncultic imperatives that the prophets have long recognized as an integral part of any relationship with Yahweh (7:9–8:17). This exhortation begins with a series of commands (7:9b-10) and concludes with a similar list of obligations (8:16-17) that summarily reechoes the starting point in its near-verbatim repetition of certain key phrases (e.g., "render true judgments," 7:9bα; 8:16bβ; "do not devise evil in your hearts," 7:10b; 8:17aα). The urgency of these demands is predicated on the prophet's presupposition that Judah now stands at a decisive turning point in its history. This presupposition is expressed in brief narration which explains that the exile was Yahweh's angry reaction to Judah's unwillingness to heed the preexilic prophets (7:11-14), and that Yahweh has now decided to give Judah another chance (8:14-15a).

The exhortation thus basically combines ethical commands with narration that serves as their motivation (7:9-14; 8:14-17). It is interrupted by material of a different but closely related sort (8:1-13). A series of five prophetic speeches (8:1-8) is interjected to provide the pivot on which the interrupted narration turns from the record of Judah's past failures (7:11-14) to the promise of a better future (7:14-15a). The first two speeches (8:2-3) describe the recent developments that have created the possibility of a new future for Judah (→ 8:1-8). Yahweh has had a change of heart, so that his anger against Judah has become transformed into zeal for their welfare (8:2; cf. 7:12b). Moreover, this attitudinal change is outwardly evident in that he has returned to dwell in Jerusalem (8:3), where his cult has been reestablished and his temple is being rebuilt (cf. 8:9b). According to the last three speeches (8:4-13), Yahweh is so pleased with the potential of even such partial progress that he cannot help but bring the entire process of restoration to its completion. The exhortation to obey Yahweh's ethical demands (7:9-14; 8:14-17) is also interrupted by another exhortation with a different but closely related aim (8:9-13). Framed by the repeated invitation to "let your hands be strong" (8:9aα², 13bβ), this exhortation encourages its audience to maintain the same level of loyalty to the temple rebuilding project that the prophets of the restoration have thus far elicited from them (8:9). This request for their continued support is motivated by a description of the growing peace and prosperity that the rebuilding project has thus far brought with it, and by a description of the complete reversal in Judah's fortunes that therefore promises to materialize (8:10-13a).

The relationship between the two exhortations is shown by the way in which they are analogously structured and by the repetition of key words and phrases. Just as the exhortation to obey Yahweh's ethical demands ends in 9:16-17 by repeating some of the same commands with which it began in 8:9-10, the exhortation to support the temple's reconstruction likewise ends in 8:13bβ by repeating the same invitation with which it began in 8:9aα², to "let your hands be strong." Just as the concluding repetition of this invitation in 8:13bβ is preceded by the admonition to "fear not" in 8:13bα, the concluding repetition of commands in 8:16-17 is likewise preceded by the admonition to "fear not" in 8:15b. Moreover, the measure of "peace" $(šālôm)$ that has already been achieved (8:10; RSV "safety"), as well as the increase of "peace" that is thereby promised (8:12aα¹), is explicitly associated with the "peace" that accompanies the keeping of Yahweh's ethical commands (8:16bβ).

These links show that the concerns of the overarching exhortation to obey Yahweh's ethical commands (7:9–8:17) and the concerns of the interjected exhortation to support the temple's reconstruction (8:9-13) converge in

8:15b-17. In the light of the prophetic interpretation of Judah's recent past, as this interpretation is expressed in various ways throughout 7:7–8:15a, any authentic commitment to the temple rebuilding project must also include a larger commitment to Yahweh's ethical demands, as these have been revealed through the prophetic tradition. The restoration is not just a return to the kind of situation that existed in preexilic times, when Judah failed to realize fully the nature of either the cultic or the ethical demands of Yahweh, and Yahweh thus brought about Judah's destruction.

The restoration instead signals the emergence of a new kind of situation characterized by a fundamental change on Yahweh's part, which similarly calls for a fundamental change on Judah's part. Yahweh now intends to work only for their welfare, but they must take him up on his offer, both cultically and ethically. The people of Bethel would thus be well advised not just to take note of the rebuilding project by no longer fasting to commemorate the temple's destruction, but also to redefine the full range of their commitments, so as to identify with the restoration in its total significance.

The prophetic speech in 8:19 succinctly and summarily concludes all that precedes it. The initial question about a fast observed in Bethel (7:2-3) is finally answered, but in terms of the new future that the prophet's historical review (7:7, 11-14; 8:14-15a) has shown to lie ahead for the entire "house of Judah" because of what the restoration shows about Yahweh's intentions for Judah (8:1-13). The directive to "love truth and peace" (8:19b) recapitulates with these key terms two dominant themes that permeate the prophet's whole reply (for "truth" see 7:9bα; 8:3bα, 8bβ, 16bα; for "peace" see 8:10bα, 12aα, 16bβ).

In its overall structure this section represents a process of prophetic reeducation that the "people of the land" and some of the priests are to undergo (7:5a), in order to grasp the full meaning of the new developments in Jerusalem. In coming to understand the need for radical changes in their old religious habits, the people of Bethel set a precedent for many others besides themselves — regardless of whether the old religious habits are observances that developed during the exile at places other than Bethel, vestigial remnants of preexilic Israelite practices, or pagan non-Israelite customs. The same process will be repeated by people from many other cities (8:20-21) and will eventually be repeated by people from many other nations as well (8:22-23).

The style of this section is characterized by a pattern of interruptions that is evident in its distinctive use of the prophetic word formula. At the outset the date citation is interrupted by this formula (→ 7:1, Structure). Then, as if to follow this precedent, each succeeding subunit is in turn interrupted by material that is introduced with the prophetic word formula. The progress of the oracular inquiry, which would normally entail a direct answer to the initial question, is interrupted at 7:5 by the prophet's counterquestions. The prophet's review of Judah's past, which begins with his final counterquestion in 7:7 and continues in 7:11, is interrupted by the commencement of the exhortation in 7:9. As the exhortation becomes interwoven with the historical review, it is in turn interrupted by the block of material that focuses specifically on the progress of the restoration (8:2-13). Each of these interruptions is introduced by the prophetic word formula (7:5, 8; 8:1). Finally, the same formula also marks the end of these interruptions, when the prophetic discourse at last shifts back to the business of answering the initial question (8:18).

This section's use of the prophetic word formula also has another noteworthy feature. There is a systematic alternation between its biographical expression in the third person (i.e., "the word of Yahweh came to *Zechariah*," 7:1, 8) and its autobiographical expression in the first person (i.e., "the word of Yahweh came to *me*," 7:4; 8:18), as well as one occurrence of the formula without any designation of the revelation's recipient in either first or third person (i.e., "the word of Yahweh came . . . ," 8:1; note that the *RSV* has supplied "to me," although there is nothing to indicate any such first person indirect object in the underlying Hebrew).

On the one hand, this alternation clearly differentiates the prophet from the anonymous narrator with regard to both perspective and rhetorical stance. The prophet is using the inquiry of the people from Bethel as an occasion for reeducating "the people of the land and the priests" concerning the overall significance of the restoration, but the narrator is retrospectively recounting the prophet's involvement in this whole process in order to raise similar issues with those who read this text. On the other hand, however, this difference is simultaneously blurred by the way in which the prophetic word formula is also repeatedly used, regardless of whether it is expressed in the third or first person, to interrupt one rhetorically distinctive sort of prophetic discourse with another.

The tension between these two patterns of usage makes it difficult to get a clear impression, at any given point, of who is speaking to whom. There are three different frames of rhetorical reference in this section. First, the prophet is addressing his contemporaries, as he gives an answer to the oracular inquiry. Second, as he speaks to them, he also describes what the preexilic prophets used to say to their contemporaries. Finally, as the incident of the oracular inquiry is recounted, the narrator addresses the readers of the text. The narrative style of this section seems intended first to differentiate and then to efface these frames of rhetorical reference, and thus to imply that although such distinctions are real, they do not make any real difference. As the prophet speaks to his contemporaries, they are in effect hearing the words of the preexilic prophets; and as the narrator addresses the readers of the text, they are in effect hearing the words of Zechariah. The prophetic word formula, which occurs where this rhetorical ambiguity is most dense, thus fails to identify any particular recipient of the revelation: "The word of Yahweh came . . ." (8:1).

As far as temporal perspective goes, there is a similar distinction without any real difference. The prophet situates his addressees during the time after the temple's foundations were relaid but before the reconstruction was finished (8:9). The narrator situates the revelation to Zechariah somewhat more precisely, on a particular date "in the fourth year of King Darius" (7:1), but this date is approximately the same point in time. There are thus two decidedly different perspectives here, but in every major respect they converge. Whether the incident of the oracular inquiry from Bethel is considered from the relatively narrow and subjective standpoint of those immediately involved in the events, or whether it is considered from the relatively broad and objective standpoint of those at some distance from the events, the issue is basically the same one that the preexilic prophets first perceived.

The issue is whether the people will share the prophetic vision of what the worship of Yahweh implies. If they will see the temple as a sign of Yahweh's call to lead a whole new way of life, they will become incorporated into a new world order that works for their welfare. If the people's commitment to the rebuilding project, based on this awareness of its significance, remains strong enough to bring the temple to completion, the status claimed for it by Zechariah and his small interest group will be widely acknowledged by everyone. It will eventually be recognized by all Jews, and by people of all nations everywhere, as a sign of the knowledge and presence of Yahweh, the one true God (8:20-23).

Genre

' This section is generically complex because it draws on elements from various types of prophetic speech and literature. Its overall form is ultimately defined, however, by the relationship between its two main parts. By virtue of the (→) prophetic word formula in the introduction (7:1), the whole section can be characterized as a report of a prophetic revelation. The revelation in question is of course one that originates in the conduct of an oracular inquiry, but because of the complicated relationship between the role of the prophet and the role of the narrator (→ Structure), this section is not simply a report of an oracular inquiry (like, e.g., → Hab 2:1-5).

The part of this section that actually narrates the request of the delegation from Bethel shares the third person perspective expressed by the narrator in the introduction (7:1-3), but the part that narrates the prophet's answer shares the first person perspective expressed by the prophet in the autobiographical versions of the (→) prophetic word formula (8:18-19; cf. 7:4-7). This difference implies that the revelation communicated by this text in its final form is the result of subsequent reflection on the prophet's initial report of the inquiry, not just a reiteration of the prophet's reply to the inquiry. It is thus best described as a REPORT OF A PROPHETIC REVELATION that can be further characterized, with respect to its material content, as a revelation concerning the larger significance of a reply to an oracular inquiry.

Setting

The final form of this section presupposes a succession of interrelated settings. The actual conduct of an oracular inquiry presumably underlies this text. Such divination practices are fairly well documented in preexilic times, and coming to the sanctuary with a question seems to be in accord with the previously common custom of "seeking Yahweh." (The phrase *ḥlh 'et-pĕnê yhwh* ["to entreat Yahweh's favor"] is used in 7:2b, rather than such technical terms as *bqš* ["inquire"], *šʾl* ["ask"], or *drš* ["seek"]; but the technical terminology is used along with this phrase in 8:21aβ.)

Following the conduct of the inquiry, the prophet may well have composed an autobiographical memoir of this event to record the outcome in a form that would enable it to be studied by others as well as himself. This possibility is suggested by the occurrences of the prophetic word formula in the first person, and by their close association with those parts of this section that recount the posing of the initial question and the reply it eventually received (7:4; 8:18). Finally, we must also suppose a situation in which the prophet's memoirs were studied and subjected to the kind of further reflection that this text is now designed to express. Zechariah could have carried out such a retrospective reconsideration of his own earlier work, but the final predominance of the third person perspective (7:1) suggests that the retrospection was done by someone else. Both the composition of the prophet's memoirs and their recomposition into the present document would have taken place in a scribal setting where the mantic arts and sciences were studied.

Intention

This text aims to involve its readers in an incident that happened around 518 BCE, during the interim period after the temple had begun to be rebuilt but before it was finished. Readers are invited to imagine, from two different but convergent perspectives, how the prophet Zechariah responded to a question posed by a group from Bethel who had not yet grasped the full implications of the temple's reconstruction. By this means readers can vicariously undergo the reeducative process through which this group came to realize what the restoration would mean for them.

For readers of the same interim period this text would have provided some incentive to support the rebuilding project. After the temple's completion, the same text would have helped readers to understand this institution, which they could then take for granted, by having them imagine it from the standpoint of a time when its existence was highly contingent. In the wake of the temple's final destruction, this text still confronts readers with the issue of whether their commitment to cultic institutions is matched by a concomitant commitment to the ethical demands of the God whom these institutions supposedly serve. It continues to identify God as one who creatively renews the world, in a way that enables God's own people to avert the historical consequences of their sins and begin anew, and in a way that all peoples can eventually recognize as beneficial for them too.

INTRODUCTION TO A REPORT OF A PROPHETIC REVELATION, 7:1

Structure

I. Date citation initiated with specification of regnal year:
   in King Darius's fourth year   7:1a
II. Prophetic word formula (in third person)   7:1bα
III. Date citation concluded with specification of day and month   7:1bβ
   A. Citation proper: in the fourth day of the ninth month   7:1bβ^1
   B. Elaboration identifying the name of the month: Chislev   7:1bβ^2

The introduction to 7:1–8:23 resembles the introductions to the two preceding sections of Zechariah (1:1, 7), as well as the introductions to the various sections of Haggai (1:1; 2:1, 10; cf. 2:20). The two basic elements that they all have in common are (1) the citation of the Persian emperor's regnal year and (2) the use of the prophetic word formula to initiate the reporting narration of the section as a whole. Other elements are sometimes added, such as the enumeration of the month (and sometimes in addition the enumeration of the day), the name of the month, and the identification of the prophet's father. There is also some variation in the way these elements are combined.

In contrast with other such introductions, this one seems to be distinguished by its emphasis on the fact that Darius is "the king" (*hammelek;* cf. Hag 1:1); by its omission of any reference to Zechariah as "the son of Berechiah, son of Iddo, the prophet" (cf. Zech 1:1b, 7b); by its explicit identification of the month in question as "Chislev"; and by the way it places the prophetic word formula between the citation of the regnal year and the citation of the month and day, rather than after all such information. Some of these variations are related to the material content of 1:7–8:23, as it fits into the thematic progression of the book as a whole, and some are related to the overall stylistic pattern of this section.

It is emphasized that Darius is "the king" because the ensuing report is about a delegation that came from the city of Bethel to make an oracular inquiry at Yahweh's sanctuary in Jerusalem. Bethel was formerly a royal sanctuary of the northern kingdom, and after the overthrow of Samaria it was incorporated into Assyrian and Babylonian imperial provinces. Bethel had not generally been under Jerusalem's jurisdiction for centuries, but in making oracular inquiry there the people of Bethel were in some sense recognizing its jurisdiction — perhaps only because some of the returning exiles, whose allegiance would naturally be directed toward the homeland of their ancestors, had previously resettled there (Ezra 2:28). Such recognition would be predicated on the common acknowledgment of Persian hegemony in general, and on the common acknowledgment of Darius's kingship in particular. It would therefore be part of the great reversal brought about by the new world order fashioned by the Persians, the design of which the prophet attributes to Yahweh (Petersen, *Haggai,* 281-82).

In this introduction Zechariah is no longer identified by his full title, "the son of Berechiah, son of Iddo, the prophet," as he is in previous introductions (1:1, 7), in order to show that this section (7:1–8:23) is materially dependent on the preceding sections (1:1-6; 1:7–6:15). Both Zechariah's basic identity as an authentic prophet of Jewish descent and the basic nature of his message regarding the significance of the temple are established in the preceding sections. The treatment and interpretation of the issue that arises in 7:1–8:23 thus follow from principles that are previously laid down in 1:1-6 and especially in 1:7–6:15 (→ Book as a Whole, Structure).

The position of the prophetic word formula in the middle of the date citation has caused some commentators considerable consternation (e.g., Meyers and Meyers [*Haggai,* 382], following Mitchell [p. 195], conclude that "the text as it stands [is] in error"). Such positioning is stylistically consistent, however, with the pattern of interruption that characterizes this section as a whole. The prophet's reply to the oracular inquiry is begun in 7:4-7, interrupted in 7:8–8:17, and concluded in 8:18-23; and the exhortation that interrupts this reply is similarly begun in 7:9-14, interrupted in 8:1-13, and concluded in 8:14-17. The date citation also begins in 7:1a, gets interrupted with the prophetic word formula in 7:1bα, and concludes in 7:1bβ. Even the apparently superfluous identification of the ninth month as Chislev fits this pattern. Just as the conclusion to the prophet's reply in 8:19 is given a further elaboration in 8:20-23, so also the conclusion to the date citation in 1:7bβ^1 is given a further elaboration in 1:7bβ^2 (→ 7:1–8:23, Structure).

Genre

Such verses are sometimes loosely called headings because they obviously resemble in some ways the superscriptions of other prophetic books; and they are sometimes called introductory formulas because they consist of formulaic elements. As noted above, however, the prophetic word and date citation formulas are here combined so as to initiate reporting narration. The elements of the (→) prophetic word formula thus assume a narrative function here, which stands in contrast with the way this formula is typically used in (→) prophetic superscriptions, so that it is not integrally connected with whatever it introduces (Tucker, 57-58). The formulaic components of 7:1 are thus not combined into a generically independent sort of heading, like a prophetic superscription. This verse is rather an integral part of the REPORT OF A PROPHETIC REVELATION that it serves to introduce (→ 7:1–8:23, Genre).

Setting

This type of introduction indicates a setting in which the records of earlier prophetic activity were being subjected to retrospective reflection and reinterpretation.

Intention

This introduction sends readers into the immediately following account of an oracular inquiry with a particular orientation. They are to view the action from the standpoint of an authoritative narrator, who retrospectively perceives the prophet's reply as having a significance that transcends the immediate circumstances in which it originated.

Bibliography

G. Tucker, "Prophetic Superscriptions and the Growth of a Canon," in *Canon and Authority* (ed. G. W. Coats and B. O. Long; Philadelphia: Fortress, 1977) 56-70.

REPORT OF AN ORACULAR INQUIRY CONCERNING THE CONTINUATION OF A PUBLIC FAST, 7:2-7

Structure

I. Request for oracular inquiry	7:2-3
A. Sending of a delegation from Bethel to Jerusalem	7:2-3a
1. The delegation itself	7:2a
a. Sender: Bethel	7:2aα
b. Those sent to inquire	7:2aβ
1) An individual: Sharezer	7:2aβ^1
2) A group: Regem-melech and his men	7:2aβ^2
2. The twofold purpose	7:2b-3a
a. To entreat Yahweh's favor	7:2b
b. To question the temple priests and prophets	7:3a
B. The question they intend to pose	7:3b
1. Basic statement: should I mourn and fast in the fifth month?	7:3bα
2. Qualifying clause: as I have done for many years	7:3bβ
II. Oracular response	7:4-7
A. Introduction: prophetic word formula	7:4
B. Response proper	7:5-7
1. Yahweh's instructions to the prophet	7:5a
a. Command to convey a response: say!	7:5aα
b. Designated addressees	7:5aβ
1) The people of the land	7:5aβ^1
2) The priests	7:5aβ^2
2. What the prophet is to say to them: a series of three counterquestions	7:5b-7
a. Two questions concerning practices related to the fast in question	7:5b-6

       1) First question (formulated positively in the
           perfect): concerning another fast in addition   7:5b
          a) Introductory temporal clause   7:5b$\alpha\beta^1$
             1) Basic statement: when you fasted
                and mourned . . .   7:5bα^1
             2) Temporal modifiers   7:5b$\alpha^2\beta^1$
                (a) Time of year: in fifth and
                   seventh months   7:5bα^2
                (b) Duration: for seventy years   7:5bβ^1
          b) Question proper: was it for me that
            you fasted?   7:5bβ^2
       2) Second question (formulated negatively
          in the imperfect): concerning consumption
          in general   7:6
          a) Introductory temporal clauses   7:6a
            (1) First clause: when you eat . . .   7:6aα
            (2) Second clause: when you drink . . . 7:6bβ
          b) Question proper: do you not eat and drink
            for yourselves?   7:6b
    b. Third question concerning the nature of such
       counterquestions   7:7
       1) Question proper: are these not the issues
          raised by Yahweh through previous prophets?   7:7a
       2) Concluding temporal clauses   7:7b
          a) Basic statement: when Jerusalem was
            inhabited and prosperous   7:7bα
          b) Elaboration: (when) the surrounding cities,
            the Negev, and the Shephelah were
            inhabited   7:7bβ

    This unit is a narrative that commences with the sending of a group to Jerusalem, where they are to "entreat" *(lĕhallôt)* Yahweh, which in this case specifically involves posing a question to the priests and prophets of the recently reestablished cult of Yahweh (Ezra 3:1-6) regarding the continuation of a certain fast (Zech 7:2-3). Some have supposed that in v. 2 "Bethel" refers not to the city but rather to the god of the same name, here combined as a theophoric element with "Sharezer" to form a compound personal name (e.g., J. Wellhausen, *Die kleinen Propheten* [4th ed.; repr. Berlin: de Gruyter, 1963] 186). This is philologically possible, but in view of the emphasis in this unit on Jerusalem's "surrounding *cities*" (v. 7b), and in view of the way this whole section concludes with the prediction that "inhabitants of many *cities*" will come to Jerusalem and do just what this delegation is doing (8:20b-21), the point seems to be that this group is representing a particular city.

    The fast in question, since it had been kept "in the fifth month" for "the past seventy years" (vv. 3b, 5b), seems to have commemorated the destruction of the first Jerusalem temple (2 Kgs 25:9; Jer 52:12-13). Such a fast would not have been observed by people native to Bethel because this city had not been

under Jerusalem's jurisdiction for centuries. As a royal sanctuary of the northern kingdom, it had been a rival to Jerusalem (1 Kgs 12:26-33); and shortly before the overthrow of Jerusalem by the Babylonians the sanctuary at Bethel
had been destroyed by King Josiah of Judah (2 Kgs 23:16-20). This fast had
presumably come to be observed in Bethel by refugees from Judah, who fled
there in the wake of Jerusalem's destruction by the Babylonians, while their
compatriots were taken into exile. Now that returned exiles were beginning to
rebuild the Jerusalem temple, and some had resettled in Bethel (Ezra 2:28), it
was time to reassess the relationship between the Jewish community there and
the restoration going on in Jerusalem.

The issue implicit in their question about the fast is whether the restored
temple signals the kind of fundamental change that would obviate the need to
keep mourning their former loss. Also at issue is whether the new polity represented by the restoration could claim continuity with the precedents set during
the reigns of David and Solomon, when the First Temple was constructed, and
north and south were both under Jerusalem's jurisdiction. If Yahweh has indeed acted decisively in bringing about the return of the exiles, and if the restoration of the old royal sanctuary signals Yahweh's creation of a new age,
there is no need to fast any longer. Hence they are going to request an oracular
word from Yahweh himself.

They are concerned only with this one custom of their particular locality,
and they intend to use as their intermediaries both the priests and the prophets
of the Jerusalem sanctuary (v. 3a). The oracular reply that they receive, however, comes not from the priests and the prophets but only from one of the
prophets (v. 4). It is addressed not just to the delegation from Bethel but to "all
the people of the land and the priests." It concerns not just the fast of the fifth
month but the fast of the seventh month as well (v. 5), which probably commemorated the murder of Gedaliah, the descendant of David whom the Babylonians had appointed governor (Rudolph, 144; Jer 41:1-3; 2 Kgs 25:25). The
prophet is thus using the question of the people from Bethel as an occasion to
reeducate other people similarly situated, both priestly and lay, concerning the
larger issues that underlie this and other such fasts.

The prophet does not answer the initial question directly, but he instead
poses some counterquestions that expand on its main theme. He first asks
whether all this mourning has actually been motivated by a desire to serve
Yahweh (v. 5b). The next question widens the matter still further to encompass not only the people's ritual abstention from food for a time but also their
whole pattern of consumption at any and all times. (Note the shift from perfect verbs in v. 5b to imperfect verbs in v. 6.) The general terminology of
"eating" (*'kl*) and "drinking" (*šth*) includes both the ritual consumption of
food that is now being done once again in the context of sacrificial worship
and the ordinary consumption that takes place in daily life outside this ritual
context. Having thus redefined the issue in the broadest terms, the prophet
asks if the overall relationship between patterns of daily life and patterns of
ritual expression does not betray a self-concern that has little or nothing to do
with Yahweh's present intentions for his people. The real issue, then, is
whether the way in which they have ordered their lives, as they have lived

422

through the consequences of Judah's overthrow, shows any true discernment, on their part, of Yahweh's will.

The prophet's final question (v. 7) serves to conclude this unit and to link it with the following one. It expands the temporal perspective, which has thus far been limited to the past "seventy years" of the exile itself (v. 5b), to include the preexilic period, when Jerusalem and the outlying rural and urban areas were inhabited and prosperous. The question asserts that there is some continuity between the kinds of issues the prophet has just raised and the kinds of things that the preexilic prophets used to say. It also looks forward to the upcoming list of commands in 7:9-10, characterizing them also as the kinds of things that the preexilic prophets used to say, although their contemporaries ignored them. This unit ends so as to suggest that the kind of cultic issue raised by the people from Bethel cannot be resolved without considering the larger issue of the relationship between cult and ethics, in the light of the historical experience of Judah's destruction and the exile.

Genre

As a narrative that basically consists of a request for an oracular inquiry and at least the beginnings of a reply, this unit bears the stamp of a REPORT OF AN ORACULAR INQUIRY.

Setting

This account reflects the actual procedure of an oracular inquiry, but it is not in itself shaped by that procedure. This tenuous relationship with the oracular inquiry is evident from the way in which the narrative shifts from the commissioning of the delegation to the revelation of the reply, leaving out any description of the practicalities that were involved. By what means was the inquiry conducted? How did the reply to an oracular inquiry, which the priests were originally intended to help conduct, end up being addressed to them instead? After the oracular reply was revealed to the prophet, under what circumstances did he communicate it to those who had requested it? The readers are not told.

The report thus does not relate all major aspects of the incident, let alone the details, but focuses only on those aspects of it that gave rise to subsequent reconsideration of its deeper implications. The occurrence of the prophetic word formula in its first person, autobiographical variation suggests that the report came to be shaped in this way by the prophet himself, as a result of retrospective reflection on his earlier involvement in the event itself. The record of such reflections would have been produced in a scribal setting, where scholars interested in prophetic matters could study it.

Intention

The incident of the oracular inquiry is reported in a way that draws the reader into the process of retrospective reflection on its deeper implications. Just as the prophet asked the delegation questions that would lead them to probe the issues underlying their concern, and just as the prophet recounts the event so as to relate the significance that it subsequently assumed for him, the reader is similarly led to ponder the point of Yahweh's rather devious response to the straightforward question of the folks from Bethel.

REPORT OF A REVELATION CONCERNING THE REJECTION OF THE DEMANDS MADE BY YAHWEH THROUGH THE PROPHETS, 7:8-14

Structure

On the one hand this unit is the continuation of its predecessor (7:2-7), as it keeps up a narrative sequence that begins in 7:7. There it is said that the preexilic prophets spoke certain words when the land was inhabited and prosperous. This unit goes on to give some examples of what those prophets used to say (vv. 9-10). It then complicates the plot by telling how the people failed to heed these words (vv. 11-12a), and brings this conflict to its conclusion by describing how Yahweh therefore scattered them, and the land became just the opposite of how it was when the story began: uninhabited and desolate rather than inhabited and prosperous (v. 14b; cf. 7:7). Within this unit itself, there is no explicit identification of the people to whom it refers. The reader must bring from the foregoing unit an awareness that they are the people who historically inhabited the region around Jerusalem.

On the other hand, the intrusion of the prophetic word formula at 7:8 seems to mark a new beginning, which makes the relationship between the speech of Yahweh in vv. 9-10 and the historical narrative in vv. 11-14 altogether ambiguous. If the exemplary set of torah commands in vv. 9-10 is read within the time frame established by 7:7, they illustrate the kinds of things that the preexilic prophets used to say. If they are read as the beginning of a whole new unit, as suggested by the occurrence of the prophetic word formula in v. 8, they appear to constitute a word from Yahweh that Zechariah is to proclaim to his contemporaries. In this case the unit would consist of an exhortation addressed to the recipients of the oracular reply (vv. 9-10), which is made more compelling by the succinct narration of what happened when Judah rejected such demands in the past (vv. 11-14).

The compositional structure of this section as a whole plays a great deal on such uncertainties (→ 7:1–8:23, Structure), and in the final analysis this ambiguity remains unresolved. In any case the main complication in the narrative is not simply the people's failure to follow Yahweh's rules. This failure is emphatically linked with their imperceptiveness (vv. 11b-12aα), which is in turn linked with their unwillingness to be guided by the prophets' interpretation of their historical situation. As Yahweh's divinely inspired messengers (v. 12aβ), the prophets could discern what obedience to such rules entailed in any given set of historical circumstances. It was thus not simply disobedience that led to the catastrophe of exile, but also the people's failure to share the prophetic vision (vv. 13-14).

Genre

The ambiguity in the structure of this unit leads to ambiguity regarding its generic classification. The revelation received by Zechariah could perhaps be in the overall form of a narrative, whose first episode recounts a kind of prophetic exhortation (vv. 9-10), and whose subsequent episodes recount its rejection (vv. 11-12a) and the consequences (vv. 12b-14). Or it could be in the form of a prophetic exhortation, whose commands are motivated by a history of Judah's rejection of the prophets, in which the exile is explained as Yahweh's angry reaction. In either case the narrative interprets past events in terms of Yahweh's agency, so as to guide present behavior. The narrative element itself can thus be characterized as a PROPHETIC HISTORICAL EXEMPLUM, showing that Yahweh's demands can be fulfilled only by heeding the prophetic interpretation of what they entail. If the commands in vv. 9-11 are not to be regarded as part of the historical narrative, vv. 9-14 have the overall form of a PROPHETIC EXHORTATION that is motivated by such an exemplum.

In either case the genre of the unit as a whole is defined in terms of the relationship between the (→) prophetic word formula in 7:8 and the type of material found in 7:9-14, not on the form of 7:9-14 alone. The unit is thus best described as a REPORT OF A PROPHETIC REVELATION that can be further characterized, with respect to its material content, as a revelation concerning a prophetic exhortation or a revelation concerning a prophetic historical exemplum (cf. Mason, "Some Examples," 229-31; also *Preaching,* 212-21).

Setting

The element of the exemplum, whether it encompasses vv. 9-14 or only vv. 11-14, presupposes the kind of setting in which historiography was practiced. Such periodization and such sweeping evaluation on the basis of prophetic ideals are also evident in larger works like the Deuteronomistic History and the Chronicler's History. This unit presents a brief digest of the conclusions reached in these much more detailed investigations, so that this information could be utilized in analyzing the theological implications of the practical question raised by the delegation from Bethel.

The form of this unit itself, whether it is an exemplum containing an exhortation or an exhortation containing an exemplum, was primarily shaped by the exigencies of the oracular inquiry itself. The content of the exemplum, however, harks back to the scribal setting in which the prerequisite historical study was carried out. As indicated by the prefaced prophetic word formula, this unit was eventually incorporated into the written record of the inquiry, which was then subjected to further study in the same scribal setting, in order to produce the present text.

Intention

This unit is aimed at those who harbor doubts about the prophetic claims regarding the significance of the temple-rebuilding project. Zechariah and his colleagues have discerned that Yahweh is taking the initiative in the restoration, creating a new world order that is radically different from the one in which his people had so tragically existed heretofore, and yet also acting in continuity with his precedent-setting establishment of the Davidic dynasty. Those who fail to share this vision will risk repeating the tragic pattern of the past, and thus be unable to accomplish in their own day what faithfulness demands in any and every age.

REPORT OF A REVELATION URGING RENEWED COMMITMENT TO YAHWEH AND THE RESTORATION, 8:1-17: PART I, 8:1-8

Since 8:1-17 is a relatively long and complex unit, the discussion here will focus only on 8:1-8, and 8:9-17 will be discussed separately below. This separation is only for the sake of convenience and should not obscure that both 8:1-8 and 8:9-17 belong together as parts of a larger entity.

Text

Since the main verbs in vv. 2-3 are perfects, they should be translated with some English past tense, or with the present perfect, rather than with the present or future: *qinnē'tî,* "I have shown zeal" (*RSV* "I am jealous"); and *šabtî,* "I have returned" (*RSV* "I will return").

Structure

1. First speech: Yahweh's changed attitude
toward Jerusalem — 8:2
   a. Introduction: messenger formula — 8:2aα
   b. Speech proper: I have shown great zeal
      for Zion — 8:2aβb
2. Second speech: the renewed manifestation
of Yahweh's presence in Jerusalem — 8:3
   a. Introduction: messenger formula — 8:3aα^1
   b. Speech proper — 8:3aα^{2}b
      1) Yahweh's actions — 8:3aα^{2}β
         a) With respect to the sanctuary:
            I have returned to Zion — 8:3aα^2
         b) With respect to the city:
            I will dwell in Jerusalem — 8:3aβ
      2) Naming indicative of changed status — 8:3b
         a) With respect to Jerusalem:
            "The Faithful City" — 8:3bα
         b) With respect to Yahweh's sanctuary
            on Mt. Zion: "The Holy Mountain" — 8:3bβ
3. Third speech: the intergenerational repopulation
of Jerusalem — 8:4-5
   a. Introduction: messenger formula — 8:4aα
   b. Speech proper — 8:4aβ-5
      1) Concerning the old: they will again
         occupy the public places — 8:4aβb
      2) Concerning the young: the streets will
         be filled with them playing — 8:5
4. Fourth speech: the disparity between the
perspectives of Yahweh and the people — 8:6
   a. Introduction: messenger formula — 8:6aα
   b. Speech proper — 8:6aβbα
      1) From the people's perspective: it may
         seem too good to be true — 8:6aβ
      2) From Yahweh's perspective: it hardly
         seems so — 8:6bα
   c. Conclusion: oracle formula — 8:6bβ
5. Fifth speech: the culmination of the restoration — 8:7-8
   a. Introduction: messenger formula — 8:7aα
   b. Speech proper — 8:7aβ-8
      1) What Yahweh will accomplish — 8:7aβ-8a
         a) The salvation of his scattered people — 8:7aβb
         b) Their return to live in the midst
            of Jerusalem — 8:8a
      2) The outcome of the process — 8:8b
         a) A renewed relationship — 8:8bα
            (1) With respect to the people:
                they will be mine — 8:8bα^1

Like all the units of 7:1–8:23, this unit is marked off by the introductory prophetic word formula (8:1). The body falls into two main parts. First comes a series of five short prophetic speeches (8:2-8), which collectively describe the restoration as an unfinished historical process in which Yahweh has initiated a creative and innovative pattern of divine activity. Then follows a parenetical address (8:9-17) in which the prophet, speaking on Yahweh's behalf, urges the people to lose their fear of responding to this divine initiative and to participate actively in the culmination of this historical process.

Each speech in vv. 2-8 begins with the messenger formula, "thus says Yahweh of hosts" (but "hosts" is lacking in v. 3aα[1]), which by virtue of being repeated five times comes to function as a kind of refrain. Each speech is thus distinctly separated from the others, while at the same time this marked repetition of a common element also indicates that they belong collectively together in a series. When one examines the content of these speeches within this formal framework, it becomes evident that each speech describes a discrete phase within a sequence of five phases, which together constitute a unified historical process (cf. Mittmann).

The main verbs of both the first speech (v. 2) and the second (v. 3) have a perfect rather than an imperfect form (→ Text), and they thus describe the two phases of the process that have already taken place. The first (v. 2) describes an attitudinal change on Yahweh's part: his "great wrath" *(ḥēmâ gĕdôlâ)* has been transformed. As a force in world history, it was previously directed against his own people (cf. the reference in 7:12b to his "great anger" [*qeṣep gādôl*]). Now, however, it serves to motivate his "great zeal" *(qin'â gĕdôlâ)* on their behalf, and has thus become redirected toward their enemies.

The second phase (v. 3) includes both a particular act of Yahweh and its beginning to be recognized as such. Yahweh has returned to Jerusalem, and has once again begun to "dwell" *(škn)* there, so that the site of the sanctuary is now an authentic representation of his presence in the city. The naming motif, conventionally used in some prophetic discourse to describe the public recognition of a divine act (e.g., Isa 1:26; 35:8; 58:12; 62:4, 12; Jer 33:16), is here used to suggest that there is an element of recognition in the very way the people are talking about recent developments. They are beginning to realize that Jerusalem may again become the home base of Yahweh's people and the center of his worship, but this time the people's loyalty will be characterized by true faithfulness, and their worship by true holiness.

The main verbs in the last three speeches (8:4-5, 6, 7-8) include two imperfects and a participle, rather than perfects. These speeches thus describe the three phases of the historical process that lie in the future. Because of Yahweh's change of heart and the people's incipient response (vv. 2-3), Jerusalem can eventually develop from the kind of provisional settlement that it has been since the exiles' return into a viable urban center. Even the most vulnerable segments of the population, the very old and the very young, will thrive and be amply accommodated (vv. 4-5).

The fourth phase focuses on the attitudes of the participants in the historical process. As the prophetic speech in v. 6 compares the tenor of Yahweh's involvement with the tenor of the people's involvement, once the restoration has gotten well underway, it further develops the theme of Yahweh's attitudinal change, which is initially described in v. 2, and the theme of the public recognition of Yahweh's action, which is initially described with the naming motif in v. 3b. The comparison suggests that although it may well feel strange for this mere "remnant" to be playing a central role in the creation of a new world order, they should not let such stage fright scare them away from full participation in the drama. They should consider the matter from Yahweh's perspective rather than from their own, for although the prospect may seem strangely frightening to them, it is strangely wonderful to him.

In the fifth and final phase of the process (vv. 7-8) Yahweh will extend the restoration process to encompass all his people everywhere, so that as citizens of the new Jerusalem they may come to "dwell" there (*wĕšāknû bĕtôk yĕrûšālāim*, v. 8a), just as he "dwells" there (*wĕšākantî bĕtôk yĕrûšālāim*, v. 3aβ). The relationship between Yahweh and his people will then be fully restored in all its integrity.

The relationship of this series of prophetic speeches to its surrounding context is somewhat ambiguous. On the one hand it continues the story that Zechariah has been telling the delegation from Bethel, to provide the background against which to reconsider the meaning of their question (7:7-14). The story left off in 7:14 with Yahweh's description of the exile as the result of his wrath; and it picks up again in 8:2-3 with Yahweh's description of his return to Jerusalem as the result of his changed attitude. By means of the speeches in 8:4-7 Yahweh then takes the story into the future, all the way to its climax.

On the other hand, the occurrence of the prophetic word formula in 8:1 suggests the beginning of a new unit, in which these prophetic speeches are somehow related to the succeeding parenesis (8:9-17). The introduction to the exhortation in 8:9 characterizes the addressees as "those hearing *these words* (*'ēt haddĕbārîm hā'ēlleh*) in these days from the mouth of the prophets." In relation to the parenesis in 8:9-17 the preceding speeches are thus identified as examples of what the pro-restoration prophets have recently been saying, in order to encourage support for the completion of the temple's reconstruction.

The compositional structure of this section as a whole plays a great deal on such uncertainties (→ 7:1–8:23, Structure), and in the final analysis this ambiguity remains unresolved. In order to reinforce and even extend the double entendre, so that these speeches can be read as the words of the restoration prophets in general, or as the words of Zechariah in particular, or even as the words of the narrator to the reader, the prophetic word formula in 8:1 does not designate any recipient of the revelation to which it refers, and thus ends on an elliptical note: "The word of Yahweh came . . ." (→ 7:1–8:23, Structure).

Genre

Each of the speeches in this section begins with the (→) messenger formula and goes on to describe either an act of Yahweh himself or a consequence of his action that portends the well-being of his people. Each may thus be individually described, and together they may be collectively described, as a PROPHECY OF SALVATION. Together they serve to substantiate the following prophetic PARENESIS (→ prophetic exhortation) in 8:9-17, which generically dominates the entire unit. The unit as a whole, by virtue of the introductory formula in 8:1, is a REPORT OF A PROPHETIC REVELATION that consists of prophetic parenesis.

Setting

The individual subunits of 8:2-8 may once have existed as independent prophetic speeches, which were subsequently collected into the present series (Beuken, 156-83; Rudolph, 142-52). If so, however, it is difficult to say much about their original setting, other than the obvious fact that it must have been in the prophetic circles that were associated with the restoration. The series, whether it was composed as such (Petitjean, 363-83) or made up of previously existing speeches, seems designed not only to make certain claims about the involvement of Yahweh in current events, but also to engage the emotional response of the audience so as to enhance these claims. This combination of functions suggests a setting where historical study and reflection were pursued, and where there was also some consideration given to the problem of effectively communicating the results of such study and reflection, in order to influence public behavior (cf. Mason, *Preaching,* 221-28).

Intention

This passage aims to give the impression of standing in the middle of a historical process that is gathering considerable momentum, and to imply that no one should fail to join in. Although this process is centered in the restoration of Jerusalem and its royal sanctuary, it encompasses all of Yahweh's scattered people, wherever they may be, and not just the returned exiles.

Bibliography

S. Mittmann, "Die Einheit von Sacharja 8,1-8," in *Text and Context (Fest.* F. C. Fensham; ed. W. Claassen; JSOTSup 48; Sheffield: JSOT Press, 1988) 269-82.

REPORT OF A REVELATION URGING RENEWED COMMITMENT TO YAHWEH AND THE RESTORATION: PART II, 8:9-17

Since 8:1-17 is a relatively long and complex unit, 8:1-8 is discussed separately above, and the discussion here will focus only on 8:9-17. This separation is only for the sake of convenience and should not obscure the fact that 8:1-8 and 8:9-17 belong together as parts of a larger entity.

Structure

(b) Prohibitions	8:17a
α. Do not devise evil in your heart	8:17aα
β. Do not love any false oath	8:17aβ
(3) Summary conclusion: for all these	
things I hate	8:17bα
b) Oracle formula	8:17bβ

The part of this unit discussed here is predicated on the possibility of entering into the unfolding historical process that is described in 8:1-7 (→ 8:1-17, Part I). In the following parenetical speech (8:8-13) the prophet thus exhorts the people to engage the process forcefully ("let your hands be strengthened," vv. 9aα² and 13bβ), as he also admonishes them not to be afraid to do so ("fear not," v. 13bα). These directives serve to encourage support for the temple rebuilding project (v. 9b), and are grounded in the observation that things have improved since the project was inaugurated. Previously, because of social conflict, there was neither economic security nor personal safety (v. 10). Now that the reconstruction is underway, the city enjoys the prospect of increasing fertility, economic viability, and overall well-being (vv. 11-12). This change has come about because the inauguration of the rebuilding project signaled a reversal in Yahweh's intentions toward his people, marking a shift from his governance of a world order that destined them to punishment and curse to his re-creation of a new world order that destined them for salvation and blessing (vv. 11-13).

The second parenetical speech (8:14-17) is linked to the first (8:7-13) by a reiteration of the admonition, "fear not" (vv. 15b, 13bβ). This whole passage serves to reinforce the motivation of the foregoing entreaty (note the subordinate conjunction kî [RSV "for"] with which v. 14 begins). Its directives are likewise predicated on Yahweh having changed his intentions from evil to good (vv. 14aα²βb-15; cf. vv. 11, 13). At the same time 8:14-17 also extends the challenge that has been issued in 8:9-13. The people are encouraged not only to maintain their support of the temple's reconstruction but also to commit themselves to a degree of faithfulness that their preexilic predecessors failed to achieve. They are thus presented with an exemplary list of rules (vv. 16-17), much like the rules that the preexilic prophets urged on their contemporaries without success (cf. 8:9b-10), so that they can avoid all that Yahweh "hates" (śn', v. 17bα). The prospect of their faithfulness is not rooted in their being by nature any different from their ancestors, but on their newfound recognition of Yahweh's creative and relentless desire to foster their well-being. Because he has dared to make a new beginning in history, so can they.

Genre

In large part 8:9-17 could be described as a (→) prophecy of salvation, but all the elements of this type are structurally subordinated to the commands and prohibitions in vv. 9aα², 13b, and 15b, and serve to motivate them. On the whole 8:9-17 is thus best described as prophetic PARENESIS (→ prophetic exhortation). The prophecy of salvation in 8:2-8 also plays a subordinate role to the parenetical passage in 8:9-17, providing both an introduction and a rationale for the orders around which the latter is organized. The bulk of the whole unit, i.e., 8:2-17, is thus basically prophetic parenesis. The unit as a whole, by virtue of the introductory formula in 8:1, is a REPORT OF REVELATION that consists of prophetic parenesis.

Setting

Parenesis based on prophecy of salvation was typically one form that the reply to an oracular inquiry might take. It is therefore possible that this unit reflects something of the incident that originally underlies this whole section (7:1–8:23), in which the prophet responded to the question posed by the delegation from Bethel (7:2-3). In its present form, however, this unit is shaped by subsequent stages of reflection on the records of this incident, through which its larger significance was elaborated for a wider audience (cf. Mason, *Preaching,* 228-32).

Parts of this unit reflect the prophet's own reconsideration of the event, through which the reply to the people from Bethel was extended to become paradigmatic for "all the people of the land and the priests" (7:5a). This reconsideration was cast in the form of a direct address to the prophet's contemporaries (8:9), thus showing that the issue raised by the people from Bethel also became the subject of public oratory urging the whole community — both those who returned from Babylon and those who never went — to support the temple rebuilding project.

In its final form this unit reflects still another stage of reinterpretation, in which this prophetic public address has been recast in a form that allows it to take on significance for readers, who are not necessarily direct participants in the events of the restoration. This shift in function is primarily evident in the introductory prophetic word formula (8:1), as it relates to both this unit as a whole (→ 8:1-17, Part I, Structure) and this section as a whole (→ 7:1–8:23, Structure).

Intention

The immediate aim of this unit is obviously to gain support for the temple rebuilding project, but this is only one aspect of its overall purpose. Such support is elicited within the context of a larger goal, which is to gain widespread commitment to a particular prophetic vision of where Judah stands in relation to their preexilic past and to the postexilic world situation.

Although the Second Temple is a reincarnation of its predecessor, it does not signify a reversion to the preexilic status quo. It rather signifies a reversal of the preexilic situation, with respect to both Yahweh's intentions toward his people and their capacity for a potentially positive response. Both the new world order that Yahweh is now creating and the new form that Judah is consequently taking work to the people's advantage, unlike the old world order and their old national status. They need only share the prophetic interpretation of this unfolding historical drama, and of what is required for them faithfully to play their part in it.

REPORT OF A REVELATION CONCERNING A CHANGE IN THE PATTERN OF RELIGIOUS OBSERVANCES, 8:18-23

Structure

a. Basic statement   8:23aα²bα
  1) When: in those days when they
     take hold . . .   8:23aα²
  2) Who: ten men from the nations of
     every tongue   8:23aβ
  3) What they will do: take hold of the robe
     of a Jew   8:23bα
b. Elaboration: what they will say   8:23bβ
  1) Request for permission to accompany
     Jewish travelers to Jerusalem:
     let us go with you . . .   8:23bβ¹
  2) Motivation: we have heard that God
     is with you   8:23bβ²

This unit is the conclusion to what began in (→) 7:2-7. In v. 19 there is at last a definite answer to the question posed in 7:3b regarding the continued observance of the fifth-month fast. The answer that finally comes, however, is formulated in light of the intervening material. The tendency to broaden the scope of the reply, which is already evident in the reference in 7:5b to an additional fast in the seventh month, reaches its culmination here with the inclusion of yet two more fasts: one in the tenth month, commemorating the initiation of the Babylonian siege of Jerusalem; and another in the fourth month, commemorating the end of the siege with a breach of the city walls (2 Kgs 25:1-4; Jer 39:1-2; 52:4-7). All liturgies of lamentation, locally observed in commemoration of any aspect of Judah's overthrow, are thus affected. The answer does not deal directly with the yes-or-no question of whether such fasts should continue to be kept, but instead prescribes their transformation into a round of feasts.

The immediately following command in v. 19b, to "love truth and peace," links this directive concerning the fasts with the principal imperatives and dominant themes in the preceding parenesis (7:9–8:17). Yahweh's affinity for "truth" *('ĕmet)* is indicated in the command to "speak the truth" *(dabbĕrû 'ĕmet)* in 8:16a, in the prospect of renewing the covenant "in truth" *(bĕ'ĕmet; RSV* "in faithfulness") described in 8:8b, in the characterization of Jerusalem as "the city of truth" *('îr hā'ĕmet; RSV* "the faithful city") in 8:3bα, and in the command to render "true judgment" *(mišpaṭ 'ĕmet)* in 7:9bα. Yahweh's affinity for "peace" *(šālôm)* is likewise indicated in the command to render "peaceable judgment" *(mišpaṭ šālôm)* in 8:16bβ, and in the prospect of a "sowing of peace" *(zera' haššālôm)* described in 8:12aα. The command in v. 19a thus ties together every aspect of the parenetic material that runs throughout 7:8–8:13.

This command also shows the same kind of rhetorical reversal that is evident in the directive concerning the fasts. The preceding parenesis concluded with the admonition that the people *are not* to love what Yahweh specifically hates (8:17aα); in v. 19a they are conversely told that they *are* to love what Yahweh generally values. This link with the conclusion of the preceding parenesis shows that the rationale for the transformation of the fasts into feasts lies in the previously described transformation of Yahweh's relationship with his people (8:1-8), and in the previously described transformation of Judah's destiny, that Yahweh's initiative has now made possible (8:11-13a). The substitution of feasts in place of these fasts is thus part of the overall pattern of reversal. They are no longer to think only negatively, in terms of specific things they *are not* to do, in order to avoid repeating their historical failure to be faithful. Now they are also to think positively, in terms of general ideals they *are* to realize, in order to participate in the new future made possible by Yahweh.

In effect, the reply to the oracular inquiry of the people from Bethel asks all the similarly situated "people of the land" to abandon the pattern of local religious observances that has grown up during the exile in favor of the cultic calendar of the restored sanctuary in Jerusalem. Such a change requires more than a mere substitution of one set of holidays for another, however. It signifies a radical shift in their worldview, their understanding of their own history as a people, and their overall pattern of life.

The speeches in vv. 20-23 put this shift in a more universal perspective. In vv. 20-22 the recognition of the Jerusalem sanctuary, which is implied in the solicitation of prophetic advice there by the people of Bethel, is described as a precedent that will be followed by people of many other cities and nations. In v. 23 it is further envisioned that the status of Jerusalem will eventually be recognized by at least some people from every ethnic group and nation in the world. Even if they do not actually become Jews, many will nevertheless take the kind of active interest in Judaism that shows their tacit recognition of Jerusalem as the authentic sanctuary of the one true God.

Genre

This unit is basically the reply to the oracular inquiry reported in 7:2-7, and even the parts of it that are not directly in response to the question about fasting are nevertheless concerned with the practice of coming to the sanctuary to solicit revelation. The unit is therefore related generically to the REPORT OF AN ORACULAR INQUIRY (→ 7:2-7, Genre). In the final analysis, however, the record of the oracular inquiry has been reformulated in order to apply the principles expressed in the reply to a wider range of circumstances, above and beyond those that originally led to the conduct of the inquiry (cf. Mason, *Preaching,* 232-34). This reformulation is particularly evident in the relationship between the introductory (→) prophetic word formula and the body of the unit itself, but also in the progression in the referential purview of the three speeches, from "the house of Judah" in v. 19, to people from many cities and nations in vv. 20-22, to people from every nation in v. 23. The pericope can thus be described as a REPORT OF A PROPHETIC REVELATION, recognizing that the revelation in question derives from the reply to an oracular inquiry.

Setting

→ 7:2-7, Setting.

Intention

This unit aims to summarize and conclude the three strands that are interwoven in this section as a whole: the story of the oracular inquiry, the contrast between the preexilic and postexilic periods as theologically distinct historical epochs, and the elicitation of support for the temple rebuilding project. At the same time it also aims to authenticate the prophetic claims regarding the significance of this project by suggesting that these claims will eventually win recognition in the court of world opinion, and that they have indeed already begun to do so.

Chapter 5

THE FOURTH MAJOR SECTION OF THE BOOK (9:1–11:17) AND ITS INDIVIDUAL UNITS

THE CRISIS OF THE HELLENISTIC AGE VIEWED FROM ZECHARIAH'S PERSPECTIVE, 9:1–11:17

Structure

I. Superscription: *maśśā'*	9:1aα^1
II. Main body	9:1aα^2–11:17
A. Prophecy promising Yahweh's intention to secure a place among the nations for his people and his temple	9:1aα^2-8
B. Directives guiding the people's response to this prospect	9:9–11:3
1. Call to rejoicing: a king will come to reign in peace	9:9-10
2. Exhortation to resist the external threat of foreign enemies and the internal threat of bad leadership	9:11–11:17
a. Basic formulation	9:11-12a
1) Statement of what Yahweh has done: I have freed your captives	9:11
2) Command for the people to respond: return from captivity	9:12a
b. Elaboration	9:12b–10:12
1) Statement of what Yahweh is doing: I am making a double restoration — your territorial integrity and your productivity	9:12b-17

2) Exhortation for the people to respond: ask rain from Yahweh, who makes the earth fertile, solves the land's leadership problem, and reunifies Israel	10:1-12
3. Cry of alarm: a crisis in leadership is underway	11:1-3
C. Symbolic actions showing that Yahweh will raise up a bad leader to bring the present order to an end	11:4-17

Scholars have not reached much agreement regarding either the delineation of the basic units in the core of this section (9:11–10:12) or the dating of the various units throughout the entire section (Otzen, 11-34; Hanson, *Dawn*, 287-90). Preoccupation with the problem of delimiting the individual units and assigning them to their respective historical situations has often led scholars to ignore or play down the questions of whether this section has any coherence and, if so, how to characterize its overall composition. (Cf., e.g., how Sæbø [*Sacharja 9–14*, 309-17] and Elliger [pp. 143-44] wrestle with these issues.)

In reaction to this tendency toward fragmentation some scholars have begun to trace the thematic patterns created by recurrent phrases, images, and motifs that permeate this section as a whole (Lamarche, 7-71; Willi-Plein, 95-104; Hanson, "Zechariah 9"; idem, *Dawn*, 286-354; Butterworth, 166-212). The results of these more holistic approaches have been just as divergent, however, as the kinds of historical analysis whose limitations they are attempting to overcome. For example, Lamarche finds that themes appear in chiastic patterns, while Hanson finds that they follow the sequence of a mythic archetype. There are undoubtedly recurrent phrases, images, and motifs in this section of the book that relate its various parts thematically to one another. But the explication of their patterns is not a sufficient basis, in and of itself, on which to describe the overall compositional form of 9:1–11:17.

The inadequacy of tracing thematic patterns can be demonstrated with respect to Hanson's analysis. He has divided chs. 9 and 10 into two separate units, arguing that each shows a sequence of mythic motifs characteristic of a particular generic form, which he calls the divine warrior hymn (*Dawn*, 292-334; → Genre). The issue is not whether such motifs are in evidence, but whether they constitute the basic organizing principle of the compositional form. When the sequence of mythic motifs is simply assumed to be the dominant feature, some very real formal differences are obscured, and some alleged similarities become rather forced in order to make both texts fit the pattern. For example, Hanson identifies both 9:9 and 10:12 as examples of the "victory shout" motif. If this is the case, why is this motif expressed in the former instance with a command and the same motif in the latter instance with a statement? The former can plausibly be characterized as a kind of victory shout (→ 9:9-10, Genre); but to make the latter fit the same description stretches this category very far indeed.

Moreover, the statement in 10:12, which Hanson identifies as an expression of the "victory shout" motif at the end of the chapter, is virtually identical in form and content with the statement in 10:6a, which Hanson identifies as an expression of the "ritual conquest" motif in the middle of the chapter. In 10:6a

441

Yahweh's intention to strengthen Judah is expressed with the verb *wĕgibbartî* ("I will strengthen") plus the nominal object, "the house of Judah"; and in 10:12 Yahweh's corresponding intention to strengthen Ephraim is expressed with exactly the same verb, *wĕgibbartî*, plus the pronominal object "them." What, precisely, makes a statement of Yahweh's intention to strengthen his people into a description of either ritual conquest or victory? Why does the same statement count in one case as an expression of the former, and in another case as an expression of the latter? There are many similar problems in Hanson's description of the structure of 9:1–10:12.

The kind of structural analysis undertaken here attempts to overcome such problems and to go beyond the limitations of a purely thematic approach, trying also to discern the conventional rhetorical structures around which the themes of this section are organized and through which they are expressed. The difference is most immediately evident with regard to (→) 9:11–10:12. When one examines the text of this passage from such a perspective, the basic rhetorical paradigm appears to be the twice-repeated pattern of a statement about Yahweh's activity (9:11, 12b) combined with a command telling the people how they might appropriately respond (9:12a; 10:1aα). There is much else in 9:11–10:12, but it all serves either to elaborate on these two basic statements about Yahweh's activity or to elaborate on the motivation for following these two basic commands. In other words, this passage coheres as an exhortation based on prophetic claims about divine involvement in human affairs.

Even if Yahweh is described throughout 9:11–10:12 in terms of the mythic archetype of the divine warrior, as Hanson has doubtless shown, such description functions here as a means of persuading the audience to accept the claims that are being made about Yahweh's involvement in the present situation, and to follow the commands that describe an appropriate response. The same can be said, mutatis mutandis, about the kind of analysis made by Lamarche. One should first note that many of the chiastic patterns identified by him are questionable (Butterworth, 169-70, 180-82); but even if some such patterns are evident, they function in this context to undergird the more dominant structure of subunits containing oracular statements (9:11, 12b-17) followed by subunits initiated with commands (9:12a; 10:1-12).

When one recognizes that 9:11–10:12 is basically an exhortation, this recognition in turn affects the way in which one views 9:9-10 and 11:1-3 in relation to their context. The composition of these two units is also based fundamentally on commands. There is some variation in the form of the commands — feminine singular in 9:9, masculine plural in 9:12a and 10:1aα, and masculine singular in 11:1-2a — variation which suggests that 9:9–11:3 may consist of material from several different sources. Nevertheless, once the basically hortatory nature of 9:9–11:3 is recognized, this section as a whole begins to take some shape. There is an initial prophecy that makes claims about the nature of Yahweh's involvement in the current international situation (9:1aα^{2}β-8), followed by a long passage that serves to elaborate persuasively on this claim and its implications for the people's collective behavior (9:9–10:12). In conclusion there is a report of a prophet's attempt to dramatize the outcome of a negative response to Yahweh's initiative (11:1-17). The entire section is entitled "a *maśśā*'" (*RSV* "an oracle"), i.e., a reinterpretation of a prophetic revelation from an earlier historical situation in light of a new but somewhat similar situation (→ Genre).

The first unit (9:1aα²βb-8) makes the general assertion that Yahweh is actively involved in international affairs, so as to secure a place among the nations for his people and his temple. More specifically, Yahweh is currently active in forces emanating from Syria (9:1aα²β-2a), which are destined to overrun Phoenicia and Philistia (9:2b-7a), but will only enhance Judah's control over Philistine territory and reinforce the security of Jerusalem (9:7b-8). The main part of this section (9:9–11:3) unfolds the implications of Yahweh's intentions in greater detail, as it also persuades the audience to share its perception of the situation and to involve themselves in the divine plan. This unfolding does not on the whole have the form of a narrative, and of its four main units (9:9-10, 9:11–10:12, 11:1-3, and 11:4-17) only the last (11:4-17) is basically a narrative. Several of these units are made up partly of narrative (e.g., 9:14-17; 10:8-12), however, as is the introductory unit, 9:1-8 (i.e., in 9:3-8). This narrative substructure imputes a quasi-narrational progression to the overall sequencing of the first four main units (9:1aα²β-8, 9:9-10, 9:11–10:12, and 11:1-3), to which the truly narrational final unit (11:4-17) then becomes the conclusion.

The action of Yahweh described in 9:1aα²β-8 brings with it, first, the joyful and welcome prospect of a new king (9:9-11). The description given in (→) 9:9-10 is in itself somewhat ambiguous with regard to just what kind of king this might be, but in any case he is characterized as someone who will play the role of Yahweh's agent in establishing an era of world peace, in which all Israel can face a new future. This action will enable the process of restoration, including the old northern kingdom as well as Judah, to continue (9:11–10:12).

Yahweh is taking the historical initiative that will enable his people to emerge from their present problematic situation, which is figuratively tantamount to drought-stricken captivity (9:11-12a). If they respond in kind, they will find that Yahweh has in store for them the "double restoration" of both their liberty and their productivity (9:12b-17). The prospect of freedom from foreign enemies, so that Yahweh's people can enjoy the blessings of security and prosperity, is already evident in the successful preliminary efforts of Yahweh's people to defend themselves against the Greeks (9:13-17). If they seek such blessings from Yahweh on the basis of the prophet's true revelation, they will come to see that their local leaders are both the main cause of their present problems and the main impediment to Yahweh's plan for changing the situation (10:1-2).

Because Yahweh's people are largely free from external threats, they can afford to concentrate on the pressing internal problem of their misled and hence misleading local authorities (10:1-2). Yahweh's plan has therefore come to include the removal of these leaders and the emergence of new leadership in Judah (10:3-4). The new kingship (9:9-10), combined with this new local administration, will not only result in the transformation of Judah, but will also make it possible for the northern kingdom to be restored in some form (10:3-

12). The present ineffective leadership is thus being put under attack (11:1-3); and however traumatic this process may be, it should be seen as a positive development within the context of Yahweh's larger, long-range plans for his people.

The concluding narration of prophetic symbolic action (11:4-17) shows that Yahweh may modify his plans in reaction to an initially negative response, but he will keep his intentions from being ultimately frustrated. He has commissioned a prophet to demonstrate the inherent ineffectiveness of the present arrangement (11:4-17), which has blocked Yahweh's intention to make the international situation work to his people's advantage, as well as his intention to include the north within the restoration. If the present exploitative leadership cannot be displaced through the political process, Yahweh will bring down the entire world order that allows such leadership to hold power (11:4-11), even if the previously prophesied return of north-south fraternal coexistence (10:6-12) is foreclosed in the process (11:12-14). Yahweh will raise up the most tyrannical leader they have ever had (11:15-17), and thereby foster the self-destruction of the present arrangement.

This section does not describe a particular course of events in linear fashion, but it is nevertheless structured so as to disclose Yahweh's involvement in a particular historical process, part of which has already happened and part of which remains to be seen. It attempts to give its readers a sense of being caught up in this process, recognizing that despite Yahweh's efforts to order the world for their benefit, their leaders have kept them from realizing the blessings of security and prosperity that he intends for them. The people are advised to acknowledge the tragic reality of their current situation, in which their present derelict leaders are destined to be violently overthrown, and yet to see this inevitability as a hopeful sign of Yahweh's eventually bringing them to the new future that he has all along had in mind for them.

Genre

Attempts to describe the compositional form of "Deutero-Zechariah" may be divided into three categories. The first approach, represented by Sæbø, employs the kind of form criticism that is altogether subservient to tradition history. He attempts to distinguish the more conventionally formulated and hence older prophetic speeches from the less conventionally formulated and hence more recent additions, and on this basis he traces the traditio-historical development of the text. The second approach, represented by Hanson, employs a different kind of form-critical analysis. On the basis of a recurring cluster of mythic motifs, he identifies parts of chs. 9–14 as variations on a generic form called the divine warrior hymn. The third approach, represented most recently by Larkin, attempts to define the literary form of this part of Zechariah on the basis of its interpretive references and allusions to other biblical texts. Each of these approaches has its shortcomings.

The sort of analysis to which Sæbø subjects all of Zech 9–14 can be illustrated by his treatment of 9:1-8 (*Sacharja 9–14,* 135-75). First he removes all the connectives joining expressions that are otherwise syntactically self-standing, thus breaking the text down into its most elemental subunits (vv. 1a + 2, 3-6a, 6b-7, and 8). He identifies vv. 3-6a as the original core of this unit because its formulation is typical of a prophecy of punishment against a foreign nation. He deduces that vv. 6b-7 were subsequently added to give further specificity to the original statement. Still later vv. 1a + 2 and v. 8 were added to frame and thereby recontextualize vv. 3-7, reactualizing the basic prophecy so that it could still function as a prophecy of punishment against a foreign nation in a different setting. Nearly all of this traditio-historical development took place in the process of oral transmission; v. 1b was added in the process of producing a fixed written text.

This approach is problematic in three main respects. First, there is no sound basis on which to atomize the text in this fashion. The narrative descriptions of prophets in action show that prophetic speeches did not need to be long in order to be effective, but they do not suggest that prophetic rhetoric typically consisted of nothing but short, bald assertions. There is no a priori reason to fragment 9:1-8 in this way, and no reason to suppose more generally that the subunits into which Sæbø has atomistically divided the text could ever have had the status often claimed for them, as discrete and independently existing prophetic sayings.

Second, the reconstruction of each unit's tradition history in such speculative detail does not measurably improve our understanding of the rhetorical conventions that inform either the individual units or the larger entities that they comprise. In the case of 9:1-8, for example, Sæbø's analysis leads to the conclusion that this unit can be classified as a prophecy of punishment against a foreign nation, but this classification is evident without going into anything like the kind of traditio-historical reconstruction that he has undertaken (→ 9:1-8, Genre). Although Sæbø's approach puts great emphasis on the traditio-historical process through which the various subunits supposedly coalesced to form each unit, and through which the various units supposedly coalesced to form each section of the present text, the description of this process appears not to shed much light on its outcome. In the final analysis the various sections of Zech 9–14, which Sæbø takes to be chs. 9–10, 11, 12–13, and 14, can be described only as literary compositions characterized by their heterogeneous tendencies, anthological style, and sporadically recurrent themes (*Sacharja 9–14*, 309-17). Again, these are characteristics that have long been noted without having to trace any underlying textual growth process (cf. Petersen's description of Zech 9–14 in terms of a literary "montage" [*Zechariah 9–14*, 23-27]).

Third, Sæbø's approach presupposes that the traditio-historical development of this prophetic text could only have happened in one particular way, and this presupposition becomes a Procrustean bed on which the text is forced to lie. Some prophetic texts may indeed have developed through a process of augmenting prophetic speeches as they were orally transmitted, and then literarily connecting these speeches to form a written text. Other sorts of transmission and redaction are also conceivable, however, ranging from the possibility that the text was written from scratch to the possibility that the text was based on older traditions without directly incorporating any material from them, etc.

445

If form criticism is going to provide a firm basis for traditio-historical reconstruction, it must begin by analyzing the final form of the text. Only on this basis can one ask whether previously existing traditions may have informed the present text, how they may have figured in its composition, and to what extent (if any) they may now be recovered.

Hanson's approach is closely tied to the question of whether, and to what extent, Zech 9–14 may be characterized as apocalyptic. The general tenor of this section is sometimes loosely characterized as "apocalyptic," and Hanson's identification of 9:1-17 and 10:1-12 as examples of the divine warrior hymn is intended to define these parts of this section more precisely as proto-apocalyptic texts, whose basic structural features are characteristic of the initial stage in the transition from prophecy to apocalyptic (*Dawn,* 300-315). Reasons for questioning Hanson's approach to the structural analysis of this material are given above (→ Structure); and reasons for delimiting the individual units of 9:1–11:17, in a way that does not recognize his identification of 9:1-17 and 10:1-12 as separate textual entities, will emerge from the more detailed analysis of the individual units presented below. Here it should simply be noted that since the structure of the material in 9:1–10:12 cannot really be described in terms of an adaptation of the divine warrior hymn, 9:1–11:17 cannot be said to show an apocalyptic tendency in the sense defined by Hanson. Whether this section is apocalyptic in some other general sense is perhaps debatable, but it does not have many of the features that have generally been thought to be characteristic of apocalyptic literature.

The question of this section's apocalyptic nature turns largely on the issue of whether its description is eschatological, and whether eschatological description should be regarded as by definition apocalyptic. The description in 9:1–11:17 probably does not deserve to be called eschatological (→ Setting). In any case, whether or not 9:1–11:17 should be called apocalyptic in a general sense, it does not have the literary form of an apocalypse (→ 12:1–14:21, Genre).

The third approach to the generic classification of Zech 9–14, represented by Larkin, grows out of work done previously by Delcor and Mason. These scholars have observed that the language of 9:1–11:17 is loaded with allusions to other biblical texts, particularly other prophetic texts. Mason has argued that the function of these allusions is exegetical, and has characterized them as reinterpretive references affirming the fulfillment of previous prophetic predictions ("Some Examples," 353). It is not clear whether Delcor and Mason see such reinterpretation as the main communicative purpose of 9:11–11:17, or whether they see it as ancillary to some other communicative purpose. Larkin, however, argues explicitly that this section is an anthology of texts composed as "mantological exegesis" of other texts, building on Fishbane's description of these chapters as comprising a "mantological anthology" of such exegetical texts (pp. 511-24). On closer examination this conclusion seems to be overstated, but it nevertheless illuminates an important feature of this part of Zechariah, which points toward a more adequate definition of its genre.

First it must be noted that a good many of Delcor's so-called references to other prophetic texts are rather tenuous. In 9:1–11:17 he finds more than twenty examples of such references ("Sources," 386-87), but in the vast majority of cases the two texts have little more in common than a word or phrase. In many cases the similarity is hardly remarkable, as when enemy troops are described in both Zech 10:5 and Ezek 38:15 as consisting of "riders on horses" (*rōkĕbê sûsîm*). Even in the most striking cases of a common word or phrase there is often not really any expression of a common idea or image. For example, the rather rare word *hărēgâ* ("slaughter") appears twice in Zech 11:4-17 as part of the construct phrase *ṣō'n hahărēgâ* (v. 4 [*RSV* "flock doomed to slaughter"] and v. 7 [*RSV* "flock doomed to be slain"]); and it also occurs twice in Jeremiah (7:32; 19:6) as part of the construct phrase *gê' hahărēgâ* ("valley of slaughter"). In the phrase from Zech 11:4-17 this word indicates the fate of sheep when shepherds are derelict, but in the phrase from Jeremiah the same word is used in coining a new name for the places near Jerusalem called Topheth and Hinnom, to indicate the punishment that Yahweh will inflict on Judah for practicing child sacrifice there. It is difficult to conclude that, simply by virtue of this common word, Zech 11:4-17 contains anything amounting to a reinterpretive commentary on either Jer 7:32 or Jer 19:36 (cf. Fishbane, *Biblical Interpretation*, 286-87).

Mason thus rightly looks for rather more substantial links between Zechariah and other prophetic texts. For example, he instead connects the same phrase from Zech 11:4-17, *ṣō'n hahărēgâ*, with Jer 12:3, the only remaining occurrence of the word *hărēgâ*. As a case of a possible reference in Zechariah to another prophetic text, this is certainly more plausible. These two texts not only have the somewhat unusual word *hărēgâ* in common; they both also use it in the context of pastoral imagery relating to the fate of the "flock" (*ṣō'n*). Yet there are still some notable differences. In Jer 12:3 the "flock" in question are the wicked, and the term "slaughter" is used to describe the well-deserved punishment that the prophet asks Yahweh to inflict on them; but in Zech 11:4-17 the "flock" in question are the people of Yahweh as a whole, and the term "slaughter" is used to describe the undeserved consequences of their being badly governed (cf. Mason, "Some Examples," 348-49).

Even in one of Mason's parade examples, in which he draws a connection between Zech 10:1-2 and the prophecy concerning the drought in Jer 14, the similarity is also rivaled by the dissimilarity. In both of these texts the concept of Yahweh as the giver of rain is associated with a condemnation of false divination (cf. in particular 10:1-2 and Jer 14:14, 22), using such pejorative terminology as *qesem/qōsmîm* (*RSV* "divination"/"diviners") and *hāzâ/hăzôn šeqer* (*RSV* "see lies"/"lying vision"). In this case both texts truly share a common concept, and yet each uses it in the expression of a quite different message. In Jer 14 a lack of rain causes a famine (vv. 2-6), which is portrayed as Yahweh's punishment of his people, thus making liars out of the prophets who have predicted that no such thing would befall them (v. 13). In contrast Zech 10:1-2 describes the rain as available in due season, thus testifying to Yahweh's beneficent intentions toward his people despite their having been led astray by leaders dependent on false divination (→ 9:11–10:12, Part I). It is difficult to see how the latter amounts to any kind of exegesis or reinterpretation of the former.

In addition to these relatively tangential connections between Zechariah and other prophetic texts, Delcor and Mason have adduced some more extended parallels, particularly between Zech 11:4-17 and parts of Ezekiel. For example, the metaphorical pastoral terminology in this unit reechoes many turns of phrase from Ezek 34:1-31; and the imagery relating to the sword of Yahweh in Zech 11:17 (cf. 13:7-9) resonates with similar imagery in Ezek 21:6-22 (*RSV* 1-17). In such cases there may well be some kind of direct intertextual relationship, but even in these extended parallels the dissimilarity is also as great as the similarity.

Larkin attempts to define more precisely the basis on which one text may be characterized as an exegetical reinterpretation of another (pp. 35-37). It is not enough to show that one text plays on the other by using the same phraseology or imagery. One must also show that one text aims to resolve a cognitive problem posed by the other, and was thus composed to answer a divinatory question by literary means. Although it may not be possible to determine conclusively that each unit of a passage like Zech 9:1–11:17 is related to some other text in this way, it may nevertheless be possible to show that the entire passage was designed to be an anthology of such exegetical texts. If so, the inconclusive cases do not weaken the hypothesis that this part of Zechariah is basically mantological exegesis.

This approach represents a considerable advance in theory, but in practice Larkin does not manage to get far beyond the kind of observations made by Mason. In some cases her approach does appear to provide a basis for making finer distinctions — as when she discounts the possibility that the negative reference to "shepherds" in 10:3 is a reinterpretive exegesis of Ezek 34:7-10 (p. 93). In other cases, however, she ends up in much the same place — as when she simply reaffirms Mason's suggestion that Zech 10:2 is an exegetical reinterpretation of Jer 14:14 (pp. 87-88), which is problematic for reasons discussed above.

Even in one of Larkin's most strongly argued analyses, the same difficulty is evident. She claims that the report of symbolic action in Zech 11:4-14 is a mantological reinterpretation of the somewhat similar report in Ezek 37:15-28 because one of the prophet's two staffs *(maqlôt)* corresponds so closely in use and significance with both of Ezekiel's two sticks *('ēṣîm)*. Although these two texts use different terms for their respective symbolic objects, these objects have similar physical shapes that lend them to the same sort of dramatic action. In both texts the objects are to be "taken" *(lqḥ)* and handled "one at a time" *('aḥad)*. Ezekiel is to inscribe each of his two sticks with a motto, indicating that one stands for the southern representation of Israelite identity, and that the other stands for the northern representation of basically the same Israelite identity. He is then to hold both sticks together, showing that north and south will eventually be restored and reunified. The prophetic protagonist of Zech 11:4-14 is similarly to name one of his staffs "Union," and then to break it, showing that it is no longer possible for the north to be restored along with the south. The description in 11:4-14 thus presents a "negative image" of the description in Ezek 37:15-28 (pp. 118-19).

If there were nothing more to the matter, this conclusion might be warranted. Larkin, however, does not fully take account of the other staff mentioned in Zech 11:4-14, the one named "Grace." Yahweh tells the prophet to break this staff, showing the annulment of "the covenant I had made with all the peoples." This is an important part of the report in 11:4-14, no less prominent than the breaking of the staff representing the north-south reunion, but nothing in Ezek 37:15-28 really corresponds to it. Larkin suggests that the reference to the "covenant of peace" in Ezek 37:26 is somehow parallel (pp. 128-29), but this is a covenant between Yahweh and his own people, not a covenant between him and "all the peoples." In other words, the symbolic action in Zech 11:4-7 serves precisely to relate the general situation of the world at large with the particular situation of Yahweh's own people, but the symbolic action in Ezek 37:15-28 has hardly any international dimension at all. It is thus difficult to describe Zech 11:4-7 as simply a "negative image" or inversion of Ezek 37:15-28.

Moreover, Zech 11:4-14 explicitly relates the issue of north-south reunion to the problem of Judah's bad leadership. This problem is forthrightly addressed elsewhere in Ezekiel (e.g., in Ezek 34), but not in Ezek 37:5-28. Zech 11:4-14 thus deals with the topic of north-south reunion in a way that is diametrically opposed to Ezek 37:15-28, and in the process it gives complementary consideration to other topics that Ezek 37:15-28 never really takes up. On the whole Zech 11:4-14 does not have much in common with Ezek 37:15-28, although they certainly resemble each other in one admittedly striking respect. How can Zech 11:4-14 be said to resolve a cognitive problem posed by Ezek 37:15-28, if they present even the one topic they do share in totally different terms? There may be a direct intertextual connection between Zech 11:4-11 and Ezek 37:15-28, but not of a sort that can be characterized as mantological exegesis.

Larkin's argument, that this section shows an anthological pattern in its overall design, is similarly problematic. She does not clearly explain what constitutes an anthological pattern (pp. 36-37), and neither does Fishbane (pp. 495, 515, 520-21), from whom she appropriates this concept. For Larkin it seems to boil down to the claim that the individual units have the kind of thematic or formal interconnections that show a deliberate literary arrangement, and hence a scribal or wisdom provenance (pp. 105-6, 139). One may readily grant this section's deliberate literary arrangement (→ Structure), but it does not follow that it has the form of an anthology (→ 1:7–6:15, Genre). The nature of the literary arrangement is better described in other terms (see below).

From the kind of data adduced by Delcor, Mason, and Larkin, and from similar data adduced by others (e.g., Meyers and Meyers, *Zechariah 9–14*, 35-45), it is difficult to conclude that 9:1–11:17 was composed primarily for the purpose of reinterpreting the oracles of other prophets. These observations nevertheless show something important, namely, that this section of Zechariah was produced by someone steeped in the study of certain prophetic texts who could therefore draw allusively on the common fund of traditional terminology and imagery established by a growing prophetic corpus. In other words, it shows that this section of Zechariah was produced by a scribal group that studied prophetic records (→ Setting).

Zech 9:1–11:17 is generically diverse, as it consists of a prophecy of punishment against foreign nations (9:1-8), whose implications are developed by a prophetic call to rejoicing (9:9-10), a long prophetic exhortation (9:11–10:12), a mock sentinel report (11:1-3), and a report of a prophetic symbolic action (11:4-17). As the foregoing structure analysis shows, this diversity does not make for incoherence, but rather serves to develop a coherent line of thought. Many scholars have thus rightly been unwilling to characterize the organization of this section in terms of mere juxtaposition. The approaches taken thus far, however, have done little more than map out the thematic affinities linking its various parts. Because of their shortcomings the approaches surveyed above have provided some basis on which to grasp the overall continuity of 9:1–11:17 with respect to its content, but the question of whether this section has any overall integrity with respect to its form has scarcely been addressed. Do its generically diverse constituent units combine to form a particular kind of composition? Or, to put it another way, is there anything generic about the way these various genres work in concert?

Zech 9:1–11:17 alludes to other prophetic texts, but only in order to express a prophetic message of its own, which was promulgated under the name of Zechariah. In determining the genre of this section it might therefore be appropriate to look into its connection with the prophecies explicitly attributed to him (i.e., those in 1:7–6:15 and 7:1–8:23) and to ask whether 9:1–11:17 might have been produced by a student of these particular prophetic texts. In this light it is appropriate to consider the significance of the superscription in 9:1aα[1], which labels this section as a *maśśā'* (→ 9:1aα[1]).

According to Weis, this is a generic term that is applicable to prophetic speeches, to sections of a work of prophetic literature, or even to prophetic literary works in their entirety. It consists typically of such elements as (a) oracular speech of Yahweh disclosing how his will is becoming manifest in human affairs; (b) directives concerning behavior or attitudes that are appropriate as a response to Yahweh's initiative; and (c) a grounding of these directives in human acts or events that reveal Yahweh's activity or purpose. Such a combination of elements serves typically to explain how some previously communicated revelation of the divine will is being manifest in human affairs, in order for the audience to realize the theological significance of current developments and react to Yahweh's initiative in accord with his will. When a *maśśā'* is a section of a prophetic work, as 9:1–11:17 is a section of Zechariah, it functions typically as a reinterpretation of prophetic material found elsewhere in that work (Weis, 252-54, 274-75).

Weis's analysis of the overall structure of 9:1–11:17 (pp. 165-91) is somewhat different from the one presented above (most notably in his exclusion of 11:4-17), as is his view of how this section relates to the (→) book as a whole. Despite such disagreements in detail, both analyses converge in recognizing that this section consists primarily of statements expressing prophetic reports and announcements, combined with commands spelling out the implications of these statements for the audience's collective behavior. By virtue of the way in which they are combined, the generically diverse units of 9:1–11:17 assume the rhetorical profile of a MAŚŚĀ'. As a *maśśā'* 9:1–11:17 serves a purpose that is typical of this genre: to reinterpret the prophetic material to which it was appended.

This section may be a reinterpretation of previously communicated revelation in more than one sense. It probably contains prophecies that existed in some other form prior to their redaction into the present text. This probability is suggested by the generic diversity of its individual units, by the fact that some units might make sense outside their present context as independent ($\rightarrow$) prophetic speeches (particularly 9:1aα²β-8) or as an independent ($\rightarrow$) prophetic report (i.e., 11:4-17), and by such rhetorically divergent tendencies as the above-mentioned variation of the command forms in 9:9–11:3 ($\rightarrow$ Structure), which is only partly functional in relation to the present compositional form of the text ($\rightarrow$ 9:11–10:12, Parts I and II, Structure). If 9:1–11:17 is indeed a redactional composite, the redaction would in itself constitute a reinterpretation of the earlier prophecies out of which it was composed. It is difficult to say anything about the nature of this reinterpretive process, however, in view of the irresolvable problems that have emerged from all attempts to date the various units of this section, treating them individually and in relative isolation from one another.

In any case 9:1–11:17 is also a *maśśā'*, or reinterpretive explanation of an earlier revelation, in the sense that it harks back to the prophecies of Zechariah in 1:7–6:15 and 7:1–8:23, reapplying the prophet's insights concerning the restoration to the events of a later time (Mason, "Relation," passim). Just as Zechariah saw Yahweh's creative hand at work in the advent of the Persians, making it possible for Judah to be transformatively restored, this prophecy sees a similar creative possibility in the advent of some new royal rule. Just as Zechariah saw the diaspora of both the north and the south as parts of a single process being reversed by Yahweh, so does this prophecy — although this prophecy also describes an evolving awareness that this goal may not be fully realized within the present world order. Just as Zechariah saw the reconstruction of the Jerusalem sanctuary as the essential element of the community's restoration, this prophecy sees the defense of the Jerusalem sanctuary as essential for the community's ongoing survival. Just as Zechariah identified new leadership as the basis for the community's adaptation to the new world situation, this prophecy also focuses on the need for a kind of compatibility between the world order and the local leadership as a prerequisite for the security and prosperity of Yahweh's people. Just as Zechariah continually reasserted Yahweh's plan to restore and transform Judah in the face of developments that seemed to deny or contradict any such plan, so does this prophecy.

In sum, 9:1–11:17 expresses a view of Yahweh's involvement in the events of its time, which corresponds typologically with Zechariah's view of Yahweh's involvement in the events of the prophet's time. It is not an exegetical commentary on previous sections of Zechariah, but a prophecy in its own right, which is inspired by the prophecies previously recorded in 1:7–6:15 and 7:1–8:23. The typological correspondences between chs. 1–8 and 9-11 do not emerge simply as a result of their being juxtaposed. They are also embodied in the design of 9:1–11:17 itself, as a fundamental influence on the way this section was shaped (see further the discussion of typology in

451

Fishbane, *Biblical Interpretation,* 350-79). They were created in the process of combining a variety of materials into the compositional form of a *maśśā',* including previously existing prophecies (such as 9:1-8) and prophetic reports (such as 11:4-17) that were either traditionally associated with Zechariah or thought to be compatible with his views, as well as redactional material (e.g., the rather artificial connectives joining the various parts of 9:11–10:12).

Setting

Such texts were evidently produced by scribal groups that preserved and studied the records of earlier prophets to gain revelatory insight into the events of their own day. Conclusions reached through such study might be expressed in the redactional reformulation of previously existing prophetic material from a variety of sources, including material taken from traditionally preserved records relating to the prophet in question, as well as material anonymously produced by members of the scribal group themselves. Conclusions reached from the study of prophetic records might also be expressed in the form of an original composition by some member of a scribal group. In either case the results of scribal investigation and reflection were formulated and promulgated in the name of the prophet being studied, and either incorporated into or appended onto the book bearing that prophet's name, as an extension of that prophet's work.

This kind of *maśśā'* uses the records of various prophetically interpreted events as the basis for a prophetic interpretation of other events. It thus relates one historical situation to another by showing that they have in common the same pattern of divine involvement in human affairs. This relationship implies that the setting of a *maśśā'* is appropriately described not just sociologically in terms of the kind of group that produced it but also historically in terms of a specific time. This implication in turn brings up the issue of a possible date, not for any of the various parts of 9:1–11:17 in whatever form they may originally have existed — a quest that has generally proved fruitless — but rather for the whole composition of 9:1–11:17 in its finished form. To what particular time does 9:1–11:17 reapply Zechariah's insights regarding Yahweh's involvement in the developments of the early Persian period?

This particular way of putting the question at least precludes the kind of position represented by Otzen (pp. 117-23; cf. Horst, 206-7), who has argued that this part of Zechariah includes two preexilic prophecies, one reflecting the cultic role of the king in Josiah's time (9:1–10:12) and the other presenting an allegorical retrospective on the time of Zedekiah (11:1-17). A wide range of possibilities is still left open, however. At one end of the spectrum lies the kind of position represented by Meyers and Meyers, who have argued for a mid-fifth-century composition reflecting the Greco-Persian struggle for control of the Levant (*Zechariah 9–14,* 26-29; cf. Lamarche, 148; and Jones, "Fresh Interpretation," 241-59); and toward the other end lies the position represented by Mitchell (pp. 277, 293), who has argued for a late-fourth- or early-third-century composition reflecting the conquest of Alexander the Great and the subsequent struggles among his successors for control of Syria-Palestine (cf.

452

Elliger, 143; Chary, 137-38). Some scholars even continue to maintain that this section was written in the second century under the Maccabeans (e.g., Treves). Although the range of possibilities can be somewhat narrowed by limiting the question to the date of the final form, one must nevertheless confront the problematic feature of the text that gives rise to such a wide range of possibilities in the first place: the historical vagueness with which it describes Yahweh's actions.

This mode of description is often characterized as eschatological, and some scholars have approached the issue of dating 9:1–11:17 in terms of how to deal with eschatological language, reaching rather disparate conclusions. For example, Childs has claimed that such language has no particular historical horizon in view and that any attempts to date it are thus in principle inappropriate (p. 482). Hanson, however, has claimed that although the text describes cosmic rather than earthly developments, using mythic rather than historical terms, it nevertheless has a historically identifiable usage. In contrast with the classical prophetic language of preexilic times, which explicitly related divine activity to political events, such eschatological language provided relatively marginalized visionary groups with categories in which to formulate a theological critique of their hierocratic rulers, and served this function in the sectarian polemics of the early postexilic period ("Zechariah 9," 49-50).

Such proposals raise the question of whether the description in 9:1–11:17 is indeed eschatological. The definition of eschatology is a complex matter (Larkin, 9-27), over which there may be some reasonable difference of opinion, but in any case Yahweh is not described here as performing any acts that are different in kind from those generally ascribed to him in preexilic prophecy. He is influencing the fate of nations, raising up a new king, empowering his people to defend themselves against foreign enemies, fomenting a critical attitude toward faithless and hence derelict leaders, and commissioning a prophet to dramatize his dissatisfaction with bad leadership, so that his sanctuary will be protected, his people will dwell secure in a productive land, the dispersed northern tribes will have the same opportunity as the southern tribes to regain their place, and the whole community will be well governed. The possibility is envisioned that Yahweh may ultimately have to bring down the present world order (i.e., the "covenant made with all the peoples" in 11:10) in order to realize his basic purpose (→ 11:4-17), but this eventuality is not actually described. The course of events thus remains firmly on this side of such an eschaton, and on a largely earthly plane.

The prominence of mythic motifs and stereotypical language, to which Hanson rightly calls attention, does mean that certain developments are portrayed less specifically than is often the case in preexilic prophecy, in terms that might generally apply to Yahweh's providential acts on behalf of his chosen people, to save them from their traditional enemies as well as from themselves, at any time in Israel's history. Some may want to call this eschatological, but the difference is not stark enough to be qualitative. The description in 9:1–11:17 does indeed lack historical specificity, but this lack of historical specificity does not make it ahistorical. This unit outlines a this-worldly course of events with broad but nevertheless discernible contours (→ Structure).

Because the text is based on a typological analogy between Zechariah's time and its own, it invites being read in terms of a typological analogy between its own time and still later times, and even in terms of a typological analogy between its own time and the last times. This text nevertheless requires some consideration of how it applies Zechariah's insights to its own time, precisely in order to guide any further typological application of its insights to the events of a later time, or of the end time.

Although there seems to be a growing recent trend toward a fifth-century date (e.g., Lamarche, 148; Hanson, *Dawn*, 353-54; Lacocque, 139-44; Meyers and Meyers, *Zechariah 9–14*, 26-29; Petersen, *Zechariah 9–14*, 2-3 and passim), three aspects of the historical process described in 9:1–11:17 point toward the early Hellenistic rather than the Persian period: (1) the advent of a king whom Yahweh would use to usher in an era of world peace; (2) the prominence of an expanded concept of restoration that includes the remnant of the northern kingdom, and treats the prospect of its being somehow reunited with the restored southern kingdom as a real but unrealized possibility; and (3) the reference in 9:13b to Yahweh's demonstrated capacity to enable his people to withstand the Greeks. Taken together, these three aspects of the historical description in 9:1–11:17 suggest that this section of Zechariah was produced toward the end of the fourth century (ca. 330-300 BCE).

The terms in which the coming king and his reign are characterized in (→) 9:9-10 are borrowed from the traditional language with which the ideal Davidic monarch was conventionally and hyperbolically described in preexilic times. In that historical context there was of course a considerable discrepancy between this ideal and the reality of any given reign, as is generally the case with any such ideal, but it nevertheless functioned as a real norm for kingship. It described the responsibility bequeathed by David to his successors, to follow the example of their dynasty's founder by playing a dominant role in the maintenance of regional stability, so that Yahweh's people could enjoy the fruits of peace (cf. Ps 72). For this reason the ideal could be adapted to another historical context and become metaphorically applicable to Judah's first Persian imperial overlord, who was described as playing the role of Yahweh's "messiah" (e.g., Isa 44:28–45:3) precisely because he approximated this ideal, at least in contrast with the former Babylonian kings. Such language, even when metaphorically used, thus indicates the anticipation of some new royal regime that has a real political possibility of establishing a peace that is "universal," at least relatively so in comparison with its predecessors.

Zech 9:9-10 is in itself ambiguous, and could refer either to some new imperial overlord or to a new Davidic king. In its present literary context, however, where it serves to describe only one part of a larger historical process that comes after the time of Zechariah himself, it is difficult to imagine that this unit could describe the prospect of either a new Persian emperor or the restoration of the Davidic dynasty in Judah. The kind of widespread peace that prevailed during the middle of the reign of Darius I (522-486), during which Zechariah helped the restoration of Judah to reach relative completion, would not reappear until the decade in which Alexander the Great briefly exerted direct control over the entire east (333-323). As long as Persia and Greece were locked in a struggle for control of the Levant during the intervening century and a half, there would have been no real prospect of a Persian king who could establish peace to the same extent as Darius (see P. Briant, "Persian Empire," *ABD* 5:239-44). In the context of such struggle between the two superpowers, there would likewise have been no real prospect of a Davidic king of Judah who could establish even the more circumscribed kind of regional stability to which his preexilic predecessors might have aspired.

Once this struggle was finally resolved by Alexander, however, the prospect of such a peace would have reemerged, albeit for only a short time. Upon Alexander's premature death his generals briefly maintained the idea of designating someone to succeed him, before finally deciding instead to divide his empire among themselves (M. Hengel, "The Political and Social History of Palestine from Alexander to Antiochus III [333-187 B.C.E.]," in *The Cambridge History of Judaism,* vol. 2: *The Hellenistic Age* [ed. W. D. Davies and L. Finkelstein; Cambridge: Cambridge University Press, 1989] 45-52). In its present literary context the language of 9:9-10 thus reflects the kind of situation that existed during the reign of Alexander and shortly thereafter, as long as his reign provided a model for the continuation of his empire. This is not to say that 9:9-10 refers directly either to Alexander himself or to any subsequent pretender to his throne, but only that it expresses a realistic expectation of being ruled by the kind of king that he was. As noted above (→ Structure), the description of the historical process in 9:1–11:17 also extends to encompass the eclipse of this expectation, as it concludes with a sign of the eventual collapse of the same world order that brought such a ruler to power (11:10; → 11:4-17). This reversal reflects the fact that such expectation proved illusory by the end of the fourth century.

It also seems unlikely that a concept of restoration, which included the reunification of the northern kingdom with a restored Judah, would have gained much currency under the Persians. The reunification of the north with the south was an aspect of the Deuteronomic ideal, expressed at least as far back as the seventh-century reign of Josiah. Although Zechariah was obviously concerned primarily with Judah and Jerusalem, he nevertheless may have conceived the overall process of exile and restoration rather broadly, so as to include the north as well as the south (e.g., 2:2; 8:13). Despite such well-established precedents, the whole idea seems to have been a dead letter throughout the Persian period. The fifth and fourth centuries were instead characterized by a tendency toward mutual exclusion between north and south, born of friction between the returned Babylonian exiles, who dominated the restoration of Judah, and the inhabitants of the territory formerly occupied by the northern kingdom, who regarded themselves as descendants of the Israelites (e.g., Ezra 4:1-4; 5:1-5; Neh 4:1-23). Moreover, the dynamics of local administration under the Persians seem only to have aggravated and reinforced this opposition, rather than to have encouraged its elimination (e.g., Ezra 4). The kind of regrouping that followed Alexander's destruction of Samaria, combined with the tentative efforts of Alexander's generals to redefine the structure of local administration, would provide a more plausible context for the restoration to be conceived in terms of the revived ideal of the north's reunification with Judah (Hengel, 38-43), and a more plausible context in which to describe this eventuality as a real and desirable opportunity that was not seized (Zech 11:14; → 11:4-17).

Last but not least, there is the overt reference to Greece in 9:13b. Attempts have repeatedly been made to eliminate it by emendation, but no convincing text-critical reasons for doing so have ever been adduced. Other ingenious ways of getting around the fact have thus been proposed, such as redefining the phrase *běnê yāwān* (lit. "the children of Javan") rather vaguely, so that it ceases to refer specifically to the Greeks (e.g., Baldwin, for whom it refers to "distant, unknown peoples on the edge of civilization" [p. 169]; cf. Weis, 183-86), but such proposals have not been very convincing. Otzen argues that this phrase refers to Greek mercenaries in the Egyptian armies that attacked Judah in the late seventh century, but he can produce no plausible parallel case of an enemy host's being named for a subgroup within it (pp. 45-50). Meyers and Meyers have similarly suggested that this reference reflects the considerable extent to which the fifth-century tension between Persians and Greeks had a direct affect on Judah (*Zechariah 9–14,* 148), but 9:13b describes neither opposition between the Greeks and the Persian rulers of the Jews, nor opposition between the Greeks and the Jews acting as surrogates for their Persian rulers, but rather opposition between the Greeks and the Jews themselves. Despite all such attempts to evade the obvious implications of this verse, it is difficult to avoid the conclusion that it means just what it seems to say: Yahweh has enabled Jerusalem to resist direct threats from the Greeks (→ 9:11–10:12, Part I, Text).

Greek rule brought with it not only the promising possibility of a new world peace from which Judah could benefit (9:9-10) but also the threatening possibility that Jerusalem might be forcefully subjected to Greek control, as Samaria had been by Alexander. During the final decades of the fourth century Jerusalem managed to avoid this fate, while also asserting a degree of autonomy, if only because it was somewhat removed from the main theater of military action, i.e., from the armies marching repeatedly back and forth along the coast between Egypt and Syria. Judah seemed immune to being negatively affected by this conflict, until Ptolemy I overran Judah several times in an attempt to extend his control northward from Egypt to Syria. The prophetic statement in 9:13b, regarding Yahweh's demonstrated intention to protect the city from the Greeks, would accurately reflect the situation that briefly existed between the time when Alexander first entered Syria-Palestine and the forays of Ptolemy I.

I therefore propose that a group of mantic scribes in Judah, who studied the records of Zechariah's prophecies now preserved in 1:7–6:15 and 7:1–8:23, produced the *maśśā'* in 9:1–11:17 sometime during the final decades of the fourth century. By this means they gained some understanding of Yahweh's involvement in the events of their time and attempted to communicate this insight to their contemporaries. The mantic scribes that produced this text thus shared a perception that was widespread throughout the Near East soon after the death of Alexander, which viewed his achievement as a turning point in world history, and thus viewed the subsequent establishment of an ongoing Hellenistic hegemony as the dawning of a new era. This perception was reflected in the custom that became common among Jews and non-Jews alike by the end of the fourth century, and that persisted for centuries afterward, of numbering years from the foundation of the Seleucid dynasty (E. J. Bickerman, *Chronology of the Ancient World,* rev. ed. [London: Thames and Hudson, 1980] 71-72; S. Zeitlin, *The Rise and Fall of the Judaean State* [2nd ed.; Philadelphia: Jewish Publication Society, 1962] 47-48).

Intention

Because this section of Zechariah expresses such strong criticism of Judah's leadership, which by implication extends to include an oligarchical ruling class, its intention has often been described in terms of the partisan polemics that are generally thought to have pervaded postexilic Judaism (M. Smith, 75-146; cf. Hanson, *Dawn,* 280-86, 350-54). This text may well have lent itself to functioning in this way, as it hardly purports to be objectively neutral or disinterested, but it does not have the form of a polemic. It therefore cannot simply be identified with some particular interest group, as if were only a manifesto stating their partisan viewpoint. It would be equally reductionistic to read Ray Bradbury's *Martian Chronicles* as propaganda from the pro-NASA lobby.

This text presents a prophetic view of Judah's situation in the final decades of the fourth century, based on an analogy between the impact of Persia's succeeding Babylon as Judah's imperial ruler and the impact of Greece's succeeding Persia. In terms of this analogy Judah still exists in a kind of captivity. Just as the coming of the Persians portended release and restoration for Judah, the coming of the Greeks promises to extend and deepen this process to include further liberation and the restoration of northern Israel as well. Like the Babylonian exile, the present oppression of Judah is due as much to the unfaithfulness and irresponsibility of their own leaders as it is to the imperialism of their conquerors.

This section of the book aims to convince its audience that there is hope of a change for the better because Yahweh is now transforming both the world situation and the leadership of his own people, in much the same way that he did during the time of Zechariah. Because of the leaders' intransigence, this transformation may turn out to be radically different in some respects from what was initially envisioned; and the situation will only get worse before it gets any better. There are nevertheless signs that things will eventually improve, in accord with Yahweh's relentless efforts to restore peace and prosperity to his people.

Bibliography

M. Fishbane, *Biblical Interpretation in Ancient Israel* (Oxford: Clarendon, 1985); P. D. Hanson, "Zechariah 9 and the Recapitulation of an Ancient Ritual Pattern," *JBL* 92 (1973) 37-59; D. R. Jones, "A Fresh Interpretation of Zechariah IX–XI," *VT* 12 (1962) 241-59; M. Treves, "Conjectures concerning the Date and Authorship of Zechariah 9–14," *VT* 13 (1963) 196-207.

THE SUPERSCRIPTION: *MAŚŚĀ'*, 9:1aα[1]

Text

The translation of *maśśā'* is notoriously difficult. Although "oracle" *(RSV)* and "burden" (KJV) are both time-honored alternatives, depending on how the etymology is understood, neither begins to capture what this term denotes in this particular context. The following analysis of this unit confirms Weis's suggestion that here it means something like "interpretation of revelation" (pp. 275-76; → 9:1–11:17, Genre). In other words, a revelation received in an earlier time is being reconsidered here in order to discern both the nature of Yahweh's involvement in the present situation and the appropriate response. Because the meaning of *maśśā'* in this particular context cannot be easily captured in a single English word or phrase, I leave it untranslated.

Structure

Some have wanted to construe *maśśā'* as a noun in construct relationship with the immediately following phrase, *děbar-yhwh* ("the word of Yahweh"), so that the heading would read something like "the *maśśā'* of Yahweh's word" (e.g., Hanson, "Zechariah 9," 41; Lamarche, 36). This reading is improbable because *maśśā'* is almost always found in construct relationship with nouns or noun phrases indicating the subject matter or theme of the prophecy that it designates, rather than with other prophetic terms like *děbar-yhwh* (e.g., Isa 13:1; 15:1; 17:1, 19:1; 21:1; 23:1; 30:6; Nah 1:1). It is perhaps possible to see a construct relationship between *maśśā'* and *děbar-yhwh* in the two other collocations of these two terminological expressions, (→) Zech 12:1aα[1] and Mal 1:1. In both of these cases, however, it is also more likely that they are in apposition. Moreover, since it is generally characteristic of prophetic superscriptions that they are grammatically and otherwise independent of the main body (Tucker, 57-58), to see these two terms in a construct relationship here would leave the third person masculine singular pronominal suffix of *měnūḥātô* ("his resting place") without any antecedent in the main body of the prophecy itself. The superscription of this section of the book thus appears to consist of a single word.

Genre

This is a PROPHETIC SUPERSCRIPTION that serves to indicate the relationship between the prophetic material in the main body of this section (9:1aα[2]βb–11:17) and preceding prophecies of Zechariah.

458

Setting

Such superscriptions were the creation of scribal groups that were concerned with the preservation and divinatory study of the records of prophetic revelation.

Intention

This superscription shows that the following prophecy is meant to extend and reapply the earlier prophetic insights of Zechariah, in order to perceive what Yahweh is presently doing and how the people should respond.

Bibliography

G. Tucker, "Prophetic Superscriptions and the Growth of a Canon," in *Canon and Authority* (ed. G. W. Coats and B. O. Long; Philadelphia: Fortress, 1977) 56-70.

YAHWEH PROMISES TO MAINTAIN THE PLACE OF HIS PEOPLE AND OF HIS TEMPLE AMONG THE NATIONS, 9:1aα^2-8

Text

The translation of vv. 1aα^2-2 is difficult, and it consequently varies widely among commentators and English versions, as does the arrangement of these verses in relation to the superscription and to v. 3. I have already discussed the issue of the extent of the superscription ($\rightarrow$ 9:1aα^1, Structure). For reasons that will become apparent below in the discussion of this unit's structure, these verses are to be translated and arranged in relation to v. 3 as follows:

(1aα^2b) Yahweh's word is in the land of Hadrach,
and in Damascus is his resting place;
for Yahweh has his eye on [all] humankind,
as well as on all the tribes of Israel.
(2) Hamath falls within its borders,
as do Tyre and Sidon.
Because she was so very wise,
(3) Tyre built herself a rampart.
She heaped up silver like dust,
and gold like the dirt of the streets.

Structure

I. Description of Yahweh's emergence on the
   international scene $9:1a\alpha^2$-$2b\alpha$
   A. Basic statement: in terms of his Syrian center
      of activity $9:1a\alpha^2\beta$
      1. Hadrach: locus of his word's agency $9:1a\alpha^2$
      2. Damascus: his resting place $9:1a\beta$
   B. Explication: in terms of his overall purview $9:1b$
      1. Its universal scope: humanity in general $9:1b\alpha$
      2. Its particular focus: all the tribes of Israel $9:1b\beta$
   C. Elaboration: in terms of the initial extent of
      his involvement $9:2a$-$b\alpha$
      1. Northward: to Hamath $9:2a$
      2. Southward: to Tyre and Sidon $9:2b\alpha$
II. Description of Yahweh's subsequent activity
    among the nations $9:2b\beta$-8
    A. At the southernmost point of his initial sphere of
       action: his punishment of Tyre $9:2b\beta$-4
       1. Reason for punishment: accusation of hubris $9:2b\beta$-3
          a. Motivation for Tyre's offenses: her great
             "wisdom" $9:2b\beta$
          b. The offenses themselves $9:3$
             1) Delusions of inviolability $9:3a$
             2) Overacquisitiveness $9:3b$
       2. Announcement of punishment $9:4$
          a. Yahweh's actions $9:4a$
             1) He will dispossess her $9:4a\alpha$
             2) He will throw her wealth into the sea $9:4a\beta$
          b. Consequences of Yahweh's actions:
             Tyre will be destroyed by fire $9:4b$
    B. Beyond Yahweh's initial sphere of action: from Tyre
       to the punishment of Philistia $9:5$-7
       1. Repercussions of Tyre's punishment on
          Philistine cities $9:5$-$6a$
          a. Its effect on their morale $9:5a$
             1) Ashkelon: fear $9:5a\alpha^1$
             2) Gaza: anguish $9:5a\alpha^2$
             3) Ekron: hopelessness $9:5a\beta$
          b. Consequences for their civic life $9:5b$-$6a$
             1) Gaza: no king $9:5b$
             2) Ashkelon: not inhabited $9:5c$
             3) Ashdod: populated by aliens $9:6a$
       2. Philistia's punishment $9:6b$-7
          a. Yahweh's direct actions against them $9:6b$-$7a\alpha$
             1) He will put an end to their arrogance $9:6b$
             2) He will do away with their voracity $9:7a\alpha$

The consensus of scholarly opinion holds that 9:1-8 forms a more or less self-contained unit, but there is little unanimity regarding its internal structure. Many commentators have tried to link the thematic progression with a particular course of historical events. Hanson has shown the inappropriateness of this approach, and proposes instead that this unit contains the first two episodes of a completely eschatological recapitulation of the divine warrior myth: the divine warrior wins the battle (vv. 1-7) and secures his temple (v. 8; "Zechariah 9," 37-39, 50-51). Sæbø identifies vv. 1-2, 3-6a, and 8 as three originally separate prophecies (the second of which was subsequently expanded by the addition of vv. 6b-7) that were secondarily edited into the present unit (*Sacharja 9–14*, 170-75). Lamarche sees vv. 1-2bα, 2bβ-4, 5-7aαβ, and 7aγ-8 arranged in an abb´a´ chiastic pattern (pp. 38-42); but cf. the critique and alternative of Butterworth (pp. 168-77). These differing analyses are all based on thematic contrasts that are indeed evident in the text. The question is how these thematic contrasts are conceptually organized in relation to one another.

The organization of this unit is conceptually programmatic. Yahweh's activity in the arena of international affairs is first described in relation to a particular topographical starting point: the Syrian cities of Hadrach and Damascus (v. 1a). His influence there is described in terms of both the dynamic agency of his "word" and the concrete territoriality of "his resting place." The bounds of his activity extend initially beyond these cities, northward to include Hamath (v. 2a) and southward to include the Phoenician cities of Tyre and Sidon (v. 2bα). From this point of departure Yahweh moves southward to the cities of Philistia (vv. 5-7), and then eastward to the site of his temple in Judah (v. 8a). Each territorial shift of his "resting place" is accompanied by a "word" describing his activity vis-à-vis that area (vv. 4, 5b-7, 8b).

Both the initial paradigmatic description of Yahweh's international involvement (vv. 1aα2-2bα) and the subsequent description of its unfolding throughout the Levant (vv. 2bβ-8) are predicated on Yahweh's capacity to oversee all that happens on earth (vv. 1b, 8b). He initially has his "eye" (*'yn*)

461

on "all humanity," as well as on "all the tribes of Israel" (v. 1b; so Otzen, 236). With the totality of the world situation and of his people's history in view, he deals with the surrounding nations in a variety of ways to assure that his people keep their place in the world and that the temple site — where the worldwide scope of his "eye" is symbolically represented (4:10b) — remains inviolate. The goal of his international activity is thus motivated by the double focus with which his "eye" sees all (v. 8b).

This unit is developed so as to play on the different but interrelated meanings of the territorial term "resting place" *(měnûḥâ)*. It can refer to a stopping point on a journey (Num 10:33), and hence to the final destination the long journey to the promised land, i.e., the land itself, where Yahweh's people can live in peace (Deut 12:9; 1 Kgs 8:56; Ps 95:11). It can also refer to the place where Yahweh's divine kingship has its earthly representation, i.e., his sanctuary (Ps 132:8, 14; 1 Chr 28:2; cf. Isa 66:1). Yahweh's various modes of involvement with each of the areas on his itinerary are actualizations of these three senses of this term.

The Syro-Phoenician starting point of Yahweh's activity (vv. 1-4) is his "resting place" in the first sense, i.e., the place where he has temporarily ceased from being on the move and from which he picks up and starts out anew. The effect of his temporary presence there is generally neutral, but it also neutralizes any threat that a particular city, like Tyre, might pose for his people. The Philistine midpoint of his journey (vv. 5-7) is his "resting place" in the second sense, i.e., the area designated as a place where his people can live in safety. In order to create such a safe place for them to live, the remnant of the Philistines will, like the Jebusites, be incorporated but not wholly integrated into the body politic of Yahweh's people (v. 7; cf. Josh 15:63; Judg 1:21; 3:5; 1 Kgs 9:20). Jerusalem, the destination of Yahweh's journey (v. 8), is his resting place in the third sense, i.e., the site of his temple. The goal of his involvement there is to secure the territorial integrity of his sanctuary.

Genre

This unit primarily describes the punishment that will be directed against Tyre and Philistia. In the former case the accusation of hubris (vv. 2bβ-3) precedes and is formally distinct from the announcement of Tyre's destruction (v. 4). In the latter case the element of accusation is incorporated within the announcement of punishment as the object of the punitive action that Yahweh will take: He will put an end to their predatory behavior (v. 7aα). The combination of these two elements is typical of the PROPHECY OF PUNISHMENT AGAINST A FOREIGN NATION, and identifies this unit as belonging to this genre (so Sæbø, *Sacharja 9–14*, 172; Petersen, *Zechariah 9–14*, 41 and passim).

This particular example of the genre involves two nations rather than just one. In addition to the typical accusation and announcement of punishment there are also other compositional elements. Divine punishment is described in a context that also describes Yahweh's influence over foreign areas that are not singled out for punishment (i.e., Syria, v. 1aα²-b), as well as

Yahweh's promise to maintain the security of Jerusalem (v. 8a). The function of this example of the genre is thus not just to describe Yahweh's disfavor toward his enemies in a way that entails or implies his favor toward his own people (→ Zeph 2:5-7, Genre), but also to relate such description to a larger, more general concept of how Yahweh is involved in international affairs.

Setting

Prophecies of punishment against foreign nations functioned in a variety of closely related settings that were all concerned in some way with international affairs. They could be spoken to the representatives of foreign nations by prophets of Yahweh, who either journeyed abroad to meet them or received them as envoys from abroad, in order to influence foreign authorities. Such prophecies could be intended for a general audience, providing a prophet with a means of expressing his views on the theological significance of some international development. They could also be spoken by prophets of Yahweh to their own people, in order to describe the usually favorable impact that Yahweh's action against a foreign nation would have on them, so as to inform and reassure them. (See the essays by Hayes and Raabe.)

With regard to this text, the third of these possibilities seems most applicable and thus warrants a somewhat more detailed discussion. In the preexilic period prophecies against foreign nations were often pronounced when the community was threatened militarily, in the context of either a communal complaint liturgy conducted under royal auspices or the king's public preparations for battle (→ Zeph 2:5-7). In the postexilic period, when Judah had neither a king nor a standing army, this practice seems to have been adapted to the new and different conditions. Nehemiah reports that the provincial leaders, who attacked his efforts to restore Jerusalem (Neh 4:1-2 [*RSV* 7-8]), had commissioned prophets to intimidate him (6:12b, 14b). Conversely, when their efforts failed, Jerusalem's enemies were made aware that the restoration was accomplished "with the help of our God" (6:16). These incidents suggest that something similar to the preexilic practice of prophesying against foreign foes persisted, but on occasions related to the local leadership's attempts to exercise whatever political influence it might have in the midst of regional conflict, or when they deployed the militia (Jdt 6:2; cf. Neh 4:3-17 [*RSV* 9-23]; 1 Macc 3:44-60).

In this particular case it appears that international developments in the Syro-Phoenician area and in Philistia have undermined the security of the Judeans, calling into question their overall place in the world of imperial society and threatening the temple site on which their communal identity is centered. This unit may well have once existed as an independent prophetic speech, spoken in reaction to some such development prior to its incorporation into its present literary context, but this development is not described specifically enough to be directly identified with any particular events known from other sources. In view of this prophecy's historical vagueness the various attempts to determine its original date, with which the history of scholarship is littered, have been in vain (e.g., Delcor, "Allusions,"; Kraeling; Malamat; cf. Hanson, "Zechariah 9," 37-39). When 9:1-8 is read within its present literary context as describing part of the larger historical process with which this section as a whole is concerned, its outline of events can nevertheless be assigned an approximate date (→ 9:1–11:17, Setting).

Intention

This prophecy affirms that Yahweh is at work in several impending international developments. He is demonstrating his influence on Syrian cities, bringing about the overthrow of Tyre, and fomenting the dissolution of the Philistine city states, all in order to ensure the security of his temple in Jerusalem and of his people's place in the world.

Bibliography

M. Delcor, "Les Allusions à Alexandre le Grand dans Zach. 9:1-8," *VT* 1 (1951) 110-24; J. H. Hayes, "The Usage of Oracles against Foreign Nations in Ancient Israel," *JBL* 87 (1968) 81-92; E. G. H. Kraeling, "The Historical Situation in Zech. 9:1-10," *AJSL* 41 (1924) 24-53; A. Malamat, "The Historical Setting of Two Biblical Prophecies on the Nations," *IEJ* 1 (1950-51) 149-59; D. L. Peterson, "The Oracles against the Nations: A Form-Critical Analysis," in *Society of Biblical Literature 1975 Seminar Papers* (ed. G. MacRae; 2 vols.; Missoula, Mont.: Scholars Press, 1975) 1:39-61; P. R. Raabe, "Why Oracles against the Nations?" in *Fortunate the Eyes That See* (*Fest.* D. N. Freedman; ed. A. H. Bartelt et al.; Grand Rapids: Eerdmans, 1995) 236-57.

YAHWEH PROMISES ROYAL LEADERSHIP THAT LIVES UP TO THE DAVIDIC IDEAL, 9:9-10

Structure

I. Twofold call to rejoice	9:9aα
A. First call	9:9aα¹
1. Command: rejoice greatly!	
2. Epithet of direct address: daughter of Zion	
B. Second call	9:9aα²
1. Command: shout aloud!	
2. Epithet of direct address: daughter of Jerusalem	
II. Motivation	9:9aβ-10
A. Advent of a king	9:9aβb
1. Basic statement	9:9aβ
a. Single description of his advent: he comes to you	9:9aβ¹

Willi-Plein joins Alonso Schökel and Sicre Diaz in opposing the vast majority of commentators, who recognize 9:9-10 as a separate unit. Willi-Plein includes these verses in a larger unit, 9:9-13, because of the second person feminine singular direct address that continues through v. 13 (pp. 47-48), while Alonso Schökel and Sicre Diaz define 9:9-15 as a unit on the basis of the war-peace theme that permeates these verses. Both analyses rightly point to elements of continuity, which are relevant to defining the relationship between 9:9-10 and 9:11–10:12 within the context of this section as a whole (→ 9:1–11:17, Structure), but there are also other elements of discontinuity that indicate a break after v. 10 (→ 9:10–10:12, Part I, Structure). Several see the main division in this unit as falling between v. 9 and v. 10 (e.g., Lamarche, 45-46; Hanson, "Zechariah 9," 53). There is a shift at v. 10, from third person description to first person speech of Yahweh; but this difference is not systematically maintained throughout v. 10. Third person description resumes in v. 10b. There is a more fundamental contrast between the commands in v. 9aα and the various kinds of description in vv. 9aβ-10 that collectively serve to provide the motivation for them.

The populace of Jerusalem, collectively personified as one of the city's daughters, are urged to rejoice over the prospect of a king, who has victoriously won his right to rule. This call to rejoicing echoes the similar call in 2:14 (*RSV* 10), the addressees of which are likewise personified as "the daughter of Zion." The previous call exhorted the exiles to see the return to Jerusalem as a manifestation of Yahweh's divine presence, and of his intention to create a safe place for his people among the nations. The present call also exhorts its addressees to see the advent of a new king as a manifestation of the same presence and intention (cf. Petersen, *Zechariah 9–14*, 57-58).

The description of this king conforms in every respect to the Davidic ideal. Both the celebratory riding of a donkey and the tempering of triumph with humility are in accord with images that became stereotypes of a messianic ideal (Gen 49:11a; Ps 45:5 [*RSV* 4]), and in combination they evoke the ceremonial pattern of Solomon's coronation (1 Kgs 1:33, 38, 44). Yahweh's destruction of weaponry is one of the hallmarks of his theophany in the royal sanctuary (Ps 46:9-10 [*RSV* 8-9]), signifying his election of the Davidic king (Ps 2:6). The scope of the disarmament, encompassing both north and south (Ephraim and Jerusalem, v. 10a), evokes David's short-lived but formative achievement of joining both Judah and Israel into a united kingdom (2 Sam 2:10b-11; 5:1-5). To rule victoriously and in peace over an empire of cosmic dimensions is the mythic destiny of the Davidic dynasty (Ps 72:7-8; 89:21-26 [*RSV* 20-25]).

Genre

Following Elliger (pp. 149-50), Sæbø classifies this unit as the speech of a herald (*Heroldwort*), i.e., the speech of a *mĕbaśśēr*, "one who bears [good] tidings" (*Sacharja 9–14*, 175-88). He compares it with such texts as Nah 2:1 (*RSV* 1:15), Isa 40:9-10, and Isa 52:7-10, with which it indeed has some similarities. Regarding the kinds of speeches that generally pertain to the function of heralds, however, four different but closely related forms need to be more carefully distinguished: (1) what someone in authority would say in commissioning a herald to go and report the tidings of a momentous event (e.g., 2 Sam 18:21); (2) what a sentinel would say to announce the approach of a herald bearing tidings (e.g., 2 Sam 18:24-27); (3) what a herald would say to communicate these tidings (e.g., 2 Sam 18:31; 1 Kgs 1:42-53; Ps 68:12-13a [*RSV* 11-12a]); and (4) what would be said in reaction to the tidings communicated by a herald (e.g., 2 Sam 1:20).

These different types of speeches are so closely related that the distinction between them could conceivably become somewhat blurred, particularly when adapted by prophets for a derivative function. For example, if one assumed that a herald was bringing good tidings, the sentinel's announcement of his approach might include some reference to the news of victory. Such blurring is evident in the examples cited by Sæbø, but it is nevertheless possible to distinguish (→) Nah 2:1 (*RSV* 1:15) and Isa 52:7-10 as speeches of the second type, and Isa 40:9-10 as a speech of the first type.

As 2 Sam 1:20 shows, a victory celebration was typically an activity led by the women of a city in reaction to the good news brought by a herald, not an activity led by the herald himself (cf. Exod 15:20; Jdt 15:13; also Ps 68:13b [*RSV* 12b]). The commands to rejoice that dominate this unit, expressed in feminine singular form and addressed to the feminine personification of Jerusalem, show that this is a stylized version of a speech of the fourth type. It is thus not strictly comparable with the texts cited by Sæbø. Its genre is more aptly characterized as a call to rejoicing than as the speech of a herald. The inclusion of oracular speech (v. 10) in the motivation of these commands indicates a prophetic adaptation of this genre, i.e., a PROPHETIC CALL TO REJOICING (→ Zeph 3:14-15, Genre).

Setting

The call to rejoicing itself originated in the context of the victory celebration (→ Zeph 3:14-15, Setting). Prophets borrowed this convention and employed it more generally in the context of prophetic public oratory, in order to interpret various kinds of developments that were not necessarily of an overtly military nature in terms of a victory over forces opposed to Yahweh.

Intention

In this particular case the form is used to celebrate the inauguration of some new king's rule, which will manifest those aspects of the Davidic ideal evoked here, thus bringing an era of peace that will extend from Jerusalem to encompass both Judah and northern Israel, finally reaching to the ends of the earth. The stereotypical description in this unit is ambiguous, in and of itself, with regard to just what kind of king this could be. Such language might apply to one of David's successors in preexilic times, to one of the emperors that imposed their rule over Judah in postexilic times (cf. the application of the term "messiah" to Cyrus in Isa 44:28–45:3), or to a late postexilic pretender to the restored Davidic throne (e.g., Pss Sol 17). This ambiguity is largely resolved when this unit is considered in relation to the rest of Zech 9:1–11:17, as describing part of the historical process outlined in this section as a whole (→ 9:1–11:17, Setting), but this prophecy nevertheless remains open to further figurative and typological interpretation (cf. Matt 21:5; John 12:15).

THE CRISIS OF THE HELLENISTIC AGE VIEWED FROM ZECHARIAH'S PERSPECTIVE, 9:11–10:12; PART I, 9:11–10:2

Since 9:11–10:12 is a relatively long and complex unit, the discussion here will focus only on 9:11–10:2, and 10:3-12 will be discussed separately below. This separation is only for the sake of convenience and should not obscure the fact that 9:11–10:2 and 10:3-12 belong together as parts of a larger entity.

Text

In 9:11a the perfect verb *šillaḥtî* is to be translated "I have set free" (*RSV* "I will set free"). Similarly, the verbs in 9:13b are perfects coordinated with the preceding perfects in 9:13a, not *waw*-consecutive perfects coordinated with an initial imperfect. Both *'ôrartî* and *śamtî* should therefore be treated as frequentative perfects (GKC §112h) and translated with some English past or

467

perfect progressive tense, such as "I have kept brandishing/wielding" (*RSV* "I will brandish/wield"), or the like.

The structure analysis below will be based on the following rendering of the very difficult passage in vv. 15aβb-17a:

(15aβ-b) They will eat,
        and they will subdue sling-stones.
    They will drink,
        and they will be boisterous, as when drinking wine;
    They will be full as a wine bowl,
        [and overflow] as corner ducts of an altar.
  (16) Yahweh their God will save them on that day,
        as the flock of his people.
    For like jewels in a crown,
        they [will serve as] his ensign on the earth.
  (17) What goodness and beauty will be theirs!

For the translation of *hāmû* in v. 15aβ² as "be boisterous" (*RSV* "their blood"), see R. L. Smith (p. 258). With respect to the kind of imagery in v. 16b, which this translation evokes, cf. Isa 11:12; 62:3.

Structure

I. Exhortation to respond to Yahweh's action:
first person speech of Yahweh   9:11-12a
  A. Description of what Yahweh has done:
    addressed to Jerusalem   9:11
    1. Designation of addressee: with second person
       feminine singular pronoun   9:11aα
    2. Yahweh's action   9:11aβb
      a. Its motivation: blood of your covenant   9:11aβ
      b. Action itself: I have set your captives free
         from the waterless pit   9:11b
  B. Directive describing the people's response   9:12a
    1. Command (masculine plural): return to the
       fortress!   9:12aα
    2. Designation of addressees: captives of hope   9:12aβ
II. Exhortation to respond to Yahweh's action   9:12b–10:12
  A. Description of what Yahweh is doing   9:12b-17
    1. Generally stated: first person speech of Yahweh
       addressed to Jerusalem   9:12b
      a. When: today   9:12bα¹
      b. What: I promise double restoration   9:12bα²β¹
      c. To whom: to you   9:12bβ²
    2. Specifically narrated   9:13-17
      a. Yahweh has joined in his people's struggle

b. Consequences of reliance on them: the people are
like sheep without a shepherd   10:2b
c. Reason to rely on Yahweh instead: he promises
to take care of the bad shepherds/leaders   10:3-12

There is little unanimity on the division of the text here. The main issue seems to be whether there is a break of some kind at 10:1. Despite considerable differences in other respects, Hanson ("Zechariah 9," 40-41), Sæbø (*Sacharja 9–14,* 188-214), and Petersen (*Zechariah 9–14,* 70-71) agree in seeing a new unit at this point, as do Willi-Plein (p. 48) and Butterworth (pp. 75-76). R. L. Smith, however, raises the possibility of a unit extending from 9:16 through 10:2 (p. 259), and both Lamarche (pp. 47-63) and Otzen (pp. 216-18) propose that 10:1 should be linked with the immediately preceding verses. The absence of a clear break at 10:1 raises acutely the question of how 9:11-17 and 10:2ff. are related.

There is likewise little agreement regarding the way in which the material following 9:10 should be subdivided, but the disagreement surrounding 10:1 is symptomatic of the main problem. How can one formally and materially account for the command that initiates this verse, to "ask for rain," except in connection with the similar masculine plural command in 9:12a, as well as the statement in 9:11b of Yahweh's intention to free his people from a lack of water? Otherwise it is quite anomalous. Sæbø points out that 10:1-2 does not really fit the category of a prophetic admonition (*Mahnwort*), into which many commentators have put it (*Sacharja 9–14,* 208-14), and Hanson admits that these verses do not really fit the scheme of the divine warrior hymn, into which he tries to force 10:1-12 (*Dawn of Apocalyptic,* 325). Such problems show the need to approach the complexities of this material along the lines proposed by Lamarche and Otzen, looking for the overarching rhetorical and thematic connections between 9:11-17 and 10:1-12, as well as discontinuities that mark the subdivisions of this material.

The unit 9:11–10:12 is a sprawling one that is not altogether self-contained. It commences with a second person feminine singular pronoun, whose antecedent can only be the "daughter of Zion/Jerusalem" in 9:9a, thus showing some continuity with the preceding unit (9:9-10). It also initiates the development of pastoral imagery concerning shepherds and flocks (9:16a; 10:2b-3), which obviously extends into the rest of this section, thus showing some continuity with the following units in ch. 11. This unit therefore cannot stand on its own, but must be seen in relation to the overall context of this section (9:1–11:17) as a whole. There are nevertheless some definite indications of a rhetorical shift at 9:11 and 11:1, as well as some rhetorical patterns that give a loose coherence to the material between these two points.

Although this unit initially maintains the precedent of directly addressing its audience as a feminine personification of Jerusalem (9:11-13), there is a change in the formulation of its directives. Unlike the commands of 9:9, which are feminine singular imperatives, the commands in 9:12a and 10:1aα are masculine plural imperatives. This shift in gender and number corresponds with a transition in the overall tenor of the description, from portraying Yahweh's people as women leading a victory celebration in (→) 9:9-10 (cf. Exod 15:20-21; Jdt 15:12-13) to portraying them as men fighting a battle in 9:11–10:12.

Although the bulk of the material in this unit is third person description, the pivotal position occupied by the commands and other second person markers shows that the rhetorical stance of direct address, which is emphasized at the outset but subsequently muted, is never entirely abandoned. There is a shift from being directly addressed in first person speech of Yahweh (9:11-12) to being directly addressed in third person speech about Yahweh (10:1), but the style of this material is generally characterized by indiscriminate alternation between these two modes of prophetic discourse. The addressee throughout is Jerusalem, personifying in this case the reunified empire of David, encompassing both the southern kingdom (Judah) and the northern kingdom (Ephraim/Joseph). There is thus a decisive shift at 11:1, where Lebanon is directly addressed with the heretofore unused masculine singular imperative form *pĕtaḥ* ("open!").

The overall coherence of 9:11–10:12 is evident not only in these rhetorical demarcations of its external borders but also in the pattern of its internal organization. The basic shape of this pattern is initially and compactly outlined in 9:11-12a. First comes Yahweh's description of his activity (9:11), and then a command directing the people to make the appropriate response (9:12a). In accord with the covenant relationship between Yahweh and his people, which was sealed from the beginning in blood (Exod 24:8) and maintained throughout their history by the blood of the faithful, Yahweh has acted to secure the release of his people from their captivity and their barrenness. (The verb in v. 11b is a perfect, indicating action that is completed; → Text.) Thus they should again prepare themselves to fight for their freedom and prosperity. The people are addressed as *'ăsîrê hattiqwâ* (*RSV* "prisoners of hope"), thus showing that although they are presently still captive to their oppressors, they nevertheless have hope of deliverance because of the initiative that Yahweh has taken.

The same structure is evident, but on a much larger scale, in 9:12b–10:12. First comes Yahweh's description of his activity (9:12b), then a command directing the people to make the appropriate response (10:1aα). Each of these elements is elaborated to an extent that seems rather baroque in comparison with the terseness of 9:11 and 9:12a, respectively, but the relationship between them is nevertheless basically the same as the relationship between 9:11 and 9:12a. Yahweh states that he is presently making a "double" *(mišneh)* restoration. (The verb *'āšîb* in v. 12b is an imperfect, in contrast with the perfect verb in v. 11a, thus indicating action that is in progress.) The ensuing narration in 9:13-17 elaborates on this promise, describing the "double" aspect of Yahweh's activity so as to show the appropriateness of the response that is commanded in 10:1aα.

The promise that Yahweh makes "today" *(hayyôm,* 9:12b) is being fulfilled through an already instigated plan of action (note the perfect verbs in v. 13; → Text), which will reach its culmination "on that day" *(bayyôm hahû',* v. 16). He has joined his people's struggle against the Greeks (9:13), and they are being empowered by his presence to win and celebrate the victory (9:14-15).

Finally, as the flock that Yahweh shepherds (9:16a), and as the earthly representatives of Yahweh's kingship (9:16b), his people will enjoy the blessings of fertility (9:17). The two episodes of the narrative, the struggle (9:13-15) and its outcome (9:16-17), are linked by the imagery of plentiful food. The festive consumption of food and wine as part of the victory celebration (9:15) progresses naturally to the plentiful provision of grain and new wine that results from the restoration of peace (9:17).

In view of the "double" nature of Yahweh's total involvement in the international situation, as both a warrior who defends his people militarily and a benefactor who blesses them with bountiful living, it is appropriate for them to respond not only by taking an overtly defensive stance against their foes (9:12a), but also by asking Yahweh for rain (10:1aα). The divine warrior manifest in the thunderstorm (9:14) is identical with the creator of the rain clouds and showers (10:1aβ). The God who gives the victory feast (9:15), and who provides ample grain and new wine (9:17b), also gives "vegetation in the fields" (10:1bβ). By also asking Yahweh for rain, the people show their recognition of his full identity.

The coherence of this unit, as a pair of exhortations (9:12a; 10:1-12) based on two statements of Yahweh's purpose (9:11, 12b-17), is thus predicated on the concept that both the Jewish community's capacity to defend itself against external foes and its capacity to prosper agriculturally are integrally associated in the recognition of Yahweh's present purpose for them. Although this concept is fully elaborated in 9:12b–10:12, it is already implied in the imagery of 9:11-12a, where the condition of captivity is metaphorically described in terms of a "waterless pit" (*bôr 'ên mayim bô*, v. 11bβ). The command to "return" (*šûbû*, v. 12a) thus includes a transition not only from oppression to sociopolitical liberty but also from waterless infertility to rain and growth galore.

Within this overarching rhetorical and conceptual framework, the unit takes a somewhat different turn at 10:1. Up to this point the emphasis has been on the people's joining Yahweh in his struggle against their external foes, but now the emphasis shifts to their joining his struggle against the internal threat of corrupt leadership. A transition is thus made in 10:1-2 from the description of peace and plenty in 9:16, with which the narration of the battle against the external foes concludes, to the narration of a similar battle in 10:3-5 + 7, describing the fulfillment of Yahweh's promise to punish the corrupt leaders of his people (10:3).

This transition turns on the double meaning of the term *š'l* ("ask") in 10:1. The command to "ask Yahweh for rain" can have in Hebrew much the same connotation that it has in English, i.e., to pray to Yahweh, petitioning him for rain, so that the crops will grow. The word *š'l* is also a technical term, however, that refers to divination. The command thus more specifically connotes, in addition, the making of an oracular inquiry concerning the time when the spring rains will come. Such an oracular inquiry would be motivated by a concern to know how to cultivate the crops already planted, so that they would mature to their fullest fruition.

The issue underlying the command to "ask Yahweh for rain" is thus not only whether they recognize Yahweh as the creator who gives life and growth,

472

but also whether they depend on the right means of divination, which can truly tell them how Yahweh is moving toward the fulfillment of his purpose. The command in 10:1 is thus elaborated in 10:2a in terms of a contrast between "asking Yahweh" and divination by other means: "teraphim" (cf. Ezek 21:26 [*RSV* 21]), idolatrous mediums (*qôsmîm; RSV* "diviners"; cf. Deut 18:10; 2 Kgs 17:17), and dream interpretation (cf. Jer 23:26-28). By virtue of this contrast the command overtly urges the people to accept a particular kind of prophetic guidance. This urging establishes a point of thematic contact between this section of the book (9:1–11:17) and the preceding section (7:1–8:23), where recognition of the authentic prophetic guidance that comes through oracular inquiry is also the issue (7:2-3).

In 10:2b the problem of bad leadership is introduced as it is related to the problem of false divination. Precisely because of the leaders' failure to rely on the proper prophetic guidance, the people founder aimlessly like wandering sheep without a shepherd. In order for the people to reap the full harvest of the crop already planted in their struggle with their external foes, they must recognize the prophetic claim that Yahweh is also concerned with the internal threat of bad leadership, and contend with this problem as well. If they show that they recognize this in the way they "ask Yahweh" (10:1), he will "answer" (*'nh,* 10:6b) them by bringing them successfully through the conflict of developing new leadership (10:3-5), and by restoring the scattered descendants of the northern tribes as he restored the remnant of Judah (10:6-12).

Genre

Because this unit consists basically of commands, preceded by statements of Yahweh on which they are based, and followed by further statements that serve as the rationale and motivation for them, it is largely (→) parenesis (cf. the recurrent identification of sermonic elements in Sæbø's analysis [*Sacharja 9–14,* 175-229 passim]). There are large blocks of material that are not of an overtly parenetical nature (9:13-17; 10:2-12), but they are formally subordinated to the parenetical elements. (Note the subordinate conjunction *kî,* "for," at 9:13 and 10:2.) This passage can thus be characterized as PROPHETIC EXHORTATION. In this particular case the predication of the commands on oracular statements shows that the function of this text is not simply to persuade the addressees to follow its directives, but also to convince them of certain revelatory claims about the nature of Yahweh's involvement in their present situation, on which the directives are based. An exhortation formulated in this way is particularly suited to serve as part of a *massā'* (→ 9:1–11:17, Genre).

Setting

This passage is informed by the conventions of prophetic hortatory speech that were used in any number of public situations: the temple, the streets, the city gates, etc. Precisely because they are Deuteronomistic texts, Jer 17:19-27,

18:1-11, and 22:1-9 probably reflect the idea of the prophet's public role that became predominant during the exile and afterward. The prophets of postexilic times, like some of their preexilic predecessors, had the function of critically assessing the policies of the central authorities in Jerusalem (e.g., Ezra 5:1-2).

This passage is concerned with the theological perceptions that determine how the community in general, as well as its leaders in particular, will respond to a crisis situation. The crisis in question is explicitly identified with the opposition of the Greeks (Zech 9:13b), but it is difficult to identify the specific historical context of this unit by considering it in isolation from the rest of the surrounding section (→ 9:1–11:17, Setting).

Intention

A prophetic voice directs itself to addressees who are beset by both the hostility of enemies and the lack of effective leadership, offering prophetic guidance that promises hope of deliverance from this crisis. Their hope lies not only in the general prophetic perception that Yahweh is fighting for them, governing the forces of both nature and history in their favor. It also lies in the more specific prophetic perception that Yahweh is accomplishing a grand plan, of which the Judean restoration itself was only the initial phase. He intends to complete the process of "return" and "restoration" (*šwb*, 9:12) by not only ensuring that Judah continues to maintain at least the kind of geopolitical integrity that was achieved under the Persians, but also by extending the process to include the return and restoration of the scattered northern tribes, so that the territoriality and social security of his people will be comparable to the status they enjoyed in the time of David.

THE CRISIS OF THE HELLENISTIC AGE VIEWED FROM ZECHARIAH'S PERSPECTIVE, PART II, 10:3-12

Since 9:11–10:12 is a relatively long and complex unit, the discussion here will focus only on 10:3-12; 9:11–10:2 has been discussed separately above. This separation is only for the sake of convenience and should not obscure the fact that 9:11–10:2 and 10:3-12 belong together as parts of a larger entity.

Text

The structure analysis given below assumes a translation of 10:8-9 that differs somewhat from the *RSV:*

> (8) I will signal for them and gather them in,
>   for I have redeemed them;
>   and they will be as many as they were

(9)   when I began sowing them among the peoples
and nations far away.
They will remember me and, with their children,
they will live and return.

Structure

I. Exhortation to respond to Yahweh's action: first person speech of Yahweh	9:11-12a
A. Description of what Yahweh has done: addressed to Jerusalem	9:11
B. Directive describing the people's response	9:12a
II. Exhortation to respond to Yahweh's action	9:12b–10:12
A. Description of what Yahweh is doing	9:12b-17
B. Directive describing the people's response	10:1-12
1. Directive proper	10:1
a. Command: ask Yahweh for the spring rains	10:1aα
b. Elaboration on Yahweh's nature: he creates rain and gives growth	10:1aβb
2. Motivation	10:2-12
a. Reason not to ask through various idolatrous intermediaries: their revelations prove to be false	10:2a
b. Consequences of reliance on them: the people are like sheep without a shepherd	10:2b
c. Reason to rely on Yahweh instead: he promises to take care of the bad shepherds/leaders	10:3-12
1) Oracle of Yahweh	10:3-12a
a) Prophecy of punishment against the leaders of the people	10:3a
(1) Basis for punishment: I am angry with the shepherds	10:3aα
(2) Announcement of punishment: I will take care of the he-goats	10:3aβ
b) Rationale for their punishment: prophecy of salvation for the people	10:3b-12a
(1) Announcement of salvation for the house of Judah	10:3b-5
(a) Basis for salvation: Yahweh takes care of his flock	10:3bα
(b) His care for Judah	10:3bβ-5
α. Yahweh's action: he will make them his warhorse	10:3bβ
β. Results of Yahweh's actions	10:4-5
aa. Enhanced materiel and personnel	10:4

	aa) The waters defeated	10:11a
	bb) Imperial power	
	defeated	10:11b
γ. Summary conclusion		10:12b
	aa. Yahweh's action: I will	
	make them strong	10:12bα
	bb. Result: they shall glory	
	in his name	10:12bβ
2) Oracle formula		10:12b

The above discussion of the overall structure of this unit (→ 9:11–10:12, Part I, Structure) showed that all the material in 10:2-12 is subordinate to the command in 10:1. Reliance on the proper means of divining Yahweh's times and purposes will inevitably pit the people against their leaders, whose ineffectiveness is due to reliance on improper means of divination (10:2). The material in 10:3-12 serves to promote the people's acceptance of prophetic guidance and their opposition to the current leadership. This passage explicates the prophetic claim that Yahweh's intention to punish the current leadership is part of his ongoing plan to complete the restoration of Israel.

The compatibility of these two goals is underscored by playing on the double meaning of the verb *pqd*. This word is used to describe Yahweh's intention to "punish" the leaders for their faithless and ineffective governance (*'epqôd*, 10:3aβ) and to describe his "care" for his people (*pāqad*, 10:3bα), thus emphasizing that these are two aspects of one and the same action on his part. The overthrow of those who are presently in authority is not a sign of Yahweh's disfavor, but rather something that he is bringing about for the people's welfare. By joining the opposition to these authorities, the people are participating in Yahweh's grand design.

The overall shape of this grand design is sketched out in 10:3bβ-12, first with respect to what it entails for Judah (10:3bβ-5), and then with respect to what the enhancement of Judah's status also entails for the descendants of the northern tribes, i.e., Ephraim/Joseph (10:6-12). His "strengthening" of Judah (*gibbartî*, 10:6aα[1]) involves his similarly "strengthening" Ephraim (*gibbartîm*, 10:12aα). Both aspects of the plan are partly described with the same kind of battle imagery that appears in 9:13-15. Yahweh "will make Judah like his proud steed in battle" (10:3bβ). They "shall be like mighty men *(gibbôrîm)* in battle" (10:5aα[1]), and Ephraim also "shall become like a mighty warrior *(gibbôr)*" (10:7aα). The empowerment that is similarly described in such military terms serves different ends in each case.

Judah is divinely empowered to be victorious (10:5) in the struggle for good leadership. The pileup of images in 10:4a connotes the ample provision of military materiel, but it also builds up to the conclusion in 10:4b that "out of [Judah shall come] every ruler." The cornerstone, the tent peg, and the war bow are all key items on which the strength and stability of a larger entity somehow depends. In the process of Yahweh's displacing the current rulers, Judah will provide Yahweh's people with rulers that can head the body politic with this kind of strength and stability.

477

When the scope of the description is broadened to include Ephraim, the temporal perspective is also extended to include the many generations that have passed since the northern tribes existed as such, and the many that may yet pass before Yahweh finally accomplishes his purpose for them (note *běnêhem* [*RSV* "their children"] in both 10:7b and 9b). Ephraim is empowered (10:7a) to realize this purpose of Yahweh, which is to gather them (10:8) and bring them back home (10:10), as part of the same process through which he has reversed his rejection of Judah and begun to restore them (10:6). The scattering of Israel, which began with the destruction of the northern kingdom in the eighth century and continued with the destruction of the southern kingdom in the sixth century, thus becomes comparable to a great "sowing" (*zr'*, 10:9aα; *RSV* "scatter"), from which the resulting harvest is now being reaped in the process of restoration (Baldwin, 176).

From this spatially and temporally expanded viewpoint, the great historical process of restoring all Israel is typologically compared with Yahweh's victory over two great enemies from the past. This restoration harks back to his overthrow of the Assyrians (10:11bα), who had originally destroyed the northern kingdom and scattered its people, and back to his defeat of the Egyptians (10:11bβ) in the course of freeing Israel from slavery and bringing them into the land. Through the imagery of combat with the sea (10:11a) these two victories are metaphorically related with Yahweh's cosmogonic victory over the watery forces of chaos (cf. Ps 74:12-17; 89:10-13 [*RSV* 9-12]). This aspect of Yahweh's control of the waters complements the foregoing description of him as the God manifest in the thunderstorm (9:14) and the giver of rain (10:1). The recurrence of water imagery thus serves to reinforce the link between the two major blocks of material in 9:12b-17 and 10:1-12 that is primarily established by the recurrence of the military imagery.

Genre

Although the bulk of the material (10:3b-12) in this passage has the characteristics of a (→) prophecy of salvation, it is all explicitly subordinated to the initial statement of Yahweh's intention to punish the leaders of Judah (10:3a; note the subordinate conjunction *kî* [*RSV* "for"] with which 10:3b begins). The overall effect is somewhat similar to the way in which a (→) prophecy of punishment against a foreign nation describes Yahweh's punishment of his people's foes so as to convey a message of salvation to the people themselves. Here, conversely, the extensive description of what Yahweh is doing for both Judah and Ephraim serves to explicate his motivation for punishing their leaders.

Hanson rightly emphasizes the predominance of the threats that are directed against the leaders in 10:1-3a over the description of the people's salvation in 10:3b-12, but he problematically identifies this formally dominant element as a "*rîb* oracle" (*Dawn*, 328-31), citing Isa 59:15b-20, 63:19b–64:2, and 66:15-16 as examples of the same generic type. All these texts do have some thematic commonalities, but they are formally quite disparate, and it is not clear how they are related to other texts that have been adduced as definitive expressions of the *rîb* or "lawsuit" pattern, such as Ps 50 and Mic 6:1-8 (K. Nielsen, *Yahweh as Prosecutor and Judge* [JSOTSup 9; Sheffield: JSOT Press, 1978] 27-42; → covenant lawsuit).

It is difficult to see any direct reflection of such a trial speech here. There is simply an announcement of punishment in 10:3a, preceded by material in 10:2 that amounts to an accusation justifying the punishment: Because of reliance on false divination, the people are in effect leaderless (v. 2), and Yahweh will therefore eradicate such leadership because he cares for his people (v. 3). This combination of elements is characteristic of the PROPHECY OF PUNISHMENT, and this passage may be classified as such, provided we keep in mind that it also serves as the motivation for the command in 10:1 in the larger scheme of the PROPHETIC EXHORTATION in (→) 9:13–10:12 as a whole.

Because of the way in which this passage is subordinate to this larger scheme, here the conjunction *'al-kēn* (*RSV* "therefore") — which typically joins the accusation with the announcement of punishment in a prophecy of punishment — instead connects the cause of the accusatory behavior (v. 2a) with its consequences (v. 2b). This deviation is due to the exigencies of the transition from a focus on Yahweh's external foes to a focus on his internal opponents, with which the compositional structure of the unit as a whole is at this point concerned.

Setting

A prophecy of punishment against an individual or group of individuals was often delivered in the context of a confrontation between the prophet and the person(s) against whom it was directed (e.g., Jer 20:1-6; Amos 7:10-17), or it could also be communicated secondhand by someone representing the prophet (1 Kgs 14:5-11). Here, however, nothing indicates that this prophecy of punishment against the leadership of Judah was ever communicated directly to them in such a confrontation. This text functions more to explain to the people the underlying significance of their leaders' impending demise than to inform the leaders themselves. The setting of this passage would thus be no different from the setting of the exhortation that makes up this unit as a whole (→ 9:11–10:12, Part I, Setting).

Intention

This text aims for the addressees to understand the prospective removal of those who govern them as an act of divine deliverance, and for them to support it accordingly. It militates against the assumption that leaders and people are so closely identified that corrupt leadership would inevitably provide Yahweh with sufficient grounds on which to overthrow the people along with them (e.g., Mic 3:1-12), and that any change of leadership would therefore be a disaster for the people. In order to contend persuasively with this assumption, Yahweh's punishment of the leaders is described as motivated by his compassion for the people, and is compared favorably with such great acts of deliverance as his overthrow of the Assyrians at Nineveh, the exodus from Egypt, and his defeat of the forces of chaos in creation.

THE LOSS OF THE LEADERS IS MOCKINGLY MOURNED, 11:1-3

Structure

I. Directive		11:1
A. Order		11:1a
1. Command: open your doors!		11:1aα
2. Addressee: Lebanon		11:1aβ
B. Consequence: that fire may devour your cedars		11:1b
II. Twofold call to lamentation		11:2
A. First call		11:2a
1. Call proper		11:2aα
a. Command: wail!		11:2aα^1
b. Addressee: cypress		11:2aα^2
2. Motivation		11:2aβ
a. The cedar has fallen		11:2aβ^1
b. The glorious trees are ruined		11:2aβ^2
B. Second call		11:2b
1. Call proper		11:2bα
a. Command: wail!		11:2bα^1
b. Addressees: oaks of Bashan		11:2bα^2
2. Motivation: the thick forest has been felled		11:2bβ
III. Twofold report of lamentation		11:3
A. First report		11:3a
1. Report proper: hark the shepherds' wail!		11:3aα
2. Explication: their glory is despoiled		11:3aβ
B. Second report		11:3b
1. Report proper: hark, the lions' roar!		11:3bα
2. Explication: the jungle of the Jordan is laid waste		11:3bβ

Several commentators do not see 11:1-3 as a unit separate from the preceding material (e.g., Lamarche, 56-63; Rudolph, 199-200; Lacoque, 162-63; Alonso Schökel and Sicre Diaz, 1188-90). Their view is based on well-taken observations regarding many points of continuity between 11:1-3 and 9:11–10:12, as well as between 11:1-3 and 9:1-10. The many interconnections between 11:1-3 and the rest of this section, most of which are discussed immediately below, suggest that this pericope plays a pivotal role in the compositional structure of (→) 9:1–11:17 as a whole.

While 11:1-3 is tightly related to its surroundings, it is nevertheless differentiated from them as well. There is a considerable shift in the rhetorical stance. From 9:9 the addressee has been Jerusalem personified, who first represents just Judah but who eventually comes to represent Ephraim as well. The primary form of direct address has been feminine singular (9:9, 11-13), supplemented with masculine plural (9:12a; 10:1aα). Now, however, the addressee is Lebanon, and the primary form of direct address is masculine singular (11:1a, 2a), also supplemented by masculine plural (11:2b). Up to this point the overall mood has been one of rejoicing and hope, but now there is a change — at least ostensibly — to a mood of mourning and despair.

Even though 11:1-3 has much in common with the foregoing material, such discontinuities indicate that these commonalities are being given a distinctively different twist here. This is also the case with regard to the following material. The "despoiling" *(šdd)* of the shepherds' glory (11:3a) is obviously connected with the two episodes concerning the worthless shepherds in 11:4-17, but the two treatments of this common theme are just as obviously quite different. For one thing, the convention of direct address is abandoned altogether in 11:4-17. As a unit, 11:1-3 thus cannot be completely separated from its context, but it is distinguished from the material on either side to such an extent that it deserves independent consideration (Ollenburger, 817).

This unit describes three successive phases of a crisis in leadership, using three different metaphors cast in three rhetorically different forms. In moving through these three phases an allusively symbolic landscape is traversed, as each description conjures up a set of thematic associations with the preceding material from this section.

There is a geographical progression, somewhat like the one in 9:1aα²βb-8, that descends from the peaks of Lebanon (v. 11a) southward, first to the heights of Bashan (v. 2bα) and then to the Jordan Valley (v. 3bβ). This topography resonates immediately with the preceding reference to Gilead and Lebanon as the locale to which Yahweh will return the descendants of the northern tribes (10:10b). Lebanon and Bashan are characterized as regions heavily forested with stands of cedar, cypress, and oak (11:1-2); and the Jordan Valley is likewise characterized as an area of lush growth (11:3b). Such description echoes the previous imagery of flourishing grain and vegetation in the fields (9:17–10:1) — but here the productivity of the land is being devastated rather than restored.

The reference in 11:3bβ to a particular river, i.e., the Jordan, also harks back to the naming of the Nile in 10:11aβ. The devastation of the area along the Jordan is thus associated with the drying up of the Nile, which in turn associates the Jordan with the motif of victorious combat with the sea (10:11aα), won by Yahweh, the God of the rain and the storm (9:14; 10:1). This connection is reinforced by the use of a particular term to connote the Jordan's lush growth *(gĕ'ôn,* v. 3b; *RSV* "jungle"), which is also used with a somewhat different connotation to refer to the "pride" of Assyria in 10:11bα. The "laying waste" *(šdd)* of the Jordan is therefore similar to the defeat of all those powers for which "sea" and "river" are metonyms, which represent the forces of chaos.

The three phases of the crisis in leadership unfold against this backdrop. The general area, into which Yahweh's restoration of Israel will eventually overflow, is being subjected to reversals of two different sorts. Although this area will eventually become part of Israel's homeland, it is now being deprived of precisely those blessings of fertility that were previously associated with their homecoming, and it is now being visited with precisely the same kind of punishing defeat that was previously associated with Yahweh's treatment of their enemies.

The crisis is first portrayed in terms of someone's opening the gates of a mountain fortress, so as to let assaulting enemies enter (11:1). The directive that calls for this entry to happen initially sounds like the order a sentry might give from the wall to get the guards below to open the gates at the approach of some friendly troops — only in this case it turns out that the troops are not friendly. The directive thus invites the attackers' entrance and is in effect a call to surrender. (The ironic force of this advisory is not unlike the ironic force of the calls to worship in Amos 4:4a.) The sentinel turns out to be working for the other side!

Next comes the reaction to the destruction. The cedars, which were the object of the attack described in the first phase (v. 1b), have now fallen (v. 2aβ). Another kind of tree, the cypress, is therefore urged to cry out in lamentation (v. 2aα). The "oaks of Bashan" are also urged to do the same, because the whole forest lies devastated (v. 2b). This call to lamentation has the same ironic tone as the command in the first phase because it is spoken by the same voice. How could the traitorous sentry, who was instrumental in allowing the destruction to happen, be sincere in inviting its survivors to mourn?

Finally, it is reported that some have complied with the call to lamentation that was issued in the second phase. The sound of their wailing has been heard (v. 3). The mourners are first characterized as shepherds lamenting the loss of "their glory" (*'addartām*), i.e., their flock and their pasturage (v. 3a). This metaphor quickly gives way to another, as the mourners are also characterized as lions roaring because the thickets of their habitat have been destroyed (v. 3b). The juxtaposition of the two figures, which are analogous with respect to their outcry over deprivation, invites the identification of the wailing shepherds with the roaring lions. This identification suggests that the shepherds have been more like predators than protectors, and that they are more upset by their own loss of a resource to exploit than by any damage done to the flock's own well-being. The report of the shepherds' mourning in v. 3 thus evokes about as much pity as the news of how traumatically Idi Amin's ouster affected him. This unit is concisely formulated as a highly ironic reversal of the main features of 9:1–10:12. The prophetic voice no longer addresses Zion, the center of Yahweh's plan of restoration, but the area that has been located on the periphery of that plan (10:10b). It does not describe the pacification of outlying areas that have traditionally been outside Israel's territory (9:1-8), but the aggravation of conflict in outlying areas that have often been within Israel's control. It does not call for the addressees to fortify themselves, so that deliverance may result (9:12); it instead calls for them to open their fortress, so that destruction may result. The fate that is envisioned for them is not any different from, but rather identical with, the fate foretold for Tyre: both are to be "devoured by fire" (11:1b; cf. 9:4b). The addressees are not invited to rejoice at the prospect of an ideal leader who brings them peace and plenty (9:9-10), but to lament their exploitation by opportunistic leaders who have brought only conflict and dearth.

The overall effect of such a reversal is twofold. First, it portrays the overthrow of any leadership — even bad leadership — as a crisis with genuinely negative effects on the people as a whole. Petersen emphasizes only this aspect of this unit's message and hence concludes that "the poem seems to encourage acceptance of the status quo" (*Zechariah 9–14*, 84). This reading does not reckon fully with the force of the ironic reversals, which add another aspect. Despite the trauma of being caught up with others in the coming crisis, Yahweh's people are invited to welcome their inclusion in it. Particularly when the effect on Judah is seen in the light of the larger historical context (9:1–10:13), it ironically seems to be a necessary and inevitable part of the restoration process. The loss of leadership is lamentable because it leaves the people vulnerable, but it is nevertheless an integral part of Yahweh's plan for their salvation.

Genre

Commentators have long noted the taunting tone and the mournful elements of this passage, and form critics have attempted to systematize these observations by classifying 11:1-3 as a (→) mock dirge (*Spott[leichen]lied;* Elliger, 154), mock lament (*Spottklage;* Horst, 250-51), ironic (→) taunt (Hanson, *Dawn,* 335), etc. Sæbø has noted (*Sacharja 9–14,* 233) that there is actually no lamentation here, but rather an invitation to lament (*Aufforderung zur Klage*), based on a prophetic adaptation of the formulaic call to communal complaint (*Aufruf zur Volksklage*).

Sæbø's criticism of previous classifications is well taken, but his own proposal accounts only for the form of 11:2, not for the form of the whole unit. There is indeed an element of (→) call to communal complaint in v. 2, but it does not dominate the structure of the text. This element is subsumed within a conventional pattern of speech that derives from the role of the sentinel.

The sentinel's task includes keeping watch as a sentry on a city wall, on a watch tower, or on the outskirts of a military encampment, so as to monitor the approach of all parties (2 Sam 13:34; 18:24b-25a; 2 Kgs 9:17-20). It also involves gathering reports brought by travelers concerning things that have happened farther away (Isa 21:6-7), and even doing some reconnaissance in order to obtain such reports (1 Sam 14:16; Jer 48:19). The sentinel might proclaim various directives, of an ominous or hopeful sort, depending on the nature of the news (Jer 6:17; 31:6; Isa 52:8-9). If there is any word of some serious impending threat, the sentinel might be the one to raise the alarm or call for communal complaint (Ezek 33:2-3; Jer 48:19-20; cf. Joel 2:1-11, 15-17). The sentinel's report is thus usually of an advisory nature, even if it simply relays information without explicitly including any warnings or directives.

This unit combines three sorts of expressions that typically pertain to the role of a sentinel: a sentry command (v. 1), a (→) call to communal complaint (v. 2), and a (→) report of a regional disturbance (v. 3). All three are used ironically, however. The sentry command does not serve to protect the fortification but renders it defenseless. The call to complaint is not made in order to avert impending destruction but in response to destruction that has already happened. Finally, the report of a regional disturbance does not serve to warn its audience about a situation somewhere else, which may come to affect them adversely, but to warn them about the adverse conditions of their own situation. The unit may thus be generically classified as a MOCK SENTINEL REPORT, used for prophetic purposes (→ Nah 3:13-17, Genre).

Setting

The sentinel report itself originated in the context of military operations and civil defense. Prophets borrowed this convention and employed it — though not necessarily in the ironic fashion that is evident here — in the context of prophetic public oratory (→ Nah 2:1-11 [*RSV* 1:15–2:10]; Hab 1:5-11). When used in this derivative way, the sentinel report could serve to interpret situations of social conflict, whether or not they were of a particularly military nature, as situations falling within the prophet's divinely commissioned purview.

Intention

This text aims to make its audience vulnerable to the possibility of losing their present leadership as they undergo a crisis. They are to be open to this prospect, even though it will be traumatic for everyone concerned, because the leaders have served more for their own advantage than for the welfare of all.

TWO SYMBOLIC ACTIONS SHOWING THAT YAHWEH WILL RAISE UP A DERELICT RULER TO BRING THE PRESENT ORDER TO AN END, 11:4-17

Structure

I. Report of a prophetic symbolic action	11:4-14
A. Yahweh's command to perform a symbolic action	11:4-6
1. Introduction: thus said Yahweh my God	11:4a
2. Speech of Yahweh	11:4b-6
a. Command: be shepherd of the flock doomed to be slaughtered	11:4b
b. Explication: prophecy of punishment	11:5-6
1) Accusation	11:5

b) Result of the prophet's action	11:11
(1) The covenant is annulled	11:11a
(2) The exploiters recognize the revelatory significance of the prophet's act	11:11b
2) As it affects Yahweh's people	11:12-14
a) The prophet disposes of his wages	11:12-13
(1) Payment of the wages	11:12
(a) He requests payment	11:12a
(b) He is paid thirty shekels of silver	11:12b
(2) Yahweh's directive concerning the wages	11:13
(a) He commands the prophet to hand them over to the temple	11:13a
(b) The prophet complies	11:13b
b) The prophet destroys his insignia	11:14
(1) His action: I broke my second staff Union	11:14a
(2) His intention: to annul the brotherhood between Judah and Israel	11:14b
II. Report of a speech of Yahweh	11:15-17
A. Introduction: Yahweh said to me . . .	11:15a
B. Speech proper	11:15b-17
1. Command to perform a prophetic symbolic action	11:15b-16
a. Command proper: again take the implements of a worthless shepherd	11:15b
b. Motivation: prophecy of punishment	11:16
1) Announcement of punishment basically stated: I am raising up a shepherd	$11{:}16a\alpha^1$
2) Elaboration on the worthlessness of the shepherd	$11{:}16a\alpha^2 b$
a) Characteristics negatively stated: he does not . . .	$11{:}16a\alpha^2 b\alpha$
(1) Care for the perishing	$11{:}16a\alpha^2$
(2) Seek the wandering	$11{:}16a\beta^1$
(3) Heal the maimed	$11{:}16a\beta^2$
(4) Nourish the healthy	$11{:}16b\alpha$
b) Characteristics positively stated: He does . . .	$11{:}16b\beta$
(1) Devour the fat ones' flesh	$11{:}16b\beta^1$
(2) Tear off their hoofs	$11{:}16b\beta^2$
2. Condemnations	11:17
a. Lamentation	$11{:}17a\alpha$
1) Woe cry	$11{:}17a\alpha^1$
2) Object: twofold epithet	$11{:}17a\alpha^1\text{-}2$
a) My worthless shepherd	$11{:}17a\alpha^1$
b) My flock deserter	$11{:}17a\alpha^2$

b. Curse: affecting arm and right eye   11:17aβb
  1) May the sword smite them   11:17aβ
  2) May they atrophy   11:17b

This autobiographical report has two main episodes. In the first (11:4-14) Yahweh commands the prophet to perform a symbolic action (11:4-6), and the consequences of his complying with that command are then described (11:7-14). In the second episode (11:15-17) there is only another command to perform a symbolic action (11:15), without any indication of whether the prophet complies with the command or what its consequences are. The consequences intended by Yahweh are nevertheless indicated in the rest of Yahweh's speech to the prophet (11:16-17). The implication of this juxtaposition is that the second symbolic action will be performed and will have its intended effect, just like its predecessor. In the first episode the prophet is ordered to "become a shepherd" (11:4). The nature of the leadership role thus described, as far as this particular context is concerned, becomes evident as the narrative unfolds. First, it is a role that the prophet can play while also acting in a specifically prophetic capacity. Moreover, the prophet is instrumental in getting rid of three others, who are also called "shepherds," in just one month (11:8a); and in the face of the ensuing conflict the prophet himself also renounces his position (11:8b). It thus appears that several can play this "shepherd" role at the same time, and also that someone can assume the role for a time and then relinquish it, depending on the dynamics of the political interaction among all those who are in the same position. Finally, the one who serves in this capacity is apparently entitled to remuneration of some sort (11:12).

Since the term "shepherd" is an epithet that is often applied to kings, it is sometimes assumed that this passage is about the assumption of kingship (e.g., Meyer, 228-29). Although the term is particularly appropriate for kings, it can also refer to the entire class of those who govern (e.g., Mic 5:4 [*RSV* 5]; Isa 63:11; Nah 3:18). In view of this rather more general usage, and in view of the particular set of characteristics that are attributed to the "shepherd" role in this particular context, it seems unlikely that kingship as such is at issue here. In view of the parallelism between "shepherd" and "king" in 11:6, however, it also seems likely that these "shepherds" are a group whose responsibility for governance is somewhat analogous to that of a king.

The group in question thus seems to have at least some quasi-official recognition. The power that they exercise is largely socioeconomic power since they are characterized with respect to their actions as the "buyers" *(qōnîm)* and "sellers" *(mōkrîm)* of the flock (11:5a; cf. the expression "traffickers [*kĕnaʿănîyê*] in the flock" in 11:7 and 11:11 [LXX]). They therefore serve a function somewhat similar to the prominent counselors who advised Joshua, the high priest, in the time of the restoration (3:8a), so that he could in turn give "peaceable counsel" (*ʿăṣat šālôm* [*RSV* "peaceful understanding"]; 6:13bβ) to Zerubbabel, the governor (so also Redditt, 685).

This narrative puts the politically charged actions of the prophet in the foreground without providing any direct description of the overall political situation in the background. It is therefore difficult to see how the advisory role assumed by the prophet relates to any of the various structures of leadership that Judah might have had at various times during the postexilic period. In any case the prophet temporarily assumes the position of a minor minister or adviser, for which prominent men with considerable socioeconomic influence are qualified, in some kind of governmental arrangement. At the same time he acts as a prophet, thus playing much the same role that Zechariah and Haggai played in relation to the dual leadership of Zerubbabel and Joshua (Ezra 5:1-2), which also occasionally involved prophetic symbolic action (→ 6:9-15 and Hag 2:10-19).

Yahweh commissions the prophet to assume this role because the very life of the Jewish community is threatened by a crisis, which their leaders are exploiting for their own economic advantage without showing any concern for the people's overall welfare (11:4b-5). The involvement of the prophet in this particular way is part of Yahweh's plan to change this situation, even if it means bringing about the collapse of the world order that engenders and perpetuates such exploitation. Humanity in general will thus be consigned to suffer the same abuse at the hands of their leaders that the Jews have suffered from their leaders, in order to bring this intolerable situation to a head (11:6).

Combining political influence with symbolic action, the prophet is able to make a stab at improving the situation (11:7). He quickly manages to eliminate some of the objectionable leaders (11:8a), but the consequent opposition brings him and the rest to an impasse (11:8b). The prophet then renounces his position, recognizing the inevitability of the present situation's proceeding tragically to its own self-destruction (11:9). By breaking one of his shepherd's staffs, allegorically named "Grace," he interprets his resignation as a sign of Yahweh's rejection of the current world order, which the prophet describes as Yahweh's "covenant *(běrît)* with all the peoples" (11:10; cf. Gen 9:8-17). The legitimacy of this international arrangement is now called into question by the failure of the Jewish leaders to make it work for the welfare of the community as a whole. The prophet believes that these leaders well understand the message from Yahweh, which his symbolic breaking of the staff is meant to convey (Zech 11:11).

The prophet thus tests their willingness to act in accord with their understanding as he poses the issue of whether they think it appropriate to pay him for his brief stint of public service. In paying "a princely sum" (11:13) to one of their own class, while ignoring the oppressive effects of their self-enrichment on "the inhabitants of the land" (11:5), they in effect deny the prophetic indictment. The prophet then complies with Yahweh's instructions to give the money away, and breaks his other shepherd's staff, allegorically named "Union" (11:13-14). He thereby interprets their rejection of his revelation as an act that forecloses the restoration of fraternal coexistence for Judah and Israel, although this restoration was previously prophesied (→ 9:11–10:12, Parts I and II, Structure). Because of their refusal to change their economically exploitative ways, the eclipse of the present order will not allow this historic opportunity to be seized after all.

In the second episode (11:15-17) the prophet is again commanded to perform a symbolic action that is similarly related to the leadership role of a

488

"shepherd." This time, however, he himself is not to assume such a role by again actually "becoming a shepherd" (rĕʿēh, 11:4b). He is rather to take up the unspecified insignia of a "shepherd" (qaḥ lĕkā kĕlî [RSV "take the implements"], 11:15b) — items perhaps not unlike the allegorically named pastoral staffs in the previous episode — in order to portend the fate of someone else. It is this person, rather than the prophet himself, who actually occupies the position of leadership. With such props the prophet is to enact the emergence of a ruler so derelict that the crisis described in 11:4-14 will be brought to the breaking point (11:16). Because the present world order is inherently incapable of providing Judah with some semblance of just local governance, Yahweh is calling forth the kind of local leader who will precipitate the collapse of the overall arrangement, a leader who will suffer the consequences of his own malfeasance in the process (11:17).

Genre

This unit has been called an allegory (e.g., Otzen, 146-51; Caquot, 45-55; Meyer, 25-40), and on this basis some have speculated about the various historical figures that the characters in the story might stand for. The narrative does contain a description of the allegorically named staffs, which are used in order to dramatize the significance of the prophet's rejection by his fellow leaders. It is thus in part a (→) report of allegorically interpreted events, but this element of allegory does not make the narrative itself an allegory on the whole. The same sort of problem arises with respect to the suggestion that this is a parable (e.g., Mitchell, 303). This unit tells how certain events take on a double meaning, but such meaning derives from the prophetic actions that are described in the story, not from the telling of the story itself. The narrative may be said to contain parabolic elements, but the narrative itself is not in the form of a parable.

Hanson describes this unit as a "commissioning narrative" that has been given a typically postexilic "ironic thrust . . . alien to the original genre" (*Dawn*, 341), i.e., the prophet is to become a shepherd only to mock the shepherds. It is not quite clear what Hanson intends by this label or by the assertion that such irony was originally alien to the form. Commissioning is obviously involved, in the sense that the prophet is ordered by Yahweh to undertake a particular course of action, but this kind of order does not in itself necessarily define the generic type. Such orders are evident in prophetic texts of different sorts (→ commission to prophesy). Hanson may intend comparison with (→) prophetic vocation accounts, such as Isa 6:1-13, Jer 1:4-10, and Amos 7:14. Nothing in this unit, however, suggests that its commands encompass the overall calling and career of the prophet, as is typical of the vocation account genre. As for a typically postexilic ironic thrust, it is difficult to see how the irony here differs from the irony in similar commissions given to preexilic prophets. For example, Hosea is commanded to get married only in order to demonstrate that Yahweh and Israel are headed for divorce (Hos 1–3).

The narrative of this unit is entirely concerned with the performance of a prophetic symbolic action. It consists of Yahweh's commands to the prophet to perform such actions (Zech 11:4, 13a, 15); speeches of Yahweh to the prophet, explaining what their performance signifies (11:5-6, 16-17); reports of what the prophet does to comply with Yahweh's commands and of how the witnesses respond (11:7-8, 10-12, 13b-14); and speeches of the prophet to the witnesses, explaining the significance of their response (11:9; cf. 11:11b). The unit as a whole can thus be aptly characterized as a REPORT OF PROPHETIC SYMBOLIC ACTION (Elliger, 160-61; Sæbø, *Sacharja 9–14,* 312; Alonso Schökel and Sicre Diaz, 1191-92; Petersen, *Zechariah 9–14,* 88-90).

This particular example of the genre has a somewhat distinctive feature. As noted above, it consists of two episodes, one in which the prophet's compliance with Yahweh's command is reported (11:4-14), and one in which the command alone is given without any report of the prophet's compliance (11:15-17). Although most reports of prophetic symbolic action include some indication of the prophet's compliance with Yahweh's command to perform the act, there are also examples of the genre that do not explicitly contain this element (cf., e.g., Ezek 4:1–5:17), and in this case a report of symbolic action that does contain a report of compliance is serially linked with one that lacks it (note *'ôd* [*RSV* "once more"], Zech 11:15bα). The report that does describe the prophet's compliance thus becomes a kind of prologue to the report that does not.

The first episode differs pointedly from the second not only in this regard, but also in describing the recognition of the symbolic action's intended significance by those who witness its performance (11:11b). The account in 11:4-14 thus authenticates the prophet's proven ability to mediate true revelations through efficacious signs, showing that this is acknowledged even by those who reject his message, as a prelude to whatever is claimed in this regard by the account in 11:15-17. The report of a prophecy that is beginning to be fulfilled is thus linked with the report of a prophecy that has not yet begun to be. Such sequencing substantiates the likelihood that the historical process, which is seen to be already underway in 11:4-14, will actually culminate in accord with what is described in 11:15-17.

Setting

Prophets could perform a wide variety of symbolic actions in a wide variety of contexts. One might, for example, perform a skit while conducting an oracular inquiry prior to battle, as Zedekiah did using a pair of metal horns as a prop (1 Kgs 22:11); or one might contract marriage and conceive children, making a public spectacle of his domestic life, as Hosea did in order to exemplify the deteriorating relationship between Yahweh and Israel (Hos 1–3); or one might make a toy model of a city under siege, as Ezekiel did in order to demonstrate how a prophecy of punishment would take effect (Ezek 4:1-3).

In this particular case the symbolic action is somewhat similar to Hosea's marriage because it involves the assumption of a real social role. The prophet is to take on the responsibilities of a local civic leadership position. At the same time, the symbolic action here is also comparable to the skit performed by Zedekiah and the toy model built by Ezekiel, for it also involves the enactment of allegorically mimetic gestures with symbolic objects, both before and after the prophet's brief tenure as a public official. These kinds of gestures were usually carried out so as to become matters of public attention. Meyer argues that a text with this particular mixture of action and meaning could not possibly describe a prophetic symbolic action that was really meant to be performed, or ever actually was performed (p. 227). He gives no reasons for such an a priori judgment, however. In view of the fact that a prophet could typically undertake symbolic actions involving either sort of representation, why could a prophet not also undertake a symbolic action combining both sorts? There is no reason to question the text's verisimilitude in this regard. Redditt claims similarly that the action reported here is altogether imaginary, "since the prophet could not actually carry out God's instructions to rule and depose other rulers" (p. 680), but he likewise gives no reasons for such a conclusion. Why would a prophet be precluded from actually assuming the kind of leadership role that "shepherds" play in this particular context? If the other "shepherds" could create political conditions that would lead the prophet to renounce his position, why could the prophet not also have been instrumental in creating political conditions that would lead to the ouster of three persons holding similar positions?

Reports of symbolic actions generally served to convey information about the prophet's deeds and their significance beyond the immediate circle of close associates and direct eyewitnesses. These reports would have been composed and circulated in order to broaden the prophet's audience, and also to preserve records of such events. The records could then be studied and used for divinatory purposes. The prophet who performed a sign may or may not have belonged to the group that made a report and kept a record of it. In this particular case the fact that the report is also an autobiographical memoir suggests that the prophetic actor did belong to this kind of group. Since this prophet is not explicitly identified as Zechariah, it is likely that this is a story about some other prophetic figure from another time, which was incorporated into the traditions concerning Zechariah because this anonymous prophet played the same kind of quasi-official active role in public affairs that Zechariah had played.

Intention

Some have supposed that this unit describes a purely imaginary incident ($\rightarrow$ Genre; also Lacocque, 174). In light of the way in which the first episode historically substantiates the prophetic force of the second, however, it is unlikely that its intention is fictional. Moreover, in comparison with other narratives of the same genre, this one does not appear to be unrealistic. One can always raise the issue of whether things actually happened just as they are reported, but such questions cannot mitigate the probability that this narrative at least

491

purports to describe something that actually happened (Sæbø, *Sacharja 9–14*, 243; Jones, "Fresh Interpretation," 257-59).

The composition is designed so that its audience will accept what is prophesied in Yahweh's final speech to the prophet, namely, that things are bound to get worse before they get any better. Yahweh is raising up the most oppressive leader imaginable, so that the system which fosters such oppressive leadership will be destroyed. The claim that the disintegration of this system is Yahweh's doing is warranted by the outcome of the prophet's previously performed symbolic acts. They have shown that within the present system the local leaders are inevitably more beholden to powerful economic interests than to their own people, and that they are constitutionally incapable of putting the common good ahead of their own self-interest. Yahweh will therefore rid his people of this form of leadership by bringing down the international order, of which it is an integral part. In the process Yahweh will also bring to an end the present sociopolitical form of his people's existence among the nations, which allowed the remnants of the old southern and northern kingdoms to aspire to a common identity. To perceive Yahweh's hand at work in these developments is to regard them as a historical turning point, beyond which there lies an as yet indiscernible future.

Bibliography

S. Amsler, *Les actes des prophètes* (Essais bibliques 9; Geneva: Labor et Fides, 1985); idem, "Les prophètes et la communication par les actes," in *Werden und Wirken des Alten Testaments* (*Fest.* C. Westermann; ed. R. Albertz et al.; Göttingen: Vandenhoeck & Ruprecht: Neukirchen-Vluyn: Neukirchener, 1980) 194-201; A. Caquot, "Brèves remarques sur l'allégorie de pasteurs en Zacharie 11," in *Mélanges bibliques et orientaux en l'honneur de M. Mathias Delcor* (AOAT 215; ed. A. Caquot, S. Légasse, and M. Tardieu; Kevelaer: Butzon & Bercker; Neukirchen-Vluyn: Neukirchener, 1985) 45-55; G. Fohrer, "Die Gattung der Berichte über symbolische Handlungen der Propheten," in *Studien zur alttestamentlichen Prophetie (1949-1965)* (BZAW 99; Berlin: Töpelmann, 1967) 92-112; idem, *Die symbolischen Handlungen der Propheten* (2nd ed.; ATANT 54; Zurich: Zwingli, 1968); L. V. Meyer, "An Allegory concerning the Monarchy: Zech. 11:4-17, 13:7-9," in *Scripture in History and Theology* (*Fest.* J. C. Rylaarsdam; ed. A. L. Merrill and T. W. Overholt; PTMS 17; Pittsburgh: Pickwick, 1977) 225-40; P. Redditt, "The Two Shepherds in Zechariah 11:4-17," *CBQ* 55 (1993) 676-86; D. Stacey, *Prophetic Drama in the Old Testament* (London: Epworth, 1990); A. S. van der Woude, "Die Hirtenallegorie von Sacharja XI," *JNSL* 12 (1984) 139-49.

Chapter 6

THE FIFTH MAJOR SECTION OF THE BOOK (12:1–14:21) AND ITS INDIVIDUAL UNITS

TO PROTECT HIS PEOPLE YAHWEH WILL CREATE A NEW WORLD, 12:1–14:21

Structure

Most scholars agree that 12:1–14:21 is a compositional entity of some kind, and that the three main components of this entity are 12:1–13:6, 13:7-9, and 14:1-21. Beyond this, however, there is little unanimity with respect to either what kind of entity this is, or how these three components are interrelated and subdivided. At one end of the spectrum some see this text as little more than a pastiche of fragmentary phrases, whose juxtaposition is organized but loosely planned (e.g., Childs, 482-85). In line with such a tendency many commentators would, for example, dislocate 13:7-9 from its present context to read it in connection with 11:17, where Yahweh's sword is also being wielded against a "shepherd" (e.g., Chary, 194-96; Rudolph, 212-15; Mason, 110; Hanson, *Dawn,* 338-39; and even *NEB*). At the other end of the spectrum some see 12:1–14:21 as a relatively well-integrated composition (e.g., Lamarche, 72-104; Baldwin, 187-208; Sæbø, 252-309; Alonso Schökel and Sicre Diaz, 1194-1203; Butterworth, 212-37), though perhaps as a result of redactional work on originally disparate prophetic speeches. Even among scholars of the latter tendency there is little unanimity regarding either the nature of this literary integrity or the delineation of the parts out of which the whole is composed.

Some attempts to analyze the structure of this section as a whole have relied primarily on the identification of rhetorical patterns, focusing on such factors as the frequent repetition of the formulaic phrase *bayyôm hahû'* ("on that day") and the alternation between first and third person in the description of Yahweh's actions (e.g., Sæbø, 252-309; Willi-Plein, 56-121; Butterworth, 212-37). Other attempts have relied primarily on the identification of thematic patterns (e.g., Lamarche, 72-104; Hanson, *Dawn*, 369-80). Neither approach, however, has managed to grasp the basic organizing principle of the compositional form. It has generally been overlooked that the main body of this section is basically narration, one sign of which is the periodic reiteration of the formulaic indicator of narrative continuity, *wĕhāyâ* ("and it will happen that . . ."). No catalogue of rhetorical and thematic patterns will therefore suffice, in and of itself, as a description of the structure of this text. The rhetorical and thematic patterns must both be seen in terms of how they function as elements of narration (cf. Petersen, *Zechariah 9–14*, 160-61). The following analysis thus aims to identify the subunits of this section as parts of a story telling what is bound to happen.

This story has a somewhat unusual beginning (12:2) and midpoint (13:7-9). The main body of this section is largely made up of narration but not entirely. The narrative unfolds from an initial announcement of what Yahweh intends to accomplish in the context of the nations' aggression against Jerusalem, the capital city of his people's homeland in Judah (12:2); and it is interrupted at 13:7-9 by a speech of Yahweh that is not formally part of the narrative but that nevertheless provides information that is crucial for its overall progression — a phenomenon that has well-established precedents at 2:10-17 (*RSV* 6-13) and 4:8-10a in the second major section of Zechariah (→ 1:7–6:15, Structure). The initial announcement in 12:2 and the interrupted narration with which it is elaborated in 12:3–14:21 together form the main body of this section, which is entitled by the superscription in 12:1.

The superscription first of all identifies this text as a prophetic revelation from Yahweh that is based on the reinterpretation of earlier prophecies (i.e., a *maśśā'* [*RSV* "oracle"]; → Genre; also → 12:1). The heading then goes on to specify that this revelation is universal in scope. It is concerned with the destiny of Yahweh's people as a whole, i.e., with "Israel" as they have existed in various forms throughout their history, and not just with the form in which they presently exist as "Jerusalem and Judah." Moreover, this revelation's concern with "Israel" is expressed in terms of Yahweh's purpose for all creation. Two particular aspects of Yahweh's role as creator are singled out, corresponding to the respective emphases of the two main parts of the narrative. Yahweh is first characterized as "the one who stretched out the heavens and founded the earth" (cf. Gen 1:1-10); and it is precisely this attribute that comes to the fore in Zech 14:1-21, where Yahweh is described as remodeling the cosmic relationship between heaven and earth. Yahweh is also characterized as "the one who formed the human spirit within them" (cf. Gen 2:4b-7); and it is precisely this attribute that comes to the fore in Zech 12:2–13:6, where Yahweh is described as reforming the "spirit" that animates his people (12:10; 13:2b). The superscription thus programmatically joins the two main segments of the narrative, 12:2–13:6 and 14:1-21, under the rubric of what Yahweh finally intends to do with and for his people, acting in his capacity as creator of the world; and 13:7-9 is the pivotal connection between these two main segments of the narrative.

The initial announcement of Yahweh's purpose is formulated so that the ensuing narrative begins in medias res. Yahweh's purpose is expressed in terms of how he intends to influence the outcome of an attack against Jerusalem by the surrounding peoples, once the attack has been launched. He will send Jerusalem's enemies reeling, as if they have drunk too much from a cup containing a strong and bitter potion (v. 2a), but Judah will inevitably suffer some negative side-effects as the dazed and beaten armies stagger drunkenly away from the city (v. 2b; → 12:2–13:6, Part I, Text). Yahweh's intention for his people is thus not defined in ideal or abstract terms. It is occasioned by the impending reality of a particular situation. As the narrative unfolds, it becomes evident that this situation has come to typify the conditions of the world order under which Yahweh's people must live, and that his response to this situation will therefore typify what he will do about their overall predicament. The world order has come to be characterized by international instability and conflict, which continually puts Yahweh's people at a disadvantage and threatens their existence. Yahweh will therefore transform the world order so as to remove opposition from other nations and secure his people's existence, but in the process they will inevitably suffer the negative side-effects of such a cataclysmic change.

The narrative that proceeds from the initial statement of Yahweh's purpose is introduced by the formulaic phrase *wĕhāyâ bayyôm hahû'* . . . ("and it will happen that on that day . . ."). Following this precedent, the recurrence of this phrase in its entirety indicates the beginning of new episodes at 12:9, 13:2, and 13:4. The recurrence of either *wĕhāyâ* . . . ("and it will happen that . . .") by itself, or *bayyôm hahû'* ("on that day") by itself, is a partial reprise of the phrase marking a new episode, which indicates the beginning of a new phase of narration within an episode (cf. Sæbø, *Sacharja 9–14*, 254-68). The narrative in 12:3–13:6 is divided by these stylistic features into four episodes, and all but the last of these four episodes are further subdivided into various phases. The first episode, 12:3-8, has four phases (vv. 3, 4-5, 6-7, 8); the second, 12:9–13:1, has three phases (12:9-10, 11-14; 13:1); the third, 13:2-3, has two phases (vv. 2, 3); and the fourth, 13:4-6, consists of a single phase, as it is not subdivided in this way. The reiteration of the oracle formula *nĕ'um yhwh* (*RSV* "says Yahweh"), at 12:4aα and 13:2aα, near the beginning of the first episode (12:3-8) and of the third episode (13:2-3), is another stylistic feature that groups the four episodes into two pairs, 12:3-8 + 12:9–13:1 and 13:2-3 + 13:4-6. The first part of the story should thus be read in terms of how these two pairs of episodes correspond (→ 12:2–13:6, Part III, Structure).

Zech 12:3–13:6 is a story of Yahweh's frustrated attempts to counter the international threat to his people's existence, in accord with his stated intention in 12:2, without radically changing the nature of the world order. He first tries to redress the imbalance and alter the dynamics of the situation without altering its underlying structures (12:3–13:1), but this turns out not to resolve one of its most problematic aspects (13:2-6). Yahweh begins by enabling his people to be victorious over all attacking nations and to overcome their divisive tendencies through uniting against their common enemies (12:3-7). As a result they develop a new polity for more effective internal governance, corresponding to their capability for more effective defense against external foes, whose authority is divinely legitimated through victory in much the same way that the authority of the judges once was. According to this polity the city of Jerusalem exercises kinglike rule over Judah, and the descendants of David provide divine guidance as prophetlike intermediaries with direct access to Yahweh (12:8; → 12:2–13:6, Part I, Structure).

In order to keep this leadership structure strong for the purpose of self-defense, but also to keep it from becoming callous and overbearing with regard to both its enemies and its own subjects, Yahweh will inspire the ruling classes with compassion and prayerfulness. Yahweh's action will foster among them a keen and constant awareness of the high human cost of the people's security, an awareness that will spread as it is expressed in rites of mourning throughout the entire population. The ruling classes will thus be motivated to make use of the means provided by Yahweh for purification and forgiveness (12:9–13:1; → 12:2–13:6, Part II, Structure).

The problem with this arrangement is that it leaves the issue of communication with Yahweh in considerable confusion. If members of the Davidic family have direct access to Yahweh, then there is no need for prophets of a more conventional sort. Because the access of conventional prophets is somewhat less direct, they are likely to make conflicting claims that may well misrepresent Yahweh. In comparison with the superior prophetlike authority claimed for the house of David, by virtue of their having become "like God" (12:8b), such prophecy is tantamount to idolatry as a distortion of the divine reality. Despite Yahweh's efforts to remove it, as part of his attempt to purify the land of all foreign and idolatrous influences, conventional prophecy will persist as a dysfunctional phenomenon. Prophets will continue to operate, although they themselves will no longer remain convinced of their own validity; they will thus become a source of social disruption (13:2-6; → 12:2–13:6, Part III, Structure).

The narrative in 12:3–13:6 describes a best-case scenario for the outcome of the conflicted situation in which Yahweh's people live under the conditions of the current world order. It shows that the kind of sociopolitical form that defines their mode of existence, as one nation or people among many others, has become intractably flawed. The problem can be remedied to some extent, but without radical changes in the world order it cannot be resolved. Under present conditions Yahweh's people can be empowered to defend themselves against enemy nations, and in the process they can develop a more humane and harmonious polity for the governance of their own society. But even if they incorporate into this polity the best characteristics of the two sociopolitical forms in which they have mainly existed, the charismatic legitimacy of the tribal league and the stable continuity of the monarchy, and even if their leadership becomes as much "like God" as is humanly possible, the prophetic role of representing Yahweh to his people and to the world will remain inherently incapable of being authentically fulfilled.

Matters will thus inevitably come to the kind of impasse envisioned at the end of (→) 11:4-17, which can only be broken by Yahweh's creating the conditions under which the present world order will self-destruct, so that a new world order can begin to emerge. In 11:15-17 it is imagined that Yahweh will start this process by precipitating a loss of leadership, first raising up a bad "shepherd" and then fomenting his demise. In (→) 13:7-9 a somewhat different situation is described, for the leader is contrastingly characterized as a "shepherd" with whom Yahweh is not loathe to associate (13:7a). The overall situation nevertheless requires the same kind of action on Yahweh's part, and he therefore expresses again his intention to precipitate a loss of leadership (13:7b). Yahweh's ultimate intention is to restore the integrity of the relationship between him and his people (13:9b), but the realization of this intention will entail their coming through a terrible ordeal in which many of them will also be lost (13:8-9a).

The nature of this ordeal and its outcome is more specifically described in the second segment of narrative (14:1-21). Narration is resumed in 14:1a with a statement that resembles in form the initial announcement of Yahweh's purpose in 12:2, and reechoes in content the formulaic phrase *wĕhāyâ bayyôm hahû'*, which begins each new episode in 12:3–13:6. The opening statements in 12:2a and in 14:1a have the same basic syntax: *hinnēh* ("behold" or "lo") plus a noun modified by a participle. In 12:2a this syntactical structure expresses the particular and relatively limited intention with which Yahweh begins his course of action, to improve his people's situation by reforming it within the old world order; but in 14:1a this same syntactical structure signals a return to the theme of the "day" (*yôm;* cf. 12:3, 9; 13:2, 4; etc.) on which he will act to realize his now more profound and far-reaching intention, to improve their situation by transforming it through the creation of a whole new world order.

This process is described as the rest of the story unfolds. Like the narration in 12:3–13:6, the narration in 14:1-21 is divided into several episodes by the periodically recurring formulaic phrase *wĕhāyâ bayyôm hahû';* and these episodes are in turn subdivided into phases by the reiteration of either *wĕhāyâ* by itself or of *bayyôm hahû'* by itself. The first episode, 14:1-5, is not overtly subdivided in this way (v. 4a contains the phrase *bayyôm hahû',* but in the middle of a sentence); the second episode, 14:6-7, has three phases (vv. 6, 7a, 7b); the third episode, 14:8-12, has three phases (vv. 8, 9a, 9b-13); and the fourth and final episode, 14:13-21, has five phases (vv. 13-15, 16, 17-19, 20, 21).

Yahweh creates the conditions under which the old world order will self-destruct by bringing all the nations against Jerusalem and allowing them to take the city (vv. 1-2). He intervenes only in time to rescue the remaining half of the survivors that have not been taken into exile. When he finally does intervene, however, his action is decisive and dramatic. Just as the sea was "split" *(bq')* to provide a way of escape for his people in their exodus from Egypt, the Mount of Olives will be "split" to provide a way through which they can flee from the catastrophe, protected by Yahweh's accompanying hosts (vv. 3-5; cf. Exod 14:21; Neh 9:11; Ps 78:13, etc.; → Zech 14:1-21, Part I, Structure). This exodus, however, ironically leads away from the promised land, and it is not clear whether the people will ever get back.

As it turns out, the separation and dislocation of the Mount of Olives is only the beginning of a radical restructuring of the cosmos (vv. 6-7), through which Yahweh will restore Jerusalem to a more secure place in a better world (vv. 8-12). The most fundamental dichotomy of the old creation, the distinction between heaven and earth, is effaced in the new creation. As this fundamental spatial difference disappears, the fundamental temporal distinctions of the diurnal and seasonal cycles will also disappear (→ 14:1-21, Part I, Structure). Jerusalem will become the center of the new creation, from which the manifestation of Yahweh's control over the watery forces of chaos flows continually and unvaryingly in a life-giving stream. Since there will no longer be any real difference between heaven and earth, there will no longer be any need for national rulers to serve as earthly representatives of Yahweh's heavenly kingship, and he himself can rule directly over all the earth. In this capacity he will create a new Jerusalem, bringing his people back to dwell in the area coextensive with its old walls, but making the city immune to the threat of international conflict (→ 14:1-21, Part II, Structure).

The lingering dynamic of international conflict will then be rooted out of the new creation in the final phase of the nations' war against Jerusalem (vv. 13-15). They will be totally defeated, and their survivors will be incorporated into the community of Yahweh's people by joining in the annual celebration of the Feast of Booths (vv. 16-19). Yahweh's people will then still exist as a community that is set apart by their role as representatives of his holiness, but they will also be a community whose distinctive identity as Yahweh's holy people no longer requires them to draw any invidious distinctions between themselves and the Gentiles (vv. 20-21; → 14:1-21, Part II, Structure).

Genre

As discussed with respect to 9:1–11:17, scholars have recently approached the form-critical analysis of "Deutero-Zechariah" in three different ways, represented by the work of Sæbø, Hanson, and Larkin. The shortcomings of each approach, identified above in connection with 9:1–11:17, are also evident in connection with 12:1–14:21.

Sæbø's analysis (*Sacharja 9–14*, 252-309) again subjects the text to unwarranted atomization, identifying fragmentary subunits from which he reconstructs a highly speculative tradition and redaction history, which yields only meager conclusions regarding the form of the resulting composition (→ 9:1–11:17, Genre).

Hanson's relocation of 13:7-9, so that it follows immediately on 11:17, prevents him from facing squarely the question of the compositional form of 12:1–14:21. He nevertheless deals with this issue more systematically than has previously been the case. Much of Zechariah has been loosely described as apocalyptic, and Hanson has tried to define more precisely the criteria for applying this term to such material, and to identify a literary genre whose formal features also meet these criteria. As a result he concludes not only that this section is apocalyptic material in a general sense, but also that both 12:1–13:6 and 14:1-21 more specifically have the generic form of an apocalypse (*Dawn*, 368-69).

Hanson focuses on the mode of divine action, and he distinguishes apocalyptic from prophecy primarily on this basis. He argues that prophecy tends to describe Yahweh as acting within history through human agents, but that apocalyptic tends to describe Yahweh as acting outside history, or as intervening directly at its end. In the transition from prophecy to apocalyptic there is a resurgence in the use of ancient mythic traditions to portray divine action, particularly with regard to the Israelite version of the ancient Near Eastern combat myth, expressed in a form that Hanson calls the divine warrior hymn. For Hanson the literary form of apocalypse is thus to be defined as an adaptation of the divine warrior hymn, in which its mythic motifs cluster in various patterns to portray Yahweh's eschatological deeds (*Dawn*, 300-315).

There is no question about the prominence of mythic divine warrior motifs in 12:1–14:21, but Hanson's approach is problematic in two major respects. First, there is the question of whether the sequencing of such motifs is actually the main organizing principle of the compositional form in either 12:2–13:6 or 14:1-21, where Hanson has seen such sequencing to be the sole structural device. The detailed analysis of these units, which is presented below, has not found that the compositional form of either unit can be adequately described as an adaptation of the divine warrior hymn (→ 12:2–13:6, Part I, Genre; 14:1-21, Part I, Genre; 9:1–11:17, Genre; Hab 3:1-19, Genre). Second, although such motifs are used in Zech 14:1-21 to describe divine action that clearly becomes eschatological, it is questionable whether this is the case in 12:2–13:6 (→ 12:2–13:6, Part I, Genre).

Neither 12:2–13:6 nor 14:1-21 has the form of an apocalypse as defined by Hanson because neither has a structure that can be described as the adaptation of the divine warrior hymn for purposes of eschatological description. One might conceivably call 14:1-21 apocalyptic material in the more general sense defined by Hanson because of the way it uses mythic motifs to describe divine actions that are truly eschatological in the root sense of the word. Even so, his analysis of various particular actions in terms of various particular motifs does not withstand close examination (→ 14:1-21, Part I, Genre). Hanson has nevertheless put his finger on one aspect of the very complex matter of Zechariah's place in the transition from prophecy to apocalyptic (see North), a matter that deserves further consideration but can only be treated here in a highly schematic fashion.

One should first note that the emergence of apocalyptic cannot be explained in relation to prophecy alone (see J. Z. Smith; cf. Larkin, 27-31). Crucial aspects of its development can nevertheless be described in terms of a transformation undergone by prophecy. If the vision of Yahweh enthroned among the heavenly council is used as a rough index of the transition from

500

prophecy to apocalyptic, the prophetic end of the continuum might be defined with reference to the form in which this vision is found in the commissioning of Isaiah in Isa 6:1-13, and the apocalyptic end with reference to the form in which much the same vision is found in *the* Apocalypse, i.e., the book of Revelation. The transition from prophecy to apocalyptic might then be schematically defined in terms of such contrasts as these: (1) In Isaiah the prophet readily recognizes the significance of what he sees, but in Revelation an angelic interpreter must explain what is seen to the seer. (2) In Isaiah the possibility of salvation is described in terms of a turning point in world history, but in Revelation it is described in terms of the end of world history. (3) In Isaiah the prophet's role requires him to clarify the direct correspondence between heavenly and earthly developments, the existence of which is simply assumed; but in Revelation the seer's role also requires him to establish that there is such a direct correspondence because its existence is no longer simply assumed. (4) In Isaiah the vision report is one among many forms of revelation that together make up the whole book, but in Revelation the vision report has been extended to become the form of virtually the whole book, or of at least whole sections of the book. The emergence of revelatory literature that is apocalyptic in a general sense may be plotted at some point along the continuum defined by these two extremes, whenever texts seen in terms of such contrasts appear to look more like Revelation than like Isaiah. Texts should be more specifically identified as having the generic form of an apocalypse, however, only when their overall compositional form becomes, on the whole or in large part, made up mostly of vision reports or some similar reports of heavenly revelation.

When one sees the emergence of apocalyptic from prophecy in this way, it is difficult to identify any particular combination of traits as marking the transition, and any determination of the stage at which the term "apocalyptic" may appropriately be used is to some extent arbitrary. It is thus more important to be clear about where one is drawing the line than to quibble over the precise point at which it is proper to do so. The emergence of the apocalypse as a distinct literary form, however, is a development that can be specified with somewhat greater precision. Texts can be identified as apocalypses when their overall form assumes the kind of shape outlined in the following definition: "An apocalypse is a genre of revelatory literature with a narrative framework, in which a revelation is mediated by an otherworldly being to a human recipient, disclosing a transcendent reality which is both temporal, insofar as it envisages eschatological salvation, and spatial insofar as it involves another supernatural world" (Collins, "Introduction," 9; cf. idem, *Daniel,* 2-14).

With regard to Zechariah as a whole, two parts of the book contain material that fits somewhere along the continuum described above. In several of the visions in 1:7–6:15 the significance of things seen is explained to the prophet by an angelic interpreter (1), but these vision reports do not resemble Revelation in any of the three other respects (→ 1:7–6:15, Genre). In 14:1-21 salvation is described so as to entail both the end of world history (2), at least in its present form, and a redefinition of the correspondence between heaven and earth (3); but the revelation is not mediated by an angelic being (1), and the literary form is neither all of one piece nor even partly based on a vision report

(4). On the basis of such traits both 14:1-21 and some of the visions in 1:7–6:15 may perhaps be appropriately called apocalyptic in a general sense, depending on where one wishes to draw the line (→ 1:8-17, Genre), but neither 12:2–13:6 nor any part of 9:1–11:17 fits this description. None of Zechariah can be said to have the generic form of an apocalypse, if this form bears any resemblance to what is described in the definition cited above. In any case 12:1–14:21 has an overall form of an altogether different sort that, despite Hanson's considerable efforts, still remains to be satisfactorily identified.

Larkin's approach to the generic classification of Zech 9–14, based on the earlier work of Delcor and Mason, has been supplemented with the similar study by Witt. Delcor, Mason, and others have noted that this section of Zechariah often reechoes earlier prophetic texts, and have therefore suggested that it somehow serves to reinterpret these earlier texts. Larkin and Witt have argued more strongly and systematically, though in somewhat different ways, that such reinterpretation is the primary function of the compositional units in 12:1–14:21, both individually and collectively.

Much like Larkin (→ 9:1–11:17, Genre), Witt has identified one or more prophetic texts as "precursors" for each unit of 12:1–14:21, and has asserted that these units are basically commentaries on the earlier prophetic texts to which they allude (pp. 28-29). He describes the combination of these units to make up the final form of the text as a process of "anthologization," a concept appropriated from the work of Delcor ("Sources," 409-10) and Fishbane (pp. 495, 515, 520-21), which Larkin also utilizes (pp. 36-37). Witt, however, distinctively defines "anthologization" as a process comparable with the way in which the various books of the Bible were gradually acknowledged as canonical (pp. 117-22). Understood thus, anthologization contrasts with the intentional procedure of redaction, as a process based on the rather more intuitive "recognition over time by the community that certain texts and traditions are best understood when collected together in one unit" (p. 117, n. 206).

The work of these scholars has helped to highlight an important characteristic of chs. 9–14: their overall allusiveness in relation to earlier mantic texts (→ 9:1–11:17, Genre). Despite the considerable refinements made by Larkin and Witt, some further distinctions need to be made regarding the nature and extent of the various ways in which the composition of one text may be informed by its association with another text. For example, both Witt (pp. 31-41) and Larkin (p. 156) identify 12:1b-6 as a commentary on Deut 28:28. Witt (pp. 51-58) also identifies Zech 13:2-6 as a commentary on Amos 7:14, and Larkin (pp. 171-72) grants this possibility. In both of these cases there is indeed an intertextual relationship, but each is of a different sort; and in both cases the very fact of an intertextual relationship does not necessarily mean that the later text from Zechariah was necessarily composed as a commentary on the earlier text from another document.

Deut 28:28 is related to Zech 12:4 because they both use the very same collocation of four words. A particular phraseology is used in Deut 28:28 to describe part of the punishment that Yahweh will inflict on his people if they prove unfaithful, and also in Zech 12:4 to describe how he will deal with Jerusalem's attackers. In both cases he will "smite" *(ykh)* them with *šiggāʿôn* ("madness"), *'iwwārôn* ("blindness"), and *timmāhôn* ("confusion, panic"). The similarity is pronounced enough to suppose that 12:4 somehow reechoes Deut 28:28, but is the former therefore some kind of commentary on the latter?

Witt and Larkin claim that Zech 12:4 amounts to a reversal of the covenant curse described in Deut 28:20-28, through which the curse is averted from Israel and instead becomes inflicted on their enemies. In the overall context of Deut 28:15-35, however, one would be hard-pressed to argue that the three maladies named in Deut 28:28 epitomize the curse any more than the approximately twenty-five other maladies that are also listed. In Zech 12:4-5 these three maladies are treated as afflictions directed specifically against troops mounted on horses. Although defeat is mentioned in the context of Deut 28:28, no explicitly martial elements in the surrounding description correspond to the "horses and riders" of the passage from Zechariah. Deut 28:28 and Zech 12:4 do indeed have some striking similarities, but even at first glance they also have some differences which suggest that the latter cannot be characterized as simply a reversal of the former.

This suggestion is further borne out by a more detailed comparison. In both texts the three maladies collectively describe not the covenant curse itself but a disorienting loss of perception. In Deut 28:20-35 this loss of perception is indeed part of what the covenant curse entails, but only part; and in the overall description of the curse it functions specifically to emphasize the effect of the various horrors that Yahweh will force Israel to see. In Zech 12:4-5 this same theme serves a quite different function, as it figures prominently in a contrast between the impaired perceptiveness with which Yahweh will afflict the enemy troops, thus keeping them from recognizing their strategic opportunities, and the insight attained by the Judeans when Yahweh beholds them in a favorable light, thus enabling them to recognize that Yahweh is strengthening the defenders of Jerusalem (→ 12:2–13:6, Part I, Structure). The use of a common terminology indicates that these two texts are both dealing with the same theme, but they use the same theme in two very different ways that can hardly be described as one's reversal of the other. Moreover, the theme they have in common is not the covenant curse but the loss of perception. In one text this loss of perception plays a part in developing the larger theme of the covenant curse, but in the other text there is nothing to indicate that this is similarly the case.

In sum, the distinctive terminology in Deut 28:28 cannot be said to epitomize the covenant curse described in that part of Deuteronomy, with which Yahweh threatens to punish his people for their infidelity; nor can the use of the same terminology in Zech 12:4 be said to indicate a reversal of this theme, so that the enemies of Yahweh's people are threatened with the same punishment instead. It is therefore misleading to describe the latter passage as a commentary on the former. That they use the same collocation of words can be better explained as a case of the former's simply borrowing from the latter some distinctive terminology that is apt for its own descriptive purposes.

The connection between Zech 13:5 and Amos 7:14 affords an example of a different and more significant kind of intertextual relationship. Here there is reason to believe that the former contains a deliberate citation of the latter.

Moreover, in view of the way in which Zech 13:4-5 also plays on other texts (i.e., Gen 4:1-2; 25:25), this citation can be more convincingly described as a reversal of Amos 7:14, and moreover an ironic one, that as such constitutes a basic element in the composition of Zech 13:2-6 (→ 12:2–13:6, Part III, Structure). In this case the intertextual connection is much stronger than the connection between Deut 28:28 and Zech 12:4, for it amounts to more than just borrowed terminology, as the reference to Amos 7:14 is an integral part of the compositional form of Zech 13:2-6. It does not necessarily follow, however, that this reference is therefore the most definitive element in this subunit's compositional form. Even in this case it would be an exaggeration to say that 13:2-6 is designed to be a commentary on Amos 7:14. It would be more accurate to say that 13:2-6 plays on Amos 7:14 to reinforce its own somewhat different main point.

These two examples, taken from the more than twenty allusions identified by Delcor, Mason, Witt, and Larkin, show the importance of the observations made by these scholars and others (see Meyers and Meyers, *Zechariah 9–14,* 35-45) regarding the overall allusiveness of 12:1–14:21, but they also show the rather limited conclusions that one can draw from such observations. It is evident that this section of Zechariah was produced by someone steeped in the study of sacred texts, whose compositions could therefore draw on such texts and be influenced by them in a wide variety of ways. The composition of a new text might be informed by the study of earlier texts in a relatively incidental way, as illustrated by the use in 12:4 of descriptive terminology borrowed from Deut 28:28; or it might be informed by such study in a relatively substantial way, as illustrated by the use in Zech 13:2-6 of ironic antitypes based on Amos 7:14, Gen 4:1-2, and Gen 25:25. Even when the influence is substantial, however, this does not necessarily mean that the new text is wholly given over to the reinterpretation of the earlier text. Inspired by the precedents of earlier texts, the new text may still be devoted primarily to expressing a message of its own. It is therefore somewhat inaccurate to characterize such a text as a commentary on other texts, and to ascribe to it a primarily exegetical function (→ Zech 9:1–11:17, Genre). Since 12:1–14:21 is presented as the final addition to the book of Zechariah, the scholarly work on its intertextuality not only shows how its message generally makes allusions to earlier texts, but also raises the more crucial question of how its message is particularly related to the foregoing sections of the book. It suggests that 12:1–14:21 was produced by someone who studiously read 1:7–8:23 and 9:1–11:17 (→ Setting).

As for the anthological nature of 12:1–14:21, for Larkin this appears to mean only that the whole has some deliberate literary arrangement. It does appear that 12:1–14:21 is deliberately arranged (→ Structure), but it would be inaccurate to describe this phenomenon in terms of an anthology (→ 1:7–6:15, Genre; 9:1–11:17, Genre). Witt's distinctive approach to anthologization also raises another issue that has lately come to the fore, particularly since the work of Childs: the question of whether the composition of a text like 12:1–14:21 can be described in terms of a canonical process. I discuss this issue more extensively in connection with the composition of the (→) book as a whole. Suffice it to point out here that, if the relationship between earlier prophetic texts and 12:1–14:21 cannot be described in terms of the analogy between canonical text and commentary, there is little basis on which to suppose that 12:1–14:21 would have taken shape through a canonization-like process involving the establishment of such a relationship. In any case it is difficult to imagine how the design and production of a text like 12:1–14:21 could have resulted from anything resembling the kind of selection and ordering through which the various books of the Bible were gradually and intuitively recognized as having their special status. Composition and canonization may well have become interrelated at some point, but this interrelationship would not necessarily make them processes of the same sort.

Like the immediately preceding section of Zechariah, 12:1–14:21 is a generically diverse text that is designated by its superscription as a (→) *maśśā'*. Like 9:1–11:17, this section begins with a (→) prophecy of punishment against foreign nations (12:1–13:6; cf. 9:1-8). Beyond this common starting point, however, the two texts differ in several major respects. In this section the initial prophecy against the nations is further developed by the addition of two (→) prophecies of salvation, the first of which (13:7-9) is relatively brief and the second (14:1-21) relatively extended, thus making prominent use of a generic form that is not found in 9:1–11:17. Moreover, the main body of 9:1–11:17 is based primarily on commands, which makes it a basically hortatory or parenetical composition; but the main body of 12:1–14:21 consists basically of narration (→ Structure). With regard to the genre of this section the main question is whether this particular combination of genres is itself generic. A superscription identical to the superscription of 9:1–11:17 raises the additional consideration of whether 12:1–14:21 should also be categorized as a *maśśā'* (→ 9:1–11:17, Genre). If so, further comparison with 9:1–11:17 makes it necessary to explain how such different components may combine so differently to form the same genre.

In line with the conclusions reached above regarding the allusiveness of 12:1–14:21, I discard the idea that this section is a mantological anthology, and turn to consider Weis's proposal that this section is basically the same kind of *maśśā'* as 9:1–11:17 (pp. 191-98). In his view 12:1–14:21 is, like the preceding section, part of a prophetic work that serves to reinterpret prophetic material found elsewhere in that work, distinguished by the following combination of elements: (a) a disclosure of how Yahweh's will is becoming manifest in human affairs, expressed in a form containing oracular speech of Yahweh; (b) directives concerning behavior or attitudes that are appropriate as a response to Yahweh's initiative; and (c) a grounding of these directives in human acts or events that reveal Yahweh's activity or purpose (pp. 252-54, 274-75; → 9:1–11:17, Genre; also → 9:1aα[1] and 12:1). The structural analysis presented above agrees with Weis in seeing the two oracular statements in 12:2 and 14:1-5 as disclosures of how Yahweh's will is becoming manifest in human affairs, and in seeing the narration in 12:3–13:6 and 14:6-21 as elaborations on these two basic statements (a). The analysis here differs from his, however, with respect to what constitutes the directive elements (b) and how they are grounded (c).

Weis identifies the commands in 13:7 as the directives that are characteristic of the *maśśā'* form. This analysis is problematic in view of the way these commands serve as the basis for the following statements disclosing Yahweh's actions in 13:8-9, and in view of the way these brief disclosure statements in 13:8-9 are parallel to the extensive disclosure statements in 12:2–13:6 and 14:1-21, because it makes this section's disclosure statements generally dependent on its commands. As Weis himself notes (p. 167), a *maśśā'* is typically characterized by a relationship between these two elements that is just the opposite, in which the directives are instead dependent on the disclosure statements.

It is also problematic to see the commands in 13:7 as the directives that are characteristic of a *maśśā'* because these commands are not really addressed to the audience of the composition. They rather constitute an apostrophe, in which Yahweh addresses his sword and commands it to take action. Their function is to announce the action of Yahweh, much like the direct statements to this effect in 13:8-9, although their formulation is considerably different (→ 13:7-9, Structure). Such commands thus do not serve the purpose that is typical of the directives in a *maśśā'*, which is to inform the attitude or behavior of the audience so that they will respond appropriately to Yahweh's initiatives.

This problem is resolved when the directives that are definitive for the *maśśā'* are identified not with the commands in 13:7 but with other elements of direct address found elsewhere. The second person forms in 14:1-5 are not commands but rather form part of the narration. They nevertheless serve to describe for the audience a course of action that they are to take, in the event that they should find themselves in the kind of situation described at the beginning of 14:1-21. The appropriate thing to do in response to Yahweh, if one is among the few who were neither killed nor enslaved in the destruction of Jerusalem, is to flee by the way of escape that he will open up (14:5a; → 14:1-21, Part I, Text). In comparison with the commands that are more typical of the *maśśā'*, this sort of directive through narration is relatively oblique, but it nevertheless plays much the same advisory role (→ 14:1-21, Part II, Intention).

In considering the grounding of this directive to flee, one is also led to consider how this section is related to the rest of Zechariah. The directive in 14:5a, to flee the site of the ruined city, is grounded in the hope that the course of events will unfold in the way that the narrative describes, so that Yahweh will establish a new Jerusalem as he also creates a whole new world. It is prudent to risk the dangers of abandoning the site because there is both a promise of divine protection (14:5b) and a prospect of eventual return and restoration (14:10-11). The probability of such promises and prospects is in turn grounded in the overall relationship between 12:1–14:21 and the preceding parts of Zechariah, as this section recapitulates and extends the prophetic insights expressed in previous sections. This observation brings up the question of how 12:1–14:21 fulfills its characteristic function as a *maśśā'* forming part of a prophetic book, which is to reinterpret prophetic material found elsewhere in that book.

The thematic connections linking chs. 9–11 and chs. 12–14 with each other, and with chs. 1–8, are multifaceted (Mason, "Relation"), but the main links can be outlined as follows. The first unit of narrative, 12:2–13:6, recounts the fulfillment of 9:1–11:17. It describes a particular event as the beginning of a process in which the kind of deliverance described in 9:1–10:12 is coming to pass, but in which the kind of impasse described in 11:1-17 will also be reached. As Jerusalem is attacked by foreign enemies, Yahweh will enable Judah to defend the city; and in the crucible of this conflict he will also effect a transformation in his people's polity, to purge their irresponsible and incompetent leaders, and to provide them with a more faithful and effective form of leadership (12:2–13:1; cf. 9:1–11:3). Because old patterns of civil and religious leadership are reinforced by the ways of the present world order, however, they will persist so as to keep Yahweh's efforts at reform from full realization (11:1-17; cf. 13:2-6).

The oracle in 13:7-9 marks the actualization of the kind of crisis that is prospectively envisioned at the end of 9:1–11:17. In 11:4-17 Yahweh commissions the prophet to dramatize his intention first to raise up and then to depose a tyrannical leader (11:15-17), in order to precipitate the collapse of the world order that engenders such leadership, because previous leaders did not respond favorably to the reforms initiated through his prophet (11:4-14). At the conclusion of 9:1–11:17 this crisis is described as more or less inevitable, but its full realization remains eventual. In 13:7-9, however, Yahweh signals that now is the time for this critical loss of leadership to take place.

Zech 12:1–13:9 thus recapitulates 9:1–11:17, arriving in 13:7-9 at much the same ominous point on which 9:1–11:17 concludes in 11:15-17. 14:1-21 carries the story forward, recounting what 9:1–11:7 seems finally to call for but does not actually describe: the emergence of a whole new world order in which international conflict is no longer the dominant force, so that Yahweh's people are no longer dominated by others, and their own leaders are no longer given any opportunity to misrule them. In order for this new world to emerge, however, all must suffer the cataclysmic demise of the old world. The progression of the narrative in 14:1-21 thus reverses the progression of the narrative in 12:2–13:6. The latter begins with Jerusalem's being successfully defended by Yahweh against enemy attack and ends without the full realization of his efforts to transform his people's existence under the limitations of the old world order. In contrast the former begins with Yahweh's allowing Jerusalem to be destroyed and ends with his successful efforts to transform his people's existence through the creation of a new world order.

The plausibility of this reversal depends on its being at least partly comparable to something that Yahweh has achieved before. The story in 14:1-21, telling how Yahweh will allow Jerusalem to be destroyed so that it can be purified and restored, thus takes as its precedent the concept of exile and restoration described in chs. 1–8. Yahweh has previously demonstrated his capacity to do such a thing while effecting a transition from one dispensation to another under the conditions of the old world order. He can therefore be trusted to carry out his stated intention to do something similar to secure his people's welfare as he brings into being a whole new world order. Jerusalem's destruction and the immense attendant suffering mark the start of the creative process through which Yahweh is making all things new. It is thus appropriate for those left by Jerusalem's destroyers to flee in hope (14:5a).

Despite being made up mostly of units that are generically quite different from those in 9:1–11:17, 12:1–14:21 also shows the rhetorical profile of a MAŚŚĀ'. As such, 12:1–14:21 is a reinterpretation of 9:1–11:17 and 1:7–8:23. 12:1–14:21 is not a commentary on these earlier texts but a prophecy in its own right. It is a reinterpretation in the sense that it describes Yahweh's involvement in the events of its own time in terms of typological correspondences with his involvement in the events of earlier times, in accord with the patterns of divine action described in 1:7–8:23 and 9:1–11:17. These typological correspondences do not emerge coincidentally from the juxtaposition of 12:1–14:21 with the other sections of Zechariah but are embodied in both the composition of the individual units and the way they are combined to form a *maśśā'* (see further the discussion of typology in Fishbane, 350-79).

This section may also be a reinterpretation of earlier revelation in the sense that it contains prophecies that existed in some other form prior to their incorporation into the present text. This possibility is suggested by the fact that the individual units retain recognizable generic structures of their own in addition to the *maśśā'* form that they assume in combination. 14:1-5 is a subunit that might make some sense as an independent prophetic speech outside its present literary context, and it also shows the rhetorical conventions of direct address that are characteristic of live prophetic speech (→ 14:1-21, Part II, Setting). Many commentators have suggested that 11:17 and 13:7-9 might have originally formed a single prophecy describing the violent overthrow of a "shepherd" by means of Yahweh's "sword," whose parts have been assigned their present respective positions in 9:1–11:17 and 12:1–14:21 in order to link these two sections of the book. If 12:1–14:21 is indeed a redactional composite, formed by the combination and augmentation of previously existing prophetic materials, the redaction itself would constitute a reinterpretation of these earlier prophecies. In view of how little can be said about the original historical settings of the individual units, however, it is difficult to say much about the nature of this reinterpretive process.

As a *maśśā'* 12:1–14:21 combines generically diverse prophecies, perhaps based on earlier oracles that were traditionally associated with Zechariah, so as to describe the same patterns of divine action evident in both the record of the prophet's own words (1:7–8:23) and an earlier reinterpretation of that record (9:1–11:17).

Setting

This kind of text was composed in scribal groups that produced such documents through their study of prophetic traditions. By studying the records of what earlier prophets had said about Yahweh's involvement in past events, members of these groups could reach some conclusion regarding Yahweh's involvement in contemporary events, a conclusion that they expressed in the form of a *maśśā'*. Because such texts are conceived in terms of an analogy between their own time and earlier times, based on their authors' apprehension of the same pattern of divine activity in both past and present events, their settings should be specifically described in historical terms if possible, as well as generally described in sociological terms (→ 9:1–11:17, Setting).

The foregoing literary analysis determines to a considerable extent how the historical questions are to be framed. In view of the fact that 12:1–14:21 coheres in a recognizable generic form, the question of date is first raised with respect to this section as a whole. It may also be raised secondarily with respect to the (→) individual units, to whatever extent they themselves afford any basis for an answer. In view of the disparate and hence meager results that past efforts to date the individual units have yielded (Otzen, 26-34, 184-212 passim), however, it would seem more promising to focus instead on the more crucial issue of a date for the composition as a whole.

Because of the way in which 12:1–14:21 is related to 1:7–8:23 and 9:1–11:17, as both a reinterpretation of insights attributed expressly to Zechariah (1:7–8:23) and an extension of a previous reinterpretation of the same sort (9:1–11:17), it probably follows them chronologically, just as it follows them in the present literary sequence. If 9:1–11:17 was composed in the early Hellenistic period, sometime during the final decades of the fourth century (→ 9:1–11:17, Setting), this date would therefore constitute the terminus a quo for the composition of 12:1–14:21. Recent opinion has tended to favor a fifth- or early-fourth-century date, while Judah was still under Persian rule (e.g., Hanson, *Dawn*, 353-54, 400; Lacocque, 139-44; Meyers and Meyers, *Zechariah 9–14*, 26-29; Petersen, *Zechariah 9–14*, 4-5 and passim); but an early Hellenistic date is more probable, not only because of the way 12:1–14:21 is related to other sections of the book in its present literary context but also because this text reflects the kind of events that most likely took place at this time.

Many have said that the events described in this section are eschatological, and some have therefore sought to describe its historical setting by supposing that the use of such eschatological language definitively identified certain partisan groups (e.g., Plöger, 78-96; Hanson, *Dawn*, 280-86). This approach is problematic because its assumption that eschatological language can be exclusively or even primarily identified with one kind of partisan group or another is doubtful. Even if one granted this assumption, however, its applicability in this particular case would be questionable because the description in this section is not entirely eschatological. 14:1-21 recounts events that cross the present bounds of space and time, but 12:2–13:6 portrays events so as to remain within these bounds (→ 12:2–13:6, Part I, Genre; also 12:2–13:6, Part III, Setting). Although the narration in 12:1–14:21 moves beyond history, it begins within history. An investigation of its historical setting can therefore begin by asking what kind of historical developments this text wishes to transcend.

The first episode of the narrative (12:2-8) reflects certain changes in the internal administration of Judah and its capital city, Jerusalem, or it at least envisions the possibility of such changes. A notable feature of this new polity is the prominent role assigned to the descendants of David, a role that is theologically quite significant. These innovations have occasioned a good deal of speculation in attempts to identify them with particular historical developments that can be reconstructed from other biblical texts and extrabiblical sources (e.g., Plöger, 93-96; Hanson, *Dawn*, 399-400; Meyers and Meyers, *Zechariah 9–14*, 354-59; Petersen, *Zechariah 9–14*, 117-18). In view of how generally these changes are described here, and in view of what sketchy information the other sources provide, however, this approach very quickly reaches a point of diverging and hence diminishing returns. If more were known about the structures of local administration in postexilic times, it might be possible to put the changes described in 12:2-8 into some kind of developmental perspective. As it is, however, the description of external events provides better clues for the determination of this text's historical setting.

This section takes as its point of departure an attack on Jerusalem by foreign enemies, and it proceeds to consider this eventuality from two different perspectives. The first narrative segment (12:2–13:6) analyzes the implications of Yahweh's enabling the city to fend off such attacks by rallying Judah to its defense, showing that even if the sociopolitical structure of Yahweh's people is decisively transformed in the process, they could not satisfactorily adapt to a world in which such conflict is the norm. With Yahweh's grace they may develop a new form of leadership and governance, one that will foster in them a capacity to cope sensitively and prayerfully with the high human cost of being continually embattled, but they will be torn by dissent over how Yahweh himself is to be prophetically represented. By contrast, the second narrative segment (14:1–21) analyzes the implications of Jerusalem's not being able to withstand an attack by foreigners, showing that even such a tragic eventuality could signal the start of a more far-reaching transformation, radically changing both the order of creation and the sociopolitical form of Yahweh's people. By this means Yahweh would remove both the external and the internal impediments to their serving him faithfully in peace and security.

Neither segment of narrative is a direct description of any particular foreign assault on Jerusalem, but together they reflect Judah's entering a phase of its history that was generally characterized by such attacks. This text reflects on the historical experience of Jerusalem's having withstood foreign enemies, admitting that the internal changes initiated in the process were a rather mixed blessing, and looking forward to the likelihood that they could not continue to defend themselves. As a *maśśā'* this section focuses on the question of how the survivors should react in the event that Jerusalem is finally destroyed by foreign foes (→ Genre). 12:1–14:21 thus presupposes a historical situation that bears little resemblance to the Persian period, when Jerusalem is not known to have been directly threatened by enemy attacks. (The account in Neh 4:1-17 [*RSV* 7-23] describes hostility against Judah from all sides but also pointedly emphasizes that this did *not* result in their enemies actually making any move against Jerusalem.) Its context is closer to, but still different from, the very beginning of the Hellenistic period, when Jerusalem was still not directly threatened by the increasing conflict in the surrounding area (→ 9:1–11:17, Setting). 12:1–14:21 reflects conditions that emerged soon afterward, as the empire of Alexander the Great — which remained intact for only a short while following his death — began to break up. Ptolemy I then made a series of forays from Egypt into Judah, which culminated in his finally taking Jerusalem sometime toward the end of the fourth century (V. Tcherikover, *Hellenistic Civilization and the Jews* [tr. S. Applebaum; Philadelphia: Jewish Publication Society; Jerusalem: Magnes, 1959] 55-58). This section of Zechariah was composed by someone for whom such developments were already a real and imminent prospect.

I thus propose that the *maśśā'* in 12:1–14:21 was produced toward the end of the fourth century by mantic scribes who studied the records of Zechariah's prophecies now preserved in 1:7–6:15 and 7:1–8:23, as well as the prophecy reinterpreting this record now appended to it as 9:1–11:17. By this means they gained some understanding of Yahweh's involvement in the events of their own time and attempted to communicate this insight to their contemporaries.

Intention

The intention of this section has sometimes been described in terms of some postexilic partisan viewpoint, but I have already indicated the problems with such an approach (→ Genre). Because 12:1–14:21 describes the demise of leadership associated with political innovations in Judah, in the context of a defeat that is part of Yahweh's plan, it could well have been used for purposes of partisan polemic. It is not actually in the form of a polemic, however, and its overall perspective is broader than any one partisan viewpoint. It would therefore be reductionistic to read the text only in this way (→ 9:1–11:17, Intention).

This section presents a prophetic view of Judah's situation toward the end of the fourth century when Judah became caught up in the chaos of Alexander's disintegrating empire. Based on Judah's past historical experience, as perceived through the lens of Zechariah's prophecies, the coming of the Greeks had first seemed largely like another restoration (→ 9:1–11:17); but in view of subsequent developments seen through the same lens, it began to seem more like another exile. They again found themselves trapped in a form of historical existence that could be transformed only through its destruction. They knew from past experience that such transformations were possible, but this time it seemed that none of the forms in which they had existed before could provide them with a model adequate to the reality of the world situation. In continuity with their past experience they nevertheless reaffirmed the possibility of a new future, even if this meant that Yahweh would redefine the conditions of reality in the process.

This text advises its audience not to despair the prospective loss of the form in which they have existed as Yahweh's people for some two hundred years now, as a minority group of the Persian empire with a tenuous geopolitical base around the restored royal temple in their old capital city. This loss would indeed be a disastrous crisis, but there is ultimately no need for them to fear it or succumb to it. Yahweh's purpose in such an event can be seen in accord with the pattern of his involvement in the exile and restoration, as previously discerned by Zechariah, even though the present crisis threatens their existence much more radically than the Babylonian exile. Now they are threatened with losing all vestiges of their status as a people, as such status has been defined by the ways of the world since time began. According to the pattern, however, their existence will nevertheless be restored in some new form. Yahweh will even re-create the world in order to make such a restoration possible.

Because the Passion narratives of the New Testament's four Gospels are laced with allusions to Zechariah in general, and with allusions to these last chapters of the book in particular (F. F. Bruce, "The Book of Zechariah and the Passion Narrative," *BJRL* 43 [1961] 336-53), this section is sometimes rather loosely described as consisting of messianic prophecies, so as to imply that messianic expectation is its main thrust. Several qualifications are in order, however, if such terminology is not to obscure either the significance of these texts in their own right or the way in which they provided one of the important bases for the early church's christology. First and foremost, the term *māšîaḥ* ("anointed one" or "messiah") does not appear, nor is the concept as such operative, anywhere in the book of Zechariah. Because the term "messianic prophecy" tends to suggest otherwise, it can be fundamentally misleading, even when used as a general or provisional indication of what this part of the book is all about.

Second, although the book of Zechariah is on the whole concerned with the question of how Judah's postexilic polity can continue to serve as the sign of Yahweh's divine kingship, just as the Davidic monarchy did in preexilic times, it attributes this symbolic capacity to the continuity of the restored temple with its royal predecessor, not to any continuity in Davidic rule as such. In chs. 1–8 the divine legitimation of local leadership is thus contingent on how the governorship and high priesthood function in relation to the restored temple complex (→ 1:7–6:15, Structure); and in chs. 9–14 Yahweh's sanctuary in Jerusalem remains the crucial means of signifying his divine kingship, as the pattern and personnel of both imperial hegemony and local leadership undergo change (9:8; 14:9-11). In Zechariah the primary manifestation of God's kingship is not the appearance of some local leader, Davidic or otherwise, but rather the persistence of Jerusalem as Yahweh's royal sanctuary as the world situation undergoes even the most radical transformations.

Third, the verses from Zechariah that the Gospels construe in reference to various incidents in Jesus' last days do not in their primary frame of reference pertain either to one and the same person or to one and the same course of events. For example, in 12:10b the phrase *'ăšer dāqārû* ("whomever they have wounded"; → 12:1–13:6, Part II, Text), which John 19:37 cites in connection with Jesus' crucifixion, describes a personification of the casualties inflicted as Jerusalem is besieged. Similarly, the striking of the shepherd and the scattering of the sheep in Zech 13:7b, which are taken in Matt 26:31 and Mark 14:27 to portend the demoralizing effect of Jesus' death on his disciples, describe the drastic actions that Yahweh will take against his own people, in order to catalyze the transformation of a threatening world situation (→ Structure above; also 13:7-9 below). When these verses are read in context, however, the one who is wounded is not the same figure as the shepherd who is struck, and the suffering of the former is not directly identified with the suffering of the latter.

Once these qualifications are noted, one can ask whether there is any basis in the text itself for the kind of christological reading that is given in the Gospels. The main impetus for such a reading comes from the way in which chs. 1–8 are related to chs. 9–14. Because the book sees typological connections between events of the Persian restoration and events of the early Hellenistic period when both are viewed through the lens of Zechariah's prophetic insights, readers are invited to draw similar typological connections between past events described in the book and events of their own day by similarly viewing both through this same lens. The typological dimension of the relationship between the text and its readers creates a secondary frame of reference that is grounded in the text itself, but one that readers also play an active role in constructing. On this basis the early Christian community could read Zechariah in terms of the momentous events that were happening to them.

A typological connection between one set of events and another depends on the perception that the pattern of divine action within these two sets of events is fundamentally the same, although any two sets of events will also obviously differ in many respects. In drawing a typological connection this fundamental similarity may be underscored in a manner that generalizes such differences away or loses sight of them altogether. For example, in chs. 1–8 the roles of Zerubbabel and Joshua are clearly distinguished, and their interrelationship is carefully defined, in order to present a viable model of local leadership for the early Persian period. As chs. 9–14 develop their extended typological analogy between events of the early Persian and early Hellenistic periods, however, this distinction is no longer maintained. This aspect of the analogy is drawn in terms of a more general category, in which those serving various sorts of local leadership functions are all lumped together under the rubric of "shepherds."

When the Gospels draw a typological analogy between events described in Zechariah and Jesus' death and resurrection, the perception that both share the same pattern of divine action leads to a similar phenomenon. As Zechariah is applied to a new historical situation, various roles that are clearly distinguished in the text are coalesced to form a composite in terms of which Jesus' role can be understood. The Evangelists see Jesus' Passion in terms of this scenario derived from Zechariah: The persistent problem of bad local leadership shows the whole world order, of which such leadership is an integral part, to be inherently and intractably flawed. This chronic instability has reached a critical point at which the identity and historical existence of Yahweh's people is threatened. Yahweh therefore sends a good leader to suffer at the hands of the bad leaders the fate that they themselves deserve, in order to bring down this system of local government and precipitate a radical transformation in the world order.

By virtue of this fundamental typological similarity, based primarily on an analogy between the roles of Jesus and the "shepherd" of Yahweh described in 13:7, Jesus also comes to assume other roles that are distinguished from one another in the text itself, but are nevertheless generalized in applying them to him: one who is pierced (12:10b); one who, as a descendant of David, is "like

God" (12:8); and the king sent by God, who has come to bring in an era of world peace (9:9-10). The figure of the Davidic heir divinely born to rule thus begins to be identified with the figure of the good shepherd who suffers for the redemption of God's people and the whole world — a process of identification that eventually leads the early church to bestow on Jesus the royal Davidic title of *māšîaḥ* precisely because of his suffering.

This section of Zechariah is "messianic" only in the very limited sense that it invites, but does not necessarily require, this kind of typological reading.

Bibliography

J. J. Collins, *Daniel; with an Introduction to Apocalyptic Literature* (FOTL 20; Grand Rapids: Eerdmans, 1984); idem, "Introduction," in *Apocalypse: The Morphology of a Genre* (*Semeia* 14; Missoula, Mont.: Scholars Press, 1979) 1-20; M. Fishbane, *Biblical Interpretation in Ancient Israel* (Oxford: Clarendon, 1985); O. Plöger, *Theocracy and Eschatology* (1959; tr. S. Rudman; Oxford: Basil Blackwell, 1968) 78-96; J. Z. Smith, "Wisdom and Apocalyptic," in *Religious Syncretism in Antiquity* (ed. B. Pearson; Missoula, Mont.: Scholars Press, 1975) 131-56; R. Tournay, "Zacharie XII–XIV et l'histoire d'Israël," *RB* 81 (1974) 355-74; D. A. Witt, "Zechariah 12–14: Its Origins, Growth and Theological Significance" (Diss., Vanderbilt University, 1991).

THE SUPERSCRIPTION, 12:1

Text

→ 9:1aα^1, Text.

Structure

I. Heading: a *maśśā'*	12:1aα^1
II. Elaboration: parallel terms in apposition	12:1aα^{2}b
A. The word of Yahweh concerning Israel	12:1aα^{2}β
B. Expanded oracle formula	12:1b
1. Oracle formula proper	12:1bα^1
2. Expansion: two participial clauses modifying Yahweh	12:1bα^{2}β
a. First clause: who stretches out the heavens and founds the earth	12:1bα^2
b. Second clause: who forms the spirit of humanity within them	12:1bβ

Some have supposed that *dĕbar-yhwh* ("the word of Yahweh") stands in a construct relationship with the initial term, *maśśā'* (*RSV* "oracle"), so that the superscription would open with the heading: "the *maśśā'* of Yahweh's word" (e.g., Lamarche, 73; Rudolph, 216). This reading is unlikely in view of two considerations. First, in other contexts where the term *maśśā'* stands in construct relation with other substantives, these are almost invariably indications of its content rather than additional technical terms for prophetic revelation, such as *dĕbar-yhwh* (e.g., Isa 13:1; 15:1; 17:1; 19:1; 21:1; 23:1; 30:6; Nah 1:1). There are only two other places where *maśśā'* might conceivably be in a construct relationship with *dĕbar-yhwh*, Zech 9:1 and Mal 1:1; but in both cases it is more likely that the latter is in apposition to the former (→ Zech 9:1aα¹, Structure; Mal 1:1, Structure). Second, the possibility of parallelism between *dĕbar-yhwh* and the following phrase *nĕ'um-yhwh* (lit. "oracle of Yahweh"; *RSV* "thus says Yahweh") is more definitely pronounced than the possibility of a construct relationship between *maśśā'* and *dĕbar-yhwh* because it is stylistically reinforced by the parallelism between the two participial clauses modifying *nĕ'um-yhwh*. It is thus more probable that *maśśā'* stands alone without any modifiers, and that both *dĕbar-yhwh* and *nĕ'um-yhwh* are in apposition to it.

By using here the same heading that is used in 9:1, the author establishes a link between 9:1–11:17 and 12:1–14:21. This link is reinforced by placing *dĕbar-yhwh* in apposition to *maśśā'* and further expanded by modifying *dĕbar-yhwh* with the prepositional phrase *'al-yiśrā'ēl* ("concerning Israel"). This section of the book resembles not only 9:1–11:17 in being a *maśśā'* that is generally concerned with the efficacious "word of Yahweh" (9:1). It also resembles the foregoing section in being specifically concerned with "Israel" in the larger sense, including the descendants of those who survived the destruction of the northern kingdom, also called "Israel" in a more particular sense, as well as the successors to the southern kingdom of Judah (note the references to "Ephraim" in 9:10, 9:13, and 10:7, "the house of Joseph" in 10:6, and "Israel" in its more particular sense in 11:14). This link with the foregoing material makes 12:1–14:21 a sequel to 9:1–11:17, so that its description of Yahweh's transformation of "Jerusalem and Judah" becomes the culmination of the history of Yahweh's people as a whole.

Just as the first phrase in apposition to *maśśā'* (v. 1aα²β) reaches backward retrospectively to establish continuity with 9:1–11:17, the second phrase in apposition to *maśśā'* (v. 1b) reaches forward prospectively to foreshadow Yahweh's characteristic modes of action in 12:2–14:21. The oracle formula *nĕ'um-yhwh* is reiterated at several points as 12:2–14:21 unfolds (12:4aα; 13:2aα, 7aβ, 8aα). Yahweh's identification as "the one who stretches out the heavens and founds the earth" (v. 1bα²) looks forward to his redefinition of the structure of the cosmos, which is described in 14:1-21; and his identification as "the one who forms the spirit of humanity (*RSV* 'man') within them" (v. 1bβ) similarly looks forward to his reformation of the "spirit" (12:10a and 13:2b) that animates and motivates his people, and is described in 12:2–13:6. The two kinds of creativity that are attributed to Yahweh in the last part of the superscription (v. 1b) are thus chiastically linked with the two main parts of the ensuing narration, each of which describes his acting in one of these two capacities:

515

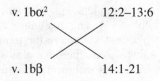

v. 1bα²   12:2–13:6

v. 1bβ   14:1-21

Genre

This is a PROPHETIC SUPERSCRIPTION that serves to indicate the way in which the following prophetic material in the main body of this section (12:2–14:21) is related to both the preceding prophecies of Zechariah (1:7–8:23) and the preceding reinterpretation of Zechariah's prophecies (9:1–11:17). As a (→) *maśśā'* 12:2–14:21 is a reinterpretation of these earlier revelations in view of changed conditions (Weis, 275-76).

Setting

Such superscriptions were the creation of scribal groups that were concerned with the preservation and divinatory study of the records of prophetic revelation.

Intention

This superscription shows that the following prophecy is meant to extend and reapply the earlier prophetic insights of Zechariah and of his previous reinterpreters, in order to perceive what Yahweh is presently doing and how the people should respond.

Bibliography

G. Tucker, "Prophetic Superscriptions and the Growth of a Canon," in *Canon and Authority: Essays in Old Testament Religion and Theology* (ed. G. W. Coats and B. O. Long; Philadelphia: Fortress, 1977) 56-70.

NEW LEADERSHIP MAKES DEFENSE MORE EFFECTIVE AND PROPHECY MORE UNCERTAIN, 12:2–13:6: PART I, 12:2-8

Since 12:2–13:6 is a relatively long and complex unit, the discussion here will focus only on 12:2-8. 12:9–13:1 and 13:2-6 will be discussed separately below. This separation is only for the sake of convenience and should not obscure the fact that these three pericopes constitute a larger entity.

Text

The syntax of v. 2b has seemed troublesome to some commentators, and various textual alterations have been proposed to make it less so, resulting in a difference of opinion with regard to whether Judah is here characterized as joining Jerusalem's enemies in the attack (Otzen, 261-62; Sæbø 89-92; cf. the opinions surveyed and the alternative proposed by Petersen, *Zechariah 9–14*, 107-8, 111-12). The Targums and Vulgate provide some versional support for this possibility, but their readings may well have arisen from an attempt to harmonize v. 2b with 14:14a, where Judah is indeed said to fight against Jerusalem. It is difficult to understand 12:2b in this way because in the immediate context Judah is explicitly described as fighting Jerusalem's attackers (v. 6b), and there is no reason to suppose that this results from any switch in Judah's role.

Moreover, there is not as much of a syntactical problem as some have supposed. In view of how the preposition *'al* is elsewhere used to denote the relationship between a cup and the one to whom it is passed, both literally (Gen 40:21) and figuratively (Lam 4:21), it is not difficult to assume — as grammatical conventions would normally dictate — that the noun *sap* from the clause in v. 2a is the antecedent for the pronominal subject of the clause in v. 2b. The latter clause would thus indicate, as the *RSV* translation suggests, that the "cup of reeling" will also be passed to Judah in the course of the attack on Jerusalem, i.e., in terms of this imagery some of the cup's contents will inevitably spill out onto Judah as well. In other words, as Yahweh repels the nations' attack against Jerusalem, some of the force directed against the attackers will negatively affect Judah, as the territory from which the attack is launched.

Structure

I. Basic statement of Yahweh's purpose	12:2
A. Introductory interjection: *hinnēh* (*RSV* "behold")	12:2aα^1
B. Basic statement proper	12:2aα^2b
1. Yahweh's punishment of the nations:	
I am making Jerusalem a cup of reeling	12:2a$\alpha^2\beta$
2. Negative side-effect on Judah: this will happen	
as they attack Jerusalem	12:2b
II. Elaboration	12:3–13:6
A. The attack of the nations will in the long run prove	
beneficial for Judah and Jerusalem	12:3–13:1
1. Yahweh will enable Jerusalem to defend	
itself victoriously	12:3-8
a. Introduction: and it will happen that . . .	
(*wĕhāyâ*)	12:3aα^1
b. Narration of what will happen	12:3aα^2-8
1) Yahweh will punish the nations	12:3aα^2b
a) Formulaic introduction: on that day	12:3aα^2

b) Description of Yahweh's action
metaphorically in terms of his making
Jerusalem a heavy stone: the nations
will hurt themselves in trying to lift it   12:3aβb
2) Yahweh's attack on the nations will
conversely strengthen his people   12:4-5
  a) Formulaic introduction: on that day   12:4aα^1
  b) Oracle formula: says Yahweh   12:4aα^2
  c) Description of Yahweh's action   12:4aβ-5
    (1) Action initiated: I will strike every
horse with panic, and its rider
with madness   12:4aβ
    (2) Action developed: described
metaphorically in terms of eyesight   12:4b
      (a) With respect to the house of Judah:
I will open my eyes upon [them]   12:4bα
      (b) With respect to enemy forces:
I will strike every horse . . .
with blindness   12:4bβ
    (3) Action concluded: Judah will
recognize that Yahweh is
strengthening the besieged
defenders of Jerusalem   12:5
3) Yahweh will give victory to his people   12:6-7
  a) Formulaic introduction: on that day   12:6aα^1
  b) Description of Yahweh's action   12:6aα^2-7
    (1) Basic statement in metaphorical
terms of his making the clans of
Judah a burning fire: they will
consume the attackers of Jerusalem
while the city remains intact   12:6aα^{2}b
    (2) Explanation of why Yahweh will use
Judah to defeat Jerusalem's attackers:
to keep the city's inhabitants from
any overbearing sense of superiority   12:7
4) Yahweh will protect Jerusalem   12:8
  a) Formulaic introduction: on that day   12:8aα^1
  b) Description of Yahweh's action   12:8aα^{2}b
    (1) Yahweh's initiative:
he will protect . . .   12:8aα^{2}β
    (2) Result of Yahweh's initiative:
a transformation described by simile   12:8b
      (a) With respect to the weakest
among Jerusalem's inhabitants:
they will become like David   12:8bα
      (b) With respect to the house of
David: they will become . . .   12:8bβ

Commentators have generally recognized that 12:2-8 forms an integral part of the larger literary entity in 12:2–13:6 (though some have reckoned 12:9 to be the conclusion of this subunit rather than the beginning of the next subunit; → 12:1–14:21, Structure). Scholarly discussion has been concerned with the separation of the so-called original material from a whole host of glosses that were supposedly added to make up the present text (e.g., Elliger, 168-69; Plöger, 82-83; Lutz, 11-21). The theme of Jerusalem's being attacked by the nations obviously has various traditional antecedents and parallels (as reflected in, e.g., Isa 29:1-8; Mic 4:11-13; Joel 4:9-16 [*RSV* 3:9-16]), and the treatment of this theme in 12:2-8 may well show the influence of earlier prophetic traditions (Lutz, 33-146). The claim that inconsistencies in the present text show it to be a hodge-podge of original material and subsequent additions is not very convincing, however. The contrast between "the peoples round about" (*hā'ammîm sābîb*, vv. 2b, 6b) and "all the nations of the earth" (*kōl gôyê hā'āreṣ*, v. 3b), as well as the similar contrast between Yahweh's striking the enemies' horses with "panic" (*timmāhôn*, v. 4a) and his striking them with "blindness" (*'iwwārôn*, v. 4b) have both been cited in this regard, as well as the concern with Jerusalem on the one hand and with Judah on the other (vv. 2b, 5), and even the mixed metaphors of the "cup of reeling" (*sap-ra'al*, v. 2a) and the "stone of weightiness" (*'eben ma'ămāsâ*, v. 3a). Such terminological variations may indeed betray a multiplicity of traditional influences, but in view of how they now fit together in the overall composition of this text, they do not show the kind of inconsistency that would warrant the analysis of any different textual sources or layers here.

This part of 12:2–13:6 falls into two sections: the initial programmatic statement in 12:2 and its elaboration in 12:3-8. In v. 2a Yahweh's intention to punish the surrounding nations is metaphorically described in terms of their being made to drink from a cup whose contents will make them stagger drunkenly; and Jerusalem is figuratively identified as the cup. Such imagery is commonplace, and though the term used here for the cup *(sap)* is different from the term that is most often used elsewhere *(kôs)*, its metaphorical function is the same (cf. Isa 51:17-23; Jer 25:15-19). Zech 12:2b supplies further information. Because Jerusalem's negative impact on the nations will materialize in reaction to their attack on the city (v. 2bβ), there will inevitably be negative side effects on Judah, too (v. 2bβα). Although Jerusalem is the enemy's primary target, the enemy must invade Judah in order to reach Jerusalem, and Judah must therefore feel the effects of their being forced back (→ Text).

Verses 3-8 offer an impressionistic description of the course of events through which the enemy nations will be made to "reel," and through which the disadvantage of Jerusalem's being under attack will be reversed in the victorious transformation of Judah and Jerusalem. The redescription of the attackers in rather universal terms, as "all peoples" (v. 3a) and then "all the nations of the earth" (v. 3b), in contrast with their more limited initial characterization as "all the peoples round about" (v. 2a), provides the first hint that there may be more at stake here than mere regional hegemony. On one level this is simply a battle between Judah and its neighbors, but on another level it also represents a struggle that will eventually have worldwide or perhaps even cosmic implications. This episode begins to draw out these implications as it unfolds in four phases: vv. 3, 4-5, 6-7, and 8.

In the first phase (v. 3) Yahweh enables Jerusalem to repulse the attack without any help from Judah. Jerusalem's strength is metaphorically described in terms of its having the inertia of a stone so sharp and weighty that the attackers will be crushed and wounded in attempting to dislodge it (Petersen, *Zechariah 9–14,* 112). In the second phase (vv. 4-5) Yahweh continues his defense of the city by disabling the enemies' mounted troops as he also expands the scope of the action to include Judah. These two developments are treated as interrelated events by connecting them metaphorically in terms of eyesight. The disorientation inflicted on the enemy mounts is extended to include blindness, and in the process Yahweh casts his beneficent eye upon Judah (v. 4bα; cf. 9:1b), so that Judah becomes perceptive enough to realize that Jerusalem's strength derives from Yahweh's efforts on the city's behalf. This realization leads into the third phase (vv. 6-7), in which Judah is motivated by it to become involved in the struggle as Yahweh's agent in the defense of Jerusalem. Judah's attack on Jerusalem's enemies is metaphorically described in terms of a burning fire that devours the foe as if they were wood and straw, thus dispersing the siege and leaving the city intact (v. 6).

The third phase concludes with a description of Yahweh's motivation in thus allowing the victory finally to be decided by Judah's intervention from without, rather than by Jerusalem's continuing to mount an effective defense from within (v. 7). A new element is also introduced at this point, as the distinction between the house of David and the inhabitants of Jerusalem becomes a factor in the narrative's development, in addition to the distinction previously made between Judah and Jerusalem. The reader has been prepared for this emerging focus on the Davidic "first family," as the narration of the foregoing phases has gradually introduced familial terminology in reference to Judah.

Judah is first mentioned without any qualification (v. 2b). In the second phase (vv. 4-5), however, as Yahweh begins to envision a more active role for Judah, they are described in v. 4 as a tribal family, i.e., "the house of Judah" *(bêt yĕhûdâ).* As Judah comes to see that Yahweh is the source of strength for Jerusalem's defenders (v. 5), the "house of Judah" is further described in terms of its constituent "clans" mobilized into a militia *('allūpê yĕhûdâ).* This characterization connotes the old Israelite tribal system that was transformed by the innovation of the monarchy with its capital in Jerusalem (e.g., 2 Sam 5:1-10). By continuing such terminology into the third phase of the narration, with another reference in v. 6 to the *'allūpê yĕhûdâ* and an even more archaizing reference in v. 7 to the *'ohālê yĕhûdâ* ("tents of Judah"; cf. 1 Kgs 12:16), the way is paved for a consideration of some further innovations at this turning point in the history of Yahweh's people, in the way the royal family (the *bêt-dāwîd*, "house of David") relates to the inhabitants of the capital city, and in the way they both relate to the surrounding "house of Judah."

Yahweh has assigned Judah the decisive role in the victorious defense of Jerusalem precisely in order to show that his consequent change of Jerusalem's status in the narrative's fourth and final phase, by assigning to the city and to the Davidic family even more significant roles than they have ever played before (v. 8), is not at Judah's expense. The rationale given for Yahweh's enabling Judah to win the day, expressed in terms of his not letting the "glory" *(tip'eret)* of either the Davidic house or Jerusalem's inhabitants grow excessive (v. 7), thus foreshadows the climactic transformation in the significance of the city and its royal family. The Davidic king was once imagined to stand in relation to God as his vice-regent, and the entire populace was correspondingly imagined to stand in an analogous subordinate relation to the Davidic king. Now, however, Yahweh is assigning the city of Jerusalem to play collectively a role like the role once played by the Davidic king, and the royal family will consequently play a part that is higher than their previously viceregal role (Petersen, *Zechariah 9–14*, 119-20). Jerusalem represents the angelic host of Yahweh, into which Judah is incorporated as a tribal militia, with quasi-divine Davidic leadership in command (12:8b; cf. Josh 5:13-15). This role entails a certain symbolic subordination for Judah, but also a kind of symbolic complementarity that in effect puts it on a politically equal footing with Jerusalem.

Genre

Hanson has argued that the dominant motifs of this opening part of ch. 12 show it to be a variation on the form of the divine warrior hymn, comparable with the particular form of this genre evident in Ps 48, adapted for the distinctive purpose of describing an eschatological battle (*Dawn*, 355-68). This proposal is problematic in several respects. First, although some similar motifs do indeed make Zech 12:1-8 and Ps 48 comparable with respect to content, this fact does not necessarily make them comparable with respect to compositional form. For example, both texts express the idea that Yahweh will make Jerusalem unconquerable, but the function of this common element in Ps 48 is entirely different from its function in Zech 12:1-8. In Ps 48 this idea provides the basis on which it evokes the praise of Yahweh from its audience, but there is no evidence of any such rhetorical strategy in Zech 12:1-8. Conversely, in 12:1-8 this idea is expressed in oracular speech of Yahweh, a compositional element that is altogether absent from Ps 48. This formal difference raises the issue of whether there is actually any such genre as the divine warrior hymn, if it can be defined only in terms of a formulaic cluster of motifs with no distinctive form of its own (→ Zech 9:1–11:17, Genre; 14:1-21, Part I, Genre; Hab 3:1-19, Genre).

Moreover, it is questionable whether the mythic imagery of the divine warrior is being used here to describe a battle that can rightly be called eschatological. It would be more accurate to say that the narrative describes a particular event in a way that also universalizes it. The narrative relates an attack on Jerusalem by certain neighboring nations, treating this event as a general case of Jerusalem's being attacked by any and all foreign enemies. Yahweh defends his people from this particular attack (12:4-6) and in the process redefines their sociopolitical form, so that they can defend themselves against all such attacks (12:7-8). Yahweh previously transformed the sociopolitical form of his people in precisely the same way, and for largely the same reason, when he bound a band of refugees together in a tribal league, when he recast the tribal league into a monarchy, and when he restored the exiled remnant of the southern kingdom as a community centered around the Second Temple. His action in 12:1-8 is on the same historical plane and on the same historical continuum and is no more eschatological than these earlier actions of roughly the same sort. The narrative in this section will eventually show that the world situation now requires some more drastic action on Yahweh's part ($\rightarrow$ 12:1–13:6, Part III), and 14:1-21 will therefore go on to describe the battle that brings the old era to its final close (14:13-15). The battle described in ch. 14 is eschatological in a proper sense of the word, but the battle described in ch. 12 is not. The latter is only the prelude to the former. Hanson's description of this text as a divine warrior hymn adapted for the purpose of eschatological description is thus not adequate as a definition of its genre.

Sæbø has described 12:2–13:6 as a composition that is virtually sui generis (pp. 274-76). Petersen has described it as a "montage" (*Zechariah 9–14*, 109-10). Such proposals reflect the conclusion that the three subunits in this section (i.e., 12:2-8, 12:9–13:1, and 13:2-6) are difficult to classify generically, and that the section itself is based only on the impressionistic juxtaposition of these generically unclassifiable subunits. Certain generic conventions are evident, however, in both the subunits and the section as a whole.

Westermann describes this part of ch. 12 as a ($\rightarrow$) prophecy of salvation. He argues that 12:2-8 belongs to a subcategory of the prophecy of salvation, which describes the deliverance of Yahweh's people so as to entail the destruction of the nations (pp. 195-96, 207). But the relationship between these two aspects of the text is exactly the opposite, and to perceive this difference is to gain an insight on which a more adequate generic classification can be based. This text is basically an announcement of the punitive action that Yahweh will take against the nations, and this punitive action against the nations is described so as to entail something that is beneficial for the people of Yahweh. In the final analysis 12:2-8 is thus better characterized as the initial and definitive part of an extensive PROPHECY OF PUNISHMENT AGAINST A FOREIGN NATION — in this case foreign nations in general — that takes up all of 12:2–13:6 ($\rightarrow$ 12:2–13:6, Parts II and III, Genre).

The reason for Yahweh's animosity toward the nations is not overtly explained. No formal accusation is lodged against them, although an accusation is typical in other examples of this genre, and even the fact of their aggression is described rather obliquely in the initial statement of Yahweh's purpose (v.

2). This initial part of 12:2–13:6 nevertheless provides an indirect explanation of Yahweh's motivation, thus assuming a function similar to the role of the accusation. The problem is not just that the neighboring nations have unfairly ganged up on the people of Yahweh, thus provoking him to retaliate. Such aggression also jeopardizes the way in which Judah and Jerusalem have served as a sign of Yahweh's agency in the world. Yahweh is therefore enabling Judah and Jerusalem to repulse the enemy attack, so as to begin a transformation in their capacity to serve this particular theological purpose.

Setting

→ 12:1–13:6, Part III.

Intention

This text identifies a certain historical eventuality as the occasion for Yahweh to work a change in the polity of postexilic Judah, thus legitimizing that change. This historical eventuality is the deliverance of Jerusalem from an attack of neighboring peoples through Judah's rallying to the city's defense. The concomitant change in polity entails a decisive shift from the concept that governed the postexilic status quo, namely, that the temple and the leaders associated with it can take the place of David, and the city of Jerusalem can take the place of all Israel, in representing Yahweh's divine kingship over creation. This concept ascribes great importance to the idea of direct continuity between the restored temple and its predecessor founded by the Davidic dynasty, but relatively little importance to Davidic descent itself (→ 1:7–6:15). As a result of what Yahweh has done to defend the city, this concept is about to change. All the inhabitants of Jerusalem, including both leaders and people, will now take the place of David; and all of Judah will in effect take the place of Jerusalem, the city of David. This change in their status also makes it possible for leaders of Davidic descent to resume a role of special importance, but not the same kind of role that they played in preexilic times. It instead opens up a new category of theological significance to which they may attain, the possibility of becoming "like God" (→ 12:2–13:6, Part III, Intention).

Bibliography

H.-M. Lutz, *Jahwe, Jerusalem und die Völker* (WMANT 27; Neukirchen-Vluyn: Neukirchener, 1968); C. Westermann, *Prophetic Oracles of Salvation in the Old Testament* (tr. K. Crim; Louisville: Westminster/John Knox, 1991).

NEW LEADERSHIP MAKES DEFENSE MORE EFFECTIVE AND PROPHECY MORE UNCERTAIN, 12:2–13:6: PART II, 12:9–13:1

Since 12:2–13:6 is a relatively long and complex unit, it is being discussed part by part for the sake of convenience, focusing here on 12:9–13:1. 12:2-8 has been discussed above, and 13:2-6 will be discussed below. This separation should not obscure the fact that these three pericopes comprise a larger entity.

Text

Regarding the crux in 12:10aβ, the proposal of Jones (*Haggai,* 161-62) represents a step in the right direction, at least as far as the specifically text-critical and grammatical aspects of the matter are concerned, although his overall interpretation of this clause has not won much acceptance. Along with most modern commentators he has recognized that *'ly* ("to me"), the reading of the first prepositional phrase that is attested in the vast majority of Masoretic mss., is preferable on text-critical grounds to the variant *'lyw* ("to him"). In addition he has rightly seen that the immediately following phrase, *'ēt 'ăšer,* is more likely to be syntactically independent from *'ēlay* than in apposition to it. (For details see M. Delcor, "Un problème de critique textuelle et d'exégèse: Zach 12:10 et aspicient ad me quem confixerunt," *RB* 58 [1951] 191-96.) Instead of the sort of conventional rendering represented by *RSV* "they shall look on him whom they have pierced," Jones thus proposes: "they shall look unto me (Yahweh) touching (those) whom they (the nations) have slain."

This proposal remains problematic in two respects. First, the relative pronoun *'ăšer* probably does not have a plural sense here because the ensuing clause (v. 10b) describes the people as mourning over an individual (*'ālāyw,* "over him") rather than a group. Jones's suggestion that this is a collective reference to the slain is not convincing (Baldwin, 190-91). Second, without any explicit indication that "the nations" are specifically the subject of the verb *dāqārû* (*RSV* "they have pierced"), it is more likely that this verb has the same subject as the immediately preceding verb *wĕhibbîṭû* (*RSV* "they look"), i.e., "the house of David and the inhabitants of Jerusalem," or that the subject somewhat more ambiguously includes both "the house of David and the inhabitants of Jerusalem" and "the nations" previously mentioned in v. 9. Jones's syntactical and text-critical proposals can be followed, while also avoiding these two problems, by ascribing to *'ăšer* a singular but indeterminate sense, and by acknowledging that the inclusion of "the nations" in the subject of *dāqārû* can at best be rather implicit.

Verse 10aβbα might thus be translated: "they shall look to me regarding whomever they have wounded, and they shall mourn for him." In other words, in reaction to each of the battle's casualties, explicitly including those that Yahweh's people have inflicted on the enemy nations and implicitly including those that the enemy nations have inflicted on them, Jerusalem will look to Yahweh. There is no reason to suppose that Jerusalem has suffered any self-inflicted casualties, but both the indeterminateness of the relative pronoun and the ambiguity regarding the subject of *dāqārû* give rise to this possibility, leaving it open to exploitation as this text is reinterpreted in other contexts. Because of the way this possibility was realized in later reapplications of this text to a particular historical figure (i.e., Jesus in John 19:37), modern scholars have also read the text in this way. Zech 12:10 has thus been seen as a description of Jerusalem's remorse over the tragic results of their vendetta against some leader or prophet, and scholars have speculated about the historical identity of this person (Larkin, 166-70). In context, however, 12:10 seems simply to portray Jerusalem's reaction to all the killing in which their side has just participated (12:4-9; cf. Petersen, *Zechariah 9–14*, 121).

Structure

I. Basic statement of Yahweh's purpose: to make Jerusalem
a "cup of reeling" for the nations   12:2

II. Elaboration   12:3–13:6

   A. The attack of the nations will in the long run prove
beneficial for Judah and Jerusalem   12:3–13:1

     1. Yahweh will enable Jerusalem to defend
itself victoriously   12:3-8

     2. Jerusalem's sense of loss will become the means
of their purification and forgiveness   12:9–13:1

       a. Introduction: and it will happen that . . .
(wĕhāyâ)   12:9aα

       b. Narration of what will happen   12:9aβ–13:1

         1) Yahweh will affect Jerusalem's
perception of their casualties   12:9aβ-10

           a) Formulaic introduction: on that day   12:9aβ

           b) Description of Yahweh's action   12:9b-10

             (1) Yahweh's initiative   12:9b-10aα

               (a) He will seek to destroy
Jerusalem's attackers   12:9b

               (b) He will pour out a spirit of
graciousness and supplication   12:10aα

             (2) Result of Yahweh's initiative   12:10aβb

               (a) Jerusalem's inhabitants will
look to Yahweh regarding each
of the dead and wounded   12:10aβ

               (b) They will react sorrowfully   12:10b

                 α. With a mournful outcry as
for the death of an only child   12:10bα

                 β. With bitter outcry as for the
death of a firstborn child   12:10bβ

         2) Mourning will extend to every family
in the land   12:11-14

a) Formulaic introduction: on that day   12:11aα
b) Description of the extent of mourning   12:11aβ-14
    (1) With respect to Jerusalem in
        particular: it will be as great as
        the mourning for Hadad-rimmon
        in the plain of Megiddo   12:11aβb
    (2) With respect to the land in general   12:12-14
        (a) Basic description in terms of
            families: every family shall
            mourn by themselves   12:12a
        (b) Further specification in terms of
            each family in general and its
            women in particular   12:12b-14
            α. With respect to certain
               families in particular:
               identified by patronym   12:12b-13
               aa. House of David   12:12bα
                 α) House of David
                   in general   12:12bα^1
                 β) Their women
                   in particular   12:12bα^2
               bb. House of Nathan   12:12bβ
                 α) House of Nathan
                   in general   12:12bβ^1
                 β) Their women
                   in particular   12:12bβ^2
               cc. House of Levi   12:13a
                 α) House of Levi
                   in general   12:13aα
                 β) Their women
                   in particular   12:13aβ
               dd. Shimeites   12:13b
                 α) Shimeites in general   12:13bα
                 β) Their women
                   in particular   12:13bβ
             β. With respect to the
               remaining families   12:14
               aa. Remaining families in general 12:14a
               bb. Their women in particular   12:14b
3) Forgiveness and purification will
   become possible   13:1
   a) Formulaic introduction: on that day   13:1aα^1
   b) Description of a future development
      metaphorically in terms of a fountain   13:1aα^{2}b
     (1) Its emergence: a fountain will
        be opened   13:1aα^2
     (2) Its beneficiaries   13:1aβ

(a) House of David		13:1aβ^1
(b) Inhabitants of Jerusalem		13:1aβ^2
(3) Its purpose		13:1b
(a) For sin		13:1bα
(b) For impurity		13:1bβ
B. The possibility of Yahweh's being misrepresented		
will remain		13:2-6
1. Yahweh will attempt to rid the land of		
idolatrous practices		13:2-3
2. Prophecy will persist as a problematic profession		13:4-6

In 12:9–13:1 the narration begun in 12:2-8 continues to unfold through another episode (note that v. 9 begins with *wĕhāyâ bayyôm hahû*'), progressing here through three phases (12:9-10, 12:11-14, and 13:1) toward the concluding episodes in 13:2-6 (Petersen, *Zechariah 9–14*, 120-28). A number of commentators include 13:1 in the next part of 12:2–13:6, but the recurrence of *wĕhāyâ bayyôm hahû*' at 13:2 shows a fundamental division there, rather than at 13:1 (→ 12:1–14:21, Structure). Like 12:2-8, this part of the story maintains a dual focus on Yahweh's external policy toward the nations (12:9) and its implications for the internal affairs of Yahweh's own people (12:10–13:1). 12:9–13:1 also resembles 12:2-8 in beginning with a programmatic statement of Yahweh's intentions vis-à-vis the nations (v. 9; cf. v. 2); but unlike v. 2, which heads and stands apart from the narration that follows in 12:3-8, v. 9 is incorporated within the narration of 12:9–13:1. 12:9 reiterates the announcement of Yahweh's purpose in 12:2, as it also reformulates it more expansively in view of the longer and wider global perspective that has gradually opened up in 12:3-8 (→ 12:2–13:1, Part I, Structure). With respect to the immediate situation Yahweh intends to repulse the neighboring nations' siege of Jerusalem and to rout them out of Judah. Stated more broadly, his intention with respect to the more long-range situation is to "destroy all the nations that come against Jerusalem" (v. 9).

The focus then shifts immediately to the aftermath of the battle, as the first phase of the narration continues with a description of how Yahweh's recently evident long-range intention to protect Jerusalem will affect its people's ongoing existence (v. 10). Yahweh will not only keep the city of David outwardly unassailable; in the process he will also foster an inward change in the predominant attitude. Acting in his capacity as creator, Yahweh will "pour out" *(špk)* on them a new "spirit" *(rûaḥ;* cf. 12:1b; also Ps 33:6; Amos 5:8, etc.) characterized by "graciousness" or "favorableness" *(ḥēn; RSV* "compassion") and by "supplication" *(taḥănûnîm).* The positive but rather general fruits of this particular spirit are more concretely exemplified in the immediately ensuing description of the way the city of Jerusalem will react whenever the fighting comes to an end. Rather than gloat over their defeated enemies, they will look to Yahweh regarding each of the dead and wounded (→ Text). This concern for the enemy dead and wounded, as well as for their own, illustrates what *ḥēn* or "graciousness" entails in this particular context; and their looking to Yahweh regarding the casualties similarly illustrates what *taḥănûnîm* or "supplication" entails in this particular context. Instead of a victory celebration, rites of mourning will therefore be observed (v. 10b). Every casualty will be mourned by the people of Jerusalem as if they were the firstborn or the only child of each family.

The second phase of the narration (12:11-14) describes both the magnitude of this grief (v. 11) and the extent to which it will spread and permeate all strands of Judah's social fabric (vv. 12-14). With respect to the magnitude, it is unclear whether the comparison with "the mourning of Hadad-rimmon in the plain of Megiddo" refers to a Canaanite ritual for a dying-and-rising weather god, or to an Israelite day of mourning observed annually in commemoration of the death of King Josiah (2 Chr 35:23-25; Meyers and Meyers, *Zechariah 9–14*, 343-44). In any case the point of the comparison is that Jerusalem's mourning for the casualties in the siege will easily compare with the mass mourning on even such great occasions of grief as these.

The conduct of this mourning is then formally schematized in terms of families in a hierarchy encompassing not just Jerusalem but "the land" as well (*hā'āreṣ* is the subject of the verb *wĕsāpĕdâ* ["mourn"] in v. 12a). This hierarchy extends from "the house of David" to other representatives of Judah's first families, finally including all the other families. The reason for the Davidic family's position at the top of the list is obvious from what has earlier been said regarding their promotion in status (12:8), and the inclusion of "the house of Levi" singles out the priestly families for special consideration. The references to two other specific families, identified by the patronyms of Nathan and Shimei, are rather ambiguous because several historically different and genealogically significant persons have borne these names. In view of this ambiguity both the reason for the specification of these two families and the significance of the hierarchy's overall arrangement remain obscure. It is nevertheless clear that the mourning is emphatically described as affecting not only Jerusalem collectively but also Judah's social units individually, emanating outward and downward from Jerusalem to encompass every single familial subdivision within "the clans of Judah" (12:5-6). The separate mention of the women in each family reflects their specialized role in mourning rites (e.g., Jer 9:16-25 [*RSV* 9:17-26]; Meyers and Meyers, *Zechariah 9–14*, 346).

The third phase of the narration (13:1) describes a development that emerges as a consequence of the event described in the two preceding phases (12:9-10 and 12:11-14) and typifies the kind of care that Yahweh will continue to provide for his people under such conditions. Because of their involvement in the killing and their contact with the dead and wounded, the people have become both morally and ritually impure (cf. Num 31:19). They thus stand in need of cleansing and forgiveness not only for the sake of their own well-being but also for the sake of maintaining the holiness of the sanctuary.

Such cleansing and forgiveness result from both the inward attitudinal inclination toward "graciousness" and "supplication," with which Yahweh will inspire them (v. 10aα), and the outward behavioral indication of an intention to cultivate this tendency, which entails a ritual of washing with water (cf. Num 19:16-20). According to 13:1 the means of performing this ritual will also be provided through the kind of action that only Yahweh can perform, acting again in his capacity as creator of heaven and earth (12:1). After Yahweh has inspired the Jerusalem community to make supplication (v. 10aα) and they have consequently "looked to" Yahweh (v. 10aβ), a spring will well up supplying water for the ritual aspects of keeping the holy city pure.

Genre

This part of 12:2–13:1 is more concerned with how Yahweh takes care of his own people than with how he treats other nations. It nevertheless describes his care of his own people in terms of what he will do for them as a consequence of his enabling them to defeat an attack of neighboring nations (12:2-8), and it explicitly generalizes Yahweh's actions in this particular situation into a typical pattern of how he will care for his people whenever they are attacked by any nation (12:9). 12:9–13:1 thus shows itself to be a continuation of the PROPHECY OF PUNISHMENT AGAINST A FOREIGN NATION begun in 12:2-8 (→ 12:2–13:1, Part I, Genre). This genre tends to describe Yahweh's unfavorable actions toward an enemy in a way that implies or entails his conversely favorable actions toward his own people (→ Zeph 2:5-7, Genre). Here this tendency is heavily accentuated while still retaining the basic form of the genre.

Setting

→ 12:1–13:6, Part III.

Intention

This text envisions the mode of existence that will become necessary for Yahweh's people, given that they are entering an era characterized by the continual attacks of foreign nations on Jerusalem, and given that their relationship with Yahweh will thus be primarily a matter of his defending them from these attacks. To have hope in such a time they must walk the fine line between not becoming numb to the high casualties, whether inflicted by them on their enemies or inflicted by their enemies on them, and not succumbing to the despair that any realistic sense of the human cost might well engender. Yahweh will therefore use Jerusalem to foster a deep sense of compassion throughout Judah as a whole so that they can fully acknowledge the grievousness of their situation. At the same time Yahweh will also use Jerusalem to give them both the desire and the ritual means of turning to him. Thus their expression of grief can be constructively transformed into a way of renewing their communal integrity and their relationship with him as they are purified and forgiven.

NEW LEADERSHIP MAKES DEFENSE MORE EFFECTIVE AND PROPHECY MORE UNCERTAIN, 12:2–13:6: PART III, 13:2-6

Since 12:2–13:6 is a relatively long and complex unit, it is being discussed part by part for the sake of convenience, focusing here on 13:2-6. 12:2-8 and 12:9–13:1 have been discussed separately above. This separation should not obscure the fact that these three pericopes comprise a larger entity.

Text

The *RSV* translation of v. 5b obscures some of its allusions to the story of Cain in Gen 4. Zech 13:5bα states not only that the prophet in question is a "tiller of (the) soil" (*'ōbēd 'ădāmâ;* cf. Gen 4:2), but also that he is a "man" (*'îš*), thus reinforcing the connection made in Zech 13:5bβ with the etymological explanation of Cain's name given by Eve in Gen 4:1, "I have gotten a man *(qānîtî 'îš).*" The *RSV*'s translation of Zech 13:5bβ avoids this connection altogether by making a completely conjectural textual emendation. A rough translation of the MT might read: "for humanity [or Adam] has gotten possession of me *(hiqnanî)* since my youth." This rendering of *hiqnanî* attempts to capture in English something of the wordplay that is involved in using here the hiphil of the same verb whose qal form *qānîtî* ("I have gotten") is used in Gen 4:1. It does not adequately convey other connotations that *qnh* may have, however, such as "redeem" and even "create."

Structure

I. Basic statement of Yahweh's purpose: to make Jerusalem a "cup of reeling" for the nations	12:2
II. Elaboration	12:3–13:6
A. The attack of the nations will in the long run prove beneficial for Judah and Jerusalem	12:3–13:1
1. Yahweh will enable Jerusalem to defend itself victoriously	12:3-8
2. Jerusalem's sense of loss will become the means of their purification and forgiveness	12:9–13:1
B. The possibility of Yahweh's being misrepresented will remain	13:2-6
1. Yahweh will attempt to rid the land of idolatrous practices	13:2-3
a. Introduction: and it will happen that . . . (*wĕhāyâ*)	13:2aα¹
b. Narration of what will happen	13:2aα¹-3
1) Formulaic introduction: on that day	13:2aα¹
2) Oracle formula: says Yahweh of hosts	13:2aα²
3) Description of Yahweh's action	13:2aβ-3

a)	With respect to idols	13:2aβ
	(1) Yahweh's initiative: I will cut off their names from the land	13:2aβ¹
	(2) Result of Yahweh's initiative: they will be remembered no more	13:2aβ²
b)	With respect to prophets and the spirit of impurity	13:2b-3
	(1) Yahweh's initiative: I will remove them from the land	13:2b
	(2) Result of Yahweh's initiative: expressed conditionally	13:3
	(a) Protasis: if anyone again pretends to prophesy . . .	13:3aα¹
	(b) Apodosis: the reaction of his father and mother	13:3aα²b
	α. They shall condemn him to death because of his lies	13:3aα²β
	β. They shall pierce him when he prophesies	13:3b

2. Prophecy will persist as a problematic profession — 13:4-6
   a. Introduction: and it will happen that . . . *(wĕhāyâ)* — 13:4aα¹
   b. Narration of what will happen — 13:4aα²-6
     1) Formulaic introduction: on that day — 13:4aα²
     2) Description of prophecy's loss of integrity — 13:4aβ-6
       a) Prophets will be ashamed of their revelations — 13:4aβ
       b) Manifestations of this development — 13:4b-6
         (1) They will not don a hairy mantle in order to deceive — 13:4b
         (2) They will deny their calling — 13:5
         (3) They will admit to receiving the stigmata of parental rejection — 13:6

Some commentators reckon the final part of 12:2–13:6 to begin at 13:1, but the phrase *wĕhāyâ bayyôm hahû'* ("and it will happen on that day . . .") at 13:2 marks the start of this subunit as a distinct episode. The recurrence of this formula at 13:4, together with the use of the oracle formula *nĕ'um yhwh ṣĕbā'ôt* (*RSV* "says Yahweh of hosts") in 13:2, shows that the compositional form of 13:2-6 mimics the compositional form of 12:2–13:1, which similarly marks off its two main subdivisions with *wĕhāyâ bayyôm hahû'* (at 12:3, 9) and similarly establishes a link with 12:1 by reiterating *nĕ'um yhwh* in the first of its two main subdivisions (12:4; → 12:1–14:21, Structure). This mimicry with respect to form is matched by mimicry with respect to content, as 13:2-6 describes in its two episodes (vv. 2-3, 4-6) an ironic reversal of what is described in 12:2-8 and 12:9–13:1, caricaturing the way in which prophecy will become dysfunctional when the previously described transformation of Yahweh's people is complete.

Zech 13:2-3 describes two actions of Yahweh so as to parody the two main actions of Yahweh described in 12:2-8 and 12:9–13:1. In 12:2-8 Yahweh strengthens his people's attachment to the land, so that they can make a great name for themselves (i.e., attain "glory") and be seen to embody a true likeness of God. Conversely, in 13:2aβ Yahweh severs the attachment of the *'ăṣabbîm* (*RSV* "idols") to the land, so that their names will be forgotten and they will be seen as false likenesses of God. (To "cut off the names of the idols" is virtually the converse of giving "glory" to Judah and Jerusalem because of the way *tip'eret* ["glory"] and *šēm* ["name"] share the same semantic field; see, e.g., Deut 26:19; Isa 63:14; Jer 13:11; 33:9; 1 Chr 22:5; 29:13.) In 12:9–13:1 Yahweh repels danger from without as he pours out a spirit that unifies extended families in mourning for their wounded enemies as if for their own children, and thus makes his people pure. Conversely, in 13:2b-3 Yahweh expels danger from within as he drives out the prophetic manifestation of a spirit that divides immediate families by leading parents to treat their own children as mortal enemies, thus making his people impure. In the context of such a parody prophecy emerges on a par with idolatry as something that inherently misrepresents Yahweh. This discrediting of prophecy will happen only as a consequence of what Yahweh has accomplished in 12:2–13:1, however. When he has wrought this change in the leadership, making the "the house of David" his more or less direct representatives in the world (12:8b), conventional prophecy's relatively indirect and hence potentially mistaken mode of representation will no longer be warranted (Bič, 155; Mason, *Haggai,* 121-22).

In 13:4-6 prophecy is portrayed as a phenomenon that will continue but as something disreputable. Prophets will still have revelations, but they will be "ashamed" of them (v. 4a). This shamefulness is described in terms of three antitypes (vv. 4b-5), comparing such prophets in variously negative ways with Jacob (v. 4b), Amos (v. 5a), and Cain (v. 5b). In conclusion there is a brief dialogue showing the gruesome consequences such prophets will suffer (v. 6).

Jacob put on skins to imitate the "hairy mantle" of his older brother Esau (*'adderet śē'ār;* cf. Gen 25:25) so that his blind father Isaac would give him the blessing to which Esau was entitled as the firstborn (Gen 27:1-40). By characterizing prophecy in terms of "donning a hairy mantle to deceive" (Zech 13:4b), the text allusively categorizes prophecy as deception while also holding out the possibility that it might at least be the kind of deception that — like Jacob's — nevertheless proves instrumental in the fulfillment of Yahweh's divine promise. By stating that the prophet will *not* play the role of Jacob, however, the text also discounts this possibility in the very process of conjuring it up.

A similar irony is also evident in v. 5, as the text moves from a description of the prophet's future role in terms of what he will do, to a description of this role in terms of what he will say. His initial words are exactly the same as those spoken by the prophet Amos in response to the command of Amaziah, priest of Bethel, to leave the royal sanctuary and stop prophesying there (Amos 7:10-17). Amos says *lō' nābî' 'ānōkî* (lit. "not prophet I") and follows this phrase with an alternative description of his social role: "for I am a herder" (*kî bôqēr 'ānōkî,* 7:14). Amos's reply is subject to a variety of interpretations, but in any case it is a disclaimer regarding his categorization as a *nābî'* ("prophet") that somehow provides him with a basis on which to assert that he is nevertheless possessed and duly commissioned by Yahweh: "Yahweh took me *(wayyiqqāḥēnî)* . . . and Yahweh told me *(wayyō'mer 'ēlay),* 'Go prophesy *(lēk hinnābē')*'" (7:15).

Here the prophet, similarly confronted by his own family (v. 3) and his own shame (v. 4a), makes the same disclaimer as Amos (v. 5a) and similarly follows it with an alternative description of his social role (v. 5b). Like Amos, this prophet describes himself in terms of a rural occupation; but in this case it is the rural occupation of the infamous character Cain: a "tiller of the soil" (*'ōbēd 'ădāmâ;* cf. Gen 4:2bβ). Unlike Amos, who was divinely possessed at some point in his adult life, this prophet resembles Cain in being humanly possessed "from his youth" (→ Text). Unlike Amos, who was sent by Yahweh from his own land to another particular place in order to serve a definite purpose, this prophet resembles Cain in being uprooted from the land by Yahweh in order to wander aimlessly (Zech 13:2b; cf. Gen 4:12).

This comparison with Cain leads into the concluding exchange between an unidentified questioner and the prophet in v. 6. As the killer of his brother Abel, Cain was the cause of familial strife (Gen 4:3-11); and this theme, which has been previously introduced by describing prophecy as a source of familial discord (Zech 13:3), is resumed here. Many commentators have attempted to explain the "wounds" *(makkôt)* that are the subject of this dialogue with reference to the self-mutilation once customary among certain types of Canaanite prophets (1 Kgs 18:28) and to identify the place where these wounds are received as a temple where sacred prostitution was practiced in devotion to Canaanite gods (reading *bêt mě'ahăbāy* as "house of my lovers" [*RSV* "house of my friends"]). These wounds, however, are not self-inflicted; and any reference to sacred prostitution here — even if such a thing ever existed — is extremely tenuous indeed.

It would seem more plausible to read v. 6 in light of its immediate context, so that the wounds mentioned here are the ones conditionally threatened in v. 3, i.e., the wounds that the prophet's parents would inflict if he were to prophesy. This reading is reinforced by ascribing to the term *bêt* ("house") the same familial connotations that it has throughout this whole passage (12:4, 8, 10, 12-14), so that the phrase *bêt mě'ahăbāy* is understood as "the house of those who love me," i.e., the home of the prophet's parents (Mitchell, 339). In other words, the dialogue in v. 6 indicates that public reaction to the prophet's disfigurement will constrain him to confess that he has been attacked by his own family and has thus suffered the previously announced consequences of continuing to play this now inherently defective role.

Genre

By virtue of its formal parallels with 12:2–13:1, 13:2-6 shows itself to be joined with 12:2-8 and 12:9–13:1 in a larger compositional entity (→ Structure; also → 12:1–14:21, Structure). These two preceding subunits are characterized by an initial description of Yahweh's action vis-à-vis the nations (12:2-4a, 9) before turning to a description of Yahweh's concomitant action vis-à-vis his own people (12:4b-8; 12:10–13:1). In 13:2-6 this same pattern is evident. Here there is a shift in emphasis, moving from the primarily military theme of battle and its aftermath in 12:2–13:1 to the primarily religious theme of revelation in 13:2-6. Despite this thematic transition the same formal precedent is followed, as Yahweh's activity is first described in relation to the international sphere and then in relation to the local sphere.

This subunit initially mentions Yahweh's treatment of the international religious influences impinging on his people (v. 2a) before then turning to focus on his concomitant treatment of a singularly important aspect of their own religious tradition, i.e., prophecy (vv. 2b-6). The term *'ăṣabbîm* ("idols"), with which the primary objects of Yahweh's punishment are characterized, denotes the images with which the gods of other nations are typically represented, including the gods of such historically prominent antagonists as the Philistines (1 Sam 31:9) and the Babylonians (Isa 46:1; Jer 50:2) in particular, but also the gods of all foreign peoples in general (Pss 106:34-36; 135:15). Yahweh's intention, to "cut off the names of the idols from the land" (Zech 13:2a), is thus consistent with his general international policy of keeping enemy forces out of the land (12:2-6, 9). His concomitant intention, to "remove the prophets . . . from the land" (13:2b), is also consistent with his general intention to reform the polity of Jerusalem in relation to Judah (12:7-8), so as to engender within his people a spiritual dynamic leading them to purity (12:10–13:1). Prophecy is thus conversely characterized as the manifestation of a "spirit of impurity" (13:2b).

As the conclusion to 12:2–13:6, 13:2-6 is composed of the same basic generic elements as 12:2-8 and 12:9–13:1. It continues the pattern of these two preceding subunits, describing how Yahweh will reform his own people in the process of protecting them against enemy forces, and thus joins them in forming part of the same extended PROPHECY OF PUNISHMENT AGAINST A FOREIGN NATION (→ 12:2–13:6, Parts I and II, Genre).

Setting

It is conceivable that 12:1–13:6 was based on previously existing prophetic sayings of some sort, as various scholars have maintained (e.g., Elliger, 168-69; Plöger, 82-83); but if so, these original antecedents are not sufficiently recoverable to make any speculation about their original setting worthwhile or even possible. In view of the fact that the subunits of 12:2–13:6 are generically indistinguishable from this section as a whole, it only makes sense to inquire about the setting of 12:1–13:6 as such.

Hanson (*Dawn*, 357-58) and others (e.g., Plöger, 84-86; Mason, "Some Examples," 343-44) have rightly noted that it is problematic to identify "the one whom they have pierced" (12:10) with the death of some specific person known from other sources. A better approach is to locate this composition both socially and historically on the basis of its literary type and on the basis of its function within this section of the book (12:1–14:21) and within the book as a whole.

Prophecies of punishment against foreign nations were typically used in three closely related social contexts, all of which were concerned in some way with international affairs. (1) In preexilic times they were typically proclaimed in anticipation of military conflict as part of the preparations made in either the cult or the royal court (→ Zeph 2:5-7, Setting). In postexilic times, in view of the fact that Judah no longer had a king in command of a standing army, this practice was adapted to situations in which the local authorities had to deal with threatening political opposition from outside the community or to deploy the militia in self-defense (→ Zech 9:1-8, Setting). In this context Yahweh's condemnations of his people's enemies functioned primarily as a means of assuring his people that he would protect them, but such prophecies might also convey warnings directed to Yahweh's people. (2) Prophecies of punishment might also be proclaimed directly to the representatives of foreign nations, when they were visited by prophets of Yahweh or received as envoys to the land of Yahweh's people, in order to persuade foreign leaders to change their policies. (3) Prophecies against foreign nations might also provide a form in which prophetic reflection on the significance of international events might persuasively commend itself to a rather more general audience (see Hayes, Raabe).

In this particular case the first and third of these contexts seem to be relevant. This unit is not really concerned with deterring the attack of the nations on Jerusalem but rather with the implications of such attacks for the people of Yahweh. This text takes as its point of departure a reference to a specific event, when Jerusalem was attacked by neighboring nations (12:2), which suggests that it could have been proclaimed on this occasion in order to assure its audience that Yahweh would protect them. This possibility is not mitigated either by the admission that Yahweh's intervention will have negative side-effects for his own people, or by the realism with which the high human cost of Judah's self-defense is described. The rhetorical capacity to reinforce hope is only enhanced by such realistic truthfulness.

The reference to this real event is largely used, however, as a basis on which to generalize hypothetically about the way in which Yahweh will henceforth deal with any and all such events (12:3–13:1); and the text goes on to describe the problematic complications that seem inherent to this particular form of divine providence under present world conditions (13:2-6). This text not only affirms that with Yahweh's help his people can survive the continual attacks of other nations; it also probes the theologically problematic significance of the continued existence of Yahweh's people as one nation among many others under the conditions of the present world order. It is possible that 12:1–13:6 may have been proclaimed to the people of Jerusalem in the thick of the battle to which it initially refers. It seems more likely, however, that 12:1–13:6 belongs to the third category mentioned above and was thus composed for purposes of theological reflection on the broader implications of this development.

In any case this text makes a claim about the nature of Yahweh's involvement in a particular event and about the way in which this event will therefore turn out. The description of Yahweh's participation in this instance is then expanded into a model of his relationship with his people for the indefinite future. Regarding the event in question, the text says only that Jerusalem is attacked by an armed force from neighboring nations. Since the text provides no other historically specific information, it would be pointless to speculate about just which attack this might be on the basis of what is said in this unit alone.

The text also envisions that the relationship between the city of Jerusalem and the surrounding area of Judah will change in the course of the conflict. This change seems to entail the incorporation of both Jerusalem and Judah into a single body politic in which Jerusalem rules Judah, but the inhabitants of Judah have the same status as the citizens of Jerusalem. The prospect of such a development implies that the text was composed at a time when Jerusalem and Judah were not as closely or as cooperatively interrelated. In view of how little is known about the development of Judah's political organization in postexilic times, however, this fact alone does not provide a sufficient basis on which to determine even an approximate historical location for this text.

On the basis of the sparse information gleaned from 12:1–13:6, regarding both the general nature of the event that gave rise to its composition and the general political conditions of its time, nothing more specific can be said about the setting of this unit itself. These data nevertheless provide some important information that, in conjunction with data from the other units in this section, can be used to draw a somewhat more definitive conclusion with regard to the social and historical location of (→) 12:1–14:21 as a whole.

Intention

With high irony 13:2-6 describes how conventional prophecy will be displaced when Yahweh brings about the previously described transformation in the polity (12:2-8) and spiritual ethos (12:9–13:1) of Judah and Jerusalem. When Jerusalem becomes "like David" and thus assumes the role of the king in representing Yahweh as his earthly vice-regent, the house of David will also become "like God" (12:8). This means, among other things (→ 12:2–13:6, Part I), that the house of David will assume a role with the same kind of directly revelatory significance that became ascribed to the figure of Moses, with all that this ascription implies. Moses could virtually impersonate God because he spoke with Yahweh "mouth to mouth" (Num 12:6-8) and knew him "face to face" (Deut 34:10). It might be necessary to designate additional intermediaries for such subsidiary purposes as helping Moses to convey his prophetic insights more articulately (Exod 4:10-16) or helping Moses to share the burden of leadership (Num 11:16-17, 24-25), but the ancillary function of interpreting Moses' prophetic insights was ideally dispersed throughout the people as a whole (Num 11:26-30). This text envisions the assumption of this specifically Mosaic prophetic role by the house of David, so that Yahweh's people as a whole assume the more general prophetic role of ancillary intermediaries, thus obviating the necessity for any other kind of prophetic role.

Prophecy of other kinds will persist, but only as a phenomenon without any positive theological significance, whose effects will be antithetical to even its own traditional ideals. It will become the sort of negative deception that destroys Israelite identity, rather than the kind of positive deception originally practiced by Jacob in order to create Israel. It will only promote social dissolution as its distorted revelations become a source of familial discord. Past prophets heroically bore the stigma of being persecuted for the truth's sake. Future prophets, of the sort ironically portrayed here, will make a ridiculous spectacle of the stigmata received for their lying, provoking violence from even the members of their own families who would naturally be most inclined to give them love and support. Although prophecy has distinguished Israelite precedents, it will become tantamount to a foreign idolatrous influence because it engenders the kind of impurity that — just like foreign armies — can lead to the loss of the land (cf. Ezek 14:6-11; Ps 106:34-41; Lev 18:26-29).

Bibliography

J. H. Hayes, "The Usage of Oracles against Foreign Nations in Ancient Israel," *JBL* 87 (1968) 81-92; D. L. Petersen, *Late Israelite Prophecy* (SBLMS 23; Missoula, Mont.: Scholars Press, 1977) 33-38; idem, "The Oracles against the Nations: A Form-Critical Analysis," in *Society of Biblical Literature 1975 Seminar Papers* (ed. G. MacRae; Missoula, Mont.: Scholars Press, 1975) 1:39-61; P. R. Raabe, "Why Oracles against the Nations?" in *Fortunate the Eyes That See* (*Fest.* D. N. Freedman; ed. A. H. Bartelt, A. B. Beck, C. A. Franke, and P. R. Raabe; Grand Rapids: Eerdmans, 1995) 236-57.

YAHWEH WILL MAKE HIS PEOPLE A LEADERLESS REMNANT, TO TEST THEM AND TO RENEW HIS COVENANT WITH THEM, 13:7-9

Structure

I. Apostrophe addressed to Yahweh's sword: speech of Yahweh	13:7
A. Initiation of speech proper	$13:7a\alpha\beta^1$
1. Vocative: O sword	
2. Command: awake!	
3. Parallel phrases indicating the target of the sword's action	$13:7a\alpha^2\beta^1$
a. Against my shepherd	$13:7a\alpha^2$
b. Against the man associated with me	$13:7a\beta^1$
B. Oracle formula: says Yahweh of hosts	$13:7a\beta^2$
C. Resumption of speech proper	13:7b
1. Command further specifying the sword's action: strike!	

    2. Object: the shepherd

    3. Parallel clauses describing the intended result   13:7bα²β

       a. The sheep may be scattered   13:7bα²

       b. I will turn my hand against the little ones   13:7bβ

II. Narration of what will be accomplished by the wielding

of Yahweh's sword: speech of Yahweh   13:8-9

A. Initiation of speech proper   13:8aα¹

    1. Narrative introduction: and it will happen that . . .

      (wĕhāyâ)

    2. Narration of what will happen: phrase setting the

      scene of the action: in the whole land

B. Oracle formula: says Yahweh   13:8aα²

C. Resumption of speech proper: continued narration

of what will happen   13:8aβ-9

    1. Action initiated: described in terms of how the

      flock fares in relation to the land   13:8aβ

      a. With respect to two-thirds: they shall be cut

        off and perish   13:8aβ¹

      b. With respect to one-third: they shall remain   13:8aβ²

    2. Action developed: the fate of the surviving one-third,

      described metaphorically in terms of assaying   13:9a

      a. What Yahweh will do: I will put them into

        the fire   13:9aα

      b. The double effect of this deed   13:9aβ

       1) I will refine them as one refines silver   13:9aβ¹

       2) I will test them as gold is tested   13:9aβ²

    3. Action concluded: restoration of the covenant

      relationship between Yahweh and the survivors   13:9b

      a. The two parties approach each other   13:9bα

       1) The people's initiative: their representative

         will call on my name   13:9bα¹

       2) Yahweh's response: I will answer him   13:9bα²

      b. The two parties form their relationship   13:9bβ

       1) Yahweh owns them: I will say,

         "he is my people"   13:9bβ¹

       2) The people own Yahweh:

         their representative will say,

         "Yahweh is my God"   13:9bβ²

This brief oracle has two main parts. The first part (v. 7) is a rhetorical apostrophe, in which Yahweh addresses his sword and directs it against someone identified as a "shepherd," thus describing the way in which he will cause his people to suffer both a loss of leadership and the devastating consequences. The second part (vv. 8-9) is a narrative in which Yahweh describes how this crisis will eventually have a positive effect on his people's relationship with him.

The image of Yahweh as a warrior wielding a sword is generally used to symbolize the realization of his purpose through some human military force. The rhetorical device of the apostrophe emphasizes that the human military force, symbolized by the sword, is activated by the direct command of Yahweh. Various forms of the same verbal root ('wr), from which the command to "awake" (so RSV) or "be roused" derives, can be used to describe both a human warrior's action with a weapon in battle (e.g., 2 Sam 23:18; cf. Zech 9:13) and Yahweh's acting by human military means (e.g., Isa 13:17; Jer 50:9; Joel 4:7 [RSV 3:7]). As the command for the sword to "strike the shepherd" is paired with Yahweh's description of his own hand's negative impact on the less powerful, the military force represented by the sword is even more overtly identified in terms of divine instrumentality.

The overall mode of description in v. 7 thus emphasizes Yahweh's direct responsibility not only for the demise of the leader himself but also for the devastating effect of this loss on the rest of the community. The objects of Yahweh's action are, moreover, characterized so as to suggest that his militancy toward them is somewhat surprising. Yahweh intends to eliminate a leader whom he calls not just a shepherd but "*my* shepherd" (*rō'î*) and also "the man closely associated with me" (*geber 'ămîtî;* RSV "the man who stands next to me"). Yahweh thus seems to be turning against someone who formerly enjoyed his approval and confidence, or someone who appeared to do so. This leader enjoyed an at least pro forma designation as Yahweh's chosen ruler.

The fate of the people is described in two phases. First they are described as a single group (i.e., "the flock" [*haṣṣō'n*]; RSV "the sheep") whose cohesiveness will be destroyed by Yahweh's depriving them of their leader; and then they are described as a multiplicity of individuals left defenseless (*hṣ'rym;* RSV "the little ones"), whose vulnerability Yahweh will exploit. Such terms are generally used to indicate a relationship of dependency on Yahweh, through which he exercises his care for his people; but here they indicate a dependency of which Yahweh appears to take advantage. Descriptive categories that usually connote Yahweh's favor toward people are thus turned inside out to express his disfavor. This reversal has the same kind of rhetorical force as the observation supposedly made by St. Theresa, that if this is the way God treats his friends, no wonder he has so few of them.

Such an observation admits that a relationship with God is often antagonistic, but it also implies that this antagonism can eventually be somehow constructive and even beneficial. A similar rhetorical strategy becomes evident in vv. 8-9 as Yahweh's action is further described in terms of a process of elimination that leaves one-third of his people to be refined through a trial by fire. It will be costly for Yahweh's people to undergo such purification, but in the end their relationship with him will be renewed with integrity by mutual consent. The replacement of the "shepherd" by another leader is not explicitly described, but the relationship between Yahweh and the survivors is renewed through the intermediation of an unnamed representative who personifies them and acts on their behalf (Petersen, *Zechariah 9–14,* 132).

Genre

Although this oracle largely describes Yahweh's action against his own people, he does not take this course in response to their wrongdoing or infidelity. They are not accused of anything that would warrant such a reaction on his part, either explicitly or implicitly. This is therefore not a (→) prophecy of punishment. The two-part form first identifies an impending disaster as the work of Yahweh (v. 7) and then recategorizes it more specifically as Yahweh's means of purifying and restoring the covenant (vv. 8-9). It is claimed that Yahweh's admittedly harsh treatment of his own people is ultimately intended for their own good. This text is thus basically a PROPHECY OF SALVATION (cf. R. L. Smith, 283), although in terms of material content it strains this generic classification to the breaking point.

Setting

This unit reflects an impending crisis that threatens to leave Yahweh's people decimated and without their designated leadership, but which nevertheless opens up a rather favorable prospect for them in the long run. As a prophecy of salvation it might have been addressed directly to a particular audience in some public place, to alert them to the significance of things currently happening (e.g., Jer 28:2-4); or it might have been received privately by a prophet, to become part of a message that he could communicate in less direct ways (e.g., Jer 33:10-11). In view of how this passage redactionally connects 9:1–11:17 with 12:1–14:21, by recapitulating the motif of the sword-struck shepherd with which 11:15-17 concludes (→ Book as a Whole, Setting), it is possible that 13:7-9 came to serve this literary purpose without ever having existed independently as a prophetic speech.

This unit casts its description in only the most stereotypical terms that could conceivably apply to any of the various social contexts in which Israel or Judah existed during any period of biblical history. Yahweh's sword is usually the symbol of an outside force, but it can also connote the use of force against any insiders who might be characterized as Yahweh's enemies (e.g., "the wicked" in Ps 17:13). There is thus not even any clear indication of whether the threat to the "shepherd" comes from the external attack of enemies, as part of the conflict described in the preceding unit (→ 12:1–13:6), or whether it comes from internal rebellion.

One can say little more about the social or historical situation of this text as long as it is considered in isolation from its overall literary context. The question of its setting can be further addressed only in the process of determining the setting of this entire section of the book in view of how 13:7-9 functions in relation to (→) 12:1–14:21 as a whole (notwithstanding such speculations as those of Cook).

Intention

The impending crisis, caused by Yahweh's removal of the established leadership, will create a remnant that he will test severely in order to reform and restore his covenant with his people.

Bibliography

S. L. Cook, "The Metamorphosis of a Shepherd: The Tradition History of Zechariah 11:17 + 13:7-9," *CBQ* 55 (1993) 453-66.

YAHWEH WILL ONE DAY MAKE JERUSALEM THE CENTER OF A NEW WORLD ORDER RULED DIRECTLY BY HIM, 14:1-21: PART I, 14:1-7

Since 14:1-21 is a relatively long and complex unit, it will be discussed in two parts for the sake of convenience. Zech 14:1-7 will be discussed here, and 14:8-21 will be discussed separately below. This separation should not obscure the fact that these pericopes together comprise a larger entity.

Text

In v. 5aα the *RSV* is based on an emendation of *wĕnastem* ("and you shall flee") to *wĕnistam* ("and it shall be stopped up"), but there is no basis for abandoning the MT here, and to do so obscures the way in which repetition is rhetorically functional in this passage (→ 14:1-21, Part II, Structure). The MT should thus be retained, reading "you shall flee (by) the valley." In v. 5bβ there is ample support in both Masoretic mss. and ancient versions for the *RSV* to favor "with him" *('immô)* over the predominant Masoretic reading "with you" *('immāk).* In view of the way v. 5b forms a counterpart to v. 1 in the overall structure of 14:1-5 (→ Structure), however, the latter is nevertheless preferable for stylistic reasons, so that this subunit begins and ends with the same kind of feminine singular direct address (Meyers and Meyers, *Zechariah 9–14,* 430-31).

There is undoubtedly some textual confusion in v. 6b, but since the versions afford so little help, it is best to stay with the MT as far as possible. When v. 6 is seen to describe not the new order of creation itself but the transition from the old order to the new (→ Structure), the MT becomes far less problematic than is often supposed. The statement *lō' yihyeh 'ôr* ("there will be no light") in v. 6bα can be seen not as a statement that contradicts v. 7 by saying that darkness will reign, but as a description of how the very basis for the old order's distinction between day and night will cease. With only slight emendation in v. 6bβ, changing the initial *yod* of both *yqrwt* and *yqp'wn* to a *waw* (according to the *Qere* for the latter word), this phrase can be seen to describe a similar state of affairs with respect to the seasons. V. 6b thus reads: "there shall not be any light, nor any cold or frost." Just as the lack of light destroys the difference between light and dark, thus obviating the basis for any diurnal distinction between day and night, the lack of cold and frost similarly destroys differences in temperature and precipitation, thus obviating the basis for any seasonal distinction between summer and winter.

Structure

I. The day of Yahweh's coming is the day of Jerusalem's
   rescue from their coming defeat   14:1-5
  A. Jerusalem will be defeated   14:1-2
    1. Summary introduction: addressed to Jerusalem   14:1
      a. Announcement: Yahweh has a day that is coming   14:1a
      b. Implication for Jerusalem: your spoil will be
         divided in your midst   14:1b
    2. Elaborating narration   14:2
      a. Yahweh's action: I will gather all the nations
         against Jerusalem for battle   14:2aα
      b. Result of Yahweh's action   14:2aβb
        1) Description of general situation: the city
           will be taken   14:2aβ^1
        2) Description of specific details   14:2aβ^{2}b
          a) Buildings: houses will be plundered
          b) People
            (1) Women in particular:
               they will be ravished
            (2) Population in general   14:2b
              (a) Half will go into exile   14:2bα
              (b) Half will not be cut off   14:2bβ
  B. Yahweh will come   14:3-5
    1. Elaborating narration continued   14:3-5a
      a. Yahweh's action on that day of battle   14:3-4aα
        1) He will go forth to fight the nations   14:3
        2) His feet will stand on the Mount of Olives   14:4aα
      b. Result of Yahweh's action   14:4aβ-5a
        1) With respect to the site   14:4aβb
          a) The Mount of Olives will be split in
            two by a great valley running east-west   14:4aβ
          b) The two parts of the Mount of Olives
            will be displaced, one to the north
            and the other to the south   14:4b
        2) With respect to the remaining people:
          direct address   14:5a
         a) Initial description: you will flee
            by the valley . . .   14:5aα

Several scholars have found the integrity of ch. 14 to be superficial and have therefore attempted to distinguish various glosses and subsequent additions from a supposedly original version of this chapter, or to identify the various once independent oracles out of which it was supposedly pieced together (e.g., Elliger, 177-79; Horst, 249-52; Plöger, 89-91). As Lutz has shown, the themes and imagery of this part of Zechariah do indeed have various parallels and traditional antecedents. These may well indicate that this text is representative of a particular tradition, but they do not necessarily indicate that this text itself went through stages of traditio-historical development. Textual elements deemed extraneous in the various reconstructions of their supposedly original forms seem less so when one begins with the final form of the text.

Petersen rejects any continuity of narrative action between vv. 1-3 and vv. 4-5 (pp. 140-43). This seems to overestimate the individuating effect of the future time formula ("on that day") that recurs throughout this section. Vv. 4-5 are indeed distinguished from vv. 1-3 by this formula, and are thus divided into two episodes, but they are nevertheless interrelated. This interrelationship is shown by the fact that the formula in v. 4a modifies a verb with an ambiguous third person masculine singular pronominal subject. Without the antecedent announcement of Yahweh's coming day in v. 1a, readers of vv. 4-5 would not know what day "that day" refers to, nor would they know who would stand on the Mount of Olives. Similarly, without the theophanic description of Yahweh's intervention in vv. 4-5, readers of vv. 1-3 would never get beyond the general description of Yahweh's "fighting against the nations" to any specific description of what this would entail. This example indicates the way in which the various subunits of ch. 14 are generally related to each other in a narrative progression (as Petersen himself seems finally to admit [*Zechariah 9–14*, 160-61; cf. Lacocque, 204; Alonso Schökel and Sicre Diaz, 1195; Butterworth, 222-34]).

Zech 14:1-21 begins with an announcement of the coming day of Yahweh (v. 1a), from which a narrative description of "that day" unfolds in four episodes: 14:1-5, 14:6-7, 14:8-12, and 14:13-21 (→ 12:1–14:21, Structure). The first of these episodes (14:1-5) concerns primarily the fate of the inhabitants of Jerusalem "on that day" and is addressed directly to them. It begins and ends with second person feminine singular forms (vv. 1b, 5bβ; → Text), indicating the commonplace personification of the city as a feminine character. These feminine singular direct address forms are complemented by second person plural forms in v. 5, referring to the inhabitants of the city collectively. The remaining episodes (14:6-21) put what will happen to Jerusalem in the larger context of Yahweh's re-creation of heaven and earth. As the narrative description broadens its scope to encompass the effects of Yahweh's action on the entire cosmos, there is a corresponding shift in rhetorical stance to encompass a broader audience. The second person direct address in 14:1-5, which singles out Jerusalem's inhabitants, gives way at 14:6 to the more inclusive and less specific third person narration, which continues all the way to 14:21.

In the opening episode (14:1-5) the coming day of Yahweh is first of all identified as a time when Jerusalem will be despoiled (v. 1b). As the story unfolds, this day is further described as part of a larger course of events that Yahweh will set in motion. He will gather all the nations into a vast coalition, so that they will attack and destroy the city, taking one half of its survivors into exile but leaving the other half destitute (v. 2). This crisis will provide Yahweh with an occasion to intervene directly, attacking the nations (v. 3) and defending the remainder of his people (vv. 4-5). Yahweh's intervention is described in terms of an upheaval emanating from the Mount of Olives toward the four points of the compass. As he takes his stand on the mountain, it splits in two. A valley then appears, running from the east to the west, as one half of the mountain moves to the north and the other half to the south (v. 4). The valley provides the surviving population of Jerusalem with a way of escape (v. 5aα) through which they will flee as the inhabitants of Jerusalem once fled the similar upheaval of an earthquake centuries ago, "in the days of Uzziah, king of Judah" (v. 5aβ). As they leave the site of Jerusalem, Yahweh and all his protecting heavenly host will come with them (v. 5b; → Text; cf. Exod 13:21; Deut 33:2).

The geographical details are an important part of the description in vv. 4-5. In v. 4aα² the Mount of Olives is situated with two phrases. The first, 'al-pěnê yěrûšālaim, describes its spatial situation, indicating that the Mount of Olives is located "before Jerusalem" or "in front of Jerusalem." The second, miqqedem, can describe either a spatial or a temporal situation, thus ambiguously indicating not only that the Mount of Olives is located "on the east" of Jerusalem (so RSV; cf. Gen 2:8; 12:8), but also that this position was its location "formerly" (cf. Isa 46:10; Mic 5:1 [RSV 2]; Ps 77:12 [RSV 11]). This ambiguity insinuates that the location of the Mount of Olives in relation to Jerusalem may be somewhat provisional. The immediately following description of the upheaval, in which the Mount of Olives is split and its two halves then displaced, is thus briefly foreshadowed in a way that also suggests that this cleavage may portend an even more drastic reshaping of the earth yet to come (i.e., in 14:10).

Verse 5aα is obscure, perhaps because the text is disturbed (for details see F. M. Abel, "Asal dans Zacharie XIV 5," RB 45 [1936] 387-92), but in any case it associates the people's path of escape with mountainous terrain. In terms of this passage's geographical frame of reference, v. 5aα thus indicates that their route leads them to the north (note that north is designated in v. 4b not just by ṣāpônâ but by hāhār ṣāpônâ, lit. "toward Mount Zaphon" [RSV "northward"]), in which case they would initially head eastward through the newly created valley to reach this destination, in contrast with a route that would take them either westward through the valley toward the sea (note yāmmâ, lit. "seaward" [RSV "to west"], in v. 4aβ) or southward toward the Negev (note negbâ [RSV "south"] in v. 4b).

Jerusalem's survivors are thus to flee over a landscape loaded with both mythic and historical connotations as they recapitulate two typological patterns. In heading for the hills they are running the risk of a direct confrontation with chaos, which typically breaks out through the mountains to the north. In Zechariah Babylon is identified as the archetypal enemy from the north (Zech 2:10 [RSV 6]; 6:8). In fleeing as they once fled from "the earthquake in the days of Uzziah" they are acknowledging that the present crisis resembles a great natural catastrophe from the past that came to be regarded as a portentous sign of Yahweh's "roaring from Zion" (Amos 1:1-2). This catastrophe, too, was a manifestation of Yahweh's "sword" (Amos 9:1a; cf. Zech 13:7), but one from which it was supposed to be impossible to "flee" (Amos 9:1b-4). Yahweh's intervention is thus ironically presented as a rescue from exile (Zech 14:2b) that is tantamount to a return to Babylon. It is an escape through the earthquake-split mountain, like the escape of their forebears from Egypt through the wind-split sea (→ 12:1–14:21,

Structure), but an exodus that will only (v. 5a) lead them to a closer encounter with chaos.

This irony suggests that the situation will have to get much worse before it gets any better, thus reinforcing the overall impression that at the end of the narrative's first episode much remains unresolved. First, in reaction to the nations' conquest of Jerusalem, Yahweh has begun to battle them (v. 3), but the outcome of this conflict has not been described. Second, Yahweh has caused a great earthly dislocation in one particular place, with ramifications that suggestively tend toward upsetting the four corners of the world (vv. 4-5), but it is not yet clear whether this dislocation portends any similar but more extensive upheaval affecting the rest of the earth. Finally, Yahweh has provided a way for the remainder of Jerusalem's population to flee the destruction (v. 5), but the difference between their destiny and the fate of their compatriots taken into exile seems not very great, and Yahweh has not indicated whether he ever intends anything better for them, such as returning to Jerusalem and resettling there. The resolution of these matters is the function of the narrative's subsequent episodes.

The second episode (14:6-7) begins to resolve the question of whether the splitting of the Mount of Olives portends anything greater in the same vein. The reshaping of the earth's terrain at one place (14:4) is but the prelude to Yahweh's redefinition of the whole order of creation, starting in the second episode with such fundamental temporal distinctions as day versus night and summer versus winter (14:6-7), and eventually including in the third episode the spatial reshaping of the earth's terrain everywhere (14:8-10a).

Verse 6b describes the disappearance of the elemental bases on which the old order marked time (→ Text). Without light, day can no longer be distinguished from night by the alternation of light and dark (v. 6bα); without cold and frost, summer can no longer be distinguished from winter by changes in temperature and precipitation. The old order thus comes to an end with a reversal of the first principles that were laid down "in the beginning" (Gen 1:1-5a) and ratified after the flood (Gen 8:22).

In Zech 14:7 a new creation emerges that is not defined in terms of such fundamental distinctions (Hanson, *Dawn,* 376-78), but that is nevertheless described paradoxically in terms of categories derived from them. The clause *wĕhāyâ yôm 'eḥād* has a double sense that is only partly conveyed by the *RSV* translation. The phrase *yôm 'eḥād* not only indicates that, in contrast with the old order's alternation of day and night, the new order will have something like "continuous day." It also reechoes the formulaic refrain with which the account of each day of creation concludes in Gen 1:1–2:4a, explicitly quoting from the conclusion to the account of the first day: "and there was morning, and there was evening, *one day*" (Gen 1:5b; note also the recurrence of the same word for "evening" [*'ereb*] in Zech 14:7b). The end of the old order's fundamental distinctions (v. 6) thus marks "day one" of the new creation (v. 7aα2), which has neither day nor night (v. 7aβ2) but is nevertheless paradoxically described in terms of "continuous day" (v. 7aα2). Similarly, although the new order has neither morning nor evening, it is paradoxically contrasted with the old order in terms of there being light "at evening time" (v. 7b).

The narrator's aside in v. 7aβ[1] suggests that the collapse of the old order's most fundamental temporal distinctions also entails the collapse of its most fundamental spatial distinction, i.e., the separation on "day two" of heaven from the area that eventually becomes the earth (Gen 1:6-8). The eternal light of "continuous day" is a condition with which Yahweh is familiar (for this sense of yd' in the niphal ["be known"] see Exod 21:36; Prov 14:33; 31:23; etc.) as it definitively characterizes the state of his dwelling in heaven (Pss 139:13 [*RSV* 12]; 76:5a [*RSV* 4a]; Ezek 1:26-28a; Dan 2:22; cf. Isa 60:19-20; Ps 104:2; Rev 22:5; 1 Tim 16:6; 1 John 1:5). In the new creation heaven and earth are thus in effect merged.

Genre

The whole of 14:1-21 is an extension of 14:1-5. The generic form of the entire unit is thus realized on the basis of the possibilities defined by 14:1-5. Jeremias includes 14:1-5 among the texts that he classifies as theophanies (pp. 23-24, 134; cf. Sæbø, 285-98), in which case 14:1-21 might be described as an extended theophany. This classification is problematic, however, because it is not clear from Jeremias's own definition whether a theophany is entitled to consideration as a distinct genre. He calls the theophany a *Gattung,* but he defines it in terms of formulaic themes and motifs that tend to cluster in the context of various compositional forms, without ever constituting an independent form of their own. Even the oldest and most original examples of the theophany are incorporated into victory songs (e.g., Judg 5:4-5). It would therefore be better to regard the theophany as a descriptive topos that can function in a variety of generic contexts, rather than as a genre in itself. 14:1-5 does indeed contain theophanic motifs, such as the shaking of the earth at the advent of Yahweh (cf. Pss 18:8 [*RSV* 7]; 68:8-9 [*RSV* 7-8]; Hab 3:6; etc.), but such a clustering of motifs does not in itself provide a sufficient basis for generic classification.

Hanson regards 14:1-21 as an apocalypse based on an adaptation of the conflict myth, in which hymnic description of Yahweh as the divine warrior plays a definitive part (*Dawn,* 369-83). The issue of whether all or part of 12:1–14:21 can appropriately be described as an apocalypse is discussed above (→ 12:1–14:21, Genre). Hanson's claim that 14:1-21 conforms to the pattern of the conflict myth in general, and to the pattern of the divine warrior hymn in particular, remains to be considered here with respect to the portion of 14:1-21 that is thus far under consideration (i.e., 14:1-7). He argues (1) that the nations' attack on Jerusalem in vv. 1-2 represents the threat of chaos, a basic element of the conflict myth pattern expressed atypically here in the adapted form of a "salvation-judgment oracle" (p. 371); (2) that the Mount of Olives is split in two (vv. 4-5) in order to form a "processional way" for the celebration of Yahweh's triumphant return to Jerusalem, reminiscent of the highway formed by the leveling of the earth in Isa 40:3-4, in accord with the pattern of the divine warrior hymn (pp. 374-76); and (3) that the new creation that begins to be described in Zech 14:6-7 represents both the peace *(šālôm)* that follows

Yahweh's victory, in accord with the same patterns, and the motif of revealed cosmic secrets that is characteristic of apocalyptic (pp. 376-81). Each of these points is questionable.

Motifs and themes derived from the conflict myth, and from its characterization of Yahweh as the divine warrior in victorious combat with chaos, are obviously evident here, as they are throughout much of 12:1–14:21. The question is whether they inform the compositional structure of the text in the way that Hanson supposes. The very status of the divine warrior hymn as a distinctive generic pattern is as dubious as the status of the theophany, and for precisely the same reasons. Hanson defines these patterns in terms of a cluster of formulaic elements, which have no independent existence as such (pp. 300-316). The same motifs and themes that appear here can also be found in compositions with a wide variety of rhetorical forms, some of which are quite different in their overall shape from the kind of narration that characterizes 14:1-21 (e.g., in vv. 12-17 of Ps 74, which is a complaint; in vv. 39-42 of Deut 32:1-43, which is a type of didactic poem; and in Ps 97, which is a hymn in the proper sense, with a call to praise in v. 12). The clustering of formulaic motifs and themes thus does not provide a sufficient basis, in and of itself, on which to define the divine warrior hymn as a distinct genre (→ Zech 9:1–11:17, Genre; 12:1–13:6, Part I, Genre; Hab 3:1-19, Genre).

Moreover, even if these descriptive elements were to form the kind of generic pattern envisioned by Hanson, the text of 14:1-7 does not actually conform to this pattern in the way that he claims. (1) In this case chaos is something that Yahweh wields, rather than something that he combats. Chaos is thus manifest not only in the attack of the nations caused by Yahweh (vv. 1-2), but also more pointedly in the measures that he subsequently takes to rescue part of his people from defeat (v. 5; → Structure). (2) The path through the valley created by the splitting of the Mount of Olives (v. 4) is hardly a "processional way" for the divine warrior's triumphant return to Jerusalem. In order to save that part of his defeated people who were not "cut off" (v. 2b), Yahweh fights (v. 3) and provides them with a way of escape (v. 5), but he does not yet win any victory. The path through the valley is thus rather the route through which the straggling survivors, accompanied by Yahweh and his hosts (v. 5b), leave Jerusalem in defeat. (3) The new creation that begins to be described in vv. 6-7 is thus not a result of victory already achieved, but a sign of Yahweh's intention to pursue it. Even the new creation remains conflicted (14:13-15). Finally, the narrator's aside in v. 7 serves not to identify the design of the new creation as secret knowledge imparted to the reader but to identify it with the heavenly reality already familiar to Yahweh (→ Structure). This text thus cannot be made to fit the Procrustean pattern of the conflict myth or the divine warrior hymn as described by Hanson, and its genre must therefore be defined on some other basis.

As in the case of (→) 12:1–13:6, Sæbø identifies 14:1-21 as a composition that is virtually sui generis (pp. 307-9), and Petersen identifies it as a "montage." Such proposals reflect the conclusion that the various subunits of this section are difficult to classify generically, and that the section itself is based only on the impressionistic juxtaposition of the generically unclassifiable subunits — although Petersen grants that there is more of a narrative progression in 14:1-21 than in 12:1–13:6 (*Zechariah 9–14*, 160-61). Generic conventions are evident, however.

When only the initial announcement (14:1) and the first two episodes of the elaborating narration (14:2-5, 6-7) are taken into account, the generic form of 14:1-21 remains ambiguous. Several possibilities emerge from the interplay of the basic elements in the first episode and from the way in which one of these elements is further developed in the second episode. 14:1-5 begins by announcing that Yahweh will bring all the nations together to attack Jerusalem. Such an announcement suggests a (→) prophecy of punishment, but since there is not the faintest indication that Yahweh is acting in response to any misdeeds on the part of his people, this classification would not be altogether apt. In bringing the nations to attack Jerusalem, Yahweh rather appears to be creating a pretext on the basis of which he can then turn and attack them. If the main theme of the narration turns out to be Yahweh's antipathy toward the nations attacking Jerusalem, 14:1-21 might be considered a (→) prophecy of punishment against a foreign nation, but thus far in the story it remains unclear whether this is indeed the main theme.

Such classification would be consistent with the way in which the upheaval on the Mount of Olives is described, as an action of Yahweh that both threatens Jerusalem's attackers and creates an escape route for the survivors not taken into exile, because prophecies of punishment against foreign nations typically describe the actions taken by Yahweh against the nations as conversely redounding to the advantage of his own people. If, however, the main purpose of this upheaval is Yahweh's deliverance of his own people, through a process of cosmic renewal that begins on the Mount of Olives (14:1-5) and extends to encompass the whole of creation (14:6-7), 14:1-21 might be better described as a (→) prophecy of salvation. Form-critical classification must acknowledge that 14:1-21 resembles all three of these genres in some respects, but it remains to be seen whether 14:1-21 belongs in the final analysis to any one of these generic categories, or to some other category (→ 14:1-21, Part II, Genre).

Setting

→ 14:1-21, Part II, Setting.

Intention

Zech 14:1-7 shows that 14:1-21 is addressed to the inhabitants of Jerusalem, asking them to consider the eventuality of their city's destruction by an army representing all the nations of the world. It induces them to imagine this eventuality in a particular way, and to act accordingly. First, the audience is to see the destruction of Jerusalem as part of Yahweh's larger purpose for them, and not simply as his handing them over to their foes. The goal of Yahweh's plan is thus far indefinite, but he clearly does not intend for Jerusalem's enemies to remain victorious. Moreover, the audience is to think of how they might act if they should find themselves among the survivors not taken into exile. They should be prepared to flee by whatever path is opened to them through these cataclysmic events because Yahweh and his heavenly host will protect them through the chaotic process by which the whole creation is being renewed. Their abandonment of the city will make it possible for them to have a radically new future as part of this process.

Bibliography

J. Jeremias, *Theophanie* (WMANT 10; Neukirchen-Vluyn: Neukirchener, 1965); H.-M. Lutz, *Jahwe, Jerusalem und die Völker* (WMANT 27; Neukirchen-Vluyn: Neukirchener, 1968).

YAHWEH WILL ONE DAY MAKE JERUSALEM THE CENTER OF A NEW WORLD ORDER RULED DIRECTLY BY HIM: PART II, 14:8-21

Since 14:1-21 is a relatively long and complex unit, it is being discussed in two parts for the sake of convenience. Zech 14:8-21 will be discussed here, and 14:1-7 had been discussed separately above. This separation should not obscure the fact that these pericopes together comprise a larger entity.

Text

However one deals with the text and translation of vv. 10b-11, the rhetorically significant threefold recurrence of the verb *yšb* should be neither eliminated by emendation nor lost altogether in translation. The *RSV* renders it "remain" in the first instance, "be inhabited" in the second, and "dwell" in the third. Each of these is an adequate rendering in and of itself, but this variation loses the effect of the repetition, which is to emphasize that Jerusalem's population will be restored through a process that is precisely the reverse of their previously having abandoned the city (→ Structure).

Structure

I. The day of Yahweh's coming is the day of Jerusalem's
rescue from their coming defeat 14:1-5
II. The day of Yahweh's coming marks the beginning of
a new creation 14:6-7
III. Jerusalem will become the center of Yahweh's reign
over the new world order 14:8-12

A. Both Jerusalem and Yahweh will assume central
positions   14:8-9
 1. Jerusalem's assumption of a topographically
 central position   14:8
   a. Introduction: and it will happen that . . . *(wĕhāyâ)*   14:8a
   b. Narration of what will happen
     1) Formulaic temporal indication: on that day
     2) Description
       a) With respect to cosmic space:
Jerusalem will become the source of
the world's life-giving water
       b) With respect to cosmic time: this will
continue during both summer and winter   14:8b
 2. Yahweh's assumption of a politically central position   14:9
   a. Introduction: and it will happen that . . .
(wĕhāyâ) $14:9a\alpha^1$
   b. Narration of what will happen $14:9a\alpha^2b$
     1) With respect to Yahweh's role: he will
become king over all the earth $14:9a\alpha^2\beta$
     2) With respect to Yahweh's attributes   14:9b
       a) Formulaic temporal indication:
on that day $14:9b\alpha^1$
       b) Description $14:9b\alpha^2\beta$
         (1) Attribution of uniqueness to
Yahweh's nature $14:9b\alpha^2\beta^1$
         (2) Attribution of uniqueness to
Yahweh's name $14:9b\beta^2$
B. Jerusalem's position will be secure:
narration continued   14:10-12
 1. Jerusalem's relative advantage over all the
 surrounding territory   14:10-11
   a. The nature of this advantage   14:10a
     1) The whole land will be leveled into a
plain from Geba to Rimmon on the south $14:10a\alpha$
     2) Jerusalem will be elevated $14:10a\beta$
   b. The consequences of this advantage   14:10b-11
     1) Jerusalem will dwell on her site   14:10b
       a) General statement $14:10b\alpha^1$
       b) Further specification: the site defined
in terms of landmarks $14:10b\alpha^2b$
     2) People will dwell in her and not be
threatened by the ban of destruction   14:11a
     3) Jerusalem will dwell in security   14:11b
 2. The plague with which Yahweh will protect
 Jerusalem from enemy attack   14:12
   a. Definitive introduction: this is the plague . . .   14:12a
   b. Definitive characteristics of the plague   14:12b

do not come to worship Yahweh in Jerusalem	14:17aα²-18
a) Described with respect to the families of the earth in general: there will be no rain on them	14:17aα²b
b) Described with respect to the families of Egypt in particular: they shall suffer the same fate	14:18
2) Summary conclusion: this will be a punishable sin both for Egypt and for all the nations . . .	14:19
C. Jerusalem and Judah will become the sanctuary of Yahweh open to all: narration continued	14:20-21
1. The domain of holiness will be redefined	14:20a
a. Formulaic temporal indication: on that day	14:20aα¹
b. Description: bells of the horses will bear the inscription, "holy to Yahweh"	14:20aα²β
2. The temple will be as the altar area	14:20b
a. Introduction: and it will happen that . . . (wĕhāyâ)	14:20bα¹
b. Narration of what will happen: the pots in Yahweh's house will be like bowls before the altar	14:20bα²β
3. Jerusalem and Judah will be as the temple	14:21
a. Introduction: and it will happen that . . . (wĕhāyâ)	14:21aα¹
b. Narration of what will happen	14:21aα²bβ¹
1) With respect to pots in Jerusalem and Judah (positively expressed)	14:21aα²β
a) Basic statement: everyone shall be holy to Yahweh	14:21aα²
b) Result clause: so that all who sacrifice may come and take from them and cook in them	14:21aβ
2) With respect to traders in Yahweh's house (negatively expressed): there will be none	14:21bαβ¹
c. Formulaic temporal indication: on that day	14:21bβ²

The third episode of the narration (14:8-12) continues the description of the new creation begun in the second episode (14:6-7), describing the place of Jerusalem in the new world order so as to resolve the question left dangling at the end of the first episode (14:1-5) regarding the fate of the survivors who escape (→ 14:1-21, Part I, Structure). Jerusalem will become the central point from which water wells up to quicken the earth (v. 8a; cf. Ezek 47:1-12), thus taking the place of Eden in the old order (Gen 2:10-14). The supply of water will not be threatened by any seasonal variations (v. 8b) — there are, after all, no more seasons (14:6) — thus indicating that the forces of natural chaos represented by the unruly waters will come under Yahweh's control. Yahweh will thus assume the role of king over all the earth (v. 9) and begin to use his power over nature to shape the history of this new world order. He will first secure a position of relative advantage for Jerusalem by leveling the terrain of all the earth, so that the site of the city will be elevated above its surroundings (v. 10a). Jerusalem will thus become the central point of reference with respect to the two most elemental aspects of earthly existence, water and land. Just as the streams of life-giving water flow out from the city along the east-west axis (v. 8a), the land drops off along the axis extending northward toward Geba and southward toward Rimmon (Meyers and Meyers, *Zechariah 9–14*, 442-43). Yahweh will then repopulate the city within well-defined bounds corresponding to its former walls (v. 10b; Meyers and Meyers, *Zechariah 9–14*, 444-47).

Thus protected, Jerusalem will never again have to face the threat of total destruction (v. 11a) and will therefore dwell in security (v. 11b). In contrast with the threefold recurrence of *nws* ("flee") in 14:5, emphasizing the survivors' departure from the ruined old Jerusalem, there is a threefold recurrence of *yšb* ("be inhabited") in vv. 10b-11 (→ Text), correspondingly emphasizing their return to repopulate the restored new Jerusalem. The threat of another enemy siege is not yet precluded, even in the new world order over which Yahweh reigns as sole king, but the inviolability of the new Jerusalem is assured by the plague with which Yahweh intends to afflict any peoples who would dare to attack (v. 12).

In the fourth and final episode of narration (14:13-21) Yahweh's conflict with the nations comes to a head. This conflict was begun under the conditions of the old order (14:3-4) and interrupted by Yahweh's efforts to create an escape for the survivors and to establish a new world in which they might dwell secure (14:5-12). It is now resumed and resolved under the conditions of the new order. Yahweh unleashes two forms of chaos on the enemy forces. First, a "great panic" will spread internal divisiveness so pervasively, contaminating the morale of every area but Jerusalem itself, that Judah will even become antagonistic toward Jerusalem (vv. 13-14a). Imbued with this panic, the nations will attack each other and defeat themselves collectively; and their material wealth can then be taken as spoil (v. 14b). Second, there will be an outbreak of a plague like the one that Yahweh was previously prepared to inflict on enemy soldiers (v. 12), disabling even their horses and beasts of burden (v. 15).

As a result of the nations' defeat, a new social order can emerge based on universal acknowledgment of Yahweh's kingship and corresponding closely to the new natural order already created. Just as the foregoing description of the new natural order continues to picture it paradoxically in terms of such fundamental distinctions as day versus night, even though it transcends these distinctions (→ 14:1-21, Part I, Structure), the new social order is also paradoxically described in terms of the national distinctions that it transcends. Egypt is singled out as one of Israel's archetypal foes, only to reaffirm that they are categorically in the very same position as the rest of the Gentiles (vv. 18-19). Just as the difference between day and night will be effaced by the heavenly reality of eternal light (14:7), the differences between the nations will be effaced by their common recognition of Yahweh's divine kingship over all the earth, expressed through their all worshiping him under the same name (14:9, 16). This common recognition is based on the reality of the ecological relationship between the two roles of Yahweh as head of both the natural order and the social order. As a consequence of any nation's not fulfilling the main obligation of the social order, they will suffer a breakdown in their relationship with the natural order: they will be cut off from the life-giving water (14:8), i.e., they will receive no rain (14:17).

For the Jews of postexilic times the Feast of Booths was a preeminent affirmation of their identity as Yahweh's covenant people (Neh 8:13-18), and the inclusion of the nations in the celebration of this pilgrimage festival thus implies that the fundamental distinction between Yahweh's people and all others will in effect also be — like the other fundamental distinctions of the old order — effaced (Harrelson, 91-95). Each of the nations is described as a "family" (mišpĕḥâ), implying that they all belong to a single community. This does not mean, however, that in the new world order Yahweh's people will no longer have any distinctive part to play. They will have a function in relation to the community of nations, analogous to the function of their priests in the old order.

The new role played by Yahweh's people becomes apparent as the new order, in further contrast with the old, is described in terms of a redefined realm of holiness (14:20-21). The distinction between sacred and profane is not altogether transcended, but rather restructured in such a way that it can no longer serve as a basis for establishing or reinforcing any invidious distinction between the people of Yahweh and the Gentiles (cf. Harrelson, 93-96). This restructuring is initially indicated by a reversal in the status of horses. They have previously been characterized as part of the enemy forces, and hence as objects of the plague with which Yahweh will strike his people's foes (14:15). Now, however, they are described as wearing some distinctive sort of livery (harness bells?), which contrastingly puts them within the purview of Yahweh's holiness (14:20a). In other words, the new world order will finally entail a radical change in the status of the nations vis-à-vis the holiness of Yahweh, which extends to encompass even their domestic animals. The severity of Yahweh's punishment of the nations was previously described in terms of its including even those domestic creatures on the border between human society and the rest of the natural order (14:15), and his efforts to bring them into a formal relationship with him are now seen as equally far-reaching (14:20a).

This change in the domain of holiness is described in terms of shifts in three rather broadly defined concentric spatial categories. First, there is the central area immediately around the altar, where sacrifices and other related rituals are performed under the direction of the priests. Second, there is the area that lies outside this inner sanctum but remains within the temple precincts, where the foods involved in various kinds of sacrifices and offerings are cooked and consumed by priests and people. Third, there is the area that lies completely outside the temple precincts but also stands in relationship to it. Worshipers periodically come from this third area to enter the second area within the temple precincts, where they can encounter the holiness of Yahweh by consuming the foods from the rituals performed in the first area around the altar. They then leave the second area and return to the third, to realize within the profane realm of ongoing everyday life the implications of their having encountered the holy within the temple precincts.

According to the old order, the first two areas were enclosed within the temple precincts of Jerusalem so that the third area included the rest of the city and the surrounding territory of Judah. The other nations further afield were not included at all, and in principle they lay outside the sphere of Yahweh's holiness altogether. According to the new order, however, each category will be broadened to include the area that formerly lay on its outer perimeter, so that the third area will be extended to include all nations. The area around the altar and the area within the temple precincts will thus be combined within the category that formerly included only the area around the altar, so that "the pots in the house of Yahweh will be as the bowls before the altar" (14:20a). The rest of Jerusalem and the surrounding territory of Judah will then fall within the category formerly occupied by the temple precincts, as the area where the food from sacrifices and offerings can be cooked and consumed (14:21a). This change would leave the other nations in the category formerly occupied by Jerusalem and Judah, as the area from which worshipers would come, and to which they would subsequently return (14:16-17). The new status to be assumed by Jerusalem and Judah, as the sacred precincts of the new order, implies that all the inhabitants of Jerusalem and Judah will assume a role analogous to the role played by the priests in the old order. They will mediate Yahweh's holiness to the nations, just as the priests formerly mediated Yahweh's holiness to them (cf. Exod 19:6a).

The final statement describing the new world order, that "there will no longer be a trader *(kĕna'ănî)* in the house of Yahweh" (14:21b), is significant in light of both the implied displacement of the priestly role and the previous references to *kĕna'ănîm* (*RSV* "traffickers") in 11:7a and 11:11 (LXX). When Yahweh himself is king of all the earth (14:9), when he is recognized as such by all the nations (14:16), and when holiness is restructured so that his people collectively assume the priestly role (14:20-21a), the temple will no longer provide any institutional power base for the kind of "traffickers" that can exploit the international situation at the expense of Yahweh's people (→ 11:4-17). The statement in 14:21b may also play on the other meaning that the term *kĕna'ănî* can have, i.e., "Canaanite." From a postexilic viewpoint the Canaanites were archetypal foreigners in relation to Israel (Meyers and Meyers, *Zechariah 9–14*, 489-92). As this old distinction is transcended and yet paradoxically also redefined in the new world order, none of the people who come into the temple from outside Jerusalem and Judah will be a foreigner or "Canaanite" as such. The temple will no longer serve as a basis for making such invidious distinctions (cf. Isa 56:3-8).

Genre

The various generic possibilities that appear in the first two episodes of the narrative in 14:1-21 (→ 14:1-21, Part I, Genre) are finally resolved here in its last two episodes. It becomes evident that Yahweh does not bring the nations to attack Jerusalem because of any particular misdeed on the part of his own people, and likewise that he does not then turn against the nations because they overplay the aggressive role that he has assigned them. This is thus not a (→) prophecy of punishment directed against either Yahweh's people or the other nations.

In bringing the nations to defeat Jerusalem, and then bringing the nations in turn to suffer defeat, Yahweh is creating the kind of situation in which the old world order will self-destruct. His ultimate purpose is to establish a new world order, in which such conflict is not endemic. His main motivation is to provide for his own people the kind of social identity that no longer threatens to dissolve, in the kind of world that no longer consigns them to an inevitably disadvantaged position. He does not mean to secure the place of his own people at the expense of the other nations, however. The birth of the new world order will require suffering on their part, but no more than it requires from Yahweh's own people. Yahweh's people will assume a more central role but not a superior role, as Yahweh himself rules directly over all alike (14:9). The other nations' participation in the new world order will be enforced (14:17-19), but the obligations it imposes on them are hardly oppressive (14:16). Thus the new world order will also be more beneficial for them in the long run.

In the final analysis 14:1-21 is a PROPHECY OF SALVATION. Westermann relegates 14:1-21 in large part to a subcategory of this genre, which he defines as describing Yahweh's deliverance of his own people through the destruction of the other nations (pp. 195-96, 211-12). Such categorization, however, does not do justice to 14:1-21 on the whole, which instead describes Yahweh's deliverance of his own people in a way that costs both them and the nations great suffering but in the end also benefits both. This is a prophecy of salvation for the nations as well as for the people of Yahweh.

Setting

Prophecies of salvation were typically designed for address to a live audience, whether in private to individuals concerning their own fate (e.g., Jer 34:4-6) or in public to representatives of the people concerning their common fate (e.g., Isa 7:7-9; Jer 28:2-4). Signs of such direct address are evident in the second person pronouns and verbs of 14:1-5 (→ 14:1-21, Part I, Structure). The narration in 14:6-21 is a continuation of the story begun in 14:1-5, and thus the whole chapter is, in effect, directly addressed to the inhabitants of Jerusalem. Since it observes the conventions of the prophecy of salvation as a form of prophetic speech, 14:1-21 could conceivably have been addressed to a live audience on some public occasion. Since it also describes Yahweh's acts of deliverance in largely eschatological terms, however, it is difficult to gain any specific information from the text itself regarding the particular historical events that might have occasioned it.

It is also possible that 14:1-21 might never have existed as an independent prophetic speech, and that it was instead composed as the conclusion to this section of the book. This possibility is suggested by the close correspondence between Yahweh's acts of deliverance in his new creation (as described here in 14:1-21) and his attempts to deliver his people under the conditions of the old world order (as described in 12:1–13:6). The same possibility is also suggested by the way in which the design of this new creation removes precisely those aspects of the old world order that limited what Yahweh could do for his people under its aegis. If 14:1-21 was composed for this purpose, the form of the prophecy of salvation and the attendant convention of direct address would both have been apt elements from which to form a *maśśā'* (→ 12:1–14:21, Genre).

Intention

This latter portion of 14:1-21 continues to guide the imagination of its audience, the people of Jerusalem, as they think through the implications of the destruction with which they are presently threatened. It moves them from entertaining the general possibility that a new world might emerge out of this crisis to considering the specific form that this new world might take, and from envisioning the primary changes in the natural order to outlining the secondary changes in the social order (→ 14:1-21, Part I).

Yahweh's characteristic mode of action is to create the fundamental natural and social conditions that make radical historical change possible, thus implying that the realization of this new world will require the audience to act on Yahweh's initiative, although there is no explicit exhortation to this effect. Otherwise the kind of suffering and destruction described here could hardly be creative. If they would like to move beyond the insecurity and abuse that have come to be their lot, as a result of the international conflict inherent in the old order, they should therefore imagine the impending crisis in terms of the old order's death throes, and should seize any opportunities the crisis affords to reestablish Jerusalem and Judah as a kind of priestly people within the community of nations, living continually on earth in the direct light of Yahweh's heavenly kingship.

Bibliography

W. Harrelson, "The Celebration of the Feast of Booths according to Zech xiv 16-21," in *Religions in Antiquity: Essays in Memory of E. R. Goodenough* (ed. J. Neusner; Studies in the History of Religions [Supplements to *Numen*] 14; Leiden: Brill, 1968) 88-96; C. Westermann, Prophetic Oracles of Salvation in the Old Testament (tr. K. Crim; Louisville, Ky.: Westminster/ John Knox, 1991).

MALACHI

Bibliography

E. Achtemeier, *Nahum–Malachi* (IntCom; Atlanta: John Knox, 1986); L. Alonso Schökel and J. L. Sicre Diaz, *Profetas: Comentario,* vol. 2 (NBE; Madrid: Cristiandad, 1980); S. Amsler, "Malachie," in Amsler, R. Vuilleumier, and A. Lacocque, *Aggée, Zacharie 1–8, Zacharie 9–14, Malachie* (CAT 11c; Neuchâtel: Delachaux & Niestlé, 1981); J. G. Baldwin, *Haggai, Zechariah, Malachi* (TOTC; London: Tyndale, 1972); R. D. Blake, "The Rhetoric of Malachi" (Diss., Union Theological Seminary [New York], 1988); H. J. Boecker, "Bemerkungen zur formgeschichtlichen Terminologie des Buches Maleachi," *ZAW* 78 (1966) 78-80; J. J. Collins, "The Message of Malachi," *TBT* 22 (1984) 209-15; K. Elliger, *Das Buch der zwölf Kleinen Propheten,* vol. 2 (3rd ed.; ATD 25/2; Göttingen: Vandenhoeck & Ruprecht, 1956); J. Fischer, "Notes on the Literary Form and Message of Malachi," *CBQ* 34 (1972) 315-20; B. Glazier-McDonald, *Malachi: The Divine Messenger* (SBLDS 98; Atlanta: Scholars Press, 1987); F. Horst, "Maleachi," in T. H. Robinson and Horst, *Die Zwölf Kleinen Propheten* (2nd ed.; HAT 14; Tübingen: Mohr [Siebeck], 1954); M. Krieg, *Mutmassüngen über Maleachi* (ATANT 80; Zurich: Theologischer Verlag, 1993); T. Lescow, *Das Buch Maleachi* (AzT 75; Stuttgart: Calwer, 1993); idem, "Dialogische Strukturen in den Streitreden des Buches Maleachi," *ZAW* 102 (1990) 194-212; S. L. McKenzie and H. N. Wallace, "Covenant Themes in Malachi," *CBQ* 45 (1983) 549-63; R. Mason, *The Books of Haggai, Zechariah, and Malachi* (CBC; Cambridge: Cambridge University Press, 1977); J. M. O'Brien, *Priest and Levite in Malachi* (SBLDS 121; Atlanta: Scholars Press, 1990); D. L. Petersen, *Zechariah 9–14 and Malachi* (OTL; Louisville: Westminster/John Knox, 1995); E. Pfeiffer, "Die Disputationsworte im Buche Maleachi," *EvT* 19 (1959) 546-68; P. L. Redditt, *Haggai, Zechariah, Malachi* (NCB; Grand Rapids: Eerdmans, 1995); A. Renker, *Die Tora bei Maleachi* (FThSt 112; Freiburg: Herder, 1979); H. Graf Reventlow, *Die Propheten Haggai, Sacharja, und Maleachi* (ATD 25/2; Göttingen: Vandenhoeck & Ruprecht, 1993); W. Rudolph, *Haggai, Sacharja 1–8, Sacharja 9–14, Maleachi* (KAT 13,4; Gütersloh: Mohn, 1976); E. M. Schuller, "The Book of Malachi," *NIB* 7:843-77; J. M. P. Smith, "Malachi," in H. G. Mitchell, Smith, and J. A. Bewer, *A Critical and Exegetical Commentary on*

Haggai, Zechariah, Malachi and Jonah (ICC; Edinburgh, T. & T. Clark, 1912); R. L. Smith, *Micah–Malachi* (WBC 32; Waco: Word, 1984); P. A. Verhoef, *Haggai and Malachi* (NICOT; Grand Rapids: Eerdmans, 1987); G. Wallis, "Wesen und Struktur der Botschaft Maleachis," in *Das ferne und nahe Wort* (*Fest.* L. Rost; ed. F. Maass; BZAW 105; Berlin: Töpelmann, 1967) 229-37; E. Wendland, "Linear and Concentric Patterns in Malachi," *BT* 36 (1985) 108-21.

Chapter 1

THE BOOK AS A WHOLE

Structure

I. Superscription   1:1
II. Main body   1:2–3:24 (*RSV* 1:2–4:6)
  A. Introduction   1:2-5
  B. Exhortation   1:6–3:24
    1. Prophetic questioning regarding various
       aspects of cultic corruption   1:6–2:16
      a. Questioning of the priests with regard to . . .   1:6–2:9
        1) Their deficient administration of
           sacrificial offerings   1:6-14
        2) Their deficient instruction   2:1-9
      b. Questioning of the people with regard to . . .   2:10-16
        1) The marriage of husbands to wives who
           serve foreign gods   2:10-12
        2) The unfaithfulness of husbands that
           threatens established marriages   2:13-16
    2. How such ways began to be changed   2:17–3:24
      a. Call to turn from speaking against Yahweh
        to serving him rightly   2:17–3:12
        1) Accusation: you speak words that
           trouble Yahweh   2:17
        2) Call to respond to the manifestation of
           Yahweh's justice   3:1-12
      b. Report of a positive response to Yahweh's call   3:13-24
        1) Accusation: you speak words that
           oppose Yahweh   3:13-15
        2) Report proper   3:16
          a) Interaction between Yahweh and those
            who fear him   3:16abα

b) Result of this interaction: a book of
remembrance was written . . .   3:16bβ
3) Speech of Yahweh explicating these
developments   3:17-24
a) Those who fear him will fare well,
in contrast with evildoers, on the day
when he acts   3:17-21
b) The law of Moses is to be remembered,
as Elijah comes to reconcile parents
and children in preparation for that day   3:22-24

With respect to the literary form of Malachi three main issues need to be resolved. The first issue is Malachi's relation to the preceding material in the Book of the Twelve. There are various theories of interdependence between Malachi and the last two sections of Zechariah (e.g., Rudolph, 218-19; Mason, 139; Petersen, 2-3), or of interdependence between Malachi, Haggai, and Zechariah (e.g., Pierce; Krieg, 229-44), which would in effect deny Malachi the status of an independent book. If this is the case, Malachi should not be treated separately but as part of Zechariah.

The second issue is whether Malachi's distinctive assertion plus question-and-answer style is the definitive factor in the book's overall organization. Building on the observations of earlier scholars regarding the centrality of this stylistic trait, Pfeiffer divided the main body of Malachi into a series of six units, each of which is defined primarily in terms of the assertion plus question-and-answer format (1:2-5; 1:6–2:9; 2:10-16; 2:17–3:5; 3:6-12; and 3:13-21 [*RSV* 3:13–4:3]). On the basis of this common factor Pfeiffer also identified them all as examples of the same genre, the (→) prophetic disputation. Pfeiffer's work has been tremendously influential, not only in the sense that many scholars still agree with him, but also in the sense that his initial premise remains accepted even by those who disagree with his conclusions. Various scholars have subsequently quibbled with Pfeiffer's classification of these units as disputations, but nearly all have continued to assume that the main body of Malachi is a series of six units, each of which is defined primarily in terms of the same assertion plus question-and-answer format, and all of which therefore belong to one and the same genre. This set of assumptions, however, has led to a scholarly impasse that now calls them into question (see below).

Third, there is the issue of how 3:22 (*RSV* 4:4) and 3:23-24 (*RSV* 4:5-6) relate to the rest of the book. It is frequently claimed that these verses are appendices, added either as an afterthought to Malachi itself (e.g., J. M. P. Smith, 81-82; Petersen, 227-28), or as a conclusion to the Book of the Twelve (e.g., Nogalski, 209-10; Bosshard and Kratz, 39-45), or as a conclusion to the entire prophetic section of the canon (e.g., Rudolph, 290-93; Lescow, *Buch Maleachi*, 168-74). Two arguments are generally adduced in support of such claims. Following Pfeiffer, many allege that 3:22 and 3:23-24 differ in form from the preceding parts of the book. The preceding parts are all supposed to be of the same genre (such as the disputation) because they share the assertion plus question-and-answer format, while 3:22 and 3:23-24 are assumed to be of a different genre because they do not share this same format. Also, it is often alleged that 3:22 and 3:23-24 differ in content from the rest of the book, as they introduce terminology and themes that have only the most superficial antecedents in the foregoing text and are thus better explained as additions from a later time (e.g., Mason, 159-61; R. L. Smith, 340; Reventlow, 160-61).

The formal aspect of this third issue is greatly affected by the resolution of the second issue. If the main body of Malachi does not consist of six units that are all based on the assertion plus question-and-answer format and hence all of the same genre, the status of 3:22-24 becomes an open question. Depending on how the structure analysis of the main body is reconfigured, 3:22-24 may no longer appear to consist of appendices but may instead be seen as an integral part of the book's final unit.

With regard to the first of these three main issues, various theories are now being developed about the nature of the Book of the Twelve as a literary entity. These theories often link Malachi with Zechariah (Nogalski, 210-12), or with Haggai and Zechariah (e.g., Pierce; House, 96-108; Lescow, *Buch Maleachi*, 159-62), into a block of material whose growth figures prominently in the redactional process through which the Book of the Twelve was composed. It is reasonable to suppose that the Book of the Twelve is not just a random collection of prophetic books, and that some rhyme or reason underlies its overall organization. The attempts that have thus far been made to discover its organizing principles are still inconclusive, however, and some of the preliminary conclusions are highly dubious.

As an example of what is often wrong with a holistic approach to the Book of the Twelve in general, and to Haggai through Malachi in particular, one may cite the conclusions drawn from the fact that Malachi's superscription (1:1) includes the same technical term *(maśśā')* as the superscriptions of the last two sections of Zechariah (Zech 9:1aα[1]; 12:1). From this phenomenon some have deduced that there must be some interdependence between Malachi and either or both of these sections of Zechariah (→ Mal 1:1), but this is not necessarily the case if this term is not used in quite the same way in all three instances. What if Malachi has a superscription that is not of the same sort as Zech 9:1aα[1] and 12:1, and what if Malachi is thus not a *maśśā'* in the same sense as Zech 9–11 and 12–14?

The present investigation has found (→) Zechariah to be a prophetic book that is fundamentally different in kind from Malachi, which makes Malachi not so readily comparable with it in part or on the whole, even with respect to their use of the same technical term for revelation. Zechariah is a prophetic book that has two additions, each of which is a *maśśā'* (→ Zechariah, Book as a Whole, Genre), but Malachi is a prophetic book that is itself a *maśśā'* (→ Genre). Holistic approaches to the Book of the Twelve often connect ostensibly similar textual features across various literary boundaries without sufficiently considering either the nature of the boundary or whether each instance of the ostensibly similar feature might be differently explained in relation to its own context. Without prejudging the potential fruitfulness of this line of research, I must say that there is as yet no convincing reason to deny Malachi separate consideration as a prophetic book in its own right (→ 1:1, Genre).

With regard to the second of the three main issues listed above, most scholars continue to work with Pfeiffer's concept of a series of six units, all based on the assertion plus question-and-answer format and all belonging to the generic category of the prophetic disputation. A few, however, have gradually begun to recognize the inadequacy of this concept. Boecker quickly noticed that in most instances the questions did not really contend with the assertion, but rather served to provide some pretext for substantiating it or to elicit some other kind of explanation, etc. (pp. 193-227). He therefore proposed that each of Pfeiffer's six units be called a *Diskussionswort* rather than a disputation (p. 79). Wallis similarly observed that the identity of the addressees is not the same in every case, and that the relationship between the addressees and the oracular speaker is also variable. He therefore proposed that each of Pfeiffer's units be more generally called a *Streitrede* instead of a disputation.

Graffy then raised a much sharper objection, noting that Malachi's assertion plus question-and-answer pattern did not really fit the scenario that had been imagined by earlier form critics (particularly Begrich) in their definitions of the prophetic disputation. They had supposed that this form of speech emerged from a prophet's face-to-face contention with a live audience, and that it therefore entailed a summary statement of the audience's opinion followed by the prophet's attempt to refute it (pp. 2-17). Graffy noted that "the speeches of Malachi begin with an initial statement by God or the prophet, which is followed after a question of the people by a full explanation." He therefore concluded that "they are of a different genre from the disputation speech, which begins with a quotation of the people's words, which is then refuted. Their aim is to convince the listeners of the initial stated point, not to reject the listeners' quoted opinion" (p. 22).

O'Brien has taken a somewhat different approach, noting that although the assertion plus question-and-answer format is a prominent stylistic feature in Malachi, this does not necessarily make it the definitive factor for determining the genre of any particular unit or the genre of the book as a whole. She follows Achtemeier's suggestion that the book is cast in the form of a court case, "tried before the priest in the temple, with the prophet playing the role of the priest in his imagination" (p. 172), and she builds on Harvey's analysis of Mal 1:6–2:9 in terms of a covenant lawsuit (*rîb;* p. 66; see further Gemser, Huffmon, and Nielsen). Using Pfeiffer's pericopes as the basic building blocks, O'Brien (pp. 63-80) reconfigures them into one great covenant lawsuit consisting of a prologue (2:1-5), a series of five accusations (1:6–2:9; 2:10-16; 2:17–3:5; 3:6-12; 3:13-21), a final admonition (3:22), and a final ultimatum (3:23-24).

O'Brien analyzes the five accusation units in terms of a common set of elements, some or all of which occur in various configurations in each unit: interrogation, indictment, declaration of guilt, ultimatum, etc. Such flexibility at first appears to have a considerable advantage over the kind of analysis that woodenly reduces each unit to the assertion plus question-and-answer format, but it finally proves to be problematic in much the same way. Comparison of the units on the basis of assertion plus question-and-answer format eventually breaks down because these common factors can differ in function from unit to unit. Comparison of the units on the basis of O'Brien's cluster of common factors also eventually breaks down because each of the supposedly comparable common elements can also differ in function from unit to unit.

For example, the portions of the text that O'Brien labels indictments have at least two different functions. In some cases they serve to describe offenses (e.g., 1:7-10a; 2:11) for which a penalty is announced (1:10b-14; 2:12), and in other cases they serve to describe behavior from which the people are urged to cease and desist (e.g., 2:8-12; 2:14-16). O'Brien seems to be aware of these differences, but she does not address the question of how they can be encompassed within one and same genre. In summing up, she seems to have only the former function in view: "Using this [rîb] form, the prophet makes clear his conviction that Israel stands under punishment for covenant violation" (p. 79).

Although O'Brien has refuted Pfeiffer's claim that the assertion plus question-and-answer format is the definitive factor for identifying the genre of Malachi's individual units as disputations, she continues to share his assumptions that a similarly shared common format provides a basis on which to delimit the individual units, and that they must all thus belong to one and the same genre (pp. 80-81). Because of the limitations that are still evident in O'Brien's much more nuanced attempt to work with these assumptions, however, the assumptions themselves appear to be dubious.

As a stylistic trait with a variable function, the assertion plus question-and-answer format is not only a questionable basis on which to determine the genre of the text. It is also a questionable basis on which to establish the units of textual analysis (Nogalski, 183). Even if the genre of such units is defined very flexibly, they all cannot finally be made to fit the same generic description. This is evident not only in the way that O'Brien must devise such ad hoc labels as "preliminaries" to cover such extraneous elements as 1:6a and 2:10a, but also from the fact that the narration in 3:16 is a completely anomalous element for a rîb, an element that remains largely unexplained (pp. 76-77). In comparison with the theories of disputation and polemic (whether *Diskussionswort*, *Streitgespräch*, or *Streitrede*), the theory of covenant lawsuit turns out to be only a somewhat more comfortable Procrustean bed.

Starting from roughly the same point as O'Brien, Lescow and Krieg move in an altogether different direction. If Pfeiffer's assertion plus question-and-answer based units are all too heterogeneous to be forced into the same generic mold, perhaps their heterogeneity can be explained in terms of different surface variations on the same underlying ideal generic form. Thus Lescow and Krieg suppose both that each of these units had a common original form and that the series subsequently underwent redaction to produce the present text.

In Lescow's view each unit was originally a torah speech, delivered in response to a request for an authoritative teaching applicable to a particular set of circumstances. The series was established by collecting and organizing a group of such speeches that was then subjected to three different redactional processes. In the first of these redactions, which profoundly transformed the nature of the entire series, each torah speech was reworked into a topical sermon *(Themapredigt)* with the primarily didactic intent of establishing the general underlying principle represented by the more specific and occasional torah speech. In the second redaction additional commentary was inserted at key points, and in the third redaction miscellaneous glosses were added here and there. As a result the final composition was shaped so as to develop a line of thought in the progression from unit to unit, while also establishing nonlinear thematic connections among some of the units at various points (*Buch Maleachi*, 145-56).

Krieg somewhat similarly imagines a group of originally didactic expressions that were subsequently redacted for homiletical purposes. In his view, however, this group of didactic expressions was not made up of once independently existing speeches but was rather a literary composition to begin with. It originally comprised several stanzas, each consisting of an assertion, a rhetorical question, an explication, and a substantiation. Together they formed a work of philosophical lyric poetry *(Gedankenlyrik)* that served the catechetical purposes of the Jerusalem temple staff (pp. 25-102). The original composition was then transformed into a homiletical work, not by developing each of the original didactic lyrics into a sermon, but by recasting the whole group of them into a four-section sermonlike argumentative response to a conflict-ridden schism in the Jerusalem priesthood (pp. 103-36).

At first glance the approach represented by Lescow and Krieg seems to solve the problem encountered by Pfeiffer and O'Brien. If similar compositional elements appear to have different functions, this can be explained by relegating the differing functions to different stages of compositional development. For example, one can see the question-and-answer element as reflecting a particular kind of rhetorical situation in the original form of the text and a different kind of rhetorical situation on the redactional level. When one compares the views of Lescow and Krieg, however, it becomes apparent that their approach does not really get beyond the limitations noted in the foregoing critique of Pfeiffer and O'Brien. Their views diverge with respect to what constitutes the original didactic layer of the text and what constitutes the secondary homiletical layer, and also with respect to the function attributed to such commonalities as the question-and-answer element on each of these levels. On the original level Lescow regards the question-and-answer as a reflection of the interchange between the prophet giving a torah speech and the person who requests it ("Dialogische Strukturen," 210-11), but on the same level Krieg regards it as a reflection of inductive thinking on the poet's part (pp. 87-102).

We thus come by a different route to the same impasse that was encountered in O'Brien's work. The heterogeneity of the various parts of Malachi cannot be encompassed by any one generic form, not even by supposing that there was originally a pristine ideal form to which all the heterogeneity secondarily accrued. Generally speaking, problems of interpretation cannot be solved by substituting a hypothetical ideal text for the real text. This is especially true in the particular case of Malachi, since its real text affords no explicit criteria for determining what an earlier version of the book might have looked like, or whether there ever was an earlier version (→ Setting).

Petersen (pp. 31-32) makes a proposal that in effect returns to Pfeiffer's starting point, while also taking into account some of the lessons learned in the various attempts to refine and modify Pfeiffer's analysis. Petersen reaffirms that Malachi is definitively characterized by the recurrence of a distinctive stylistic device, in which the prophetic speaker directly quotes his addressees and then reacts to this quotation. Petersen concludes from his review of research, however, that any description of Malachi's literary form must also reckon with the fact that this recurrent device does not in every case have the same rhetorical function. He suggests that Malachi may be compared with a Hellenistic diatribe, in which speakers or writers would typically mimic dialogue with an imagined other party in order to argue forcefully. For Petersen the comparison is apt precisely because in the diatribe this stylistic trait can have a variety of rhetorical functions, as it serves to underscore the author's points in several different ways.

Petersen has made a strategic attempt to break out of the present scholarly impasse, but his proposal is problematic in two respsects. First, although there is no a priori reason why a Hebrew composition might not be generically comparable with a Hellenistic literary form, particularly in the cosmopolitan cultural context of the Persian period, a valid cross-cultural comparison of this sort would have to be demonstrable in more ways than one. Malachi can perhaps be compared with the diatribe in one major respect, namely, the stylistic trait of quoting an imagined dialogue partner. Malachi does not really compare with this genre, however, in other major respects. For example, a diatribe is a form of expression that attempts to develop an argument. The logic of the diatribe is typically more tortuous than syllogistic, as it often draws false inferences only to discredit them and thereby show true reasoning. The main rhetorical purpose of the diatribe is nevertheless to advance a particular line of thought (S. K. Stowers, "Diatribe," *ABD* 2:191). The overall literary form of Malachi can hardly be defined in such terms. As Petersen himself admits, "One searches in vain for a compelling architectonic scheme, whether driven by redaction-critical, literary-critical, or canonical-critical perspectives, to explain the order of all the diatribes" (p. 32). Judging from his analysis of the individual units, the same is true for them. In most cases one searches in vain for the progressive argumentation that characterizes a diatribe. Although Malachi is stylistically similar to the diatribe, the comparison evidently does not provide a basis on which to discern the compositional integrity of this book.

Second, Petersen still assumes that stylistic uniformity entails generic uniformity. He therefore continues to work with the same units that Pfeiffer defined on the basis of this same assumption, although Petersen attempts to describe in different terms what the generic uniformity is. In view of the impasse to which this assumption has repeatedly come, however, it must now be abandoned. One can no longer assume that Malachi's stylistic consistency shows the text to be generically uniform in all its main parts. Nor can one assume what often seems to be a corollary of this view: that generic diversity among the individual units would prevent the whole book from having any compositional integrity (→ Genre).

When these presuppositional constraints are removed, Pfeiffer's series of generically identical units can be replaced by a generically varied configuration of somewhat differently delineated units. After an introduction (1:2-5) that may still be called a prophetic disputation, the rest of the book (1:6–3:24) divides into two sections. The first section (1:6–2:16) consists of two speeches, one addressed to the priests (1:6–2:9) and the other to the people (2:10-16), regarding practices that profane the cult. The speech to the priests and the speech to the people are structurally parallel in form. Both begin with a prophecy of punishment (1:6-14; 2:10-12) announcing the penalty that is already in effect (1:10-14; 2:12) for a practice that profanes the cult (1:6-9; 2:10-11). Both conclude with a prophetic call to repentance (2:1-9, 13-16) urging the addressees to behave in a way that avoids profanation of the cult.

The second section (2:17–3:24) consists of two speeches addressed to the people as a whole (2:17–3:12; 3:13-24) regarding the cynical attitude that is evident in popular discourse. The first speech (2:1–3:13) is a prophetic call to repentance, urging the people to turn away from the attitude expressed in such discourse and to contribute fully to the support of the newly reformed temple cult. The second (3:13-24) is a prophetic report of how one group actually did turn from cynical talk and then began to engage the covenant traditions in a way that fostered the development of a deeper relationship with Yahweh and a deeper sense of their identity as people of the covenant.

This overview of Malachi's structure brings us to the third of the issues listed above, the status of 3:22 and 3:23-24 in relation to the main body of the book. With respect to form, the claim that these are appendices has largely been based on their apparent difference from the units defined by the assertion plus question-and-answer format. Since the status of these units has become dubious, however, the issue can no longer be approached in this way. 3:22 and 3:23-24 cannot be relegated to the status of appendices just because they fail to fit the generic mold that is supposedly normative for all units in the main body, for no one particular generic mold is in fact normative for all units in the main body. It is rather a question of whether and how these verses form an integral part of the final unit that tells how a group turned from speaking against Yahweh (3:13-24).

In this last unit of the book the action narrated in 3:16 is explicated by a speech of Yahweh that extends from 3:17 through 3:24. The first part of this speech (3:17-21) elaborates on the initial action reported in 3:16a, and the second part of this speech (3:22-24) elaborates on the subsequent action reported in 3:16b (for details → 2:17–3:12, Structure; and 3:13-24, Structure). Considerations of form thus suggest that 3:22 and 3:23-24 should no longer be regarded as appendices.

This conclusion regarding the formal structure of the final unit suggests that the status of 3:22-24 should be reconsidered from the standpoint of content as well. The claims of thematic discontinuity between these verses and the preceding parts of the book have been greatly overstated. Some of the relatively minor points of alleged terminological discrepancy are discussed below (→ 3:13-24, Structure). Here we will consider, in relation to the thematic development of the book as a whole, the larger issues posed by the concluding references to the law of Moses and the prophet Elijah.

Prior to 3:22 there has been no mention of Moses or Horeb, or of "statutes and ordinances" *(ḥuqqîm ûmišpāṭîm)*, or of "all Israel" *(kol-yiśrā'ēl)*. All these terms, however, serve only to specify a set of other more general and more basic terms that do have direct antecedents in the preceding text. The main thrust of this verse is to "remember" *(zkr)* the "law" *(tôrâ)* that is "commanded" *(ṣwh)* by Yahweh, which harks back to 2:1-9 and to 3:16. In 2:1-9 Yahweh gives the priests a "command" *(ṣwh)* to give true "instruction" *(tôrâ)*. In 3:22 Yahweh therefore exhorts the people to receive what he has previously ordered the priests to give. The priests' recognition of their responsibility, to give "instruction" *(tôrâ)* based on Yahweh's "command" *(ṣwh)*, is predicated on the authority of traditions relating to their patronymic ancestor, Levi; the people's recognition of their responsibility to accept the "law" *(tôrâ)* based on Yahweh's "command" *(ṣwh)* is predicated on the authority of traditions relating to the ancestral figure of Moses. These are but two sides of the same traditional coin, however, since Moses was traditionally regarded as a Levite (Exod 2:1) authorized by Yahweh to delegate priestly duties to a clan within the tribe of Levi (Exod 28:1; cf. Deut 33:8-11).

There is a difference, however, between the way in which the priests are traditionally supposed to give instruction and the way in which the people are now urged to receive it. The priests were to give instruction orally, with the goal of maintaining the "fear" *(yr')* of Yahweh, the recognition of his "name" *(šm)*, and a sense of his presence *(pnym;* 2:5-7). Now, however, the people are to "remember *(zkr)* instruction" (3:22a) by means of a book that has been written for the purpose of such "remembrance" *(zkr)*, but still with the goal of maintaining the "fear" *(yr')* of Yahweh, the recognition of his "name" *(šm)*, and a sense of his presence *(pnym;* 3:16b; → 3:13-24, Structure).

Mal 3:22 thus expresses from the standpoint of the people a concept of *tôrâ* that is basically the same as the one expressed in 2:1-9 from the standpoint of the priests, while also expanding this concept on the basis of the new development that is reported in 3:16b (cf. Renker, 98-122). The exhortation to "remember the law of my servant Moses" is consistent with the way the theme of torah is developed in the book as a whole, so as to show a change in the way that torah is imparted, from the giving of oral instruction to the reading and interpretation of a written document.

Prior to 3:23-24 there has been no mention of Elijah the prophet, and some have argued that he thus appears here *ex machina,* and that there are no antecedents for his role of "turning the hearts of the fathers to their children, and the hearts of the children to their fathers." The two concluding verses should thus be understood as an addition to Malachi, perhaps reflecting the intergenerational cultural conflict of the Hellenistic age (e.g., Mason, 160-61). The removal of intergenerational discord, however, is a theme whose development permeates nearly every unit of the book, both metaphorically in terms of the people's relating to Yahweh as their father and literally in terms of the intergenerational relationships among the people themselves.

In 1:6-14 the priests are accused of not honoring Yahweh as a son honors his father (1:6). In 2:1-9 Yahweh threatens to chastise the priests' "offspring" *(zr')* on account of their fathers' failings (2:3a), and the priests are also charged with falling short of the ideal represented by their patriarchal forefather, Levi

569

(2:8-9). In 2:10-12 questions are raised about the people's being unfaithful both to God their father and to the "covenant of our fathers" (2:10). In 2:13-16 Yahweh's disapproval of divorce is rooted in his desire to keep the next generation faithful (i.e., to have "godly offspring" [zerā' 'ĕlōhîm], 2:15a). In 2:17–3:12 Yahweh's messenger will purify the "sons of Levi," thus calling them back to the ancient traditions of their priestly forefather (2:3b-4), and the people are urged not to be like their forefathers in being unfaithful to Yahweh (3:7a). By the time the reader gets to 3:13-24 the hearts of the fathers are being turned to the children and vice versa, so that Yahweh promises to spare those who turn to him "as a man spares his son who serves him" (3:17b).

Elijah's role as the reconciler of generations is thus consistent with a theme that is pervasive in the book. This theme is developed in a way that states and then reverses the pattern of one generation's being unfaithful to their forebears, and thus visiting the consequences of their infidelity on their children. The changed way of imparting torah has already begun to reverse this tendency, and the appearance of Elijah thus serves to continue and reinforce a process that is already underway.

The other main aspect of Elijah's role, i.e., his being sent to show that Yahweh is about to act (3:23), is also based on previous developments, although its antecedents are not so all-pervasively evident in every part of the text. Elijah assumes this role as a result of the overall progression in the characterization of Yahweh's representatives, a progression that is evident from a changing pattern in the terms used to describe them and their functions.

In the first section of the book (1:6–2:16) Yahweh's representatives are called "priests" (kōhănîm), and they are described as having an unrealized prophetic potential. A priest is ideally a "messenger of Yahweh" (mal'ak yhwh, 2:7b), but at this stage the priest does not actually do what such messengers typically do. They do not disclose how Yahweh is about to act, but only give "true instruction" about the norms of covenant observance affecting all areas of life, including but not limited to the cult. In giving their oral teaching they are to "guard knowledge" (šmr da'at), i.e., to be faithful custodians of the traditions on which true instruction is based (2:7).

In 2:17–3:12 a "messenger of Yahweh" is described in terms of these same priestly functions. In purifying the priesthood and the cult he is to enforce the covenant in accord with ancient tradition (3:3-4). In addition certain prophetic functions are also attributed to this representative of Yahweh. He is "sent" (šlḥ) by Yahweh (3:1aα; cf. Isa 6:8; Jer 1:7; Ezek 2:3-4; etc.); and in being sent he discloses that Yahweh is about to act (Mal 3:1aβ), i.e., that Yahweh is "drawing near for judgment" (qrb lĕmišpāṭ, 3:5).

In 3:13-24 the returning Elijah assumes these particular prophetic traits without also assuming any of the priestly ones. He is explicitly described as a "prophet" (nābî') who is "sent" (šlḥ) by Yahweh (3:23a), and in being sent he discloses that Yahweh is about to act on the coming day of judgment (3:23b; cf. 3:17aβ, 19aα, 21bα). In the final unit of Malachi the priestly function of giving tradition-based "instruction" (tôrâ) is still operative, but it appears in a different guise. The covenant is now enforced not through oral instruction but through the interpretation of a book, which serves as a means of both remembering the tradition and discerning the difference between what is "just" (*ṣdq; RSV* "righteous") and what is "wicked" (*rš'*; 3:17-21).

The role of Elijah is thus described in terms of a three-phase progression in which priestly and prophetic functions are developmentally interrelated. In the first phase the priestly function of giving instruction is described as having prophetic potential but not actually serving any prophetic function (2:1-9). In the second phase this priestly function is conflated with the prophetic function of signaling that Yahweh is about to act (2:17–3:12). In the third phase, as a result of the events reported in 3:16, the priestly function becomes differentiated from the prophetic function represented by Elijah, but it has also been transformed by having been conflated with the prophetic function in the second phase. As the priestly function progresses from oral teaching to the reading and interpretation of a book, it takes on a prophetic dimension. It does not thereby usurp the prophetic function, but rather complements it. Priestly instruction still attempts to articulate the norms of covenant observance on the basis of tradition, but this is now informed by the traditionally prophetic function of discerning how Yahweh is about to act (cf. Meyers, 230-36).

The prophetic function has also been transformed in the progression from the second to the third phase. In the second phase (2:17–3:12) the prophetic function is exercised simply by reading the signs of the times. On this basis a purge of the priesthood (3:3-4) appears to be a sign that Yahweh will soon judge the society as a whole (3:5). In the third phase (3:13-24) the prophetic function is still exercised in this way, but the attempt to discern Yahweh's actions is also informed by the precedents established by past prophets like Elijah. Yahweh's involvement in present events can be discerned through the reactualization of Elijah's past prophetic insights, in which Elijah will (as it were) reappear.

When examined in the light of the book as a whole, the material in 3:22-24 not only forms an integral part of the final unit but also leads the thematic development of the book to its climax. Therefore these verses can hardly be appendices. They are rather an essential part of what the book of Malachi has to say. They are necessary for its explanation of how the priestly teaching of written torah comes to be prophetic.

The bulk of the book (1:6–3:24) is a paradigmatic example of priestly teaching in a prophetic mode. On the one hand it is priestly teaching in the sense that its overall concern is to promote adherence to some form of the law of Moses. In 1:6-14 priests and people are urged to quit violating the rule that prohibits offering blemished animals for sacrifice (1:8a, 13b-14a; cf. Lev 22:17-25; Deut 15:21). In Mal 2:10-16 moral principles analogous to convenantal norms, principles appropriate to the current situation, are developed with regard to intermarriage (2:11b; cf. Deut 7:3) and divorce (Mal 2:14-16; cf. Deut 24:1-4). In Mal 2:17–3:12 the people are urged to pay the tithes that are stipulated for the maintenance of the cult (3:8-10a; cf. Lev 27:30; Num 18:21-24), in anticipation of Yahweh's coming to enforce various other covenantal rules (Mal 3:5) regarding sorcerers (Deut 18:10), those who commit adultery and swear falsely (Exod 20:14, 16; Deut 5:18, 20), those who oppress the hireling in his wages (Lev 19:13), and those who oppress the widow, the orphan, or the sojourner (e.g., Deut 24:17). On the other hand Mal 1:6–3:24 is also prophetic in the sense that it consistently casts this priestly teaching in conventional forms of prophetic speech, thus actualizing its interpretation of the law in relation to the perceived involvement of Yahweh in the contemporary situation (cf. M. Fishbane, *Biblical Interpretation in Ancient Israel* [Oxford: Clarendon, 1985] 332-34).

In the context of the main body (1:2–3:24) this prophetically actualized teaching of the law (1:6–3:24) is introduced by a prophetic disputation (1:2-5) defending the claim of Yahweh's love for Israel against the view that such claims are meaningless because there is no tangible sign of any such love. The prophetic voice responds by pointing to Israel's neighbor, Edom, as an example of what would happen if Yahweh really did not have any love for his people. In that case they would have been destroyed without any hope of restoration. The very fact of Israel's survival, in the form of a restored if struggling Judah, is a tangible sign of Yahweh's constant love (3:6). Seen in this context, the prophetically actualized teaching of the law (1:6–3:24) is an additional sign of Yahweh's love, his gift to the people of Israel to aid and ensure their ongoing survival from generation to generation.

In the context of the book as a whole this message is attributed to a prophetic intermediary called *mal'ākî*. It has long been debated whether this is a proper name or a common noun (Glazier-McDonald, 27-29), and whether it is also some kind of reference to the "messenger" whom Yahweh promises to send in 3:1 (e.g., G. Fohrer, *Introduction to the Old Testament* [tr. D. Green; Nashville and New York: Abingdon, 1968] 469). Regardless of whether the prophetic intermediary is designated with a proper name or a common noun, it is likely that this designation plays on the convention of naming prophets in superscriptions so as to associate the intermediary with the development of the *mal'āk* ("messenger") theme within the text. This does not necessarily mean that the intermediary is to be identified with the person or being that Yahweh is sending to purge the priesthood (3:1). This is not the text's only reference to a messenger of Yahweh (cf. 2:7).

The *mal'ākî* ("my messenger") of 1:1 is not a direct reference to either the *mal'ak yhwh* ("messenger of Yahweh") in 2:7 or the *mal'ākî* in 3:1, but it can be seen in the light of the way the messenger theme is developed in the book as a whole. As noted above, this term first describes the unrealized prophetic potential of the priesthood (2:7b), and then describes a figure who integrates the roles of priest and prophet, thus fulfilling the priesthood's prophetic potential (3:1). As the book comes to an end, the prophetic role is clearly differentiated in the figure of Elijah, but no one is as clearly assigned the now prophetically significant priestly role. This is because the book itself now stands as a demonstration of what it would mean to play this role. The prophet whose revelation is recorded in this text is thus the priestly teacher whose role is defined by the development of the messenger theme (→ 1:1).

Genre

Scholars have scarcely addressed the question of the book's genre as such. They have generally assumed that Malachi consists of a series of units that are all of the same genre, and that the genre of the book is simply the same as the genre of all its units, whether disputation (Pfeiffer, 567-68), covenant lawsuit (O'Brien, 63-80), diatribe (Petersen, 31-32), etc. One can no longer assume, however, that the units are generically homogeneous; and this raises the question of whether the generically heterogeneous units are collectively configured in accord with any particular generic convention on the level of the book as a whole.

Lescow (*Buch Maleachi,* 149-55) and Blake (pp. 81-92) regard the overall character of the book as homiletical or parenetical, and Krieg has more specifically characterized it as preaching that attempts to contemporize and actualize the text on which it is based (pp. 103-28). The views of Lescow and Krieg are based on what they perceive to be the nature of the redactional process to which the original units of the text have been subjected, while Blake's view is based on the nature and compositional arrangement of the final form of the text. In the present study I am methodologically opposed to the views of Lescow and Krieg, and I reach conclusions that are materially different from Blake's on the basis of an approach similar to his. Nevertheless, I agree with these other scholars in their general characterization of the main body of Malachi. The generically diverse units comprise two sections (1:6–2:16; 2:17–3:24) that are both prophetic exhortations, designed to persuade their audience to accept certain ideas and to motivate them to change their behavior in specific ways. These exhortations point to certain observable developments as signs of a renewal process that Yahweh has undertaken, and urges the audience to think and act so as to participate in this divine initiative and reach its goal. The introduction (1:2-5) under which these two exhortations are subsumed focuses more on disabusing the audience of a particular attitude than on changing their behavior, but its mode of persuasion is basically the same.

The superscription (1:1) specifically characterizes the main body of the book as a *maśśā'*. Weis finds this to be a genre term for both a type of prophetic speech and a type of prophetic literature. It is flexibly defined in terms of a cluster of basic elements that are found in most examples: (1) oracular speech of Yahweh; (2) reports of past and/or present events; and (3) commands and/or prohibitions directly addressed to the audience, sometimes in oracular speech and sometimes in the prophet's own words. However arranged, this combination of elements serves to explain how some previously communicated expression of the divine will is now being realized, or is about to be realized, in the realm of human affairs. The *maśśā'* is thus a revelation that serves to interpret the present applicability of a previous revelation, giving the audience guidance concerning an appropriate response on their part (Weis, 273-74).

In the case of Malachi the last unit (3:13-24) is a report based on the events that are narrated in 3:16. The other units are all parenetical, being based on commands. All of the units include oracular speech of Yahweh, although

573

there is great variety in the way it is combined and alternated with the prophet's own words. The main body of the book thus exhibits all the elements typical of the MAŚŚĀ', and in combination they serve the basic function that is typical of this genre, which is to identify the contemporary events in which Yahweh is at work and guide the people's involvement in them. (Cf. Weis's analysis, pp. 199-203, which notes the parenesis but misses the report.) But what is the previous revelation whose interpretation provides the basis on which to make such an identification?

As noted above, the book is largely a prophetic reactualization of rules from the law of Moses, designed to show that the priestly interpretation of such rules can be prophetically divinatory. The previous revelation actualized by Malachi's *maśśā'* is thus some form of the Pentateuch. This revelation is described as the book of the law that Yahweh commanded Moses at Horeb (3:22), which certainly associates it with Deuteronomy. Malachi's concept of tradition also extends to include patriarchal legends from other sources of the Pentateuch (e.g., 1:2-3; 2:4-5, 12), as well as laws from the Priestly Code (see above). It thus seems that for Malachi "the law of Moses" includes much of what eventually became incorporated into the Pentateuch, but not necessarily all of the Pentateuch in its final form (O'Brien, 85-112).

Setting

Several scholars have attempted to decide whether Malachi and its constituent units originally had an oral or written setting by drawing some conclusion from the nature of the assertion plus question-and-answer format alone (e.g., Fischer, 318; Lescow, "Dialogische Strukturen," 210-11). This is not a sufficient basis on which to deal with the issue, however, because the rhetorical imputation of questions to the audience is equally well suited to both a speaker's interaction with a live audience and a writer's interaction with his or her readers. Rather, it is necessary to consider the genre of each unit in relation to the genre of the overall compositional context.

Although Malachi is obviously a written document, it adheres consistently to the conventions of prophetic speech. The entire main body of the book, in every unit and section, is patterned on compositional forms that could have been — and often were — spoken orally. This does not necessarily mean that any of Malachi's component parts ever existed as independent speeches, because there is no explicit indication that this was the case, and their forms can all be very well explained in terms of how they fit into their present literary context. It is nevertheless significant that, even if the main body of Malachi were literarily composed from scratch along with its superscription, the main body differs markedly from the superscription by consistently addressing readers in accord with the conventions of prophetic speech.

When one considers this formal difference in relation to the *mal'ak yhwh* theme, the perspective of the superscription stands in relation to the perspective of the main body as theory stands in relation to praxis. The superscription's authorial voice speaks as one who recognizes in theory what an authentic messenger of Yahweh is, and can thus designate the main body as a revelation mediated by such a figure. The main body's prophetic voice develops a definition of this role as it also demonstrates what being a messenger of Yahweh entails, i.e., the prophetic reinterpretation of torah traditions. Other glimpses of a prophet playing much the same role can be caught in (→) Zech 7:1–8:23 and (→) Hag 2:10-19, where it also appears that prophets are reinterpreting torah traditions (Meyers, 230-31). These three examples show that this kind of prophetic activity could be undertaken under various conditions and for various reasons. Malachi reflects a setting in which the theory and practice of such torah reinterpretation were studied. This would be a scribal setting in which priests were schooled in exercising what had come to be a prophetic aspect of their vocation.

Attempts have repeatedly been made to identify Malachi with various partisan movements in Second Temple Judaism and to situate it within the conflicts that then surrounded the status of various priestly groups (Berquist, 121-25; O'Brien, 1-26; Redditt, "Book of Malachi," 241-44). These attempts have thus far elicited little agreement among scholars, for although Malachi obviously reflects tensions within the postexilic community regarding the priestly administration of the temple cult and various marriage practices, etc., the text does not define these issues in terms that allow them to be readily identified with the narrative descriptions of community conflict in Ezra-Nehemiah (contra Dumbrell). For example, both (→) 2:10-12 and Ezra 9:1–10:44 treat the issue of intermarriage between Jews and foreigners, but in somewhat different ways. Similarly, both (→) Mal 2:17–3:12 and Neh 13:10-13 treat issues regarding the administration and upkeep of the temple cult, but there is not enough information to connect these two episodes directly with each other.

Since Malachi's description of the cult presupposes that the temple has been rebuilt (3:10), it definitely reflects a situation later than the time of Haggai and Zechariah. A terminus ad quem can thus be set toward the end of the sixth century. Beyond this it can be said that Malachi generally reflects a milieu in which the postexilic community was struggling with issues like those portrayed in Ezra-Nehemiah, but it does not necessarily reflect the same time period. A terminus a quo cannot be defined with any certainty, but various considerations suggest a date sometime from the late sixth to mid-fifth century (e.g., Hill); there is no particular reason to follow Krieg (pp. 193-227) in dating this book as late as the second century.

Intention

Malachi is designed to show how torah can be interpreted prophetically so as to guide the community through difficult times, turning its tendency to cynicism back toward hope. Malachi's starting point is the brute historical fact that a vestige of Israel has survived both the trauma of exile and at least the onset of the throes of restoration. This fact is a mysterious given that stands as a sign of Yahweh's constant love for his people. Beyond this Malachi focuses on the nexus of cultic and family life as the key to the community's survival and prosperity.

First, the torah regarding acceptable sacrifices is reinterpreted to call the priests to account for not properly fulfilling their responsibilities and for allowing the people to be irresponsible in their cultic obligations. Similarly, the torah regarding intermarriage and divorce is then reinterpreted to call the people to account for both contracting and dissolving marriages in ways that threaten the community's survival as a religious minority.

Second, the torah regarding tithes is reinterpreted to urge the people to abandon their cynicism and contribute fully to the maintenance of the cult, motivated by the ripple effects that are being generated by Yahweh's drastic reform of the priesthood. This reform portends a wider moral renewal of society at large, in accord with the torah's norms for a just social order, as well as the eventual economic viability of both cult and society. The abandonment of cynicism is further motivated by the emergence of a vital pattern of communal existence among those who have tentatively moved in this direction, a pattern that entails prophetic reinterpretation of the Mosaic torah tradition in written form, reading it in the light of what can be learned from such past prophets as Elijah concerning the initiatives that Yahweh holds in store.

Modern readers are similarly confronted with the mysterious historical fact that God's people have retained their identity as such to this day, even in the process of disdaining and abusing it, while other peoples have lost their identity. From this starting point Malachi suggests the possibility of now reactualizing torah traditions in a way that is analogous to their reactualization in the text, so as to guide the modern covenant community through its difficult times and turn its tendency to cynicism back toward hope. To this end modern prophetic reinterpreters of torah may focus not only on the nexus between cultic and family life but also on any other aspects of communal existence that are now crucial in order for God's people to survive, prosper, and serve the common good. Their primary motivation is the ongoing vitality of the now familiar pattern of communal existence, which entails prophetic reinterpretation of the Scriptures, reading them in the light of what can be learned from past prophets concerning the initiatives that God holds in store.

Bibliography

J. L. Berquist, "The Social Setting of Malachi," *BTB* 19 (1989) 121-26; E. Bosshard and R. G. Kratz, "Maleachi im Zwölfprophetenbuch," *BN* 52 (1990) 27-46; W. J. Dumbrell, "Malachi and the Ezra-Nehemiah Reforms," *RTR* 35 (1976) 42-52; B. Gemser, "The *Rîb*- or Controversy-Pattern in Hebrew Mentality," in *Wisdom in Israel and in the Ancient Near East* (*Fest.* H. H. Rowley; ed. M. Noth and D. Winton Thomas; VTSup 3; Leiden: Brill, 1955) 120-37; A. Graffy, *A Prophet Confronts His People* (AnBib 104; Rome: Biblical Institute Press, 1984); J. Harvey, *Le plaidoyer prophétique contre Israël aprés la rupture de l'alliance* (Scholasticat de l'Immaculée Conception; Paris: Desclée de Brouwer, 1967); A. Hill, "Dating the Book of Malachi: A Linguistic Reexamination," in *The Word of the Lord Shall Go Forth* (*Fest.* D. N. Freedman; ed. C. L. Meyers and M. O'Connor; Winona Lake, Ind.: Eisenbrauns, 1983) 77-89; P. R. House, *The Unity of the Twelve* (JSOTSup 97; Sheffield: Almond, 1990); H. Huffmon,

"The Covenant Lawsuit in the Prophets," *JBL* 78 (1959) 285-95; E. H. Meyers, "Priestly Language in the Book of Malachi," *HAR* 10 (1987) 225-37; K. Nielsen, *Yahweh as Prosecutor and Judge* (JSOTSup 9; Sheffield: JSOT Press, 1978); D. F. J. Nogalski, *Redactional Processes in the Book of the Twelve* (BZAW 218; Berlin: de Gruyter, 1993) 182-212; R. Pierce, "Literary Connectors and a Haggai-Zechariah-Malachi Corpus," *JETS* 27 (1984) 277-89; idem, "A Thematic Development of the Haggai-Zecharia-Malachi Corpus," *JETS* 27 (1984) 401-11; P. L. Redditt, "The Book of Malachi in Its Social Setting," *CBQ* 56 (1994) 240-55; A. van Selms, "The Inner Cohesion of the Book of Malachi," in *Studies in Old Testament Prophecy* (ed. W. C. van Wyk; *OTWSA* 13-14; Potchefstroom, South Africa: OTWSA, 1975) 27-40; R. Weis, "A Definition of the Genre *Maśśā'* in the Hebrew Bible" (Diss., Claremont Graduate School, 1986).

Chapter 2

THE SUPERSCRIPTION (1:1)

Text

Concerning the translation of *maśśā'* (*RSV* "oracle"), → Zech 9:1aα[1], Text.
With regard to the other problematic element in the superscription, Petersen
(p. 165) argues for the LXX reading, *angelou autou* ("his messenger"), which
can hardly be taken as a proper name. He prefers this to MT *mal'ākî,* which has
traditionally been regarded as a proper name ("Malachi") but can also be understood as a common noun ("my messenger"). On the principle of *lectio
difficilior* the MT would seem to be preferable. In either case the convention of
naming a prophet in the superscription is played on in such a way that the
"name" becomes a cipher for a role that is subsequently developed in the main
body of the book, described initially in third person form as "Yahweh's [i.e.,
his] messenger" (2:7b) and subsequently in first person form as "my [i.e.,
Yahweh's] messenger" (3:1a).

Structure

I. Title: *maśśā'*	1:1aα[1]
II. Expansion	1:1aα[2]b
A. Basic term: the word of Yahweh	1:1aα[2]
B. Qualifying phrases	1:1aβb
1. Designation of addressees: to Israel	1:1aβ
2. Designation of intermediary: by the hand of *mal'ākî*	1:1b

The initial term in this and other such superscriptions (i.e., Zech 9:1aα[1];
12:1) is often treated as if it were in a construct relationship with the ensuing
noun or noun phrase, in which case the opening of this verse would be translated: "the *maśśā'* of the word of Yahweh . . ." (so *RSV*). It is unlikely, however, that this technical term for a type of revelation would be in a construct relationship with another such technical term. In other contexts the word *maśśā'*

occurs only in construct relationship with words that describe the content or subject of the revelation (e.g., Isa 13:1; 15:1; 17:1; 19:1; 21:1; 23:1; 30:6; Nah 1:1). In support of the claim for a construct relationship here the superscriptions of Zech 9–11 and 12–14 are often adduced as parallel examples. In these cases too, however, it is unlikely that *maśśā'* is in a construct relationship with *děbar-yhwh* ("the word of Yahweh"), not only because of the way *maśśā'* is generally used in the other contexts listed just above, but also for other reasons relating to its use in these particular contexts ($\rightarrow$ Zech 9:1aα[1]; 12:1). This superscription thus has two basic parts, one consisting of the term *maśśā'* itself, and the other consisting of a noun phrase in apposition to it: "the word of Yahweh to Israel by the hand of *mal'ākî*."

Regardless of whether *mal'ākî* should be understood as a proper name or a common noun ($\rightarrow$ Text), it should be noted that there is a designated intermediary here ("by the hand of *mal'ākî*"). This is an important consideration in view of various claims that have been made about the status of this book in relation to Zech 9–11 and 12–14. Some have argued that Malachi has a superscription like these two additions to Zechariah, and that this similarity entails some kind of interdependence among these three blocks of material (e.g., Rudolph, 218-19, 253; Mason, 139). It is true that all three of these superscriptions contain the term *maśśā'*, but it is questionable whether they all use this term in the same sense ($\rightarrow$ Book as a Whole, Genre; Zech 9:1–11:17, Genre; Zech 12:1–14:21, Genre). Moreover, Mal 1:1 differs significantly from Zech 9:1aα[1] and 12:1 precisely because these latter examples do not designate any intermediary (Glazier-McDonald, 25-26; Petersen, 166). In this respect Mal 1:1 is more comparable with Nah 1:1, which similarly uses *maśśā'* in the main title and names the intermediary in an elaboration on the main title, than with either of these superscriptions from Zechariah.

Mal 1:1 not only designates the intermediary. It also emphasizes the intermediary's agency by specifying that the word of Yahweh was revealed *běyad mal'ākî* ("by the hand of *malā'kî*"). The phrase *běyad* is used a couple of times in connection with other prophets (e.g., Isa 20:2; Jer 50:1), but it is particularly used in connection with Haggai (1:1; 2:1, 10), a prophet who is also called Yahweh's *mal'āk* ("messenger," Hag 1:13). Like the word of Haggai, the word of this *mal'ak yhwh* is described as being forcefully effective in urging the people to a particular course of action ($\rightarrow$ Hag 1:1-15a; Mal 2:17–3:24 [*RSV* 2:17–4:6]).

The message of Malachi is directed "to Israel." As the book unfolds, it becomes evident that the prophetic voice is actually addressing only Judah under the conditions of the postexilic era. The Judeans are pointedly described, however, as descendants of Jacob (1:2; 2:12), thus showing that the Judeans are here conceived as the surviving heirs of Israel as a whole.

Genre

This is a PROPHETIC SUPERSCRIPTION that introduces Malachi as a ($\rightarrow$) *maśśā'* consisting of a separate book, comparable in this regard with the superscription of Nahum. It stands in contrast with the superscriptions that head Zech 9–11 and 12–14, which introduce each of these texts as a *maśśā'* appended to the preceding portions of Zechariah. Some have argued that the status of Malachi as a separate book is a fiction, devised merely in order to provide the composite Book of the Twelve with a requisite twelfth book (e.g., G. Fohrer, *Introduction to the Old Testament* [tr. D. Green; Nashville and New York: Abingdon, 1968] 469). The designation of the intermediary as *mal'ākî* may perhaps fictively play on the convention of prophets being named at the head of prophetic books, but for internal reasons relating more to the composition of Malachi itself than to such external numerological considerations (→ Book as a Whole, Structure). If the superscription of Malachi is a fiction, it is nevertheless fundamentally different from the convention with which Zech 9–11 and 12–14 are introduced; the latter superscriptions present these texts as reinterpretations of revelations once received by a prophet named Zechariah. Even as a fiction Mal 1:1 serves to distinguish the book of Malachi from the book of Zechariah and must therefore be taken seriously as an indication that Malachi has a message distinct from the message of Zechariah.

A prophetic superscription usually distinguishes the perspective of the book's anonymous author from the perspective of the prophet under whose name revelations are recorded therein. In this case, however, the convention has been modified. If the LXX reading is preferred (→ Text) these two perspectives are distinguished, but the prophet is designated in terms of a functional role ("his messenger") instead of a proper name. If the MT reading is preferred the prophet is named, but with a "name" that in effect characterizes the voice of the superscription as speaking from the same perspective as the prophetic voice in the main body. The authorial voice uses in the superscription the same oracular convention ("my messenger") that the prophetic voice uses in the main body (3:1a). The MT shows a more unusual variation on the conventions of superscriptions, for it virtually collapses the distinction in perspective between the superscription and the main body, thereby conflating the authorial role of the superscription and the prophetic role of the main body. In either case the superscription identifies the prophetic voice of the main body as an effective demonstration of the role about which it is also speaking. In the case of the MT, the author of the superscription is further identified as one who speaks from the same prophetic consciousness as the prophetic voice in the main body (cf. the similar effect of the narrative structure in Haggai; → Haggai, Book as a Whole).

Setting

Such superscriptions were the creation of scribal groups concerned with the preservation, study, and ongoing reinterpretation of the records of prophetic revelation.

Intention

This superscription introduces the book of Malachi as a representation of a particular type of prophetic role, a role that is both played by the prophet who speaks throughout the book and defined by the thematic progression within the book. This prophetic role is characterized as one that authoritatively reinterprets the revelatory traditions of priestly torah in order to provide effective guidance for the community as they struggle to order their common life in a way that is consistent with their history as the people of the God of Israel.

Bibliography

G. Tucker, "Prophetic Superscriptions and the Growth of a Canon," in *Canon and Authority* (ed. G. W. Coats and B. O. Long; Philadelphia: Fortress, 1977) 56-70.

Chapter 3

THE INTRODUCTION (1:2-5)

Structure

2) Described with respect to the future:
    a hypothetical case   1:4-5
    a) Condition: if Edom should express
        any intentions of a restoration   1:4aα
    b) Consequences: Yahweh's statement of
        what would happen as a result of any
        attempt to realize such intentions   1:4aβb
        (1) Introductory messenger formula   1:4aβ^1
        (2) Statement proper   1:4aβ^{2}b
           (a) Edom's attempt:
              they may build . . .   1:4aβ^2
           (b) Yahweh's reaction to Edom's
              attempt: I will tear down . . .   1:4aβ^2
           (c) Public reaction to Edom's failure
               due to Yahweh's opposition   1:4b
              α. They will coin new epithets
                 for Edom   1:4bα^1
              β. The epithets themselves   1:4bα^{2}β
                 aa. The wicked country   1:4bα^2
                 bb. The people with whom
                    Yahweh is angry forever   1:4bβ
           (d) The effect of this eventuality
               on Israel (direct address)   1:5
              α. Their perception of it:
                 your own eyes shall see . . .   1:5a
              β. Their reaction to it: you
                 shall say . . .   1:5b

In this unit Yahweh first asserts his "love" (*'hb*) for Israel (v. 2aα), then poses a question that such an assertion might evoke from the audience (v. 2aβ), and finally answers this question in terms of a comparison between Yahweh's treatment of them and his treatment of the nation that they have traditionally regarded as a "twin" people, i.e., Edom. The Edomites were recognized as a nation that, like Israel, owed possession of their land to Yahweh's generosity (Deut 2:4-5); but because they rejected the status that was theirs by right, as "older brothers" of the Israelites, Yahweh has come to treat them as his enemies (vv. 2b-3a; *śn'*, RSV "hate"; cf. Gen 25:19-34). In the historical context presupposed by this unit, Yahweh's negative attitude toward Edom is evident from the fact that they have been destroyed and left without the hope of being restored in any way (vv. 3b-4). This implies that Yahweh's positive attitude toward Israel is conversely evident from the fact that, although they have likewise been destroyed, Yahweh has given them the hope of restoration. Yahweh's love for his people is manifest in the current international situation, as it affords the possibility of this hope being realized before their very eyes (v. 5).

The rest of the book proceeds to address the main problems that stand in the way of this realization, particularly the laxness that keeps the restored sacrificial cult from regaining its viability (1:6–2:16). Yahweh promises to send a "messenger" in order to resolve these problems (2:17–3:15), and this begins to have the intended effect (3:16-24 [*RSV* 3:16–4:6]). Such is the eventuality foreshadowed implicitly by this introduction as a concrete manifestation of Yahweh's "love" for Israel.

Genre

This unit makes a claim about Yahweh and then begins to substantiate this claim in the face of public skepticism toward it. This skepticism is not necessarily based on a directly antithetical view, but only on the view that such claims are not self-evident and thus need to be substantiated. The substantiation itself, however, takes the form of an argument based on antitheses (Snyman, 436-38).

In view of the fact that Israel has been destroyed, it is certainly not self-evident that Yahweh still loves his people. This does not necessarily mean that he hates them; it could also mean that he is totally indifferent, that he is no longer in control of world affairs, etc. By establishing some basis for comparison in the case of Edom, and thus getting some idea of what it would mean for Yahweh not to love his people's closest relatives, the speaker can get the audience to see, conversely, what Yahweh's love for his people might entail in this particular historical situation.

There has been some debate over the proper term for such an argumentative form. Pfeiffer called it a disputation, but Boecker has objected that nothing is technically under dispute here (pp. 78-79). Rather, the grounds for the prophet's initial assertion are being probed. With regard to the way the argument works, Boecker's point is well taken. There is no battle between two diametrically opposed views here, as is often the case in prophetic disputations (e.g., Jer 28:1-17). The prophet's initial assertion is nevertheless questioned in a way that could conceivably lead to an antithetical conclusion.

Graffy (p. 22) has observed that a disputation typically involves a prophet's stating a popular view and then taking issue with it, and that this unit does exactly the opposite. It states the prophet's view, with which the people then take issue, only to be quickly refuted. He therefore suggests that this unit not be considered a disputation, but Murray has pointed out that despite this formal reversal the speech still attempts to refute a popular attitude antithetical to the view of the prophet, and may thus be fairly compared with texts that go about doing this otherwise (Murray, 111-12). It can therefore be described as a PROPHETIC DISPUTATION.

Setting

As a type of prophetic speech this genre originated in the context of a prophet's confrontation with an individual or a group, in which the prophet took issue with an opposing view held by the addressee(s) (Graffy, 118-24).

Such a form would easily lend itself to fictional adaptation, in which case it might be used to anticipate and discredit the hypothetically conceivable objections to a prophetic claim, rather than to dissuade some group or person from an already held opposing view.

The genre of prophetic disputation was originally an oral convention, and there is no formal reason why a speech like 1:2-5 could not have had an oral setting (Reventlow, 134). It is nevertheless difficult to suppose that such an example of the genre, whose content serves primarily to provide a point of departure for the book as whole, could ever have been an independently existing prophetic speech (Fischer, 315-16). The introductory function of 1:2-5 is evident in a number of ways. For example, in characterizing its audience with reference to their eponymous ancestor, Jacob, and his brother, Esau, this unit sets a precedent that is maintained throughout the book. The priests are subsequently characterized with reference to their eponymous ancestor, Levi (2:4-6; 3:3); membership in the community is defined in terms of dwelling among "the tents of Jacob" (2:12); and the people are addressed as "children of Jacob" (3:6). This unit materially serves to substantiate in general and negative terms the questionable claim of Yahweh's love for Israel, a claim that is further substantiated in more positive and specific terms as the rest of the book unfolds. Such features suggest that this unit was originally composed as the introduction to the book.

The rhetorical situation is fictional, in the sense that this unit is addressed to the readers of the text rather than to a group that was once actually assembled on a particular occasion. The rhetorical situation is nevertheless realistically defined with respect to an actually existing historical situation. The text would hardly be persuasive if Judah and Edom had not in fact suffered similar defeats, and if Judah did not really have prospects of restoration more promising than those of Edom. The outlook of the text can thus be historically located sometime late in the sixth century BCE. At that time Judah's restoration had progressed to the point of rebuilding the Jerusalem temple but had not yet attained full viability; and Edom's future remained uncertain because it had just recently suffered defeat, either by the Babylonians in the sixth century or perhaps by the Nabateans in the fifth century (Glazier-McDonald, 34-41).

Intention

This unit aims for its readers to see the general conditions of the early postexilic period, during which Judah was still struggling to restore itself, in a theologically positive light. The exile could have meant not only that Judah was finished but also that Yahweh was finished with Judah, as is now apparently the case with their historically similar neighbors, the Edomites. But the brute fact that Judah survived and now knows the possibility of restoration tangibly signals that Yahweh continues to love his people as he continues to govern the world.

Bibliography

G. J. Botterweck, "Jakob habe ich lieb — Esau hasse ich: Auslegung von Malachias 1,2-5," *BibLeb* 1 (1960) 28-38; A. Graffy, *A Prophet Confronts His People* (AnBib 104; Rome: Biblical Institute Press, 1984); A. Herranz, "Dilexi Jacob, Esau autem odio habui," *EstBib* 2 (1941-42) 559-83; D. F. Murray, "The Rhetoric of Disputation: Re-examination of a Prophetic Genre," *JSOT* 38 (1987) 95-121; S. D. Snyman, "Antitheses in Malachi 1,2-5," *ZAW* 98 (1986) 436-38.

Chapter 4

THE FIRST MAJOR SECTION
OF THE BOOK (1:6–2:16)
AND ITS INDIVIDUAL UNITS

Structure

587

Most commentators divide this section of the book into two units, 1:6–2:9 and 2:10-16. This division is based on the correct observation that these two pericopes have different addressees, the former being directed to the priests and the latter to the people of Judah as a whole. This is indicated by a rhetorical shift from the second person masculine plural ("you priests!"), which has been in effect throughout 1:6–2:9, to first person plural at 2:10. At this point the prophetic voice begins to speak in terms of "we," and the "we" in question is "Judah." This encompasses the people as a whole, including but not limited to the priests. Second person masculine plural forms reappear in 2:13, but since the shift from priests to people is already well established, this continues to encompass Judah as a whole ("you people of Judah"; cf. Ogden, passim).

The division of the text into these two units is also largely based, however, on Pfeiffer's analysis of each as a self-contained prophetic disputation (pp. 557-60, 664-67), which emphasizes that both are basically designed to refute an objection (1:6bβ^2; 2:14a) that is raised against an initial assertion (1:6abβ^1; 2:10+13; Pfeiffer even excises 2:11-12 in order to make 2:10-16 fit this pattern more neatly!). The shortcomings of the thesis that Malachi consists of a series of prophetic disputations is generally discussed above (→ Book as a Whole). Here it can be shown in greater detail that when 1:6–2:9 and 2:10-16 are considered as two members in such a series, the more prominent generic patterns that define this section of the book become obscured.

The pattern of making an assertion and then quoting a question raised by the audience is a characteristic trait of Malachi's style, but this pattern does not always have the same function vis-à-vis the other elements of the text, and it is not always the most basic aspect of the compositional structure. In 1:6-14, for example, the questioning (1:6bβ^2-9) serves to elaborate on an accusation that is directed against the priests, charging that they in effect dishonor Yahweh's name (1:6bβ^1); while in 2:13-16 the ostensibly similar questioning (2:14a) has the quite different function of introducing an explanation (2:14b) of why Yahweh does not favorably accept the people's sacrificial offerings (2:13b). In each case the questioning not only has a different function but is also subordinated to some other quite different compositional element. When these questionings are taken out of context and used as a basis on which to compare 1:6–2:9 and 2:10-16, the more salient differences between these two pericopes are ignored, as are the more basic compositional structures of this section of the book.

Both the speech addressed to the priests in 1:6–2:9 and the speech addressed to the people in 2:10-16 are subdivided by a similar device, a kind of introductory subheading that signals a transition from one type of discourse to another. In the case of the priests, they have previously been accused of dishonoring Yahweh's name by the way they conduct sacrifices (1:6-9), and Yahweh's rejection of their offerings has been identified as their punishment for this offense (1:10-14). At 2:1 a phrase ("and now this command is for you!") introduces a passage that recommends fidelity to the priestly tradition of "true instruction" (2:5-9) as an alternative to remaining under this curse (2:1-4). In the case of the people of Judah, they have previously been accused of profaning Yahweh's sanctuary by the intermarriage of Jewish men with women who worship other gods (2:10-11), and Yahweh's removal of each man's legal and cultic standing has been identified as the penalty for this offense (2:12). At 2:13 a phrase ("and this you also do!") introduces a passage that identifies divorce as another reason for Yahweh's rejection of offerings and recommends fidelity in marriage as an alternative to remaining in this lamentable state (2:14-16).

This section of the book thus consists of two complementary addresses, one directed to the priests (1:6–2:9) and the other directed to the people as a whole (2:10-16), both of which are concerned with practices that in different ways profane the cult and thus render it inefficacious. Both of these addresses are subdivided into two analogous parts. Both begin with a prophecy of punishment (1:6-14; 2:10-12) identifying the dysfunction of the cult as the penalty imposed by Yahweh for these practices; and both conclude with a prophetic call to repentance (2:1-9; 2:13-16) urging the addressees to change the practices that have alienated Yahweh from his worshipers.

Genre

This section of the book is generically complex, but in a way that assumes a definite rhetorical pattern: a twice-repeated sequence of (→) prophecy of punishment plus (→) prophetic call to repentance. As noted above, the prophecies of punishment in 1:6-14 and 2:10-12 do not serve primarily to announce that Yahweh will bring some future doom on those to whom they are addressed. Rather, they identify the unfortunate circumstances in which the addressees now find themselves as a punishment of Yahweh, a punishment that will continue indefinitely if they persist in violating the cult's holiness. The prophecies of punishment thus provide the basis on which the calls to repentance in 2:1-9 and 2:13-16 are predicated, and their plea to turn from cultic profanation is the overall main thrust of 1:6–2:16. This section may therefore be described as a PROPHETIC EXHORTATION.

Setting

As shown, for example, by Jer 17:19-27 and 22:1-9, prophets might make speeches of this sort in a public place, whether addressed to an individual such as a king (22:1-9) or to the leaders and people at large (17:19-27). Even if these examples are both Deuteronomistic fictions, they would nevertheless reflect this convention of prophetic oratory with some verisimilitude.

It is therefore possible that the two addresses in this section were delivered orally, either singly or in combination, before being recorded and edited into their present literary context. This is not necessarily the case, however. They could also have been composed literarily as fictional examples of such prophetic speeches. Utzschneider has argued that this is the case with respect to Mal 1:6–2:9, but his evidence is not conclusive. He maintains that a tightly

589

organized inner structure (pp. 23-41) and a web of outer intertextual allusions (pp. 42-74) are mutually confirming indications of an originally literary composition, but both of these criteria are problematic. This part of Malachi is indeed a well-crafted verbal construct, but there is no reason to suppose that literary compositions have any monopoly on this trait. As the above analysis shows, the carefully balanced rhetorical structure of this section is precisely in accord with the conventions of prophetic oratory. One therefore cannot conclude, simply on the basis of its well-wrought structure, that this or any text was originally a literary composition.

Utzschneider also considers the way in which the distinctive terminology and themes of 1:6–2:9 echo similar terminology and themes in some nine other texts. He concludes that such connections indicate the literary dependence of Malachi on previously existing documents such as Deuteronomy and Ezekiel. In many cases, however, the common words and phrases are part of a priestly formulaic vocabulary that any text concerned with cultic matters might well use. For example, references to "the priests" *(hakkōhănîm),* "food" *(leḥem),* and "Yahweh's table" *(šulḥan yhwh)* occur in Mal 1:6-7 and also in Ezek 44:6-7, 15-16. Malachi could perhaps be echoing Ezek 44, but such terminology is hardly unique to either text. Why does its recurrence in Malachi and Ezekiel necessarily indicate the literary dependence of either text on the other? Utzschneider makes a couple of theoretical points that are very well taken: prophetic literature is not always produced by the redaction of prophetic speeches, and writing is not necessarily a secondary form of prophetic expression. He has not shown conclusively, however, that these theoretical points apply in the case of Mal 1:6–2:9.

In sum, this section could have been produced by the transcription or redaction of previously spoken prophecy, or it could have been composed as a literary representation of such a prophecy. There is no evidence that would strongly argue in favor of either alternative. In the final analysis the reader must take account of the fact that this section, although it is obviously part of a written document, nevertheless consistently follows the conventions of live prophetic speech.

Intention

This section of the book addresses an audience composed of both priests and laypersons, looking at the problem of a dysfunctional cult first from one perspective and then from the other. It aims for them to see Yahweh's rejection of their worship as a condition for which they are jointly responsible and which can only be reversed by a concerted effort on the part of the priests to perform the sacrificial rituals properly, and by a similarly concerted effort on the part of the people to reorder their domestic life in two crucial respects: to penalize intermarriage with the forfeiture of one's right to legal representation and cultic participation, and to refrain voluntarily from divorce. It is necessary for them to take these measures if the cult is to regain its integrity, and it is necessary for the cult to regain its integrity if the community is going to survive and prosper.

Bibliography

H. Utzschneider, *Künder oder Schreiber? Eine These zum Problem der "Schrift-prophetie" auf Grund von Maleachi 1,6–2,9* (BEATAJ 19; Frankfurt: Peter Lang, 1989).

YAHWEH HOLDS THE PRIESTS ACCOUNTABLE FOR BEING DERELICT IN THEIR ADMINISTRATION OF THE SACRIFICIAL OFFERINGS AND THUS PROFANING HIS NAME, 1:6-14

Structure

I. Accusation of the priests	1:6-9
A. Basic statement (speech of Yahweh): a contrastive analogy describing how respect is shown to people in positions of honor but not to Yahweh	1:6
1. Speech proper	1:6abα
a. Statements concerning two ways in which respect is shown to certain human beings	1:6a
1) In terms of family relations: a son honors a father	1:6aα
2) In terms of social class: a servant honors a master	1:6aβ
b. Questions claiming that respect is not analogously shown to Yahweh	1:6bα
1) In terms of family relations: Yahweh compared with a dishonored father	1:6bα¹
2) In terms of social class: Yahweh compared with a dishonored master	1:6bα²
2. Expanded speech report formula	1:6bβ¹
a. Speech report formula: says Yahweh of hosts	
b. Accusatory designation of addressees: to you, O priests, who despise my name	
B. Elaboration on the basic statement	1:6bβ²-9
1. Further definition of the charge	1:6bβ²-8a
a. Yahweh's twofold response to questions imputed to the priests	1:6bβ²-7
1) First response	1:6bβ²-7aα
a) Imputation of a question to the priests: but you say, "How have we despised your name?"	1:6bβ²
b) Yahweh's reply: by offering polluted food on my altar	1:7aα
2) Second response	1:7aβb

b. Speech report formula: says Yahweh of hosts   1:10bα[2]
c. Refusal of the priest's offerings: I will not
    accept [them] . . .   1:10bβ
B. Basis for rejection: contrastive analogy between the
pure worship of Yahweh offered abroad and the
impure worship offered at home   1:11-14
  1. Description of Yahweh's cult as practiced abroad:
     speech of Yahweh   1:11
     a. Speech proper   1:11abα
       1) Yahweh's greatness is recognized
         internationally   1:11aα
       2) Yahweh is rightly worshiped in every
         (other) place   1:11aβbα
         a) Form in which he is worshiped
           everywhere: incense and a pure offering   1:11aβ
         b) Reason for such practice: his greatness
           is recognized internationally   1:11bα
     b. Speech report formula: says Yahweh of hosts   1:11bβ
  2. Description of Yahweh's cult as practiced in Israel:
     twofold speech of Yahweh directly addressed
     to the priests   1:12-13
     a. First speech   1:12-13aα
       1) Speech proper: concerning the effects
         of the bad attitudes expressed in the
         priests' words   1:12-13aα[1]
         a) First case   1:12
           (1) Effect: you profane [my name]   1:12a
           (2) Words expressing a bad attitude   1:12b
             (a) Yahweh's table is polluted   1:12bα
             (b) Its food is to be despised   1:12bβ
         b) Second case   1:13aα[1]
           (1) Words expressing a bad attitude:
             what a weariness this is!
           (2) Effect: demonstration of disdain
             for Yahweh
       2) Speech report formula: says Yahweh
         of hosts   1:13aα[2]
     b. Second speech   1:13aβb
       1) Speech proper: concerning the priests'
         unacceptable practices   1:13aβbα
         a) Statements describing such practices   1:13aβ
           (1) You bring what has been taken by
             violence, or is lame, or is sick   1:13aβ[1]
           (2) You make this your offering   1:13aβ[2]
         b) Rhetorical question expressing rejection
           of such offerings: shall I accept that
           from your hands?   1:13bα

This unit is part of a larger address to the priests that also includes the next unit (2:1-9). The two units are thus closely interrelated, but they differ in focusing on somewhat different concerns (McKenzie and Wallace, 550, n. 3). The first part of this address (1:6-14) is concerned with how the priests fail to "honor" *(kbd)* Yahweh, as a son "honors" his father (1:6bα[1]), because they have in effect "despised his name" *(bzh šm)* by allowing defective sacrifices to be offered (1:6bβ[2]-14). The second part is concerned with how the priests fail to "honor" *(kbd)* and "fear" *(yr')* Yahweh, as a servant "honors" and "fears" his master (1:6bα[2]), because they have in effect "dishonored his name" *(lō' ntn kābôd lšm;* RSV "not give glory to the name"; 2:2) by giving defective "instruction" *(tôrâ)* that shows no "fear" *(yr')* of him (2:5-8). Even as 1:6-14 and 2:1-9 differ from each other in this way, they are linked by the analogy in 1:6 that serves to introduce both units and by the conclusion in 2:9 that likewise serves to link both units thematically. Because of the priests' defective instruction (2:1-9), Yahweh "despises" *(bzh)* them, just as they have "despised" *(bzh)* him (1:6-14; → 1:6–2:17, Structure).

This unit has two main parts: an accusation addressed to the priests (1:6-9), and an announcement of the punishment that Yahweh is imposing because of this offense (1:10-14). The accusation is basically that the priests "despise the name" *(bzh šm)* of Yahweh (v. 6bβ[1]). This charge is further defined by responding to two questions imputed to the priests. They have in effect despised Yahweh's name because they have offered defective sacrificial victims on his altar and have thus treated it despicably (v. 7). The response this gets from Yahweh is just about as favorable as the response that a similarly second-rate gift would get from the governor (v. 8). No wonder the community is not thriving.

On the basis of this charge, which asserts that the sacrifices performed by the priests are in effect useless (v. 10a), Yahweh announces that he will no longer accept any such sacrifices (v. 10b). He then proceeds to rub it in by unfavorably contrasting the purity of the cult wherever else he is worshiped and the cultic impurity that is fostered by the priests of his own home sanctuary (vv. 11-13; on the vexed interpretation of v. 11, see the bibliography below). The priests are not the only ones to blame for this, however. The people themselves bring the defective and hence less valuable animals that the priests then wrongly allow them to sacrifice, even though they could afford to bring acceptable animals. Such "cheating" *(nkl)* among the Yahweh worshipers in their own homeland stands in stark contrast with the reverence shown by Yahweh worshipers in the diaspora, and thus brings on Yahweh's curse (v. 14).

Genre

Many follow Pfeiffer (pp. 557-61) in describing this unit as part of a (→) prophetic disputation that takes up all of 1:6–2:9. Elements of the disputation genre are indeed evident in this text, particularly in the questions and answers of vv. 6bβ²-9, but they do not constitute its fundamental structure. They rather serve to explicate the accusation in v. 6bβ¹ (Murray, 112-14), which in turn provides the basis for the announcement of punishment in vv. 10-14. O'Brien (pp. 64-65) regards this unit as part of a larger (→) covenant lawsuit that covers all of 1:6–2:9, but if violation of the covenant were the main concern here, why would this theme be missing from the accusation, to be brought up only as an appendage to the announcement of punishment (2:4-5; → 2:1-9)? This unit combines elements of accusation (1:6-9) and announcement of punishment (1:10-14) in a way that is not particularly legal (→ Book as a Whole, Genre). This combination is rather the definitive characteristic of a PROPHECY OF PUNISHMENT.

Setting

Prophets might deliver such speeches in direct encounter with the priests at whom they were targeted (e.g., Amos 7:16-17, where the accusation similarly entails direct discourse imputed to the accused; cf. Hos 4:4-10). This unit, like prophecies of judgment in general, thus might have originated as a prophecy spoken in such a confrontational context — perhaps as part of a larger address to the priests including 2:1-9 — that was subsequently incorporated into its present literary context. This text fits so programmatically into the (→) book as a whole, however, that it might also have originated as an integral part of the literary composition to which it now belongs. There is no evidence that would argue conclusively for one of these alternatives over the other.

In any case, because 1:11 describes the "burning of incense" *(qṭr)* and the presentation of a "pure offering" *(minḥâ ṭĕhôrâ)* to Yahweh as a worldwide practice, this unit appears to reflect a historical situation in which the principle of legitimate sacrifice in Jerusalem alone had not yet been accepted by the majority of Jews. It is debatable whether these phrases refer to the sacrificial worship of Yahweh by Jews in the diaspora (Glazier-McDonald, 55-61; see also the bibliography below), but there is some evidence that temples existed in the diaspora from the time of the exile on (e.g., Ezek 11:16), and that their legitimacy was a live issue during the latter half of the sixth century.

Intention

This unit cites the priests for allowing many of the people to defraud the temple by presenting blemished animals for sacrifice and for thereby allowing the sanctuary to become impure. Yahweh thus rejects both the priests' ministrations and the people's offerings, so that the cult might as well cease to operate. To continue in this fashion will only alienate Yahweh and run the risk of incurring his curse.

Bibliography

J. G. Baldwin, "Mal 1:11 and the Worship of the Nations in the Old Testament," *TynBul* 23 (1972) 117-24; D. F. Murray, "The Rhetoric of Disputation: Re-examination of a Prophetic Genre," *JSOT* 38 (1987) 95-121; M. Rehm, "Das Opfer der Völker nach Mal 1,11," in *Lux tua veritas (Fest.* H. Junker; ed. H. Gross and F. Mussner; Trier: Paulinus, 1961); J. Swetnam, "Malachi 1,11: An Interpretation," *CBQ* 31 (1969) 200-209; T. C. Vriezen, "How to Understand Malachi 1:11," in *Grace upon Grace (Fest.* L. J. Kuyper; ed. J. I. Cook; Grand Rapids: Eerdmans, 1975) 128-36.

YAHWEH'S COMMAND CALLS THE PRIESTS BACK TO THEIR TRADITIONAL ROLE OF GIVING TRUE INSTRUCTION, 2:1-9

Structure

I. Command of Yahweh addressed to the priests	2:1-4
A. Introduction identifying this type of speech and its addressees	2:1
B. Command proper	2:2-3
1. Announcement of a curse against the priests that is already taking effect because of their intransigence	2:2
a. Twofold protasis describing the priests' failure to redress their deficiencies	$2:2a\alpha^1$
1) First condition: if you will not listen . . .	
2) Second condition: if you will not lay it to heart to give glory to my name . . .	
b. Speech report formula: says Yahweh of hosts	$2:2a\alpha^2$
c. Twofold apodosis describing the consequences of the priests' inaction	$2:2a\beta b$
1) Described in terms of partial misfortune: I will send the curse on you	$2:2a\beta^1$
2) Described in terms of total reversal of fortune	$2:2a\beta^2b$

	1) On the part of the priest: his lips should guard knowledge	2:7aα
	2) On the part of the people: many may seek instruction from his mouth	2:7aβ
	b. Rationale: for he is the messenger of Yahweh of hosts	2:7b
B.	Consequences of violating the Levitical covenant	2:8-9
	1. Yahweh's accusation of the priests	2:8
	a. Accusation proper	2:8abα
	1) In terms of the primary priestly function entailed by the Levitical covenant	2:8a
	a) With respect to the priests themselves: you have turned aside from the way	2:8aα
	b) With respect to their guidance of the people: you have caused many to stumble by your instruction	2:8aβ
	2) In terms of the overall relationship: you have corrupted my covenant with Levi	2:8bα
	b. Speech report formula: says Yahweh of hosts	2:8bβ
	2. Announcement of punishment	2:9
	a. Description of punishment: I have made you despised and abased before all the people	2:9a
	b. Twofold rationale	2:9b
	1) Negatively expressed: you have not kept my ways	2:9bα
	2) Positively expressed: you have shown partiality in your instruction	2:9bβ

This unit is part of an address to the priests that also includes the forego-ing unit (1:6-14). Continuity with the preceding unit is indicated by the intro-ductory reference to the priests' not giving "honor" (*kbd; RSV* "glory") to Yahweh's "name" (*šm,* 2:2a), thus reiterating the introductory reference in the preceding unit to their failure to "honor" *(kbd)* Yahweh by despising his "name" (*šm,* 1:6). A link is also established by reiterating in 2:1-9 two of the thematic notes on which 1:6-14 concludes: the theme of "curse" (*'rr,* 1:14a; 2:2b) and the theme of "fearing" *(yr')* either Yahweh or his name (1:14b; 2:5). Despite this continuity and linkage, a turning point is also indicated at 2:1 by the combination of the adverb "now" (*'attâ*) and the clause "this command is for you" (*'ălêkem hammiṣwâ hazzō't*). This heading points forward to the in-troduction of two new interrelated themes: "covenant" (*bĕrît,* 2:4-5a, 8) and "instruction" (*tôrâ,* 2:6-9). This unit thus explores additional implications of matters that have already come up in the preceding unit.

The first basic part of this unit (2:2-4) is the "command" *(miṣwâ)* that is introduced by the heading in 2:1. There is really no command as such, but only a tacit directive that is implied in Yahweh's stated intention to punish the priests if they do not turn away from the offenses they are accused of in the preceding unit. If they do not try to "give honor" (*ntn kbd; RSV* "give glory") to Yahweh's "name" *(šm)*, and thus turn away from those practices that show in effect how they "despise" *(bzh)* his "name" *(šm)*, Yahweh will inhibit them and their descendants from fulfilling their priestly role (2:2-3). A call to repent is thus implied, and it is authenticated as a true command of Yahweh by the consequences that will immediately ensue from either heeding or not heeding it (2:4a). If the priests do not heed this call, they will remain under Yahweh's curse until the priesthood itself becomes defunct (2:2-3). Conversely, if they do heed it, the curse will turn to blessing, and the traditional priestly role and function will remain intact.

The priesthood's proper role and function are described in terms of Yahweh's "covenant with Levi" (2:4b). The second part of this unit (2:5-9) describes the nature of this relationship (2:5-7) and the consequences of its having presently gone awry (2:8-9), so as to reinforce Yahweh's stated intention to maintain it if possible (2:4b) and thereby reinforce the motivation for the priests to heed the tacit call to repent. The special responsibility of the priests is to model the "fear" *(yr')* of Yahweh (2:5-6). They must rightly discharge this responsibility if the community is to "turn from iniquity" *(šwb mē'āwōn)*, and thus have "life and peace" *(haḥayyîm wĕhaššālôm)* as the priests walk with Yahweh "in peace and uprightness" *(bĕšālôm ûbĕmîšôr)*. This is the kind of fear that a servant shows his master (1:6bα), and it is manifest primarily in each priest's being careful to give "true instruction" *(tôrat 'ĕmet)* and to "keep knowledge" *(šmr da'at)*, and also in the people's corresponding recognition of the priest as an authentic "messenger of Yahweh" *(mal'ak yhwh)*.

The priests have violated the terms of Yahweh's covenant with Levi by giving instruction unfairly. They have caused many to make mistakes, and Yahweh has thus caused them to lose their credibility with the people (2:9). It is implied that they could reverse this situation by reverting *(šwb)* to the proper role and function of the priesthood, thus regaining their capacity to keep the people turning *(šwb)* from evil (2:6b).

In Ezra-Nehemiah a distinction is systematically drawn between Aaronid priests and Levites, and many interpreters have supposed that such a distinction is similarly operative in Malachi, particularly in this unit. This supposition has been driven more by a desire to relate Malachi directly to the historical developments described in Ezra-Nehemiah than by rhetorical analysis of how the terms *kōhēn* ("priest") and *lēwî* ("Levi," "Levite") function in this context. Since the priests are being addressed here in terms of whether they live up to the ideals of Yahweh's "covenant with Levi," it is evident that in this context priests and Levites are virtually the same (cf. O'Brien, 66, 83, 143-44, and passim). This conclusion may pose problems for various theories regarding the evolution of the priesthood in the postexilic period (O'Brien, 1-26), but this is not the only case in which Malachi deals — in its own distinctive way — with themes that are also prominent in Ezra-Nehemiah (→ Book as a Whole, Setting; 2:10-12, Structure).

Genre

Several commentators agree with Pfeiffer (pp. 557-61) in describing this unit as part of a (→) prophetic disputation that takes up all of 1:6–2:9, but O'Brien (pp. 64-66) describes it as part of a (→) covenant lawsuit that also extends from 1:6 through 2:9. Whether or not this unit is considered in conjunction with 1:6-14, however, there is nothing particularly disputational or legal about it (→ Book as a Whole, Genre). It rather consists of an oracular "command" that is obliquely but still forcefully expressed in a conditional formulation (2:1-4): "If you do not change the evil ways that have already brought misfortune on you, you will suffer even greater misfortune. (So you had thus better change your ways.)" This directive is then reinforced by describing it in terms of a venerable tradition that has become inoperative but could conceivably regain its rightful role in the life of the community (2:5-9). This entails turning away from the offenses that are described in the preceding unit (1:6-14) and turning toward the positive role model that is described here in terms of Yahweh's covenant with Levi. This unit is thus a PROPHETIC CALL TO REPENTANCE predicated on the accusation and announcement of judgment that comprise the (→) prophecy of punishment in the preceding unit.

Setting

Raitt views this genre as the adaptation of an important part of a covenant renewal ceremony, in which the covenant mediator called for the people's renewed affirmation of their relationship with Yahweh on the basis of covenant law. The prophets supposedly took this manner of speaking and put it to a more general use. Even if the texts that are crucial for this hypothesis (e.g., Exod 19:1-6) do indeed reflect genuinely early tradition rather than later Deuteronomistic influence, it is nevertheless evident that the majority of textual examples adduced by Raitt from both early and late periods do not explicitly involve covenant terminology or concepts. It seems more likely that calls to covenant renewal would thus have constituted a special case of a more general phenomenon, rather than the paradigm from which all examples of the call to repentance subsequently derived.

In this case covenant terminology is explicit, but it is used in a highly idiosyncratic way that is unique to Malachi (McKenzie and Wallace, 550-52) to describe the traditional responsibilities that priests must rightly fulfill if they are to play their proper social role. Such terminology thus does not establish any link between this particular call to repentance and a broadly based tradition of covenant renewal formularies. The prophetic call to repentance could occur in a cultic context, perhaps in connection with a covenant renewal liturgy but also in connection with a communal complaint liturgy (e.g., Joel 2:12-14). It could be spoken to a group gathered in the sanctuary, but not as an integral part of the liturgy (e.g., Jer 26:1-6). It could also be spoken in a public place on an occasion that was not directly related to any cultic celebration (e.g., Jer 17:19-27; Jonah 3:4; cf. Jer 11:6). In this case the priestly addressees are of course defined in terms of their association with the cult, but this does not necessarily mean that they were addressed in a liturgical context or on a cultic occasion.

This unit, like prophetic calls to repentance in general, might have originated as a prophecy spoken in one of these public contexts — perhaps as part of a larger address to the priests including 2:1-9 — that was subsequently incorporated into its present literary context. This unit fits so programmatically into the (→) book as a whole, however, that it might also have originated as an integral part of the literary composition to which it now belongs. There is no evidence that would argue conclusively for one of these alternatives over the other.

Intention

This unit confronts the priests with the consequences of their laxness with regard to the criteria for acceptable offerings. By letting the people sacrifice unfit animals they have fostered a kind of falsehood that has had drastically negative social effects; and they have gravely compromised their traditional role, which is to give true instruction in such matters. The priests are also confronted with an ideal model of their role, which they have fallen far short of but to which they might nevertheless still aspire. By these two means they are indirectly urged to change their ways for the better.

Bibliography

J. Botterweck, "Ideal und Wirklichkeit der Jerusalemer Priester," *BibLeb* 1 (1960) 100-109; T. M. Raitt, "The Prophetic Summons to Repentance," *ZAW* 83 (1971) 30-49; K. A. Tångberg, *Die prophetische Mahnrede: Form- und traditionsgeschichtliche Studien zum prophetischen Umkehrruf* (FRLANT 143; Göttingen: Vandenhoeck & Ruprecht, 1987).

YAHWEH HOLDS THE PEOPLE ACCOUNTABLE FOR BEING UNFAITHFUL IN MARRIAGE AND THUS PROFANING HIS SANCTUARY, 2:10-12

Structure

I. Accusation of unfaithfulness	2:10-12
A. Definition of the offense	2:10
1. Rhetorical questions establishing grounds for faithfulness	2:10a
a. Do we not all have one father?	2:10aα
b. Has one God not created us?	2:10aβ

601

Both this unit and the succeeding unit (2:13-16) form part of a larger speech to the people of Judah ($\rightarrow$ 1:2–2:16, Structure). This unit is linked with its successor by the way in which the initial questions in 2:10 introduce themes that are picked up again only in 2:13-16, such as the "oneness" (*'ḥd*) of God (vv. 10a, 15aα) and the intergenerational aspect of the covenant relationship (vv. 10b, 15aβ).

Scholars readily acknowledge such links but disagree about whether and how 2:10-12 and 2:13-16 are related with respect to their content. Some have argued that the terminology regarding family relationships is entirely or largely figurative, since the unit is introduced with the metaphor of God as "father of us all" (e.g., Ogden). Two subsequent phrases, "the daughter of a foreign god" in v. 11b and "the wife of your youth" in vv. 14-15, are thus construed as referring not literally to categories of women but figuratively to such things as non-Yahwistic cults and traditions from the time when Israel was young, etc. When real women have thus been banished from the scene, the meanings of two key verbs are called into question. The verb *b'l* (v. 11b) normally means "marry" when a woman is its object; but if "the daughter of a foreign god" is not literally a woman, then this verb might well have one of its other meanings. Similarly, the verb *šlḥ* (v. 16a) would probably mean "divorce" in connection with "being faithless" (*bgd*) to a married woman, but if "being faithless to the wife of one's youth" means something like not adhering to tradition, then this verb might well have one of its many other meanings.

When the interpretation proceeds in this vein, the nature of the relationship between 2:10-12 and 2:13-16 becomes uncertain. Although most scholars regard marriage as the common concern of both units, some do not think that divorce is the issue in 2:13-16 (e.g., van der Woude, 66-71), and some do not even see marriage at issue anywhere in 2:10-16 (e.g., Ogden; Petersen, 205-6; cf. O'Brien, "Judah as Wife and Husband"). The whole matter becomes even more complicated when other contingencies are introduced. Some scholars maintain that both 2:10-12 and 2:13-16 are aimed at one particular group within Judah, assuming that the same people are implicated in the practices condemned by both units, while others maintain that each unit has a different group in view. Some hold that polygyny was still customary in the early postexilic period, and that this fact conditions whatever is said here regarding marriage, while others hold that this practice had become obsolete or very rare by this time, and is thus a negligible consideration here (Hugenberger, 84-123). There has also been considerable debate about how 2:13-16, if it is concerned with divorce, relates to the apparent provision for divorce in Deut 24:1-4 (Hugenberger, 48-83), and to the roughly contemporary attempts by Ezra and Nehemiah to dissolve marriages between Jewish men and foreign women (Ezra 9:1–10:17; Neh 13:23-30).

As a way into this thicket of problems, one may observe that the metaphorical use of familial terms to describe relationships between divine and human beings does not necessarily mean that the same terms are metaphorical when used to describe relationships between human beings. Given the precedent of describing the Jews in general as "Yahweh's children" and Jewish men in particular as "Yahweh's sons" (1:6; cf. 2:10aα [on which see below]), it is likely that the phrase "daughter of a foreign god" correspondingly designates a non-Jewish woman who worships a different god. From this particular metaphorical use it does not necessarily follow that the phrase "the wife of your youth" must also be metaphorical, since it could hardly be metaphorical in just the same way.

There are rather clear indications that the familial terminology is not metaphorical when it is used to describe relations on a human level. The penalty that is invoked on Judah for doing something (i.e., *b'l*) with a woman who worships a foreign god is formulated in terms of what should happen to each "man" (*'îš*) who does it (v. 12). When *b'l* is used in v. 11b to describe what an individual man does with an individual woman, and when the penalty for this is defined in terms of how it affects his standing in the community as a whole (v. 12; see below), this verb probably means "marry" in a literal sense. Similarly, in vv. 14-15 the faithless relation between a man and "the wife of his youth" is problematic because it impedes the goal of "godly offspring" (*zera' 'ĕlōhîm*, 2:15b), i.e., a new generation that will maintain their relationship with Yahweh their God as his "children" (1:6; 2:10a). If the state of the relationship is negatively evaluated in terms of how it affects the children of the next generation — and even the most figurative reading seems constrained to admit that the reference to children is a literal one here (e.g., Ogden, 271) — the relationship in question is likely to be marriage in the literal sense. In the context of concern for the integrity of the marriage relationship, which pervades vv. 14-15, it is likely that the verb *šlḥ* in v. 16 refers similarly to divorce in a literal sense.

The two units, 2:10-12 and 2:13-16, are thus linked by their common concern with the negative effects of two different practices on the people's covenant relationship with Yahweh: intermarriage between Jewish men who worship Yahweh and foreign women who worship some other god (2:10-12), and divorce of couples that have been married for some time (2:13-16). The text neither says nor implies anything about polygyny, and its view of intermarriage and divorce is thus not predicated on the normativeness of either polygyny or monogamy. Whether a man has one or more wives, the covenant with Yahweh is negatively affected when any wife worships another god and when a man divorces any wife.

Similarly, the text says nothing about whether intermarriage and divorce are endemic among one and the same segment of the population. It simply asserts that both are common in Judah. They are not interconnected here in the same way that they are ostensibly interconnected in Ezra 9:1–10:17 and Neh 13:23-30, as there is nothing to indicate that divorce or separation is necessarily the penalty for intermarriage. They may nevertheless be interconnected in the sense that a man who suffers the penalty for intermarriage (see below) could conceivably also suffer the consequences of divorcing his wife (→ 2:13-16). In general, however, the text applies broadly to those cases that fall into either category, whether or not there might also be a few cases that fall into both categories. With regard to the questions of how this text relates to the issue of divorce as it is raised in Ezra 9:1–10:17 and Neh 13:23-30, see below; and with regard to how this text relates to the divorce law in Deut 24:1-4, see the discussion of the next unit (→ 2:13-16, Structure).

The initial introductory question (v. 10aα) asserts that the people of Judah have a common bond as children of "one father." In view of previous references to Jacob as their human forefather (1:2) and to Yahweh as their divine father (1:6), this assertion grounds their identity in both their history as the people of Israel and their relationship with the God of Israel. The second question (v. 10aβ) puts this whole matter into a larger context by grounding Yahweh's status as Israel's father in his role as their creator. Since Israel is only one among the many peoples that Yahweh created, this situates Yahweh's distinctive relationship with his own people in the broader context of his relationship with all humanity.

The third question (v. 10b) asserts that an ideal of mutual faithfulness grows out of Israel's status as a distinctive branch of the human family, and that the people of Judah are presently falling far short of this ideal. They are heirs of a long-established covenant relationship between Yahweh and his own people that both distinguishes them from other nations (Exod 19:5-6) and serves as a sign of Yahweh's intention to bless all those whom he created (cf. Gen 1:27-28; 9:1; 12:2-3). They stand accused of "profaning" *(ḥll)* this "covenant of the fathers" *(běrît 'ābôt)* by committing an "abomination" *(tô'ēbâ)* that "profanes" *(ḥll)* the Jerusalem sanctuary. This abomination is the intermarriage of Jewish men with women that worship the gods of other nations (v. 11).

This kind of intermarriage threatens the integrity of the covenant community because their common loyalty to the worship of Yahweh alone is now the main force that binds them together. If individual Jewish families have divided loyalties in this regard, the ties that bind all Jewish families together as a people are thereby weakened. If a Jewish husband's faithfulness to Yahweh is compromised by his faithfulness to his wife, the holiness of the cult of Yahweh is profaned by the husband's participation in it. Some commentators have claimed that this proscription of intermarriage contradicts the principle stated in v. 10aβ, that all peoples were created by one God. This is not necessarily the case, however. It is quite possible to recognize and even honor the common humanity of all peoples without countenancing the kind of intermarriage that would result in the total assimilation of minority groups. Particularly in the postexilic situation, it would have been necessary for the Jewish community to maintain a strong sense of their own identity as the people of Yahweh by drawing a sharp distinction between themselves and the nations that worship other gods, precisely in order for there to be a holy people whose continuing existence would serve as a sign of Yahweh's intention to bless all nations.

The appropriate penalty for any man who marries the worshiper of a foreign god (2:12) is thus to lose standing in the two social processes that now primarily define the community: the legal process in which a man has a "witness" (*'ēd,* so *RSV* and *BHS*) who "answers" (*'ōneh*) for him (on the meaning of these terms see O'Brien, *Priest and Levite,* 69-72); and the cultic process in which a man has a priestly intermediary who assists in "bringing" (*maggîš*) his offering to Yahweh. The offender will lose his right to both legal representation and cultic participation.

In this unit intermarriage with foreign worshipers of a god other than Yahweh is regarded as a particularly serious matter, not because it involves crossing the kind of identity boundary that social groups of all sorts are generally anxious to maintain, but because it compromises the holiness of the cult on which the integrity of the community now chiefly depends. Intermarriage per se is at issue in Ezra 9:1–10:17 and Neh 13:23-30, where it gets treated in a rather different way. In these two episodes the community's leaders order marriages with foreign women to be annulled so that the men can maintain full participation in the cult. Here marriage with a foreign woman is not deemed problematic in itself, but rather marriage with a woman who worships a foreign god. This could presumably be either a non-Jewish woman who does not upon marriage become a convert to the cult of Yahweh, or a Jewish woman who participates in the cult of a god other than Yahweh (Collins, 212). Here it is also conversely assumed that the marriages will be maintained, and that the men should therefore lose their right to cultic participation.

This difference does not necessarily provide any basis on which to order this unit chronologically in relation to the events portrayed in Ezra 9:1–10:17 and Neh 13:23-30. This unit might reflect a change in the attitude toward intermarriage, from the policy reflected here to the policy that was enforced in the time of Ezra and Nehemiah, or vice versa. It could also, however, reflect an alternative or dissident view contemporaneous with the policy of Ezra and Nehemiah.

Genre

According to Pfeiffer (pp. 564-66) this unit forms part of a (→) prophetic disputation that includes all of 2:10-16, and according to O'Brien (*Priest and Levite,* 66-72) it forms part of a (→) covenant lawsuit (*rîb*) that likewise extends from 2:10 to 2:16. Whether or not this unit is considered in conjunction with 2:13-16, however, there is nothing particularly disputational or legal about it (→ Book as a Whole, Genre). It simply combines an accusation (2:10-11) with an announcement of punishment (2:12) to form a PROPHECY OF PUNISHMENT. It is a somewhat unusual example of this genre because it contains no oracular speech of Yahweh, but the punishment that is invoked is nevertheless described as an act of Yahweh. Although it reports no speech of Yahweh, it still makes a prophetic claim.

Setting

Prophets might deliver such speeches in direct encounter with a group representing the people as a whole (e.g., Jer 7:1-2, 13-15). Like prophecies of punishment in general, this unit thus might have originated as a speech delivered in such a confrontational context — perhaps as part of a larger public address including 2:1-9 — that was subsequently incorporated into its present literary context. This unit fits so programmatically into the (→) book as a whole, however, that it might also have originated as an integral part of the literary composition to which it now belongs. There is no evidence that would argue conclusively for one of these alternatives over the other.

Intention

As it invokes the penalty of losing the right to legal representation and cultic participation, while also claiming divine sanction for this penalty, this text is intended to deter the marriage of Jewish men with women who worship gods other than Yahweh.

Bibliography

→ 2:13-16.

THE PEOPLE OF JUDAH ARE URGED
NOT TO BE UNFAITHFUL TO YAHWEH
BY SEEKING DIVORCE, 2:13-16

Text

The sense of 2:15-16 is notoriously difficult. The analysis given below (→ Structure) assumes the following rather conservative and literalistic rendering of the MT, in contrast with the somewhat conjectural translation of the *RSV,* because in view of the most recently available information from the Qumran scrolls the MT remains the preferred reading (R. Fuller, "Text-Critical Problems in Mal 2:10-16," *JBL* 110 [1991] 53-57).

(15) . . . and not one thing has he [i.e., Yahweh] ever done half-spiritedly! And what does the one God seek? Godly offspring. So keep your spirit up, and let no

one be unfaithful to the wife of your youth. (16) "If one hates and divorces," says Yahweh the God of Israel, "he covers his garment with violence," says Yahweh of hosts. So keep your spirit up, and do not be unfaithful.

With regard to v. 16 I follow Hugenberger (pp. 48-76). With regard to v. 15 I go my own way, based on the following assumptions: (1) that v. 15 continues the statement begun in v. 14, which explains why Yahweh rejects the people's offerings; (2) that such an explanation would probably not shift into an interrogative mode in v. 15aα without the kind of explicit interrogative marker that shows such a shift in v. 15aβ; (3) that the *maqqeph* joining *lō'* ("not") with the noun *'eḥād* ("one") precludes the possibility of *lō'* modifying the verb; (4) that although *lō'-'eḥād* agrees with the third person masculine singular verb *'āṣâ* ("he did/made"), it is semantically impossible for *lō'-'eḥād* to be the subject; (5) that since Yahweh is the only third person masculine singular referent in vv. 14-15aα[1], Yahweh is also the most probable antecedent for the third person masculine singular pronominal subject of this verb, which in turn makes *lō'-'eḥād* its object; (6) that for the same reason Yahweh is also the most probable antecedent for the third person masculine singular pronominal suffix on the prepositional form *lô* ("to him") in v. 15aα[2]; (7) that since Yahweh's animating vitality is due to his having *rûaḥ* ("spirit"; e.g., Ps 104:29b-30a), the expression *šě'ār rûaḥ lô* ("his having a residue of spirit") probably refers to his being somewhat diminished in this regard, in which case v. 15aα asserts that Yahweh could never be thus diminished; and (8) that *hā'eḥād* ("the one") can only be the subject of the participial clause in v. 15aβ, and as such it should be identified not with the *lō'-'eḥād* of v. 15aα but with the *'ēl 'eḥād* ("one God") of 2:10aβ. For further discussion of the issues surrounding these assumptions see Hugenberger's exhaustive review (pp. 124-67), as well as the articles by Rudolph and Locher listed in the bibliography below.

Structure

of Yahweh): the man who hates and divorces has
done violence to others and to himself 2:16a
b. Exhortation: keep up the spirit and avoid
being unfaithful! 2:16b

This unit is part of a larger address to the people of Judah that includes the foregoing unit (2:10-12). It is implicitly linked with its predecessor by the way it picks up themes mentioned in 2:10 but left untreated in 2:11-12, including the oneness of God and the intergenerational aspect of the covenant relationship. It is also explicitly linked with 2:10-12 by its introduction: "and this is a second thing you do" (*RSV* "and this again you do"). This signals a transition from the subject of intermarriage to another closely interrelated but nevertheless different subject, which turns out to be divorce (→ 2:10-12, Structure). Although this unit stands in continuity with 2:10-12, there is nevertheless something new and different in 2:13-16, marked not only by the thematic transition from one kind of marital problem to another but also by the new theme of the *rûaḥ* ("spirit"), both divine and human.

According to the description in v. 13aα^2b the people recognize that Yahweh has rejected them because their sacrifices evoke no sign of his favor, but they do not understand why this is so. In vv. 14-16 they are given the underlying reason for this unfortunate situation, as they are also exhorted to act in a way that might change it for the better. The explanation generally identifies Yahweh's rejection of the people's offerings as his reaction to their practice of divorce (vv. 14b-16), as it more specifically considers two different aspects of this reaction (vv. 14b-15, 16).

First, Yahweh's negative reaction is attributed to the direct negative effect of divorce on him. Marriage is defined not only as a relationship between husband and wife but also as a relationship in which Yahweh is directly involved as a "witness" (*'d*). The marriage relationship thus takes on the nature of a lasting covenant; and because divorce violates this covenant, it becomes a kind of "unfaithfulness" (*bgd*). A man who divorces his wife is thus being "unfaithful" to her as his covenant partner, and is at the same time being "unfaithful" to Yahweh. Yahweh does not undertake the witnessing of marriages in any "half-spirited" way (→ Text), but gives it his all so that lasting marriages will bring forth a new generation that is faithful (i.e., "godly offspring," v. 15aβ). The people are thus urged to commit themselves to the maintenance of their marriages with the same fullness of spirit that characterizes Yahweh's own commitment (v. 15b).

Second, the problem of divorce is analyzed not only in terms of how it negatively affects the woman and Yahweh but also in terms of how it negatively affects the man himself (v. 16). He lets himself be subject to the disaffection that can happen as a couple grows older, and the love that generally characterizes a husband's attitude toward the "wife of his youth" (*'ēšet n'r*) thus gives way to "hate" (*śn'*). When a man divorces his wife for this reason, he "covers his garment with violence" (v. 16a). This figure is obscure, but it can probably be compared with other texts in which clothes metaphorically become the emblem of an attitude that a person assumes (Pss 73:6; 109:18; Jer

2:34; Hugenberger, 73-76). A husband who divorces his wife thus wears, as it were, a sign of the "violence" *(hāmās)* he has thereby done to others, which in turn negatively affects both his image in the community and his own self-image. The people are therefore urged again to commit themselves to marriage with the same fullness of spirit that characterizes Yahweh's own commitment (v. 16b).

The question of how this unit relates to the law of divorce in Deut 24:1-4 has been much discussed (Hugenberger, 76-81). It is difficult to make any direct comparison of these two texts, however, because this unit does not address the question of divorce in terms of its legality. Deut 24:1-4 is actually more concerned with the remarriage of a formerly divorced woman than with the initiation of divorce itself, but it nevertheless shows that a husband was allowed to divorce his wife for good cause. Mal 2:13-16 seems to assume that divorce of some sort is a legal option, and neither prohibits nor condemns divorce outright. It rather attempts to persuade the people of Judah to take care of their marriages and not to let the bonds of affection between husband and wife deteriorate, so that they will not resort to divorce lightly. It attempts to deter divorce not by making it a punishable offense but by describing its negative effects on the parties directly involved — including Yahweh himself — and on the community at large. Since Deut 24:1-4 and this unit do not stand in direct opposition to each other, it is possible that Deut 24:1-4 could have been in effect as the law of the postexilic community when this prophecy was promulgated. This is not necessarily the case, however, for although this unit seems to presuppose that divorce of some kind is legal, it does not necessarily presuppose either the same grounds for divorce or the same legal procedure that is spelled out in Deut 24:1-4.

Genre

According to Pfeiffer (pp. 564-66) this unit forms part of a (→) prophetic disputation that includes all of 2:10-16, and according to O'Brien (*Priest and Levite,* 72-73) it forms part of a (→) covenant lawsuit *(rîb)* that likewise extends from 2:10 through 2:16. Whether or not one considers this unit in conjunction with 2:13-16, however, there is nothing particularly disputational or legal about it (→ Book as a Whole, Genre). It does not argue with a contrary view held by the people, nor does it sentence them to a penalty for having committed some offense. They are already suffering the negative consequences of their actions, albeit unwittingly, and this unit explains the cause as it also urges them to avoid such actions. It is thus basically an exhortation, and since it exhorts the people to turn away from a kind of self-destructive behavior (although it does not use such telling terms as *šwb*), it has the nature of a PROPHETIC CALL TO REPENTANCE (cf. Tångberg, 137-38).

Setting

→ 2:1-9, Setting.

Intention

This unit urges the people of Judah to reconsider the practice of divorce not from the perspective of its legality but from the perspective of its negative effects on all concerned, including Yahweh and the community at large. The dissolution of the family will result in the dissolution of the community, and the dissolution of these human relationships will in turn result in the dissolution of their relationship with Yahweh — which is already evident in the cult's failure to attain its proper beneficial function. They can change this situation by fostering among themselves a spirited commitment to maintaining the covenant of marriage, the same kind of spirited commitment that Yahweh has shown in maintaining the covenant with his people.

Bibliography

G. J. Botterweck, "Schelt- und Mahnrede gegen Mischehen und Ehescheidung," *BibLeb* 1 (1960) 179-85; B. Glazier-McDonald, "Intermarriage, Divorce, and the *bat-'ēl nēkār:* Insights into Mal 2:10-16," *JBL* 106 (1987) 603-11; G. P. Hugenberger, *Marriage as a Covenant* (VTSup 52; Leiden: Brill, 1994); C. Locher, "Altes und Neues zu Maleachi 2,10-16," in *Mélanges Dominique Barthélemy* (ed. P. Casetti, O. Keel, and A. Schenker; OBO 38; Fribourg: Éditions Universitaires; Göttingen: Vandenhoeck & Ruprecht, 1981) 241-71; J. M. O'Brien, "Judah as Wife and Husband: Deconstructing Gender in Malachi," *JBL* 115 (1996) 241-50; G. S. Ogden, "The Use of Figurative Language in Malachi 2.10-16," in *Issues in Bible Translation* (ed. P. C. Stine; UBSMS 3; London: United Bible Societies, 1988) 265-73; W. Rudolph, "Zu Maleachi 2,10-16," *ZAW* 93 (1981) 85-90; A. S. van der Woude, "Malachi's Struggle for a Pure Community: Reflections on Malachi 2:10-16," in *Tradition and Re-interpretation in Jewish and Early Christian Literature* (*Fest.* J. C. H. Lebram; ed. J. W. van Henten et al.; Leiden: Brill, 1986) 65-71.

Chapter 5

THE SECOND MAJOR SECTION OF THE BOOK (2:17–3:24 [*RSV* 2:17–4:6])

Structure

611

Many commentators follow Pfeiffer (pp. 561-64, 566-67) in delineating 2:17–3:5, 3:6-12, and 3:13-21 as the basic units in this section of the book. This is problematic in two respects. First, 3:6 can hardly mark the beginning of a new unit because with respect to form it is explicitly subordinated to the foregoing announcement of judgment by the conjunction *kî* ("for"), and with respect to content it provides an explication for the foregoing announcement of judgment in 3:5 (cf. Baldwin, 245). Second, these subdivisions take no account of the way in which 3:16 introduces something altogether unprecedented in both this section and the book as a whole. At this point there is a shift from prophetic speech to narrated action (B. S. Childs, *Introduction to the Old Testament as Scripture* [Philadelphia: Fortress, 1979] 496-97). This narration is very brief (3:16), and the text quickly reverts to prophetic speech (3:17-24). The report in 3:16 is not just an aside, however. It marks a major turning point because the prophetic speech in 3:17-24 continues from 3:16, not from the prophetic speech that precedes 3:16 (Nogalski, 184-85, 206).

When 3:6-12 is recognized as a continuation of 2:17–3:5, the rhetorical profile of this section of the book begins to emerge. It consists of two units (2:17–3:12; 3:13-24), both of which begin with accusations regarding the people's "words" (*dĕbārîm*, 2:17; 3:13-15). Beyond this initial similarity, however, the two units develop in different but closely interrelated ways (cf. Alonso Schökel and Sicre Diaz, 1215). The accusation of speaking against Yahweh in 2:17 is followed in 3:1-12 by a call to respond to a coming manifestation of Yahweh's justice (3:1-7a), so as to turn from the kind of attitude and the behavior that underlie this way of speaking (3:7b-12). By contrast, the similar accusation in 3:13-15 is followed in 3:16-24 by a report of how some of the people began to make this kind of change, no longer speaking against Yahweh in the way that had led him to reject them, but speaking with one another in a way that now leads him to "heed and hear" (*qšb wšmʿ*) them (3:16). The report in 3:16 is followed by a speech of Yahweh in 3:17-24, which explains that those making this change have begun a process of interaction with Yahweh that will eventually lead to their salvation.

It is frequently claimed that 3:22 and 3:23-24 are appendices, added either as an afterthought to Malachi itself (e.g., J. M. P. Smith, 81-82; Petersen, 227-28), or as a conclusion to the Book of the Twelve (e.g., Nogalski, 209-10; Bosshard and Kratz, 39-45), or as a conclusion to the entire prophetic section of the canon (e.g., Rudolph, 290-93). Two arguments are generally adduced in support of such claims: (1) that 3:22-24 differs in form from the preceding parts of the book because the preceding parts are all of one particular genre (such as the disputation), and 3:22-24 is not of that same genre; and (2) that 3:22-24 differs in content from the rest of the book, as it introduces terminology and themes that have no more than superficial antecedents in the foregoing text, and are thus better explained as additions from a later time (e.g., Mason, 159-61; R. L. Smith, 340; Reventlow, 160-61).

The main points of the argument concerning content have been discussed above, where I have shown that the material in 3:22-24 stands in direct continuity with the thematic development of the (→) book as a whole. In addition, I mention two more minor points of detail here before turning to consider the question of how this material fits into the structure of this section. In support of the claim that 3:22 and 3:23-24 are appendices, some argue that the phrase "all Israel" *(kol-yiśrā'ēl)* shows 3:22 to have a different perspective from the rest of the book, which only has Judah in view. Some also similarly argue that the phrase "day of Yahweh" *(yôm yhwh)* shows 3:23-24 to have a different perspective from the rest of the book, which refers instead to "the day when I act" *(hayyôm 'ăšer 'ănî 'ōśeh;* 3:17aβ, 21bα) or "the day that is coming" *(hayyôm habbo';* 3:19aα; e.g., J. M. P. Smith, 85).

Although 3:22 refers to "all Israel" *(kol-yiśrā'ēl),* there is no radical disparity between this terminology and the references to Judah elsewhere in the text (2:11). Judah's identity is defined in terms of descent from Jacob (1:2) and in terms of dwelling within "the tents of Jacob" (2:12). In this case Judah is thus conceived as representing "all Israel" (cf. 1:1).

The use of the phrase *yôm yhwh* similarly indicates no radical disparity between 3:23-24 and the foregoing descriptions of this "day" in somewhat different terms. The phrase "day of Yahweh" is not a *terminus technicus* so precise that it cannot be subject to any phraseological variation whatsoever. In Zeph 1:14-18, for example, which is a locus classicus on "the day of Yahweh," one finds not only the phrase *yôm yhwh* (1:14aα) but also such phrases as *yôm 'ebrat yhwh* ("the day of Yahweh's wrath"; 1:18aβ[1]; cf. Isa 13:9b). In and of themselves, the phraseological differences between Mal 3:23 and 3:17-21 can hardly be taken to indicate radically different concepts of "the day of Yahweh."

Since no considerations of content separate 3:22-24 from the rest of the book, I now turn to consider this issue from the standpoint of literary form. With respect to the individual units thus far considered, I have shown that 1:2–3:21 cannot be divided into a series of units that are all of the same genre, whether the genre be prophetic disputation, covenant lawsuit, prophetic torah, etc. (→ Book as a Whole). The concluding verses of Malachi thus cannot be relegated to the status of appendices just because they fail to fit the generic mold that is supposedly normative for the book as a whole, for no one particular generic mold is in fact normative for the book as a whole. The form-analytical issue posed by 3:22-24 is thus not defined in terms of how the structure of this passage differs from the supposedly common structure of 2:17–3:5, 3:6-12, and 3:13-21, because these parts of the text do not form a series of units that each has a common structure. The issue is rather defined in terms of whether and how 3:22-24 forms an integral part of the prophetic speech that proceeds from the narration in 3:16.

In 3:16 two different kinds of action are reported. 3:16a describes inter-action among some of the people and Yahweh. Those who fear Yahweh confer among themselves, and Yahweh responds positively. The first part of the ensu-ing speech of Yahweh (3:17-21) describes the course of events that is set in motion by this interaction. A relationship with Yahweh is established, charac-terized by a dynamic of repentance, on the basis of which he will eventually save them and destroy the wicked, thus refuting the allegations that the people were initially accused of making in 3:13-15.

Mal 3:16b describes the writing of a book that will inform the people's corporate memory (→ 3:13-24, Structure). For those who have turned from speaking against Yahweh (3:13-15) to the positive interaction described in 3:16a, this book serves to keep them in the "fear" (yr') of Yahweh by deepen-ing their "discernment" (ḥšb; RSV "thought") of his nature (i.e., his "name" [šm]). The second part of the ensuing speech of Yahweh (3:22-24) gives fur-ther information about this book and the process of identity formation that its "remembrance" (zkr) engenders. The hitherto untitled book is first identified as the "law of Moses" (3:22). The "discernment" process (ḥšb) on which its God-fearing readers embark is then characterized in two ways. It involves looking for signs of Yahweh's activity (3:23), and this in turn involves partici-pation in a process of intergenerational repentance and reconciliation, so that the people do not fall back into their history of chronic infidelity (3:24; cf. 3:7) and thus suffer the imposition of Yahweh's ban.

Mal 3:22-24 thus appears to be an integral component of 3:13-24 with respect to form as well as content. As part of the speech of Yahweh in 3:17-24, 3:22-24 explicates the action that is narrated in 3:16b, just as 3:17-21 ex-plicates the action that is narrated in 3:16a. This analysis is not materially af-fected by the textual variant that appears in some LXX mss., in which the or-der of 3:22 and 3:23-24 is reversed. Every version of the text includes both subunits, and in any combination they relate to the other parts of this unit in virtually the same way, even if their order according to the MT is reversed. By ending in this way Malachi may also provide a suitable ending for the Book of the Twelve or for the prophetic section of the canon, but in view of how 3:22-24 forms an integral part of this unit in the context of this section and the book as a whole, there is no reason to assume that this concluding passage or any part of it was designed primarily for either of these other pur-poses.

Genre

This section consists of two units with different generic shapes. The first (2:17–3:12) is a (→) prophetic call to repentance, and the second (3:13-24) is a (→) prophetic report. These two units complement each other in a way that re-inforces the call to repentance.

614

In the (→) prophetic call to repentance (2:17–3:12) the people are urged to turn from speaking against Yahweh and to begin paying their full share toward the maintenance of the temple cult. The impetus for this change is an imminent purge of the priesthood, conducted by someone who is claimed to be sent by Yahweh. This reform signals that Yahweh is bringing the entire society to justice, starting from the cult. As the people begin to change their ways, they will begin to share in what Yahweh is accomplishing. By establishing the temple's economic viability, they will take part in a larger process through which Yahweh is working for their enjoyment of the fruits of justice.

In the prophetic report (3:13-24) some of the people abandon the kind of words that provoke Yahweh's rejection and begin to converse in a way that gains his favor. By making this change they also begin to engage their traditions in a new way, using the book of the law of Moses to inform their corporate memory, and using its interpretation as a means of discerning Yahweh's actions. This group thus opens themselves to further and deeper involvement in Yahweh's work of bringing the world to justice. They embark on a process that extends from generation to generation, through which all those who fear Yahweh will eventually be reckoned righteous and will finally be saved.

Mal 3:13-24 provides a concrete example of the kind of change that 2:17–3:12 is calling for. In the prophetic report at least some of the people do turn from speaking against Yahweh, thus reorienting themselves onto a path of repentance with salvific potential. At the same time, however, it is a more general example. At issue in 3:13-24 are not specific cultic practices but only the general way in which people interact in engaging the tradition. As this section progresses from one unit to the other, it moves from the specific to the general, as it also moves from the potential to the actual. The prophetic report thus provides a substantiating warrant for doing not just what 2:17–3:12 calls for but the *kind* of thing that 2:17–3:12 calls for. In the final analysis the dominant tone is parenetic, and this section may therefore be described as a PROPHETIC EXHORTATION.

Setting

→ 1:6–2:16, Setting.

Intention

This section addresses a malaise perceived to be prevalent in the early postexilic Jewish community, a malaise reflected in the way the people commonly speak. Their words reflect an attitude of hopelessness because of the general disarray in both cultic institutions and socioeconomic relations. Yahweh himself seems indifferent to the situation, and there is thus no use in trying to be conscientious in matters of either religion or morals.

In an attempt to counter this attitude the people are offered an incentive to full participation in the religious life of the community, defined in terms of its two main overlapping aspects. On the one hand they are urged to fulfill their cultic obligations by offering acceptable animals for sacrifice and by paying the full share of their tithes. On the other hand they are also presented with the example of a group that has begun to read and discuss the story of the covenant's origins, to understand how their common life might be better ordered on the basis of the covenant.

In both cases the people's participation is elicited in response to initiatives taken by Yahweh. Their cultic obligations deserve reconsideration because of a reform that is underway, a purge of the priesthood that is being carried out in Yahweh's name. This is the sign of a much more extensive renewal process that Yahweh is instigating, in which they can begin to take part by contributing their full share toward the temple's upkeep. Yahweh's involvement in such a process is evident in the potential that an economically viable temple cult holds for the community's overall prosperity.

The practice of reading and interpreting the law of Moses also deserves their consideration because of the vitality that it is demonstrating in the face of the current malaise. This, too, is a sign of the great renewal process that Yahweh has undertaken, in which the people can begin to take part by pondering the meaning of the tradition and thereby attempting to discern what Yahweh is presently asking of them. Yahweh's involvement in such a process is evident in the potential that this mode of identity formation holds for the community's survival through space and time.

Bibliography

E. Bosshard and R. G. Kratz, "Maleachi im Zwölfprophetenbuch," *BN* 52 (1990) 27-46; J. Nogalski, *Redactional Processes in the Book of the Twelve* (BZAW 218; Berlin and New York: de Gruyter, 1993) 182-212.

YAHWEH CALLS THE PEOPLE FROM SPEAKING AGAINST HIM TO SERVING HIM RIGHTLY, 2:17–3:12

Structure

I. Accusation of troublesome speech   2:17
  A. Accusation proper: you have wearied Yahweh
     with your words   2:17aα
  B. Explanation   2:17aβb
     1. Imputation of a question to the people: you say,
        "How so?"   2:17aβ¹
     2. Answer to this question   2:17aβ²
        a. By saying that Yahweh favors evildoers   2:17bα
        b. By asking where the God of justice is   2:17bβ

II. Call to respond to the manifestation of Yahweh's justice:
speech of Yahweh   3:1-12
  A. Announcement of coming judgment   3:1-7aα
    1. The appearance of a messenger   3:1-4
      a. The messenger's purpose   3:1
        1) Yahweh is sending him to prepare his way   3:1abα
        2) His coming marks a renewal of the covenant
and manifests the true source of delight   3:1bβ
      b. The role of the messenger   3:2-4
        1) Rhetorical questions describing the day of
his coming as almost unbearable   3:2a
        2) Explication   3:2b-4
          a) What he can be compared with:
two similes   3:2b
            (1) Like a refiner's fire   3:2bα
            (2) Like fullers' soap   3:2bβ
          b) What he will do (expanding on one of
the similes): he will purify the sons
of Levi as silver and gold are refined   3:3a
          c) Effects of what he will do   3:3b-4
            (1) The cult will be efficacious   3:3b-4a
              (a) The priests will make offerings
rightly   3:3b
              (b) The offerings of Judah and
Jerusalem will be pleasing
to Yahweh   3:4a
            (2) As it was before   3:4b
              (a) In days of old   3:4bα
              (b) In former years   3:4bβ
    2. The appearance of Yahweh himself   3:5-7aα
      a. Yahweh's purpose: I will draw near
for judgment   3:5aα¹
      b. Yahweh's role   3:5aα²b
        1) Role proper: a witness   3:5aα²
        2) Those against whom he is quick
to witness   3:5aβbα
          a) Those who specifically . . .   3:5aβ
            (1) Practice sorcery   3:5aβ¹
            (2) Commit adultery
            (3) Swear falsely
            (4) Oppress the wage laborer, the
widow, and the orphan   3:5aβ²
            (5) Thrust aside the sojourner   3:5bα
          b) Those who generally do not fear me   3:5bβ
      c. Explication in terms of past relationship
between Yahweh and the people   3:6-7aα
        1) On Yahweh's part: I have not changed   3:6a

    b) Positively stated in terms of worldwide
        recognition: all the nations will call
        you blessed, for you will become a
        land of delight   3:12

    The initial accusation (2:17) shows that this unit mainly concerns a widespread malaise that is reflected in the way the people speak of Yahweh's involvement in their present situation. Evildoers seem to prosper by their wrongdoing, which leads many to say that Yahweh "delights *(ḥpṣ)* in them" (v. 17bβ[1]), and that he is ineffective in maintaining "justice" (*mišpāṭ*, v. 17bβ[2]). The rest of this unit (3:1-12) attempts to disabuse the people of this negative attitude by first announcing that Yahweh's "justice" (*mišpāṭ* [*RSV* "judgment"], v. 5aα[1]) will soon begin to be manifest in a reform of the cult (3:1-4), a reform that will in turn result in a moral renewal of society at large (3:5). The people are then urged to take part in this process by conscientiously resuming their full participation in the cult, so that Yahweh's blessing will emanate from the temple into the socioeconomic dimension of their daily life (3:6-11). It will thus become evident that Yahweh's "delight" *(ḥpṣ)* lies in good things, not in wrongdoing (3:12).

    The overall process has two phases. Yahweh will first "send a messenger" *(šlḥ mal'āk)* to prepare for his coming (3:1a), and then Yahweh himself will "draw near for judgment" *(qrb lĕmišpāṭ,* 3:5). The syntax of 3:3b makes it difficult to tell whether the messenger sent by Yahweh is further described here as *mal'āk habbĕrît* ("messenger of the covenant"), so that his coming as enforcer of the covenant is contrasted with Yahweh's coming as "the Lord *(hā'ādôn)* into his temple" (so, e.g., Petersen, *Late Israelite Prophecy,* 42); or whether the messenger's coming is described in terms of his becoming "the lord" of Yahweh's temple, which is also "his" (i.e., the messenger's) in the sense that he controls its administration (so, e.g., Wallis, 231); or whether *mal'āk habbĕrît* is used here as an epithet for Yahweh himself, not to be confused with the messenger sent by Yahweh, so that Yahweh comes into his own temple as "Lord" and "messenger of the covenant" after he has sent another "messenger to prepare the way" (so, e.g., Glazier-McDonald, *Malachi,* 130-42). This matter is further complicated by the fact that *mal'āk* could refer to a heavenly being rather than a prophetic figure, an "angel" whose epiphany would be tantamount to the disclosure of Yahweh's own presence (van der Woude, 293-99).

    The first phase may thus entail the coming of the messenger sent by Yahweh as something altogether distinct from the subsequent coming of Yahweh himself; or it may entail the coming of this messenger as a preliminary manifestation of Yahweh's presence in the temple, prior to a more complete manifestation of Yahweh's power as judge and enforcer of the covenant in the wider society. In any case the first phase demonstrates something with regard to the "covenant" *(bĕrît),* a relationship between Yahweh and his people that has previously been defined as cultically based (2:10-16), a relationship that in turn depends on the maintenance of a subsidiary covenant between Yahweh and the Levitical priests (1:6–2:9). The first phase also demonstrates something with regard to the "delight" *(ḥpṣ)* that the people might take in the state of their relationship with Yahweh (3:12b), if they were not under the mistaken impression that he "delights" in evildoers (2:17bβ).

In the first phase the covenant will begin to be restored by reforming the lax and corrupt group on which the integrity of this relationship chiefly depends, i.e., the priests. By showing that Yahweh "takes no delight" in them (1:10bα; *RSV* "has no pleasure"), it will become evident that he generally takes no delight in wrongdoing, and the way will then be prepared for a more comprehensive demonstration of this fact in the second phase (3:5). The purge of the priesthood will not be easy, for harsh measures will be necessary in order to get them sacrificing rightly again (3:2-4). Once this first phase is accomplished, however, Yahweh's judgment will in the second phase begin to take effect against those who, by their transgressions of the various covenant norms, show that they do not "fear" him (*yr'*, 3:5; cf. 1:6bα^2; 2:5).

The people are then reminded that, in view of their past history, their present unfortunate situation is not likely to be the result of any change on Yahweh's part, but is rather more likely to be the result of their failure to fulfill their covenant obligations. Indeed, their very survival shows that Yahweh characteristically continues to be merciful despite their characteristically continuing to be unfaithful (3:6-7aα). They are thus urged to respond in kind to the initiative that Yahweh is presently taking. In response to his sending a messenger and thereby reforming the cult, so that the priests will administer its sacrifices properly (3:1-4), the people are to cease from "robbing" *(qb')* Yahweh, i.e., to cease from not paying their full "tithe" *(ma'ăśēr)* for the temple's upkeep and from not presenting worthy offerings *(tĕrûmâ,* 3:8b; cf. 1:13b-14). As the temple begins to acquire enough of a food surplus to have an economically viable foundation, the curse (3:9; cf. 1:14; 2:2aβ) will abate and Yahweh will conspicuously bless their agriculture with prosperity (3:10-12).

Genre

As several scholars have observed (e.g., Pfeiffer, 561-62, 566-67), there are elements of (→) prophetic disputation in this unit. These do not, however, constitute its basic structure. The unit as a whole does contend with the popular opinion that is summarily described at the outset in 2:17, but not by arguing for its antithesis. This unit rather points to an imminent reform of the cult (3:1-4) as the beginning of a process that will eventually demonstrate how false this opinion is (3:5-7a), and urges the people to begin taking part in this process by contributing fully to the cult as it undergoes reform (3:7b-12). They will thus discover that their cultic laxness is symptomatic of their overall laxness in fulfilling their covenant obligations toward Yahweh, and that this laxness — rather than any moral indifference on Yahweh's part — is the cause of their current malaise. By turning away from laxness toward their cultic obligations they will begin to participate in the process by which Yahweh is extending the reinforcement of covenant norms to all areas of society, thus reversing the tendency toward injustice and cursedness so that justice and blessedness will prevail.

This unit does not attempt to refute a popularly held opinion. It rather attempts to get the people to change their ways with respect to their cultic participation, thus reacting positively to a harsh purge of the priesthood as a development divinely sanctioned by Yahweh. They will thereby begin to discover how false the popular opinion is and eventually change other aspects of their behavior that are also rooted in it. The operative term is *šwb* ("return," 3:7aβ). This unit is therefore a PROPHETIC CALL TO REPENTANCE (cf. Tångberg, 138-39; Collins, 213).

Setting

→ 2:1-9, Setting.

Intention

This unit aims for its audience to see a purge of the priesthood as a sign that Yahweh does not approve of wrongdoing, and that he is a God who works for justice. They are urged to contribute fully to the upkeep of the temple, thus recognizing the validity of the cult as it is being reformed. In this way they will begin to turn from their overall unfaithfulness to covenantal norms and to reverse the overall negative effects of this on their common life. They will begin to participate in Yahweh's efforts to establish justice in accord with covenantal norms and cooperate in his efforts to foster the positive effects of this on their common life.

Bibliography

→ 2:1-9, Bibliography; also B. Glazier-McDonald, "*Mal'ak habbĕrît:* The Messenger of the Covenant in Mal 3:1," *HAR* 11 (1987) 93-104; B. V. Malchow, "The Messenger of the Covenant in Mal 3:1," *JBL* 103 (1984) 252-55; D. L. Petersen, *Late Israelite Prophecy* (SBLMS 23; Missoula, Mont.: Scholars Press, 1977) 42-45; A. S. van der Woude, "Der Engel des Bundes: Bemerkungen zu Maleachi 3,1c und seinem Kontext," in *Die Botschaft und die Boten* (*Fest.* H. W. Wolff; ed. J. Jeremias and L. Perlitt; Neukirchen-Vluyn: Neukirchener, 1981) 289-300.

THOSE WHO FEAR YAHWEH TURN FROM SPEAKING AGAINST HIM AND ARE THUS DESTINED FOR SALVATION, 3:13-24 (*RSV* 3:13–4:6)

Structure

I. Accusation of contentious words: speech of Yahweh	3:13-15
A. Accusation proper: your words have been stout against me	3:13a
B. Explanation	3:13b-15
1. Imputation of a question to the people: you say, "How have we spoken against you?"	3:13b
2. Answer to this question: you have said that . . .	3:14-15
a. It is pointless to serve God, and worthless to keep his charge and walk earnestly before him	3:14
b. We now deem the arrogant blessed, since evildoers not only prosper but when they put God to the test they also escape	3:15
II. Reaction of those who feared Yahweh	3:16-24
A. Narration: report of what they did	3:16
1. Interaction involving Yahweh and those who feared him	3:16abα
a. They spoke with one another	3:16a
b. He heeded and heard them	3:16bα
2. Result of this interaction: a book of remembrance was written in Yahweh's presence for those who feared him and thought on his name	3:16bβ
B. Speech of Yahweh explicating these developments	3:17-24
1. Explication of the interaction involving Yahweh and those who feared him	3:17-21
a. Description of their destiny	3:17-18
1) Outcome on the day when Yahweh acts	3:17
a) They will be my special possession	3:17a
b) I will spare them as a man spares his son who serves him	3:17b
2) Its effect in the meantime: regaining the capacity to distinguish . . .	3:18
a) Between the righteous and the wicked	3:18a
b) Between one who serves God and one who does not	3:18b
b. Contrast of the fate of evildoers and the destiny of those who fear Yahweh on the day when he acts	3:19-21
1) Announcement: behold, the day is coming, burning like an oven!	3:19a
2) Consequences of this day	3:19b-21
a) For all the arrogant and evildoers:	

The initial accusation (3:13-15) shows that this unit mainly concerns a widespread malaise that is reflected in the way the people speak of their present situation. Evildoers seem to prosper by their wrongdoing, which leads many to say that there is no point in "serving" (*'bd*) Yahweh or in trying to keep his ordinances (3:14), and that the "arrogant" (*zēdîm*) and the evildoers (*'śh rišʿâ*) are thus most fortunate (3:15). The rest of this unit (3:16-24) describes how some of the people began to turn away from such speech, thus reversing the dynamic in which despair and inaction keep reinforcing each other. By mutually encouraging one another this group shows the "fear" (*yr'*) of Yahweh and the concern for his "name" (*šēm*) that Yahweh has so far found lacking (1:6, 11; 2:2, 5), thus gaining the favorable recognition by Yahweh (3:16bα) that has so far eluded them (1:10b; 2:13b). This interaction establishes a relationship in which those who fear Yahweh become his "special possession" (*sĕgûlâ*, 3:17a), because they "serve" (*'bd*) him as a son serves his father (3:17b; cf. 1:6; 2:10). On the basis of this relationship it will soon become evident that there is a reason to "serve" (*'bd*) Yahweh, and that the "righteous" (*zēdîm*) and the "evildoers" (*'śh rišʿâ*) are not so fortunate after all.

Because of their positive response Yahweh will "spare" (*ḥml*) those who fear him "on the day when he acts" (3:17), i.e., at the time when he "draws near for judgment" (*qrb lĕmišpāṭ*, 3:5). On them the "sun of righteousness" shall dawn, imparting to them health and vigor (3:20). The "arrogant" (*zēdîm*) and the "evildoers" (*'śh rišʿâ*), however, will be consumed like stubble burned by fire (3:19). As those who fear Yahweh come to be reckoned righteous (*ṣdq*, 3:20; cf. 3:18a), they will share in Yahweh's victory over the wicked (3:21).

In turning away from the kind of cynical speech that is targeted in 3:13-15, those who do so show that they fear Yahweh, and thus begin the process of conversion that finally destines them for salvation. In order to encourage such conversion, Yahweh will send the prophet Elijah (3:23). He will foster the kind of intergenerational fidelity to covenant traditions (3:24a) that is necessary for both a properly functioning sacrificial cult (2:3-7) and a well-ordered society (2:10, 13-16), thus preparing the people to face the day of Yahweh.

A "book of remembrance" (*sēper zikrôn*, 3:16b) plays a similar part in this process. Most interpreters regard this as an aide mémoire for Yahweh, analogous to other heavenly books in which the names of the righteous and the wicked are inscribed (e.g., Exod 32:32-33; Isa 65:6; Dan 12:1b), so that Yahweh can distinguish those who are to be spared from those who are not on the day when he acts. It is doubtful, however, that the book mentioned here has this function. Yahweh's heavenly book is never called a "book of remembrance," as this book is, but rather a "book of life" (*sēper ḥayyîm*, Ps 69:29 [*RSV* 28]), a "book of truth" (*kĕtāb 'ĕmet*, Dan 10:21), etc. A "book of remembrance" is rather a document that records memorable deeds for human beings on earth. In Est 6:1 King Ahasuerus has such a book *(sēper zikrōnôt)* read "in [his] presence" *(lipnê hammelek)* and is thus reminded of Mordecai's still unrewarded past loyalty to him; and in Exod 17:14 Yahweh orders Moses to write "in a book" *(bassēper)* a "remembrance" *(zikrôn)* of Israel's victory over the Amalekites, so that Joshua will be reminded of Yahweh's intention to blot out Amalek. The "book of remembrance" in Mal 3:16b has a similar function (Nogalski, 207-9).

Although this book is written "in [Yahweh's] presence" (*lĕpānāyw; RSV* "before him"), this does not necessarily mean that it is located in heaven. This phrase could also refer to the earthly sanctuary where Yahweh's presence is manifest. Moreover, this book is not a record of God-fearers' names written for Yahweh, but a record written "for God-fearers" *(lĕyir'ê yhwh)* who are "pondering his [Yahweh's] name" *(ḥōšĕbê šĕmô)*. It is thus a document used in the sanctuary to remind worshipers of the traditions concerning Yahweh, so that they will continue to fear Yahweh and reflect on the implications of his reputation. The book plays a role that is similar to the coming of Elijah, serving in the meantime as an incentive to the same process of conversion that the prophet will encourage.

Nogalski (pp. 209-10) has suggested that the document in question is the book of Malachi itself. This is unlikely in view of the way in which 3:17-24 serves to explicate the actions reported in 3:16 (→ 2:17–3:24, Structure). Just as 3:17-21 explicates what is narrated in 3:16a, 3:22-24 explicates what is narrated in 3:16b. The command in 3:22, to "remember" *(zkr)* the law of Moses, is thus probably a catchword reference to this "book of remembrance" *(sēper zikrôn)*. Since the document is described in terms of what Yahweh commanded for "all Israel at Horeb," it probably includes the traditions now contained in Deuteronomy (e.g., Deut 5:2-3), but it is probably not limited to Deuteronomic traditions (O'Brien, 85-112). This document will serve as a repository of the tradition that needs to be engaged through interpretation, in order to live the kind of repentant life that will lead to salvation. The book of Malachi is rather a model of the kind of interpretation that is conducive to living such a life (→ 2:17–3:24, Structure; Book as a Whole, Structure).

Genre

Although the initial questioning in 3:13-15 is reminiscent of a (→) prophetic disputation (Pfeiffer, 362-64), this does not in the final analysis define the structure of this unit as a whole, nor even the structure of the introduction in 3:13-15. In the context of the unit as a whole 3:13-15 functions as an accusation, which is subsequently juxtaposed with a brief report (3:16). This juxtaposition implies that the report narrates the reaction to the accusation. Although there is much else in the speech of Yahweh that forms the rest of the unit (3:17-24), it all serves to explicate one of the two things that are reported in 3:16.

One block of this material (3:17-21) draws out the future implications of the interaction described in 3:16a. This segment of the text is basically a (→) prophecy of salvation, as it promises a favorable destiny to those who fear and serve Yahweh in contrast with those who do not. Another block of material (3:22-24) draws out the future implications of the book whose production is described in 3:16b. This segment of the text is basically a (→) prophetic exhortation, as it urges the people to heed this "book of remembrance" as an incentive to repentance until Elijah comes.

Although the text is generically heterogeneous in this way, its various generic elements function so as to reinforce the basic structure of an accusation (3:13-15) combined with a report of the reaction to this accusation (3:16), and of the developments that are thereby set in motion (3:17-24). This stands in contrast with the previous unit (2:17–3:12), where a similar accusation (2:17) introduces a prophetic call to repentance (→ 2:17–3:12, Genre). 2:17 describes speech that is symptomatic of an attitude, from which the people are called to repent (3:1-12). 3:13-15 describes speech that is symptomatic of a similar attitude, from which some of the people actually did begin to repent (3:16-24). This unit is therefore basically a report of how some of the people began to heed a call to repentance, of the sort that is found in the previous unit. By this response those who fear Yahweh are entering into a process of repentance. This process is to be continually repeated until the time when the words and deeds of the prophet Elijah are reactualized (3:23-24a), thus showing that their salvation is at hand.

This unit may be described as a PROPHETIC REPORT, an adaptation of the (→) report genre that is prophetic in two senses. First, it treats a prophetic theme, as it narrates a positive response to a prophetic call to repentance. Second, it does so in a prophetic way, using oracular speech of Yahweh to elaborate on the third person description of the narration itself.

Setting

The report genre might have been adapted for prophetic purposes in the same kind of popular setting that gave rise to stories of prophetic feats (Long, 347-48), or in the same kind of academic setting that gave rise to prophetic historiography (→ Haggai, Book as a Whole, Setting). In this case the report is not an integrated narrative but a composition with a narrative sequence that is implied in the juxtaposition of accusation with reportage. This, along with the close compositional dependence of this unit on its predecessor (→ 2:17–3:24, Structure) would suggest that this text was composed through a redactional process, in roughly the same eclectic way and in basically the same mantic scribal context in which prophetic history was typically composed.

Intention

This unit aims to show that the previous prophetic call to repentance (2:17–3:12) had been effective, so that when the people were again accused of speaking against Yahweh (3:13-15; cf. 2:17), those who feared Yahweh began to discuss among themselves how they should change their ways. Their positive response, based on their anticipation of the messenger sent by Yahweh and guided by the book of the law of Moses, provides readers with a model of how to relate to Yahweh in anticipation of the coming of Elijah, on the day when Yahweh finally draws near for judgment.

Bibliography

G. J. Botterweck, "Die Sonne der Gerechtigkeit am Tage Jahweh: Auslegung von Mal 3:13-21," *BibLeb* 1 (1960) 253-60; B. O. Long, "2 Kings iii and Genres of Prophetic Narrative," *VT* 23 (1973) 337-48.

GLOSSARY

GENRES

APOCALYPSE (Apokalypse). A genre of revelatory literature with a narrative
framework, in which a revelation is mediated by an otherworldly being
to a human recipient, disclosing a transcendent reality which is both temporal, in that it envisages eschatological salvation, and spatial, in that it
involves another, supernatural, world.

The two main subgenres are apocalypses with or without an otherworldly journey. The point at issue here is not the presence or absence of a single motif, since the otherworldly journey provides the
context for the revelation and determines the form of the work (cf.
1 Enoch 1–36; *2 Enoch; 3 Baruch*). All the Jewish apocalypses which
are not otherworldly journeys have a review of history in some form
and may be conveniently labeled "historical" apocalypses (cf. Daniel;
the *Animal Apocalypse* and *Apocalypse of Weeks* in *1 Enoch;* 4 Ezra;
2 Baruch).

The genre functions to provide a view of the world that will be a
source of consolation in the face of distress and a support and authorization for whatever course of action is recommended, and to invest this
worldview with the status of supernatural revelation.

The genre is attested in Persian and Greco-Roman literature as
well as in the Jewish and Christian corpora. Apocalypses generally presuppose a crisis of some kind, but the specific kind of crisis may vary
widely.

CALL TO COMMUNAL COMPLAINT (Aufruf zur Volksklage) A directive addressed to a community threatened by some catastrophe, such as famine,
plague, or enemy attack, to assemble for a liturgy of communal (→)
complaint. Such a call typically consists of: (1) one or more imperatives
rousing the community and calling for their participation, either in the
rite itself or in various activities associated with it; (2) direct address of

627

the group(s) involved; and (3) a motivating description of the crisis that occasions their assembling for a communal complaint liturgy. The overall intent is for the community to join in prayer to Yahweh, asking him to keep the crisis from developing into a disaster. In actual practice the call to communal complaint was presumably broadcast loudly in public by some kind of crier, and in several respects it thus resembles the (→) sentinel report.

This genre is frequently adapted for use in various kinds of prophecies, where it serves purposes other than actually convening the community for communal complaint, such as calling the audience's attention to the complaint-worthy crisis situation with which a prophecy is concerned. The most fully developed example of the call to communal complaint is Joel 1:2-14. Other examples include Isa 14:31; 32:11-14; Jer 6:26; 25:34; 49:3; Zeph 1:11; and Zech 11:2.

COMMISSION TO PROPHESY (Beauftragung zum Prophezeien) An adaptation of the conventional way in which a superior gives an authoritative charge to a subordinate, used for the specific purpose of describing the mission of a prophet. A commission might be ordinarily addressed by a military commander to an envoy (e.g., 2 Sam 11:18-21), by a king to a royal official (e.g., 2 Kgs 19:2-7), by a person of means to a servant (e.g., Gen 32:3-5), or by a prophet to an emissary (e.g., 2 Kgs 9:1-3; 1 Kgs 14:7-11). The mission of a prophet can be similarly described in terms of receiving an authoritative charge but from Yahweh rather than another human being. With respect to form, a commission would normally include commands or specific instructions depending on the particular role that the superior intends for the subordinate to play. In the case of a prophetic commission the form tends to include such commands from Yahweh as "go!" "speak!" and "prophesy!" (e.g., Amos 7:15), as well as an oracle that the prophet is thereby directed to convey to some individual or group (but cf. 1 Kgs 19:15-16). The oracle is often introduced by a (→) messenger formula ("thus says Yahweh"), characterizing the prophet specifically as Yahweh's designated messenger (e.g., 1 Kgs 12:23-24; 21:18-19).

This particular adaptation of the commission does not occur as an independent genre but as an element in narratives about prophets. In this context it is often prefaced by the (→) prophetic word formula: "the word of Yahweh came to x . . ." (e.g., 1 Kgs 12:22-24; 21:17-19). It thus becomes part of a stock scene that is commonly described in (→) prophetic history (e.g., Hag 2:1-9, 20-23), in the (→) report of a prophetic revelation (e.g., Jer 2:1-3), and in the (→) prophetic vocation account (e.g., Isa 6:9-10; Jer 1:4-10; Ezek 3:4-11).

COMPLAINT (Klage als Beschwerde, Beschwerdeklage, Bittklage, Anklage) A type of (→) psalm to be sung or recited by cultic personnel on behalf of persons in distress, who are complaining to Yahweh about their situation and petitioning him for deliverance. Some complaints are particularly designed for the use of individuals, in which case the distress is of a sort that typically befalls individuals, such as getting sick, being guilty of some sin, being prosecuted for some offense, losing wealth or social standing, being persecuted by personal enemies, etc. Other complaints are particularly designed for the use of entire communities, in which case the distress is of a sort that typically befalls communities, such as famine, plague, attack by enemies, etc.

A plea for deliverance from distress is the complaint's definitive element. In addition, a complaint may include any and all of the following elements, though not necessarily in this order: invocation of Yahweh; description of distress; confession of guilt or, conversely, protestation of innocence; affirmation of confidence in Yahweh; curse of enemies; and vow of sacrifice.

Complaints were sung or recited on behalf of the individual or community in the context of complaint liturgies. For an individual this liturgy typically involved coming to the sanctuary with family and friends, offering the appropriate sacrifices, and praying the complaint. Other practices might also be involved, such as the individual's remaining at the sanctuary overnight, or, in the case of certain sicknesses, being diagnosed by the priests, etc. A communal complaint liturgy typically involved an assembly of the community at a sanctuary or other public place (→ call to communal complaint) in order to perform ritual acts of repentance, pray the complaint, and perhaps initiate an oracular inquiry as to what might be done to remedy the situation (→ report of an oracular inquiry). Prophets sometimes officiated at communal complaint liturgies, in which case the complaint might take the form of a (→) prophetic complaint.

COVENANT LAWSUIT (Bundesrechtsstreit, Prozess um den Bund, Prozess um das Bundesrecht) A commonly used but highly problematic genre classification, based on the supposition that because some prophetic texts are thematically concerned with Israel's violations of covenant laws and because they describe Yahweh's reaction metaphorically with the imagery of legal process, they therefore have the form of a lawsuit *(rîb)*. The form is said to consist of such elements as: (1) preliminary motions; (2) judge's interrogation; (3) indictment; (4) declaration of guilt; (5) threat and/or condemnation; and (6) ultimatum (→ Malachi, Book as a Whole, Genre and Bibliography).

DIRGE (Leichenklage, Leichenlied) An expression of grief over someone's death, at the funeral or on some other memorial occasion, uttered in simple stereotypical forms by associates and relatives of the deceased (e.g., Jer 22:18; 2 Sam 3:33-34) and in more elaborate poetic forms by gifted individuals or professional mourners (e.g., 2 Sam 1:19-27; cf. Jer 9:16-18 [*RSV* 17-19]). In its more elaborate forms the dirge typically bewails the loss of the deceased, celebrates his or her merits, and urges those present to take part in the mourning.

DREAM INTERPRETATION (Traumdeutung) A speech formulated in response to a (→) dream report, usually corresponding in its main elements to the various aspects of the dream described in the report but sometimes based on a rather free-form allegorization of the dream. Such a speech generally reflects the social role of a professional dream interpreter.

DREAM REPORT (Traumbericht) A type of (→) report, formulated in either first or third person, designed to recount the principal elements of a dream experience. There is typically an introduction identifying the dreamer, the locality, and other circumstantial factors, as well as a conclusion that often includes the reaction of the dreamer or the subsequent fulfillment of the dream.

HISTORICAL STORY (Historische erzählte Geschichte) A (→) story that is mainly concerned with recounting and explaining a particular event. The historical story may contain mythical, legendary, or fictional elements, but when such elements are present they are subservient to the primary intention of recounting and interpreting an event that actually happened. In recounting a single event the historical story differs from other kinds of historiographical compositions that cover a whole series of events or an entire epoch. The historical story also differs from the (→) report, which similarly describes a single event but without the relatively well-developed plot that is characteristic of the story.

HISTORY (Geschichtsschreibung) An extensive, continuous, written account of a particular time in the past, composed as the result of an investigation in which the author surveys, evaluates, and interprets the existing sources of information in light of concerns generated by the author's own contemporary situation. The quality of the account depends on the nature of the existing sources of information and the extent of their availability to the author, whether they be oral traditions or written documents, firsthand observations or vague memories, artifactual remains or the still observable effects of events on the sites where they happened. The criteria by which sources are evaluated can vary considerably depending on the social and cultural background of the author. (Ancient and modern historians differ considerably in this regard, as do historians from the same time and place but with different ideological assumptions.) The author's interpretation is often expressed in the way the historical narrative is thematically organized and chronologically periodized. Historians generally intend to document and reflect on the past in order to understand, legitimate, or variously define the social institutions and main developments of their own time. Since historiography presupposes literacy, it developed in Israel primarily among scribes who served as advisers to the royal government.

HYMN OF PRAISE (Hymnus, Loblied) A type of (→) psalm whose form is basically defined by the combination of (1) a call to praise or worship and

(2) a description of Yahweh's praiseworthy attributes and/or deeds. It may also include (3) blessings and (4) petitions. The function of the hymn of praise is to extol Yahweh while also involving the congregation in the activity of worship. Hymns often reflect in their content the kind of liturgical setting in which they were performed, i.e., generally sung by choirs with instrumental accompaniment in the context of a procession or dance, with the congregation sometimes making an antiphonal response.

INSTRUCTION (Instruktion, Unterweisung) A type of discourse that gives guidance on matters of traditional concern to an individual or group. Such discourse is produced by someone in a position of civil, religious, or administrative authority through reflective study of the traditions in question. The content thus may vary depending on the nature of the traditions that are studied, whether laws, cultic practices, or aphoristic wisdom, etc. The form may likewise vary, though instruction tends to be expressed in a predominantly imperative mode. The most clearly defined examples of the genre are instructions given by scribes concerning wisdom traditions (e.g., Prov 1–9; 22:17–24:22; → wisdom instruction), but there are also priestly and prophetic adaptations of this kind of didactic discourse (→ priestly torah, prophetic instruction).

LAMENTATION (Volksklage, Untergangsklage) A lyric bewailing the disaster, defeat, or destruction that has befallen a community. The lamentation may have been recited or sung as part of a public assembly held in the wake of the catastrophe, at which the community was called to such activities as mourning, fasting, repentance, and prayer for the survivors' salvation (e.g., Joel 1:13-14; 1 Sam 7:5-6; Judg 20:26). In its more elaborate forms the lamentation typically contrasts the formerly happier conditions with the present desolation, urges the community to express their grief, and prays for the survivors' situation not to worsen. Examples prominently include Lam 1; 2; 4; and 5.

MAŚŚĀ' A Hebrew genre term that is difficult to translate, referring to both a type of (→) prophetic speech and a type of prophetic literature. In the latter capacity it can designate either a section of a prophetic book (e.g., Zech 9:1–11:17; 12:1–14:21; Isa 21:1-10) or an entire prophetic book (e.g., Nahum, Habakkuk, and Malachi).

As a genre of prophetic speech the *maśśā'* typically consists of (1) reports or announcements of Yahweh's acts or intentions, combined in various ways with (2) description of human acts or events, so as to show that Yahweh's involvement is manifest in the realm of human affairs, and (3) directives describing appropriate ways of thinking and/or acting in response to such divine activity (e.g., Isa 21:1b-10). Such a prophetic speech would serve to clarify uncertainty concerning Yahweh's involvement in a particular situation, as well as the consequent uncertainty regarding an appropriate response. It might therefore be de-

fined as an exposition of a prophetic revelation, and a phrase like *maśśā'
mô'āb* (Isa 15:1a) might be paraphrased as "prophetic exposition of
Yahweh's revealed will concerning Moab." Oracular inquiries may have
typically been answered in the form of a *maśśā'* with the three elements
identified above (e.g., as is apparently the case in Isa 14:28-32). A
maśśā' of this sort is very similar to a (→) prophetic sentinel report (cf.
Isa 21:8-10 and Hab 2:1-5; report of an oracular inquiry).

As a genre of prophetic literature the *maśśā'* typically uses much
the same combination of elements in order to reinterpret a previously
communicated revelation. Its form is defined by (1) citation of a previously communicated revelation either within the *maśśā'* itself or in the
surrounding literary context; (2) additional prophetic discourse, including at least some oracular speech of Yahweh, disclosing the divine will
or action; (3) reports of past and/or present human acts or events, showing the continuity of Yahweh's involvement in both the past situation to
which the previous revelation was addressed and the present situation to
which the *maśśā'* itself is addressed; (3) directives addressed to the audience, describing appropriate ways of thinking and acting in view of how
the previous revelation continues to take effect. Such a prophetic literary
composition would serve to clarify uncertainty as to whether previous
claims regarding the nature of Yahweh's involvement in human affairs
are still in effect, or whether Yahweh's designs have altered as historical
circumstances have changed, and to clarify the consequent uncertainty
regarding an appropriate response. A *maśśā'* of this sort might be defined
as a prophetic reinterpretation of revelation, and a phrase like *maśśā'
nînĕwēh* (Nah 1:1a) might be paraphrased as "prophetic reinterpretation
of a previous revelation concerning Yahweh's will for the city of
Nineveh."

Used in this way, the term *maśśā'* designates a type of prophetic
book. When it stands alone as the superscription to a section of a prophetic book (e.g., Zech 9:1aα[1]; 12:1aα[1]), this term indicates that the section is a reinterpretation of the foregoing material in the book, which in
its entirety constitutes the previous revelation that the section serves to
reinterpret.

MOCK DIRGE (Satirische Leichenklage, Satirische Leichenlied) A prophetic adaptation of conventions for mourning the death of an individual, used
  with reference to a figure that represents or personifies a community or
  nation, in order to identify the catastrophe faced by them as an act of
  Yahweh. Because it treats the figure as an individual, this type of prophetic speech basically resembles a (→) dirge, which was typically sung
  or recited at someone's funeral (e.g., 2 Sam 1:19-27; 3:33-34). Because
  this figure also stands for a community or nation, however, there is often
  a blurring of the distinction between a dirge and a (→) lamentation,
  which was typically sung or recited when a group gathered to mourn a
  catastrophe affecting the people as a whole (e.g., Lam 1; 2; 4; and 5).
  The dirge serves to mourn a death that has already happened, but

632

the prophetic adaptation of the genre can serve the purpose of announcing a fatal catastrophe that Yahweh will soon bring about. The funeral song is sung in advance, as it were, suggesting that the people represented by the figure for whom it is sung are as good as dead (e.g., Amos 5:1-3). The dirge sometimes includes eulogistic description of how the deceased person lived honorably and died heroically, etc. (e.g., 2 Sam 1:19-27; 3:33-34). The prophetic adaptation of the genre can instead feature mock-heroic characterization of the representative figure as one who has in effect lived so as to deserve death (e.g., Isa 14:4-23). The dirge sometimes includes exclamations of sorrow, descriptions of mourning, and calls for members of the funeral party to participate in the expression of grief. The prophetic adaptation of the genre can ironically substitute expressions of joy on the part of those who are witnessing the demise of "the deceased."

MOCK SENTINEL REPORT (Satirischer Wächterruf) An adaptation of the (→) sentinel report in which its basic elements, announcements of impending developments and directives for appropriate reactions, are played on for a variety of rhetorical effects. For example, in one case (Nah 3:13-17) the "impending" development is a defeat that is virtually complete, so that the ensuing commands to take defensive measures only underscore the hopelessness of the situation. In another case (Zech 11:1-3) the directives are, in effect, commands to welcome destroyers and find positive potential in the destructive campaign that they have waged. This genre is used in prophetic discourse but is not necessarily a (→) prophecy in the strict sense.

OATH (Eid, Schwur) A pronouncement that binds the oath taker to a particular attitude, belief, or course of action by invoking the sanctions of a deity.

ORACLE (Orakel) A divine revelation communicated through a human intermediary. Such a revelation may be communicated in response to an inquiry conducted by an intermediary (→ report of an oracular inquiry), in which case there may be some formal divinatory procedure involved, but an intermediary may also receive a revelation spontaneously without its having been solicited.

The intermediary was often a prophet, in which case the oracle could take the form of a (→) prophecy, particularly a (→) prophetic vision report (e.g., 2 Kgs 8:7-15; cf. 1 Kgs 22:19-23). A prophet might make oracular inquiry by conducting a kind of complaint liturgy on behalf of those soliciting the oracle (prophetic complaint) and then wait however long it might take for Yahweh to reply (e.g., Jer 42:1-22; cf. Hab 2:1-5).

The intermediary might also be a priest or some other kind of diviner. A priest might make oracular inquiry by casting the sacred lots, Urim and Thummim (e.g., 1 Sam 14:36b-42), or by similarly manipulating some other divinatory object (e.g., an "ephod," as in 1 Sam 23:6-14), to determine the deity's answer to a direct question, in which case the oracle would simply take the form of a positive or negative reply. If the intermediary were a "seer" *(hōzeh)*, like Balaam (Num 22:7–24:25), the oracular inquiry might involve making a sacrifice, going out to a high place to receive the revelation, and returning with the deity's reply (23:1-6), or alternatively sacrificing on the high place where the revelation was to be received (23:28–24:1); and the oracle could take the form of a prophecy (23:7-10, 18-24) or vision report (24:3-9, 15-22). If the intermediary were some other kind of diviner, like Daniel, the oracle could take still other forms, such as a (→) dream interpretation (e.g., Dan 2:36-45).

The human intermediary was commonly regarded as a more or less direct representative of the deity, as shown by the fact that he or she could speak in the first person on the deity's behalf. Many oracles do not use such first person forms, however, and many oracles also mix statements made by the prophet about God, which speak of the deity in the third person, indiscriminately with statements made by the prophet in the name of God, which speak for the deity in the first person.

ORDER (Anordnung, Befehl) A speech directly expressing what one person wills for some other person(s) to do, think, or feel. An order may be positively stated in the form of a command or negatively stated in the form of a prohibition.

PARENESIS (Paränese) An address directed to an individual or group, which attempts to persuade the addressee(s) to act or think in a particular way. Parenesis is based primarily on imperatives and other similar directives and may thus be formulated either positively in terms of commands or negatively in terms of prohibitions. Parenesis differs from the closely related genre of (→) order, which similarly consists of commands and prohibitions, by the addition of the persuasive rationale with which its parenetic imperatives are usually supported, often expressed in the form of motive or *kî* clauses. Parenesis that is positively formulated, in the sense that it is based entirely or primarily on commands, is called exhortation; and parenesis that is negatively formulated, in the sense that it is based entirely or primarily on prohibitions, is called admonition. Parenesis is a staple form of priestly, prophetic, and sapiential discourse, and is thus subject to a wide variety of variations depending on the particular setting.

PRIESTLY TORAH (Priesterliche Unterweisung) A priestly adaptation of the genre of (→) instruction, based on the reflective study of cultic traditions, giving guidance to an individual or group with regard to religious practices and lore. When priestly torah is given in response to an inquiry concerning a particular rule or custom, the response of the priestly authorities is often expressed in the form of a simple positive or negative pronouncement (e.g., Hag 2:11b-13; cf. Zech 7:2-3; Mal 2:7). Related genres include (→) prophetic instruction and (→) wisdom instruction.

PROPHECY (Prophezeiung) Any form of communication based on a claim regarding the nature of God's involvement in human affairs, or a claim regarding the outcome of events because of God's involvement, made by a person recognized as having the capacity to make such claims. Prophecies may originally have been written or oral (prophetic speech), and they may or may not be expressed in oracular form, i.e., in the form of a direct revelation from the deity (oracle). The many genres of prophecy are expressed in a variety of different forms, concerned with a variety of different issues, and intended for a variety of different rhetorical effects. Among the most common and important are the (→) prophecy of punishment, the (→) prophecy of salvation, and the (→) prophetic exhortation.

PROPHECY OF PUNISHMENT (Prophetische Strafankündigung) A type of (→) prophetic speech that announces disaster to an individual or group because of some offense against Yahweh. Such a prophecy typically contains (1) an accusation directly addressed to an individual or a group, which confronts them with their offense; and (2) an announcement of punishment that describes the disaster to which Yahweh is subjecting them. The announcement of punishment is typically formulated in the first person, as oracular speech of Yahweh, and typically identified as such by a (→) messenger formula, kōh 'āmar yhwh ("thus says Yahweh") or by a similar (→) speech report formula. The announcement of punishment is often explicitly linked with the accusation by lākēn ("therefore"), showing that the disaster is understood to be a consequence of the offense. Examples addressed to individuals include 1 Sam 2:27-36; Amos 7:14-17; Jer 20:1-6. Examples addressed to groups include Amos 2:1-3; 4:1-3; Hos 2:7-9. The form is fairly flexible. In many cases the order of the two definitive elements is reversed (e.g., Isa 3:1-11; Jer 2:26-28; Amos 9:8-10), and the stylistic details can vary considerably (e.g., Zeph 1:2-18). The prophecy of punishment serves primarily to make its addressees aware of the offense they are committing and to inform them of its consequences. This genre can also serve to explain a disaster that has already happened as the consequence of an offense committed by its addressees (e.g., Mal 1:6-14).

PROPHECY OF PUNISHMENT AGAINST A FOREIGN NATION (Prophetische Strafankündigung gegen ein Fremdvolk) A variant form of the (→) prophecy of punishment, more specifically characterized by its being directed against a foreign nation. Prophets might deal directly with the representatives of foreign nations (e.g., 2 Kgs 5:1-27; 8:7-15), in which context this genre might not have differed appreciably in form or function from an ordinary prophecy of punishment. When directed against an enemy of Israel or Judah, however, this genre was often only fictively addressed to the enemy nation and actually spoken in the presence of an Israelite or Judahite audience (e.g., 1 Kgs 19:20-28). In such cases the punishment announced for the foreign nation might be described not so much in terms of its disastrous consequences for them as conversely in terms of its beneficial consequences for the audience (e.g., 1 Kgs 20:28). The announcement of punishment concerning the enemy nation thus might include elements of an announcement of salvation for the people of Yahweh, to be overheard (as it were) by them (e.g., Zeph 2:5-7, 8-11), so that the prophecy of punishment against a foreign nation functioned for Israel or Judah virtually as a (→) prophecy of salvation.

This genre could also serve a purpose more general than identifying a particular event as Yahweh's punishment of a particular foreign nation. Some examples, either singly (e.g., Zech 9:1aα^2-8) or in series (e.g., Zeph 2:5-7, 8-11, 12-15), describe Yahweh's involvement in a larger international context.

PROPHECY OF SALVATION (Prophetische Heilsankündigung) A type of (→) prophetic speech announcing that health, peace, prosperity, restoration, etc., is coming to an individual or a group as a manifestation of Yahweh's favor. It typically consists of (1) an announcement of salvation stating Yahweh's intention to bestow salvation on a particular individual or group; and (2) a statement grounding this announcement of salvation in some attribute or prior act of Yahweh. The prophecy may be directly addressed in the second person to the individual or group that Yahweh intends to save, or it may refer to them in the third person. The announcement of salvation is typically formulated in the first person, as oracular speech of Yahweh, and typically identified as such by an introductory (→) messenger formula, kōh 'āmar yhwh ("thus says Yahweh"), or other similar (→) speech report formula. The statement of Yahweh's intention, which basically constitutes the announcement of salvation, may also be extended by a more detailed description of what Yahweh is accomplishing or what the good outcome will eventually be. The form of this genre is very flexible. In many cases the order of the two definitive elements is reversed, and the stylistic details can vary considerably. Examples include Jer 28:2-4; 31:2-6; 34:4; Amos 9:11-15; Zeph 3:18-20.

PROPHETIC CALL TO REJOICING (Prophetischer Aufruf zur Freude) A type of (→) prophetic speech based on an adaptation of the way in which women were customarily called to lead the celebration when victorious troops returned home in triumph. Commands in feminine form invited the women of the community, who could be addressed as the "daughters" (bānôt) of the victorious people, to "rejoice" (gyl, 'lz, rw', rnn, śmḥ, etc.), i.e., to lead the singing and dancing (Exod 15:20-21; Judg 11:34; 1 Sam 18:6-7). Such commands were predicated on an announcement of the victory that had been won (2 Sam 1:20).

In the prophetic adaptation of this convention Israel or Judah is collectively addressed as the personification of one such "daughter" (i.e., as the *bat ṣîyôn/yĕrûšālaim* ["daughter of Zion/Jerusalem"]), who is urged with feminine singular commands to "rejoice." Such commands are followed by an announcement of an action of Yahweh, characterized as the result of his having fought for his people. The victory has already been won, but its still unfolding effects are yet to be fully realized. Examples include Zeph 3:14-17 and Zech 9:9-10. The (→) prophecy of salvation is a closely related genre.

PROPHETIC CALL TO REPENTANCE (Prophetischer Aufruf zur Umkehr)
A prophetic adaptation of the conventions of (→) parenesis, formulated positively as (→) prophetic exhortation or negatively as prophetic admonition, in which the directives specifically urge the addressees to reverse a pattern of behavior that is self-destructive and/or offensive to Yahweh, and the rationale for doing so is to avert the disastrous consequences that Yahweh will keep in force or bring about if they fail to change their ways. This genre may be expressed entirely or partly in oracular speech of Yahweh, but in any case its force is predicated on a claim about the nature and consequences of Yahweh's involvement in the situation to which it is addressed, thus showing it to be a type of (→) prophecy. Examples include Zeph 2:1-4; Mal 2:1-9, 13-17.

PROPHETIC CHARGE OF FAILURE TO REPENT (Prophetischer Angriff gegen Umkehrverweigerung) An accusation consisting of (1) a prophetic claim that a group's pattern of behavior is opposed to Yahweh's purpose; and (2) an assertion that they have not reversed this pattern of behavior. These two elements are often connected by an adversative conjunction such as *wĕlōʾ* ("but not") or *ʾākēn* ("but nevertheless"). The group's unwillingness to change their ways is thus attributed, at least implicitly, to their unwillingness to accept the prophetic assessment of their situation. The charge of failure to repent may have been a rhetorically distinct element within more complex forms of prophetic public address (e.g., Jer 7:25-26) rather than an independently existing form of (→) prophetic speech. For example, in a (→) prophecy of punishment the accusation may be more specifically formulated as a charge of failure to repent (e.g., Jer 15:5-9; 25:1-14); and such a charge may also form part of a (→) prophetic exhortation (e.g., Zeph 3:1-7).

PROPHETIC COMPLAINT (Prophetische Klage als Beschwerde, Prophetische Beschwerdeklage, Prophetische Bittklage, Prophetische Anklage)
A prophetic adaptation of the (→) complaint genre, used when a prophet officiates at the recitation of the prayer for deliverance in a communal complaint liturgy. The prophetic complaint basically resembles the communal complaint, except that the voice and role of the prophet as the intermediary between Yahweh and the community are reflected in the formulation of some or all of the constitutive elements, particularly the description of distress or the plea for deliverance (e.g., Hab 3:2-19a).

Sometimes the prophetic role is evident in the inclusion of an oracular speech of Yahweh (e.g., in Ps 12, where it serves to ground the affirmation of confidence).

PROPHETIC COMPLAINT ABOUT THE FULFILLMENT OF A PROPHECY (Prophetische Klage über die Erfüllung einer Prophezeiung) A type of (→) prophetic complaint occasioned by a turn of events that seems problematic in view of a previously promulgated prophecy. It may be that what was prophesied seems to have been confirmed partly in the course of events, but not entirely (e.g., Jer 15:10-18); or that a prophecy which has long proved true now seems to be invalidated (e.g., Ps 89); or that a prophecy has come to pass but in a way that raises moral questions about the nature of divine justice (e.g., Hab 1:2-17), etc. In any case a quote from the previous prophecy is included within the complaint itself as part of the description of distress. The plea for deliverance and the affirmation of confidence express the hope that Yahweh will intervene so as to remedy the situation, whether by completing the fulfillment of a partially realized prophecy (Jer 15:10-18), renewing the fulfillment of a once realized prophecy (Ps 89), rectifying the injustice incurred in the fulfillment of an already realized prophecy (Hab 1:2-17), etc. In the context of communal complaint liturgies such complaints addressed the community's tendency to lose confidence in their prophetic leaders when previous prophecies proved problematic. In the context of scribal activity such complaints could also serve as case studies for theological reflection on the nature of prophecy.

PROPHETIC DISPUTATION (Prophetisches Disputationswort, Prophetisches Streitgespräch) A type of (→) prophetic speech based on adaptation of a convention of public debate involving representatives of two or more contending opinions. Such debate could occur among sages (e.g., as portrayed in Job), in legal proceedings (e.g., as reflected in Gen 31:36-43), between prophets (e.g., Jer 28:1-11), etc. Prophets adapted this convention in order to contend with popular opinions contrary to their own claims regarding Yahweh's involvement in particular historical situations. In this adaptation there is actually no exchange between speakers but only the reflection of such an exchange. The prophet makes a summary statement of the popular attitude and then takes issue with it. These two basic elements may be ordered and expressed in a wide variety of ways, but in taking issue with popular opinion the prophet usually employs oracular speech of Yahweh. Examples of this genre are typically addressed directly to the audience, suggesting that prophets delivered such speeches orally in some public arena (e.g., Mic 2:6-11; Hag 1:2-11; cf. Jer 7:4-15; 26:1-7). The genre also lends itself easily to written use, however, as a means of developing an argument addressed by writers to readers. It is therefore difficult to tell whether some of the texts in this form are speeches transcribed from oral tradition or written fictive representations of such speeches (e.g., Mal 1:2-5). It is particularly difficult to make such a distinction in Deutero-Isaiah, where this genre is especially prominent.

PROPHETIC EXHORTATION (Prophetische Ermutigung) A prophetic adaptation of (→) parenesis that is positively formulated, consisting of (1) commands with (2) supporting rationale often expressed in the form of motive or *kî* clauses. (An analogous adaptation of parenesis that is negatively formulated, and hence based on prohibitions, would conversely be termed *prophetic admonition [Prophetische Ermahnung]*.) In this particular adaptation of the genre the supporting rationale may be predicated on claims about the nature of Yahweh's involvement in the situation of the addressee(s), and oracular speech of Yahweh may also characterize the formulation of the command and/or the rationale, thus showing the exhortation to be a type of (→) prophecy. In prophetic exhortation the rationale for the commands often takes the form of a particular genre of prophecy, such as a (→) prophecy of punishment (e.g., Zeph 1:7-10, 11-18) or a (→) prophecy of salvation (e.g., Zeph 3:14-20; Hag 2:3-9).

PROPHETIC HISTORICAL EXEMPLUM (Prophetisches geschichtliches Beispiel) A type of (→) prophetic speech that describes Yahweh's involvement in the past so as to teach something about his involvement in the present. To this end the following elements are combined in a variety of ways: (1) direct address inducing the audience to learn theologically from the past; (2) narration or report of some past event(s); (3) interpretation of the past event(s) as a type of divine activity that recurs within or still impinges upon the present. This generic form is evident in texts originally composed for lyrical recitation (e.g., Deut 32; Ps 78), texts into which older prophetic traditions have been redactionally incorporated (e.g., Nah 1:2–2:11 [*RSV* 1:2–2:10]), and texts written as prophetic literature (e.g., Zech 1:2-6).

The prophetic historical exemplum resembles the (→) prophetic symbolic interpretation of a past event, which also deals with the present theological significance of the past; but this genre differs from the latter by virtue of its more overtly didactic form and content.

PROPHETIC HISTORY (Prophetische Geschichtsschreibung) A type of literary narrative that is both historiographical and prophetic. It is historiographical in the sense that it presents the results of the writer's investigation of a particular time in the past based on the writer's survey of previously existing sources of information, sources that are evaluated and interpreted in light of the writer's contemporary situation (→ history). It is also prophetic in the sense that the writer purports to discern God's involvement in past situations, in a way that sheds light on God's involvement in the writer's contemporary situation (→ prophecy). Readers are thereby provided with a model for imagining how God might be analogously involved in their own historical situation. The prophetic intention of this genre is primarily evident in the writer's characterization of the narrator as someone with prophetic consciousness. Prophetic history was produced by scribal groups concerned with studying the records of public affairs and prophetic revelations so as to gain prophetic insight regarding the management of public affairs in their own time. The prophetic book of Haggai provides a good example of this genre.

PROPHETIC INSTRUCTION (Prophetische Instruktion, Prophetische Unterweisung) A prophetic adaptation of the genre of (→) instruction, based on the reflective study of prophetic traditions, giving guidance to individuals or groups concerning the ongoing significance of past prophecies and other prophetic lore (→ Zeph, Book as a Whole, Genre). Related genres include (→) priestly torah and (→) wisdom instruction.

PROPHETIC INTERROGATION (Prophetische Vernehmung, Prophetische Untersuchung) An adaptation of the rhetoric of inferential questioning, which pertains primarily to various kinds of wisdom discourse, for the prophetic purpose of confronting a group or individual with a revelation requiring a reassessment of attitude or behavior. This type of rhetoric combines propositional statements with rhetorical questions whose answers depend on inferences drawn from such statements.

In wisdom discourse inferential questioning may be the predominant element in a speech constituting a more or less independent textual unit, such as a proverb (e.g., Prov 18:14; 20:6; 27:4) or an exchange in a dialogue (e.g., Job 26:2-14). Inferential questioning may also form part of a kind of speech in which it does not predominate (e.g., Job 9:4-12; 36:22-23). It may concern purely pragmatic or specifically theological matters, and it may be formulated either impersonally or in second person direct address.

Prophets would often provoke their audience with accusatory or confrontational questions (e.g., Isa 7:13; 22:1b, 16; Jer 4:30; Ezek 18:2, 25, 29; cf. Pss 50:16; 52:3 [*RSV* 1]), and inferential questioning could serve as one way of pursuing this rhetorical strategy (e.g., Amos 3:8; Isa 50:7-9). In prophetic discourse inferential questioning usually serves to foster an assessment of some claim about the nature of Yahweh's involvement in human affairs (→ prophecy), and its confrontational nature may be emphasized by its being formulated in second person direct address (e.g., Nah 1:9). Prophetic interrogation can be the predominant generic element in a more or less independent textual unit (e.g., Nah 1:2-10), but it may not have been an independently existing form of (→) prophetic speech.

PROPHETIC PROMISE (Prophetisches Versprechen) A statement of Yahweh's commitment to act in a certain way or bring about a specific situation, usually but not always formulated in the first person as an oracular speech of Yahweh. Such a promise may be the essential performative element of an (→) oath spoken by a prophet (e.g., 1 Kgs 17:1), and it may also form part of the announcement of salvation in a (→) prophecy of salvation (e.g., 2 Kgs 20:5-6). The prophetic promise may also have been an independently existing type of (→) prophetic speech, used particularly with reference to the well-being of a king or royal dynasty. The independent existence of this genre is suggested by the fact that such prophetic promises are quoted in various kinds of historical reporting by the narrator (e.g., 1 Kgs 3:10-14; 2 Kgs 10:30) or by a character within the narrative (2 Sam 5:2b; 2 Kgs 22:18b-20; 1 Chr 22:8-10), and by the fact that a prophet could be commissioned to deliver a message from Yahweh basically consisting of such a promise (e.g., Hag 2:21b-23).

PROPHETIC PSALMODY SCRIPT (Prophetischer Psalmengesangstext) A text containing a (→) psalm with annotations reflecting an understanding of psalmody as a prophetic activity. Such annotations primarily take the form of a (→) superscription, but they can also appear at various places within the body of the psalm and at its conclusion.

The annotations sometimes associate the psalm with a particular person, situating it within either the general circumstances or a specific event of his or her lifetime. Since most of the information about this person is usually preserved in other texts, this kind of annotation usually creates intertextual connections. The psalm is illuminated by identifying its otherwise anonymous speaker with someone whose words or deeds are known from these other sources; and these other sources are conversely illuminated by imagining the psalm as the utterance of someone described in them.

Annotations of this kind are historiographical in the sense that they attempt to view the psalm in light of what is actually known from extant documentation about a particular person's words or deeds. In ancient historiography, however, speeches were conventionally composed as fictional representations of what a particular person might well have said on a given occasion. Psalms were historiographically identified as speeches of particular persons in accord with this same convention, on a similarly fictional basis.

The annotations also provide information about the nature of the psalm and the manner of its liturgical rendition. Much of this information is expressed in technical terminology whose meaning is no longer clear, such as the enigmatic *selâ* found at various places within the body of many psalms. In any case this terminology generally reflects the conventional ways in which psalmody was performed in the Second Temple.

Taken together both kinds of annotations reflect an understanding of the Second Temple's liturgy as a reactualization of the conditions under which preexilic prophets served as intermediaries between Yahweh and the people, both in proclaiming Yahweh's oracles to them and in interceding to Yahweh on their behalf. A text annotated for use in such a liturgical context served not only as a libretto for the Second Temple's psalmodists, who performed the psalm as a reactualization of what a past prophetic figure had once proclaimed or prayed. It also served as revelatory scripture for the scribes of the Second Temple period, who subjected it to mantic exegesis. They drew typological correspondences between Yahweh's involvement in the situation described in the psalm and Yahweh's involvement in the situation faced by the person named in the annotation. Such typological correspondences provided them with a model for drawing further typological correspondences between Yahweh's involvement in the situation described in the psalm and Yahweh's involvement in their own situation. Hab 3:1-19 is the most notable example outside the Psalter.

PROPHETIC REPORT (Prophetischer Bericht) An adaptation of the (→) report genre that recounts a past event so as to communicate the narrator's prophetic insight regarding Yahweh's involvement in that event. In Mal 3:13-24 (*RSV* 3:13–4:6), for example, such insight is in effect communicated by the juxtaposition of the reporting statement in 3:16 with the prophetic speeches in 3:13-15 and 3:17-24. A related genre is (→) prophetic history.

PROPHETIC SENTINEL REPORT (Prophetischer Wächterruf) A prophetic adaptation of the (→) sentinel report, implying metaphorical comparison of the prophet's role with the sentinel's role (e.g., Isa 21:6-10; 52:7-10; Jer 6:17; Ezek 3:17-21; 33:2-9; Mic 7:4, 7; Hab 2:1) in which the prophet similarly announces contemporary developments that affect the community's welfare and gives directives concerning appropriate responses that the community might make. In keeping with the specifically prophetic function of this genre the contemporary developments are interpreted as signs of Yahweh's involvement in the situation, and the directives are given as indications of Yahweh's will for the community under such circumstances. Examples include Nah 2:1-11 (*RSV* 1:15–2:10) and Hab 1:5-11.

PROPHETIC SPEECH (Prophetische Rede) A type of (→) prophecy defined in terms of the rhetorical conventions characterizing the verbal interaction of a prophet with a live public audience. Narrative accounts of prophetic activity portray recurrent rhetorical patterns of prophetic speech making, sometimes directed to an individual but more often to a group. These same patterns are often evident in prophecies without any narrative context, thus showing that such prophecies were originally oral and subsequently written down, or that they were composed as written imitations of originally oral forms. Direct address is generally implied and often explicitly indicated by use of the second person. Since narrative accounts of prophets' words and deeds typically use the third person, and thus avoid direct address, they are not usually classified as prophetic speeches, even though some examples of such narratives may be appropriately classified as prophecies and may also have originally been orally recounted. Prophetic speeches may or may not be expressed in oracular form, i.e., in the form of a direct revelation from the deity (oracle), and prophetic speeches may include oracular elements without consistently distinguishing between statements made by the prophet about Yahweh, which speak of the deity in the third person, and statements made by the prophet in the name of Yahweh, which speak for the deity in the first person.

PROPHETIC STORY (Erzählte prophetische Geschichte) A type of (→) historical story in which a prophetic figure plays a central role, recounting the event so as to communicate the narrator's insight regarding Yahweh's involvement in it (e.g., 1 Kgs 12:1-20; 22:1-37). Related genres are (→) prophetic history and (→) prophetic report.

PROPHETIC SUPERSCRIPTION (Prophetische Überschrift) A type of (→) superscription prefixed to a prophetic book or section of a prophetic book. Of the fifteen biblical books that are prophetic, in the sense that they are named after a particular prophet, four begin with an introduction rather than a superscription (i.e., Ezekiel, Jonah, Haggai, and Zechariah). The others are headed by superscriptions that consist basically of a (→) title naming the prophet with whom the book is associated. (The superscription of Malachi constitutes a special case in that it is not clear whether a prophet is actually being named or whether the convention of naming a prophet is instead being played upon [→ Mal 1:1].)

These superscriptions are of two main types. The first type uses the distinctive terminology of the (→) prophetic word formula, $děbar$ $yhwh$ $'ăšer$ $hāyâ$ $'el$ x ("the word of Yahweh that came to x"), e.g., Hos 1:1; Joel 1:1; Mic 1:1; Zeph 1:1. The second type uses other terminology for prophetic revelation, such as $ḥāzôn$ ("vision" or "revelation"), $děbārîm$ ("words"), or (→) $maśśā'$ (RSV "oracle"). The first two of these terms are usually bound with the name of the prophet in a construct phrase, as in $dibrê$ x ("words of x," e.g., Jer 1:1; Amos 1:1) and $ḥăzôn$ x ("vision of x," e.g., Isa 1:1; Obad 1:1; Nah 1:1b).

The term $maśśā'$, however, does not occur in construct relationship with the name of the prophet. In one case (Zech 9:1aα[1]) it stands alone without any modifiers, heading an appendix to the book of Zechariah that develops the insights of the prophet already named in the foregoing part of the book (Zech 1:1; 1:7; 7:1). In one case (Hab 1:1) it stands alone as the object of a relative clause naming the prophet. In another case (Nah 1:1a) it forms a construct phrase with the name of a city (i.e., "Nineveh"), thus describing the main theme of the prophecy (i.e., the fate of Nineveh). In this last instance the term $maśśā'$ also stands in apposition with another term for prophetic revelation that is in turn modified so as to name the prophet: $sēper$ $ḥăzôn$ $naḥûm$ ("the book of Nahum's vision"; Nah 1:1b). In two other cases $maśśā'$ similarly stands in apposition with other terms for prophetic revelation, such as $děbar$ $yhwh$ ("the word of Yahweh") and $ně'um$ $yhwh$ ("the oracle of Yahweh"), which in turn have modifiers designating the prophetic intermediary (Mal 1:1) or further specifying the scope and theme of the prophecy (→ Zech 12:1).

With respect to a prophetic book in its entirety, a prophetic super-scription thus serves primarily to entitle the document as a prophetic revelation of some kind and to name the prophet in whom the revelation originated. With respect to a section within a prophetic book, a prophetic superscription may likewise serve both of these functions (e.g., Isa 2:1; Hab 3:1); but since the prophet has already been named in the initial superscription, it may only serve to entitle the following section of the book as a particular type of revelation (e.g., Zech 9:1aα^1; 12:1).

Prophetic superscriptions may also include other kinds of information, such as the prophet's genealogy and place of origin; the people with whom the revelation is primarily concerned; and the historical context of the revelation as defined by specific dates, references to particular events, or the kings in whose reigns the prophet was active.

PROPHETIC SYMBOLIC INTERPRETATION OF A PAST EVENT (Prophetische symbolische Auslegung eines Ereignisses aus der Vergangenheit) A type of (→) prophetic speech in which the present theological implications of a past event are metaphorically described using allegorical or mythical symbolism. The following elements combine in various ways to form this genre: (1) report of a past event; (2) metaphorical interpretation of the event by means of allegory or mythical allusion; and (3) description of the still unfolding consequences. The symbolism serves to elucidate the nature of Yahweh's involvement in the ongoing historical process, but the elucidation may result more from the interplay of these three elements than from the second element in itself. Examples include Ezek 17:2-24; 24:2-14; and Nah 1:11-14.

This genre resembles the (→) prophetic historical exemplum, which also deals with the present theological significance of past events, but the latter differs from the former in several respects. The prophetic historical exemplum has a more didactic form and content, and does not depend to the same extent on metaphorical comparison to make its interpretive point.

PROPHETIC VISION REPORT (Prophetischer Visionsbericht) A type of (→) report that describes what a prophet sees, and sometimes also simultaneously hears, in an extraordinary experience charged with revelatory significance. Such reports are mostly in first person autobiographical style, and typically consist of (1) an introductory statement that the prophet has "seen" something, using some active form of the verb r'h, or that the prophet "was made to see" something by Yahweh, using a hiphil form of the same verb; this terminology of "seeing" is sometimes accompanied by similarly formulaic terminology relating to visual perception, such as the phrase *nś' 'ênayim* ("to lift the eyes"); (2) a transition to the description of the vision itself, using the phrase *wĕhinnēh* ("and behold!"); and (3) a description of what the prophet has seen (and perhaps also heard), with some indication that the figures on the field of perception are revelatory. With regard to this last factor there is great variety. The scene may range from things bizarre (e.g., the flying scroll in Zech 5:1-4) to things quite ordinary (e.g., a man with a surveyor's tool in Zech 2:5-10 [*RSV* 1-5]), but they are invariably assumed to show something about Yahweh's involvement in human affairs. The revelatory nature of the scene is often obvious because the figures in it are superhuman beings (e.g., the heavenly chariots in Zech 6:1-8), or because the scene itself is heavenly or supramundane (e.g., Isa 6:1-13; Ezek 1:1-28; Zech 3:1-10). But even the most ordinary objects of human daily life, like a basket of fruit (Amos 8:1-2) or a boiling pot (Jer 1:13), can take on revelatory significance when Yahweh himself shows them to the prophet or speaks to the prophet about them, or when an angelic being appears to interpret them (e.g., the horns in Zech 2:1-4 [*RSV* 1:18-22]).

The prophetic vision report may be compared with the (→) report of a prophetic revelation, in that the former focuses on the reception of a revelation that is primarily visual, while the latter analogously focuses on the reception of a revelation that is primarily verbal. This focus on the reception of the vision does not serve to emphasize the subjective aspects of any religious experience giving rise to the prophet's perception, for virtually no information is given regarding the extent to which the visionary experience is paranormal, or whether it may be more specifically attributed to hallucination, trance, daydream, etc. The focus on the reception of the vision serves rather to emphasize the prophet's capacity to recognize the authenticity of what is seen, as a revelation that is truly from Yahweh. The vision report thus models for its audience how to be similarly discerning in recognizing the prophet as an authentic mediator of a true revelation.

The prophetic vision report is also closely related to the (→) report of an oracular inquiry, since a prophet seeking to divine God's purpose in a particular situation would often receive a reply in the form of a vision (e.g., 1 Kgs 22:13-23; 2 Kgs 8:7-15; Jer 38:21-23).

PROPHETIC VOCATION ACCOUNT (Prophetisches Berufungsbericht) A variation on the (→) report of a prophetic revelation in which the revelation received is the (→) commission to prophesy that inaugurates the prophet's career (e.g., Amos 7:15; Jer 1:4-10; Ezek 1:1-3:11).

PSALM (Psalm) A poem designed for use in the liturgies of Israelite and Judahite cults at various places in preexilic times and at Jerusalem in the Second Temple period. On the basis of differing forms and liturgical functions psalms are divided into various genres, including the (→) hymn of praise and the (→) complaint. Each of these genres has significant marked variations. With regard to the complaint, for example, variations include the individual complaint, the communal complaint, and the (→) prophetic complaint.

REPORT (Bericht) A brief, self-contained narrative, usually in third person style, about a single event or situation in the past. In contrast with the

(→) story, the report shows little appreciable development of plot or characterization. The report also differs from a mere statement of fact, however, in its rather more developed description of action. Reports can vary considerably in content, setting, and intention. For example, the types of report related to prophecy prominently include (→) report of an oracular inquiry, (→) report of a prophetic symbolic action, (→) report of a prophetic revelation, and (→) prophetic vision report.

REPORT OF A PROPHETIC REVELATION (Bericht einer prophetischen Offenbarung) A type of (→) report that describes a prophet's private reception of a message from Yahweh, found in both first person autobiographical and third person biographical forms. It typically begins with (1) the (→) prophetic word formula in the form of either narration (*hāyâ/wayhî děbaryhwh 'el x/'ēlay lē'mōr . . .* ["the word of Yahweh came to *x*/to me, saying . . ."]; e.g., Ezek 6:1-10; Zech 4:8-10; 6:9-15) or superscription (*děbaryhwh 'ăšer hāyâ 'el x/'ēlay lē'mōr . . .* ["the word of Yahweh which came to *x*/to me, saying . . ."]; e.g., Jer 14:1-10; cf. 30:1-3); and it typically continues with (2) a quotation of the message, which can be virtually any kind of prophecy. Such reports may also include specific information about the conditions under which the revelation was received, such as the date and historical circumstances (e.g., Jer 34:8-22; Ezek 14:1-11; Zech 1:1-6). Several prophecies can be incorporated into a single report and thus be treated as a single revelation (e.g., Zech 1:7–6:15), in which case intervening actions involving the prophet may be briefly described (e.g., Jer 32:1-44; 35:1-19).

In any case this type of report remains primarily focused on the private reception of prophetic revelation and thus stands in marked contrast with other generic forms that focus instead on the public communication of prophetic revelation to the individual or group for which it was intended. These other generic forms include both the kinds of narratives that typically give a more developed account of a prophet's words and deeds, such as (→) prophetic story (e.g., 1 Kgs 20:1-43; 22:1-38), and the kinds of prophecies that typically use some kind of (→) speech report formula, like the (→) messenger formula, thus showing that their communication is presupposed. This characteristic focus on the reception of revelation does not serve to emphasize the subjective aspects of any religious experience on which prophetic intermediation may be based, about which virtually no explicit information is given. It rather serves to emphasize the prophet's capacity to recognize the authenticity of the prophecy quoted in the report as a revelation that is truly from Yahweh. The report thus models for its audience how to be similarly discerning in recognizing the prophet as an authentic mediator of a true revelation.

REPORT OF A PROPHETIC SYMBOLIC ACTION (Bericht einer prophetischen symbolischen Handlung) A type of (→) report that describes a prophet's involvement in an action understood to be a symbolic dramatization of the prophetic message. Such reports are found in both third person biographical and first person autobiographical forms (e.g., Hos 1:2-3; cf. 3:1-2). They typically describe (1) the prophet's initial apprehension of Yahweh's command to perform the symbolic action (→ commission to prophesy), (2) the prophet's subsequent compliance with this command, and (3) the significance of the symbolic action, usually in the form of an oracular message from Yahweh that accompanies or follows the performance (e.g., Isa 20:1-6; Hag 2:10-19).

Some examples of this genre do not explicitly describe Yahweh's command to perform the symbolic action (e.g., 1 Kgs 11:29-39; 22:11), so that they resemble in form a (→) prophetic report. In such cases the symbolic action is usually still accompanied by an oracular speech of Yahweh interpreting its significance, and the action itself is therefore implicitly understood to have been instigated by Yahweh. Other examples do not explicitly describe the performance of the symbolic action (e.g., Ezek 4:1-8ff.), so that they resemble in form a (→) report of a prophetic revelation. In such cases there is often some implicit indication that the action was or would be performed, either in the formulation of the report itself (e.g., Zech 6:9-15) or in the surrounding context (e.g., Zech 11:15-17 in relation to 11:4-14). In still another variation, the performance of the symbolic action itself is explicitly described but not the delivery of the oracular message stating its significance (e.g., Jer 13:1-11), in which case the performance of the former implies the performance of the latter.

REPORT OF AN ORACULAR INQUIRY (Bericht eines Gottesbescheides) A type of (→) report that describes (1) the attempt of a priest, prophet, or some other kind of intermediary to seek a revelation from God; and (2) the revelation received in response to this inquiry. Such an attempt might be made at the request of another person, particularly a community leader, in order to determine how to manage a particular situation in accord with God's will (e.g., Jer 21:1-14). The inquiry might also be undertaken on the initiative of the intermediary alone (e.g., Hab 2:1-5). In some cases of priestly oracular inquiry a response would be determined by casting the sacred lots, Urim and Thummim (e.g., 1 Sam 14:36b-42), or by means of an "ephod" (e.g., 1 Sam 23:6-14). A response might also be apprehended by a prophet under the influence of music (e.g., 2 Kgs 3:4-20). In most cases, however, there is no explicit description of how the deity's response is divined by the human intermediary. The response generally comes in the form of an oracle spoken by Yahweh or a vision disclosed by Yahweh (e.g., 2 Kgs 8:7-15; cf. 1 Kgs 22:19-23). Reports of oracular inquiries may be incorporated as individual scenes into extended narratives, in which case a description of the oracle's fulfillment (e.g., 1 Kgs 14:1-18) or rejection (e.g., Jer 42:1–43:13) is sometimes included; or they may be juxtaposed as relatively self-contained units with other kinds of material in prophetic books (e.g., Zech 7:2-7 in relation to 7:8–8:23).

REPROOF SPEECH (Tadelnde Rede) A speech based on a type of disciplinary rhetoric that characterizes the wisdom traditions of domestic life, public affairs, and scribal learning. Reproof *(ykḥ)* basically involves calling someone to account for a kind of behavior that has negative consequences, either as a precondition for changing this behavior and thereby averting the consequences, or as a precondition for suffering the consequences and thereby providing an instructive example of how not to behave. A parent might reprove a child (Prov 1:25), citizens might reprove one another or their leaders "in the gate" (Amos 5:10; Isa 29:21), and a teacher might reprove a student (Prov 5:12-13).

The rhetoric of reproof consists basically of (1) a maxim describing either a kind of good behavior with positive consequences or a kind of bad behavior with negative consequences, and (2) direct address characterizing a person or group as suffering the negative consequences of their deeds, thus implicating the addressee(s) in either violation of the former kind of maxim or confirmation of the latter kind. Such rhetoric can play a subsidiary role in various sorts of discourse, for example, in the dialogue between Job and his three friends (e.g., Job 6:25-26; 19:5-6; 32:12), and as the basis for the accusation in a (→) prophecy of punishment (e.g., 1 Sam 15:22-23). Reproof speech is discourse in which these two basic elements predominate, sometimes including other elements that emphasize or vary the rhetorical force of the maxim and/or the implicating direct address (e.g., Hab 2:6aα^2-8, 9-11, 12-14, 15-17, 18-20).

SENTINEL REPORT (Wächterruf) The kind of speech by which a sentinel keeping watch over a group advises them or their leaders of developments concerning the common welfare. Sentinels might be posted on a city wall or tower, on the outskirts of a military encampment, or on the border of an area being scouted by military reconnaissance. From such a vantage point they would convey announcements of messengers approaching and armies advancing or returning, etc. (e.g., 2 Sam 13:34; 18:24b-25a; 2 Kgs 9:17-20), along with directives concerning any measures that might be appropriately taken in view of what they saw happening (e.g., Jer 6:17; 31:6). The role of a prophet is often metaphorically compared with the role of a sentinel (e.g., Isa 21:6-10; 52:7-10; Jer 6:17; Ezek 3:17-21; 33:2-9; Mic 7:4, 7; Hab 2:1), and the sentinel report is thus adapted for prophetic use (→ prophetic sentinel report; mock sentinel report).

STORY (Erzählte Geschichte) A narrative with a relatively well-developed plot, i.e., a narrative that creates interest in its description of action by first arousing and then resolving tension as it progresses through a series of events or situations. The tension is created by complications arising from the unfolding relationship between the action and the setting in which the action takes place, and from the unfolding personality and personal relationships of the characters involved in the action. A story has narration that is relatively more complex than, for example, a (→) report, which similarly describes action but does not develop the plot to a similar extent.

SUPERSCRIPTION (Überschrift) A statement prefixed to a text that may be either a literary work in its entirety (e.g., Amos 1:1 in the case of a prophetic book); or a section of a literary work (e.g., Prov 10:1a in the case of Prov 10:1–24:34); or an individual composition in a collection of such compositions (e.g., as in the case of many psalms in the Psalter). A superscription sometimes gives a (→) title for the text to which it is prefixed, but it may contain various other things in addition to or instead of a title, such as information about a person with whom the text is be associated, including his or her name, hometown, and genealogy, as well as important dates or events in his or her lifetime; terms characterizing the form, content, or function of the text, along with related information concerning its transcription or recitation; etc. A superscription differs from an introduction in that the latter is an integral part of the composition that it opens and is thus not an independent genre while the superscription stands rather more apart from the text that it heads.

TAUNT (Verspottung, Verhöhnung) A derisive utterance insinuating that one person, group, or thing is inferior to another. Taunts have no fixed formulation but are defined by their function and intention in the context of a battle of words between opponents (e.g., 1 Sam 17:43-44; 1 Kgs 12:10b; 20:11; Isa 23:15-16; Jer 22:14-15).

TITLE (Titel) A word or concise phrase that names a literary composition, often using terminology that categorizes the composition as a particular type of literary work and identifying the person with which it is traditionally associated. A title usually heads the composition that it names as its (→) superscription or as an element within its superscription.

WISDOM INSTRUCTION (Weisheitsinstruktion) A scribal adaptation of the genre of (→) instruction, based on the study of such wisdom traditions as aphoristic lore, giving guidance concerning the attitudes and conduct that are appropriate for the well-educated in general and for those entering the scribal profession in particular (e.g., Prov 1–9; 22:17–24:22). Related genres include (→) priestly torah and (→) prophetic instruction.

WOE ORACLE (Weheruf) A type of speech used by prophets to criticize and/or announce punishment upon a person or group. Woe oracles can occur individually (Isa 1:4; 10:5) or in series (Isa 5:8-24). The woe oracle consists typically of (1) the exclamation *hôy* ("woe"); (2) a participle denoting the criticized action, or a noun negatively characterizing the object(s) of criticism; and (3) a conclusion variously consisting of threats (Isa 5:9, 13-14, 24; 28:2-8), accusations (Ezek 13:3-9; 18:19), rhetorical questions (Isa 10:3-4; Amos 6:2), etc. The woe speeches in Hab 2:6b-20 are often classed as woe oracles, but they are better understood as examples of the (→) reproof speech (Hab 2:6-8, Genre).

FORMULAS

CHALLENGE FORMULA (Herausforderungsformel) The phrase *hinněnî 'ēlayik* ("behold, I am against you"), characteristically part of the (→) prophecy of punishment in Nahum (e.g., 2:14 [*RSV* 13]; 3:5), Jeremiah (e.g., 21:13), and Ezekiel (e.g., 5:8; 13:8, 20). Such a formula reflects the context of a duel (1 Sam 17:45).

FUTURE EVENT FORMULA (Zukunftereignisformel) Various stock phrases using the terms *yôm* ("day") or *'ēt* ("time") to indicate an indefinite future time, such as *bayyôm hahû'* ("on that day"), *bā'ēt hahî'* ("at that time"), and *hinnēh yāmîm bā'îm* ("behold, the days are coming"). These phrases are often used in a (→) prophecy whose fulfillment is envisioned as a development discontinuous with the present course of events. Such language may be used in describing eschatological events but does not in itself necessarily indicate that the description is eschatological.

MESSENGER FORMULA (Botenformel) The phrase *kōh 'āmar yhwh* ("thus says Yahweh") used to designate a (→) prophecy, or some part of a prophecy, as a verbal revelation from Yahweh. This phrase is rooted in the customary way of sending a message orally from one person to another person or group by means of a third party. The sender of a message would insert his or her name into the formula, "thus says *x*," in commissioning the messenger (e.g., Gen 32:5; 45:9); and the messenger would repeat the formula when delivering the message to its recipient (e.g., 2 Kgs 18:29; Num 22:15). When adapted for prophetic purposes, the use of this phrase connotes that the prophet's communication of a revelation is analogous to the customary practice of delivering a message, and that the prophet's role as an intermediary is thus more specifically characterized as the role of Yahweh's messenger. In contrast with the (→) prophetic word formula, which focuses primarily on the prophet's reception of a revelation from Yahweh, the messenger formula focuses primarily on the communication of the revelation to its intended recipient(s).

ORACLE FORMULA (Orakelformel, Gottesspruchformel) The phrase *ně'um yhwh* ("utterance of Yahweh") found typically at almost any juncture in virtually any kind of (→) prophecy, designating the prophecy as verbal revelation from Yahweh. Though this formula is often translated "says Yahweh," it is actually formulated as a noun phrase rather than a verb phrase. Unlike the (→) messenger formula and other prophetic variations on the (→) speech report formula, which are otherwise quite similar, the oracle formula does not narrate or report the revelation in any strict sense. It is thus a kind of tag line that functions more like a (→) superscription or subscript.

PROPHETIC WORD FORMULA (Prophetische Wortereignisformel) The noun phrase *děbar-yhwh* ("word of Yahweh"), used in combination with the verb phrase *hāyâ 'el* plus the name of a prophet ("came to *x*"), either as a predicate to create an introductory sentence of narration ("the word of Yahweh came to *x*"), or as a relative clause to create a (→) prophetic superscription ("the word of Yahweh that came to *x*"). In both forms this formula can be used to introduce whole prophetic books or sections of prophetic books, as well as individual instances of a (→) report of a prophetic revelation. In contrast with the (→) messenger formula and other prophetic variations on the (→) speech report formula, which focus primarily on the communication of a prophetic revelation to its intended recipients, the prophetic word formula focuses primarily on the prophet's reception of a prophetic revelation from Yahweh.

SPEECH REPORT FORMULA (Redeberichtsformel) A phrase consisting of a nominal or pronominal subject plus a verb of saying, usually *'mr,* used with a quotation as its object in the narration of direct discourse. In the prophetic adaptation of this formula "Yahweh" or "Yahweh of hosts" *(yhwh ṣĕbā'ôt),* etc., is the subject; and the quoted speech is thereby designated as oracular speech of Yahweh. The prophetic adaptation of this formula is very similar to the (→) messenger formula, and it similarly focuses on the communication rather than the reception of prophetic revelation, but it does not necessarily imply that the prophet is acting specifically as Yahweh's messenger.